WITHDRAWN

Stafford Library
Columbia College
1001 Rogers Street
Columbia, Missouri 65216

AMERICAN LAW YEARBOOK 2004

ISSN 1521-0901

AMERICAN LAW YEARBOOK 2004

AN ANNUAL SOURCE PUBLISHED
BY THOMSON GALE AS A
SUPPLEMENT TO
WEST'S ENCYCLOPEDIA OF
AMERICAN LAW

Detroit • New York • San Francisco • San Diego • New Haven, Conn. • Waterville, Maine • London • Munich

American Law Yearbook 2004

Project Editor
Jeffrey Wilson

Editorial
Jeffrey Lehman

Editorial Support Services
Selwa Petrus

Permissions
Margaret Chamberlain, Mari Masalin-Cooper

Imaging and Multimedia
Randy Bassett, Dean Dauphinais, Lezlie Light

Composition and Electronic Capture
Evi Seoud

Manufacturing
Rhonda Williams

© 2005 Thomson Gale, a part of the Thomson Corporation.

Thomson and Star Logo are trademarks and Gale is a registered trademark used herein under license.

For more information, contact
Thomson Gale, Inc.
27500 Drake Rd.
Farmington Hills, MI 48331-3535
Or you can visit our Internet site at
http://www.gale.com

ALL RIGHTS RESERVED

No part of this work covered by the copyright hereon may be reproduced or used in any form or by any means—graphic, electronic, or mechanical, including photocopying, recording, taping, Web distribution, or information storage retrieval systems—without the written permission of the publisher.

For permission to use material from this product, submit your request via Web at http://www.gale-edit.com/permissions, or you can download our Permissions Request form and submit your request by fax or mail to:

Permissions Department
Thomson Gale, Inc.
27500 Drake Rd.
Farmington Hills, MI 48331-3535
Permissions Hotline:
248-699-8006 or 800-877-4253, ext. 8006
Fax: 248-699-8074 or 800-762-4058

Since this page cannot legibly accommodate all copyright notices, the acknowledgments constitute an extension of the copyright notice.

While every effort has been made to ensure the reliability of the information presented in this publication, Thomson Gale, Inc. does not guarantee the accuracy of the data contained herein. The Thomson Gale, Inc. accepts no payment for listing; and inclusion in the publication of any organization, agency, institution, publication, service, or individual does not imply endorsement of the editors or publisher. Errors brought to the attention of the publisher and verified to the satisfaction of the publisher will be corrected in future editions.

ISBN 0-7876-9027-9
ISSN 1521-0901

Printed in the United States of America
10 9 8 7 6 5 4 3 2 1

CONTENTS

Preface . . . . *vii*

Acknowledgments . . . . *xi*

Abortion 1
Age Discrimination 5
Aliens 6
Americans with Disabilities Act 7
In Focus
    ADA Compliance of Internet Sites 8
Antitrust Law 11
Apportionment 15
Bankruptcy 19
Bounty Hunter 24
Bribery 26
Broadcasting 27
Capital Punishment 31
Central Intelligence Agency 38
Civil Rights 39
Copyright 41
Corporate Fraud 45
Criminal Procedure 48
Discovery 51
DNA Testing 54
Double Jeopardy 55
Drugs and Narcotics 56
Education Law 59
Elections 60
Eleventh Amendment 63
E-mail 64
Environmental Law 67
Espionage 72
Establishment Clause 73
Federalism 77
Fetal Rights 78
First Amendment 79
Foreign Sovereign Immunities Act 85
Fourth Amendment 86

Freedom of Information Act 95
Freedom of Speech 97
Gay and Lesbian Rights 101
Gun Control 104
Habeas Corpus 107
Identity Theft 115
Insider Trading 116
Insurance 117
Intellectual Property 119
Internet 120
Iraq War 121
Judge 123
Jurisdiction 124
Jury 128
Kerry, John Forbes 131
Long, Russell Billiu 133
Manslaughter 135
Mine and Mineral Law 140
Miranda Rights 141
Murder 143
Obscenity 157
Oklahoma City Bombings 158
Owner 159
Partnership 161
Patents 162
Pension 163
Presidential Powers 164
Prisoners' Rights 166
Privacy 167
Privacy Act of 1974 168
Rape 171
Reagan, Ronald Wilson 172
Recuse 173
Regan, Donald T. 176

v

Right to Counsel................... 176
Right to Die 177
Securities 181
Sentencing 183
September 11th Attacks 188
Sex Offenses 193
Sexual Abuse...................... 195
Sexual Harassment.................. 198
Simon, Paul....................... 200
Sixth Amendment 200
Social Security..................... 203
Sports Law 204
Telecommunications 207
Television........................ 209
Terrorism 210
Tobacco 218
Tort Law 219
Trademarks....................... 220
Truth in Lending Act 221
Uniform Commercial Code 223

Victims' Rights 225
Voting 226
Warsaw Convention 229
Water Rights...................... 230

Bibliography *233*

Appendix (documents):
   Elections: The Bipartisan Campaign
      Finance Reform Act of 2002 255
   E-mail: The CAN SPAM Act 258
   Fetal Rights: Laci and Conner's Act... 259
   Telecommunications: Do-Not-Call
      Implementation Act 260

Glossary of Legal Terms *263*

Abbreviations *287*

Table of Cases Cited.................. *307*

Index by Name and Subject............. *311*

PREFACE

The need for a layperson's comprehensive, understandable guide to terms, concepts, and historical developments in U.S. law has been well met by *West's Encyclopedia of American Law* (*WEAL*). Published in a second edition in 2004 by Thomson Gale, *WEAL* has proved itself a valuable successor to West's 1983 publication, *The Guide to American Law: Everyone's Legal Encyclopedia*. and the 1997 first edition of WEAL.

Since 1998, Thomson Gale, a premier reference publisher, has extended the value of *WEAL* with the publication of *American Law Yearbook* (*ALY*). This supplement adds entries on emerging topics not covered in the main set. A legal reference must be current to be authoritative, so *ALY* is a vital companion to a key reference source. Uniform organization by *WEAL* term and cross-referencing make it easy to use the titles together, while inclusion of key definitions and summaries of earlier rulings in supplement entries—whether new or continuations—make it unnecessary to refer to the main set constantly.

Understanding the American Legal System

The U.S. legal system is admired around the world for the freedoms it allows the individual and the fairness with which it attempts to treat all persons. On the surface, it may seem simple, yet those who have delved into it know that this system of federal and state constitutions, statutes, regulations, and common-law decisions is elaborate and complex. It derives from the English common law, but includes principles older than England, along with some principles from other lands. The U.S. legal system, like many others, has a language all its own, but too often it is an unfamiliar language: many concepts are still phrased in Latin. *WEAL* explains legal terms and concepts in everyday language, however. It covers a wide variety of persons, entities, and events that have shaped the U.S. legal system and influenced public perceptions of it.

FEATURES OF THIS SUPPLEMENT

Entries

ALY 2004 contains 162 entries covering individuals, cases, laws, and concepts significant to U.S. law. Entries are arranged alphabetically and use the same entry title as in *WEAL* or *ALY*—when introduced in an earlier *Yearbook* (e.g., September 11th Attacks). There may be several cases discussed under a given topic.

Profiles of individuals cover interesting and influential people from the world of law, government, and public life, both historic and contemporary. All have contributed to U.S. law as a whole. Each short biography includes a timeline highlighting important moments in the subject's life. Persons whose lives were detailed in *WEAL*, but who have died since publication of that work, receive short obituary entries in *ALY*.

Definitions

Each entry on a legal term is preceded by a definition, which is easily distinguished by its sans serif typeface. The back of the book includes a Glossary of Legal Terms containing the definitions for the terms **bolded** in the text of the essays and biographies.

Cross References

To facilitate research, *ALY 2004* provides two types of cross-references: within and following entries. Within the entries, terms are set in small capital letters (e.g., FIRST AMENDMENT) to indicate that they have their own entry in *WEAL*. At the end of each entry, additional relevant topics in *ALY 2004* are listed alphabetically by title.

In Focus Pieces

In Focus pieces present additional facts, details, and arguments on particularly interesting, important, or controversial issues. These pieces are set apart from the main entries with boxed edges and their own logo.

Appendix

This section follows the Glossary of Legal Terms and features the text of documents complementary to the main entries, such as the CAN SPAM Act and the Unborn Victims of Violence Act of 2004.

Table of Cases Cited and Index by Name and Subject

These features make it quick and easy for users to locate references to cases, people, statutes, events, and other subjects. The Table of Cases Cited traces the influences of legal precedents by identifying cases mentioned throughout the text. In a departure from *WEAL*, references to individuals have been folded into the general index to simplify searches. Litigants, justices, historical and contemporary figures, as well as topical references are included in the Index by Name and Subject.

Citations

Wherever possible, *ALY* includes citations to cases and statutes for readers wishing to do further research. They refer to one or more series, called "reporters," which publish court opinions and related information. Each citation includes a volume number, an abbreviation for the reporter, and the starting page reference. Underscores in a citation indicate that a court opinion has not been officially reported as of *ALY*'s publication. Two sample citations, with explanations, are presented below.

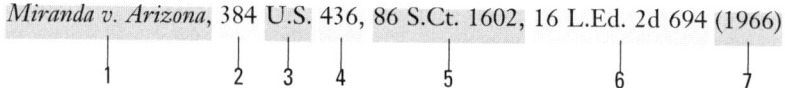

Miranda v. Arizona, 384 U.S. 436, 86 S.Ct. 1602, 16 L.Ed. 2d 694 (1966)

1 2 3 4 5 6 7

1. *Case title.* The title of the case is set in i and indicates the names of the parties. The suit in this sample citation was between Ernesto A. Miranda and the state of Arizona.

2. *Reporter volume number.* The number preceding the reporter abbreviation indicates the reporter volume containing the case. The volume number appears on the spine of the reporter, along with the reporter abbreviation.

3. *Reporter abbreviation.* The suit in the sample citation is from the reporter, or series of books, called *U.S. Reports,* which contains cases from the U.S. Supreme Court. Numerous reporters publish cases from the federal and state courts; consult the Abbreviations list at the back of this volume for full titles.

4. *Reporter page.* The number following the reporter abbreviation indicates the reporter page on which the case begins.

5. *Additional reporter citation.* Many cases may be found in more than one reporter. The suit in the sample citation also appears in volume 86 of the *Supreme Court Reporter,* beginning on page 1602.

6. *Additional reporter citation.* The suit in the sample citation is also reported in volume 16 of the *Lawyer's Edition,* second series, beginning on page 694.

7. *Year of decision.* The year the court issued its decision in the case appears in parentheses at the end of the cite.

PREFACE IX

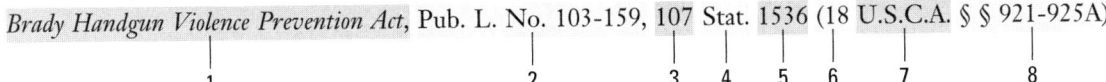

1. Statute title.

2. *Public law number.* In the sample citation, the number 103 indicates this law was passed by the 103d Congress, and the number 159 indicates it was the 159th law passed by that Congress.

3. *Reporter volume number.* The number preceding the reporter abbreviation indicates the reporter volume containing the statute.

4. *Reporter abbreviation.* The name of the reporter is abbreviated. The statute in the sample citation is from *Statutes at Large.*

5. *Reporter page.* The number following the reporter abbreviation indicates the reporter page on which the statute begins.

6. *Title number.* Federal laws are divided into major sections with specific titles. The number preceding a reference to the U.S. Code stands for the section called Crimes and Criminal Procedure.

7. *Additional reporter.* The statute in the sample citation may also be found in the *U.S. Code Annotated.*

8. *Section numbers.* The section numbers following a reference to the *U.S. Code Annotated* indicate where the statute appears in that reporter.

COMMENTS WELCOME

Considerable efforts were expended at the time of publication to ensure the accuracy of the information presented in *American Law Yearbook 2004*. The editor welcomes your comments and suggestions for enhancing and improving future editions of this supplement to *West's Encyclopedia of American Law*. Send comments and suggestions to:

American Law Yearbook
Thomson Gale
27500 Drake Rd.
Farmington Hills, MI 48331-3535

ACKNOWLEDGMENTS

SPECIAL THANKS

The editor wishes to acknowledge the contributions of the writers and copyeditors who aided in the compilation of *American Law Yearbook*. The editor gratefully thanks Matthew Cordon, Frederick K. Grittner, Lauri R. Harding, John Harper, David R. Johnstone, Jeff Lilly, Mary Hertz Scarbrough, and Scott D. Slick. Furthermore, valuable content review of entries came from: Matthew Cordon, Frederick K. Grittner, and Lauri R. Harding.

PHOTOGRAPHIC CREDITS

The editor wishes to thank the permission managers of the companies that assisted in securing reprint rights. The following list—in order of appearance—acknowledges the copyright holders who have granted us permission to reprint material in this edition of *American Law Yearbook*:

Altmann, Maria, photograph. AP/Wide World Photos. Reproduced by permission. **Anderson, Ryan,** yearbook photo. AP/Wide World Photos. Reproduced by permission. **Banks, LaShawn, hands behind back, right, with lawyer on left in front of building.** AP/Wide World Photos. Reproduced by permission. **Bryant, Kobe,** photograph, with security and lawyer following. AP/Wide World Photos. Reproduced by permission. **Conte, Victor, smiling, with vitamin stocks behind him, holding framed photo of Barry Bonds.** AP/Wide World Photos. Reproduced by permission. **Copy of the Bill of Rights,** photograph. AP/Wide World Photos. Reproduced by permission. **Court illustration of four defendants in terrorism trial, Detroit 2003.** AP/Wide World Photos. Reproduced by permission. **Davey, Joshua,** photograph. AP/Wide World Photos. Reproduced by permission. **Durst, Robert,** photograph. AP/Wide World Photos. Reproduced by permission. **Faris, Lyman,** photograph. AP/Wide World Photos. Reproduced by permission. **Favish, Allan,** photograph. AP/Wide World Photos. Reproduced by permission. **Four computer company executives sitting in front of banner announcing CAN SPAM law.** AP/Wide World Photos. Reproduced by permission. **Franklin, Daniel,** photograph. AP/Wide World Photos. Reproduced by permission. **Franklin, Gary,** photograph. AP/Wide World Photos. Reproduced by permission. **Gaiman, Neil,** photograph. AP/Wide World Photos. Reproduced by permission. **Gray Davis,** photograph. AP/Wide World Photos. Reproduced by permission. **Hernandez, Joel,** photograph. AP/Wide World Photos. Reproduced by permission. **Hnida, Katie,** photograph. AP/Wide World Photos. Reproduced by permission. **Jackson, Michael,** photograph. AP/Wide World Photos. Reproduced by permission. **Janklow, Bill,** photograph. AP/Wide World Photos. Reproduced by permission. **Lane, George,** photograph. AP/Wide World Photos. Reproduced by permission. **Luster, Andrew,** photograph. AP/Wide World Photos. Reproduced by permission. **McBride, Darl,** photograph. AP/Wide World Photos. Reproduced by permission. **McConnell, Mitch,** photograph. AP/Wide World Photos. Reproduced by permission. **McCoy, Charles, Jr.,** photograph. AP/Wide World Photos. Reproduced by permission. **Newson, Gavin, San Francisco**

mayor, photograph. AP/Wide World Photos. Reproduced by permission. **Olson, Molly left, and Olson, Jim, right,** photograph. AP/Wide World Photos. Reproduced by permission. **Peterson, Scott,** photograph. AP/Wide World Photos. Reproduced by permission. **Schiavo, Michael,** photograph. AP/Wide World Photos. Reproduced by permission. **Seibert, Patrice,** photograph. AP/Wide World Photos. Reproduced by permission. **Skilling, Jeffrey,** photograph. AP/Wide World Photos. Reproduced by permission. **Smith, Robert,** photograph. AP/Wide World Photos. Reproduced by permission. **Spector, Phil,** photograph. AP/Wide World Photos. Reproduced by permission. **Stewart, Martha,** photograph. AP/Wide World Photos. Reproduced by permission. **Suders, Nancy,** photograph. AP/Wide World Photos. Reproduced by permission. **Summerlin, War-** **ren,** photograph. AP/Wide World Photos. Reproduced by permission. **Tate, Lionel,** photograph. AP/Wide World Photos. Reproduced by permission. **The dungeon of rapist John Jamelske,** photograph. AP/Wide World Photos. Reproduced by permission. **Timberlake, Justin, staring down at Janet Jackson during Superbowl performance, 2004.** AP/Wide World Photos. Reproduced by permission. **Venn, Desmon,** photograph. AP/Wide World Photos. Reproduced by permission. **William Buffalo Tiger,** photograph. AP/Wide World Photos. Reproduced by permission. **Williams, Jayson,** photograph. AP/Wide World Photos. Reproduced by permission. **Wilson, Edwin,** photograph. AP/Wide World Photos. Reproduced by permission. **Woolston, Thomas,** photograph. AP/Wide World Photos. Reproduced by permission.

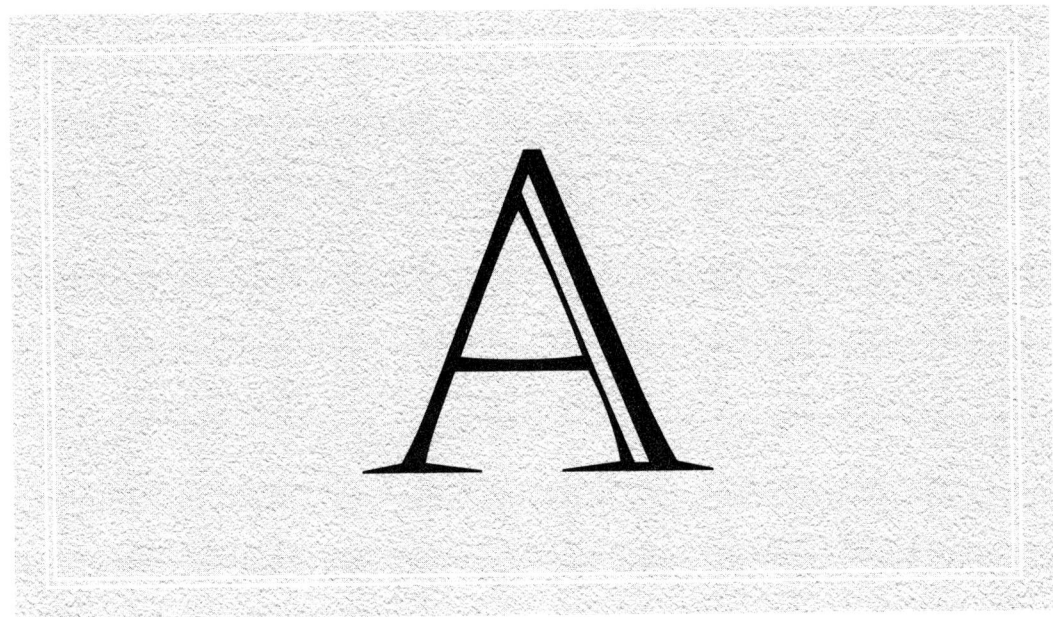

ABORTION

The spontaneous or artificially induced expulsion of an embryo or fetus. As used in legal context, the term usually refers to induced abortion.

Roe v. Wade Continues to Make Headlines Three Decades After Landmark Abortion Decision

More than three decades after the United States Supreme Court issued its decision in the abortion case of *Roe v. Wade* 410 U.S. 113 (1973), the ruling remains as controversial as ever. In 2003 and 2004, the case made headlines again when the original plaintiff, "Jane Roe," filed suit to have the case reversed. In addition, in 2004 the private papers of the late Supreme Court Justice HARRY A. BLACKMUN were unsealed. Blackmun's papers revealed that the nation's highest court very nearly overturned *Roe* in 1992.

Norma McCorvey was "Jane Roe" in the case. In 1970, McCorvey, a resident of Dallas, wanted to have an abortion. The procedure was illegal under Texas law at the time. McCorvey's attorneys, on her behalf and as a representative of all Texas women, sued Dallas County District Attorney Henry Wade. They sought a **declaratory judgment** that the Texas abortion **statute** was unconstitutional. McCorvey eventually gave birth and put the child up for adoption, but the case was allowed to proceed through the court system. On January 22, 1973, the Supreme Court issued its ruling in the case.

Blackmun wrote the 7-2 opinion. The Supreme Court ruled that a woman is constitutionally entitled to an abortion during the first trimester of pregnancy. After the first trimester, certain state interests came into play that would limit the circumstances when abortion would be appropriate. The decision was based upon guarantees found in the First, Ninth, and Fourteenth Amendments, including a constitutional right to **privacy**. A right to privacy is not specifically **enumerated** in the Constitution, but is implied therein, the Supreme Court has ruled.

McCorvey, once an advocate for a woman's right to abortion, eventually became an outspoken advocate against it. She now has a ministry devoted to pro-life issues. In 2003, she filed suit in federal district court in Texas to ask that *Roe v. Wade* be reversed. According to the district court, McCorvey sought to reopen the old **judgment** so the court could "conduct a wide-ranging inquiry into whether *Roe* is still good law in view of more recent Supreme Court decisions and the current state of scientific knowledge."

McCorvey based her request on Federal Rule of Civil Procedure Rule 60(b). That rule provides a limited exception to the finality of judgments. A request under Rule 60(b) must be made within a "reasonable time." Timeliness in bringing a 60(b) motion is important because the judicial process has as its aim orderliness, predictability, and finality.

In a decision dated June 19, 2003, Federal District Court Judge David C. Godbey denied McCorvey's request to reopen the case. Godbey stated, "Court opinions measure 'reasonable time' under Rule 60(b) in weeks or months, not in decades. Thirty years is manifestly not a reasonable time." Godbey examined the facts of McCorvey's case, and concluded that she had failed to carry her **burden of proof** that she made her motion within a **reasonable time**. Moreover, the court noted, no case "remotely close to thirty years" has ever been found to constitute a reasonable time under Rule 60(b).

Judge Godbey concluded,

Whatever else it may or may not have done, the Supreme Court's *Roe* decision thirty years ago ended *this* lawsuit between *these* parties. Whether or not the Supreme Court was infallible, its *Roe* decision was certainly final in this litigation. It is simply too late now, thirty years after the fact, for McCorvey to revisit that judgment. Other parties in other cases may be able to reexamine those issues, but not McCorvey in this case.

McCorvey has appealed the district court's decision. The Fifth **Circuit Court** of Appeals will decide the case without hearing oral argument.

Roe's author, Justice Blackmun, died in 1999. According to his wishes, Blackmun's papers were made available to the public through the LIBRARY OF CONGRESS five years after his death. Blackmun was a copious note taker. His records reveal not only an insight into the legal maneuvering and reasoning behind court decisions, but also provide an interesting insight into various personalities on the court.

Roe was released on January 22, 1973. It was ready sooner, but Chief Justice WARREN E. BURGER withheld his approval from the majority opinion for a time. Blackmun's papers indicate he believed the delay came about so that the decision would not upstage or embarrass President RICHARD M. NIXON on his second inauguration on January 20. Blackmun's extensive records indicate that initially the high court did not realize the explosive nature of the case. The fallout from *Roe* resulted in tens of thousands of angry letters to the Supreme Court, as well as threats on Blackmun's life.

Blackmun's papers also tell how Roe was nearly overturned in the 1992 case, *Planned Parenthood v. Casey* 505 U.S. 833 (1992). For a time after the oral arguments, it appeared that that the vote would be 5 to 4 against a woman's right to have an abortion. Initially, Chief Justice WILLIAM H. REHNQUIST, and Justices BYRON WHITE, ANTONIN SCALIA, CLARENCE THOMAS, and ANTHONY M. KENNEDY favored overturning *Roe*. Unexpectedly, Kennedy switched his vote.

While Rehnquist was crafting the majority opinion, Kennedy was reconsidering his stance. He sent a note to Blackmun, asking to meet. He then gave Blackmun the news that he had changed his mind. Blackmun later scribbled on a memo pad, "Roe sound." The minority became the majority.

Blackmun, a Nixon appointee, took his seat in 1970. All the justices who voted to uphold a woman's right to abortion in *Planned Parenthood v. Casey* were Republican appointees. The justices were JOHN PAUL STEVENS, SANDRA DAY O'CONNOR, DAVID SOUTER, Kennedy, and Blackmun.

Five-week-old Fetus is a "Member" of the Mother's Body for Purposes of Attempted Sexual Assault Statute

A man was convicted of sexual assault and attempted assault for inserting prescription pills into his girlfriend's vagina for the purpose of causing her to abort her five-week-old fetus. The Connecticut Supreme Court ruled that the fetus constituted a part of the mother's body and, therefore, was a member of her body within meaning of the laws criminalizing attempted aggravated sexual assault in the first degree and attempted assault in the first degree. *State v. Sandoval*, 263 Conn. 524, 821 A.2d 247 (Conn. 2003).

The case arose out of a four-year relationship between Edwin Sandoval, a 32-year-old civil engineer residing in East Hartford, Connecticut, and his girlfriend (hereinafter "the victim"), whose name and age were withheld from the legal proceedings. Their relationship began to deteriorate on August 5, 1998, when the victim informed Sandoval, a native of Peru, that she was five weeks pregnant.

Sandoval told the victim, also a native Peruvian, that he did not want her to have the baby, and urged her to have an abortion. The victim refused, and the **defendant** left. Four days later Sandoval went to the victim's home ostensibly to have breakfast, during which he asked the victim to have sex with him. She agreed. During intercourse, the victim later testified that the Sandoval forcibly shoved his fingers into her vagina, something he had never done before. The victim asked him to stop immediately, as she was experiencing sharp pain.

Sandoval ate breakfast at the victim's home again on August 10, after which the two had sex, during which he again forcibly shoved his fingers into her vagina until she complained of pain and made him quit. Still experiencing pain and some hemorrhaging at approximately 2:45 p.m. that same day, the victim went to see her obstetrician-gynecologist, Marcia Waitzman. Conducting an internal examination, Waitzman discovered two partially dissolved white pills three to four inches inside the victim's vagina.

Both pills bore the legends "Searle" and "1461." Toxicology tests later identified the pills as Cytotec, a prescription medication containing misoprostol. Misoprostol is an abortifacient that can cause a woman to suffer a miscarriage by inducing strong uterine contractions. The victim denied having inserted the pills herself. The victim did indicate, however, that Sandoval's brother worked as a physician in Peru, where misoprostol is used to induce labor and abort pregnancies.

Waitzman then called the local police department to report the incident. After the victim signed a written statement, the police procured a search warrant for Sandoval's home, where they found a plate covered with white powder residue, an emery board, a hammer, and instructions for administering medication intravaginally. The police also found three white pills bearing the names "Searle" and "1461." Lab tests confirmed that the pills were Cytotec.

Sandoval was then arrested and charged with 12 different **felony** counts, ranging from first-degree sexual assault and attempted sexual assault to **aggravated assault** and attempted assault. See Connecticut General Statutes sections 53a-70a (a)(2), 53a-70 (a)(1), 53a-60 (a), 53a-59 (a), 53a-49 (a)(2). Sandoval argued he could not be convicted on any of the charges because the fetus was the target, not the mother. But the jury was not persuaded, convicting him on seven charges of varying degrees of sexual assault and attempted assault. The trial judge sentenced the defendant to two years in prison and ten years probation. In sentencing the defendant, the judge took notice of the fact that the victim gave birth to a healthy baby in March 1999.

On **appeal**, the Connecticut Supreme Court unanimously affirmed the defendant's conviction. The Connecticut high court rejected Sandoval's argument that the state had failed to prove that he had assaulted the victim with "intent . . . to destroy . . . or disable permanently a member or organ of [her] body," as required by the laws prohibiting first-degree sexual assault and first-degree attempted assault. See C.G.S.A. §§ 53a-70a(a)(2), 53a-59(a)(2). Because the state conceded that the five-week-old fetus was not an "organ" in the victim's body, the case turned on the meaning of the word "member," a term not defined anywhere in the state's penal code.

The supreme court began its analysis by noting that both parties agreed that the word "member" as used in the statute means roughly the same as "bodily part." The court then observed that Webster's Third New International Dictionary defines the term "part" as "one of the equal or unequal portions into which something is or is regarded as divided: something less than a whole: a unit (as a number, quantity, or mass) held to constitute with one or more other units something larger: constituent, fraction, fragment, member, piece. . . ."

The court then reasoned that "as with any bodily part, a fetus constitutes physically identifiable tissue. . . . [I]mplantation of the fetus occurs within the mother's uterus, and the fetus is attached to the mother via the umbilical cord and placenta." In light of the state's compelling interest in safeguarding life and limb, the court said it was "unwilling to presume that the legislature sought to protect a person's ear, tongue, and skin but not a developing fetus living within, and physically attached to, the mother." To conclude otherwise, the court emphasized, "would not only yield an untenable result but would require us to ignore the policy that those statutory provisions were designed to implement, a result that is inconsistent with our duty to give voice to the legislative **intent** underlying those provisions."

Although the defendant contended that, because a fetus is attached to a part of the mother's body that is shed routinely every month as part of menstruation, namely, the endometrial lining of the uterus, the fetus cannot be considered a "member" of the mother's body. The court responded to this argument by pointing out that teeth, hair, and skin are also lost during the course of a person's lifetime, and had the defendant's conduct caused the victim to lose any of these parts there would be no doubt that he had committed assault as defined by the statute. Thus, the court concluded that the five-week-old fetus was a "member" of the victim's body for the purposes of the assault and sexual assault laws under which the defendant was convicted.

The Connecticut Supreme Court's opinion received mixed reviews from both sides of the abortion debate. Anti-abortion groups applauded the court's protection of the fetus, but criticized the identification of a fetus as a body part. "[The fetus] could have had a different blood type, and certainly it had different DNA," said Bill O'Brien, vice president of the Connecticut Right to Life Corporation. "Any time I hear about giving rights to fetuses, I get concerned," said Elaine Werner, executive director of the Connecticut chapter of the National Abortion and Reproductive Rights Action League. "That's the slippery slope to eroding *Roe vs. Wade*." Senior Assistant State's Attorney Timothy J. Sugrue said the decision sets a precedent for Connecticut in cases where a fetus is the target of an attack, and for other states seeking guidance in similar cases.

Federal Judge Strikes down State Ban on Partial Birth Abortions

The U.S. District Court for the Eastern District of Virginia ruled that Virginia's law banning one type of late-term abortion is unconstitutional, striking down a state law that uses language mirroring the federal ban signed into law in 2003. *Richmond Medical Center v. Hicks*, ___ F.Supp.2d ___, 2004 WL 199300 (E.D.Va. 2004). Virginia's law made illegal what opponents **call** partial-birth abortion, a procedure in which a fetus is partially delivered, generally in the second or third trimester, before being aborted. Judge Richard L. Williams found that the law "impermissibly infringe[d] on the fundamental right to choose an abortion" and endangered women's health, citing a U.S. SUPREME COURT ruling that struck down a similar law in Nebraska.

In issuing his ruling, Williams granted the motion to dismiss brought by the plaintiffs, a group of Virginia physicians, medical clinics, and health care workers who challenged a 2003 law passed by Virginia General Assembly. The law made it a Class 4 **felony** for a person to knowingly perform "partial birth infanticide." West's V.C.A. § 18.2-71.1. The **statute** defines partial birth infanticide as "any **deliberate** act that (i) is intended to kill a human infant who has been born alive, but who has not been completely extracted or expelled from its mother, and that (ii) does kill such infant, regardless of whether death occurs before or after extraction or expulsion from its mother has been completed." Persons convicted under the law faced a prison term of up to ten years and a fine of up to $100,000.

Subsection E of the Act provided a limited exception from prosecution for persons who perform the procedure to save the life of the woman:

> This section shall not prohibit the use by a physician of any procedure that, in reasonable medical **judgment**, is necessary to prevent the death of the mother, so long as the physician takes every medically reasonable step, consistent with such procedure, to preserve the life and health of the infant. A procedure shall not be deemed necessary to prevent the death of the mother if completing the delivery of the living infant would prevent the death of the mother.

Health care workers who performed the procedure to preserve the life of the mother were still subject to prosecution under the law, and the law made no distinction between persons who performed the procedure before or after the fetus had reached viability.

However, the law did distinguish between a "dilation and evacuation" procedure ("D & E"), whereby the body of the fetus is dismembered before removal from the vagina, and an "intact dilation and evacuation" procedure ("intact D & E"), where the fetus remains unharmed until removed from the vagina, at which point it may show signs of life before being aborted. According to expert medical testimony presented by the plaintiffs, D & E is the most common method of pre-viability second-trimester abortion, accounting for approximately 96 percent of all such abortions in the United States.

Doctors also testified that intact D & E's have many safety advantages over D & E's involving dismemberment. In a D & E in which the physician dismembers the fetus, sharp instruments and sharp fetal fragments may damage the woman's uterus. When the fetus remains intact during a D & E, the risks of uterine perforation, cervical rupture, infection, and retained fetal tissue are reduced. That is so because the procedure is less invasive; an intact fetus allows the physician to avoid the repeated insertion of sharp instruments into the woman's uterus, and the fetus passes through the birth canal intact.

In striking down the state law, Judge Williams relied on the U.S. Supreme Court's decision in *Stenberg v. Carhart*, 530 U.S. 914, 120 S.Ct. 2597, 147 L.Ed.2d 743 (U.S. 2000), which invalidated a Nebraska statute banning partial birth abortions. The Court said the Nebraska law was unconstitutional for two reasons: (1) because it caused all those who perform abortion procedures using the D & E method to fear prosecution, conviction, and imprisonment," thereby placing an undue burden upon a woman's right to make an abortion decision; and, (2) because it failed to contain a health exception even though substantial medical authority supported the proposition that banning intact D & E's would endanger women's health. Judge Williams found the Virginia law "unconstitutional on its face for precisely the same reasons" as *Stenberg.*.

The Virginia federal district court decision in *Richmond Medical Center v. Hicks* came less than three months after President GEORGE W. BUSH signed into law the Partial-Birth Abortion Ban Act of 2003. PL 108-105. In passing the act, which is codified at 18 U.S.C.A. § 1531, Congress made clear that it was taking aim at *Stenberg*. The public law makes specific findings that

> substantial evidence presented at the *Stenberg* trial and overwhelming evidence presented...at extensive congressional hearings, much of which was compiled after the district court hearing in *Stenberg*, and thus not included in the *Stenberg* trial record, demonstrates that a partial-birth abortion is never necessary to preserve the health of a woman, poses significant health risks to a woman upon whom the procedure is performed and is outside the standard of medical care. . . . Thus, in *Stenberg*, the . . . Supreme Court was required to accept the very questionable findings issued by the district court judge—the effect of which was to **render null** and void the reasoned factual findings and policy determinations of the United States Congress and at least 27 State legislatures.

Despite these specific Congressional findings, three separate federal district courts stopped the Partial-Birth Abortion Ban Act of 2003 from going into effect, holding that it was unconstitutional under *Stenberg*. U.S. **Attorney General** JOHN ASHCROFT vowed to **appeal** those decisions. Similarly, Virginia Attorney General Jerry W. Kilgore, who is expected to run for state governor in 2005, has said he will appeal the federal district court decision in *Richmond Medical Center v. Hicks*.

AGE DISCRIMINATION

Prejudicial treatment or denial of rights based on age.

Age Discrimination in Employment Act Does Not Cover Reverse Discrimination Claims

The Age Discrimination in Employment Act of 1967 (ADEA), 29 U.S.C.A. §§ 621 *et seq.*, outlawed discrimination by employers against employees or applicants over the age of 40. The ADEA was enacted to protect older workers from arbitrary employment practices, such as the setting up of age requirements unrelated to the ability needed for the job, and to meet the problem of the increasing numbers of older workers who are unable to regain employment after job displacement, a situation resulting in deterioration of skills, morale, and employability. The scope of the ADEA ban against age discrimination was tested in *General Dynamics Land Systems, Inc. v. Cline*, 124 S.Ct. 1236, 157 L.Ed.2d 1094 (2004). In this case the U.S. SUPREME COURT rejected the argument that the ADEA prohibited employers from favoring older workers over younger ones. In so ruling, the Court rejected the theory of reverse discrimination.

The case arose after General Dynamics and the United Auto Workers signed a collective bargaining agreement in 1997 that eliminated the company's obligation to provide health benefits to workers who retired in the future. However, the agreement granted these retirement benefits to currently employed workers who were at least 50 years old. A group of workers, including Dennis Cline, who were over 40, and thereby covered by the ADEA, but under 50, sued General Dynamics, alleging that the new terms constituted age discrimination. The plaintiffs filed a claim with the EQUAL EMPLOYMENT OPPORTUNITY COMMISSION (EEOC), which agreed that the agreement violated the ADEA. After failing to negotiate a settlement with General Dynamics, the plaintiffs filed an ADEA suit in federal district court. The court dismissed the suit, ruling that the courts had never recognized such a "reverse discrimination" claim. *Cline v. General Dynamics Land Systems, Inc.*, 98 F. Supp. 2d 846 (N.D. Ohio 2000) On **appeal** the Sixth **Circuit Court** of Appeals reversed this decision, concluding that the ADEA's language barring discrimination against "any individual . . . because of such individual's age" clearly prohibited the retirement health care benefit for older workers. *Cline v. General Dynamics Land Systems, Inc.*, 296 F.3d 466 (6th Cir. 2002)

The Supreme Court, in a 6-3 decision, overturned the Sixth Circuit decision. Justice DAVID

SOUTER, in his majority opinion, noted that the key question was what the word "age" meant. In his view, Congress sought to address discrimination that helped younger workers by hurting older workers. Souter reviewed the **legislative history** of the ADEA, pointing out that there was no evidence that "workers were registering complaints about discrimination in favor of their seniors." To the contrary, the record was filled with complaints about employment practices that forced older workers from their jobs. In sum, the ADEA "was concerned to protect a relatively old worker from discrimination that works to the advantage of the relatively young."

Souter buttressed his legislative **interpretation** by looking at societal and cultural views on age. He cited the commonplace description of U.S. "youth culture," where "younger is better." Therefore, discrimination based on age is commonly understood to "refer to discrimination against the older." If Congress had truly sought to protect younger workers it would not have ignored workers under 40.

The majority rejected three arguments advanced by Cline and the other younger workers. First, the Court rejected the claim that the ADEA's use of the word "age" must be given its natural and ordinary meaning throughout the entire **statute**. Justice Souter found that the word had different meanings in various sections of the law. The word "age" in the context of this case clearly referred to "old age" when linked with the word "discrimination." The plaintiffs advanced a second argument, noting that in a Senate floor debate a sponsor of the ADEA had commented that the law would prohibit age as a factor in the decision to hire "as to one age over the other, whichever way [the] decision went." Justice Souter dismissed the significance of this statement because it was, in all the voluminous hearings, reports and debates, the only item "going against the grain of the common understanding of age discrimination." Finally, the plaintiffs had argued that the EEOC had adopted a regulation in 1981 that was consistent with the comment made by the sponsor on the Senate floor. The Supreme Court typically grants great deference to administrative readings of statutes, as agencies are tasked with the job of enforcing these laws. However, in this case the majority refused to give the EEOC regulation any deference because the commission "is clearly wrong." Therefore, the reverse discrimination claim had no basis in the language or legislative history of the ADEA and must be dismissed.

Justices ANTONIN SCALIA, ANTHONY KENNEDY and CLARENCE THOMAS dissented. Justice Scalia argued that the EEOC reading of the law should have been followed. Justice Thomas, in an opinion by Kennedy, looked at the words of the ADEA and agreed with the plaintiffs that the common meaning of the word "age" clearly prohibited "discrimination because of an individual's age, whether the individual is too old or too young."

ALIENS

Foreign-born persons who have not been naturalized to become U.S. citizens under federal law and the Constitution.

Bush Proposal for Temporary Legal Status of Immigrant Workers

Prior to the SEPTEMBER 11TH ATTACKS in 2001, the Bush administration had launched a joint effort with Mexican President Vincente Fox to garner support for legalizing the status of illegal Mexican immigrants, a group accounting for half of the estimated eight million total U.S. illegal **aliens**. In return, Mexico would assist in tightening security along the border. President Bush's plan fell silent following the terrorist attacks, although, to the anger of many Mexican officials, border patrols were subsequently enhanced.

In January 2004, Bush again confronted the unpopular issue by openly proposing temporary legal status for *all* illegal immigrants who were employed in the United States. Gathering a group of congressional delegates, presidential cabinet members, and immigration advocates in the East Room of the White House, the president talked frankly about the problem. The immigration system, Bush said, failed to keep borders safe and did not address the candid reality of the underground economy that relied on illegal immigrants. "Reform must begin by confronting a basic fact of life and economics," stated Bush, as quoted by Elizabeth Llorente in Hackersack, New Jersey's *The Record*. "Some of the jobs being generated in America's growing economy are jobs American citizens are not filling." He went on to say that foreigners who would do the least desirable work that Americans would *not* do should not be relegated to the shadows, unprotected from abusive employers and conditions, and afraid to report crimes. Moreover, he proposed that bringing immigrants out of the shadows would provide the United States with a better accounting of the identities of those living in the country illegally. With fewer undocumented persons in hiding, law enforcement authorities could better focus their attention on the real security problems.

Referring to his proposal as the "temporary worker program," Bush offered a plan under which undocumented immigrants would be eligible for temporary legal status for three years, providing they remained employed. Although workers could renew their status for another three years, the Bush plan offered financial incentives to those who returned to their home countries. To protect against identity compromises, workers would be given biometrically encoded cards, enabling them to travel freely to and from their home countries. Under the plan, no fees for temporary status would be charged to workers entering the country, but those already in the United States would pay an unspecified fee. Employers that sponsored immigrants would need to certify that no Americans were available to fill the work vacancies.

The proposal was met with predictably mixed reviews. Supporters appreciated Bush's public acknowledgment of the economic dependency on low-paying or undesirable jobs that were hard to fill, while opponents likened the plan to an amnesty that rewarded illegal conduct. A third category of immigration advocates complained that the plan did not go far enough, holding that it failed to provide a path toward permanent residency and citizenship for illegal aliens.

Originally, support and criticism crossed party lines, but in the ensuing months, the matter began to show signs of political polarization. In May 2004, Democratic lawmakers led by Senator EDWARD KENNEDY (D-MA) and Representatives Luis Gutierrez (D-IL) and Robert Menendez (D-NJ) unveiled their own plan. The Democrats' Safe, Orderly Legal Visas and Enforcement (SOLVE) Act, introduced as S. 2381 and H.R. 4262, proposed to grant legal residency to all undocumented aliens who had resided in the United States for at least five years and who could provide **proof** of employment for 24 months. Immigrants already in the United States could become eligible by working for two years, starting with the effective date of the bill.

More specifically, the SOLVE Act proposed to grant permanent residency to persons living in the United States for five years, working 24 months, passing a background check and medical examination, and demonstrating proficiency in the English language. In contrast, the Bush proposal also required background checks, but workers would have to apply separately for residency with no special consideration. Both plans required employers to certify that U.S. citizens were not available for hire, but the SOLVE proposal added a requirement that the U.S. DEPARTMENT OF LABOR first find that employment of foreign workers would not adversely affect the wages and working conditions of U.S. workers. The key difference between the two plans was that the Democratic proposal aimed for permanent residency status of illegal aliens along with encouragement of legal immigration for their family members, while the Bush proposal for temporary status offered a tax-sheltered account for workers to **set aside** monies to return home (with workers getting credit for Social Security contributions).

Lawmakers expressed hope that a final bill could be passed before the year's congressional recess. As of 2004, there was an estimated backlog of 5.5 million persons who had applied for legal immigration benefits. The 2000 census indicated that some 500,000 to 700,000 illegal aliens were settling in the United States each year. Under the still-effective 1986 Immigration Reform and Control Act (IRCA), employment-related green cards were limited to 140,000 annually.

AMERICANS WITH DISABILITIES ACT

Supreme Court Upholds Access to the Court for Disabled Persons

Under **Title** II of the Americans with Disabilities Act of 1990 (ADA), 42 U.S.C.A. §§ 12131-12165, a person with a qualifying disability shall not "be excluded from participation in or be denied the benefits of the services, programs or activities of a public **entity**, or be subjected to discrimination by any such entity." State governments have argued that disabled persons cannot sue them for alleged violations of the ADA because the Eleventh Amendment bars lawsuits for damages against states. The Supreme Court has ruled that the ELEVENTH AMENDMENT bars such suits brought under Title I, but in *Tennessee v. Lane*, __ U.S. __, 124 S.Ct. 1978, 158 L.Ed.2d 820 (2004) the Court ruled that Title II suits that deal with access to the courts are not barred by state **sovereign immunity** under the Eleventh Amendment. The ruling, while important, leaves open whether lawsuits based on access to other state and local government facilities are permitted.

George Lane and Beverly Jones, both paraplegics, filed a federal lawsuit under Title II

ADA COMPLIANCE OF INTERNET SITES

Congress enacted the Americans with Disabilities Act (ADA), Pub. L. No. 101-336, 104 Stat. 327 (codified at 42 U.S.C. §§ 12101 et seq.) to provide "a clear and comprehensive national mandate for the elimination of discrimination against individuals with disabilities." At the time of its enactment, nearly forty-three million Americans suffered from physical or mental disabilities, and Congress recognized "unfair and unnecessary discrimination and prejudice" that existed with respect to the treatment of those persons with disabilities. Also at the time of the enactment of the ADA, the Internet was largely still in its developmental stages, and only a relatively small percentage of the American public could access this form of communication.

In the years that followed the enactment of the ADA, use of the Internet ballooned. Corporations, governmental entities, education providers, private individuals, and many others developed Web sites. By many estimates, nearly six hundred million people worldwide are now Internet users, and these numbers continue to grow. However, many individuals with disabilities have been limited in the number of Web pages they can access due to visual, auditory, or other limitations.

Title III of the ADA prohibits discrimination in places of "public accommodation." In 1996, the Justice Department issued an opinion indicating that this prohibition should extend to Internet sites. According to the opinion, "Covered entities [under the ADA] that use the Internet for communications regarding their programs, goods, or services must be prepared to offer those communications through accessible means." A number of commentators have interpreted this mandate to mean that any **entity** that is required to accommodate those with disabilities in physical places, such as buildings, are likewise required to provide accommodations on Internet sites.

As technology has improved, Web site developers have been able to include increasingly dynamic visual and audio enhancements on Internet sites. However, a disability, such as blindness or hearing impairment, can hinder a person's ability to use these sites. To allow people suffering from impairments to access these sites, a number of tools have been developed that provide alternative means to access the information available. For instance, certain programs are able to convert textual information into audio information so that those who suffer from blindness can hear the information. Likewise, voice navigation software allows those with physical disabilities to dictate commands in a manner similar to using a keyboard or mouse.

A number of state and local governments have passed bills and ordinances requiring state agencies and local governmental entities to develop Web sites that allow those with disabilities to access the sites. For example, in 1999, the Texas Legislature enacted a bill requiring all state agencies to conform "to generally acceptable standards for Internet accessibility for people with disabilities." Tex. Gov't Code Ann. § 2001.006(c) (Vernon 2000). The

IN FOCUS

---

against the state of Tennessee. They alleged that the state had violated, and continued to violate, Title II provisions. Both plaintiffs used wheelchairs for mobility. They claimed they were deprived access to the courts because of their disabilities. Lane was ordered to appear for a criminal proceeding at a second floor courtroom that had no elevator. He crawled up two flights of stairs at his first appearance, but he refused to do this at his second hearing. He also declined to be carried up the stairs by court employees. As a result, he was arrested for failing to appear. Jones, a certified court reporter, alleged she could not gain access to a group of county courthouses and had lost work and the opportunity to participate in the judicial process. The state asked the federal district court to dismiss the lawsuit on Eleventh Amendment grounds, but the court refused to grant them motion. The Sixth **Circuit Court** of Appeals upheld this ruling, which led Tennessee to **appeal** to the Supreme Court.

The Court, in a 5-4 decision, affirmed the appeals court. Justice JOHN PAUL STEVENS, writing for the majority, based the decision on the FOURTEENTH AMENDMENT. This amendment, which was enacted after the Civil War, prohibits the states from denying any citizen **due process of law**, **equal protection** of the law, or **privileges and immunities** accorded by law. Its passage signaled a major shift of power from the states to the federal government. Congress is authorized under Section 5 of the amendment to enact legislation to enforce the substantive guarantees found in its first section. Stevens cited **case law** that found Section 5 legislation reaching beyond the scope of the amendment's actual guarantees must exhibit "congruence and proportionality between the **injury** to be prevented or remedied and the means adopted to that end."

This test for congruence and proportionality had to be applied to the legislative history of the ADA. Congress could only be authorized to

JUSTICE DEPARTMENT has issued a series of documents instructing state and local governments as to how they can provide accessibility to their Web sites.

Private entities have also played a prominent role in developing standards for accessibility. The World Wide Web Consortium (W3C), a highly influential association that develops standards for Internet usage, has adopted a series of guidelines that explains how Web site developers can make Internet content available to people with disabilities. The Center for Applied Special Technology (CAST) has developed a Web site known as "Bobby" that allows developers to determine whether their Web sites conform to the W3C standards. This site is available at <http://bobby.watchfire.com/bobby/html/en/index.jsp>.

Although few people may openly question the need to provide accessibility of Web sites to disabled persons, the issue of which entities are required to provide this access has not been clearly established. In a case decided relatively soon after the ADA was enacted, the First **Circuit Court** of Appeals suggested that ADA requirements were not limited to physical places. *Carparts Distribution Ctr. v. Automotive Wholesaler's Ass'n of New England, Inc.*, 37 F.3d 12 (1st Cir. 1994). However, more recent decisions have held that certain Internet sites were not places of public accommodation.

In *Access Now, Inc. v. Southwest Airlines Co.*, 227 F. Supp. 2d 1312 (S.D. Fla. 2002), a person suffering from blindness, joined by a non-profit advocacy organization, brought a suit against Southwest Airlines. The plaintiff claimed that Southwest violated the ADA because the plaintiff could not access Southwest's site, even though the plaintiff had a voice synthesizer installed on his computer. Southwest claimed that the site was not a place of public accommodation under the ADA. The court agreed with Southwest. It found that the Internet site was not among those places contemplated in the **statute**. The ADA includes a list of twelve places of public accommodation in 42 U.S.C. § 12181(7). Each of these places corresponds with an actual physical location, according to the court. Since the plaintiffs were neither able to establish that Southwest's site was a place of public accommodation, nor to prove a connection between the site and a actual physical location, the court dismissed the claim.

Other courts have reached the same conclusion. The Eastern District of Virginia, for instance, found that an Internet chat room was not a public accommodation under the ADA. *Noah v. AOL Time Warner, Inc.*, 261 F. Supp. 2d 532 (E.D. Va. 2003). In fact, in another case in the Southern District of Florida, the court indicated that no court has ever held that a retail entity has been required to make its Web site accessible to persons with disabilities. *Access Now, Inc. v. Claire's Stores, Inc.*, No. 00-14017-CIV-MOORE, 2002 WL 1162422 (S.D. Fla. May 7, 2002)

Since plaintiffs have not had success in the courts in requiring Web site developers to make their sites accessible to disabled persons, it will likely fall on the various legislative bodies to do so. According to the court in *Access Now, Inc. v. Southwest Airlines Co.*, "As Congress has created the statutorily defined rights under the ADA, it is the role of Congress, and not this Court, to specifically expand the ADA's definition of 'public accommodation' beyond physical, concrete places of public accommodation, to include 'virtual' places of public accommodation."

include the states within the ADA's reach if it identified a history and pattern of unconstitutional discrimination against disabled persons in judicial services and public access. Justice Stevens, after surveying the legislative record, found that the "long history of unequal treatment of disabled persons in the administration of judicial services has persisted despite several state and federal legislative efforts to remedy the problem." Congress, in writing the ADA, was "justified in concluding that the difficult and intractable problem of disability discrimination warranted added … measures." Denying disabled persons such as Lane and Jones access to courtrooms deprived them of equal protection and due process of law. Moreover, it implicated the First Amendment rights of members of the public to observe criminal proceedings.

Having established the basis for Congressional revocation of state sovereign **immunity**, Justice Stevens examined whether Title II was an "appropriate response to the history and pattern of unequal treatment." He limited the scope of this inquiry to access to the courts, not to access to the various types of public buildings—hockey rinks, voting booths, public education, etc. The congressional remedy for enforcing Title II was limited, directing the states to take reasonable steps to remove architectural and other barriers. Title II requires states to make only "reasonable modifications," and in the case of older buildings, where structural change would be more difficult, states may take less costly steps. These include relocating services to more accessible sites and assigning staff to assist disabled persons with accessing services. Because of these limited and reasonable measures, Title II, as applied to access to the courts, comported with Section 5 of the Fourteenth Amendment.

Chief Justice WILLIAM REHNQUIST, in a dissenting opinion joined by Justices ANTHONY KENNEDY and CLARENCE THOMAS, argued

George Lane, shown at Brushy Mountain Correctional Complex in January 2004.

that the decision was inconsistent with prior case law on the ADA. Justice Rehnquist reiterated his belief that Congress had failed to adequately document a pattern of unconstitutional conduct by the states. In addition, the majority had wrongly equated access to the courts with access to a courtroom. In his view the Court had never said a person had a constitutional right "to make his way into a courtroom without any external assistance."

Justice ANTONIN SCALIA, in a separate **dissent**, concluded that the congruence and proportionality test should be dropped because it "is a standing invitation to judicial arbitrariness and policy-driven decisionmaking." He urged the use of a new test that would bar enforcement of federal laws against the states if the laws went beyond enforcing the provisions of the Fourteenth Amendment.

Employers Granted More Leeway in Not Rehiring Persons with Drug or Alcohol Addictions

The Americans with Disabilities Act of 1990 (ADA), 42 U.S.C.A. §§ 1201 *et seq.*, bans discrimination in employment for "qualified individuals with a disability because of the disability of such individual." The ADA has generated numerous lawsuits since its adoption, as employers and employees have sought to define the scope of the law. The Supreme Court, in *Raytheon Co. v. Hernandez*, __ U.S. __, 124 S.Ct. 513, 157 L.Ed.2d 357 (2003), examined whether an employer must rehire a lawfully terminated disabled employee who had violated workplace conduct rules. In this case, the employee was a recovering drug addict, who claimed ADA protection. The Court declined to issue a definitive ruling due to the misapplication of law by the **circuit court** but did make clear that an employer may escape **liability** in a discrimination lawsuit if it relied on a neutral policy of not rehiring employees terminated for personal conduct rules.

Joel Hernandez worked for Hughes Missile System (later acquired by Raytheon) for 25 years, until he tested positive for cocaine use. His illegal drug use violated company workplace conduct rules. The company gave Hernandez the option to resign or face being fired. He resigned, and the company placed a note in his personnel record indicating that he quit **in lieu of** being discharged for workplace misconduct. Hernandez applied to be rehired two years later, claiming to be rehabilitated. However, Raytheon had in place a policy that prohibited the rehiring of former employees who had been terminated for workplace misconduct. Therefore, Raytheon determined that Hernandez was not eligible to be rehired.

Hernandez filed a complaint with the EQUAL EMPLOYMENT OPPORTUNITY COMMISSION (EEOC), claiming he suffered discrimination barred by the ADA. Under the ADA, illegal drug use is excluded from coverage, but rehabilitated addicts are protected. The EEOC sided with Hernandez and authorized him to sue Raytheon in federal district court. In his court filing, Hernandez based his case on the disparate treatment theory of liability. This theory is based on a claim of intentional discrimination by the employer. In this case Hernandez contended that Raytheon refused to rehire him because it regarded him as either being a drug addict or because of his prior record of drug addiction.

Raytheon asked the district court to dismiss the lawsuit because it had applied a blanket company policy, which meant it applied equally to all former employees terminated for misconduct. The company claimed it had not singled Hernandez because of his drug addition. In response, Hernandez then asked the court to apply the **disparate impact** theory of discrimination liability. Under disparate impact, an employer such as Raytheon could be held liable for damages if a facially neutral policy (the no-rehire policy for misconduct) had a disproportionate impact on rehabilitated drug users under the ADA. The district court dismissed the lawsuit on the disparate treatment theory and refused to consider the disparate impact theory because it had not been raised in a timely manner. The Ninth Circuit Court of Appeals for the Ninth Circuit reversed the district court, ruling that Raytheon's no-rehire policy had a disparate impact on recovering drug addicts such as Hernandez under the ADA. In its ruling, the court professed to use the disparate treatment theory but came to its conclusion using an **element** of the disparate impact theory.

The Supreme Court, in a unanimous decision (with Justices DAVID SOUTER and STEPHEN BREYER not participating in the decision), reversed the Ninth Circuit. The question before the Court had been whether the ADA granted preferential rehire rights on disabled employees who had been lawfully terminated for violating their employer's workplace conduct rules. However, the Court never reached the question. Justice CLARENCE THOMAS, writing for the Court, concluded that the Ninth Circuit had improperly applied a disparate impact analysis to a disparate treatment claim. He stated: "Had the Court of Appeals correctly applied the disparate-treatment framework, it would have been obliged to conclude that a neutral no-rehire policy is, by definition, a legitimate, nondiscriminatory reason under the ADA." Once Raytheon had advanced this policy, Hernandez could only overcome it by producing sufficient evidence to show this policy was merely a pretext for its decision. The case was sent back to the Ninth Circuit to apply the correct legal analysis for disparate treatment.

Though the decision did not settle the broader question raised on **appeal**, the Supreme Court did make clear that applying a neutral no-rehire policy generally protects an employer from disparate treatment claims under the ADA. The decision still leaves open the possibility that a disparate impact theory might prevail if a company cannot provide a "business necessity" for the neutral no-rehire policy.

ANTITRUST LAW

Legislation enacted by the federal and various state governments to regulate trade and commerce by preventing unlawful restraints, price-fixing, and monopolies; to promote competition; and to encourage the production of quality goods and services at the lowest prices, with the primary goal of safeguarding public welfare by ensuring that consumer demands will be met by the manufacture and sale of goods at reasonable prices.

Joel Hernandez at home in Tucson, Arizona.

F. Hoffman-LaRoche, Ltd. v. Empagran, S.A.

The U.S. SUPREME COURT, on June 14, 2004, ruled that U.S. antitrust law does not apply when foreign price-fixing has no effect on domestic businesses. The case began with foreign vitamin purchasers alleging **price-fixing** by an international vitamin **cartel**. The case was closely followed by both businesses and commentators because it tested the global breadth of antitrust laws in the United States.

During the early 1990s, the Justice Departments Antitrust Division conducted an investigation regarding alleged price-fixing by an international group of vitamin producers. The investigation revealed a **conspiracy** among approximately twenty foreign companies to inflate vitamin prices used in a myriad of products. The JUSTICE DEPARTMENT convicted more than a dozen companies of this conspiracy, resulting in jail terms for several executives and substantial fines for a number of the members of the cartel.

Each of the companies implicated in the Justice Department's investigation were foreign. Moreover, none of the price-fixing activities occurred within the United States. Nevertheless, a number of foreign plaintiffs who purchased vitamins brought lawsuits against members of the cartels, alleging antitrust violations. The question has arisen in a number of cases, as to whether U.S. antitrust laws extend to foreign plaintiffs when the transactions in question did not actually take place in the United States.

In 1982, Congress amended the Sherman Anti-Trust Act, 15 U.S.C. §§ 1 **et seq.** with the enactment of the Foreign Trade Antitrust Improvements Act (FTAIA), 15 U.S.C. § 6a. This amendment renders inapplicable domestic antitrust laws to cases involving trade or commerce with foreign nations unless this conduct "has a direct, substantial, or reasonably foreseeable effect" on U.S. trade and commerce. If foreign plaintiffs are unable to establish such an effect on U.S. trade and commerce, a domestic court will not have jurisdiction to hear the dispute.

In 2001 and 2002, two federal courts of appeals heard claims, brought by foreign plaintiffs who alleged violations of the antitrust laws, against the members of the vitamin cartel. The courts took completely opposite views of the application of the FTAIA. In *Den Norske Stats Oljeselskap AS v. HeereMac Vof*, 241 F.3d 420 (5th Cir. 2001), the Fifth **Circuit Court** of Appeals found that the foreign plaintiffs had not proven that the direct effect on U.S. trade and commerce had given rise to their claims. Accordingly, the court dismissed the case for lack of jurisdiction. One year later, however, in *Kruman v. Christie's International PLC*, 284 F.3d 384 (2d Cir. 2002), the Second Circuit Court of Appeals found that even though the transactions of the foreign plaintiffs in the case took place outside of the United States, the price-fixing adversely impacted U.S. trade and commerce. Hence, the court found that the transactions indeed had a direct effect on U.S. trade and commerce, and the suit was allowed to proceed.

The case of *F. Hoffman-LaRoche, Ltd. v. Empagran, S.A.*, 542 U.S. ___ (2004) arose when a group plaintiffs representing foreign and domestic corporations filed suit in the U.S. District Court for the DISTRICT OF COLUMBIA, alleging violations of U.S. antitrust laws arising from the alleged price-fixing conspiracy. The defendants—a number of international vitamin sellers—moved to dismiss the suit, claiming that the transactions had no direct effect on U.S. trade or commerce. The district court granted the motion to dismiss, finding that the court lacked subject-matter jurisdiction over the case with respect to the claims brought by the foreign plaintiffs. *Empagran S.A. v. F. Hoffman-LaRoche, Ltd.*, No. Civ.001686TFH, 2001 WL 761360 (D.D.C. 2001).

The plaintiffs appealed to the U.S. Court of Appeals for the District of Columbia. In a lengthy opinion, the appeals court considered whether the FTAIA applies to a case involving activities that affect both foreign and domestic trade and commerce in which the plaintiffs were injured as a result of activities that occurred solely on foreign soil. Despite the fact that the foreign plaintiffs had not purchased the vitamins within the United States, the court held in their favor, finding that the defendant's anticompetitive conduct violated the Sherman Act and that the conduct had a harmful effect on U.S. commerce. *Empagran S.A. v. F. Hoffman-LaRoche, Ltd.*, 315 F.3d 338 (D.C. Cir. 2003).

The court found no "plain meaning" of the FTAIA that it could apply, nor did it find guidance in the approaches taken by the Second and Fifth Circuits. Since the court found that the language of the **statute** created ambiguities, it considered the statute's **legislative history** in reaching its conclusion. The court found that a committee report from the House of Representatives "suggests that Congress intended for **subject matter jurisdiction** to exist over the conduct of an international cartel that had an effect on domestic commerce, even if the plaintiff's claim does not arise from that domestic effect." The court also determined that Congress intended to provide a deterrence of antitrust violations when it enacted the FTAIA. Because the court found that the FTAIA permitted the foreign plaintiffs to bring the suit, it reversed the district court's **dismissal** of the suit.

Faced with a significant split within the federal courts of appeals involving an issue with international implications, the U.S. Supreme Court granted **certiorari** to hear the case. A unanimous Court ruled 8-0 (with Justice Sandra Day O'Connor not participating) for Hoffman, vacating the court of appeals' decision and remanding the case to "consider whether respondents properly preserved their alternative argument that the foreign injury here was not in fact independent of the domestic effects."

Supreme Court Limits Antitrust Lawsuits Against Phone Companies

Congress enacted the Telecommunications Act of 1996, Pub. L. No. 104-104, 110 Stat. 56, to increase competition within the industry and to end state-sanctioned monopolies. The act came in the aftermath of the breakup in the early 1980s of American Telephone and Telegraph's (AT&T) monopoly over virtually all aspects of the telephone business. AT&T settled an antitrust lawsuit in 1982 by divesting itself of its local operating companies, while retaining control of its long distance activities. Seven regional telephone companies, known as Baby Bells, were given responsibility for local telephone service. Other companies then entered the long-distance service market to compete with AT&T. The act allowed the Baby Bells to compete in the long-distance telephone market but more importantly, it permitted AT&T and other long-distance carriers, as well as cable companies, to sell local telephone service. It required the "incumbent" (preexisting) local exchange carriers (LEC), such as the Baby Bells, to share their networks with their competitors. The act also gave the Federal Communications Commission (FCC) the authority to issue regulations that would implement the local-competition provisions of the act.

The LECs and the new generation of telecommunications companies have been locked in disputes over the commitment of incumbent LECs to provide these competitors with access to their networks, as mandated by the 1996 act. These disputes have been litigated before the FCC and state public service commissions. However, a new avenue for litigation appeared to open when a New York law firm filed a **class action** lawsuit against Verizon Communications, an incumbent LEC, alleging that its failure to cooperate with the new phone companies violated antitrust provisions of the Sherman Act, 15 U.S.C.A. §§ 1 *et seq.*,. However, the U.S. SUPREME COURT, in *Verizon Communications Inc. v. Law Offices of Curtis V. Trinko, LLP*, __ U.S. __, 124 S.Ct. 872, __ L.Ed.2d __ (2004), placed a permanent roadblock in front of this type of litigation, concluding that such claims did not fall under the Sherman Act.

The Trinko law office was a local telephone service customer of AT&T, a new or "competitive" LEC, which in turn purchased "unbundled network elements" from Verizon, the incumbent LEC. Trinko filed suit in federal court, alleging that Verizon had filled the orders of AT&T on a discriminatory basis as part of an anticompetitive scheme to discourage customers from becoming or remaining customers of AT&T. Trinko contended that this behavior impeded AT&T's ability to enter and compete for local telephone service. However, Trinko only pointed to one example where Verizon allegedly limited access to its network. The FCC and the New York Public Service Commission had addressed this issue prior to the lawsuit, negotiating **consent** decrees with Verizon in which Verizon agreed to pay $3 million to the federal government, $10 million to other competitive LECs and to submit to reporting and measurement requirements that could lead to sanctions for noncompliance. The district court dismissed the Trinko lawsuit, finding that the plaintiff's allegations did not satisfy the requirements of the Sherman Act. *Law Offices of Curtis V. Trinko, LLP v. Bell Atlantic Corp.*, 123 F. Supp. 2d 738 (S.D.N.Y. 2000). The Second **Circuit Court** of Appeals reversed, leading Verizon to **appeal** to the Supreme Court.

The Court unanimously overturned the Second Circuit decision, with six justices agreeing to a majority opinion and three justices filing a concurring opinion based on another line of reasoning. Justice ANTONIN SCALIA, writing for the majority, reviewed the recent history of telecommunication law and business practices, noting the complex regulatory scheme that is divided between the FCC and state administrative bodies. Though the 1996 act's comprehensive enforcement scheme might imply that Congress sought to prevent antitrust scrutiny, Justice Scalia pointed to a provision in the law that expressly precluded such an **interpretation**. The law stated that it did nothing to impair the applicability of antitrust actions, thereby removing any doubt that LECs were not immune from Sherman Act litigation.

Justice Scalia also noted that the 1996 law did not create any new claims that go beyond existing antitrust standards. Therefore, the Trinko claim had to be analyzed to determine whether Verizon had violated any preexisting standards. The competitive circumstances of the telecommunications industry worked against the application of prior case antitrust law to the Trinko claim. For example, prior to the 1996 act Verizon was not involved in leasing its network elements to LECs. Therefore, its "prior conducts sheds no light on the motivation of its refusal to deal—upon whether its regulatory lapses were prompted not by competitive zeal but by anticompetitive malice." In addition, Verizon offered unbundled network elements to competitors, not to consumers, "and at considerable expense and effort." The prices at which Verizon provided its unbundled network elements to competitors were set by regulators at cost: "Verizon's reluctance to interconnect at the cost-based rate of compensation available under [the 1996 act] tells us nothing about dreams of monopoly."

Having found no preexisting standards to justify the allegations, Justice Scalia refused to create a new standard. This refusal was based on the regulatory complexity of the telecommunications industry. The millions of dollars extracted from Verizon by the FCC and the New York Public Services Commission, along with additional oversight, demonstrated that this course of conduct was better for society than class action lawsuits that would drive up costs and tie up companies in litigation for years. Therefore, the lawsuit must be dismissed.

Justice JOHN PAUL STEVENS, in a concurring opinion joined by Justices DAVID SOUTER and CLARENCE THOMAS, argued that the lawsuit should have been dismissed on jurisdictional grounds. Stevens contended that Trinko, as a retail phone customer, did not have standing to raise an antitrust claim was based on conduct between two LECs. Only AT&T would have had standing to sue Verizon under Stevens' analysis.

U.S. Postal Service Cannot Be Sued Under Antitrust Laws

The Postal Reorganization Act of 1971 (PRA), 39 U.S.C.A. $sect;§ 101 *et seq.*, renamed the U.S. Post Department the United States Postal Service (USPS) and removed it from the Cabinet. The law made the USPS an independent establishment of the executive branch and setup a structure for the USPS to raise postal rates. In addition, the law allowed the USPS to retain its monopoly over the delivery of letters. The special status of the USPS in the federal governance structure lead to questions as to whether it was liable under federal antitrust laws. The U.S. SUPREME COURT, in *United States Postal Service v. Flamingo Industries (USA) Ltd.*, __ U.S. __, __ S.Ct. __, __, 124 S.Ct. 1321, 158 L.Ed.2d 19 (2004), settled the matter, ruling that the USPS was immune from antitrust lawsuits.

The case arose after the USPS terminated a contract with Flamingo Industries, which manufactured mail sacks for the USPS. Flamingo filed a lawsuit in federal court alleging that the USPS had sought to suppress competition and to create a monopoly in the production of mail sacks. The district court dismissed the action, ruling that the USPS was protected from antitrust lawsuits because of governmental **immunity**. Under the **doctrine** of governmental immunity, private individuals cannot sue the federal government for damages unless Congress makes a specific exemption. In this case the court concluded Congress had not exempted the USPS from immunity. However, on **appeal** the Ninth **Circuit Court** of Appeals reversed the decision. The Ninth Circuit ruled that USPS could be liable but that it had a limited immunity from antitrust **liability** for actions taken at the direction of Congress. *Flamingo Industries (USA) Ltd. v. United States Postal Service*, 302 F.3d 985 (9th Cir. 2002). The USPS then appealed to the Supreme Court.

The Supreme Court, in a unanimous decision, reversed the Ninth Circuit and ruled that the USPS was immune from federal antitrust laws. Justice ANTHONY KENNEDY, writing for the Court, first reviewed the history of mail delivery in the United States. He pointed out that the U.S. Constitution, in Article I, § 8, specifically empowered the federal government to provide and regulate postal services. With the passage of the PRA in 1971, the USPS shed its Cabinet status and came under a new governance structure. A Board of Governors, consisting of 11 members, oversees the management of the USPS, while a separate Postal Rate Commission recommends postal rate changes to the Board of Governors. The USPS retained its right to have postal inspectors search and seize mail transported in violation of the USPS monopoly. Justice Kennedy, in reviewing these items, concluded that the USPS had "significant governmental powers, consistent with its status as an independent establishment of the Executive Branch." Though the USPS had been specifically exempted from many laws regulating federal agencies, the PRA did not address the issue of federal antitrust laws.

Because the PRA was silent on antitrust liability under the Sherman Act, 15 U.S.C.A. $sect;§ 1 *et seq.*, the Court looked at whether a general waiver of immunity contained in the PRA included antitrust laws. Justice Kennedy noted that a line of prior Supreme Court cases had held that congressional waivers of immunity should generally be interpreted liberally. A two-step analysis was set out in *FDIC v. Meyer* 510 U.S. 471, 114 S.Ct. 996, 127 L.Ed.2d 308 (1994), which Kennedy applied to the mail sack contract **controversy**. The first step was to determine if Congress had waived immunity for actions against the USPS. Justice Kennedy agreed with the Ninth Circuit that the USPS could be sued for damages under theories such as breach of contract and tort, but the Ninth Circuit had failed to look at the second step. This step required the Court to determine if the USPS was immune from substantive liability found in federal laws such as the Sherman Act.

Justice Kennedy first pointed out that the USPS retains its governmental status. Thus, the question came down to whether the USPS was a "person" under the Sherman Act. The act defines "person" to include corporations and associations and makes state governmental bodies liable. However, it was much different when it came to the federal government. It would not make sense to believe Congress intended to expose the federal government to antitrust liability. Congress had opportunities to amend the Sherman Act to include the federal government after a number of Supreme Court decisions touched on the definition of "person," yet it never did. Therefore, Kennedy concluded that the federal government was not a "person" as defined by the Sherman Act.

The sole remaining issue was whether the USPS was a person separate from the United States government. Though the PRA gave the USPS a "high degree of independence" from other federal offices, Justice Kennedy held that it was not a separate person from the United States. Moreover, the USPS did not share the goals of private enterprises, as it did not seek to make a profit but only break even. In sum, the powers of the USPS were "more characteristic of Government than of private enterprise." Therefore, the USPS was immune from Sherman Act liability.

APPORTIONMENT

The process by which legislative seats are distributed among units entitled to representation; determination of the number of representatives that a state, county, or other subdivision may send to a legislative body. The U.S. Constitution provides for a census every ten years, on the basis of which Congress apportions representatives according to population; each state, however, must have at least one representative. Districting is the establishment of the precise geographical boundaries of each such unit or constituency. Apportionment by state statute that denies the rule of one-person, one-vote is violative of equal protection of laws.

Also, the allocation of a charge or cost such as real estate taxes between two parties, often in the same ratio as the respective times that the parties are in possession or ownership of property during the fiscal period for which the charge is made or assessed.

Congressional Redistricting Incites Controversy

Efforts to redraw congressional districts generated significant **controversy** in several states in 2003 as legislators fought over the approval of various maps defining which voters fall into individual districts. Many of the debates centered on claims by members of the Democratic Party that Republican legislators were engaging in political gerrymandering in an effort to gain seats in Congress. Although several of the legislatures eventually settled on redistricting plans by the end of the year, a number of these disputes were far from resolved.

One of the more heated—and sometimes bizarre—confrontations took place in Texas, where Democratic legislators left the state on several occasions to prevent the legislature from convening a **quorum**. States are required to reapportion their congressional districts following publication of the federal census. However, unable to approve a plan during 2001, the Texas legislature required a federal district court to do so on a temporary basis until the legislature could approve a plan. *Balderas v. Texas*, No. Civ. A. 6:01CV158, 2001 WL 34104833 (E.D. Tex. Nov. 28, 2001)

The Texas legislature, which convenes exclusively during odd-numbered years for 140 day sessions, has a limited time frame in which it can enact legislation. Congressional redistricting plans introduced by Republican members of the legislature in 2003 sparked controversy among the majority of the Democratic members. Among their allegations were claims that the Republican plan was aimed toward removing minority voters from Democratic districts and placing them in Republican districts. The result, according to the Democrats, was that the Republicans could gain a stronger foothold on certain districts, thereby gaining seats for the REPUBLICAN PARTY in Congress. Republicans dismissed the allegations, saying that the plans were designed to reflect population shifts that had occurred since the 1990 census. Versions of the districting maps could have gained the Republicans an estimated five to seven seats in Congress out of the 32 congressional districts in the state.

During the 2003 legislative session, the Texas House of Representatives consisted of eighty-eight Republicans and sixty-two Democrats. The House could not convene without the presence of at least one hundred of these members. As the deadline for passing legislation in Texas approached, the members of the legislature were unable to reach a compromise on the redistricting plans. In May 2003, more than fifty of the Texas Democrats left the state, staying in a hotel in Ardmore, Oklahoma, for approximately four days. The action prevented the

Texas House from meeting, and so the body could not consider any plans during that time. Though the representatives eventually returned, the state legislature was unable to approve a plan during the regular legislative session.

The Texas Constitution allows the governor of the state to convene a special thirty-day session following the conclusion of the regular session. Governor Rick Perry, a Republican, convened a special session on June 30, 2003. After the legislature was unable to approve a plan, Perry convened yet another special session on July 28. During the second session, several Democratic members of the legislature again left the state, this time staying in Albuquerque, New Mexico, for several weeks. When the second session concluded on August 26, the legislature had once again failed to reach a compromise.

After Perry convened a third special session, the two sides were finally able to agree to a plan on October 12, though state Democrats continued to voice their disapproval. The Texas redistricting plan received preapproval by the Justice Department in December 2003, and the plan was approved by the U.S. District Court for the Eastern District of Texas in January 2004.

The controversy in Texas was indicative of the type of heated contests and contemptuous exchanges between political parties in several states considering the issue of reapportionment. Republican legislators in Colorado faced similar opposition to their state redistricting plans, prompting Democratic legislators in Oklahoma and New Mexico to threaten to draft plans that would increase the number of congressional seats for Democrats in those states. While the threats were viewed as retaliation for the actions of the Republicans in Texas and Colorado, national leaders of the DEMOCRATIC PARTY disapproved of these plans.

Controversies were not limited to Democrats and Republicans. In Maine, a plan drawn up by Democratic legislators, the state's controlling party, effectively dismantled the voter base for state representative John Eder, a member of the GREEN PARTY, who was elected in November 2002. The Green Independent Party filed suit to block the proposed plan in May 2003.

A dispute over redistricting efforts by Republicans in Pennsylvania reached the U.S. SUPREME COURT in 2003. A Republican reapportionment plan, approved in 2002, allowed the G.O.P. to gain several seats in Congress and stripped two long-standing Democrats of their offices. Democrats challenged the action, but the plan was approved by the U.S. District Court for the Eastern District of Pennsylvania in January 2003. The Supreme Court, in *Vieth v. Jubelirer*, ___ U.S. ___, 124 S.Ct. 1769, ___ L.Ed.2d ___ (2004), upheld the lower court decision and came within one vote of ruling that the courts do not have jurisdiction to consider political gerrymandering cases. The decision made clear that opponents of recent **apportionment** plans face an uphill battle in the courts.

Supreme Court Upholds Pennsylvania Redistricting Plan

States must redraw voting districts every ten years to reflect changes in population that are documented by the U.S. census. As a result, some states gain seats in the U.S. House of Representatives, while others lose representatives. State legislatures must reapportion congressional districts, a process that necessarily involves party politics. The minority party usually argues that the majority party in the legislature has unfairly drawn districts to help it elect more representatives. Sometimes, voters file federal lawsuits challenging the fairness of reapportionment, but the courts are generally reluctant to intrude. However, the U.S. SUPREME COURT, in *Davis v. Bandemer*, 478 U.S. 109, 106 S.Ct. 2797, 92 L.Ed.2d 85 (1986), ruled that political gerrymandering claims are **justiciable**, which means that courts have jurisdiction to hear such actions. The *Davis* decision did not give clear direction on how courts should analyze gerrymandering claims, and this ambiguity has made **adjudication** difficult and confusing. The Supreme Court, in *Vieth v. Jubelirer*, ___ U.S. ___, 124 S.Ct. 1769, 158 L.Ed.2d 546 (2004), came within one vote of overturning *Davis*. Though a bare majority preserved the justiciability of gerrymandering actions, the multiple opinions filed in the case again demonstrated the difficulty in conceptualizing how courts can act fairly in highly politicized litigation.

Following the 2000 census, Pennsylvania lost two of its 21 congressional seats. The REPUBLICAN PARTY controlled the state legislature and the governorship. In 2002, under pressure from national political leaders, the legislature adopted a partisan redistricting plan. A group of registered Democrats filed suit, alleging that the plan violated the Constitution's requirement of **one person, one vote**, and that it was a blatant political **gerrymander**. A three-judge panel dismissed the gerrymandering claim but agreed that the plan violated the one person, one vote requirement. The legislature then passed a modified plan for the court's approval.

The plaintiffs asked the court to redraw the districts, but the court declined. *Vieth v. Pennsylvania*, 241 F. Supp. 2d 478 (M.D. Pa. 2003). The plaintiffs then appealed to the Supreme Court on the political gerrymandering claim.

The Supreme Court, in a 5-4 decision, upheld the **dismissal** of the gerrymandering claim. More importantly, another five-vote majority comprised of Justice ANTHONY KENNEDY and the four dissenting justices, voted to retain the *Davis* precedent that gerrymandering claims could be heard by the courts. Justice ANTONIN SCALIA, writing for Chief Justice WILLIAM REHNQUIST and Justices SANDRA DAY O'CONNOR and CLARENCE THOMAS, argued that *Davis* had produced much sound and fury in the courts in the years since it was decided, and since there was "virtually nothing to show for it . . . we must conclude that political gerrymandering claims are nonjusticiable and that [the ruling] was wrongly decided."

Justice Scalia noted that political gerrymandering can be traced back to the early 1700s. The term "gerrymandering" comes from the 1812 action of Massachussetts governor Eldbridge Gerry. Gerry crafted a voting district in the shape of a salamander so as to insure the election of a member of his political party. The framers of the Constitution recognized this problem in Article 1, § 4, when it gave Congress the power to "make or alter" districts drawn by state legislatures. During the nineteenth century, Congress passed several laws that sought to impose some requirement on how states drew districts. However, such actions disappeared in the twentieth century. Nevertheless, Scalia argued that it was "generally conceded that each party would attempt to gain power which was not proportionate to its numerical strength."

In *Baker v. Carr*, 369 U.S. 186, 82 S.Ct. 691, 7 L.Ed.2d 663 (1962), the Supreme Court overturned prior case precedents that barred the courts from dealing with redistricting issues. The prior decisions had prevented the courts from entering the "political thicket," but *Baker* allowed the courts to hear cases if it could be determined that this would not intrude on the powers of the executive or legislative branches to manage their own affairs. Justice Scalia noted that *Baker* barred court intervention if the court could not develop "judicially discoverable and manageable standards for resolving" the issue. He concluded that no such standards for adjudicating political gerrymandering claims had developed in the eighteen years following the *Davis* decision and none would emerge. Therefore, *Davis* should be overruled.

Justice Kennedy, while agreeing that the Pennsylvania claims must be dismissed, refused to abandon *Davis*. He too worried that allowing courts to correct district boundaries drawn for partisan reasons "would commit federal and state courts to unprecedented intervention in the American political process." Despite this concern, Kennedy thought it best to preserve the right of courts to look at redistricting plans that might be unconstitutional, even though no clear standards exist for analyzing such claims now.

Justice JOHN PAUL STEVENS, in a dissenting opinion, argued that prior **apportionment** decisions, including *Baker*, provided courts with standards to analyze whether a redistricting plan was political gerrymandering. For example, when a district is drawn in a "peculiar shape," this might be a "symptom of an illicit purpose in the line-drawing process." In addition, the Court had developed standards in recent cases involving racial gerrymandering that could be applied to political gerrymandering.

Justice DAVID SOUTER, in a dissenting opinion joined by Justice RUTH BADER GINSBURG, contended the Court needed to make a "fresh start" and clarify the *Davis* ruling. He proposed a political gerrymandering test analogous to a test used in civil rights law where the plaintiff must put forth enough **proof** to require the state to rebut the evidence. Justice STEPHEN BREYER, in a dissenting opinion, described a set of circumstances that would conflict with "constitutionally mandated democratic requirements" and which could be analyzed using "applicable judicially manageable standards." However, he declined to describe what these standards might be.

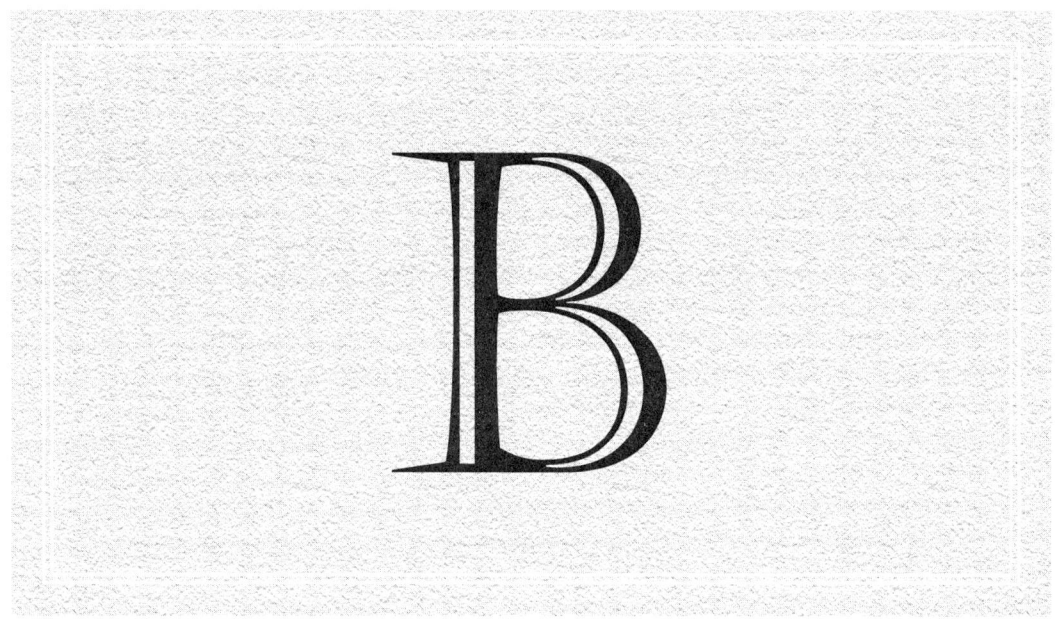

BANKRUPTCY

A federally authorized procedure by which a debtor—an individual, corporation, or municipality—is relieved of total liability for its debts by making court-approved arrangements for their partial repayment.

Debtor Must Object to Late Filing Before Case Decided on the Merits

Federal **bankruptcy** statutes and court rules govern the procedure for the various types of bankruptcy filings. Though the **debtor** seeks to use bankruptcy to avoid repaying creditors, creditors are entitled to file objections if, for example, they believe the debtor has fraudulently transferred assets prior to bankruptcy. Such was the case in *Kontrick v. Ryan*, __ U.S. __, 124 S.Ct. 906, 157 L.Ed.2d 867 (2004). However, the U.S. SUPREME COURT was not called upon to decide the **merits** of the case. Instead the Court had to rule on the effect of an untimely **objection** by a creditor when the debtor did not **contest** it until after the bankruptcy court had ruled on the merits of the objection. The Court held that the debtor could not contest the lateness of the filing once the case was decided on its merits.

The case arose out of the failed cosmetic and plastic surgery **practice** of Dr. Andrew J. Kontrick and Dr. Robert A. Ryan. In April 1997, Kontrick filed a Chapter 7 bankruptcy **petition** in which he sought a **discharge** of all of his debts except those specifically exempted by **statute**. Ryan, who was a major creditor, opposed Kendrick's discharge. He obtained three extensions of time from the bankruptcy court to file his complaint objecting to the discharge. He finally filed the complaint in January 1998. In it Ryan alleged that Kontrick had transferred property within one year of his Chapter 7 petition filing, with the **intent** to defraud creditors. Therefore, Ryan contended that Kontrick should not be discharged of his debts.

Under Bankruptcy Rule 4004 a creditor must file the objection within 60 days of the first **meeting of creditors** or obtain an extension from the court. Ryan's original complaint conformed to this rule but he filed an amended complaint in early May 1998. In this case he did not seek a court-approved time extension. Under the rules Ryan's amended complaint was clearly untimely and Kontrick had the right to contest it and ask the court to reject it from consideration. However, when Kontrick filed a response in June 1998, he did not contest the timeliness of the amended complaint but instead focused on Ryan's allegations. In this amended complaint, Ryan alleged that Kontrick had transferred money to his wife by taking his name off their joint checking account and having his salary check deposited into the account, from which Kontrick's wife paid the family's living expenses. In his June response, Kontrick admitted the transfers of his salary but denied he had intended to defraud his creditors.

In early 2000, the bankruptcy court ruled in favor of Ryan's family-account claim, acknowledging that the facts supporting the ruling were in the May 1998 amended complaint. Kontrick, with a ruling that denied discharge of his debt to Ryan in the sum of $520,000, filed a motion for reconsideration. In his motion he raised for the first time the fact that the amended complaint had been untimely. He argued that court lacked jurisdiction to make its ruling because the critical facts were contained only in the amended complaint. In his view Rule 4004 had created a mandatory, fixed time limit that prohibited the court from accepting the amended complaint no matter when the objection to its timeliness had been raised. The court rejected the motion, finding that the rule's time instructions were not jurisdictional. The court also ruled that Kontrick had waived his right to object once the court ruled on the merits of Ryan's objections. Kontrick's appeals to the federal district court and the Seventh **Circuit Court** of Appeals proved unsuccessful. The Supreme Court accepted his **appeal** because the circuit courts had divided opinions over whether Rule 4004's time instructions were jurisdictional.

In a unanimous opinion, the Supreme Court sided with the Seventh Circuit. Justice RUTH BADER GINSBURG, writing for the Court, reviewed the federal bankruptcy statutes and rules, noting that Rule 4004 was a claim-processing rule that did not "delineate what cases bankruptcy courts are **competent** to adjudicate." Kontrick, while arguing that the rule was "jurisdictional," had admitted at oral argument that this word really was used to mean a nonextendable time limit. Justice Ginsburg seized on the difference between a rule governing **subject matter jurisdiction** (does the court have the right to consider certain classes of case?) and claim-processing rules that in this case gave the creditor notice of time limits for filing and the debtor the right to raise an **affirmative defense** for a late filing. In this case Kontrick had the right to raise the timeliness issue in his June 1998 response, yet he failed to do so. Justice Ginsburg agreed with the Seventh Circuit that such an affirmative defense must be raised in an answer or **responsive pleading**. Moreover, Kontrick could have amended his June 1998 pleading at anytime before the **decision on the merits** to challenge the timeliness of Ryan's amended complaint. Therefore, the bankruptcy court had properly rejected his motion for reconsideration. Justice Ginsburg concluded that no construction of the rules would allow someone like Kontrick to "defeat a claim, as filed too late, after the party has litigated and lost the case on the merits."

Chapter 7 Attorney's Fees Must be Authorized by the Bankruptcy Court

The U.S. **bankruptcy** court system relies on the professional expertise of attorneys to guide debtors through the process. In recognition of this need, the bankruptcy statutes set out how attorneys are paid. In 1994 Congress amended the Bankruptcy Code dealing with the award of attorney's fees, 11 U.S.C.A. § 330(a)(1). The amendment required that in Chapter 7 proceedings, where a **debtor** liquidates all assets and is discharged from all debts, an attorney could not be awarded fees unless the attorney had been appointed by the trustee and approved by the bankruptcy court. Bankruptcy scholars and attorneys have repeatedly questioned the amendment, contending the change was the result of a legislative drafting mistake. The Supreme Court, in *Lamie v. U.S. Trustee*, __ U.S. __, 124 S.Ct. 1023, 157 L.Ed.2d 1024 (2003), resolved the issue. The Court upheld the provision based on rules of statutory construction and **legislative history**.

Attorney John M. Lamie represented Equipment Services, Inc. (ESI), preparing and filing a Chapter 11 bankruptcy proceeding in 1998 that sought to reorganize the corporation's debts and develop a repayment plan for its creditors, all the while allowing the business to continue. The bankruptcy court approved Lamie's representation of ESI. After he filed the **petition** he began to draw on a $5000 retainer from ESI. He earned a total of $1,325 in fees for his Chapter 11 work. However, the U.S. Trustee determined that ESI did not qualify for Chapter 11 reorganization and shifted the proceeding to Chapter 7, which mandates the cessation of the business and **liquidation** of all assets to repay creditors. Despite this shift Lamie continued to represent ESI but did not formally ask the trustee to be appointed under § 330(a)(1). When Lamie presented his bill for the Chapter 7 work, which amounted to $1,000, the trustee objected and refused to pay it from ESI's assets. The bankruptcy court agreed, and Lamie brought an action in federal district court. The district upheld the decision, as did the Fourth **Circuit Court** of Appeals. Both courts concluded that the plain language of § 330(a)(1) controlled and that Lamie could only have collected payment for his Chapter 7 work if the trustee had appointed him. By failing to apply for appointment he forfeited his right to his fees. *In re Equipment Services, Inc.*, 290 F.3d 739 (4th Cir. 2002). Lamie appealed to the Supreme Court, which heard the **appeal** to resolve a division in the circuit courts over the **interpretation** of § 330(a)(1). Two circuits lined up with the Fourth Circuit, while three other circuits found the amended section in error and allowed attorney's fees without an appointment by the trustee.

The Supreme Court unanimously agreed that the Fourth Circuit ruling was correct, with three justices filing a concurring opinion. Justice ANTHONY KENNEDY, writing for six justices, acknowledged that the amended § 330(a)(1) was ungrammatical, yet it could still be read on its face to bar fees to attorneys who have not been authorized to represent a Chapter 7 debtor. The 1994 amendment had deleted the phrase "or to the debtor's attorney" from the section that authorized payment of fees without the need for a trustee appointment. However, a subsection dealing with reasonable compensation for services retained the phrase "or attorney." Lamie and three other circuit courts argued that Congress had made a drafting error in revising this section and that "or to the debtor's attorney" had been deleted by mistake. In the face of such a drafting error the Court was advised to ignore the language of the section, which was ambiguous, and turn to legislative history.

Justice Kennedy rejected this argument, even though the **statute** was "awkward, and even ungrammatical." He concluded that the language was not ambiguous because the first part of § 330(a)(1) clearly does not list attorneys as one of the persons eligible for compensation. The subsection referring to what types of services are eligible for compensation listed attorneys but was "irrelevant" because attorneys were not part of the named classes of persons in the first part. This reading meant that the inclusion of the word "attorney" was "surplusage" in § 330(a)(1) but this did not automatically create ambiguity that required a review of legislative history.

Though Justice Kennedy found the plain meaning of the statute sufficient to uphold the lower courts, he went on to review the legislative history. He agreed that a plausible case could be made that Congress did not intend to omit attorneys from this compensation section. However, he pointed out that the National Association of Consumer Bankruptcy Attorneys (NACBA) had spotted the change prior to enactment but the association had declined to object to the deletion after bringing it to Congress's attention. This inaction coupled with the lack of interest by Congress to remedy a supposed error since its 1994 enactment led Justice Kennedy to find that Congress was aware of the change and intended to make it.

Justice JOHN PAUL STEVENS, in a concurring opinion joined by Justices DAVID SOUTER and STEPHEN BREYER, agreed that there had been a drafting error and that legislative history should be consulted. The failure of NACBA to object to this change was enough for the concurring justices to uphold the Court's reading of § 330(a)(1).

Debtors May Seek Relief from State-backed Education Loans

Under Chapter 7 of the Federal **Bankruptcy** Code, a **debtor** may be discharged of all debts, but a debtor's student loans may only be discharged if the court determines it would be an "undue hardship." 11 U.S.C.A. — 523(a)(8). State-backed student loans are subject to the undue hardship provision, but the state of Tennessee challenged the application of this provision. It argued that under the Eleventh Amendment the bankruptcy court lacked jurisdiction to consider such a **discharge**. The Supreme Court, in *Tennessee Student Assistance Corporation v. Hood*, __ U.S. __, 124 S.Ct. 1905, 158 L.Ed.2d 764 (2004), sidestepped the ELEVENTH AMENDMENT issue, but ruled that the bankruptcy courts could consider the discharge of student loan debt without treading on state **sovereign immunity**.

Pamela Hood took out students loans between 1988 and 1990 to attend school in Tennessee. The Tennessee Student Assistance Corporation (TSAC) guaranteed these loans—TSAC is a government corporation created by the Tennessee legislature. Hood filed a Chapter 7 bankruptcy **petition** in 1999. At the time of the bankruptcy filing, she had $4,100 in student loans still outstanding. However, she did not list the loans in her proceedings, and the general discharge of her debts did not cover them. Several months later, Hood reopened her petition, seeking discharge of the student loans as an undue hardship. Following the applicable rules of procedure, Hood served a summons and complaint on TSAC, notifying TSAC of her undue hardship action. TSAC asked the bankruptcy court to dismiss the complaint for lack of jurisdiction. Its argument was based on the Eleventh Amendment and sovereign **immunity**. The bankruptcy court denied this motion; the Sixth **Circuit Court** of Appeals upheld this decision. The appeals court concluded that the states had surrendered their immunity when they ratified the Constitution and its Bankruptcy **Clause**. This clause gives Congress the authority to handle all bankruptcies. *In re Hood*, 319 F.3d 755 (6th Cir. 2003).

The Supreme Court, in a 7-2 decision, ruled that the bankruptcy court could consider the undue hardship application but declined to address the Eleventh Amendment issue. Chief Justice WILLIAM REHNQUIST, writing for the majority, noted that the Eleventh Amendment does not prevent federal jurisdiction over *in rem* admiralty proceedings "when the State is not in possession of the property." Generally, *in rem* actions involve a proceeding where property, rather than a person, is a party. Rehnquist concluded that bankruptcy proceedings are similar to federal admiralty proceedings; the bankruptcy court's jurisdiction "is premised on the debtor and his estate and not on the creditors."

Rehnquist cited several cases that established that states are bound by a bankruptcy court's discharge orders, whether or not the state participates in the proceeding; states are treated like any other creditors. These cases also made clear that the bankruptcy court's *in rem* jurisdiction did not infringe on state sovereignty. TSAC agreed that states were generally bound by discharge orders, but it argued that the process for discharging student loans was unconstitutional under the Eleventh Amendment. Under — 523(a)(8), Congress made student loans "presumptively nondischargeable" and required debtors to make, in the TSAC's view, an "individualized adjudication." TSAC argued that this new individualized process was identical to a lawsuit against a state. Under the Eleventh Amendment, such an action by the debtor was barred.

Chief Justice Rehnquist rejected this argument. He emphasized that the bankruptcy court had jurisdiction based on the debtor's property. More importantly, the position of the debtor was different from a typical lawsuit. Hood was not seeking "monetary damages or any affirmative **relief** from a State," merely the discharge of a debt. Therefore, the Eleventh Amendment was not implicated in such an action.

As to the procedure that debtors must follow to seek discharge of student loans, Rehnquist acknowledged that the Bankruptcy Rules required debtors to file an "adversary proceeding" against the state. Though this label had "some similarities to a traditional civil trial," Rehnquist concluded that this specific procedure did not change the character of the underlying *in rem* jurisdiction proceeding. Moreover, even if TSAC failed to respond to the summons, the bankruptcy court still had to make an undue hardship determination. Viewed this way, the summons was "indistinguishable in practical effect from a motion." Therefore, labels and formalities contained in the procedures should not be used to prevent the bankruptcy court from making the undue hardship determination.

Justice CLARENCE THOMAS, in a dissenting opinion joined by Justice ANTONIN SCALIA, argued that bringing TSAC into bankruptcy court through a summons and complaint amounted to an **adversary proceeding** barred by state sovereign immunity.

Till v. SCS Credit Corporation

In its 2003-2004 term, the U.S. SUPREME COURT heard four different **bankruptcy** court matters. The case of *Till v. SCS Credit Corporation* 542 U.S. ____, 124 S.Ct. 1951, 158 L.Ed.2d 787 (2004), dealt with Chapter 13 of the Federal Bankruptcy Code (the Code) (11 U.S.C. §§ 1301 *et seq.*,) which governs debt reorganization and adjustment for individuals with regular income. Chapter 13 filings are the more common forms of bankruptcy proceedings, with more than 473,000 new filings in 2003 alone.

At issue in the *Till* case was the "cram down" provision under Chapter 13 (11 U.S.C. § 1325). This option allows debtors to propose a substitute, or "adjusted" repayment plan, as long as the secured creditor is provided with a **lien** securing the claim and the value of property to be distributed under the plan "*is not less than the allowed amount of such claim.*" 11 U.S.C. § 1325(a)(5)(B)(ii).

Prior to the bankruptcy filing, Mr. And Mrs. Till had purchased a truck under an installment payment agreement with SCS Credit Corporation (SCS) at an interest rate of twenty-one percent. Later, when they prepared their debt adjustment plan in bankruptcy court, the Tills proposed the amounts they would pay to each creditor per month. In addition to **principal**, they proposed to pay their creditors (including SCS) an annual interest rate of 9.5 percent. This rate of interest, referred to as the "prime-plus" or "formula rate," was reached by taking the national prime rate of eight percent and augmenting it in consideration of the risk posed to creditors by borrowers such as the Tills, whose financial position was somewhat tenuous. The bankruptcy court approved the proposed plan.

SCS filed objections in the bankruptcy court, arguing that the Tills had contracted to pay a twenty-one percent interest rate on their truck loan, and therefore, SCS was entitled to the full benefit of the contracted amount. SCS argued that the "cram down" provision of the Code guaranteed that no adjusted plan would be approved unless creditors would receive an amount "not less than the allowed amount of such claim."

The federal district court, which has jurisdiction to hear bankruptcy court appeals, reversed. Although referring to the twenty-one percent interest rate as a "coerced rate," the court nonetheless held that SCS was entitled to what it could have obtained had it foreclosed on the loan, sold the collateral, and reinvested the proceeds in equivalent loans. Since under the "cram down" provision, creditors were to receive not less than the "allowed amount" of the claim (and the claim of SCS was a loan worth twenty-one percent interest), SCS was entitled to that amount.

When the case reached the Seventh **Circuit Court** of Appeals, the ruling was modified to indicate that the twenty-one percent rate was a "presumptive rate" that could be challenged with evidence that a higher or lower rate would be more appropriate. The case was remanded to allow the parties to rebut the presumptive rate of twenty-one percent. *In re Till*, 301 F.3d 583 (7th Cir. 2002). The parties appealed once again, this time to the U.S. Supreme Court.

Writing the majority opinion for the Supreme Court, Justice JOHN PAUL STEVENS concluded that the prime-plus—or formula rate—proposed in the original bankruptcy adjusted plan, was the best one to meet the purposes of the Code. The opinion conceded that Congress gave little guidance as to which of the proposed interest rates was intended for the "cram down" provision. However, in summarizing the **intent** of the provision, the high court noted that when a **debtor** promises to make future payments, the value is less than an immediate lump sum payment. This is true because of the risk that the debtor may not be able to honor future payments, the risk of future inflation that may decrease the value of the dollar, and the fact that the creditor cannot use the money right away. The "cram down" provision empowers bankruptcy court judges to modify the rights of creditors and choose an appropriate interest rate that is sufficient to compensate creditors for the above risks. It does not doom the repayment plan. Of all the rates proposed by the lower courts, the prime-plus rate is the most effective and least costly as far as evidentiary burden, and the most familiar to all concerned.

Justice CLARENCE THOMAS wrote a separate opinion in which he concluded that the prime-plus rate more than compensated SCS. He also noted that the relevant Code provision did not require that the proper interest rate reflect the risk of nonpayment. The **dissent**, led by Justice ANTONIN SCALIA, joined by Chief Justice WILLIAM REHNQUIST and Justice SANDRA DAY O'CONNOR and Justice ANTHONY KENNEDY, voiced preference for the adoption of the "presumptive" contract rate as a starting point. The bankruptcy court would then be allowed to revise the rate in either direction, following motion by either party and an evidentiary hearing.

Yates v. Hendon

In *Yates v. Hendon*, 541 U.S. ___, 124 S.Ct. 1330, 158 L.Ed.2d 40 (2004), the U.S. SUPREME COURT held that a sole owner of a corporation could be an employee-participant in ERISA (Employee Retirement Income Security Act) pension plans. However, the court held that there must be more than just an owner and his wife as **bona fide** "employees" of the corporation. In this case, Yates's corporation had four employees, including Yates and his wife.

As a result of this ruling, the Court held that monies paid by a sole owner as repayment of a loan from a qualified ERISA pension plan could be exempt from creditors. Notwithstanding, the Supreme Court remanded the case to the Sixth **Circuit Court** of Appeals to determine two key facts that would dictate whether, in Yates's particular circumstances, repayments would qualify for such protection.

Raymond Yates, a physician, was the working owner and sole shareholder of Raymond B. Yates, M.D., P.C. The company maintained a profit sharing pension plan for its employees, with Yates serving as its administrator and trustee. As required by the Internal Revenue Code (IRC), Yates's pension plan contained a "spendthrift clause" or anti-alienation provision. In particular, the plan stated, "Except for loans to Participants as [expressly provided for in the Plan], no benefit or interest available hereunder will be subject to assignment or alienation."

In December 1989, Yates borrowed $20,000 from the plan, to be repaid at eleven percent interest. He failed to make any payments on the loan, and later extended the loan for another five years. His very first payment on the loan was in November 1996, at which time he made one payment of $50,467—the entire balance then due, including accrued interest. The lump sum payment came from proceeds on the sale of his house.

Three weeks later, creditors attempting to reach the funds repaid by Yates to his pension plan filed an involuntary **bankruptcy petition** against him in the U.S. Bankruptcy Court for the Eastern District of Tennessee. **Respondent** Hendon, the bankruptcy trustee, filed a complaint requesting that the bankruptcy court **set aside** Yates's loan repayment as a prohibited "preferential transfer" and instead pay it over to the Bankruptcy Trustee for the benefit of the creditors. Yates responded that under Bankruptcy Code Section 541(c)(2), interest from a profit sharing/pension plan could not be seized (alienated). The bankruptcy court found in favor of Hendon and the creditors, ruling that Hendon could recover the funds. The bankruptcy court held that the spendthrift provision on Yates's plan did not preclude recovery of those funds because, as sole shareholder of the business, Yates was an employer and not an employee of his business for purposes of ERISA. The U.S. Circuit Court of Appeals for the Sixth Circuit affirmed, relying on its own **case law**, which held that neither a sole shareholder nor a sole owner could be a participant in an ERISA plan. Accordingly, the Sixth Circuit ruled, Yates could not invoke ERISA provisions to block the transfer of the loan payment assets to his bankruptcy creditors. *In re Yates*, 287 F.3d 521 (6th Cir. 2002)

Justice RUTH BADER GINSBURG, writing for the Court, noted that resolution of the dispute required (among other things) **interpretation** of definitions and coverage provisions under **Title** I of the four titles comprising the ERISA. 29 U.S.C. §§ 1001 *et seq*. The Court noted that ERISA's definitions of "employee" and "participant" were uninformative. However, ERISA's text contained multiple indications that Congress intended working owners to qualify as pension plan participants. The Court noted that both ERISA and the IRC favored such an understanding, pointing to the fact that since 1962, Congress has allowed partners and sole proprietors to establish tax-favored pension plans, such as Keogh plans. Ginsburg expressly noted that under ERISA, a working owner of a company may wear two hats, as employer and employee. (29 U.S.C. § 1301(b)(1) and I.R.C. § 401(c)(4))

The high court further noted that the Sixth Circuit incorrectly read a DEPARTMENT OF LABOR provision in concluding that an individual and his spouse shall not be deemed employees with respect to a business they own because that same provision stated, *"for purposes of this section."* (Emphasis added.) (29 C.F.R. § 2510.3-3) According to the Supreme Court, the Sixth Circuit also mistakenly relied on an ERISA "anti-inurement" provision contained in 29 U.S.C. § 1103(c)(1).

In summary, the high court held that if a pension plan covered employees other than the business owner and his or her spouse, the working owner may participate on equal terms with other employees of the plan.

The Court further hinted that the lower courts should have considered whether Yates's failure to honor his repayment requirements over the years was inconsistent with the anti-inurement provision. Without expressing opinion on that matter, the high court remanded the case for the lower court(s) to address (1) whether the repayment, made just three weeks prior to the bankruptcy, became part of Yates's interest in the plan, such that it qualified for exclusion from his bankruptcy estate, and if so, (2) whether the repayment was beyond the reach of the Bankruptcy Trustee's power to recover it as a preferential transfer.

The Supreme Court's 9-0 opinion included concurring opinions from Justice ANTONIN SCALIA and Justice CLARENCE THOMAS. Justice Scalia wrote that the Court's overanalysis of the statutes was comparable to using a "sledgehammer to kill a gnat." He wrote that he would have deferred to Department of Labor guidance to reach the same conclusion. Justice Thomas, on the other hand, would have remanded with directions for the lower court to address common-law understanding of the term "employee" as used in ERISA.

BOUNTY HUNTER

Name for a category of persons who are offered a promised gratuity in return for "hunting" down and capturing or killing a designated target, usually a person or animal.

Fugitive Grandson of Max Factor Caught by Bounty Hunter in Mexico

Five months after fleeing the United States due to a **pending rape** trial, Andrew Stuart Luster, the thirty-nine-year-old great-grandson of Hollywood makeup legend Max Factor, was caught in Mexico by **bounty hunter** Duane "Dog" Chapman. Luster, who was convicted by a jury in Ventura County, California, during his absence, was returned to the United States to begin serving a prison sentence of 124 years. Chapman, on the other hand, was arrested by Mexican authorities, who view bounty hunting as a form of kidnapping. A California court later determined that Chapman should not receive the $1 million in bail that was forfeited by Luster when he fled to Mexico.

Max Factor, a legend in Hollywood, invented the "pancake makeup" worn by many stars during the 1920s. As Factor's great-grandson, Luster received a generous trust fund and had a net worth of more than $30 million by some estimates. Luster, who did not hold a job, reportedly frequented nightclubs, surfed, and seduced young women to bide his time.

Luster's legal problems began in July 2000, when a twenty-one-year-old college student told police that Luster had drugged and assaulted her. When police officers searched Luster's house, they found videotapes of Luster having sex with women who appeared to be unconscious. On one of the tapes, Luster could be heard saying, "That's exactly what I like in my room: A passed-out beautiful girl." Prosecutors maintained that Luster drugged women using gamma hydroxybutyrate (GHB) and liquid Ecstasy. The drug GHB is known as the "date rape drug" because rapists may **render** a victim unconscious by administering the drug, allowing the rapist to have sex with the victim. Authorities accused Luster of raping three women numerous times between 1996 and 2000.

Pending trial, with bail set at $1 million, Luster was detained under **house arrest** by way of electronic surveillance. His trial began in December 2002. Testimony from one of the alleged victims was damaging to Luster's defense, and prosecutors were prepared to show a videotape labeled "Shauna GHBing," apparently a reference to the drug GHB. The defense claimed that the alleged victims were merely acting, but court observers reported that the evidence was, once again, adverse to Luster's defense.

On January 3, 2003, as required to do under the court's order, Luster told his probation officer that he was leaving his home. Luster then took his dog, along with other items, and fled. Three days later, Judge Ken Riley declared Luster a fugitive, revoked his bail, and issued an **arrest warrant** for Luster. The trial continued for more than two weeks following Luster's disappearance. He was convicted on January 21 on eighty-six of the eighty-seven counts of rape, drug possession, and poisoning. About one month later, on February 18, Luster was sentenced to 124 years in prison.

Chapman, a Hawaii-based bounty hunter who claims to have captured six thousand fugitives as a bounty hunter, began searching for Luster immediately. Within days, Chapman had begun interviewing Luster's neighbors. Law enforcement officials, including California police officers and agents of the Federal Bureau of Investigation (FBI), also conducted a national search for the fugitive.

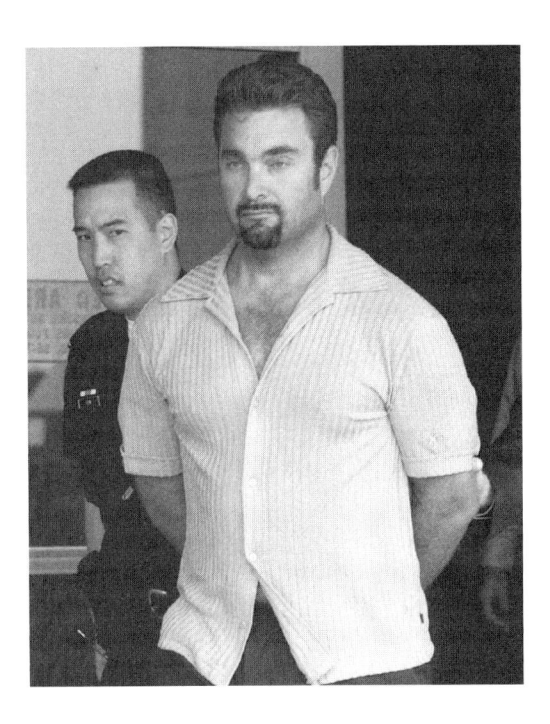

Andrew Luster, following his capture by bounty hunters in June 2003.

During his last month on the run, Luster lived in the coastal city of Puerto Vallarta, a popular resort location that attracts many American tourists. One American couple socialized with Luster in Puerto Vallarta, but upon returning to the United States, discovered that he was a fugitive. The couple provided information about Luster both to Chapman and the FBI.

Chapman arranged for his two sons and a camera crew to travel with him to Mexico to capture Luster. Hours before FBI agents were to arrive, Chapman and his crew caught Luster, detaining him after a loud fracas outside of Luster's hotel. Chapman's group, which traveled in two cars, began to leave Puerto Vallarta, but were caught outside of the town. Mexican authorities arrested the entire group, including Luster, for being in Mexico illegally. Because Mexican law treats bounty hunting as a form of kidnapping, Chapman and his group faced the prospect of criminal charges in Mexico. Ultimately, no charges were filed against Chapman or the others.

Luster was soon returned to California, where he began serving his sentence. His lawyer, Roger Jon Diamond, had sought an **appeal** of the conviction, even while Luster remained in Mexico. Luster's flight hurt his chances at the **appellate** level, as well. Under California law, a court may determine that a **defendant** has forfeited a right to an appeal by fleeing justice. Although such sanctions are not mandatory, a court is well within its power to dismiss an appeal in which a defendant "flouts the authority of the court by escaping." About two weeks after Luster's return, the Second District Court of Appeals in California dismissed Luster's appeal due to the fact that he had fled the country during the trial. (*People v. Luster*, 2d Crim. No. B166741, 2003 WL 21509182 [Cal. App. June 2, 2003]). The California Supreme Court declined to review the case in September 2003.

Although Chapman was not charged with engaging in criminal activity in Mexico, his ransom was much less than he expected for the capture. In addition to a reward offered by the FBI, Chapman sought a percentage of the $1 million in bail that Luster forfeited when he fled. Ventura County Superior Court Judge Edward Brodie declined to award any portion of the bail money to Chapman, noting, "I cannot do vigilante justice."

BRIBERY

The offering, giving, receiving, or soliciting of something of value for the purpose of influencing the action of an official in the discharge of his or her public or legal duties.

Federal Bribery Statute had Sufficient Nexus between Alleged Bribe and Federal Funds

Affirming a decision of the U.S. Court of Appeals for the Eighth Circuit, the U.S. SUPREME COURT held that 18 U.S.C.A. § 666(a)(2), which proscribes bribery of state, local, and tribal officials of entities that receive at least $10,000 in federal funds, is a valid exercise of congressional authority under Article I of the Constitution, which governs the legislative branch of the United States Government. *Sabri v. U.S.*, 124 S.Ct. 2127 (2004). The petitioner, a real estate developer who was charged with bribing a city councilman, argued that the statute was unconstitutional on its face for failure to require **proof** of a connection between the federal funds and the alleged bribe, as an **element** of **liability**. The district court agreed with him, but a divided panel of the Eighth Circuit reversed. The Supreme Court granted **certiorari** to resolve a split among the courts of appeals over the need to require connection between forbidden conduct and federal funds.

Basim Omar Sabri was a real estate developer and a commercial landlord in Minneapolis, Minnesota. During the spring and summer of 2001, Sabri was pursuing a commercial real estate project within the city's Eighth Ward. From 1993 through July 2001, Brian Herron served on the Minneapolis City Council, representing the Eighth Ward. He also served on the Board of Commissioners overseeing the Minneapolis Community Development Agency's (hereinafter "MCDA") budget. MCDA is a city agency created to fund housing and economic development programs within Minneapolis. MCDA received approximately $23 million in federal funds in the calendar year beginning January 1, 2001.

The federal government subsequently charged Sabri under a three-count indictment in the U.S. District Court for the District of Minnesota, each **count** charging him with having attempted to bribe a city official. Specifically, the indictment alleged that that (1) Sabri gave Herron $5000 in an attempt to obtain Herron's assistance in receiving regulatory approval from the city to commence the proposed real estate project; (2) Sabri offered Herron $10,000 to threaten the then property owners that the city would use its **eminent domain** powers to take their property if they did not sell to Sabri; and (3) Sabri offered to give Herron $80,000 as a 10% **kickback** in return for his assisting Sabri to obtain $800,000 in community economic development grants for the proposed real estate project.

Sabri moved to dismiss the entire indictment as unconstitutional on its face, arguing that all three counts were based on a federal law, 18 U.S.C.A. § 666, that exceeded Congressional lawmaking power. This section provides, in relevant part, that if a local government or local governmental agency "receives, in any one year period, benefits in excess of $10,000 under a Federal program involving a grant, contract, subsidy, loan, guarantee, insurance, or other form of Federal assistance," then it is a crime against the United States for any person to corruptly give, offer, or agree to give "anything of value to any person, with **intent** to influence or reward an agent of … a … local … government, or any agency thereof, in connection with any business, transaction, or series of transactions of such … government or agency involving anything of value of $5,000 or more."

For the purposes of his motion, Sabri did not **deny** engaging in the conduct alleged in the indictment. Instead, he argued that the federal government lacked power to regulate such conduct. Sabri observed that the only federal interest contemplated by the statute is the receipt of federal funding. But Sabri said that the statute does not specifically require an evidentiary connection or nexus between a defendant's bribes or attempted bribes and the federal funds received by the local governmental **entity**.

For example, Sabri contended, a **defendant** may be convicted under the law even though the law does not require any proof that the defendant's actions resulted in an unlawful misappropriation, diversion, or kickback of the federal funds. Instead, Sabri maintained, that a defendant's mere attempt to bribe or influence a state or local governmental recipient of federal funds is sufficient to trigger criminal liability under 18 U.S.C.A. § 666. Without such an evidentiary nexus, Sabri reasoned, the federal government lacks a sufficient interest to regulate what amounts to essentially local conduct that would otherwise be subject only to a state's **police power**.

In response, the prosecution answered that all corruption within state and local governments that receive federal funds affects a federal interest, whether or not the corruption directly and actually involves federal monies. The prosecution offered two alternative constitutional powers as **justification** for the statute, the Spending **Clause** (U.S.C.A. Const. Art. 1, § 8, cl. 1) and the Necessary and Proper Clause (Art. 1, § 8, cl. 18.). The Spending Clause provides that "Congress shall have Power to lay and collect Taxes, Duties, Imposts and Excises, to pay the Debts and provide for the common Defence and **general Welfare** of the United States; but all Duties, Imposts and Excises shall be uniform throughout the United States." The NECESSARY AND PROPER CLAUSE provides that "Congress shall have the Power to make all Laws which shall be necessary and proper for carrying into Execution the foregoing Powers, and all other Powers vested by this Constitution in the Government of the United States, or in any Department or Officer thereof."

The district court granted Sabri's motion to dismiss the indictment, finding that Congress had exceeded its lawmaking power under the Spending Clause (the district court did not address the validity of section 666 under the Necessary and Proper Clause). *United States v. Sabri*, 183 F.Supp.2d 1145 (D.Minn. 2002). The U.S. Court of Appeals for the Eighth Circuit reversed. *United States v. Sabri*, 326 F.3d 937 (8th Cir. 2003). Although agreeing that Congress had exceeded its Spending Clause authority, the court of appeals found that 18 U.S.C.A. 666 had been constitutionally enacted under the Necessary and Proper Clause.

Sabri appealed to the U.S. Supreme Court, which granted certiorari. Justice DAVID SOUTER, writing for a unanimous court, concluded that 18 U.S.C.A. § 666 is an instance of necessary and proper legislation. Although not every bribe or kickback offered or paid to government agents and covered by § 666(b) will be traceably skimmed from specific federal payments or show up in the guise of a **quid pro quo** for some dereliction in spending a federal grant, Souter wrote, this possibility contemplates no enforcement beyond the scope of federal interest. Nor need corruption be traceable in this fashion to affect a federal interest. It is enough, Souter said, that the statute conditions the offense on a threshold amount of federal dollars defining the federal interest, and on a bribe that goes well beyond liquor and cigars.

Souter also rejected the argument that § 666 was legislation that a majority of the Supreme Court had already held to exceed Congress's authority under the **Commerce Clause**. In *United States v. Lopez*, 514 U.S. 549, 115 S.Ct. 1624, 131 L.Ed.2d 626 (1995), and *United States v. Morrison*, 529 U.S. 598, 120 S.Ct. 1740, 146 L.Ed.2d 658 (2000), the Supreme Court struck down federal statutes regulating gun possession near schools and gender-motivated violence, respectively. In rendering those decisions, Souter noted that the Court emphasized the noneconomic nature of the regulated conduct, unlike in the instant case where Sabri's alleged conduct involved substantial sums of money.

BROADCASTING

As a verb, to transmit programs or signals intended to be received by the public through radio, television, or similar means. As a noun, the radio, television, or other program received by the public through the transmission.

Janet Jackson's Breast Exposure at Super Bowl Sparks Uproar

A stunt that resulted in the exposure of pop music star Janet Jackson's right breast during a Super Bowl halftime show in February 2004 provoked outrage among a large number of viewers, the chief of the Federal Communications Commission (FCC), and members of Con-

Janet Jackson and Justin Timberlake perform at Super Bowl XXXVIII, shortly before Timberlake ripped off part of Jackson's costume.

gress. Just over one month after the event, the House of Representatives passed a bill that would significantly increase penalties imposed on television and radio broadcasters for violating prohibitions against the transmission of indecent, **obscene**, and profane materials.

Super Bowl XXXVIII was held at Reliant Stadium in Houston, Texas, on February 1, 2004. By some estimates, ninety-nine million television viewers, along with the 71,525 in attendance, watched the game's halftime show, which is often considered an event in itself. Towards the end of the twelve-minute halftime program, Jackson and fellow singer Justin Timberlake sang a duet, during which they danced with each other in a sexually suggestive fashion. At the conclusion of the song, which included the lyric, "I'll have you naked by the end of this song," Timberlake grabbed the right breast cup of Jackson's outfit and tore it away, revealing Jackson's breast. Jackson covered herself after a momentary pause. The CBS television broadcasters and commentators did not mention the incident on the air.

Television viewers were reportedly stunned by the event, which only lasted a few seconds. A representative of TiVo, a system that allows viewers to replay live television instantly, reported that subscribers replayed those few seconds more than any moment in the company's three-year history. The event was the highlight of many evening news telecasts and morning talk shows, as well as numerous Internet sites.

Both Jackson and Timberlake claimed that the exposure was an accidental result of a wardrobe mishap. MTV, the producer of the program, and CBS, which broadcast the game and the halftime show, both claimed that they had no knowledge of plans for the stunt. Both networks immediately issued apologies. Likewise, the halftime show's sponsor, AOL, sought to distance itself from the controversy, noting that it did not produce the show.

Others expressed outrage. The FCC received more than five hundred thousand complaints from viewers, more than twice the total number of complaints in 2003. Paul Tagliabue, the commissioner of the National Football League, vowed that the NFL would change its policies regarding the selection of halftime show content for future Super Bowls. Michael Powell, the chief of the FCC, decried the incident as a "classless, crass and deplorable stunt." Members of Congress, including Representative Rob Simmons (R-Conn.), called on the FCC to investigate the circumstances behind the show.

The Super Bowl gaffe occurred at a time when government leaders had already vowed to enforce decency standards on television. Television channels that are broadcast "over the air" are forbidden from airing material that is considered indecent during the times of 6 a.m. through 10 p.m. These stations cannot air anything considered obscene at any time. Nevertheless, a series of occurrences on broadcast television in 2003 and 2004 have tested the boundaries of what is considered indecent. For instance, rock star Bono shouted a profane word during NBC's live broadcast of the Golden Globe Awards in 2003. Likewise, Actress Diane Keaton uttered an expletive at the 2004 Golden Globe Awards.

Some media entities have been fined significantly for violating these regulations. For instance, Clear Channel Communications, the largest radio chain in the United States, was fined $750,000 in January 2004 for airing sexually explicit broadcasts. The current fines for indecency, though, have not been viewed by many as particularly stringent. Licensed stations can be fined up to a maximum of $27,500 per incident for indecency. "Personalities," such as Jackson and Timberlake, can be fined up to a maximum of $11,000 per incident. A number of critics have noted that these fines are minimal, especially considering the large revenues brought in by such events as the Super Bowl, as well as the fees paid to the individual performers. Moreover, these critics note that the FCC often acts too slowly in investigating these incidents for the regulations to serve as an effective deterrent.

Both the House of Representatives and the Senate have considered bills that would increase these fines significantly. The proposal considered by the Senate would increase the fine for first-time offenses for indecency from $27,500 to $275,000, with increasing fines for repeat offenses. S. 2056, 108th Cong. (2004). Under the Senate bill, the FCC could double fines when a particular program was scripted or planned in advance or when an audience is unusually large, such as the Super Bowl telecast. The Senate Commerce Committee approved the bill on March 9, 2004.

A similar measure passed by the House would increase the fines even more. Under House Bill 3717, both broadcast companies and individual performers could be fined $500,000 per incident of indecency. The FCC would be required to act within 180 days of receipt of a complaint. Moreover, a broadcaster with three indecency violations would have its license revoked. The House approved the bill by a vote of 391 to 22 on March 11, 2004.

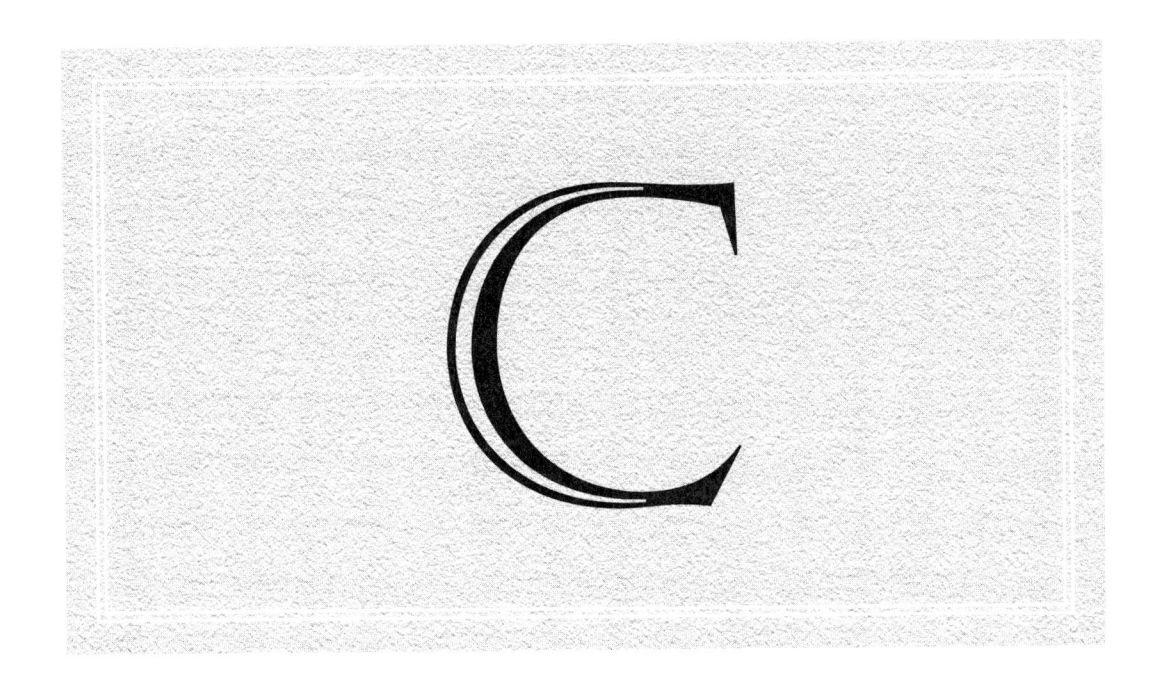

CAPITAL PUNISHMENT

The lawful infliction of death as a punishment; the death penalty.

Death Row Defendant Could not Invoke Rule Requiring Consideration of Mitigating Factors not Found Unanimously to Exist

The U.S. SUPREME COURT ruled 5-4 that a mass-murderer on death row was not entitled to invoke a 1988 decision that held in capital cases a jury instruction is unconstitutional if a reasonable juror could understand the instruction to preclude that juror from considering a mitigating circumstance that was not unanimously found to exist by all jurors. *Beard v. Banks*, ___U.S.___, ___ S.Ct. ___, ___L.Ed.2d___, 2004 WL 1402567 (2004). The Court determined that the 1988 ruling could not be retroactively applied to a case that had become final a year earlier. As a result, the trial court was ordered to conduct a new sentencing hearing consistent with the Supreme Court's opinion.

George Banks was sentenced to death for the **murder** of thirteen people in Wilkes-Barre, Pennsylvania, in 1982. His conviction and sentence were upheld by the Pennsylvania Supreme Court on direct **appeal**, *Commonwealth v. Banks*, 513 Pa. 318, 521 A.2d 1 (1987), and on appeal for state post-conviction **relief**. *Commonwealth v. Banks*, 540 Pa. 143, 656 A.2d 467 (1995). Banks then sought a **writ** of **habeas corpus** in the Middle District of Pennsylvania, which was denied. *Banks v. Horn*, 63 F.Supp.2d 525 (M.D.Pa.1999). The U.S. Court of Appeals for the Third Circuit reversed, finding that the jury instructions given during the sentencing phase were unconstitutional. *Banks v. Horn*, 271 F.3d 527 (3rd Cir. 2001). The U.S. Supreme Court reversed and remanded. *Horn v. Banks*, 536 U.S. 266, 122 S.Ct. 2147, 153 L.Ed.2d 301 (U.S. 2002). Upon **remand**, the third circuit again ruled that the sentencing phase jury instructions were unconstitutional. *Banks v. Horn*, 316 F.3d 228 (3rd Cir. 2003).

The sole issue before the third circuit on remand was whether the rule enunciated in *Mills v. Maryland*, 486 U.S. 367, 108 S.Ct. 1860, 100 L.Ed.2d 384 (U.S. 1988) is retroactively applicable to Banks's appeal. In *Mills*, the U.S. Supreme Court ruled that in capital cases a jury instruction is unconstitutional if a reasonable juror could understand the instruction to preclude that juror from considering a mitigating circumstance that was not unanimously found to exist by all jurors. It is beyond dispute, the *Mills* Court said, that in a capital case the sentencing jury may not be precluded from considering, as a mitigating factor, any aspect of a defendant's character or record and any of the circumstances of the offense that the defendant proffers as a basis for a sentence less than death, even if only one juror is persuaded as to the existence of the mitigating circumstance.

For the purposes of the third circuit appeal in *Banks*, the parties stipulated that a reasonable juror could have understood the instructions given during the sentencing phase as precluding jury consideration of certain **mitigating circumstances**. Instead, the dispute was whether the retroactivity principles articulated in *Teague v. Lane*, 489 U.S. 288, 109 S.Ct. 1060, 103 L.Ed.2d 334 (U.S. 1989) could be applied to invalidate the instructions given in *Banks*. Ac-

Jim Olson and his wife show where Olson was shot by George Banks in 1982.

cording to *Teague*, new rules of constitutional criminal procedure enunciated during habeas review will not be applicable to those cases that have become final before the new rules are announced, unless they fall within an exception to the general rule.

In determining whether an exception to the *Teague* nonretroactivity principle applied, the third circuit wrote in *Banks*, a court must first determine when a defendant's conviction became final, and then the court must survey the legal landscape to determine whether the case in question announced a new rule of **constitutional law**. If the case does not announce a new constitutional rule, then *Teague* does not apply and the rule may be applied retroactively.

A conviction becomes "final," for the purposes of *Teague*, when availability of direct appeal to state courts has been exhausted and time for filing a **petition** for writ of **certiorari** has elapsed, the third circuit said. Banks' conviction became final in October 1987, the third circuit ruled, eight months before the Supreme Court issued its decision in *Mills*. Thus, the third circuit turned to the question of whether *Mills* announced a new constitutional **rule of law**.

The third circuit concluded that *Mills* did not enunciate a new constitutional rule, but instead "represented merely an application of the well established constitutional rule that the Eighth Amendment prohibits all barriers to the sentencer's consideration of any and all mitigation evidence in the penalty phase of a capital trial." By the time that *Mills* became final in 1987, the third circuit noted, the Supreme Court had decided *Lockett v. Ohio*, 438 U.S. 586, 98 S.Ct. 2954, 57 L.Ed.2d 973 (1978), *Eddings v. Oklahoma*, 455 U.S. 104, 102 S.Ct. 869, 71 L.Ed.2d 1 (1982), *Woodson v. North Carolina*, 428 U.S. 280, 96 S.Ct. 2978, 49 L.Ed.2d 944 (1976), and at least four other cases. These cases, the third circuit said, demonstrate the Supreme Court's "unwavering recognition and insistence" that the EIGHTH AMENDMENT prohibits any barrier to a sentencing jury's consideration of mitigating evidence in a capital case, and they provide a clear indication that a jury instruction that could work to prevent a juror from considering any and all mitigating evidence, whether because of unanimity requirements or otherwise, would be constitutionally infirm.

The Supreme Court disagreed. Writing for the majority, Justice CLARENCE THOMAS performed his own *Teague* analysis.

First, Thomas wrote, *Teague* requires a determination of when the conviction became final. Here, Justice Thomas said, the ordinary rule of finality applied—the conviction became final when direct appeal in the state courts had been exhausted and the time for filing a petition for a writ of certiorari had expired or a timely filed petition had been finally denied. Under this rule, the conviction became final in 1987 before *Mills* was decided. Thomas rejected the argument that a conviction that was no longer subject to direct review nonetheless was not final for *Teague* purposes because of the state court's past discretionary **practice** of applying a relaxed waiver rule in death penalty cases. An otherwise final **judgment** is not rendered nonfinal by the possibility that the state court might, in its discretion, decline to enforce an available procedural bar and choose to apply a new rule of law, the Justice said.

Justice Thomas said that the *Banks* argument reflected a fundamental misunderstanding of *Teague*. *Teague*'s nonretroactivity principle "acts as a limitation on the power of federal courts to grant 'habeas **corpus** relief to . . . state prisoner[s].'" Federal courts must apply *Teague* before considering the **merits** of a claim, whenever the state raises the issue. The rule protects not only reasonable judgments of state courts, but also the state's interest in finality quite apart from their courts.

Second, Thomas determined that *Mills* announced a new rule that was not dictated by then-existing precedent when the conviction became final in 1987. The *Mills* rule prohibiting states from requiring jurors to find mitigating factors unanimously was not dictated or compelled by the Court's earlier decision in *Lockett*.

That decision, striking down a death penalty **statute** that prohibited consideration of aspects of a defendant's character or record as a mitigating factor, as well as its then-existing progeny, considered only obstructions to the jury's ability to consider mitigating evidence. It did not mandate the *Mills* rule, which shifted the focus from the jury to individual jurors, Thomas explained. Moreover, *Mills* governed how the sentencer considered evidence, unlike *Lockett*, which determined what evidence the sentencer may consider. Moreover, there was no need to guess whether reasonable jurists could have differed as to whether the *Lockett*, line of cases compelled *Mills*. Four Justices dissented in *Mills* on the basis that *Lockett*, did not control, and three Justices dissented in a related case on the basis that *Lockett*, did not remotely support the new emphasis on individual jurors.

Third, Justice Thomas said that the *Mills* rule did not fall within either of the two exceptions to *Teague*'s nonretroactivity rule. There was no argument that the first exception applied. The second exception, for "watershed rules of criminal procedure implicating the fundamental fairness and accuracy of the criminal proceeding," applied only to a small core of rules that were implicit in the concept of ordered liberty. The Supreme Court had yet to find a new rule that fell under that exception. Any qualifying rule would have to be central to an accurate determination of guilt or innocence, and it was unlikely that any such components of due process still remained to emerge. The *Mills* rule, Thomas continued, removed a remote possibility of arbitrary imposition of a death penalty. For example, 11 of 12 jurors could decide that several mitigating circumstances existed, but the remaining juror could force imposition of a death sentence by disagreeing as to the existence of any mitigating factors. The *Mills* rule worked narrowly, and therefore did not fall within the second *Teague* exception.

Section 1983 is Appropriate Vehicle for Challenging "Cut-Down" Lethal Injection Procedure

The U.S. SUPREME COURT ruled that a SECTION 1983 civil rights claim does not constitute the functional equivalent of a "second or successive" habeas **petition**, and thus a death row inmate was not barred from challenging the procedure by which he was scheduled to be executed. *Nelson v. Campbell*, ___U.S.___, 124 S.Ct. 2117, ___L.Ed.___ (2004). Reversing a decision of the Eleventh **Circuit Court** of Appeals, the Supreme Court held that 42 U.S.C.A. § 1983 was an appropriate vehicle for a prisoner's Eighth Amendment claim seeking a temporary stay and permanent injunctive **relief**, in connection with his challenge to a Alabama's intended use of a "cut-down" procedure to access his veins during an execution by lethal injection.

David Larry Nelson was convicted and sentenced to death for first-degree **murder** in a Jefferson County Circuit Court in Alabama. During trial, the prosecution introduced evidence that Nelson intentionally killed two persons in a 24-hour crime spree on December 31, 1977, and January 1, 1978. Over the next 25 years, Nelson filed a series of unsuccessful appeals challenging the conviction.

An execution date was scheduled for 6 p.m. on Oct. 9, 2003, at Holman Prison in Atmore, Alabama. The day before he was scheduled to die, the U.S. Court of Appeals for the Eleventh Circuit seemingly cleared the way for his execution by denying his 42 U.S.C.A. § 1983 civil rights claim, which asserted that Alabama's proposed possible use of the "cut-down" procedure to gain venous access as part of the lethal injection procedure violated the Eighth Amendment's prohibition against **cruel and unusual punishment**. *Nelson v. Campbell*, 347 F.3d 910 (11th Cir. 2003). Using local anesthetic, the "cut-down" procedure would require making a two-inch incision in Nelson's upper arm for the purpose of locating a peripheral vein to perform a central-line procedure. Before resorting to this procedure, Alabama first proposed to gain venous access through a femoral vein in Nelson's thigh, and, if unsuccessful, then through the external carotid artery in Nelson's neck, neither of which procedure Nelson challenged. It is only if venous access cannot be readily gained in those two areas that Alabama proposed to use the third alternative of the "cut-down" procedure.

Nelson appealed the Eleventh Circuit's ruling, and the U.S. Supreme Court granted him a stay of execution and a **writ** of **certiorari**. *Nelson v. Campbell*, ___ U.S ___, 124 S.Ct. 835, 157 L.Ed.2d 692 (2003). The crux of the **appeal** centers on the question whether Nelson's § 1983 action amounted to a second or successive habeas petition prohibited by 28 U.S.C.A. § 2244. This section provides in relevant part:

(2) A claim presented in a second or successive **habeas corpus** application under section 2254 that was not presented in a prior application shall be dismissed unless—

(A) the applicant shows that the claim relies on a new rule of **constitutional law**, made

retroactive to cases on collateral review by the Supreme Court, that was previously unavailable; or

(B)(i) the factual predicate for the claim could not have been discovered previously through the exercise of due diligence; and

(ii) the facts underlying the claim, if proven and viewed in light of the evidence as a whole, would be sufficient to establish by clear and convincing evidence that, but for constitutional error, no reasonable factfinder would have found the applicant guilty of the underlying offense.

Nelson previously filed a federal habeas petition on April 14, 1997, alleging error due to the trial court's failure to conduct a hearing prior to allowing him to proceed **pro se** at his 1994 re-sentencing hearing. The petition was denied by the U.S. District Court for the Northern District of Alabama, and the district court's decision was affirmed on appeal. *Nelson v. Alabama*, 292 F.3d 1291 (11th Cir. 2002). Additionally, Nelson, through his **counsel**, acknowledged that he had exhausted all available habeas **corpus** relief and that he would have to get permission from the Eleventh Circuit in order to file a second or successive habeas petition.

The Eleventh Circuit determined that Nelson's § 1983 action was the "functional equivalent" of another habeas petition, and thus barred by 28 U.S.C.A. § 2244. The court said it was bound by its own decision in *Fugate v. Department of Corrections*, 301 F.3d 1287, 1288 (11th Cir.2002), where the court ruled that the *Fugate* petitioner's § 1983 challenge to the state of Georgia's "cut down" procedure was tantamount to a second or successive habeas petition.

Justice SANDRA DAY O'CONNOR, writing for a unanimous Supreme Court, reversed. She noted that § 1983 must yield to the more specific federal habeas **statute**, with its attendant procedural requirements, where an inmate seeks injunctive relief challenging the fact of his conviction or the duration of his sentence. Such claims fall within the core of habeas corpus and are thus not **cognizable** when brought pursuant to § 1983. By contrast, constitutional claims that merely challenge the conditions of a prisoner's confinement, whether the inmate seeks monetary or injunctive relief, fall outside of that core and may be brought pursuant to § 1983 in the first instance.

Even if the Supreme Court were to accept the premise that a challenge to lethal injection constitutes the functional equivalent of a habeas proceeding, Justice O'Connor wrote, the mere fact that venous access was a necessary prerequisite to execution did not imply that a particular means of gaining such access was likewise necessary. If as a legal matter the cut-down were a statutorily mandated part of the lethal injection **protocol**, or if as a factual matter the prisoner were unable or unwilling to concede acceptable alternatives for gaining venous access, the state might have a stronger argument that granting Nelson success on the **merits**, coupled with injunctive relief, would **call** into question the death sentence itself. But that was not the case here, O'Connor pointed out, since Nelson opposed use of the cut-down procedure only if the state could not gain venous access through the femoral vein in his thigh or the external carotid artery in his neck.

Decision Requiring Jury Determination of Aggravating Factors Supporting Death Penalty was Not Retroactive

In a 5-4 decision, the U.S. SUPREME COURT held that *Ring v. Arizona*, 536 U.S. 584, 122 S.Ct. 2428, 153 L.Ed.2d 556 (2002), announced a new procedural rule, and thus did not apply retroactively to cases already final on direct review. In *Ring*, the Supreme Court held that aggravating factors that lead to the imposition of the death penalty must be determined by a jury.

Warren Summerlin was convicted of **felony murder** for killing Brenna Bailey, a delinquent account collector for Finance America. The evidence produced at trial in state court demonstrated that Summerlin brutally attacked Bailey when she visited Summerlin's Arizona home to investigate an overdue account in April 1981. Summerlin was sentenced in July 1982.

The felony-murder **statute** provided for imposition of either life imprisonment or the death penalty. Under Arizona law as it existed at the time of the defendant's conviction, the trial judge, sitting alone, determined the existence of aggravating circumstances that rendered a **defendant** eligible for the death penalty. See Arizona Statute § 13-703. The state trial judge imposed the death penalty based on a finding of two statutory aggravating factors-(1) the fact that the present crime was committed under especially cruel, heinous, and depraved circumstances, and (2) a prior felony conviction involving the use or threat of violence.

Summerlin spent almost twenty years pursuing appeals in state court, all of which proved unfruitful. Summerlin began to concurrently pursue federal remedies in 1995. While Summerlin's most recent federal habeas **petition** was **pending** before the U.S. District Court for the District of Arizona, the U.S. Supreme Court decided *Ring v. Arizona*, 536 U.S. 584, 122 S.Ct. 2428, 153 L.Ed.2d 556 (U.S. 2002).

In *Ring* the Supreme Court ruled that capital defendants, no less than non-capital defendants, are entitled under the Sixth Amendment to a jury determination of any fact on which the legislature conditions an increase in their maximum punishment. U.S.C.A. Const.Amend. 6. The SIXTH AMENDMENT right to a jury trial thus precludes a procedure whereby the sentencing judge, sitting without a jury, finds an aggravating circumstance necessary for imposition of the death penalty. As a result, Arizona statute § 13-703, pursuant to which, following a jury **adjudication** of a defendant's guilt of first-degree murder, the trial judge, sitting alone, determines the presence or absence of the aggravating factors required by Arizona law for imposition of the death penalty, violates the Sixth Amendment right to a jury trial in capital prosecutions.

Despite the holding in *Ring*, the Arizona federal district court dismissed Summerlin's **writ** of **habeas corpus**. The U.S. Court of Appeals for the Ninth Circuit, sitting **en banc**, reversed. The court of appeals began its opinion by recognizing that under *Teague v. Lane*, 489 U.S. 288, 109 S.Ct. 1060, 103 L.Ed.2d 334 (1989), new rules of criminal procedure do not apply to criminal cases that were final before the new rule was announced. According to the ninth circuit, however, *Ring* did not announce a new rule of criminal procedure.

Instead, the court said that *Ring* announced a new substantive rule for Arizona, and therefore was not subject to the strictures of *Teague*. The ninth circuit reasoned that capital murder was a separate offense under Arizona law and the aggravating circumstances that elevate a crime to capital murder were elements of that offense. Thus, *Ring* announced a substantive rule, "even if its form is partially procedural."

On **appeal** to the U.S. Supreme Court, the state of Arizona argued that the ninth circuit's decision conflicts with a decision of the Arizona Supreme Court in *State v. Towery*, 64 P.3d 828 (Ariz. 2003), which found that *Ring* imposed a procedural rule. Other state and federal courts reached the same conclusion as the Arizona Supreme Court, the state contended. This conflict has created a "morass for capital litigation" in Arizona, as death-sentenced prisoners are not entitled to **relief** under *Towery* in state courts, but may pursue relief under the ninth circuit's decision on a petition for a writ of habeas **corpus**, the state of Arizona contended.

Warren Summerlin in an Arizona Department of Corrections photograph.

The U.S. Supreme Court agreed. *Schriro v. Summerlin*, ___ U.S. ___, ___ S.Ct. ___, ___ L.Ed.2d ___, 2004 WL 1402732 (2004). Justice ANTONIN SCALIA wrote for the majority. He stated that when a decision of the Supreme Court results in a new rule, that rule applies to all criminal cases still pending on direct review. As to convictions that are already final, however, the rule applies only in limited circumstances. New substantive rules generally apply retroactively. New rules of procedure, on the other hand, generally do not. The ninth circuit agreed with the state that *Ring* announced a new rule. It nevertheless applied the rule retroactively to the defendant's case because it concluded that the rule was substantive rather than procedural.

Justice Scalia stated that a rule is substantive rather than procedural only if it alters the range of conduct or the class of persons that the law punishes. In contrast, rules that regulate only the manner of determining the defendant's culpability are procedural. Judged by this standard, the holding in *Ring* was procedural, Scalia said. *Ring* did not alter the range of conduct Arizona law subjected to the death penalty. Instead, it altered the range of permissible methods for determining whether a defendant's conduct is punishable by death, requiring that a jury rather than a judge find the essential facts bearing on punishment. Rules that allocate decision-making authority in this fashion are prototypical procedural rules.

The defendant nevertheless argued that *Ring* was substantive because it modified the elements of the offense for which he was convicted. However, *Ring* did not alter the range of conduct the statute punished, rendering some formerly unlawful conduct lawful or vice versa. The range of conduct punished by death in Arizona was the same before *Ring* as after. The Supreme Court's holding that, because Arizona had made a certain fact essential to the death penalty, that fact was required to be found by a jury, was not the same as the Supreme Court making a certain fact essential to the death penalty.

Jury Should have been Given Opportunity to Consider Evidence of Murder Defendant's Mental Retardation

The U.S. SUPREME COURT ruled that a certificate of appealability (COA) should have been issued to consider a **habeas corpus** petitioner's claim that Texas' capital sentencing scheme provided an inadequate vehicle for jurors to consider mitigating evidence of his low intelligence. *Tennard v. Dretke*, ___U.S.___, 124 S.Ct. 2562, ___L.Ed.2d___, (2004). Reasonable jurists could have found the district court's rejection of the petitioner's claim debatable or wrong under *Penry v. Lynaugh*, 492 U.S. 302, 109 S.Ct. 2934, 106 L.Ed.2d 256 (1989), which held that Texas was required, in the special issues presented to the jury, to give jurors an opportunity to consider and give effect to mitigating evidence in imposing sentence. Thus, the Fifth Circuit erred in denying a COA on the basis that the petitioner had failed to show that his low intelligence was a "uniquely severe permanent handicap" that bore a "nexus" to the crime, the Supreme Court said. Originally, the Supreme Court had coupled *Tennard* with a very similar case, *Smith v. Cockrell*, 311 F.3d 661 (5th Cir. 2002). However, that case was dismissed by joint agreement of the parties.

The case arose out of events that occurred in 1985, when 22-year-old Robert James Tennard and an accomplice robbed and killed two persons, Tennard stabbing one victim fifteen times with a knife while his accomplice killed the other victim with a hatchet. Tennard played a dominant role in disposing of the victims' stolen property. At trial, Tennard presented an alibi defense, and other evidence from which the jury might have concluded that another person could have possibly committed the murders. However, the jury found him **guilty** of capital murder and Tennard was sentenced to death. At no time did Tennard argue to the jury that his culpability was in any way diminished by mental retardation.

However, Tennard's parole officer testified that a Texas Department of Correction's (TDC) record from his prior incarceration indicated he had an intelligence quotient (I.Q.) of 67. During **cross-examination** of this witness, the state introduced the TDC record into evidence. This document appears to have been prepared approximately five years before Tennard committed the capital murder, and there is a notation providing Tennard had an I.Q. of 67. The parole officer could not say who prepared the report or conducted the I.Q. test. This is all the evidence presented at Tennard's trial with respect to his "mental retardation." The term "mental retardation" is not mentioned anywhere in the trial record.

A few years after Tennard was convicted, the U.S. Supreme Court ruled that the Eighth Amendment to the federal Constitution requires punishment to be directly related to the personal culpability of the **defendant**, and that a jury must be allowed to consider and give effect to mitigating evidence relevant to defendant's character, the defendant's criminal record, and the circumstances of the offense. *Penry v. Lynaugh*, 492 U.S. 302, 109 S.Ct. 2934, 106 L.Ed.2d 256 (U.S. 1989) (Penry I). Rather than creating a risk of an unguided emotional response by the jury, the Court in Penry I said, full consideration of any evidence that mitigates against the death penalty is essential if the jury is to give a reasoned moral response to defendant's background, character, and crime. In a subsequent decision, however, the Court ruled that the Eighth Amendment's requirement that a jury give a "reasoned moral response" to the defendant's character, crime, and record is not satisfied by a mere instruction informing the jury that it may consider evidence of **mitigating circumstances**, if the wording of the instruction prevents the jury from having a "vehicle" for expressing its opposition to sentencing the defendant to death. *Penry v. Johnson*, 532 U.S. 782, 121 S.Ct. 1910, 150 L.Ed.2d 9 (U.S. 2001) (Penry II).

The Fifth Circuit, interpreting *Penry* I, crafted new jury instructions. The instructions required that before a jury would be allowed to consider mitigating evidence concerning a defendant's low intelligence, the evidence would have to be of a kind showing that (1) the defendant suffered from a "uniquely severe permanent handicap" and that (2) the defendant's crime was directly attributable to that handicap. A person generally is considered mentally retarded if he scores 70 or below on a standard IQ test, has a school history indicating mental retardation, and is unable to function independently or care for his own basic needs.

While Tennard was appealing in lower courts, the U.S. Supreme Court issued a decision banning the executions of mentally retarded defendants. *Atkins v. Virginia*, 536 U.S. 304, 122 S.Ct. 2242, 153 L.Ed.2d 335 (U.S. 2002). Meanwhile, the Fifth Circuit rendered a decision in Tennard's **appeal**. It held that the simple fact that a defendant on trial for capital murder is labeled "mentally retarded" through trial testimony is insufficient to justify a special *Penry* I instruction informing jurors that they must give full consideration to the mitigating effect of a defendant's impaired intellectual functioning. Instead, the court of appeals said that the defendant must show that there is a nexus between the alleged mental retardation and the capital murder before the jury will be so instructed. *Tennard v. Cockrell*, 284 F.3d 591 (5th Cir. 2002)

In October 2002, the Supreme Court vacated the Fifth Circuit's decision, and remanded it with orders that the appeals court reconsider its decision in light of *Atkins*. *Tennard v. Cockrell*, 537 U.S. 802, 123 S.Ct. 70, 154 L.Ed.2d 4 (U.S. 2002). In January 2003, the Fifth Circuit ruled that *Atkins* did not apply to Tennard's case. Tennard's lawyers appealed again to the Supreme Court, which granted **certiorari** in October 2003.

Writing for a six-to-three majority, Justice SANDRA DAY O'CONNOR ruled that the Fifth Circuit's test had no foundation in the decisions of the Supreme Court. Neither *Penry* I nor its progeny screened mitigating evidence for its "constitutional relevance." The Supreme Court's decisions made clear that the meaning of relevance was no different in a capital sentencing context than any other, O'Connor wrote. Thus, the state could not bar the consideration of evidence if the sentencer could reasonably find that the evidence warranted a sentence less than death. Once this low threshold for relevance is met, Justice O'Connor said, the EIGHTH AMENDMENT requires that the jury be able to consider and give effect to a capital defendant's mitigating evidence. The Fifth Circuit's test was inconsistent with these principles.

Texas death row inmate Robert Smith, who had his death sentence commuted due to mental retardation.

In the case at bar, the Fifth Circuit invoked both the "uniquely severe" and "nexus" elements of its test, contrasting the petitioner's evidence of an I.Q. of 67 with mental retardation, and finding that the petitioner made no showing at trial that his criminal acts were attributable to his low intelligence. Neither ground, Justice O'Connor said, provided an adequate reason to fail to reach the heart of the petitioner's *Penry* claims. To say that only those features or circumstances that a federal appellate court deems severe may have a tendency to mitigate a defendant's culpability is simply incorrect. Likewise, it was wrong to require evidence that the crime was attributable to low intelligence, O'Connor continued. As stated in *Atkins v. Virginia*, impaired intellectual functioning is inherently mitigating, and nothing there suggested that a defendant must establish a nexus between his mental **capacity** and his or her crime before the Eighth Amendment prohibition on executing a mentally retarded defendant is triggered.

Turning to the substantive analysis that the Fifth Circuit should have conducted, reasonable jurists could conclude that petitioner's low IQ evidence was relevant mitigating evidence, and that the state court's application of *Penry* was unreasonable. Justice O'Connor noted that the relationship between the special issues on which the jury was instructed and the petitioner's low IQ evidence had the same essential features as that between those issues and Penry's mental retardation evidence.

Edwin Wilson enters the Federal Courthouse in 1983.

CENTRAL INTELLIGENCE AGENCY

Former CIA agent's conviction overturned after more than twenty years in prison

In 1983, Edwin P. Wilson faced trial for acting in his own best interests at the expense of his country's security. A former CIA operative, he had turned, the government maintained, into an avaricious rogue arms dealer, selling guns, massive amounts of explosives, and the training of military guerilla experts to Moammar Qadaffy, one of the top sponsors of world **terrorism** at the time and sworn enemy of the United States. Wilson and his lawyers argued in vain that he had done these things at the behest of the CIA, in order to exchange the arms for information and to have the Libyan leader's ear. Wilson was convicted and sent to prison for a total of fifty-seven years. But in late 2003, after new evidence had come to light and appeals had been filed by Wilson's lawyers, the truth became clear. Wilson had apparently been telling the truth after all, and was the victim of a government cover-up.

In the original case, the government alleged that Wilson had shipped more than twenty tons of C-4 plastic explosive on a chartered DC-8 directly to Qadaffy. Wilson was also accused of selling handguns and other small arms to Qadaffy for the purpose of assassinating his enemies in Libya and abroad, as well as supplying the expertise of former U.S. special forces soldiers (including members of the Green Berets) to train Qadaffy's people how to shape and hide the C-4 in everyday items. Wilson was living in Libya at the time, jetting around the world and living the life of a millionaire. In 1982, he was lured to New York where he was arrested by federal agents.

The Bureau of Alcohol, Tobacco, and Firearms had been investigating Wilson since 1977, and there was no doubt that he had indeed made the shipments. But Wilson argued that he had been asked to do so at the request of the government, in particular the CIA, in order to strengthen the Libyan leader and use him for U.S. interests. Wilson maintained that the C-4 was not for terrorist purposes, but to help develop Libya's oil industry. Upon examination, some aspects of the government's denials indeed seemed questionable. The sheer amount of explosives was one point. Just a pound or two of C-4 is enough to destroy a bridge or bring down an airliner. The manufacture of C-4 was therefore tightly controlled and monitored by the government. So how had one man managed to buy up twenty tons—an amount representing an entire year's output for all U.S. manufacturers combined—without the government's notice? The government also offered official denials, with officials stating in memos and under oath that Wilson had had absolutely no dealings with the CIA since 1971 and that, in fact, he was not known to them. But Wilson was a well-known figure in Washington and had many social contacts throughout the 70s with the same people who were now testifying against him. Wilson's lawyers were also not allowed to cross-examine CIA witnesses. According to the government, this would represent a dangerous breach of national security, which the court, incredibly, agreed on. This ruling naturally put Wilson's defense in an extremely disadvantageous position. The final blow was a memorandum issued by the CIA's third in command, categorically denying that the CIA had had any dealings with Wilson since his retirement in 1971.

A federal court in Virginia sentenced Wilson to ten years for selling the explosives. A Texas court found him **guilty** of arms dealing with Libya and sentenced him to seventeen more years. In addition, Wilson was convicted of attempted **murder** for allegedly plotting to kill key prosecution witnesses, and fifteen additional years were added to his sentence.

For years, Wilson's lawyer, David Adler, sought **proof** of the government's duplicity. He obtained hundreds of thousands of documents through the Freedom of Information Act. Upon examination of these documents, Adler found records of more than forty instances of Wilson being hired by the CIA for various jobs after officially leaving in 1971, including several assignments given while he was living in Libya, some coming from as high up as the CIA Inspector General. Adler filed an **appeal** in 2000. On October 29, 2003, Judge Lynn N. Hughes of the Federal District Court in Houston threw out Wilson's Texas arms dealing conviction. Judge Hughes noted that ". . . (the) government knowingly used false evidence against him," and further remarked that had the government told the truth, the jury would have found Wilson not guilty. Judge Hughes went on to publicly chastise the government's prosecutor in the case, saying that the false testimony was "presented knowingly . . . in the courtroom, with the express approval of his superiors in Washington."

In concluding the opinion, Judge Hughes wrote: "America did not defeat the Axis because it locked up Japanese Americans. America did not defeat the Soviet Union because it tried to lock up its philosophic fellow-travelers here. America will not defeat Libyan terrorism by double-crossing a part-time, informal government agent."

While only one of the three convictions has been thrown out, Wilson has served more than twenty years in prison, which Adler believes will make him eligible for parole in the other cases.

The government's reaction has been cautious. They are reviewing the ruling and deciding whether or not to appeal. Mark Mansfield, a CIA spokesman, repeated the claim that Wilson had acted alone and without government **consent** in selling explosives to Libya: "The CIA did not . . . have anything to do with his decision to sell explosives to Libya. That decision was his, and that's why he went to jail."

While he still faces various legal hurdles, including landing a parole hearing and another court battle should the government appeal, Wilson, who is reportedly in failing health, can hold out hope that his dealings with the government may be coming to an end.

CIVIL RIGHTS

Personal liberties that belong to an individual, owing to his or her status as a citizen or resident of a particular country or community.

Supreme Court Upholds Federal Four-Year Statute of Limitations

Persons who wish to pursue a civil lawsuit have a limited time in which to file their action. State and federal statutes of limitations define the time limits for filing suits; the time periods vary depending on the substantive area of law. Federal civil rights lawsuits brought under 42 U.S.C.A. § 1981, which bars racial discrimination in contracts, were governed until 1991 by state statutes of limitations that dealt with contracts. However, each state had its own time limit, which led to confusion and uncertainty. Congress remedied this situation when it passed a provision in the Civil Rights Act of 1991, Pub. L. No. 102-166, 105 Stat. 1071, which created a four-year **statute** of limitation for actions arising under federal laws enacted after December 1, 1990. Section 1981, which was originally enacted after the Civil War, was also amended in the Civil Rights Act of 1991. The Supreme Court, in *Jones v. R.R. Donnelley & Sons Co.*, __ U.S. __, 124 S.Ct. 1836, 158 L.Ed.2d 645 (2004), determined that actions filed under § 1981 were governed by the new four-year federal time period rather than state law. In so ruling, the Court rejected the argument that only new causes of action created after December 1990 could qualify for the federal **statute of limitations**.

Edith Jones and other African-American plaintiffs sued their former employee, R.R. Donnelley & Sons, alleging that the company had discriminated against them on the basis of race, in violation of § 1981, at its Chicago, Illinois, plant. The plaintiffs filed their **class action** lawsuit in November 1994, alleging that discriminatory conduct had occurred in the early 1990s. The company asked the federal district court to dismiss the lawsuit, arguing that the new federal statute of limitation did not apply. Instead, the company believed the two-year Illinois statute of limitations applied. If so, this would bar the plaintiffs' action. The district court rejected this argument, noting that Congress had amended § 1981 in its 1991 law. Therefore, under the federal statute, the district court held that the plaintiffs' lawsuit had been filed in time. *Adams v. R.R. Donnelley & Sons Co.*, 149 F. Supp. 2d 459 (N.D. Ill. 2001). Donnelley appealed to the Seventh **Circuit Court** of Appeals, which reversed the lower court. The appeals court reasoned that the new statute of limitation only applied to wholly new causes of action created by Congress. The 1991 amendments to § 1981 had "merely" redefined terms in the original law without rewriting the statute itself. The pre-existing nature of § 1981 meant that the shorter state statute of limitations applied. *Jones v. R.R. Donnelley & Sons Co.*, 305 F.3d 717 (7th Cir. 2002). The Supreme Court agreed to hear Jones' **appeal** because of a split in the circuit courts over this issue.

The Supreme Court, in a unanimous decision, rejected the Seventh Circuit court's **interpretation**. Justice JOHN PAUL STEVENS, writing for the Court, noted that the 1991 Civil Rights Act was an "act" of Congress passed after December 1, 1990. The plain language of the statute of limitations law seemed to mandate its application to § 1981 lawsuits, but Justice Stevens admitted matters were more complicated. Therefore, the Court needed to examine what Congress intended when it enacted the new statute of limitations. Justice Stevens reviewed the history of applying state statutes of limitations to federal civil rights actions and concluded that there had been many problems for litigants and the courts. Congress had appointed a study committee to recommend changes. From this initiative came the 1991 federal law creating a freestanding federal statute of limitations. Justice Stevens found that this **legislative history** supported the application of the statute to § 1981 actions. The Seventh Circuit decision, on the other hand, "subverts" the congressional goal of simplifying filing time periods. Moreover, an act of Congress that amended an existing statute was "no less an 'Act of Congress' than a new, stand-alone statute."

Justice Stevens reiterated that the Court's construction of the statute best served "Congress' interest in alleviating the uncertainty inherent in the **practice** of borrowing state statutes of limitations while at the same time protecting settled interests." In this particular case, the plaintiffs' alleged discriminatory conduct under § 1981 was "made possible" by amendments to § 1981 in 1991. Prior to the amendments, the plaintiffs could not have used §1981 as the basis of their substantive claims. Therefore, the claims arose under a law enacted after December 1990, and the federal statute of limitation clearly applied. The plaintiffs were entitled to proceed with their lawsuit.

Investigators Find Thirty-four Credible Violations of USA Patriot Act

An internal investigation by the Office of the Inspector General, an independent office within the Justice Department, revealed thirty-four credible claims for civil rights violations arising from antiterrorism legislation, known as the USA Patriot Act of 2001. The report was released both to Congress and the public in July 2003.

Following the SEPTEMBER 11TH ATTACKS in 2001, Congress enacted a **statute** entitled United and Strengthening America by Providing Appropriate Tools Required to Intercept and Obstruct **Terrorism** (USA PATRIOT) Act of 2001, Pub. L. No. 107-56, 115 Stat. 272. The legislation has been viewed by many to have indeed strengthened the federal government's ability to take actions to prevent further terrorist attacks, but it has come under criticism from civil rights advocates and government officials as having given the federal government too much power.

Section 1001 of the USA Patriot Act requires the Inspector General of the Department of Justice to designate an official to review complaints and other information regarding abuses of civil rights and civil liberties by employees and officials of the JUSTICE DEPARTMENT. This official's responsibilities and functions must be made known to the public, and the public should know how to contact the official. The official is required to submit semi-annual reports to the Committee on the Judiciary of the House of Representatives and to the Committee on the Judiciary of the Senate "detailing any abuses" of civil rights or civil liberties. Inspector General Glenn Fine appointed a special **counsel**, Scott Dahl, to oversee the reporting activities required under section 1001.

In compliance with this provision, the Inspector General established a Special Operations Branch to assist in the investigation. This branch receives civil rights complaints through mail, e-mail, telephone, and fax communications. Any complaint is reviewed by a Special Agent in Charge, along with two Assistant Special Agents in Charge. After the Special Agent Branch reviews the complaint, the complaint is entered into a database, and the branch determines what decision should be made regarding the disposition of the complaint. When an **allegation** implicates an employee or contractor of the Justice Department, the allegation is assigned to an Investigations Division field office. Other complaints are sent to the Inspector General's Office of Oversight and Review for additional investigation.

Between December 16, 2002, and June 15, 2003, the Inspector General's office received 1,073 complaints regarding violations of civil rights and civil liberties related to the USA Patriot Act. Of these complaints, 272 were within the jurisdiction of the Inspector General. These complaints ranged from allegations of excessive force or verbal abuse from offices of the Federal Bureau of Prisons; improper treatment by officials from U.S. Citizenship and Immigration

Services; and illegal searches by agents of the FEDERAL BUREAU OF INVESTIGATION (FBI).

The Inspector General also received a number of complaints that either were not within the office's jurisdiction or were simply not credible. For instance, some complaints related to illegal searches and seizures by local law enforcement officers; unfair labor practices; and improper treatment by state correctional officers. Other complaints were less credible, such as allegations from individuals claiming that the Central Intelligence Agency, or other governmental agencies, were conducting twenty-four-hour surveillance on that particular individual.

Among the complaints received, the Inspector General's office determined that thirty-four of the complaints were credible and within the office's jurisdiction. Several of the complaints related to alleged abuses by officials of the Bureau of Prisons. One investigation focused on allegations that a federal correctional officer ordered a Muslim inmate to remove his own shirt so that the officer "could use it to shine his shoes." Twenty inmates alleged similar verbal abuse by this particular officer.

Several other complaints related to allegations that agents of the FBI or other agencies conducted illegal searches of Arab-American's homes or apartments. According to one allegation, FBI agents conducted an illegal search of an Arab-American's apartment, vandalized the apartment in the process, stole items from the dwelling, and referred to the **complainant** as a terrorist. The complainant also alleged that though the FBI officials found no evidence of terrorism during the search, the agents recruited an acquaintance of the complainant to plant drugs in the complainant's apartment. According to the complainant, the agents returned to the apartment, requested another search, and arrested the complainant when agents found the drugs. Similar complaints were made regarding alleged searches by officials from the Drug Enforcement Administration (DEA) and the Immigration and **Naturalization** Service (INS).

Other allegations focused on the treatment of **aliens** following the terrorist attacks on September 11, 2001. According to the report, after the attacks, as part of the investigation, the FBI detained 762 aliens for various immigration offenses. The report notes that the FBI failed to distinguish between aliens who were the subject of the terrorism investigation and those who were not suspected of terrorist activities. The report also found that the INS did not consistently notify aliens who were detained after September 11 of the charges under which they were being held. Moreover, the report found that officials of the Bureau of Prisons shut down communications to or from the inmates who were detained upon suspicion of their involvement with the September 11th attacks.

Several congressional leaders blamed leadership within the Justice Department for the violations. According to Representative John Conyers (D.-Mich.), "This report shows there are more victims of (**Attorney General**) John Ashcroft's war on the Constitution. The attorney general appears on television nearly every week claiming to protect us, while he simultaneously dismantles our civil liberties and civil rights. Will the Justice Department ever admit that it has gone too far?" The Justice Department defended its actions, with one spokesperson noting that the department "made no apologies for finding every legal way possible to protect the American public from further attacks."

COPYRIGHT

A bundle of intangible rights granted by statute to the author or originator of certain literary or artistic productions, whereby, for a limited period, the exclusive privilege is given to that person (or to any party to whom he or she transfers ownership) to make copies of the same for publication and sale.

Federal District Court rules that DVD Copying Software is Illegal

In a decision dated February 19, 2004, U.S. District Judge Susan Illston from the Northern District of California ruled in *321 Studios v. Metro Goldwyn Mayer Studios*, 307 F.Supp.2d 1085 (N.D.Cal.2004), that 321 Studios' digital versatile disc ("DVD") copying software violated the Digital Millenium **Copyright** Act. 321 Studios, the plaintiff, sells software and instructions that make it possible to copy DVDs. Judge Illston enjoined the company from manufacturing, distributing, or otherwise trafficking in DVD circumvention software as of one week from her ruling. 321 Studios indicated it would **appeal** Illston's ruling.

The majority of defendants in the case are members of the Motion Picture Association of America ("MPAA"). These studios are the owners of copyrights in motion pictures. They also produce and/or distribute DVDs containing copyrighted material.

DVDs presently make up nearly four out of every ten sales of video and film works. The digital data on many DVDs is stored in a format called the Contents Scramble System ("CSS"). CSS requires licensure by both the DVD manufacturers and the manufacturers of DVD players.

Information on the DVDs is encrypted with CSS; DVD players equipped with CSS decrypt the information for viewing. CSS involves 31 electronic keys and algorithms to decode a DVD. The keys and algorithms are available on the Internet, albeit illegally.

321 Studios does not have CSS licensure. On April 22, 2002, 321 Studios filed a complaint in federal district court in California. The company sought a **declaratory judgment** that its DVD copying software does not violate the Digital Millenium Copyright Act ("DMCA"). In the alternative, 321 Studios asked that the DMCA be declared unconstitutional. Moreover, the company asked for a determination that its products constitute fair use under the copyright laws.

The DMCA was enacted in 1998, as part of **Title** 17 of the **U.S. Code**. One of the DMCA's provisions prohibits the circumvention of technological measures that copyright owners have employed to protect their works. Another provision prohibits the tampering with copyright management information. These provisions carry both civil and criminal penalties for their violation.

The defendants in the case sought partial **summary judgment**. According to Rule 56(c) of the Federal Rules of Civil Procedure, summary **judgment** is appropriate where the admissible evidence on file demonstrates that "there is no genuine issue as to any material fact and that the moving party is entitled to a judgment as a matter of law." In deciding a summary judgment motion, a court cannot make **credibility** determinations. Nor can it weigh conflicting evidence.

The federal court ruled that many of the issues in this case had already been decided in other cases. For example, in *Universal City Studios, Inc. v. Corley*, 273 F.3d 429, (2nd Cir. 2001), the appellate court ruled that the DMCA did not unduly burden the defendants' First Amendment rights, and that the DMCA did not unconstitutionally limit fair use. In *Corley*, the court ruled that purchasing a DVD does not authorize the purchaser to decrypt CSS.

In another case, *United States v. Elcom Ltd.*, 203 F. Supp. 2d 1111 (N.D. Cal.), the United States successfully prosecuted a case using the DMCA. The government prosecuted a company that developed and sold a product that allowed users to easily reproduce and electronically distribute electronic books. The books were intended to be read only on the computer to which they were downloaded.

In both *Corley* and *Elcom*, the courts differentiated between those who manufacture, traffic, and make of devices to circumvent encryption technology and those who use such technology. The DMCA prohibits the former, but does not prohibit the legal use of copyrighted material by consumers. Judge Illston reached the same conclusion, writing "It is the technology itself **at issue**, not the uses to which the copyrighted material may be put. This Court finds . . . that legal downstream use of copyrighted material by customers is not a defense to the software manufacturer's violation of the provisions of [the DMCA]."

321 Studios also argued that even if its circumvention of CSS is illegal, as the district court found, it could not prohibit the marketing of DVD copying software. 321 Studios said such a prohibition would violate the guarantees of free speech in FIRST AMENDMENT, because the product has some legal attributes. Illston disagreed. She found that the legal attributes of the software could not cloak its illegal aspects in First Amendment protection, "as the First Amendment does not protect commercial speech that involves illegal activity."

Moreover, regarding claims that the DMCA violates the First Amendment, Illston wrote:

> Congress enacted the DMCA after evaluating a great deal of information . . . Congress determined that the DMCA was needed to protect copyrights and **intellectual property** rights; this Court finds that the challenged provisions further important and substantial government interests unrelated to the suppression of free expression, and that the incidental restrictions on First Amendment freedoms are no greater than essential to the furtherance of those interests.

Judge Illston determined that the DMCA provisions do not unconstitutionally impinge on fair use rights. The fair use **doctrine** permits use of copyrighted material in a reasonable manner without **consent** of the copyright owner. Illston noted that plaintiffs conceded that a DVD's content may be copied in other ways than by making an exact DVD copy. "Fair use is still possible under the DMCA, although such copying will not be as easy, as exact, or as digitally manipulable as plaintiff desires."

Illston likewise rejected arguments that the DMCA was unconstitutional based upon the **Commerce Clause** or the Intellectual Property **Clause**, basing her ruling on reasoning set forth in the *Elcom* and *Corley* cases.

Judge Illston concluded that an **injunction** was appropriate in this case. The DMCA allows for injunctions "on such terms as it deems reasonable to prevent or restrain a violation." Illston enjoined 321 Studios, from seven days of the date of her order, from "manufacturing, distributing, or otherwise trafficking in any type of DVD circumvention software."

Comic Creators Fight Copyright Battle Over Oral Contract

Neil Gaiman rose from being an obscure writer of dark fantasy comics to become one of the most respected creators and world-builders in the comics field, and a best-selling fiction author as well. Todd McFarlane was a popular artist at Marvel Comics, chafing under strict company rules, who dreamed of creating and controlling his own characters, so he broke away and started his own company that grew into a publishing and toy empire. These two real-life superheroes of the comics field and former collaborators came together in a titanic court clash in 2003, the culmination of years of legal wrangling. This time, McFarlane played the role of corporate heavy, in a struggle with Gaiman over **copyright**, creator control, and the binding power of verbal agreements.

In 1994, McFarlane asked Gaiman to write an issue of McFarlane's popular *Spawn* comic. Gaiman wrote issue #9 and in the storyline created three new characters: Angela, Medieval Spawn, and Cagliostro. There was no written contract for this transaction, only a verbal agreement by McFarlane to treat Gaiman "better than the big guys do" (referring to conditions at the major comics publishing houses, which often use work-for-hire contracts in which all rights to characters created by the artists and writers become the sole property of the publisher). The Angela character especially was a big hit, so much so that a mini-series devoted to her was published. Action figures of the characters Gaiman created were produced, generating significant revenue.

At this point, around 1997, Gaiman asked that a written contract be drawn up spelling out his rights to these characters and royalty percentages. Both parties agreed to use Gaiman's con-

Author Neil Gaiman, who won a copyright suit against artist Todd McFarlane.

tracts at DC, one of his publishers, as a base to build the contract on. The two sides could not come to an agreement, however. It was then proposed that Gaiman give his rights for Cagliostro and Medieval Spawn to McFarlane's company, Image comics, in exchange for the rights to Miracleman, a property McFarlane had acquired from another bankrupt publisher. Many faxes were exchanged, comprising the only written record of these agreements. It was at this point that the relationship began to break down. McFarlane suspected that Gaiman was exaggerating the terms of his contracts with DC in order to gain more royalty payments, while Gaiman was shocked when McFarlane filed trademark applications on Miracleman, a property Gaiman was supposed to exclusively own. Gaiman also took exception to reprints of material he had authored that used his name and biography without his permission and from which he received no royalty payments. Gaiman filed suit, claiming breach of contract and seeking to claim his share of rights and revenues for the characters he created for *Spawn*.

The case was tried at Federal Court in Madison, Wisconsin, with Judge John Shabaz presiding. A twelve-member jury, all women, were seated to decide the case, which opened on October 1, 2002. The main questions put before them were: Did the conversations and faxes between McFarlane and Gaiman constitute a contract? Did Gaiman have rights to the characters he created as a guest in McFarlane's universe, or was he simply work-for-hire help who had no claim on the established milieu?

Since the agreements were verbal and much of each side's case came down to "he said, she said" testimony, much of the maneuvering by both teams of attorneys was aimed at attacking the other side's **credibility**. McFarlane's lawyers attempted to portray Gaiman as greedy, aiming to snatch a piece of a suddenly lucrative property. A note written by Gaiman to McFarlane in the script to *Spawn #9* was read: "It's your playground, I'm just in for an afternoon on the swings." McFarlane's lawyer went on,

> "Now, ten years later, Neil says he owns one of the swings and the slide and wants to be paid whenever someone goes around the merry-go-round."

However, McFarlane had the worst time of it, because under **cross-examination** his testimony held many inconsistencies with written statement he had earlier made about the specifics of his verbal contracts with Gaiman. McFarlane was also continually undermined by statements from his own employees. A glaring example of this was when McFarlane testified that Gaiman had not been forthcoming with the details of his DC contracts. But during cross-examination, a memo came to light, written by Image's executive director to McFarlane, discussing points of the DC contracts.

McFarlane appealed to the Seventh Circuit of Appeals. The court, in *McFarlane v. Gaiman*, 360 F.3d 644 (7th Cir.2004), rejected McFarlane's claims. He had argued that Gaiman had only contributed ideas, which were not protected by copyright, and that his illustrations were artistic expressions recognized as copyrightable property. Judge Richard Posner, writing for the three-judge panel, disagreed. He wrote in his decision:

> "Gaiman's contribution may not have been copyrightable by itself, but his contribution had expressive content without which Cogliostro wouldn't have been a character ... but merely a drawing."

Gaiman plans to donate the royalty payments, which will total in the millions of dollars, to a charity that defends the first-amendment rights of comic creators.

SCO Group Sues IBM, Novell, and Others Over Unix and Linux Use

SCO Group, a Utah-based company that inherited the **intellectual property** rights for the Unix computer operating system, filed a lawsuit in March 2003 against a number of companies for **copyright** infringement and misappropriation of trade secrets, along with other causes of action. Among the defendants in the multibillion dollar action, as well as other related actions, are IBM, Novell, and several other users of Unix and derivatives of the operating system.

The rather complicated history of Unix began in the 1960s, when Bell Labs joined forces with several other entities to develop a multitasking and multi-user computer operation system. The first Unix system was developed in 1969 by AT&T's Unix Systems Laboratory. Numerous companies, organizations, institutions, and individuals contributed to the operating system's development during the 1970s and 1980s. A number of companies released versions of Unix during the late 1970s and 1980s, including Microsoft (Xexix in 1980); Hewlett-Packard (HP-UX in 1982); Santa Cruz Operation, later to become SCO Group (Xenix System V in 1983); and IBM (AIX in 1986). During the 1990s, Unix and its derivatives became the most commonly used operating systems for servers on the Internet.

In 1991, Linus Torvalds—later to be known as a founder of the search engine Google—was a student at the University of Helsinki when he developed Linux. Linux is similar to Unix and became popular among developers because of its stability. The Linux source code is also free, which means that anyone can download the code and make further developments to it. Due to Linux's availability and stability, countless numbers of programmers have worked to improve the code since it was first developed. Moreover, several companies, including IBM, have adopted Linux as a standard. Both Linux and Unix are competitors of the popular Microsoft Windows NT operating systems.

AT&T sold its intellectual property rights in Unix to Novell, a well-known networking company, in 1992. Three years later, Santa Cruz Operation purchased the Unix System Source code and the Unixware 2 operating system from Novell. Caldera International, in turn, acquired these rights from Santa Cruz Operation (now known as Tarantella). In 2002, Caldera changed its name to SCO Group since most of its revenue came from the SCO products.

SCO and IBM began a partnership during the late 1990s to create a version of Unix that could run on processors developed by Intel Corporation, the world's largest computer chip manufacturer. During this partnership, SCO offered its expertise as to how to use Unix with the Intel processors. This **joint venture** failed in 2001, and IBM then focused its attention on its own operating system, known as AIX. (IBM has also worked to develop the Linux system along with others in what is known as the "open source community.")

The failed partnership eventually led SCO (under the name of Caldera International) to file a lawsuit against IBM in March 2003. The suit claimed that IBM misappropriated SCO's trade secrets, engaged in unfair competition, breached contractual obligations with SCO, and committed **tortious** interference with SCO's business. According to the suit, IBM used SCO's Unix source code in further development of the Linux operating system. SCO claimed that when Linux code was compared with Unix code, the two contained similarities that suggested that the Linux code was based on the Unix code. According to SCO's chief executive officer Darl McBride, "We're finding (Linux) code that looks like it's been obfuscated to make it look like it wasn't UnixWare code—but it was." SCO also threatened to revoke IBM's license to use AIX because IBM's system is based on SCO's version of Unix.

IBM responded to the suit in May 2003, denying each of SCO's allegations. According to IBM, SCO was seeking to "hold up the open-source community (and development of Linux in particular) by improperly seeking to assert proprietary rights over important, widely-used technology and impeding the use of that technology by the open-source community." SCO amended its complaint in June 2003 to ask for $3 billion from IBM.

The lawsuit caused concern among those involved with Linux, since if a court held that Linux contains Unix source code, users could then be held liable for infringement for its use. In May 2003, SCO sent letters to about 1,500 companies that used Linux, warning that the companies could be liable to SCO for the use of the operating system. SCO was struggling financially at the time, and some commentators viewed the lawsuit, along with SCO's letters, as a means to prompt another company to acquire SCO. The Linux community resented SCO's actions, and a rift arose between the company and others involved in the development of Linux.

IBM responded to SCO's lawsuit in August 2003 by filing a countersuit. The countersuit claimed that SCO had infringed on IBM's patents and had damaged IBM's reputation. According to the complaint, SCO had filed the suit in order to "extract windfall profits" that would aid a declining stock price.

Dan McBride, chief executive of SCO Group.

In May 2003, Novell challenged SCO's claims that SCO owned the copyright for Unix. The company asserted that the 1995 agreement between Novell and Santa Cruz Operation did not include copyrights or patent rights in Unix. However, shortly after its issuing its statement, Novell conceded that it had sold some of the rights to SCO in a 1996 amendment to the original agreement. In January 2004, Novell purchased SuSE Linux, Europe's leading Linux distributor.

SCO sued Novell, accusing the latter of slander for its statements that Novell still owned the Unix copyrights. Shortly after bringing suit against Novell, SCO added a copyright claim to its action against IBM. These subsequent actions occurred after the parties had filed a series of back-and-forth motions regarding the release of certain information. IBM responded in March 2004 by requesting a **declaratory judgment** that it had not infringed upon SCO's copyrights.

SCO followed it copyright claims by filing lawsuits against certain users of Linux. SCO alleged that the users had violated SCO's Unix copyrights by using Linux. Among the companies sued were AutoZone and DaimlerChrysler AG. These suits, along with the claims brought against IBM, Novell, and others, are not expected to be resolved for at least two to three years.

CORPORATE FRAUD

The Roundup of Enron Executives Continues

Enron Corporation began in 1985 with the merger of Houston Natural Gas and Inter-North, another natural gas company headquar-

Former Enron CEO Jeffrey Skilling speaks to reporters after pleading not guilty to 36 counts.

tered in Nebraska. In 1989, the company shifted its focus from being merely a pipeline supplier and diversified into commodities trading. Enron quickly grew over the next decade, eventually claiming its position as the #1 natural gas broker in North America and the United Kingdom. In December of 2000, Enron reached its zenith. The company announced that Jeffrey Skilling would assume the post of CEO. Enron shares, already a valuable commodity, were closing in on $100 a share. At this point, Enron ranked seventh in the list of Fortune 500 companies and looked to have an even brighter future ahead.

In August of 2001, Skilling mysteriously resigned from his CEO post, having sold off his Enron stock, netting over $60 million in profits. On October 16, Enron reported some shocking figures: A $638 million loss for the fiscal quarter and a $1.2 billion reduction in shareholder equity. A week later, the SEC began looking into the situation, upping the inquiry to a full investigation one month later. In late November, Enron's shares were worth less than $1, and on December 2, 2001, less than a year after hitting their apparent high-water mark, Enron filed for Chapter 11 protection. Thousands of employees were suddenly out of a job, and most of them, who had received Enron shares as part of their savings and retirement plans, lost their entire nest egg. What had gone so wrong, and who was responsible?

On January 9, 2002, the Justice Department announced the launch of criminal investigations into the Enron collapse. The Powers Report, the results of an investigation by Texas School of Law Dean William Powers, revealed a whole host of shady dealings and characters—almost all of them among the company's top executives and directors. Testifying in front of a House panel in February of 2002, former chief financial officer Andrew Fastow and several other Enron execs invoked the 5th Amendment against **self-incrimination**, while Skilling spoke out and flatly denied any criminal activity. As the investigation continued and arrests were made, the spotlight began to focus on Fastow and his wife, Lea. On October 31, 2002, Andrew Fastow was indicted on 78 counts of **fraud**, **money laundering**, **conspiracy**, and other charges, which was later upped to 98 counts and finally to 109. He was accused of being the prime mover behind financial schemes that shifted funds around, hid losses accrued by various divisions of the company, and lined his own pockets to the tune of $30 million. Lea Fastow, a former assistant treasurer at Enron, was charged on May 1, 2003, with tax fraud and conspiring with her husband in his money-shuffling schemes.

Throughout the rest of the year, the investigation continued, and more and more lower-level Enron executives were rounded up. Meanwhile, the Fastows were busy trying to cut a deal with government prosecutors before their scheduled April court date. While convicting Andrew Fastow was important, the information that he and others could provide could prove invaluable to the government. In the end, Fastow played his last card, and the government had their case against him. On January 14, 2004, Andrew Fastow pleaded **guilty** to two of the counts of wire and securities fraud. He agreed to serve up to a ten-year jail sentence (though the final sentence is at the discretion of the judge and might hinge on his continued cooperation) and surrender $24 million in funds. Lea Fastow pleaded guilty to tax fraud in exchange for a sentence of five months in prison and five more months of **house arrest**. In exchange, both agreed to provide information about the roles of top tier executives in the collapse of the company.

On February 19, the SEC landed another major target. CEO Jeffrey Skilling was arrested in Houston and charged with 36 counts, including violating antitrust laws, fraud, conspiracy, and insider trading. Bond was set at $5 million and Skilling was restricted to travel only within the continental United States. One of Skilling's lawyers, Daniel Petrocelli, dismissed the charges against his client as "scapegoating." In interviews, Skilling has denied all the charges, maintaining that he had no idea of the brewing financial crisis and his leaving the company when he did was simply due to being "tired." As Skilling said in testimony before Congress during the initial investigation: "It is my belief that Enron's failure was due to a classic run on the bank, a liquidity crisis spurred by lack of confidence in the company."

In March, U.S. District Judge Kenneth Hoyt rescheduled Andrew Fastow's sentencing for late October 2004. This move is designed to facilitate Fastow's continued cooperation in the investigation and is described as a typical move for a cooperating witness. Fastow will receive his final sentence after the last cases against the other executives have gone to trial.

On April 7, U.S. District Judge David Hittner rejected Lea Fastow's sentencing deal, aiming for a longer sentence of ten to sixteen months in prison. In response, Lea Fastow initially withdrew her plea and planned to send the case to trial, but she later agreed to a plea bargain and began serving a one year sentence on July 12, 2004.

Meanwhile, in mid-March, U.S. District Judge Sim Lake postponed Skilling's trial date indefinitely, as attorneys from both sides need time to sift through literally millions of documents connected to almost every financial transaction Enron made from the years 1999 to 2002. Judge Lake has ordered an update every two weeks in order to **assess** when a trial date might conceivably be set.

The interesting question is whether Skilling will be able to structure some sort of plea agreement himself—perhaps one aimed at bringing Kenneth Lay, Enron's Chairman of the Board, to trial. Lay is widely suspected of being involved with the dealings that brought Enron to its knees, and on July 8, 2004, was formally charged in an eleven-count indictment. Lay pleaded not guilty to all charges and was released on $500,000 bail. Following closely upon Lay's criminal charges, the SECURITIES AND EXCHANGE COMMISSION filed a civil complaint against Lay that sought more than $90 million in damages. Lay denied any wrongdoing.

WorldCom Woes

2003 was a busy year for MCI WorldCom (WorldCom). The previous year saw the communications giant file for Chapter 11 **bankruptcy** protection (July 2002). Less than a month before that, on June 25, 2002, the company had publicly disclosed that substantial accounting irregularities had been internally discovered, making it necessary to revise 2001 and early 2002 financial statements. WorldCom's board of directors also requested resignations from its chief executive officer, (CEO) Bernard J. Ebbers, and chief financial officer (CFO), Scott Sullivan. At the time of their resignations/terminations, Ebbers and Sullivan were embroiled—as defendants, along with WorldCom—in a major **class action** lawsuit involving alleged securities **fraud**, *Goldstein v. MCI WorldCom, et al.*. In August 2003, the U.S. Court of Appeals for the Fifth Circuit affirmed the **dismissal** of Ebbers and Sullivan in the class action suit, but retained jurisdiction over the **pending appeal** as to WorldCom. *See below.*

Two days later, on August 27, 2003, the State of Oklahoma filed **felony** charges against WorldCom and six former employees, including Ebbers and Sullivan. The fifteen-count criminal complaint, filed by the Oklahoma **Attorney General** on behalf of Oklahoma investors, **enumerated** various violations of the Oklahoma Securities Act that essentially paralleled those of the Securities and Exchange Commission (SEC). Alleging crimes that occurred between October 2000 and March 2002, the counts charged the company and employees with fraudulent representation and falsifying information to the SEC with the **intent** to inflate the value of company stocks and bonds. Meanwhile, the SEC had brought its *own* suit against WorldCom on securities fraud claims. (This case was settled in mid-2003 for $750 million.) *SEC v. WorldCom, Inc.*, No. 02-4963 (JSR), (S.D.N.Y. 2003).

But that was not the end of it all. In February 2003, a *qui tam* **civil action** (usually brought by an informer or "relator" alleging statutory violations, the penalty or fine for which is shared with the state or other **entity**) was brought against WorldCom by John Russo, a private individual. The complaint alleged that WorldCom defrauded the United States by charging inflated PICC charges (Pre-subscribed Inter-exchange Carrier Charges) as pass-through surcharges, when in fact, WorldCom had only been charged a fraction of those amounts. (Long distance companies charge PICC fees for providing outside telephone wires, underground conduits, etc., to link customers to telephone network systems.) In May 2004, WorldCom filed motion in the U.S. Bankruptcy Court for approval of a proposed $27 million settlement in this matter.

WorldCom was formed in 1983 to provide long distance services to Mississippi customers.

Under the direction of Ebbers, the company acquired sixty other telecommunications companies in a fifteen-year period. In 1998, WorldCom purchased MCI Communications Corporation, making it the second largest communications company in the world. But when it attempted a $129 billion surviving merger with Sprint in 2000, federal regulators rejected the plan.

In October 2000, WorldCom reported, for the first time, that due to bankruptcies by seventeen of its wholesale customers, it would write off $685 million in receivables. Following the announcement, WorldCom stock (on trading volumes of approximately 40 million shares) dropped in price from $25 to $21 (on trading volumes of nearly 67 million). Within a few weeks, lawsuits were filed in Mississippi, New York, and Washington, D.C. They were consolidated in March 2001 (under the *Goldstein* caption) with a certified class of all persons who purchased or otherwise acquired the securities of WorldCom during the class period of February 10 and November 1, 2000.

Goldstein v. MCI WorldCom

In the *Goldstein* consolidated case, various allegations (consisting of 110 pages and 285 paragraphs) of corporate **malfeasance** and SEC violations were directed against WorldCom and its chief officers and employees. However, only one claim of fraud was on appeal to the Fifth Circuit. That claim charged that Ebbers and Sullivan knowingly, or with severe recklessness, failed to direct the write-off of millions of dollars of uncollectible accounts. This, in turn, resulted in material misrepresentations and omissions in WorldCom's financial statements and communications with shareholders and investors, violations of the Securities Exchange Act of 1934. The case further charged that these actions, omissions, and violations were intentionally carried out for the purpose of artificially inflating WorldCom's stock in anticipation of pending merger with Sprint.

Bearing in mind the limited issue and scope on appeal, the Fifth Circuit affirmed the ruling of the district court, dismissing the claims against Ebbers and Sullivan. The appellate court agreed that the plaintiffs' complaint failed to adequately plead "scienter" (defendants' **culpable** prior knowledge) in conformity with the requirements of the Private Securities Litigation Reform Act (PSLRA), needed under Rule 9(b) of the Federal Rules of Civil Procedure. Relevant and controlling **case law** supported this conclusion. (Plaintiffs' **counsel** had requested leave to amend the complaint and cure the defect in pleading. The district court's rejection of this untimely request was affirmed on appeal, apparently premised on what the **appellate** court referred to as "'cat and mouse' class action gamesmanship" on the part of plaintiffs' counsel.)

The PSLRA requires that plaintiffs plead specific facts which give rise to a strong **inference** that defendants either intentionally or recklessly committed the alleged fraud. Pleading with specificity is also part of the federal procedural rules. A failure to adequately plead an **actionable** complaint may generally be cured by timely request for leave to amend the pleadings.

CRIMINAL PROCEDURE

The framework of laws and rules that govern the administration of justice in cases involving an individual who has been accused of a crime, beginning with the initial investigation of the crime and concluding either with the unconditional release of the accused by virtue of acquittal (a judgment of not guilty) or by the imposition of a term of punishment pursuant to a conviction for the crime.

United States v. Benitez

The U.S. SUPREME COURT in June 2004 decided a case involving a question of whether the defendant's conviction can be overturned when a judge failed to inform the **defendant** that his plea of not-guilty could not be revoked even if the judge chose to increase a plea-bargained sentence. In *United States v. Benitez*, ___ U.S. ___, 124 S. Ct. 2333, ___ L. Ed. 2d ___ (2004), the Court determined that a defendant's conviction in such a case can be overturned only if the defendant can demonstrate, with reasonable probability, that he would not have entered the plea if the error had not been committed.

Carlos Dominguez Benitez was found in May 1999 with 500 grams of methamphetamine, plus 1391 grams of a mixture of illegal substances, when Benitez tried to sell the drugs to an under-cover police informant at a restaurant in Anaheim, California. Benitez was charged with possession of the drugs with **intent** to distribute them, plus **conspiracy** to possess the drugs with the intent to distribute.

The Federal Sentencing Guidelines rate various federal crimes by assigning to the crimes a "level." Each level corresponds with a mandatory sentencing range. The level assigned for a crime can be reduced by certain mitigating factors, such as acceptance of responsibility. The Guidelines also allow a court to lower an offender's level under the so-called safety value provision, which applies when the defendant has had a minimal criminal history, the defendant did not use violence or threats of violence, the offense did not result in death or serious bodily **injury**, the defendant did not organize or lead others in committing the crime, and the defendant has provided to the government truthful information about the crime. U.S. Sentencing Guidelines § 5C1.2 (2002).

Under these guidelines, the Benitez's charges were rated a level 32. Benitez entered into a plea agreement with federal prosecutors that would have lowered his sentence by several months. Government prosecutors stipulated that Benitez's sentence should be reduced by three points for accepting responsibility for his actions. The prosecutors further agreed to a two-point reduction under the safety-value provisions. Under the plea agreement, Benitez would have been sentenced at level 27. The sentence range under level 27 would have been 70 to 87 months.

The plea agreement noted that Benitez could not have withdrawn his plea even if the judge had refused to accept the sentence recommended by the prosecutors. Benitez had previously pleaded not **guilty**, and the court held a change-of-plea hearing. At that hearing, Benitez testified that the plea bargain had been read to him in his native Spanish, and that he understood the plea agreement after discussing it with his **counsel**. However, Benitez also complained to the court several times during the hearing and before sentencing that he had not communicated with counsel immediately prior to the hearing. He also told the court that he did not understand the sentencing guidelines or its provisions, such as the safety value provision.

At this hearing, the court informed Benitez that the court was not a party to the plea bargain, that the plea bargain was not binding on the court, and that he would be sentenced to the statutory minimum of 120 months in prison if he was not eligible for the safety-value provision. However, the court did not inform Benitez that he was forbidden from withdrawing his plea should the court refuse to accept the recommendations in the plea bargain. Under Rule 11(e)(2) of the Federal Rules of Criminal Procedure, the court is required to advise the defendant of the circumstances in which the defendant may not withdraw a guilty plea.

Neither the prosecutors nor defense counsel was aware that Benitez had two prior criminal convictions under an alias. These criminal convictions raised his criminal history to a level III, whereas the prosecutors had assumed a level I history. Because Benitez had a higher criminal history level, he was not eligible for his sentence to be reduced under the safety-value provisions, and his sentencing level was a 29. This level corresponded with a sentencing range of 108 to 135 months in prison, with a mandatory minimum sentence of 120 months.

Benitez appealed his conviction to the Ninth **Circuit Court** of Appeals. Under controlling **case law**, the appellate court could reverse Benitez's conviction if it found that: (1) the district court had erred in its disposition of the case; (2) the error was "plain"; and (3) the error affected Benitez's "substantial rights." *United States v. Olano*, 507 U.S. 725, 113 S. Ct. 1770, 123 L. Ed. 2d 508 (1993). Moreover, even if a defendant could demonstrate that these conditions were satisfied, the **appellate** court could not correct the district court's error unless the decision had seriously affected the integrity, fairness, or reputation of judicial proceedings, according to the Supreme Court's standard in *Olano*.

The Ninth Circuit found that the district court had indeed committed a plain error by not following the requirements of Rule 11(e)(2). *United States v. Benitez*, 310 F.3d 1221 (9th Cir. 2001). Nevertheless, the court would not reverse the conviction unless Benitez could prove that he did not understand his rights when he entered his plea. The government argued that because his rights were explained to him in plea bargain itself, Benitez could not meet the burden of proving that he did not understand his rights. The Ninth Circuit disagreed, noting the importance of a judge's warning in **open court**. Even the fact that Benitez had said in court that he discussed the plea agreement with his counsel was not enough to convince the court that Benitez understood his rights. According to the court, the error of the judge in failing to warn Benitez of his rights served as sufficient grounds to reverse the conviction.

The Supreme Court granted Benitez's **petition** for **certiorari** on December 8, 2003. At oral arguments on April 21, 2004, the Supreme Court justices appeared to be split on the question of whether the judge's failure to warn Benitez was grounds for reversal or whether it was merely a **harmless error**. Both Justice DAVID SOUTER and RUTH BADER GINSBURG noted that the judge should have followed a written checklist of warnings that must be recited to a defendant prior to the defendant pleading guilty. Moreover, both justices also noted that the prosecutor should have advised the judge that the judge should have recited those warnings.

Other justices, including Chief Justice WILLIAM REHNQUIST, appeared to favor the government's position. Rehnquist pointed out that Benitez knew that he had two prior convictions, and that Benitez had been warned of his rights by a translator prior to the hearing. However, JUSTICE JOHN PAUL STEVENS quickly responded that the judge was still required to give the warning. According to Stevens, "The basic problem here is we're dealing with dumb defendants. That's why you have to tell them twice."

The justice came to an agreement in the end, as seven justices, including Rehnquist and Stevens, joined Souter's opinion. According to Souter, the proper test for determining whether Benitez's conviction should be overturned was whether Benitez could "show a reasonable probability that, but for the error, he would not have entered the plea." The Court remanded the case to the Ninth Circuit for a determination of whether Benitez could indeed satisfy this standard.

DISCOVERY

A category of procedural devices employed by a party to a civil or criminal action, prior to trial, to require the adverse party to disclose information that is essential for the preparation of the requesting party's case and that the other party alone knows or possesses.

Cheney v. United States District Court for the District of Columbia

The United States Supreme Court in June 2004 resolved a case involving important questions of whether a court can require a presidential advisory group, which included as a member Vice President Richard Cheney, to disseminate information about the group's activities. The Supreme Court's decision was less than definitive, however, as the Court refused to order the lower appellate court to block a District Court judge's order requiring Cheney and the advisory group to produce records.

The case of *Cheney v. United States District Court for the District of Columbia*, ___ U.S. ___, 124 S. Ct. 2576, ___ L. Ed. 2d ___ (2004) became well-known to the general public due to Justice Antonin Scalia's refusal to **recuse** himself despite having gone duck hunting with Cheney just weeks after the Supreme Court granted **certiorari** (see, this volume, Recusal: Scalia Refuses to Recuse Himself in Case Involving Cheney).

President GEORGE W. BUSH established the National Energy Policy Development Group (NEPDG) in January 2001, just days after Bush entered office. The group was established within the Executive Office of the President. The group's mission, according to Bush's memorandum that established the group, was to "develop a national energy policy designed to help the private sector, and as necessary and appropriate Federal, State, and local governments, promote dependable, affordable, and environmentally sound production and distribution of energy." *Judicial Watch, Inc. v. Nat'l Energy Policy Dev. Group*, 219 F. Supp. 2d 20 (D.D.C. 2002). The group was assigned the tasks of gathering information, deliberating, and making policy recommendations to the president by way of reports. The group's duration was limited to the end of the 2001 fiscal year.

Among those appointed to this group by Bush were Cheney and several members of Bush's cabinet. Cheney was designated to serve as the chair and was delegated authority to invite other federal government officers to participate in the group's meetings. After meeting for several months, the group issued a report in May 2001, and Bush approved the report as the National Energy Policy. The recommendations that Bush approved relied heavily on coal, oil, and nuclear energy, and called for drilling in the Arctic National Wildlife Refuge in Alaska.

The NEPDG's authority ended on September 30, 2001. The group's activities gained national attention, and several public interest organizations demanded information regarding the process of developing the energy policy. Although Bush's memorandum only mentioned officials within the government, some groups maintained that the group had contacted private industry leaders and that these private individuals had full access to the NEPDG. Most notably, evidence surfaced that the former chief executive officer of Enron, Kenneth Lay, had contact with members of the group. By the end of 2001, Enron had become embroiled in a major scandal involving its accounting and had filed for **bankruptcy**.

Judicial Watch, a nonprofit, public-interest law firm, wrote to Cheney in June 2001 to request information about the NEPDG and its activities. When Cheney refused, Judicial Watch filed a lawsuit in the U.S. District Court for the DISTRICT OF COLUMBIA. According to the lawsuit, Judicial Watch sought to enforce the requirements of the Federal Advisory Committee Act (FACA), 5 U.S.A. app. 2 (2000); the FREEDOM OF INFORMATION ACT, 5 U.S.C. § 552 (2000); the Administrative Procedures Act, 5 U.S.C. §§ 701 **et seq.** (2000); and the federal **mandamus statute**, 28 U.S.C. § 1361 (2000). The plaintiff's complaint, which was amended several times, named the NEPDG, Cheney, several members of the Cabinet, and several private individuals as defendants. In January 2002, SIERRA CLUB, another public-interest organization, filed a similar suit against many of the same defendants in the U.S. District Court for the Northern District of California. The two suits were consolidated in the District of Columbia in March 2002.

The FACA requires advisory committees to release to the public any reports, records, or other documents that are used by the committee, subject to some exceptions. One of these exceptions applies to committees that are made up entirely of full-time officers and employees of the federal government. 5 U.S.C. app. 2 § 3(2)(iii) (2000). The defendants argued that since the group was exclusively comprised of federal government officers and employees, it should not be required to release the group's documents to the public. Moreover, the defendants argued that requiring the group to release the documents would infringe upon the principle of separation of powers because the court would order the release of documents that were allegedly protected by **executive privilege**.

The District Court denied the defendant's motion to dismiss the case and ordered the defendants to comply with the plaintiff's **discovery** requests. The court determined that discovery was necessary to determine whether private individuals were indeed involved with the NEPDG. The court ordered the defendants to identify the precise reasons why the defendants objected to a particular discovery request or why a particular document or piece of information was privileged. The court required the defendants to produce the documents no later than December 9, 2002.

The defendants produced about 36,000 pages of documents, but Cheney then sought an emergency **writ** of mandamus from the U.S. Court of Appeals for the District of Columbia Circuit to protect the vice president from further discovery. Cheney argued that releasing the documents would extend "the legislative and judicial powers to compel a Vice President to disclose to private persons the details of the process by which a President obtains information and advice from the Vice President." *In re Cheney*, 334 F.3d 1096 (D.C. Cir. 2003). This, according to the petitioners, raised separation of powers concerns "of the first order." The court of appeals, however, disagreed. According to the court, any problems regarding discovery requests of privileged information could be cured by the district court. Even though the **appellate** court conceded that the plaintiffs' requests were overly broad for the purposes of proving their case, the court found that the petitioners had not satisfied the burden to obtain a writ of mandamus. Accordingly, the court dismissed the **petition** for a writ of mandamus and dismissed the **appeal**.

The Supreme Court in its June 2004 decision disagreed that the lower appellate court lacked jurisdiction to issue a writ of mandamus. *Cheney v. United States District Court for the District of Columbia*, ___ U.S. ___, 124 S. Ct. 2576, ___ L. Ed. 2d ___ (2004). According to the Court's majority opinion, written by ANTHONY KENNEDY, the Vice President was not required to assert an executive privilege for each discovery request in order to give the Court of Appeals jurisdiction to consider Cheney's petition for a writ of mandamus. On **remand**, the Court of Appeals may now consider the Vice President's separation-of-powers objections without also considering the executive privilege objections.

Though the Court did not require the Court of Appeals to ban the District Court judge from ordering the Vice President to comply with discovery, the practical effect of the Supreme Court's decision was that Cheney most likely would not have to release documents until after the November 2004 elections, if at all. Whether Cheney is required to release these documents depends upon the decision of the Court of Appeals on remand.

U.S. Courts May Order Discovery for Foreign Tribunals

Computer hardware and software companies zealously guard their **intellectual property**. When threatened with lawsuits from competitors these companies have sought to limit **discovery**, fearing disclosure of sensitive information. It was not surprising that computer microprocessor giant Intel Corporation sought to prevent its main PC rival, Advanced Micro Devices, Inc. (AMD), from using discovery involving an antitrust claim that AMD had filed with the European Commission. The commission is the **principal** European antitrust enforcement authority. The U.S. SUPREME COURT, in *Intel Corp. v. Advanced Micro Devices, Inc.*, __ U.S. __, 124 S.Ct. 2466, __ L.Ed.2d __ (2004), ruled that a U.S. district court had the authority to order discovery in this case but emphasized that such an order was not mandatory.

AMD, after filing its complaint with the commission in 2000, asked a northern California federal district court for an order requiring Intel to produce documents that were potentially relevant to its complaint. AMD alleged that Intel had abused its dominant position in Europe by using loyalty rebates, exclusive purchasing agreements with manufacturers and retailers, and price discrimination. AMD was particularly interested in documents that Intel had filed in an Alabama private antitrust case brought in 1998. It sought the federal discovery order only after the commission had declined to pursue these documents. The district court rejected AMD's request, which was grounded on a federal law, 28 U.S.C. § 1782(a). This section provides that a federal district court "may order" a person residing or "found" in the district to give testimony or to produce documents "for use in a proceeding in a foreign or international tribunal ... upon the application of any interested person." On **appeal**, the U.S. Court of Appeals for the Ninth Circuit reversed the lower court, finding that § 1782(a) did authorize release of the documents to AMD. *Advanced Micro Devices, Inc. v. Intel Corp.*, 292 F.3d 664 (9th Cir. 2002).

The U.S. Supreme Court, in a 7-1 decision (Justice SANDRA DAY O'CONNOR did not participate), upheld the Ninth Circuit ruling. Justice RUTH BADER GINSBURG, writing for the majority, concluded that § 1782(a) "authorizes, but does not require, a federal district court to provide **judicial assistance** to foreign or international tribunals or to 'interested persons' in proceedings abroad." Justice Ginsburg noted that the **legislative history** of this section revealed that Congress did not intend to restrict the provision in the ways advanced by Intel. The provision, which had been enacted in 1855, was amended in 1948 and 1964. Each time, Congress broadened the scope of the provision, removing the need for a foreign government to be a party in the U.S. action or for a judicial proceeding to be **pending** in a foreign country. Congress added language that required "a proceeding in a foreign or international tribunal." A 1964 Senate report indicated that the word "tribunal" was used to include administrative and quasi-administrative proceedings as well as judicial proceedings.

Intel had argued that AMD should not be entitled to the documents because Intel was not a party to the commission proceedings. Justice Ginsburg acknowledged this fact but found that AMD was an "interested person" because it had "significant procedural rights" and could seek **judicial review** if it disagreed with the commission's disposition of the complaint. Intel also had challenged the use of § 1782(a) because the commission proceeding was not a judicial review. Justice Ginsburg pointed out that the 1964 Senate report specifically allowed discovery for documents used by tribunals. The European Commission was an administrative tribunal that met this statutory requirement. Intel raised another issue, contending that discovery was inappropriate because the commission did not have a proceeding pending. Justice Ginsburg dismissed this claim because Congress had eliminated the requirement that proceedings be "pending." A court could issue a discovery order if a "dispositive ruling by the Commission, reviewable by the European courts, be within reasonable contemplation."

Intel had further claimed that U.S. courts could impose discovery only if the documents in question were discoverable in the foreign jurisdiction. Justice Ginsburg rejected such a "foreign discoverability" requirement but acknowledged that a district court should take this issue into account when deciding a discovery issue. However, just because a foreign country limits discovery based on its "own legal practices, culture or tradition," these reasons did not "necessarily signal **objection** to aid from United States federal courts." Although the Court ruled that AMD should be allowed to pursue its discovery request, it emphasized that district courts have the discretion to grant or **deny** such requests.

In a dissenting opinion Justice STEPHEN BREYER, argued that although § 1782(a) gives district courts broad authority to order discovery, the **statute** "must be read as subject to some categorical limits, at least at the outer bounds." He contended that the fact the European Commission did not regard itself as a tribunal should have been taken into account. In addition, he believed that since the commission did not seek the documents (nor would it under its laws), the U.S. courts should decline to grant discovery.

DNA TESTING

Mandatory DNA Testing in New Jersey Faces Court Challenges

The AMERICAN CIVIL LIBERTIES UNION (ACLU) of New Jersey filed an action in January 2004 to challenge New Jersey's program of collecting DNA samples from all criminals. The ACLU's action was the second challenge of the New Jersey law, which was enacted in September 2003.

DNA was first used to resolve a criminal case in England in 1986. In that case, police sought to match **DNA evidence** to a perpetrator from a semen stain discovered in the investigation of a rape-murder in the village of Narborough. The officers had a suspect in custody, but the DNA evidence did not match that of the man being held. Police then collected DNA samples from more than 4,582 men in the area to try to match a sample with the evidence. Though none of the samples matched, police discovered that one of the men had asked someone else to provide a sample for him. Ultimately, the man confessed to the crime. DNA has since become a **principal** means by which law enforcement officials can identify those responsible for committing certain crimes certain crimes, especially in **murder** and **rape** cases.

States in the late 1980s and early 1990s quickly developed the idea to collect DNA samples from convicted criminals in order to build vast databases of DNA information. Colorado became the first state to enact legislation establishing such a database, and by the end of the 1990s, every state in the U.S. had enacted similar legislation. Questions arose, however, regarding the scope of collecting the DNA information. Every state requires collection from those who are convicted of sex offenses, and the majority of states require collection from those who are convicted of murder and offenses against children. Some states require collection from offenders in cases involving assault, **robbery, burglary**, kidnapping, and stalking. Although mandatory DNA testing has been challenged in the courts on constitutional grounds, such testing has been uniformly upheld.

In the late 1990s, some states considered expanding the DNA databases to include samples from anyone who was convicted of a **felony**. Moreover, some proposals have called for the collection of DNA from anyone who has been arrested, much like the collection of fingerprints. Supporters of this expansion cite the growth in the use of DNA evidence and note that the expanded database would enhance the ability of law enforcement officers to identify perpetrators. Critics, however, have noted that many states have a backlog of unprocessed DNA samples and argue that expanding the number of samples will only create further accumulation of unprocessed samples. Moreover, these critics have expressed concern that the DNA could be used by entities outside of law enforcement, such as insurance companies and medical researchers.

Prior to 2003, New Jersey law only required those convicted of sex offenses and certain violent crimes, such as murder and kidnapping, to provide a DNA sample. By 2003, the state had collected a total of 11,869 samples. In September 2003, New Jersey Governor James E. McGreevey signed a new piece of legislation that expanded the database to include samples from anyone convicted of any crime, excluding some minor offenses, such as traffic offenses. The law also applies to anyone who is acquitted of a crime by reason of insanity. The new law was designed to increase the total number of samples in the state's database to approximately 140,000 within two years of the law's enactment. The legislation took effect immediately and applied retroactively to the estimated 120,000 prisoners in the New Jersey prison system.

Several critics, including the ACLU, immediately decried the expansion of the database. The legal director of the ACLU, Ed Barocas, commented, "Now a 13-year-old who shoplifts will have his DNA code collected by the government and maintained throughout his life. We're becoming more and more of a surveillance state." Criminal defense lawyers echoed the concerns, noting that the law is too broad.

Shortly after the law's enactment, judges, sheriff's departments, and other officials sent letters to thousands of individuals convicted of crimes, requesting these individuals to submit to having a DNA sample taken. One of these individuals, Ed Forchion, challenged the law in a **habeas corpus petition** in the U.S. District Court in the District of New Jersey in November 2003. Forchion, an activist for the legalization of marijuana, had been arrested more than thirty times and had just been released from prison following a conviction for dealing marijuana. His suit alleges that the law mandates an illegal search without **probable cause** and challenges the **retroactive** effect of the law. The ACLU filed a brief **amicus curiae** to support Forchion's position.

The ACLU followed Forchion's suit by filing a lawsuit in a New Jersey state court in January 2004. The plaintiffs in the case are Jamaal Allah, who was convicted of two drug offenses, and a fifteen-year-old who was placed on probation after an altercation with a police officer. The suit, filed in Mercer County, claims that New Jersey's law violates an individual's right to **privacy**, right to bodily integrity, and due process rights, and also claims that the law constitutes an ex post facto law. As of May 2004, both the state court lawsuit and the federal court action were still **pending**.

DOUBLE JEOPARDY

A second prosecution for the same offense after acquittal or conviction or multiple punishments for same offense. The evil sought to be avoided by prohibiting double jeopardy is double trial and double conviction, not necessarily double punishment.

Tribal Prosecutions Do Not Bar Federal Criminal Proceedings

Though the Fifth Amendment's **Double Jeopardy Clause** bars multiple prosecutions for the same crime, the clause does not apply when different sovereign governments try a person for a crime under their laws. For example, a police officer acquitted of assault in state court could be tried under federal civil rights laws for violating the victim's civil rights. Questions arose whether an American Indian tribal government's prosecution of a **defendant** barred the federal government from trying the defendant on federal charges. American Indian tribes are regarded under the law as sovereign entities; hence the questions over double jeopardy protection. The Supreme Court, in *United States v. Lara*, __ U.S. __, 124 S.Ct. 1628, 158 L.Ed.2d 420 (2004), ruled that tribes have the authority to prosecute members of other tribes for crimes committed on their reservations. In addition, tribal sovereignty enables the federal government to bring a subsequent prosecution for the same criminal conduct.

Billy Jo Lara, a member of the Turtle Mountain Band of Chippewa Indians, married a member of the Spirit Lake Tribe—a different tribe—and lived with his wife on the Spirit Lake Tribe reservation in North Dakota. Lara got into trouble on several occasions, leading the tribe to ban him from the reservation. He ignored the order, and when stopped by federal officers, he struck one of the officers. The Spirit Lake Tribe prosecuted him for "violence against a police officer". Lara pleaded **guilty**, and he served ninety days in jail for his crime. The federal government then charged him with the federal crime of assaulting a federal officer. The elements of the tribal and federal criminal laws were the same, which under ordinary circumstances would have triggered double jeopardy protection for Lara.

The federal government argued that "dual sovereignty" was at work here: the Spirit Lake Tribe and the federal government were separate sovereigns. Therefore, the Double Jeopardy Clause did not apply. However, this argument was complicated by the fact that Lara was not a member of the Spirit Lake Tribe. A 1990 Supreme Court decision, had ruled that an Indian tribe did not have "sovereign authority" to prosecute a nonmember Indian. Congress responded quickly, enacting a law in 1990 that authorized a tribe to prosecute members of other tribes. 25 U.S.C.A. — 1301. The law stated that it sought to enlarge the tribes' own "powers of self-government" to include the "inherent power of Indian tribes . . . to exercise criminal jurisdiction over all Indians," including nonmembers. The federal district court accepted this reading of the law; the court ruled that Lara could be prosecuted for the federal crime. The Eighth **Circuit Court** of Appeals reversed this decision, holding that the tribal court had exercised federal prosecutorial power in prosecuting Lara rather than invoking its inherent sovereign power. The court reasoned that Congress had merely delegated its own powers, which meant that the Double Jeopardy Clause barred federal prosecution. Lara could not be prosecuted twice for the same crime by two holders of federal police powers. *United States v. Lara*, 294 F.3d 1004 (8th Cir. 2002).

The Supreme Court, in a 7-2 decision, reversed the Eighth Circuit ruling. Justice STEPHEN BREYER, writing for the majority, noted that Lara's double jeopardy defense hinged on whether the source of the power to punish a nonmember Indian was based on inherent tribal sovereignty or delegated federal authority. In the Court's view, Congress intended to base the 1990 law on the tribal sovereignty. Justice Breyer concluded that Congress had the constitutional authority to "relax" restrictions placed on tribal prosecutions of nonmember Indians by the *Duro* decision. First, Congress has the authority under the **Commerce Clause** and the Treaty Clause to legislate matters involving Indian tribes. Second, the Court had long recognized that Congress could pass "legislation that both restricts and, in turn, relaxes those restrictions on tribal sovereign authority." Therefore, Congress had the constitutional authority to change "judicially made" federal Indian law. Based on this reading, the Court acknowledged that the tribe had "acted in its **capacity** of a separate sovereign." Lara's prosecution and conviction by the tribe did not bar a federal prosecution under the dual sovereignty exception to the Double Jeopardy Clause.

Justices JOHN PAUL STEVENS, ANTHONY KENNEDY and CLARENCE THOMAS filed concurring opinions, each expressing concerns over the state of tribal sovereignty **jurisprudence**. Justice Thomas contended that the topic of tribal sovereignty was confusing and ripe for a sweeping reexamination. Justice DAVID SOUTER, in a dissenting opinion joined by Justice ANTONIN SCALIA, concluded that criminal prosecution of nonmembers "necessarily rests on a delegation of federal power." Souter argued that Lara should not have been subjected to the second prosecution; when the federal governments restores authority to Indian tribes it cannot restore inherent sovereignty but merely delegate federal power.

DRUGS AND NARCOTICS

Drugs are articles that are intended for use in the diagnosis, cure, mitigation, treatment, or prevention of disease in humans or animals, and any articles other than food, water, or oxygen that are intended to affect the mental or body function of humans or animals. *Narcotics* are any drugs that dull the senses and commonly become addictive after prolonged use.

FDA Bans Ephedra

On April 12, 2004, all sales of the popular herbal stimulant ephedra were banned by the Food and Drug Administration (FDA). The FDA, after more than ten years of research and debate, banned ephedra because its use was linked to 155 deaths, along with numerous heart attacks and strokes. The FDA action was the first time it had banned an over-the-counter nutritional supplement. The ephedra-linked death in February 2003 of Baltimore Orioles pitcher Steve Bechler drew national attention to the risks associated with the stimulant, which has been used for weight loss and bodybuilding. Two manufacturers filed a lawsuit prior to the ban, but a federal judge denied the their request for an **injunction** that would have allowed sales until the lawsuit had been resolved.

Ephedra, which is also called ma huang, epitonin, and sida cordifolia, contains stimulants known chemically as ephedrine. Ephedrine alkaloids are active chemicals that are found naturally in a number of plants. Ephedrine can also be produced synthetically. Unlike organic ephedra, synthetic ephedra compounds are classified as illegal drugs in the United States. During the 1990s, more than sixty companies in the U.S. produced ephedra as a dietary supplement. Ephedra use became popular with people seeking to lose weight and with athletes who believed it enhanced their performance. Beginning in 1994, the FDA received reports on the side effects of ephedra. The side effects included heart attacks, heart palpitations, strokes, and psychosis. Under federal drug laws, the FDA requires makers of drugs to prove that they are safe. In contrast, the FDA cannot force makers of nutritional supplements to demonstrate their safety before marketing them. Instead, the FDA can remove such products if they are proven to be unsafe—only after showing that a product poses a significant health risk.

The makers of ephedra challenged claims that ephedra was unsafe. They funded the Ephedra Education Council. The group supported stronger labeling requirements, but contended that there was no scientific **proof** to show a link between the stimulant and death by stroke. The ephedra makers argued that between twelve and seventeen million people used ephedra, but only a handful of people reported serious side effects.

By the late 1990s, the FDA recognized that more evidence needed to be collected in order to judge the safety of ephedra. Its reliance on Adverse Events Reports, which only recorded claims of medical problems associated with ephedra use, would not be sufficient to prove that the supplement was a significant health risk. The FDA commissioned a study that reviewed 140 reports of serious problems with ephedra products. In November 2000, scientists at the University of California at San Francisco released the study. It revealed that forty-three of the cases were related to ephedra supplements, with forty-forty cases possibly related. In addition, ten deaths could be tied to ephedra use, and thirteen persons suffered permanent disabilities due to use of the drug. The report concluded that ephedra posed health risks to some users. Moreover, because ephedra supplements were stimulants, persons with kidney disease, high blood pressure, heart disease, overactive thyroid, diabetes, a history of seizures, or psychiatric disorders, should not use ephedra products.

The Department of Health and Human Services (HHS), which oversees the FDA, commissioned a more comprehensive study on the safety of ephedra in June 2002. Critics of ephedra argued that the government should ban ephedra, but HHS noted again that adverse reports were not sufficient evidence under federal law to support such an action. However, the scientific and medical community issued more warnings about ephedra. In October 2002, members of the AMERICAN MEDICAL ASSOCIATION testified before Congress and asked that the FDA ban ephedra. Then, on February 17 2003, the death of Oriole pitcher Steve Bechler put a prominent, human face on the issue. Bechler collapsed and died at the Oriole's spring training camp after taking three pills containing ephedra. Ten days later, HHS released the Rand Corporation study, which questioned the safety of ephedra. The study found that ephedra use was associated with higher risks of heart palpitations, tremors, and insomnia. In addition, a February 2002 report in the Annals of Internal Medicine pointed out that while ephedra products accounted for less than one percent of dietary supplement sales, these products constituted sixty-four percent of the serious side effects associated with supplements, as reported to the Centers for Disease Control and Prevention.

Based on the Rand Corporation study, HHS announced in early March 2003 that it would require warning labels on all products containing ephedra. Some makers of ephedra products stopped producing them in 2003, while others embraced the labeling requirement. However, on December 30, 2003, the FDA announced it would ban the sale of ephedra, effective April 12, 2004. The FDA concluded that ephedra products presented "an unreasonable risk of illness or injury." On the eve of the ban, two manufacturers filed a federal lawsuit in New Jersey challenging the ban. U.S. District Court Judge Joel Pisano declined to issue a **temporary restraining order** that would have allowed sales to continue during the course of litigation. The manufacturers will eventually have their day in court, but the sale of ephedra in the U.S. will remain illegal.

EDUCATION LAW

The body of state and federal constitutional provisions; local, state, and federal statutes; court opinions; and government regulations that provide the legal framework for educational institutions.

Numerous Groups Oppose Federal No Child Left Behind Act

In January 2002, President GEORGE W. BUSH signed into law the No Child Left Behind Act of 2001, Pub. L. No. 107-110, 115 Stat. 1425 (20 U.S.C. §§ 6301 **et seq.**). The act was designed as a major part of educational reform on a national level. The statute's purpose was to "ensure that all children have a fair, equal, and significant opportunity to obtain high-quality education." Although few may openly doubt that education in the United States is in need of reform, the No Child Left Behind Act has come under harsh criticism from educators, state legislators, and others who assert that the law fails to accomplish its purposes. In 2003 and 2004, some states announced that they were considering relinquishing federal funds instead of trying to meet the act's requirements.

Critics of the No Child Left Behind Act (NCLBA) have focused on three primary areas. First, educators, along with some politicians, resent the focus of the act on standardized tests and stringent qualifications for teachers. Second, state legislators and educational administrators claim that the act creates unfunded federal mandates, which has caused major budgetary problems for states and local governments. Third, some conservatives disfavor federal intrusion into the area of education, which traditionally has been an area of responsibility for the states.

Educational Requirements Under the NCLBA

The NATIONAL EDUCATION ASSOCIATION (NEA) maintains that the NCLBA has obstructed improvement of student achievement and strengthening of public schools for the following primary reasons: the act focuses on punishment of schools rather than assistance from the federal government in improving education; the **statute** mandates compliance rather than proving support for effective programs; and the NCLBA promotes privatization of education rather than teacher-led and family-oriented solutions to educational problems.

The NEA points out a number of "absurdities" that have resulted from the NCLBA. Many of the examples that the NEA cites as ridiculous results of the implementation NCLBA relate to the requirements that schools demonstrate "adequate yearly progress" (AYP) in raising test scores of students' mathematics and reading skills. In one case, a Tennessee high school that had been one of the state's highest rated was labeled as one "in need of improvement" under NCLBA standards because only 94.1 percent of the school took a standardized math test. Had three more students taken the test, the school would have received at least a satisfactory rating.

Other stories focus on the fact that a school exceeding its own state's standards can fail to meet the federal AYP standards. For instance, an elementary school in Florida scored so well under Governor Jeb Bush's education plan that it received a check for $40,000. However, under the federal standard, the school was rated so low that the school was required to allow its students to attend another school in the district. The NEA cites several other stories with similar results.

Federal Funding for the NCLBA

Several state legislators have complained that the NCLBA creates federal mandates without providing adequate funding. State legislators have been particularly harsh in their criticism of the NCLBA mandates due to budgetary concerns. The National Conference of State Legislatures insists that the NCLBA has imposed on states an estimated $10 billion in unfunded mandates. Some state and local leaders have estimated that the costs to their state programs will greatly exceed the amount—tenfold, by some estimates—of federal money provided.

Several states have become vocal in their disagreements regarding the implementation of the NCLBA. The Hawaii Legislature, for instance, approved a resolution in 2003 to ask state education administrators to forgo federal funding until Congress provides more money for the state's educational programs. Similarly, Vermont's legislature passed a law in 2003 that prohibits schools from incurring any costs under NCLBA that are not fully funded by the federal government. Other states that have engaged in formal or informal protests of the Act include Arizona, Minnesota, New Hampshire, New Mexico, and Virginia.

Supporters of the NCLBA maintain that the Act is neither unfunded nor constitutes a federal mandate. According to the Republican Policy Committee, chaired by Senator Jon Kyl (R.-Ariz.), the act cannot be considered a mandate because states are free to forgo federal assistance and decline to adopt the federal program. Moreover, this committee contends that the Act is not unfunded or underfunded, noting that several states do not currently spend their federal education funding.

Federal Regulation of Education

Some critics of the NCLBA resent the statute because they believe that the federal government should not impose itself in an area traditionally reserved to the states. The Republican-controlled Virginia House of Delegates, for instance, approved a resolution in 2003 by a vote of 98-1 asking Congress to exempt Virginia from the requirements of the NCLBA. According to the resolution, the statute marks "the most sweeping intrusions into state and local control of education in the history of the United States."

The Civil Rights Project at Harvard University conducted four studies of the NCLBA, resulting in a series of reports collectively entitled *Inspiring Vision, Disappointing Results: Four Studies on Implementing the No Child Left Behind Act*. According to one of these studies, one of the shortcomings of the act has been the federal government's refusal to work collaboratively with state and local governments. "When federalism works well there is collaboration across levels of government and federal deference to state priorities, something that has not been evident so far in the process of implementing NCLB," the report notes. "Under the Bush administration, the federal government has taken a leadership role and assertively advanced its own political and policy goals while ignoring the role of state and local governments in the policy process."

Although the level of criticism regarding the No Child Left Behind Act has grown since 2003, members of Congress and other supporters have continued their support for the implementation of the NCLBA. Many educators, including the NEA, have expressed that they will commit to meeting the goals of the statute, even if they do not agree with its specific provisions.

ELECTIONS

The processes of voting to decide a public question or to select one person from a designated group to perform certain obligations in a government, corporation, or society.

California Gubernatorial Recall Survives Numerous Legal Challenges

The California Recall Election of 2003, in which Governor Gray Davis was successfully removed from office and replaced with former bodybuilder and actor Arnold Schwarzenegger, will no doubt be remembered as an interesting chapter in the history of United States politics. Beyond all of the campaigning, the colorful and outspoken array of candidates, and the issues that spawned it, this recall drive will no doubt also be studied and referred to for years for the variety and character of the legal challenges that sought to promote or hinder it every step of the way.

In 2002, Democrat Gray Davis was elected to his second term as governor. The state of California was in the throes of the economic downturn that was affecting the entire country, and the task of balancing the state budget was the worst of the problems Davis faced. After Davis admitted that the state faced a $38 billion deficit, some people decided to act. The recall effort was begun and financed by several GOP members, most notably U.S. Representative Darrell Issa, who announced himself as a candidate to replace Davis. Mass petitions were circulated, seeking signatures that would total 12% of the votes cast in the last gubernatorial election, the minimum needed to trigger a recall vote. The petitions soon gathered almost double that number. It fell on California Secretary of State Kevin Shelley to accept the signatures and certify the election. Shelley gave counties an extra thirty-day window in which to verify the signatures and was promptly sued by the Recall Gray Davis Committee, who accused Shelley of stalling and maintained that the signatures should be verified immediately, as they came in. The 3rd District **Court of Appeal** in Sacramento agreed, and ordered that the signatures be verified within the thirty-day window in which they were received, not the one after. On July 28, 2003, Shelley confirmed that the required number of signatures had been gathered and soon after announced that the recall election would be held on October 7, 2003.

The first major challenge to the recall came from the group Taxpayers Against the Recall. Paul Kiesel, an attorney for the group, sought to have the election certification postponed, citing irregularities in the signature gathering drive. After having appeals rejected in lower courts, Kiesel appealed to the California Supreme Court. But the court voted unanimously not to review the case, and the group ran out of time for further appeals.

Next up was a challenge from the governor himself. The recall was designed as a two-part question. First, should the governor be removed from office? If voters answered yes on the first part, then they would get to choose a replacement from a second ballot. According to California election law, the candidate up for recall can't be listed on this second ballot. Davis asked the California Supreme Court to list his name on the second ballot, claiming that not doing so would violate the **equal protection** rights of those voters who wished to retain him. They also asked that the election be delayed until March 7, 2004, citing the fact that new voting machines designed to replace the old punch card systems (made infamous in Florida during the disputed presidential election of 2000) were not yet operating in all districts, effectively disenfranchising voters in those areas. Again, though, the court decided not to intervene, and election officials continued to scramble to prepare for the vote and to deal with the hundreds of people that had filed papers to be placed on the ballot.

Gray Davis, center, at a rally to fight his recall as governor of California.

But more legal maneuvering remained. On September 11, the ACLU asked the 9th **Circuit Court** of Appeals to postpone the election until March, again citing the antiquated voting machines used in some counties. They argued that the state needed time to replace the machines, and if they did not, that up to 44% of voters in the state, concentrated in six counties, could be affected. These counties, the ACLU noted, included a disproportionate number of minority voters and allowing the election to proceed using equipment that the Secretary of State had found "unacceptable" would constitute disenfranchisement. Nathan Barankin, a spokesman from the California Attorney General's office, countered by saying: "Punch cards aren't an ideal way to conduct an election . . . but they . . . (have) been used in this state for decades without Florida-like problems, and we don't see why that can't continue on October 7." But the three-judge panel that heard the case sided with the ACLU, ordering a halt to election preparations. In the ruling, the judges wrote: "the . . . defects in the system are such that approximately 40,000 voters . . . will not have their vote counted at all . . . in assessing the public interest, the balance falls heavily in favor of postponing the election for a few months."

But the pro-recall forces appealed the decision, and the court re-heard the case **en banc**. On September 23, less than twenty-four hours after hearing the case, the panel, in a unanimous decision, struck down the earlier ruling and ordered that the election preparations go forward. While agreeing that use of punch-card machines was problematic, the judges wrote "... it is merely speculative possibility ... that any such (disenfranchisement) will influence the result of the election." The judges also noted that postponing the election would be problematic because the election had effectively already begun, with 700,000 absentee ballots already mailed in that would have to be discarded if the election were postponed. The judges noted that "... a federal court cannot lightly interfere with or **enjoin** a state election."

With only two weeks remaining before the election, the ACLU declined further appeals, and the rest is a matter of history, as action film star and Republican Arnold Schwartzenegger became governor. But the success of this recall campaign has opened the proverbial can of worms for citizens of other states who may be displeased with the performance of their elected officials. The ramifications of the California recall election of 2003 will no doubt reverberate throughout the United States for many years to come.

Major Provisions of Federal Campaign Finance Law are Constitutional

After many failed attempts to address federal campaign finance reform, Congress passed the Bipartisan Campaign Reform Act of 2002 (BCRA), 116 Stat. 81, which is also known as the McCain-Feingold Law (Senator JOHN MC-CAIN, R-Arizona and Senator Russell Feingold, D-Wisconsin, were the Senate sponsors.) The law banned "soft money" contributions to political candidates and restricted corporations, labor unions, and advocacy groups from spending their funds to finance "electioneering communications" that seek to influence a federal election. Both major political parties and other groups affected by these reforms immediately challenged the BCRA. The U.S. SUPREME COURT, in *McConnell v. Federal Election Commission*, __ U.S. __, 124 S.Ct. 619, 157 L.Ed.2d 491 (2003), affirmed the key provisions of the BCRA, distancing itself from a 1976 decision that struck down campaign finance restrictions based on First Amendment principles.

The passage of the BCRA sought to correct a campaign finance system that itself had grown out of reforms in the 1970s. Congress enacted the Federal Election Campaign Act of 1971 (FECA), 2 U.S.C.A. §§ 431 *et seq.*, and amended it in 1974 during the WATERGATE scandal.

FECA attempted to limit expenditures on campaigns but the Supreme Court, in *Buckley v. Valeo*, 424 U.S. 1, 96 S.Ct. 612, 46 L.Ed.2d 659 (1976), struck down three kinds of expenditure limits contained in the 1974 law. The Court ruled that Congress could not place expenditure limits (1) on the amount that a candidate may spend from funds lawfully raised from others; (2) on the amount that individuals may spend from their own assets on their campaigns; and (3) on the amount that may be spent by an individual or a political action committee (PAC) in support of or in opposition to a candidate, but independent of that candidate. PACs are special organizations formed by labor, industry, the professions and other interest groups that are not identified with individual candidates. The Court stated that "virtually every means of communicating ideas in today's mass society requires the expenditure of money." This conclusion, which equated spending money with speech, when the money is spent for political expression, meant that this speech was entitled to the protection of the FIRST AMENDMENT. The Court found that there were two related sets of rights: the right of the speaker to make his or her opinion heard and the right of individuals to associate with each other to make a greater impact than they could individually.

This ruling created a **loophole** for lobbyists, corporations, unions and wealthy individuals, allowing them to contribute millions of dollars to PACs. By 2002 these unlimited "soft money" contributions (in contrast, "hard money" is the amount that an individual may contribute to a political candidate; federal law places strict limits on these contributions, with individuals allowed to contribute only $2000 to a federal candidate) to candidates and national parties had risen to almost $500 million. The BCRA sought to end soft money contributions because this system had given disproportionate influence to soft money contributors. Senator Mitch McConnell, R-Kentucky, along with other plaintiffs, challenged the BCRA, arguing that it violated the First Amendment under the *Buckley* decision. A federal district court upheld the major provisions of the act and the Supreme Court granted review, hearing the case in September 2003 rather than waiting for the beginning of the term in October.

The Court, in a 5-4 decision, upheld the major provisions of the BCRA. Justices JOHN PAUL STEVENS and SANDRA DAY O'CONNOR, in a joint majority opinion, ruled that the government interest in banning soft money, in-

Senator Mitch McConnell stands between his legal counsel in front of the Supreme Court.

tended to prevent "actual or apparent corruption of federal candidates and officeholders," was a "significantly important interest to justify contribution limits." That interest went beyond the "elimination of *quid pro quo*, cash-for-votes exchanges" but "extends also to **undue influence** on an officeholder's **judgment**, and the appearance of such influence."

The Court also upheld the BCRA's "express advocacy" restriction on "issue ads." The *Buckley* decision had barred corporations, unions and other groups from running ads expressly endorsing or calling for the defeat of the candidate. Interest groups have financed these commercials, supposedly to advance their causes, but they were often barely disguised ads in support of a candidate. The BCRA required that the financing of "electioneering communication" be publicly disclosed like other campaign spending, so the voters could know who was financing these ads. Justices Stevens and O'Connor rejected First Amendment arguments against this new restriction. In their view *Buckley* had been an exercise in statutory **interpretation** and not a constitutional command. They abandoned the *Buckley* interpretation because it had "not aided the legislative effort to combat real or apparent corruption." Moreover, the provision did not violate the First Amendment because "it is a regulation of, not a ban on, expression."

The four dissenting justices argued that the BCRA provisions violated the First Amendment. Chief Justice Rehnquist, in his **dissent**, did not dispute that Congress believed it needed to correct abuses but its "response, however, was too blunt." Justice ANTONIN SCALIA stated that it was a "sad day for the freedom of speech," with the Court approving a law "that cuts to the heart of what the First Amendment is meant to protect: the right to criticize the government."

ELEVENTH AMENDMENT

Lawsuit Against State to Enforce Consent Decree Does not Violate the Eleventh Amendment

The Eleventh Amendment bars individuals from suing state governments unless a state consents to such a lawsuit. The U.S. SUPREME COURT has consistently ruled that states cannot be sued for damages but they may be sued if the plaintiff seeks injunctive **relief** from the court. The state of Texas sought to extend the bar to injunctive relief. The state contended that the federal courts could not order it to carry out the terms of a **consent** decree it had signed several years before. However, the Supreme Court rejected this argument in *Frew v. Hawkins*, __ U.S. __, 124 S.Ct. 899, 157 L.Ed.2d 855 (2004), concluding that the ELEVENTH AMENDMENT could not be used to allow the state from reneging on its agreement.

The case arose over the state's administration of the federal-state Medicaid program, which provides medical services to poor people. Though state participation is voluntary, if a state joins the program it must follow federal statutes and regulations that set out specific requirements. One such requirement was the administration of an Early and Periodic Screening Diagnosis (EPSDT) program that provided healthcare services to children. In 1993, Linda Frew and a group of mothers sued Texas state officials on behalf of their children, arguing that Texas had not provided the level of services required for EPSDT. Their lawsuit was a **class action** that represented more than one million children entitled to EPSDT.

Settlement negotiations went on between the parties for three years before Texas agreed to enter into a consent decree in 1996. A consent decree is an agreement between the parties that the court embodies in an order, thereby making it capable of judicial enforcement if either party fails to live up to the terms of the decree. The 80-page decree that the judge signed provided detailed descriptions of how Texas was to implement an improved EPSDT program. Two years later, in 1998, Frew and the other plaintiffs returned to the district court, asking that the court enforce the consent decree provisions. Texas officials denied that they had failed to live up to the agreement and stated that even if they were not in compliance, the Eleventh Amendment barred enforcement of the decree. The court disagreed, issuing an order that found Texas had not complied with all the provisions of the decree and that directed the parties to submit ideas on how to correct the problems. Texas appealed to the Fifth **Circuit Court** of Appeals, which reversed the lower court. The appeals court reasoned that the Eleventh Amendment barred enforcement of the decree unless the consent decree violation also violated the federal Medicaid **statute**. In this case the terms of the consent decree went beyond binding statutory requirements. Texas provided a good enough program in spite of its violation, thus making the consent decree unenforceable. *Frazar v. Gilbert*, 300 F.3d 530 (5th Cir. 2002).

The Supreme Court, in a unanimous decision, reversed the Fifth Circuit. Justice ANTHONY KENNEDY, writing for the Court, found that the consent decree was enforceable based on a longstanding decision, *Ex parte Young*, 209 U.S. 123, 28 S.Ct. 441, 52 L.Ed. 714 (1908). This case held that a suit to **enjoin** a state **attorney general** from enforcing a state law alleged to violate the FOURTEENTH AMENDMENT was not a suit against the state and thus was not barred by the Eleventh Amendment and the **doctrine** of **sovereign immunity**. The Court avoided the **immunity** issue by creating a legal fiction: to the extent the state laws authorizing the actions of the attorney general were unconstitutional, the attorney general was stripped of his official authority, thus making him an individual who could be enjoined without regard to sovereign immunity. On the one hand, the attorney general's acts constituted state action under the Fourteenth Amendment; on the other hand, the actions were distinct from the state so as not to implicate the Eleventh Amendment. However, *Ex parte Young* only permits prospective injunctive relief.

Texas contended that the terms and entry of the consent decree were permissible under *Ex parte Young* but enforcement was not. *Ex parte Young* created only a narrow exception to Eleventh Amendment immunity involving the actions by the state. Consent decrees had the ability to bind state governments to terms that went beyond statutory commitments. Moreover, decrees tied the hands of public officials who inherit these agreements. Therefore, only state violations of the federal EPSDT law could trigger judicial enforcement.

Justice Kennedy rejected these arguments, stating that federal courts "are not reduced to approving consent decrees and hoping for compliance. Once entered, a consent decree may be enforced." He based this conclusion on the equitable powers bestowed on federal courts to remedy violations of federal law. If Texas believed that circumstances required a change in the decree, it should go back into court and request modification of the terms. It could not, however, simply ignore the decree and shield itself using the Eleventh Amendment.

E-MAIL

Actual Damage to Computer E-mail System Required in Trespass Action

Companies and government agencies must deal with commercial "spam" e-mail that enters their e-mail systems, but they also may encounter mass emails from disgruntled former employees or citizens. Companies have resorted to litigation when requests to stop sending the emails have been ignored or resisted. The Intel Corporation filed a **civil action** against a former employee, alleging that the employee's e-mails to thousands of Intel employees constituted the tort of trespass to chattels (personal property). The California Supreme Court, in *Intel Corporation v. Hamidi*, 30 Cal.4th 1342, 71 P.3d 296, 1 Cal.Rptr.3d 32 (2003), rejected this claim, finding that a trespass to personal property action will only succeed if it is shown that the e-mail damaged the companies' computer system or impaired its functioning.

Kourosh K. Hamidi had worked as an Intel engineer for four years when, in 1990, he was involved in a auto accident while on company business. He sustained chronic pain and eventually took medical leave. He also filed a workers' compensation claim, alleging that he was entitled to benefits because the accident was a work-related **injury**. Intel successfully fought the workers' compensation claim and terminated Hamidi for cause in 1995. Soon after Hamidi established Former and Current Employees of Intel (FACE-Intel) and created a website to disseminate critical information about Intel. After someone anonymously gave him information that allowed him to create an e-mail list for Intel employees, Hamidi sent out a series of e-mail messages to between 8,000 and 35,000 Intel employees. The content of the six messages was critical of Intel practices and suggested employees should consider moving to other companies. Each message contained a notice that the recipients could contact Hamidi and he would remove their names from the list. There was no dispute that Hamidi honored these requests for removal. After Hamidi resisted Intel's demands that he stop sending the messages, Intel filed suit in state court alleging that the e-mails constituted a trespass of its computer system. The trial court granted Intel an **injunction** barring further e-mail communications and the California Court of Appeals affirmed the decision.

The California Supreme Court, in a 4-3 decision, reversed the appeals court. Justice Kathryn Mickle Werdegar, writing for the majority, found that the facts alleged by Intel did not sustain the tort of trespass of chattels. Moreover, the court declined to extend this tort to encompass actions where the personal property in question has not been damaged or impaired. In the case of Hamidi, Intel's only alleged injuries were to the loss of employee productivity caused by reading and reacting to the messages and to Intel's efforts to block the messages. Though the court acknowledged these might be injuries under different theories of **liability**, they were inapplicable to a trespass action. Justice Werdegar emphasized that Hamidi was not immune from possible liability. Intel could have sued Hamidi under different theories. These included interference with prospective economic relations, interference with contract, or intentional inflection of emotional distress. In addition, Intel could have, if the facts warranted it, sued Hamidi for **defamation**, publication of private facts, or other "speech-based" torts.

The Court distinguished a series of "spam" e-mail cases where the Internet service providers (ISP's) were allowed to use a trespass to chattels theory because the great volume of the e-mail sent by spammers overburdened the ISP's computers and made the entire computer system harder to use for recipients, who were the customers of the ISP. Intel did not make any such showing here and Justice Werdegar concluded that the only alleged harm was to be found in the contents of Hamidi's messages. The trespass action required that Intel show that its physical computer network system had been injured or incapacitated. The evidence showed that the volume of Hamidi's messages was insignificant compared to e-mail spam. Absent a loss of available memory or processing power of the computer, trespass was not applicable.

The court found that when Intel set up its e-mail system and allowed employees to communicate outside of the corporation's network, it was inevitable that employees would receive non-business related e-mail. Hamidi did nothing but use the e-mail system for its intended purpose to communicate with employees, and the system worked as designed. The Court refused to create liability for unwanted, non-commercial communications. It concluded that such liability, if any, should be addressed by the legislature. In addition, the Court further found no constitutional issue at risk in this case. Therefore, the injunction had to be dissolved.

Three justices dissented, including Chief Justice Ronald George. Justice Richard Mosk, in a dissenting opinion joined by George, contended that intruding on private property, regardless of injury, was sufficient to demonstrate trespass to chattels.

Congress and States Enact Legislation to Fight Spam

During 2003 and 2004, Congress and various state legislatures considered bills designed to deter marketers from sending unsolicited bulk advertising, popularly known as spam, through e-mail messages. After Virginia enacted the toughest state anti-spam law in April 2003, Congress responded by enacting federal legislation later in the year. Some critics, however, have

Representatives of AOL, Earthlink, Microsoft and Yahoo! announce lawsuits against leading spammers in March 2004.

decried the legislation as restrictive on freedom of speech, and skeptics have noted that the legislation may not have much of an impact on how much spam an average person receives through email.

Of the estimated 7.2 billion e-mail messages sent per day in the United States, about half of them are spam messages. Although more than half of the states have enacted some form of anti-spam legislation, these statutes have been largely ineffective for a variety of reasons. Some states, such as California, require individuals who send bulk advertising messages through email to include the abbreviation "ADV" to identify a message as an advertisement. Other states have enacted statutes that **call** for harsher punishment for violators. The vast majority of state statutes provide for fines, rather than potential criminal sentences, and catching a perpetrator who sends the spam is often difficult. Moreover, many e-mails originate from overseas, making domestic legislation much weaker.

In April 2003, Virginia Governor Mark Warner approved legislation that makes distribution of certain types of spam a criminal action, punishable as a **felony**. Va. Code Ann. § 8.01-328.1 **et seq.** (Michie Supp. 2004). It is possible that a violator could be sentenced to prison for one to five years and be required to pay a significant fine. Moreover, the **statute** allows the state to seize profits and income received from the sale of spam advertising.

In order for the state to convict a person under the statute, the person must send, through a hidden e-mail identity, a certain amount of spam messages, such as ten thousand within a twenty-four-hour period. The statute is designed to reach beyond those who send messages from the state of Virginia. And significantly, the law applies to e-mail sent through Internet Service Providers that are located in Virginia, which is home to American Online. By some estimates, half of the email in the world passes through the state.

Virginia's law is considered to be the toughest among the state anti-spam laws in the United States, but several critics noted that the law would probably not be enough to curb the number of spam messages that the average user receives. Consumer groups have advocated a system whereby companies can only receive bulk advertising messages if they so request them, known as an "opt-in" system. Moreover, these groups have advocated for statutes that allow individuals to bring **class action** suits against those who send spam messages. According to these consumer groups and others, Virginia's law and similar laws in other states would be effective only if the state were successful in prosecuting perpetrators.

In December 2003, prosecutors in Virginia announced that two men had been indicted for violating the state's new anti-spam law. Both men, Jeremy Jaynes and Richard Rutowski, were

North Carolina residents when they were charged with sending thousands of spam e-mail messages containing false routing information. According to Virginia **Attorney General** Jerry W. Kilgore, the two men used the America Online computer network to send these messages, which included advertisements regarding mortgage rates, Internet history erasers, and stock schemes. Kilgore made the announcement at America Online's headquarters in Loudoun County, Virginia. Jeremy Jaynes' sister, Jessica Jaynes, was indicted on similar charges in April 2004.

Congress considered several anti-spam proposals during the early 2000s. An anti-spam bill in 2000 was approved by an overwhelming majority of the House of Representatives but was never acted upon by the Senate. In 2003, fifty-three members of Congress sponsored a similar anti-spam bill that would provide for federal regulation of unsolicited e-mail messages. Although, initially, the legislation had strong support from both Democrats and Republicans, disputes arose that led to bipartisan bickering. By December 2003, however, Congress finally enacted the law, known as Controlling the Assault of Non-Solicited **Pornography** and Marketing (CAN-SPAM) Act of 2003, Pub. L. No. 108-187, 117 Stat. 2719.

Rather than require marketers to limit e-mails to individuals who have requested such messages, Congress adopted an "opt-out" system. This system permits marketers to send bulk emails, but requires marketers to provide a link that allows recipients to block further emails. Moreover, the statute does not permit class action suits against those who infringe upon the law's requirements. Supporters claim that, on a national basis, the federal law provides the strongest protection from spam. If a person sends a request to someone who has sent spam, and the sender continues to deliver messages to the recipient anyway, the sender can be subjected to severe penalties.

A number of critics quickly responded that the law effectively rendered spam legal in the United States. According to these critics, the federal legislation will not slow down mass e-mails sent from foreign countries. Moreover, recipients will potentially have to "opt-out" to hundreds or thousands of marketers in order to prevent the marketers from sending the messages to the receivers. Thus, the critics maintain, the average e-mail recipient will still receive as many spam messages as the recipient may have received prior to the passage of the statute.

Though the federal law preempts certain state laws that attempt to regulate spam, states have continued their efforts to enact anti-spam legislation. In April 2004, the Maryland legislature passed a bill, H.D. 1320, that is similar to the Virginia bill but that provides for tougher criminal sanctions. However, detractors have commented that the Maryland law may not have much of an effect on the amount of e-mail its residents receive because no major e-mail provider is located in Maryland.

ENVIRONMENTAL LAW

An amalgam of state and federal statutes, regulations, and common-law principles covering air pollution, water pollution, hazardous waste, the wilderness, and endangered wildlife.

Local Air Quality Emission Standards Governing Miscellaneous Truck Fleets Did Not Escape Clean Air Act Pre-emption Simply because they Addressed Purchase of Vehicles

Vacating a decision of the U.S. Court of Appeals for the Ninth Circuit, the U.S. SUPREME COURT held that fleet rules adopted in California did not escape pre-emption by the Clean Air Act (CAA) simply by virtue of the fact that they addressed the purchase of vehicles, rather than their manufacture or sale. *Engine Manufacturers Association v. South Coast Air Quality Management District* 541 U.S. _____ (2004). The Supreme Court also remanded the case, indicating that at least certain aspects of the rules appeared to be preempted, but that it was appropriate that the lower courts address certain issues in the first instance. The rules cover fleets (15 vehicles or more) of public transit buses, school buses, garbage trucks, street sweepers, shuttle buses and taxis serving airports, public works trucks, and other vehicles in the area. The rules were challenged under a claim that they constituted new emission standards, and thereby preempted by federal standards.

South Coast Air Quality Management District ("SCAQMD") is the air quality management district established under the California Health and Safety Code to develop and implement a strategy for achieving and maintaining ambient air quality standards within the South Coast Air Basin. In 1999 SCAMQD released a study finding that diesel particulates are responsible for nearly 70 percent of the cancer risk from toxic air pollution in the Los Angeles metropolitan area.

The following year, SCAQMD adopted six rules (referred to hereinafter as the "Fleet Rules"), each of which mandates that when certain local operators of fleets purchase or replace their fleet vehicles, they must acquire only those specific motor vehicles that the SCAQMD has designated as meeting its standards and requirements. As a result, makers of diesel engine vehicles used in the Los Angeles metropolitan area had to gradually retrofit existing fleets or replace them with low-emission vehicles.

The Fleet Rules were challenged by Engine Manufacturers Association ("EMA") and Western States Petroleum Association ("WSPA"). EMA is a not-for-profit trade association representing the leading manufacturers of internal combustion engines used in most medium-duty and heavy-duty motor vehicles, other than passenger cars. EMA members manufacture the medium-duty and heavy-duty compression-ignition, diesel-fueled engines that are installed in certain pickup trucks and sports-utility vehicles, delivery vans, shuttle vans, and cargo vehicles, trucks, tractor-trailers, waste haulers, street-sweepers and buses, and sold throughout the United States. WSPA is a trade association organized as a nonprofit corporation under California law. Its members consist of companies engaged in the exploration, production, transportation, refining and marketing of crude oil and petroleum products, including diesel fuel.

The case came before the U.S. District Court for the Central District of California. **Counsel** for EMA and WSPA argued that section 209(a) of the Clean Air Act, which prohibits any state or local "standard relating to the control of emissions from new motor vehicles," preempts the SCAMQD's regulations requiring the purchase of cleaner-fuel vehicles by fleet operators. The parties stipulated that the case should be adjudicated on the pleadings, as no material factual disputes are **at issue**.

The court first examined the scope of the express preemption provision contained in section 209 of the CAA. Codified at 42 U.S.C.A section 7543(a), this provision states:

> No State or any political subdivision thereof shall adopt or attempt to enforce any standard relating to the control of emissions from new motor vehicles or new motor vehicle engines subject to this part. No State shall require certification, inspection, or any other approval relating to the control of emissions from any new motor vehicle or new motor vehicle engine as condition precedent to the initial retail sale, titling (if any), or registration of such motor vehicle, motor vehicle engine, or equipment. 42 U.S.C. § 7543(a).

EMA and WSPA argued that the Fleet Rules violate CAA section 209(a) because they constitute "standard[s] relating to the control of emissions from new motor vehicles or new motor vehicle engines."

The district court disagreed, holding that the Fleet Rules impose no new emission requirements on the sale of the vehicles, but rather regulate only the purchasing and leasing of vehicles. *Engine Manufacturers Association v. South Coast Air Quality Management District*, 158 F.Supp.2d 1107 (C.D.Cal.2001). The CAA expressly requires the SCAQMD to establish fleet rules regarding the purchase of new vehicles, the district court continued, and state law authorizes the SCAQMD to promulgate the rules. Moreover, the district court emphasized, a state regulation that does not compel manufacturers to meet a new emissions limit, but rather affects the purchase of vehicles, is not a "standard," and thus does not violate section 209 of the CAA.

The court next addressed the relevance of CAA section 177 to the dispute. Codified at 42 U.S.C.A. section 7507, section 177 permits states other than California to adopt California's "standards relating to control of emissions," but only so long as those standards are identical to California's. Section 177 makes clear that such states are not "authoriz[ed] ... to prohibit or limit, directly or indirectly, the manufacture or sale of a new motor vehicle or motor vehicle engine that is certified in California as meeting California standards."

According to EMA and WSPA, the Fleet Rules fail these requirements in two separate ways. First, the rules are not identical to the California standards. Their very purpose is to be more restrictive than the California standards. Second, the Fleet Rules are foreclosed by Section 177's prohibition against limiting the sale of motor vehicles. There can be no question that, in prohibiting the purchase of certain vehicles, the Fleet Rules limit indirectly the sale of a new motor vehicle that is certified in California, EMA and WSPA argued.

But the district court rejected this **interpretation**. It ruled that section 177 applies only to non-California "opt-in" states. Section 177 first identifies the circumstances under which a state may adopt California's emission standards, the district court observed, and then declares that "any such state" adopting a California emission standard is still subject to certain limitations. According to the court, the phrase "any such state" clearly refers back to the non-California "opt-in" states referenced at the outset of the section. Section 177 thus has no application to the right of SCAQMD to regulate the purchase of fleet vehicles in California, the district court concluded.

The U.S. Court of Appeals for the Ninth Circuit summarily affirmed the district court's decision in a terse, two-sentence memorandum opinion. *Engine Manufacturers Association v. South Coast Air Quality Management District*, 309 F.3d 550 (9th Cir. 2002). EMA and WSPA appealed. At oral arguments before the U.S. Supreme Court the GEORGE W. BUSH administration and the engine and petroleum industries argued that the Fleet Rules should be declared pre-empted by the CAA because of the potential economic implications for the nation. The petitioners argued that the Fleet Rules would eventually cause a splintering of the national vehicle manufacturing market, which currently provides an exemption only for one state, California. If SCAQMD's Fleet Rules are upheld, the petitioners maintained, a decentralized system could develop, with several local air districts creating their own markets based on their own rules.

Justice ANTONIN SCALIA, writing for an 8-1 majority, disagreed with the courts below. He stated that today, as in 1967 when section 209 of the CAA became law, "standard" is defined as that which "is established by authority, custom, or general **consent**, as a model or example; criterion; test." The courts below engrafted onto this meaning a limiting component, Scalia wrote, defining it as only a production mandate requiring manufacturers to ensure that the vehicles they produce have particular emissions characteristics, whether individually or in the aggregate. This confused standards with the means of enforcing standards, Justice Scalia stated.

Manufacturers can be made responsible for ensuring that vehicles comply with emission standards, but the standards themselves are separate from those enforcement techniques, the justice continued. While standards target vehicles or engines, standard-enforcement efforts that are proscribed by section 209 can be directed to manufacturers or purchasers. Justice Scalia declined to read into section 209 a purchase/sale distinction that was not to be found in the text or the structure of the CAA.

The courts below held that all six of the rules were entirely outside the pre-emptive reach of section 209 based on reasoning that did not withstand scrutiny, Justice Scalia stressed, as at least certain aspects of the rules were clearly pre-empted. However, Scalia cautioned that there were still a number of issues that might affect the ultimate disposition of the suit, including the question whether some of the rules or some applications of them could be characterized as internal state purchase decisions. These issues were neither passed on below nor presented in the **petition** for **certiorari**. As a result, Scalia said that such issues would best be addressed in the first instance by the lower courts, and **remand** thus was appropriate.

Supreme Court Delivers Mixed Ruling over Water Regulation in Everglades

Disputes over environmental regulations typically involve complaints by property owners that compliance with clean water and air standards is too burdensome. However, disputes occasionally arise between government water management districts and citizens over environmental problems allegedly caused by the government agency. Such has been the case in south Florida, where water management has been used to drain parts of the Everglades and make large tracts of land fit for human habitation. Using canals and pumping stations, the South Florida Water Management District (SFWMD) has reclaimed a large portion of Broward County. However, the Miccosukee Indian Tribe became concerned about the high phosphorus levels in this water, which ends up in a 915 square mile Everglades conservation area. The phosphorus kills fish and native flora that are essential for the endangered species living in the Everglades. The tribe finally filed suit, asking that SFWMD be forced to comply with the federal Clean Water Act, 33 U.S.C.A. — 1251 and stop pumping the polluted waters that find their way into the Everglades. The Supreme Court, in *South Florida Water Management District v. Miccosukee Tribe of Indians*, __ U.S. __, 124 S.Ct. 1537, 158 L.Ed.2d 264 (2004), issued a mixed ruling, sending the case back to district court for additional facts. In addition, the Court rejected a "unitary waters" argument that threatened to undermine water quality throughout the United States.

SFWMD operates diesel-powered pumps that take surface water runoff from agricultural, urban, and residential land and moves it uphill to a drainage canal. If SFWMD turned off the pumps, the water would back up, and the western

William Buffalo Tiger, former chief of the Miccosukee Indians, drives his airboat through the Florida Everglades.

section of Broward County would flood in just a few days. The high levels of phosphorus in the water have undercut the social good promoted by the pumping. Fertilizers used by farmers and homeowners have altered the Everglades ecosystem, which is naturally low in phosphorus. Algae and other plants foreign to the Everglades have grown with the introduction of phosphorus. The problem was recognized in the 1980s, and state and federal agencies have worked on reducing the phosphorus level. However, the Miccosukee Tribe grew impatient with these initiatives; it soon filed suit under the Clean Water Act. In the suit, the tribe sought to have the pumps turned off and the water moved from the canal into the Everglades.

The federal district court granted the Miccosukee **summary judgment** on its lawsuit, finding that SFWMD needed a permit to operate its pumping station. The court concluded that the water from Broward County and the water from the Everglades were separate bodies of water. The phosphorus-laden water had been discharged into the Everglades, which would not have occurred naturally. Therefore, the Clean Water Act applied. The court rejected SFWMD's argument that the pump had merely moved already polluted water from one place to another, which technically was not a **discharge** under the act. The act requires defined "discharge" as "any addition" of "any pollutant." SFWMD appealed to the Eleventh **Circuit Court** of Appeals, which upheld the district court ruling. The appeals court found that the water in the canal would not flow into the Everglades without the operation of the pump. The pump station was the "cause in fact" of the addition of the pollutants to the Everglades. *Miccosukee Tribe of Indians v. South Florida Water Management District*, 280 F.3d 1364 (11th Cir. 2002).

The Supreme Court, in an 8-1 decision, concluded that the lower courts had based their legal conclusions on insufficient facts. Justice SANDRA DAY O'CONNOR, writing for the majority, first rejected SFWMD's contention that the Clean Water Act did not apply because the pumping station merely passed through polluted water originating from a different source. O'Connor ruled that the mere **conveyance** of polluted water to **navigable waters** triggered the act's provisions.

O'Connor also considered an argument filed by the Bush Administration in its *amicus curiae* **brief**. The government proposed a "unitary waters" theory, which would **render** a Clean Water Act permit unnecessary. Under this reading of the **statute**, all navigable waters in the United States should be considered one body of water. Once a pollutant is present in one part of U.S. waters, then its conveyance to a different part is not a discharge of a pollutant. The Court rejected this argument, which would have dramatically restricted the Clean Water Act provisions. Justice O'Connor found that this theory conflicted with other provisions of the act and with existing regulations.

Despite the rejection of these arguments, the Court still had problems with the lower court's ruling that the drainage canal and the Everglades conservation area were separate and distinct bodies of water. O'Connor stated that if the bodies were not separate and distinct, then polluting the same body of water did not trigger the Clean Water Act. She analogized that if "one takes a ladle of soup from a pot, lifts it above the pot, and pours it back into the pot, one has not added soup or anything else to the pot." SFWMD contended that the canal and the Everglades area were one pot of water and the pump did not cause the addition of phosphorus. The Court remanded the case to the district court to consider whether this might be true. O'Connor pointed out that groundwater connections between Broward County and the Everglades might lead to the seepage of phosphorus. Other possibilities included seepage across the levees near the pumping station. On **remand**, the district court would be called on to **assess** hydrological evidence in more detail.

Environmental Groups May Not Sue to Compel Federal Agency to Take Action

Environmental groups that seek to preserve federal lands as wilderness areas have been locked in battles with other groups that want to use those lands for commercial and recreational purposes. The growing popularity of off-road vehicles (ORVs) triggered a lawsuit by environmental groups against the Department of Interior's Bureau of Land Management (BLM). The groups asked the federal courts to compel the BLM to protect wilderness areas in Utah from the damage cause by ORVs. The U.S. SUPREME COURT, in *Norton v. Southern Utah Wilderness Alliance*, __ U.S. __, 124 S.Ct. 2373, 159 L.Ed.2d 137 (2004), rejected this approach, ruling that private parties may not sue a federal agency when the agency does not have a "mandatory nondiscretionary duty" to take requested actions.

The Southern Utah Wilderness Alliance (SUWA) and other environmental groups sued the BLM over its management of 23 million acres in Utah. The acreage, which encompasses half of the state, contains large tracts of land that Congress could designate as wilderness areas. Wilderness-area designation bars commercial and recreational use; no permanent roads or man-made structures may be built in these areas, and no motorized vehicles may be operated. In 1991, two million acres were recommended for wilderness designation, but Congress has not taken action. These lands are categorized as "wilderness study areas" (WSAs) and are managed by the BLM under federal law "so as not to impair the suitability of such areas for preservation as wilderness." 43 U.S.C.A. § 1782(c). The BLM devised resource-management plans for these lands, setting allowable uses and goals for future condition of the land. ORVs were permitted to operate in these areas.

SUWA sued BLM because they claimed that the increasing use of ORVs in these wilderness study areas was disturbing soil conditions, harassing animals, and annoying nature lovers. The popularity of ORVs has risen dramatically, with 42 million people now participating in off-road travel. Sales of all-terrain vehicles doubled between 1998 and 2003. Faced with the prospect of an ever-growing presence of ORVs in these lands, the environmental groups filed suit in federal district court. They alleged that BLM had failed to follow its statutory obligations to protect the lands for future preservation as wilderness. The suit was based on a provision of the Administrative Procedure Act (APA), 5 U.S.C.A. § 706(1), that permits a private party to sue to "compel agency action unlawfully withheld or unreasonably delayed." The district court dismissed the lawsuit, but the U.S. Court of Appeals for the Tenth Circuit reversed, ruling that BLM's nonimpairment obligation was a mandatory, nondiscretionary duty for which BLM could be compelled to comply. *Southern Utah Wilderness Alliance v. Norton*, 301 F.3d 1217 (10th Cir. 2002).

The U.S. Supreme Court, in a unanimous decision, overturned the Tenth Circuit's ruling. Justice ANTONIN SCALIA, writing for the Court, admitted that ORVs have had significant negative effects on the environment. The plaintiffs had grounded their lawsuit on the BLM's failure to take action on the ORV issue, but Scalia pointed out that not all failures to act could be remedied through the APA. **Judicial review** of agency actions is limited by the APA to "final agency action." In the Court's view, a failure to act is not the same as denying a request to act. A failure to act is "simply the omission of an action without formally rejecting a request-for example, the failure to promulgate a rule or take some decision by a statutory deadline." Properly understood, a failure to act under the APA meant failing to take a "discrete" action. In addition, the only agency action that can be compelled by a court under the APA is action that is "legally required." These principles bar "broad programmatic attack[s]" and lawsuits premised on the discretionary authority of federal agencies.

Justice Scalia applied these principles to the SUWA claims and concluded that BLM's statutory obligation not to impair wilderness study areas was mandatory as an ultimate objective. However, the **statute** gave the BLM broad discretion as to how to achieve this objective. Scalia disagreed with SUWA's contention that a federal court could issue a general order compelling compliance with the statutory objective without providing specific ways in which the BLM could comply. The main purpose of the APA was to "protect agencies from undue judicial interference with their lawful discretion, and to avoid judicial entanglement in abstract policy disagreements which courts lack the expertise and information to resolve." To have granted SUWA's remedy would have been to contradict this purpose and to make the court the supervisor of the BLM. Because SUWA could not show that BLM had failed to take a discrete action required by statute, the Court concluded that the federal courts did not have jurisdiction under the APA to consider the case.

ESPIONAGE

The act of securing information of a military or political nature that a competing nation holds secret. It can involve the analysis of diplomatic reports, publications, statistics, and broadcasts, as well as spying, a clandestine activity carried out by an individual or individuals working under secret identity to gather classified information on behalf of another entity or nation. In the United States, the organization that heads most activities dedicated to espionage is the CENTRAL INTELLIGENCE AGENCY (CIA).

National Guardsman Charged with Espionage, Guantánamo Bay Chaplain is Released

On February 12, 2003, the U.S. Army arrested a twenty-six-year-old national guardsman and charged him with attempting to supply military intelligence to the al-Qaeda terrorist network. Specialist Ryan G. Anderson, a tank crewman with the 81st Armor Brigade, was scheduled to deploy in March 2003 for a one-year mission in Iraq.

Also known as Amir Abdul Rashid, Anderson faced three charges. First, Anderson was accused of knowingly giving intelligence to the enemy by disclosing to U.S. military personnel, posing as members of the al Qaeda terrorist network, information regarding U.S. Army troop strength, movements, equipment, tactics, and weapon systems; methods and means of killing U.S. Army personnel; and procedures for destroying U.S. weapons systems and equipment. Second, he was accused of attempting, without proper authority, to knowingly communicate with the enemy by oral, written, and electronic communication, allegedly telling undercover U.S. military personnel, "I share your cause; I wish to continue contact through conversations and personal meetings." Third, Anderson was accused of attempting to aid the enemy by providing undercover U.S. military personnel with sketches of the M1A1 and M1A2 tank; a computer disk containing the accused's passport photo; the accused's military identification card; a DA Form 3749 equipment receipt for weapons; and a U.S. Army motor vehicle operator's identification card.

According to military officials, Anderson attempted to contact al-Qaeda through an Internet chat room that catered to Muslim extremists. In a sting operation involving the Army, the Federal Bureau of Investigation (FBI), and the Department of Justice, he ended up communicating with an undercover operative. If convicted, Anderson could face a sentence varying from twenty years in prison to death.

A native of Lynwood, Washington, Anderson had been training at nearby Fort Lewis. Over the past seven years, military officials alleged, he had posted scores of self-revelatory messages on Internet user groups. His writings portray a young man infatuated with guns, prone to exaggeration, and eager to make sudden commitments to new religious beliefs. "I am a die-hard Christian," he wrote to a militia newsgroup in February 1996, while a freshman at Washington State University, where he graduated with a degree in military history and an emphasis on the Middle East. Eight months later, in an Islam newsgroup, Anderson wrote that after taking a course in Arab history, "Islam has literally called to me." "Help!" he wrote. "I'm looking to convert, but I don't know where to start."

Anderson eventually did convert to Islam, and military officials claim that his crimes were motivated by ideology and not money. Anderson is now being detained at a military facility at Fort Lewis. He next faces an Article 32 hearing, which is the equivalent of a civilian **grand jury**, to determine whether there is sufficient evidence to proceed with a court martial.

A month after arresting Anderson, the U.S. military dropped all criminal charges against thirty-six-year-old Muslim army chaplain Captain James Yee, who ministered to prisoners at the U.S. Naval base in Guantánamo Bay, Cuba,

Ryan Anderson in his high school yearbook photo.

where approximately six hundred prisoners are being held, most of whom are terrorist suspects captured during the U.S.-led military operations in Afghanistan. The **dismissal** of the charges against Yee marked the final collapse of the espionage case against him. The military had charged Yee with spying, mutiny, **sedition**, aiding the enemy, and espionage. He was arrested on September 10, 2003, at Jacksonville Naval Air Station in Florida as he arrived back in the United States from Guantánamo. The charges were dropped on March 20, 2004.

In dismissing the charges, Major General Geoffrey D. Miller, commander of Joint Task Force Guantánamo, which operates the **detention** center at Guantánamo Bay, cited "national security concerns that would arise from the release of the evidence" if the case proceeded. Yee will be allowed to return to his station at Fort Lewis, near Tacoma, Washington. On March 22, 2004, Yee agreed to nonjudicial punishment for lesser, unrelated adultery and **pornography** charges. He was reprimanded in writing the same day on both charges, though the reprimand was dismissed by General James T. Hill of Army's Southern Command in Florida in April 2004.

Still awaiting rulings on possible courts-martial are Air Force translator Ahmad Halabi, 24, a Syrian naturalized as a U.S. citizen, and Colonel Jackie Farr, the highest-ranking Army officer ensnared in a crackdown on suspected mishandling of intelligence at Guantánamo Bay. Halabi faces seventeen charges, the most serious being attempted espionage, for which he could get life in prison without parole. He originally faced thirty counts, some of which carried the death penalty.

The fifty-eight-year-old Farr was charged on November 29, 2003, after a spot check of his luggage allegedly uncovered classified documents. Authorities claim he was trying to remove the documents from the base following completion of his two-year tour of duty as director of the intelligence-collection operation. If convicted, Farr could face a sentence of up to seven years in a military prison.

ESTABLISHMENT CLAUSE

State Tax Law Involving Religion May Be Challenged in Federal Court

Litigants have filed numerous lawsuits in federal courts challenging state tax laws that allegedly violate the Constitution. Since the 1950s, the federal courts have never doubted their ability to hear such lawsuits, even though a 1937 law, the Tax **Injunction** Act (TIA), 28 U.S.C. $ 1341, prohibits federal courts from restraining "the assessment, **levy** or collection of any tax under State law." In *Hibbs v. Winn*, __ U.S. __, 124 S.Ct. 2276, 159 L.Ed.2d 172 (2004), the U.S. SUPREME COURT reaffirmed the jurisdiction of the federal courts to hear challenges involving tax credits authorized by state law. In so ruling, the Court permitted a taxpayer lawsuit that challenged an Arizona tax credit as a violation of the First Amendment's Establishment **Clause**.

The state of Arizona authorized income tax credits for state residents who donated money to organizations that give educational scholarships and tuition grants to children who attend private elementary and secondary schools. An individual taxpayer may receive a tax credit of up to $500 per year for donations, and a married couple filing jointly may receive a maximum credit of $625. A group of Arizona taxpayers filed a federal lawsuit challenging this scheme. They contended that scholarships and grants went to children who attended private religious schools and that the tax credits were direct contributions to organized religion. The state of Arizona, they alleged, had aided organized religion in violation of the Establishment Clause.

The state filed a motion asking the court to dismiss the federal action, citing the Tax Injunction Act as a bar to federal jurisdiction. The state contended that a federal injunction barring the state tax credit scheme would restrain the "assessment" of taxes "under State law." The court agreed and dismissed the suit but the U.S. Court of Appeals for the Ninth Circuit reversed, ruling that the TIA did not bar the lawsuit because it would not adversely affect the state's ability to raise revenue; moreover, if the tax credit scheme were ruled unconstitutional, the decision would give the state more tax revenues. *Winn v. Killian*, 307 F.3d 1011 (9th Cir. 2002).

The U.S. Supreme Court, in a 5-4 decision, upheld the Ninth Circuit's ruling. Justice RUTH BADER GINSBURG, writing for the majority, noted that Supreme Court cases reaching back to the 1950s had reviewed challenges of state tax credits without considering the TIA a "jurisdictional barrier." Arizona, while acknowledging that the TIA had not been raised in these cases, argued that the Court should not consider this silence as precedent. Justice Ginsburg rejected this argument, based on a reading of the TIA, the **legislative history** and purposes of the TIA, and prior court decisions.

Justice Ginsburg pointed out that the plaintiffs had sought an injunction barring the state from allowing taxpayers to claim the tax credit and directing the state to notify the affected organizations to pay to the state general fund any funds it had received from the state from this tax scheme. Based on this requested **relief**, did the plaintiffs seek to restrain the "assessment" of taxes, which is forbidden by the TIA? The Internal Revenue Code defined "assessment" as the "recording of the amount the taxpayer owes the Government." I.R.C. § 6203. According to Ginsburg, an assessment was "closely tied to the collection of a tax, *i.e.*, the assessment is the official recording of **liability** that triggers levy and collection efforts." When seen in this light, the term did not encompass the entire Arizona tax scheme but was limited to its "collection-propelling function." The plaintiffs did not challenge their tax assessments but the overall taxing scheme.

Justice Ginsburg also examined the history surrounding the TIA. She found that the act had been designed to restrict the jurisdiction of federal district courts over lawsuits involving the collection of state taxes from individual taxpayers. Congress restricted the ability of individual taxpayers to file lawsuits in federal court because it gave an unfair advantage to persons who could afford such litigation. Under state laws, taxpayers generally must pay the disputed tax first and litigate in state court afterward. If they prevail, they will receive refunds. Prior to the TIA, a person could file a challenge in federal court and not have to pay until the litigation had been completed. Beyond that purpose, the Court did not find any "sweeping congressional direction" to bar federal court interference in all state court tax-administration issues.

Finally, Justice Ginsburg reviewed prior U.S. Supreme Court decisions involving the TIA. She concluded that the Court had applied the TIA provisions only in cases where state taxpayers sought to use the federal courts to avoid paying state taxes. In addition, the lower federal courts had issued many cases that read the TIA as not prohibiting "third parties from pursuing constitutional challenges to tax benefits in a federal forum." Justice Ginsburg also found it revealing that many federal court decisions had reached the **merits** of constitutional challenges without even mentioning the TIA. Based on these, factors the Court found it consistent to allow the Arizona lawsuit to proceed in federal court.

Justice ANTHONY KENNEDY, in a dissenting opinion joined by Chief Justice WILLIAM REHNQUIST and Justices ANTONIN SCALIA and CLARENCE THOMAS, argued that the majority had expressed "great skepticism for the state courts' ability to vindicate constitutional wrongs." He found troubling the belief that "state courts are second rate constitutional arbiters, unequal to their federal counterparts." The dissenters believed that the TIA did bar federal court jurisdiction.

Alabama's Chief Justice Continues Fight Over Ten Commandments

Roy S. Moore, the chief justice of the Alabama Supreme Court until his suspension in August 2003, continued a struggle in federal court in 2003 to keep a monument of the Ten Commandments outside of a state judicial building. However, a federal district court in Alabama ordered its removal, and the decision was upheld by the Eleventh **Circuit Court** of Appeals. Nevertheless, a manuscript of the Ten Commandments, along with other secular displays, returned to the building in February 2004.

Moore ordered the installment of the monument on July 31, 2001. At the time, Moore indicated that it had be paid for through private funds and that officials in Alabama were aware of that the monument was going to be installed. Three months later, however, the AMERICAN CIVIL LIBERTIES UNION, along with the Americans Union for Separation of Church and State, filed a lawsuit against Moore, claiming that the display violated the Establishment **Clause** of the First Amendment to the U.S. Constitution.

The case was brought before the U.S. District Court for the Middle District of Alabama. The court, on November 18, 2002, agreed with the plaintiffs' claims and ruled that the display of the monument indeed violated the Establishment Clause. *Glassroth v. Moore*, 229 F. Supp. 2d 1290 (M.D. Ala. 2002). Even after the court gave Moore thirty days to remove the monument voluntarily, Moore refused to do so. The court then entered a permanent **injunction** that ordered Moore to remove the exhibit no later than January 3, 2002. *Glassroth v. Moore*, 242 F. Supp. 2d 1067 (M.D. Ala. 2002) Moore filed a notice of **appeal** on the same day. He requested that the court stay its injunction **pending** an appeal. The court reluctantly agreed on December 23. *Glassroth v. Moore*, 242 F. Supp. 2d 1068 (M.D. Ala. 2002)

A three-judge panel of the U.S. Court of Appeals for the Eleventh Circuit, on July 1, 2003, affirmed the district court's order. They found that Moore had indeed violated the Establishment Clause. The court admonished Moore. They held that as a high-ranking member of the judiciary, he should have known that he was required to follow a federal court's order. "The **rule of law** does require that every person obey judicial orders when all available means of appealing them have been exhausted," the court stated. "The chief justice of a state supreme court, of all people, should be expected to abide by that principle." *Glassroth v. Moore*, 335 F.3d 1282 (11th Cir. 2003)

The case returned to the federal district court in Alabama, where the court, on August 5, 2003, ordered state officials in Alabama to remove the monument. *Glassroth v. Moore*, 275 F. Supp. 2d 1347 (M.D. Ala. 2003) The court required the monument to be removed no later than August 20. However, Moore again defied the court, saying that he had no intention of removing it. Moore sought an emergency appeal to the U.S. SUPREME COURT on August 15, but the Supreme Court declined to block the federal court's ruling.

Even after the August 20 deadline passed, though, Moore continued to refuse to remove the monument. On August 23, Moore was suspended from his position as chief justice after the remaining eight justices, the governor of Alabama, and the Alabama **attorney general** disagreed with him. The monument was removed on August 27 and placed into a private storage room.

The actions of the remaining justices on the Alabama Supreme Court gave rise to a second lawsuit, which alleged that the justices unconstitutionally established religion of "nontheistic beliefs" by ordering the removal of the display. The same judge that ordered the display's removal, Myron H. Thompson, also dismissed the subsequent lawsuit against the remaining justices. *McGinley v. Houston*, 282 F. Supp. 2d 1304 (M.D. Ala. 2003) The Eleventh Circuit affirmed the **dismissal** on March 5, 2004. *McGinley v. Houston*, 361 F.3d 1328 (11th Cir. 2004)

The controversy sparked debate across the United States regarding the role of religion and religious exercise. A group consisting of hundreds of Christians convened in Washington, D.C., to protest the removal of the Ten Commandments. They claimed that the removal was ordered by "activist judges" who attacked religious freedom. Many of those who took part in the "Save the Commandments Caravan" assembled on the steps of the U.S. Supreme Court building. In November, a CNN-USA Today-Gallop poll of more than one thousand Americans showed that seventy-seven percent opposed the federal court's order to remove the Commandments from the courthouse.

Despite all of the litigation, a new display was erected at the Alabama Judicial Building that included a copy of the Ten Commandments. This document was part of a larger display of historical documents that also included the Magna Carta and the U.S. Constitution. Similar types of displays have been ruled to be constitutional in prior Supreme Court decisions. Moore remains suspended from the Alabama Supreme Court.

FEDERALISM

Federalism is a principle of government that defines the relationship between the central government at the national level and its constituent units at the regional, state, or local levels. Under this principle of government, power and authority is allocated between the national and local governmental units, such that each unit is delegated a sphere of power and authority only it can exercise, while other powers must be shared.

Supreme Court Endorses Federal Environmental Regulatory Powers

The Environmental Protection Agency (EPA) is authorized to enforce federal environmental laws, including the Clean Air Act of 1970 (CAA), 42 U.S.C.A. §§ 7401 *et seq.* The CAA includes a Prevention of Significant Deterioration (PSD) program that prohibits the construction of major air pollutant emitting facilities unless they are equipped with "the best available control technology" (BACT). Under PSD, the EPA may issue an order that bars a state from allowing construction to go forward if the state has not complied with CAA requirements. Despite these broad federal powers, the states, through their environmental regulatory agencies, make judgments on whether new construction meets the BACT standard. In *Alaska Department of Environmental Conservation v. Environmental Protection Agency*, __ U.S. __, 124 S.Ct. 983, 157 L.Ed.2d 967 (2004), the Supreme Court was called upon to decide whether the EPA had the power to block construction if it concludes state authorities have made an unreasonable BACT determination. In a major decision that limits the powers of the states, the Court ruled that EPA did have statutory authority to **overrule** a state environmental decision.

Teck Cominco Alaska, Inc. (Cominco) owned and operated the Red Dog Mine in Northwest Alaska, about 100 miles north of the Arctic Circle. The zinc mine was the largest employer in this remote area and provided 25 percent of the area's wage base. The mine began operations in 1988 after obtaining a PSD permit that allowed it to operate five 5,000 kilowatt diesel electric generators. Of these five generators, two were operated only on a standby basis. The Alaska Department of Environmental Conservation (ADEC) issued another permit in 1994, allowing a sixth generator and authorizing the mine operation to run five of the generators full time. Cominco sought to expand zinc production by 40% percent in 1996, aided by funding from the state of Alaska. It proposed adding a seventh generator and a BACT called Low Nox to limit nitrogen oxide emissions. ADEC staff concluded that a BACT called SCR would do a much better job of reducing emissions, but the ADEC leadership endorsed Cominco's proposal. Cominco's proposal assumed that one or more generators would not be running but if all seven were running the amount of annual emissions would rise by 79 tons.

The National Park Service filed an **objection** to the BACT decision in 1999, and soon after, the EPA wrote to ADEC, raising doubts about the effectiveness of the Cominco air pollution plan. ADEC then conducted another review that concluded the SCR technology was too costly for the mine; if SCR was required,

ADEC estimated that Cominco would have to raise its zinc prices by 20 percent, which would not be economically feasible. Therefore, ADEC reaffirmed its decision to issue a construction permit with the Low Nox system. The EPA protested this decision and argued that ADEC had failed to conduct a thorough economic analysis to determine whether SRC technology was too costly. The EPA issued an order in December 1999 barring ADEC from issuing Cominco a construction permit until ADEC "satisfactorily documents why SCR is not BACT" for the generators. ADEC filed suit in the Ninth **Circuit Court** of Appeals challenging this decision. While the lawsuit proceeded, ADEC granted Cominco a permit to use the additional generators but required SCR as the BACT. Cominco could have abandoned SCR if the Supreme Court had ruled in ADEC's favor. The Ninth Circuit upheld the EPA's power to issue the order against ADEC. The appeals court had the authority to determine whether a state agency had "reasoned justification" for a permitting decision. *Alaska Department of Environmental Conservation v. United States Environmental Protection Agency*, 298 F.3d 814 (9th Cir. 2002).

The Supreme Court, in a 5-4 decision, agreed with the Ninth Circuit. Justice RUTH BADER GINSBURG, writing for the majority, ruled that the federal law trumped state control of air quality issues. Though the CAA gives states the authority to determine the best ways of controlling pollution in areas that have met clean air standards, the federal government has reserved the right to intervene if it concludes the state has failed it meet these standards. In this case ADEC had ignored the recommendations of its staff for the SCR technology and had offered a **vague** economic analysis as to why SCR was too costly for the mining operations. In Ginsburg's view, ADEC's own records "showed there was scant, if any, evidentiary basis for choosing less stringent emission-reduction technology." In addition, it made no sense to believe Congress would have given the EPA "an expensive surveillance role" but then "preclude the agency from verifying substantive compliance." The majority cautioned, however, that the EPA can step in only when it believes a state has made a decision without good reason in light of the CAA objectives.

Justice ANTHONY KENNEDY, in a dissenting opinion joined by Chief Justice WILLIAM REHNQUIST and Justices ANTONIN SCALIA and CLARENCE THOMAS, argued that the Court had not given due deference to the states in regulating air quality. The decision meant "a state agency can no longer represent itself as the real governing body." The day-to-day decisions on interpreting federal environmental rules had been delegated to the states by Congress. The state of Alaska was in the best position to decide which air quality technology was right for the zinc mine in a remote part of the state.

FETAL RIGHTS

The rights of any unborn human fetus, which is generally a developing human from roughly eight weeks after conception to birth.

Unborn Victims of Violence Act

After five years of contentious political and legal disagreement, the 108th Congress finally passed legislation that expanded the legal rights of unborn infants who may be harmed as a result of assault or violence committed against pregnant women. Senator Lindsay Graham (R-SC) first introduced the bill as H.R. 1997 in 1999. The Senate passed the final version by a 61-38 vote in March 2004. President GEORGE W. BUSH signed the Unborn Victims of Violence Act into law in early April 2004. The new law effectively established two separate crimes committed against a pregnant woman: one against her and one against her unborn child. This was significant in that it represented the first time ever that federal law recognized an embryo or fetus as a distinct person. It neither affected nor altered any state law. The new federal law was alternately identified as "Laci and Conner's Law," in memory of Laci Peterson and her full-term unborn son, Conner, found murdered in California in 2002.

Notwithstanding its final passage, the law is limited in scope. It applies only to instances where harm to a fetus occurs during the commission of a federal crime against the pregnant mother. Examples of federal crimes include drug-related shootings, attacks that occur on federal lands or military bases, or terrorist attacks. Assailants may be convicted of both crimes even if they are unaware that the adult female victim is pregnant. Moreover, the law protects both viable and unviable fetuses, from conception to delivery. It expressly defines an "unborn child" as "a member of the species *Homo sapiens*, at any stage of development, who is carried in the womb." It further declares that the punishment for the separate offense to the unborn child is the same as that provided under federal law for the crime to the mother.

The final version of the law narrowly defeated an amended version introduced by Senator Dianne Feinstein (D-CA). The amendment differed from the passed version in that its language focused on harm to the *pregnancy* rather than to any unborn being, and provided only for one offense—that being against the mother. The difference was more than just a matter of semantics. "Clearly, there is a concerted effort to codify in law the legal recognition that life begins at conception," Feinstein was quoted in *Women's Health Weekly*. "If we allow that to happen today, or in any other law, we put the right to choose squarely at risk." However, other senators disagreed, noting that the final passed version expressly excluded conduct related to consensual abortions.

Laws covering fetal homicide were in effect in twenty-nine states in early 2004. Many expressly excluded the mother from culpability. But there were several high-profile cases in other states in which mothers were held liable for the deaths of their stillborn or fetal infants, especially in drug-related cases. In April 2004, Salt Lake County district attorneys agreed to drop **murder** charges against Melissa Ann Rowland for allegedly refusing a Caesarian section that likely would have saved her unborn twin son's life. Lingering questions about Rowland's mental health prompted prosecutors to agree to a plea bargain in which she pleaded **guilty** to two counts of third-degree **felony** child endangerment instead. She was sentenced to drug and mental health treatment and eighteen months probation. A few months earlier, an Hawaiian mother was charged with **manslaughter** in the death of her newborn son resulting from methamphetamine poisoning. Likewise, a California woman was sentenced to life in prison for the poisoning of her newborn through methamphetamine-tainted breast milk.

In related news, the U.S. SUPREME COURT denied **certiorari** without comment, in October 2003, of an **appeal** involving a woman convicted and sentenced to twelve to twenty years for the drug-related death of her stillborn child. *McKnight v. South Carolina*, No. 02-1741. In that case, Regina McKnight tested positive for cocaine while in the hospital. After the test, she delivered a stillborn child with drugs in its system. McKnight was convicted of homicide under South Carolina law. Evidence concluded that the near-full-term infant was viable and could have survived but for the drug poisoning.

FIRST AMENDMENT

Preliminary Injunction Against Child Online Protection Act Upheld

The U.S. SUPREME COURT affirmed a preliminary **injunction** prohibiting the enforcement of the Child Online Protection Act (COPA) because it violated the Free Speech **Clause** of the First Amendment to the federal Constitution. *Ashcroft v. American Civil Liberties Union*, ___ U.S. ___, ___ S.Ct. ___, ___ L.Ed.2d ___, 2004 WL 1439998 (2004). The Supreme Court held that the district court did not abuse its discretion in issuing the preliminary injunction, since the government failed to rebut the contention that there were plausible less restrictive alternatives to the **statute**, and because substantial practical considerations argued in favor of upholding the injunction and allowing the case to proceed to trial.

COPA, codified at 47 U.S.C.A. § 231, makes it unlawful, for commercial purposes, to knowingly post any material on the Internet that is "harmful to minors." The act defines "material that is harmful to minors" as:

> any communication, picture, image, graphic image file...or other matter of any kind that is **obscene** or that— (A) the average person, applying contemporary community standards, would find, taking the material as a whole and with respect to minors, is designed to appeal to, or is designed to **pander** to, the prurient interest; (B) depicts, describes, or represents, in a manner patently offensive with respect to minors, an actual or simulated sexual act or sexual contact, an actual or simulated normal or perverted sexual act, or a lewd exhibition of the genitals or post-pubescent female breast; and (C) taken as a whole, lacks serious literary, artistic, political, or scientific value for minors.

On behalf of all persons and organizations that publish materials on the World Wide Web, the AMERICAN CIVIL LIBERTIES UNION (ACLU) filed a motion seeking a preliminary injunction to restrain the enforcement of COPA on grounds that it violated the Free Speech Clause of the FIRST AMENDMENT. U.S. **Attorney General** JANET RENO was named as the primary **defendant** (JOHN ASHCROFT was later substituted as the defendant when he succeeded Reno as attorney general following the 2000 presidential election).

The U.S. District Court for the Eastern District of Pennsylvania held that (1) COPA would apply to any Web site that contains even some materials harmful to minors, and not merely to commercial pornographers; (2) as a content-based regulation of non-obscene sexual expression, COPA is presumptively invalid and is subject to **strict scrutiny**; and (3) the plaintiffs were likely to succeed on the **merits** if allowed to proceed.

The U.S. Court of Appeals for the Third Circuit affirmed, albeit on somewhat different grounds. *American Civil Liberties Union v. Reno*, 217 F.3d 162 (3d Cir. 2000). It held that COPA's reliance on "community standards" to identify material that is harmful to minors renders COPA unconstitutional because, given the wide reach of the Internet, it effectively requires Web businesses in the most tolerant jurisdiction to abide by the standards of the most puritanical.

The Supreme Court vacated and remanded the third circuit's decision. *Ashcroft v. American Civil Liberties Union*, 535 U.S. 564, 122 S.Ct. 1700, 152 L.Ed.2d 771 (2002). The Court held that "COPA's reliance on community standards to identify 'material that is harmful to minors' does not by itself **render** the statute substantially overbroad for purposes of the First Amendment."

On **remand**, the Third Circuit once again affirmed the district court's grant of a preliminary injunction. *American Civil Liberties Union v. Ashcroft*, 322 F.3d 240 (3d Cir. 2003). It held that COPA had a number of constitutional defects, beyond the problem of variable community standards it identified in its earlier opinion. The government petitioned for **writ** of **certiorari** on the issue of whether COPA violates the First Amendment. The U.S. Supreme Court then granted certiorari on Oct. 14, 2003.

In a 5-4 decision written by Justice ANTHONY KENNEDY, the Supreme Court affirmed. Justice JOHN PAUL STEVENS filed a concurring opinion, in which Justice RUTH BADER GINSBURG joined. Justice STEPHEN BREYER filed a dissenting opinion, in which Chief Justice WILLIAM REHNQUIST and Justice SANDRA DAY O'CONNOR joined. Justice ANTONIN SCALIA filed a separate dissenting opinion.

Kennedy said that blocking and filtering software is an alternative that is less restrictive and likely more effective than COPA's requirements. Filters impose selective restrictions at the receiving end, not universal restrictions at the source, Kennedy noted. Under a filtering regime, adults without children may gain access to speech they have a right to see without having to identify themselves or provide their credit card information. Adults with children may obtain access on the same terms simply by turning off the filter on their home computers. Above all, promoting the use of filters does not condemn as criminal any category of speech.

Filters may well be more effective than COPA for three reasons, Kennedy wrote. First, a filter can prevent minors from seeing all **pornography**, not just pornography posted to the Web from America. Second, verification systems may be subject to evasion and circumvention, for example by minors who have their own credit cards. Third, filters can be applied to all forms of Internet communication, including e-mail.

Filtering software is not a perfect solution, Kennedy continued, since it may block some materials that are not harmful to minors and fail to catch some that are. Whatever the deficiencies of filters, Kennedy concluded, the government failed to introduce specific evidence proving that existing technologies are less effective than COPA. The argument that filtering software is not an available alternative because Congress may not require it to be used carried little weight, according to Kennedy, since Congress undoubtedly may act to encourage the use of filters.

Supreme Court Clarifies Adult Business Licensing Requirements

The Supreme Court has made clear that municipal governments may restrict adult businesses trafficking in sexually oriented materials to certain areas of a city. Cities may employ a licensing scheme that requires adult business owners to apply for permission to operate. These schemes do not directly implicate the First Amendment because they address the negative secondary effects that adult businesses produce in communities. Such negative effects include lower property values and increased crime rates. However, the Court has also insisted that when a city denies a license to an adult business applicant, there must be prompt **judicial review** of the decision. In *City of Littleton, Colorado v. Z.J. Gifts D-4, L.L.C.*, ___ U.S. ___, 124 S.Ct. 2219, 159 L.Ed.2d 84 (2004), the Court clarified its thoughts on this issue, ruling that a municipal licensing **ordinance** did not need to specify a time limit for a court decision in order to satisfy "prompt" judicial review.

The city of Littleton, Colorado enacted an adult business license ordinance in 1993 that restricted where such businesses could be located. In addition, applicants would be denied a license if they were underage, filed false information, had been convicted of certain crimes, or had failed to comply with state business regulations. In 1999, Z.J. Gifts opened a store in Littleton called "Christal's" which sold adult toys, lingerie, magazines, movies and other sexually oriented material. Before the store opened to the public, city officials informed the owner that under the Littleton ordinance an adult business could not be located on this particular block. Z.J. Gifts refused to file a license application. Instead, it filed a lawsuit in federal court, alleging that the ordinance violated its rights under the FIRST AMENDMENT. Though the ordinance required city officials to make a final licensing decision within 40 days of a license application, Z.J. Gifts argued that the ordinance did not ensure that a final judicial decision was made promptly. The district court dismissed the lawsuit but the Tenth **Circuit Court** of Appeals reversed. It agreed with the business owner that the ordinance, on its face, violated the First Amendment because it did not require a prompt judicial determination. The ordinance merely noted that a rejected applicant could file an **appeal** in the state district court under Colorado's civil rules of procedure. The city appealed to the Supreme Court, which accepted review to resolve a conflict in the circuit courts of appeals over what prompt judicial review meant. *Z.J. Gifts D-4, L.L.C. v. City of Littleton, Colorado*, 311 F.3d 1220 (10th Cir. 2002).

The Supreme Court, in a unanimous decision, overturned the Tenth Circuit decision. Justice STEPHEN BREYER, writing for the Court, noted that several circuits required a prompt judicial determination, while several others merely required the ordinance to give prompt access to the courts. The city of Littleton argued that it needed to provide only prompt access to the courts and not mandate a short time limit for a court to review and **render** a final decision on the license. It pointed to a 1990 Supreme Court decision, *FW/PBS, Inc. v. Dallas*, 493 U.S. 215, 110 S.Ct. 596, 107 L.Ed.2d 603 (1990), which dealt with an adult business licensing scheme. In this case the Court spoke of the "possibility of prompt judicial review," which suggested that the scheme needed only to provide an "assurance of speedy access to the courts, not an assurance of a speedy court decision." Justice Breyer disagreed, finding that the Court's basic holding in the case emphasized the need for a judicial decision in "a reasonable period of time." Therefore, an adult business licensing scheme will fail under the First Amendment if a prompt judicial decision is not made.

Though Littleton's first argument failed, Justice Breyer found merit in its claim that a "prompt" decision did not require the city to impose a short time limit on a decision nor impose special adult business judicial review rules. The Court agreed with this position and modified its holding in *FW/PBS*, concluding that special judicial review rules do not have to be applied to adult business licensing ordinances. Justice Breyer stated that ordinary judicial review procedures sufficed "as long as the courts remain sensitive to the need to prevent First Amendment harms and administer those procedures accordingly." If the courts failed to treat such cases with sensitivity, license applicants could bring these matters to the courts for a case-by-case determination.

Justice Breyer backed up the Court's modification of its prior ruling on a number of grounds. He found that the Colorado courts had ways of preventing delay, including expedited review at the **appellate** level; in addition, he had confidence in Colorado judges "to exercise their powers wisely so as to avoid serious threats of delay-induced First Amendment harm." Moreover, judicial review would be based on an analysis of objective factors rather than on subjective determinations as to whether material was pornographic. Finally, there was no need to require the placement of "judicial review safeguards in ordinances." Breyer noted that many cities lack state-law authority to impose deadlines on state courts. Therefore, the attack on the Littleton ordinance failed. Adult business owners who were denied licenses in the future were free "to raise special problems of undue delay in individual cases as the ordinance is applied."

States May Deny Scholarships to Theology Students

The First Amendment addresses religion in both the Establishment and Free Exercise Clauses. The Establishment **Clause** bars Congress and the states (through the FOURTEENTH AMENDMENT) from passing laws that seek to promote religion, while the Free Exercise Clause prohibits government from limiting religious freedom. These two clauses are sometimes in tension with each other. Moreover, 36 state constitutions contain provisions that go beyond the FIRST AMENDMENT in barring state money for religious education. Such was the case in *Locke v. Davey*, __ U.S. __, 124 S.Ct. 1307, 158

Joshua Davey speaks to reporters outside the Supreme Court.

L.Ed.2d 1 (2004), where the U.S. SUPREME COURT upheld a college scholarship program by the state of Washington that barred theology students who wish to be become ministers from receiving the scholarships. The Court concluded that depriving these students of financial aid did not violate the Free Exercise Clause.

The Washington legislature enacted the Promise Scholarship Program in 1999 (Wash. Rev. Code § 28B.119.005 (Supp. 2004), to help academically gifted students finance their postsecondary education. The scholarships, which were worth $1,542 in 2000-2001, could be renewed for a second year. Students eligible for the program had to graduate from Washington public or private schools and either be in the top 15% of their graduating class or achieve high scores on standardized college admissions tests. In addition, the program was limited to families of students whose income was 135% of the state's median income. Students could use the scholarship to attend public and private institutions, including religiously affiliated schools, as long as they were accredited. The only program restriction was a bar to financial aid for students who sought a degree in theology, which was interpreted to mean a program that trained a person to be a minister. The restriction was based on Washington's state constitution, which bars spending on religious education.

Joshua Davey was awarded a Promise Scholarship and enrolled in Northwest College, a private Christian institution affiliated with the Assemblies of God denomination. He wanted to pursue a double major that would include business management and pastoral ministries. The pastoral ministries degree was devotional in nature and thus was excluded from the scholarship program. After he was denied the scholarship, Davey filed a civil rights suit in federal court, alleging that the restriction on devotional theology degrees violated the First Amendment and the **Equal Protection** Clause of the Fourteenth Amendment. The district court dismissed his case and he appealed to the Ninth **Circuit Court** of Appeals. The appeals court reversed the decision, finding that state had singled out religion for unfavorable treatment. The state's concerns about funding devotional theology were not so compelling as to mandate this restriction. *Davey v. Locke*, 299 F.3d 748 (9th Cir. 2002).

The Supreme Court, in a 7-2 decision, reversed the Ninth Circuit. Chief Justice WILLIAM REHNQUIST, writing for the majority, noted the frequent tension between the Establishment and Free Exercise Clauses. However, there was enough "play in the joints" that there were "some state actions permitted by the Establishment Clause but not required by the Free Exercise Clause." Davey had argued that the program was presumptively unconstitutional because it was not neutral on its face with respect to religion. Rehnquist rejected this argument, noting that the Washington law did not impose any civil or criminal penalties on any religious service or rite, nor **deny** the right of ministers to participate in civic affairs. The state "has merely chosen not to fund a distinct category of instruction."

Chief Justice Rehnquist found a significant difference between training for religious professions and secular professions. Unlike secular professions, training in devotional theology was an "essentially religious endeavor" that was "akin to a religious calling as well as an academic pursuit." The state and federal constitutions contain viewpoints that "find no counterpart to other callings or professions." In the Court's view these constitutional provisions shaped the debate over denial of funding religious education for the ministry rather than hostility toward religion. An historical review of state constitutions revealed that from the inception of the United States, there had been explicit exclusions that prohibited the use of tax funds to support the ministry. This historical tradition helped explain Washington's ban. In addition, the Promise Scholarship Program did much to support religious schools. Students could attend accredited religious affiliated schools and even take devotional theology courses without forfeiting their scholarships. Because neither the Washington law nor the operation of the scholarship programmed suggested "animus toward religion," the "denial of funding for vocational religious instruction alone is [not] inherently constitutionally suspect."

Justice ANTONIN SCALIA, in a dissenting opinion joined by Justice CLARENCE THOMAS, strongly disagreed that the program was not discriminatory against religion. In his view the law discriminated on its face because it "carved out a solitary course of study for exclusion: theology." Davey had only sought equal treatment, which was the right to use his scholarship for his chosen course of study. Scalia contended that Washington could have avoided this problem if it had limited the scholarships to public universities or only for select courses of study. The current program discriminated against a religious minority: those persons who religious beliefs were so strong that they "dedicate their study and their lives to its ministry." The Washington law was one more expression of a popular culture that displayed "trendy disdain for deep religious conviction."

Supreme Court Reverses Pledge Ruling on Standing Issue

The U.S. SUPREME COURT ruled that an atheist father lacked the right to bring a constitutional challenge, on behalf of his daughter, to the words "under God" in the Pledge of Allegiance. By an 8-0 vote, the justices overturned a controversial decision by the U.S. Court of Appeals for the Ninth Circuit, which had held that a California public elementary school violated the Establishment **Clause** of the First Amendment by allowing its teachers to lead their students in a recitation of the of the Pledge of Allegiance because it contained the phrase "under God." The ninth circuit said that the "under God" reference is a profession of a religious belief, namely, a belief in monotheism, and that the district's **practice** of teacher-led recitations was designed to inculcate a respect for the ideals set forth in the Pledge, including the religious values it incorporates. *Newdow v. U.S. Congress*, 292 F.3d 597 (9th Cir 2002).

On June 22, 1942, Congress first codified the Pledge of Allegiance as "I pledge allegiance to the flag of the United States of America and to the Republic for which it stands, one Nation indivisible, with liberty and justice for all." Pub.L. No. 623, Ch. 435, § 7, 56 Stat. 380 (1942) (codified at 36 U.S.C.A. § 1972). On June 14, 1954, Congress amended section 1972 to add the words "under God" after the word "Nation." Pub.L. No. 396, Ch. 297, 68 Stat. 249 (1954) ("1954 Act"). The Pledge is currently codified as "I pledge allegiance to the Flag of the United States of America, and to the Republic for which it stands, one nation under God, indivisible, with liberty and justice for all." 4 U.S.C.A. § 4 (1998) (**Title** 36 was revised and recodified by Pub.L. No. 105-225, § 2(a), 112 Stat. 1494 (1998). Section 172 was abolished, and the Pledge is now found in Title 4.).

The "under God" clause was added during the height of the Cold War Red Scare during which Senator Joe McCarthy (R-WI) sought to root out and expose "godless" communists in the State Department. Although Senator McCarthy was censured in December of 1954 for his tactics of leveling groundless charges of disloyalty and subversion against countless loyal Americans, the "under God" language remained, generally uncontested and uncontroversial until it was challenged on March 8, 2000, by Michael Newdow.

An atheist, Newdow objected to having his elementary school age daughter listen to her schoolteacher lead the class in the Pledge of Allegiance each morning in the Elk Grove Unified School District. Newdow contended that his daughter suffered legal **injury** when she was compelled to listen and watch her state-funded teacher in a state-funded school lead "her classmates in a ritual proclaiming that there is a God."

Newdow filed suit in the U.S. District Court for the Eastern District of California on March 8, 2000, naming the U.S. Congress and the school district as defendants. He asked the district court, among other things, "[t]o declare that Congress, in passing the Act of 1954, violated the Establishment and Free Exercise Clauses of the United States Constitution," and "[t]o demand that . . . Congress . . . immediately act to remove the words 'under God' from the Pledge. . . ." On the motion of the school district and Congress, the U.S. district court dismissed the lawsuit, ruling that Newdow had failed to state a legal claim. Newdow then appealed to the Ninth Circuit.

The three-judge panel, in a 2-1 decision, reversed. Judge Alfred T. Goodwin, in his majority opinion, found that Newdow had standing to bring the case because the lawsuit articulated an identifiable legal injury to his daughter. Turning to the **merits** of the case, Goodwin observed that the U.S. Supreme Court had already ruled that public school children could not be compelled, under the threat of punishment, to recite the Pledge of Allegiance and salute the flag. *West Virginia State Board of Education v. Barnette*, 319 U.S. 624, 63 S. Ct. 1178, 87 L. Ed. 1628 (1943).

While acknowledging that *Barnette* was decided before the 1954 Act added the words "under God" to the Pledge, Goodwin nonetheless concluded that the "under God" language had a similarly coercive effect on young and impressionable school children who are forced to watch their peers stand and recite the Pledge. It placed the school children, Goodwin said, in an "untenable position of choosing between participating in an exercise with religious content or protesting." As such, the court ruled that it violated the Establishment Clause of the FIRST AMENDMENT to the U.S. Constitution. The Establishment Clause provides that "Congress shall make no law respecting an establishment of religion."

Coming less than a year after the September 11, 2001, terrorist attacks in New York City and Washington, D.C., the Ninth Circuit's decision generated a maelstrom of disapproval across the county. The U.S. Senate condemned the decision 99-0 on the day the court released its opinion. The U.S. House of Representatives passed a similar resolution by a vote 416-3 vote.

President GEORGE W. BUSH declared that the ninth circuit was out of step with the country.

Sandra Banning, the child's mother, then filed a motion to intervene or dismiss, declaring that she had exclusive legal custody under a state-court order and that, as her daughter's sole legal custodian, she felt it was not in the child's interest to be a party to Newdow's suit. Concluding that Banning's sole legal custody did not deprive Newdow, as a noncustodial parent, of standing to object to unconstitutional government action affecting his child, the Ninth Circuit held that under California law, Newdow retained the right to expose his child to his particular religious views even if they contradicted her mother's, as well as the right to seek redress for an alleged injury to his own parental interests. *Newdow v. U.S. Congress*, 328 F.3d 466 (9th Cir. 2003)

In an opinion written by Justice JOHN PAUL STEVENS, the Supreme Court reversed. The standing requirement derives from constitutional and prudential limits to the powers of an unelected, unrepresentative judiciary, Stevens began. The Court's standing **jurisprudence** encompasses the general prohibition on a litigant's raising another person's legal rights, Stevens continued, and the U.S. Supreme Court generally declines to intervene in domestic relations, a traditional subject of state law. The extent of the standing problem raised by the domestic relations issues in this case was not apparent until Banning filed her motion to intervene or dismiss, declaring that the family court order gave her sole legal custody and authorized her to 'exercise legal control' over her daughter, Stevens stressed.

Newdow's argument that he nevertheless retains an unrestricted right to inculcate in his daughter his beliefs fails, Stevens reasoned, because his rights cannot be viewed in isolation. The case also concerns Banning's rights under the custody orders and, most important, their daughter's interests upon finding herself at the center of a highly public debate. Newdow's standing derives entirely from his relationship with his daughter, Stevens observed, but he lacks the right to challenge the Pledge of Allegiance on her behalf, since their legal interests are not parallel and, indeed, are potentially in conflict.

Nothing that either Banning or the school board has done, however, impairs Newdow's right to instruct his daughter in his religious views, Stevens wrote. Instead, Newdow requests the more ambitious **relief** of forestalling his daughter's exposure to religious ideas endorsed by her mother, who wields a form of veto power, and to use his parental status to challenge the influences to which his daughter may be exposed in school when he and Banning disagree. According to Justice Stevens, existing precedent simply does not stand for the proposition that Newdow has a right to reach outside the private parent-child sphere to dictate to others what they may and may not say to his child respecting religion.

FOREIGN SOVEREIGN IMMUNITIES ACT

Supreme Court Permits Lawsuit Against Austria to Reclaim Art Treasures

The Foreign Sovereign Immunities Act of 1976 (FSIA), 28 U.S.C.A. §§ 1602 *et seq.*, was enacted by the United States Congress to set clear standards for determining when foreign states are immune from the jurisdiction of federal and state courts. In most cases, foreign states are immune for from lawsuits, but the FSIA contains exceptions, including § 1605(a)(3). This section permits suits against foreign governments "in which rights in property taken in violation of **international law** are in issue." The American heir of an Austrian sugar magnate sought to reclaim six paintings by Gustav Klimt from the Austrian government using this section of the FSIA. The Austrian government argued that FSIA did not apply to conduct that occurred before the 1976 enactment but the Supreme Court, in *Republic of Austria v. Altmann*, __ U.S. __, 124 S.Ct. 2240, 159 L.Ed.2d 1 (2004), ruled that the law did apply. The Court stated that the art in question was had been seized by the Nazis in the 1940s and the decision could lead to other suits involving other property illegally taken during the Nazi period when the Nazis were in power.

Maria V. Altmann, now 88, was the niece and sole surviving relative of Ferdinand Bloch-Bauer, a wealthy Austrian who lived in Vienna until the Nazis seized occupied Austria in 1938. Bloch-Bauer, who died in Switzerland in 1945, had acquired six paintings by Gustav Klimt, one of which was a portrait of Bloch-Bauer's wife, Adele. Adele died in 1925 and requested in her will that her husband **bequeath** the paintings to the Austrian Gallery after his death. Bloch-Bauer, who was Jewish, fled Austria just before the Nazis occupied the country in March 1938. He made no legal arrangements to donate the paintings to the gallery. The Nazis took over his sugar company and his house and divided up his artworks. A Nazi lawyer took the six Klimt paintings. He sold three to the National Gallery and another to a Vienna museum.

With the fall of the Nazi Party in 1945, the Republic of Austria enacted a law that voided all transactions motivated by Nazi ideology. However, the new government also placed restrictions on the removal from the country of artworks central to the nation's cultural heritage. Maria Altman's brother hired a Viennese lawyer in 1947 to recover Bloch-Bauer's property, including the Klimt paintings. The National Gallery responded by asserting that Adele had bequeathed the paintings to the gallery and that Ferdinand had merely been allowed to retain possession of them during his lifetime. Believing this statement to be true, Altmann and her brother did not pursue the paintings. However, in 1998 a journalist examined gallery records and discovered that the Austrian government was aware that the Adele and Ferdinand had not donated the paintings, which in 2004 have been valued at more than $100 million. Altmann, a resident of California, sued in federal district court, asking the court to order the return of the paintings to her. Austria filed a motion to dismiss the case, arguing that it could not be sued in U.S. courts under the **doctrine** of **sovereign immunity**. Altmann argued that § 1605(a)(3) gave the court jurisdiction to hear her claims, and the district court and the U.S. Ninth **Circuit Court** of Appeals for the Ninth Circuit sided with her.

The U.S. SUPREME COURT, in a 6-3 decision, upheld this reading of the FSIA provision. Justice JOHN PAUL STEVENS, writing for the majority, noted that the key issue was whether FSIA applied to acts committed before the passage of the act in 1976. If it did not apply, then Austria could successfully assert sovereign **immunity**. Justice Stevens reviewed the history of foreign sovereign immunity in the United States courts and pointed out that until the enactment of the FSIA, the courts relied on the guidance of the Executive Branch, and specifically the State Department, to determine immunity issues. This tradition had produced no real standards and had led to case-by-case reviews that often bred confusion. Congress sought to define clear standards when it enacted the FSIA and transferred immunity determinations to the judiciary. In addition, Congress endorsed a restrictive theory of sovereign immunity that provided few

Maria Altmann in front of a reproduction of a Klimt painting her family had stolen from them by Nazis during World War II.

exceptions to a general grant of immunity to foreign governments.

Justice Stevens concluded that the FSIA applied to acts committed before the passage of the act. He based this conclusion on numerous provisions in the act that "unquestionably" applied to cases arising out of conduct committed before 1976. In addition, applying the law to "all **pending** cases regardless of when the underlying conduct occurred" fulfilled the **intent** of Congress to clarify the rules governing sovereign immunity claims and to "eliminat[e] political participation in the resolution of such claims." To hold otherwise would force courts to apply the confusing set of rules that existed prior to the FSIA. Justice Stevens also suggested that the STATE DEPARTMENT could offer its an opinion on particular cases to the courts and these this opinions "might well be entitled to deference as the considered **judgment** of the Executive on a particular question of foreign policy." The Court's decision gave Altmann the chance to proceed on the substantive **merits** of her claim.

Justice ANTHONY KENNEDY, in a dissenting opinion joined by Chief Justice WILLIAM REHNQUIST and Justice CLARENCE THOMAS, argued that it was unfair to apply the **statute** retroactively, as it diminished "a rule of fairness based on respect for expectations." Moreover, they asserted that the ruling could damage relations with foreign governments.

FOURTH AMENDMENT

Supreme Court Sets Reasonable Waiting Period for Forced Entry into House

The Fourth Amendment's protection against unreasonable searches and seizures can be traced back to English common law. Both the common law and the constitutional provision hold that an individual's house cannot be searched without a warrant. Moreover, police are expected to knock on the individual's door and announce their right to enter the home. The Supreme Court has developed **case law** for situations where police do not want to announce themselves out of concern that they will put themselves or others in danger or that evidence will be destroyed. These "no-knock" entry cases permit such a **practice** when reasonable grounds exist. Another line of cases deal with the reasonableness of officers breaking into an abode after they knock, announce their presence and get no response. The Supreme Court, in *United States v. Banks*, __ U.S. __, 124 S.Ct. 521, 157 L.Ed.2d 343 (2003), ruled that a 15-20 second waiting period between announcing and forced entry was reasonable when police feared the drug dealer would flush cocaine down the toilet or kitchen sink. The fact that the dealer was in the shower when police knocked and announced did not make the search unconstitutional.

North Las Vegas, Nevada police received information that Lawshawn L. Banks was selling cocaine out of his two-bedroom apartment. Armed with a search warrant, local police and FBI agents went to his home around 2 PM on a weekday and posted themselves at the front and back doors. The officers at the front door called out that they had a search warrant and pounded on Banks's door. The agents at the backdoor could hear the knocking. After waiting 15 to 20 seconds and hearing no response, the officers used a battering ram to knock down the front door. They then discovered that Banks had been in the shower at the time and had not heard them until they broke the door. He came out of the bathroom, dripping wet, to confront the officers. Once inside the officers found weapons and crack cocaine. He was charged with a series of drug and firearms offenses. He contested the forced entry of his apartment on Fourth Amendment grounds, but the federal district court rejected his claim. Banks then pleaded **guilty** but reserved the right to **appeal** the search. The Ninth **Circuit Court** of Appeals reversed the district court, finding that the search violated the FOURTH AMENDMENT because waiting 15 to 20 seconds before entering the apartment was unreasonable under the circumstances. In addition, the appeals court announced a set of four categories to measure the reasonableness of intrusions after knock and announcement, and listed a series of factors to take into account when placing a case into one of these categories.

The Supreme Court, in a unanimous decision, reversed the Ninth Circuit decision concerning Banks and also rejected the categorical approach developed by the appeals court. Justice DAVID SOUTER, writing for the Court, reaffirmed the obligation of police to knock and announce unless a court has authorized a no-knock entry. He also reaffirmed the Court's process for assessing the reasonableness of a search, which reviews the "totality of the circumstances." Souter noted that "it is too hard to invent categories without giving short shrift to details that turn out to be important in a given instance, and without inflating marginal ones."

In this case the Court looked at whether police had reasonable grounds to believe that Banks would dispose of the drugs before they could enter the apartment. If police can demonstrate "exigent circumstances," the Court has generally upheld the reasonableness of a forced entry. Here the government claimed that it risked losing the cocaine as evidence within a very short period if Banks was aware of their presence. Justice Souter agreed with this "danger of disposal" **justification**. In this type of case it was "reasonable to suspect imminent loss of evidence after the 15 to 20 seconds the officers waited prior to forcing their way."

Justice Souter dismissed Banks's argument that because he was in the shower the wait was too short. The facts known to the police at the time governed what a court must use in determining a reasonable waiting time. There was no evidence that the police knew Banks was in the shower and used this to justify a forced entry. In addition, a reasonable waiting time must be judged on the exigent need of the police to make sure the cocaine was not flushed away, not by how long it would have taken Banks to reach his front door. Bathrooms and the kitchens are "usually in the interior of a dwelling," so travel time to the front door was not relevant. Souter stated that there was no "reliable basis for giving the proprietor of a mansion a longer wait than the resident of a bungalow, or an apartment like Banks's." Once police determined that waiting any longer outside risked the loss of evidence, they had reasonable grounds to knock the door down.

Having concluded that the forced entry was constitutional, Justice Souter scolded the Ninth Circuit for seeking to impose categories on judging the reasonableness of knock and announce forced entries. Each case had to be viewed on the totality of its circumstances. The Ninth Circuit approach threatened to distort this analysis "by replacing a stress on revealing facts with resort to pigeonholes."

LaShawn Banks, *right*, stands with his lawyer behind the apartment where he was arrested in 1998.

Gas Tank Border Searches are Constitutional

The federal government's efforts to prevent the entry of illegal narcotics into the United States has led to aggressive policing by the U.S. customs agents. These efforts have focused mostly on border crossing points between the U.S. and Mexico. Policies for inspecting motor vehicles that seek to enter the U.S. include removing gas tanks to determine if contraband has been hidden inside. The Supreme Court's ruling in *United States v. Flores-Montano*, __ U.S. __, 124 S.Ct. 1582, __ L.Ed.2d __ (2004) upheld the legality of such searches, even when officers do not have reasonable suspicion that the vehicle contains contraband. The Court ruled that these searches do not violate the Fourth Amendment.

In 2002, Manuel Flores-Montano tried to enter the United States at the Otay Mesa port of entry in southern California. A customs inspector searched the station wagon Flores-Montano was driving and then asked him to leave the car. The automobile was driven to another inspection station where it underwent further examination. Based on sounds made by tapping on the gas tank, it was concluded that the tank seemed to be solid, so an inspector phoned a mechanic to come the station to remove the gas tank. The mechanic, who was on contract to the Customs Service, arrived thirty minutes later. He placed the car on a hydraulic lift, removed the tank, and gave it to the inspector. An inspector opened an access plate and found thirty-seven kilograms of marijuana bricks. The entire inspection process took no more than twenty-five minutes to complete.

Flores-Montano was indicted on federal drug charges; he proceeded to challenge the constitutionality of the gas tank search, arguing that under a Ninth **Circuit Court** of Appeals ruling, customs inspectors needed reasonable suspicion under the FOURTH AMENDMENT. In this case, the inspectors admitted they did not act based on reasonable suspicion. Based on this decision, the federal district court ruled that the search violated the Fourth Amendment and that the marijuana could not be used as evidence against the **defendant**. The government appealed to the Ninth Circuit, arguing that the appeals court overturn its prior decision. The appeals court reaffirmed its holding that reasonable suspicion is the proper standard for measuring the constitutionality of an intrusive automobile search. The government appealed to the Supreme Court.

The Court, in a unanimous decision, reversed the Ninth Circuit decision. Chief Justice WILLIAM REHNQUIST, writing for the Court, concluded that the Ninth Circuit had misapplied a Supreme Court decision that required reasonable suspicion for highly intrusive searches of a person. This standard had "no place in border searches of vehicles." Rehnquist noted that the government's interest in keeping out "unwanted persons and effects is at its zenith at the international border." Numerous Court decisions had emphasized that the border searches were reasonable "simply by virtue of the fact that they occur at the border." Moreover, Congress had granted the Executive branch authority to conduct routine searches ever since the formation of the U.S. government.

The case of Flores-Montano was clearly routine. Chief Justice Rehnquist cited government statistics that hiding contraband in automobile fuel tanks was a common tactic used by smugglers. From 1998 to 2003 there had been almost 19,000 drug seizures at southern California border ports of entry; more than 4,600 of these seizures were found in gas tanks, accounting for almost twenty-five percent of the cases. In addition to drugs, inspectors find persons concealed in and around gas tanks about once every ten days at the Otay Mesa port of entry.

The Court rejected Flores-Montano's claim that he had a **privacy** interest in his fuel tank. Prior decisions had permitted searches of an automobile's passenger compartment, making it "difficult to imagine" that the search of a fuel tank was more invasive. In addition, the removal and reinstallation of the gas tank did not constitute a significant deprivation of the defendant's property interests. Rehnquist found that in 2003, 348 gas tank searches did not turn up contraband; these vehicles were reassembled and the passengers proceeded into the United States. Though the interference with the motorist's property rights was "not insignificant," the removal of a gas tank was justified by the government's "paramount interest in protecting the border."

Supreme Court Fails to Resolve Automobile Search Issue

The Supreme Court has permitted police officers to search automobiles without a search warrant, based on concerns for officer safety and the preservation of evidence. In *New York v. Belton*, 453 U.S. 454, 101 S.Ct. 2860, 69 L.Ed.2d 768 (1981), the Court upheld a search of a vehicle when the **defendant** was a "recent occupant" of the auto, yet it failed to define recent occupancy. The lack of clarity over what this term meant has led state and federal courts to develop two competing definitions. The Court appeared ready to resolve the issue in *Arizona v. Gant*, __ U.S. __, 124 S.Ct. 461, 157 L.Ed.2d 308 (2003) but vacated the decision of the Arizona Court of Appeals and remanded the case. On **remand** the court was instructed to review its thinking in light of the Arizona Supreme Court's recent decision in *Arizona v. Dean*, 206 Ariz. 158, 76 P.3d 429(2003). Despite the lack of a Supreme Court decision on this issue, the facts surrounding *Gant* and the legal analysis in *Dean* illustrate the complexities of Fourth Amendment law.

In 1999, Tucson police went to Rodney Gant's house looking for drugs. He answered the door but told the officers that Gant was not home. The officers left but returned later, finding two people in the house, one of whom possessed a crack pipe. As the police processed these suspects Gant pulled his car into the driveway. The police had learned after leaving the residence the first time that Gant was wanted on an **outstanding warrant** and that his drivers license had been suspended. An officer shined his flashlight into the car but Gant stepped out of the vehicle before the police said anything to him. The officers searched his vehicle and found a handgun and a bag of cocaine. The state charged Gant with possession of cocaine and drug paraphernalia and he was convicted of the charges. Gant had failed to persuade the trial court to suppress the evidence taken from his car; the court concluded that the warrantless search had been incident to a lawful arrest. The Arizona Court of Appeals reversed, finding that the *Belton* rule applied only when the police initiated contact when the suspect was still in the vehicle. In this case Gant was already outside his car when the police approached him. Therefore, concerns about the officers safety and the destruction of evidence were inapplicable.

The Arizona Supreme Court declined to review this decision, so the state sought and was granted review by the U.S. SUPREME COURT in April 2003. Oral argument was scheduled for the fall of 2003 but the Arizona Supreme Court released its decision in *Dean* in September. The U.S. Supreme Court elected to **vacate** the *Gant* ruling because the *Dean* decision addressed the "recent occupant" issue. Once the Arizona Court of Appeals issued a new ruling it might be appealable to the U.S. Supreme Court.

The Arizona Supreme Court reviewed the conviction of Donald Dean on drug charges. Police followed Dean as he drove his vehicle around Phoenix. After police activated the overhead lights in their marked patrol car, Dean did not pull over. Instead, he drove back to his house and parked in the driveway. He jumped out of his car, leaving the keys in the ignition, and ran into his garage. Police found Dean hiding in the attic and he was arrested about two and one-half hours after jumping out of his car. Only after he was arrested did police search the car and find methamphetamine. Dean asked the Supreme Court to throw out this evidence based on *Belton*.

Justice Andrew Hurwitz, writing for a unanimous court, threw out Dean's conviction and in so doing rejected the analysis employed by the court of appeals in *Gant*. He pointed out that courts had defined the "recent occupant" requirement in two distinct ways. The *Gant* decision employed the first approach, which viewed a defendant as a recent occupant only when police had initiated contact with the suspect before he left the vehicle. The court concluded that this approach was "irrelevant to the determination whether an arrestee was a 'recent occupant' of a vehicle under *Belton*." The "appropriate inquiry" focused on when and where the arrest took place. A search would be constitutional if it was "substantially contemporaneous with the arrest and is confined to the immediate vicinity of the arrest." In Dean's case the police waited too long to search his vehicle, therefore the evidence had to be suppressed. Based on this analysis, Gant's search would likely be constitutional, as he had just stepped out of his car when police arrested him on the outstanding warrant and the search took place immediately after detaining him.

Law Enforcement Officer Can be Liable for Preparing Faulty Search Warrant

The Warrant **Clause** of the Fourth Amendment requires that a search warrant particularly describe "the place to be searched, and the persons or things to be seized." The Supreme Court, in *Groh v. Ramirez*, __ U.S. __, S.Ct., __ L.Ed.2d __ 2004 WL 330057 (2004), ruled that a search warrant that failed to describe what was to be seized was constitutionally defective, even though a description was contained in the warrant application and the supporting **affidavit**. In addition, the Court held that the law enforcement officer who prepared the defective warrant and led the search was not immune from a civil damages lawsuit for his conduct.

In February 1997, Jeff Groh, an experienced special agent with the Bureau of Alcohol, Tobacco and Firearms (ATF), received information that Joseph Ramirez was stockpiling automatic weapons, grenades, grenade launchers, and rocket launchers on his Montana ranch. Groh prepared and signed an application for a search warrant to present to the federal **magistrate** for issuance of the warrant. The application described the weaponry Groh believed was on the ranch and included a separate affidavit signed by Groh that listed the items that might be found. Groh also prepared the warrant and included this in his submission. The magistrate signed the search warrant. In contrast to the particularity found in the application and affidavit, the warrant contained nonspecific language that only mentioned the size, color and front entrance of Ramirez's home.

Groh and a team of law enforcement officers entered the Ramirez ranch and searched it for weapons. Ramirez was not at the ranch that day but his wife and children were. Groh allegedly told Mrs. Ramirez what they were looking for but she recalled being told they were looking for "an explosive device in a box." The search found no illegal weapons or explosives and no charges were filed against Ramirez. When Ramirez's attorney asked for a list of what the officers had been looking for, he was sent a copy of the pages in the warrant application.

Ramirez and his wife filed a federal civil rights lawsuit seeking money damages against Groh and the other officers who conducted the search, alleging that the officers violated their FOURTH AMENDMENT rights. The district court dismissed the lawsuit on a **summary judgment** motion, concluding that the warrant's description of the house was sufficient. The court also ruled that even if the warrant had been defective the officers were entitled to official **immunity** because the failure to describe the items to be seized was equivalent to a typographical error. The Ninth **Circuit Court** of Appeals concluded that that warrant had been defective and that all the officers except Groh were protected by qualified official immunity. The appeals court decided that Groh's drafting of the defective warrant precluded his qualified immunity, which meant that the lawsuit against Groh could proceed to the **discovery** phase and a possible trial. Groh appealed this decision to the Supreme Court.

The Supreme Court, in a 5-4 decision, upheld the Ninth Circuit. Justice JOHN PAUL STEVENS, in his majority opinion, cited the Warrant Clause's particularity requirement as an **absolute** Fourth Amendment principle. It did not matter that the application for the warrant and the affidavit of Groh contained detailed descriptions of the things to be seized. On its face, the search warrant violated the Fourth Amendment. Justice Stevens made clear that it is acceptable for a warrant to cross-reference other documents that specify what items are to be seized. As long as these documents accompany the warrant the warrant will be legal. However, in this case Groh had not attached the application or affidavit; he had placed these documents under seal to protect his informant.

Justice Stevens rejected the idea that Groh's mistake was akin to a typographical error and could therefore be excused. The majority found that the warrant was defective and the magistrate's review and signature did not "establish that he agreed that the scope of the search should be as broad as the affiant's [Groh] request." As to Groh's claim that he orally informed Mrs. Ramirez of the search items, Justice Stevens reminded Groh that in a summary **judgment appeal** Mrs. Ramirez's account must be believed. The trial court's summary judgment concluded that even if Mrs. Ramirez was to be believed, she and her husband could not prevail under the law. Therefore, Groh's oral description had no bearing on the defective warrant.

Having established the Fourth Amendment violation, Justice Stevens agreed with the Ninth Circuit that Groh could not claim immunity. A law enforcement officer will not be granted immunity if the officer violates a "clearly established" constitutional right. In this case Stevens ruled that "no reasonable officer could believe that a warrant that plainly did not comply" with the Warrant Clause was valid. In addition, the ATF had issued guidelines that warned agents that they could be held liable for executing an invalid warrant. Therefore, the lawsuit must be reinstated and returned to the district court so the Ramirez's could litigate their claims.

Justice ANTHONY KENNEDY, in a dissenting opinion joined by Chief Justice WILLIAM REHNQUIST, agreed that the warrant was defective but contended that Groh was entitled to qualified immunity because the error was one of fact, not of **constitutional law**. Groh's error was a simple oversight, as he had listed the items in the two other documents. Such a clerical mistake did not rise to a level where Groh must lose his immunity. Justice CLARENCE THOMAS, in a dissenting opinion joined by Justice ANTONIN SCALIA, concluded that the search was equivalent to a reasonable warrantless search. In his view Groh had not violated the Fourth Amendment and therefore the immunity issue did not need to come into play. However, Thomas agreed with Kennedy that Groh should have received immunity if the search was defective.

Refusing to Give Name to Police Is a Crime

The U.S. SUPREME COURT, in *Terry v. Ohio*, 392 U.S. 1, 88 S.Ct. 1868, 20 L.Ed.2d 889 (1968), ruled that police officers may **stop and frisk** a person for a **brief** time if they have "reasonable suspicion" that the person might be involved in a crime. To justify this exception to the Fourth Amendment's **probable cause** requirement, the Court emphasized that the **seizure** of the person must be limited, based on the circumstances surrounding the stop. In a concurring opinion, Justice BYRON WHITE stated that a person who was stopped was not obliged to answer questions from the police and that such a refusal did not form the basis for an arrest. Nevertheless, 20 states have enacted laws that make it a crime for persons to refuse to tell the police their names. The constitutionality of these statutes was challenged in *Hiibel v. Sixth Judicial District Court of Nevada, Humboldt County*, __ U.S. __, 124 S.Ct., __ L.Ed.2d __ 2004 WL 1373207(2004). The Court, in a 5-4 decision, upheld these laws, concluding that they did not violate the Fourth Amendment or the Fifth Amendment's right against **self-incrimination**.

The Humboldt County, Nevada, sheriffs office received a telephone call reporting that a man had assaulted a woman inside a pickup truck on a local road. An officer was dispatched to the location and found a truck parked on the side of the road. A man was standing outside the truck, and a woman was inside the passenger compartment. The officer, who believed that the man was intoxicated, asked him for identification. The man questioned why he needed to provide his name and eventually began to taunt the officer. After refusing 11 times to give his name, Larry D. Hiibel, a Nevada rancher, was arrested and taken to jail. Hiibel was charged with obstructing a police officer by failing to identify himself. He was convicted of a misdemeanor and fined $250. Hiibel appealed to the Nevada Supreme Court, arguing that his arrest violated both the Fourth and Fifth Amendments. That court upheld Hiibel's conviction and Hiibel took his case to the U.S. Supreme Court.

In a 5-4 decision, the high court rejected Hiibel's constitutional claims. Justice ANTHONY KENNEDY, writing for the majority, placed Hiibel's police stop in the context of the *Terry* decision. The police officer had reasonable suspicion to approach Hiibel and had, under Nevada law, the right to ask Hiibel to identify himself. Under this law, Hiibel only needed to tell the officer his name; he did not need to produce a driver's license or any other form of identification. As long as a person tells the officer his name or provides written identification there, is no criminal violation.

Justice Kennedy pointed out that asking questions is a central part of police investigations. Asking a suspect for identification did not implicate the FOURTH AMENDMENT because such an inquiry is a "routine and accepted part of many *Terry* stops." In addition, "Obtaining a suspect's name in the course of a *Terry* stop serves important governmental interests." Learning the suspect's name allows the police to determine whether the suspect is wanted for another offense, or has a police record. Knowing the person's identify can also clear the suspect. In Hiibel's case, police suspected a domestic assault. In these types of incidents, officers need to know "whom they are dealing with in order to **assess** the situation, the threat to their own safety, and possible danger to the potential victim."

Despite these conclusions, Justice Kennedy admitted that the Court had never ruled as to whether a suspect had to provide identification or face arrest for refusing. Prior decisions, including Justice White's concurrence in *Terry*, suggested that a person did not have an obligation to respond, but Justice Kennedy stated that those decisions were not controlling precedents. The Court ruled that requesting a suspect to identify himself was consistent with the "purposes, rationale, and practical demands of a *Terry* stop." The request in this case was a "commonsense inquiry" and not an attempt to arrest Hiibel for failing to identify himself when the investigation for domestic assault provided insufficient evidence.

Hiibel also contended that requiring him to identify himself violated his FIFTH AMENDMENT right against self-incrimination. Justice Kennedy rejected this argument, ruling that in this case the disclosure of Hiibel's name "presented no reasonable danger of incrimination." The Fifth Amendment only bars compelled testimony that is incriminating. Hiibel had failed to articulate any "real or appreciable fear" that his name would be used to incriminate him. His apparent belief that the police had no business asking questions did not rise to a constitutional violation because Hiibel could not explain how the disclosure of his name "would have been used against him in a criminal case."

In a dissenting opinion, Justice JOHN PAUL STEVENS challenged the Court's conclusion that names were usually not incriminating or would not provide "a link in the chain of evidence." He argued that a police officer would not ask the question unless the information might be incriminating. Otherwise, "the **statute** requires nothing more than a useless invasion of privacy."

Justice STEPHEN BREYER, in a dissenting opinion joined by Justices DAVID SOUTER and RUTH BADER GINSBURG, contended that even if there was no formal precedent permitting a person to refuse to identify himself, there was a "generation-old" understanding that suspects in *Terry* stops may decline to answer questions.

Highway Checkpoints Not Presumptively Unconstitutional

After the U.S. SUPREME COURT, in *Indianapolis v. Edmund*, 531 U.S. 32, 121 S.Ct. 447, 148 L.Ed.2d 333 (2000), ruled that drug searches by police at highway checkpoints violated the Fourth Amendment, lower courts have given greater scrutiny to other types of police checkpoints. The Illinois Supreme Court used *Edmund* to throw out the conviction of Robert S. Lidster for drunk driving, who was arrested at a police checkpoint. However, the U.S. Supreme Court reversed this decision in *Illinois v. Lidster*, __ U.S. __, 124 S.Ct. 885, 157 L.Ed.2d 843 (2004), finding that state court had misapplied *Edmund*. In so ruling the Court made clear that not all arrests generated by police checkpoints and roadblocks violate the Fourth Amendment's **search and seizure clause**.

The case was set in motion by a hit and run automobile accident that occurred around midnight in August 1997. A vehicle struck and killed a 70-year-old bicyclist, who had just left his shift at a U.S. Post Office, which was located in an industrial park near the highway. The driver drove off, leaving the police with little information as to who struck the bicyclist. One week later the police set up a checkpoint at the same time and place of the accident, hoping to obtain information from postal workers and others employed at the industrial park who might have been on the road the week before. Traffic was forced to slow down before the checkpoint, with up to 15 cars idling in each lane. As each vehicle reached the checkpoint, officers would ask the occupants whether they had seen anything the week before and then hand out a flyer describing the incident and asking for the public's help in solving this crime. Each stop took between 10 to 15 seconds.

Robert Lidster was driving his minivan that night and saw the checkpoint. The minivan swerved as it approached the checkpoint and almost struck a police officer. An officer smelled alcohol on Lidster' breath and pulled him over for a sobriety test. Lidster was arrested and later convicted of driving under the influence. He appealed his conviction, arguing that the police had obtained most of the incriminating evidence against him through the use of the checkpoint stop. His attorney convinced both an Illinois appeals court and the state supreme court that such a stop violated the FOURTH AMENDMENT based on the *Edmund* decision.

The Supreme Court voted unanimously to overturn the state supreme court. Justice STEPHEN BREYER, writing for the Court, concluded that the Illinois court was not bound by the *Edmund* decision, as that case addressed a much different policing function. In that case police stopped vehicles at a checkpoint, walked a drug-sniffing dog around the car, looked through the windows to examine the vehicle's interior, and arrested individuals where enough evidence was uncovered through these methods. Justice Breyer noted that the **intent** of this checkpoint was to find "evidence of ordinary criminal wrongdoing" without first establishing "individualized suspicion" of such wrongdoing. This type of checkpoint violated the Fourth Amendment because of this lack of individualized suspicion.

In the Court's view the Illinois checkpoint was much different. The purpose was not to determine whether occupants of a vehicle were committing crimes but to ask members of the public for assistance in solving a crime that had "in all likelihood [been] committed by others." In addition, the Court had approved of other police checkpoints, such as sobriety and Border Patrol checkpoints, recognizing legitimate reasons for such police actions. In this case the focus was on seeking information. Police are fully entitled to ask individuals walking down the street for assistance in an investigation, but Justice Breyer admitted that *Edmund* held that an involuntary stop of a vehicle was a "seizure" under the Fourth Amendment. He concluded, however, that the difference between a pedestrian and automobile information stop was not important enough to trigger the *Edmund* rule.

Having ruled out the application of *Edmund*, Justice Breyer applied a three-part test first detailed in *Brown v. Texas*, 443 U.S. 47, 99 S.Ct. 2637, 61 L.Ed.2d 357 (1979) to determine whether the checkpoint was constitutional. The Illinois checkpoint met the first factor, which was whether the public concern was sufficiently grave. The death of the bicyclist clearly made this a matter of grave concern. Second, the checkpoint advanced the public interest by having the police target the same location and time of night where the accident occurred. Finally, the checkpoint stops "interfered only minimally with the liberty of the sort the Fourth Amendment seeks to protect." The stops only lasted a few seconds, the occupants of the vehicles were asked a brief question and given flyers, and all vehicles were treated the same. Therefore, the checkpoint stop of Lidster was constitutional and his subsequent criminal conviction as well.

Justice JOHN PAUL STEVENS, in a concurring opinion joined by Justices DAVID SOUTER and RUTH BADER GINSBURG, agreed that *Edmund* did not apply. However, he would have remanded the case to the Illinois courts to determine whether the checkpoint stops met the three-part test of *Brown*. Stevens noted that the state courts had not addressed these factors because of their application of *Edmund*.

Police Had Probable Cause to Arrest Passenger of Vehicle in Which Drugs were Found

The Fourth Amendment's **probable cause** requirement forces police officers to justify their arrests of individuals suspected of criminal behavior. Criminal behavior that takes place in automobiles has led to cases where defendants allege that police could not reasonably find probable cause to arrest a passenger in a vehicle where drugs or other incriminating contraband are found. The Supreme Court, in *Maryland v. Pringle*, __ U.S. __, 124 S.Ct. 795, 157 L.Ed.2d 769 (2003), ruled that police had probable cause to arrest a front-seat passenger for possession of cocaine which was found behind the back-seat armrest.

A Baltimore County police officer stopped a car for speeding around 3 AM in August 1999. Three men occupied the car. Joseph J. Pringle was a front-seat passenger and Otis Smith sat in the backseat. When the officer asked the driver, Donte Partlow, for his license and registration, Partlow opened the glove compartment directly in front of Pringle to retrieve the paperwork. The officer noticed a large amount of rolled-up money in the compartment. A second squad car arrived and the officer asked Partlow if he had any weapons or narcotics in his car. He denied he had these items and agreed to the officer's request to search the car. The officer found five plastic bags of cocaine behind the back-seat armrest, which had been placed in the upright position against the seat. The three men denied owning the drugs and refused to discuss the drugs or the money. The police officers then arrested all three men and took them to the police station. Pringle eventually waived his *Miranda* warnings and confessed that the cocaine was his. He claimed he was bringing it to a party where he planned to sell it or barter it for sex. Pringle said that Partlow and Smith were not involved, so the police released them. Pringle sought to have his confession suppressed but the trial court denied the motion. A jury convicted him of cocaine possession and possession with **intent** to distribute cocaine. The court sentenced him to ten years in prison.

Pringle appealed his conviction, arguing that the police lacked probable cause to arrest him, which in turn would invalidate his confession. The Maryland Court of Special Appeals court rejected his claims but the Maryland Court of Appeals overturned the conviction. The court held that the mere **discovery** of the cocaine in the backseat area was insufficient to establish probable cause to arrest a front-seat passenger. The court said it was unconstitutional to arrest everyone until someone confesses. Maryland then appealed to the U.S. SUPREME COURT.

The Supreme Court, in a unanimous decision, reversed the Maryland appeals court. Chief Justice WILLIAM REHNQUIST, writing for the Court, noted that Maryland law authorizes police officers to make warrantless arrests where the office has probable cause to believe that a **felony** has been committed. In this case it was uncontested that the officer had probable cause to believe a felony had been committed once the five bags of cocaine had been found. The only issue was whether the officer had probable cause to believe Pringle was the person who had committed the crime.

Rehnquist emphasized that the Court in prior decisions had made clear that the probable cause standard was to be interpreted in light of the realities of police work. Probable cause was a fluid concept that is "incapable of precise definition or quantification into percentages because it deals with probabilities and depends on the totality of circumstances." Therefore, the Court would review the facts that led up to the arrest from the standpoint of an "objectively reasonable police officer."

Based on this standard the Court concluded that a reasonable officer would infer that the three occupants of the car had knowledge of and control over the cocaine. A reasonable officer could conclude that there was probable cause to arrest Pringle for possession, either as the sole perpetrator or in collusion with the other two men. Pringle argued that his arrest had been based on guilt-by-association and that his proximity to the cocaine could not, by itself, give the officer probable cause. Chief Justice Rehnquist rejected this argument, pointing out that the confined interior space of the automobile suggested that the three men shared a criminal enterprise. The quantity of drugs and the large amount of money in the car indicated drug dealing, "an enterprise to which a dealer would be unlikely to admit an **innocent** person with the potential to furnish evidence against him." None of the men initially told police who owned the cocaine, which gave the officer probable cause to arrest all of them.

Search Incident to Arrest of Driver who has Exited Vehicle does not Violate the Fourth Amendment

The U.S. SUPREME COURT ruled that a police officer's search of a vehicle incident to the arrest of the driver does not violate the FOURTH AMENDMENT to the federal Constitution, even though the police officer did not make contact with the driver while he was still in the vehicle. *Thornton v. U.S.*, 2004 WL 1144370, ___U.S.___, ___S.Ct.___, ___L.Ed.___ (2004). State and federal courts had divided on the application of the search-incident-to-arrest rule in situations where police contact is first initiated after the suspect has exited the vehicle. Some jurisdictions had required the suspect to be actually or constructively aware of police presence while still in the vehicle, while others had looked to the defendant's physical proximity to the vehicle at the time of his arrest. Still other jurisdictions had factored in the temporal proximity between the arrest and the search.

The case arose out of a traffic incident on July 21, 2001, in Norfolk, Virginia. Officer Deion Nichols, driving in an unmarked police cruiser, observed a gold Lincoln Town Car pull to the left of his vehicle, at which point it suddenly decelerated. Assuming that the driver of the Lincoln suspected that he was a police officer, Nichols pulled over to a side street and made a right turn. After the Lincoln passed him, Nichols ran a check on the tags, which revealed that the license tags had been issued to a 1982 Chevy two-door car rather than to a Lincoln Town Car.

Officer Nichols followed the Lincoln, intending to pull it over. The Lincoln was driven into a parking lot, however, before Nichols had a chance to do so. The **defendant** then parked the Lincoln and exited the vehicle. Nichols pulled in behind the defendant and exited his police cruiser. In uniform, Nichols approached Thornton and asked him for his driver's license, advising Thornton that the license tags did not match the registered vehicle.

Nichols later testified that Thornton "appeared nervous" and "right away started rambling," "licking his lips," and "sweating." Thornton told Nichols that "someone had just given him the car." "For officer safety," Officer Nichols asked Thornton if he had any narcotics or weapons on him. Thornton said no. The officer then asked him if there were any weapons or narcotics in the car. Thornton again said no. Nichols proceeded to pat-down Thornton, after obtaining permission to do so. Officer Nichols felt a "bulge" in Thornton's front left pocket. Unable to identify the bulge by touch, Nichols asked Thornton, "Do you have any illegal narcotics on you?" Thornton said that he had "a bag of weed." Officer Nichols then asked him if he could have the bag. Thornton reached into his pocket and pulled out two individual bags, one containing three bags of a "green leafy material consistent with marijuana" and the other containing a "large amount of an off-white rocklike substance consistent with crack cocaine."

At that point, Officer Nichols handcuffed Thornton and advised him that he was under arrest. Officer Nichols later testified that he then put Thornton in the back of the police car, and immediately conducted what he described as a search incident to arrest, entering the interior of the vehicle where he found a "BryCo .9-millimeter handgun" under the front driver's seat. On the way to the police station, Thornton confessed that he had "just robbed some cat out at Ocean View, and that's where he got the dope." Nichols said that Thornton confessed on his own and "without any provocation."

Based on the confession and the evidence seized during Nichols' search of the Lincoln, Thorton was convicted of possession with **intent** to distribute cocaine base and two firearm offenses. The U.S District Court for the Eastern District of Virginia sentenced Thornton to 180 months imprisonment and eight years of supervised release. At trial Thornton objected to the admissibility of the drugs and weapons, arguing that they were not lawfully obtained as a "search incident to arrest." The district court denied the defendant's motion to suppress, and the defendant appealed.

The U.S. Court of Appeals for the Fourth Circuit affirmed. *United States v. Thornton*, 325 F.3d 189 (4th Cir. 2003). The fourth circuit first observed that police searches performed without a search warrant are presumptively invalid under the Fourth Amendment to the federal Constitution. However, the court of appeals then noted that searches performed incident to arrest comprise a well-recognized exception to the warrant requirement. When an arrest is made, the court said, it is reasonable for the arresting officer to search the person arrested to remove any weapons that the arrestee might use to resist arrest or effect his escape. Otherwise, the officer's safety might well be endangered, and the arrest itself frustrated.

Moreover, the court stressed that it is entirely reasonable for the arresting officer to search for and seize any evidence on the arrestee's person in order to prevent its concealment or destruction. The area into which an arrestee might reach in order to grab a weapon or evidentiary items must, the court reasoned, be governed by a like rule. The court then reiterated the two historical rationales for the search-incident-to arrest exception: (1) the need to disarm the suspect in order to take him into custody, and (2) the need to preserve evidence for later use at trial.

In *New York v. Belton*, 453 U.S. 454, 101 S.Ct. 2860, 69 L.Ed.2d 768 (U.S. 1981), the fourth circuit wrote, the Supreme Court established the "workable rule" that "when a policeman has made a lawful custodial arrest of the occupant of an automobile, he may, as a contemporaneous incident of that arrest, search the passenger compartment of that automobile." Applying this rule, the fourth circuit concluded that Nichols' search of Thornton's vehicle was constitutionally permissible.

Thornton appealed, relying on a line of authority from the sixth circuit that modifies the *Belton* rule in cases where the defendant has voluntarily exited the automobile and begun walking away from the automobile before the officer has initiated contact with him. See, for example, *United States v. Hudgins*, 52 F.3d 115, 119 (6th Cir.1995); *United States v. Strahan*, 984 F.2d 155, 159 (6th Cir.1993). In such instances, this line of authority requires that the lawfulness of the search be evaluated by courts on a case-by-case basis, to determine the reasonableness of the police officer's conduct under the circumstances. According to Thornton, Nichols' search of him in this case was unreasonable under the circumstances because Thornton had walked far enough away from the vehicle to no longer present a threat of returning to the vehicle and seizing the weapon without Nichols first stopping him.

In a 7-2 decision, the U.S. Supreme Court affirmed. Chief Justice WILLIAM REHNQUIST, writing for the majority, rejected the notion that *Belton* was limited to situations in which the officer initiated contact while the arrestee was still in the vehicle. Nowhere in the *Belton* decision, Rehnquist wrote, did the Court rely on the fact that the officer had ordered the occupants out of the vehicle or initiated contact with them while they remained in the vehicle.

Under Thornton's proposed "contact initiation" rule, officers who decide that it may be safer and more effective to conceal their presence until a suspect has left the car would be unable to search the passenger compartment in the event of custodial arrest, thereby compromising the officer's safety and placing potentially incriminating evidence at risk of concealment of destruction, Rehnquist said. Moreover, Rehnquist emphasized that the proposed rule would **render** the constitutional limits of *Belton* unclear, requiring an officer who is approaching a suspect who has just alighted from a vehicle to determine whether the officer's presence actually signaled a **confrontation** with the suspect or whether the suspect was unaware of the officer at the time he or she exited the vehicle. *Belton* sought to eliminate such "ad hoc determinations" by police officers in the field, Rehnquist concluded.

FREEDOM OF INFORMATION ACT

Privacy Rights of Survivors Trumps Public's Right to Know

The Freedom of Information Act (FOIA), 5 U.S.C.A. § 552, gives the public the opportunity to force the federal government to disclose data. However, FOIA contains provisions that give the government the right to **deny** disclosure under certain circumstances. One such provision is § 552(b)(7)(C), which bars disclosure if the data "could reasonably be expected to constitute an unwarranted invasion of personal privacy." The Supreme Court, in *National Archives and Records Administration v. Favish*, __ U.S. __, 124 S.Ct. 1570, __ L.Ed.2d __ (2004), broadened the

Allan Favish talks to reporters outside the Supreme Court.

scope of this provision to protect not only the **privacy** of the person to whom the documents referred but also the person's family once the person has died. The decision will make the release of autopsies and photographs of death scenes more difficult.

The case arose out of the 1993 suicide of Vincent Foster in a Virginia park. Foster, a close friend of President BILL CLINTON and his wife Hillary Rodham Clinton, worked as White House deputy **counsel**. His death led to speculation by the press and political opponents of the Clintons that Foster had not shot himself with a revolver, but had been murdered as part of a political cover-up. The intensity of this speculation led to investigations of his death by the FEDERAL BUREAU OF INVESTIGATION (FBI), committees in both houses of Congress, and independent counsels Robert Fisk and Kenneth Starr. Each of these investigations concluded that Foster had killed himself. Allan Favish, a lawyer associated with Accuracy in Media who was interested in this matter, applied under the FOIA for photographs of Foster's death scene. After his request was denied, Favish filed suit in federal district court. He argued that the investigations had been "grossly incompetent and untrustworthy." Among the documents he requested were eleven photographs. Ten of the images showed Foster's body, and the other was a photo of Foster's eyeglasses. The district court agreed that the government should release the eyeglasses photo, but the court denied access to the death-scene pictures. The court balanced the Foster family's privacy interests against the public interest in disclosure. It concluded that Favish had not produced a strong explanation as to how disclosure would advance the investigation of Foster's death to trump the family's privacy interests.

The Ninth **Circuit Court** of Appeals reversed the district court. It ruled that Favish had "the right to look, a right to speculate and argue again, a right of public scrutiny." The appeals court recognized the Foster family's privacy interests, but found that the district court had improperly balanced the relevant interests. It sent the case back to the district court for a fresh analysis. The district court then ordered the release of five death-scene photographs. On subsequent **appeal** to the Ninth Circuit, the appeals court upheld the decision, this time without explanation. The court ruled that only four of the photographs should be released. The government appealed this ruling to the Supreme Court.

The Supreme Court, in a unanimous decision, overturned the Ninth Circuit ruling. Justice ANTHONY KENNEDY, writing for the Court, examined whether the release of the four photographs constituted an "unwarranted invasion of personal privacy." Favish contended the family did not have a personal privacy interest as set out in the 7(C); the only person who had an interest in the photos was Vincent Foster, but he surrendered this right when he died. Justice Kennedy rejected this argument, finding that the 7(C)'s language did not limit its reach to Foster. The exemption's "comparative breadth is no mere accident in drafting." Congress had given "special consideration" to this FOIA exemption.

Justice Kennedy noted that the Foster family did not seek to invoke the exemption "for fear that the pictures may reveal private information about Foster to the detriment of his posthumous reputation or some other interest personal to him." Instead, the family had invoked their own right to personal privacy, using the exemption "to secure their own refuge from a sensation-seeking culture for their own peace of mind and tranquility." Kennedy pointed out that the Foster family had been subject to many painful incidents since 1993, and that the leak of one death-scene photograph had been emotionally traumatic.

In interpreting the 7(C)exemption, Justice Kennedy acknowledged cultural traditions surrounding burial rites that show respect for the feelings of family members of the deceased.

These traditions, which include family control over the body and death images of the deceased, have been recognized at common law and, in Kennedy's view, formed the background for Congress's drafting of 7(C). In more practical terms, Kennedy stated that "child molesters, rapists, murderers and other violent criminals often make FOIA requests for autopsies, photographs, and records of their deceased victims." By ruling that family members have enforceable privacy interests, the Court could permit the government to deny these "gruesome requests in appropriate cases." This reading of 7(C) made sense because it was "inconceivable" that Congress would have intended to convicted felons to obtain these materials.

Justice Kennedy then examined what it meant, under 7(C), to constitute an "unwarranted" invasion of privacy. When persons apply for FOIA access they do not have to offer a reason for their requests. In this case, however, the Court concluded the general rule was inapplicable and provided a new standard. The person must first establish "a sufficient reason for the disclosure" that demonstrates a "significant" public interest in the release of the material. If that **element** is satisfied, the person must show that "the information is likely to advance that interest." In this case, the public interest in making sure the investigation had been performed properly satisfied the first element. However, Favish's reasons for seeking the photos did not advance this interest. Therefore, none of the photographs could be released.

FREEDOM OF SPEECH

The right, guaranteed by the FIRST AMENDMENT to the U.S. Constitution, to express beliefs and ideas without unwarranted government restriction.

School District Violated Constitution by Excluding Anti-Gay Viewpoint during "Diversity Week"

In a strongly worded opinion, the U.S. District Court for the Eastern District of Michigan ruled that the First Amendment to the federal Constitution protects the right of a Christian public high school student to express her religious beliefs in opposition to homosexuality during the school's 2002 "Diversity Week" program, which was designed to teach tolerance of homosexual lifestyles. *Hansen v. Ann Arbor Public Schools*, 293 F.Supp.2d 780 (E.D.Mich. 2003). The case involved a federal lawsuit filed by the Thomas More Law Center, a national public interest law firm, on behalf of student Elisabeth "Betsy" Hansen, whose religious views against homosexuality were censored and excluded from the diversity program held at the high school.

Diversity Week 2002 was held March 18-22 at Pioneer High School (PHS) in Ann Arbor, Michigan, where Hansen was a senior. For at least ten years prior to this case, PHS had been holding a "Diversity Week" of some kind. Traditionally, the week's activities included a general assembly program; panel discussions on race, religion and sexual orientation; an open microphone session for persons to air their thoughts and feelings on subjects related to the week's events; and a number of multi-cultural activities involving music and food. The panel discussions were held during class time in the school's theater, and teachers brought their classes to attend the discussions.

In preparation for the 2002 Diversity Week events, faculty advisor Sunnie Korzdorfer and Student Council President Tom Jensen sent emails asking for help in planning to all of the student organizations. The only club to respond was the Gay/Straight Alliance (GSA). The GSA asked if it could steer the sexual orientation panel. Korzdorfer agreed, and she turned over sponsorship and administration of the panel to the GSA and its co-sponsors, Parker Pennington and Rodney Mancini, two openly gay faculty advisors.

Traditionally, the race, religion, and sexual orientation panel discussions had been composed of PHS students; this was the anticipated format when Diversity Week 2002 was being planned. In fact, the student council continued with the student-composed panel format for the "race" and "religion" panels that it organized. The GSA, however, decided to change both the composition and the format of the sexual orientation panel. First, instead of presenting a panel discussion on "sexual orientation," the GSA decided to change the panel's topic to "Religion and Homosexuality." Second, the GSA decided that, instead of having PHS students as presenters, its "Religion and Homosexuality" panel would be composed of adult religious leaders from the Ann Arbor community.

Six different clerics were invited to participate in a panel discussion about religion and homosexuality. All six, including a rabbi, cited biblical authority for their view that homosexuality is a legitimate lifestyle. Hansen, a Catholic and a member of the PHS student organization, "Pioneers for Christ" (PFC), asked if she or a clerical representative designated by her could participate in the "Religion and Homosexuality" panel to convey the message that the Bible teaches that homosexuality is a sin. Hansen's request was denied, though school officials later allowed Hansen to give a two-minute speech at a separate assembly. At trial, the school attempted to show that Hansen's request had not been made in a timely fashion, but this testimony was rebutted by evidence indicating that the GSA opposed anyone participating on the panel who believed that homosexuality was an invalid lifestyle, especially a member of the PFC student organization.

The Homosexuality and Religion panel went forward without Betsy or her representative. As indicated, six pro-homosexual adult clergy and religious leaders were presenters. None of the clergy or religious leaders was Roman Catholic, nor shared Roman Catholic beliefs regarding homosexuality. Some of the clergy wore clerical garb during the panel. The panel members were held out as experts on matters of religion. The format was one of question-and-answer and was moderated by Pennington. Questions were pre-submitted by students, and Pennington decided which questions he would ask. Panelists discussed the Bible and scripture. They explained how passages referring to homosexuality had been misunderstood or mistranslated by others to mean that homosexuality was immoral or sinful or incompatible with Christianity.

Meanwhile, before Hansen was allowed to give her speech at a separate assembly, she was first required to submit the text of the speech to Korzdorfer, who called Betsy at her home on the Sunday prior to the Assembly (**i.e.**, Sunday, March 17) to "suggest" that she make the changes in the speech because the speech targeted a specific group of individuals, namely homosexuals, and described the lifestyle of that group as immoral. Betsy did not want to change her speech, but she felt she had no choice, as school policy states that it is "inappropriate behavior" for a student to refuse to comply either verbally or non-verbally with a direction or instruction of a staff member. Betsy gave a two-minute speech that omitted any reference to what she believed was the immorality and sinfulness of homosexuality.

Hansen and her mother, Constance Hansen, then filed a law suit pursuant to 42 U.S.C.A section 1983. They claimed that, through its actions during Diversity Week 2002, PHS had deprived Betsy of her FIRST AMENDMENT rights to freedom of speech and free exercise of religion. They also claimed that the school had violated the **Equal Protection clause** of the FOURTEENTH AMENDMENT and of the Establishment Clause of the First Amendment. Judge Gerald Rosen, writing for the court, found three separate constitutional violations.

First, Rosen found that the school district violated Hansen's First Amendment free speech rights by excluding her from designating a clerical participant in the Diversity Week panel on homosexuality and religion who would reflect her opinion that homosexuality was sinful and by editing her speech to remove any reference to her belief that homosexuality was wrong. The exclusion was impermissibly based on her anti-gay viewpoint, the court concluded, and the school's alleged reasons for exclusion—to stay on the topic of tolerance, to teach students to follow proper procedures, to get across minority viewpoints, and to create safe and supportive environment for gays and lesbians—were not legitimate pedagogical concerns that could overcome viewpoint discrimination. Public school districts cannot discriminate among competing points of view to be expressed at a school-sponsored event without running afoul of the Free Speech Clause, the court wrote.

Second, Rosen found that the school district violated the First Amendment Establishment Clause by sponsoring a school-event panel that featured six clergy representatives expressing their view that homosexuality was consistent with religious scripture. Under the so-called *Lemon* test, a court must apply a three-part test to evaluate an Establishment Clause claim. Specifically the court must determine (1) whether the governmental activity under scrutiny has a non-secular purpose; (2) whether the activity's primary effect advances or inhibits religion; and (3) whether the government activity fosters an excessive entanglement with religion. *Lemon v. Kurtzman*, 403 U.S. 602, 91 S.Ct. 2105, 29 L.Ed.2d 745 (U.S. 1971). Communicating a message that some churches see consistency between religion and homosexuality does not serve any secular purpose, the court said. It is also clear, the court said, that the primary effect of the panel was to impermissibly advance the idea that government preferred the religious view that homosexuality and religion were compatible. Finally, Rosen ruled that the school district became excessively entangled with religion by recruiting clergy and making arrangements for the panel.

Third, Rosen found that the school district violated the Fourteenth Amendment's Equal Protection Clause by barring Hansen from participating in the school's Diversity Week panel on homosexuality and religion or from designating a clergy member who shared her religious views on homosexuality to represent her on the panel, while at the same time allowing a gay student association to select all of the members on the panel. The school permitted the panel to go forward, Judge Rosen wrote, even though all six clergy participants shared that view that homosexuality and religion were compatible, and then the school urged Hansen to remove contrary views from her own speech given at a separate assembly during the same week.

The judge then ordered the school district to pay Hansen's legal fees of $100,000. In so doing the judge wrote that:

> This case presents the ironic, and unfortunate, paradox of a public high school celebrating "diversity" by refusing to permit the presentation to students of an "unwelcomed" viewpoint on the topic of homosexuality and religion, while actively promoting the competing view. This **practice** of "one-way diversity," unsettling in itself, was rendered still more troubling—both constitutionally and ethically—by the fact that the approved viewpoint was, in one manifestation, presented to students as religious **doctrine** by six clerics (some in full garb) quoting from religious scripture. In its other manifestation, it resulted in the **censorship** by school administrators of a student's speech about "what diversity means to me," removing that portion of the speech in which the student described the unapproved viewpoint.

GAY AND LESBIAN RIGHTS

The goal of full legal and social equality for gay men and lesbians sought by the gay movement in the United States and other Western countries.

Battle Over Gay Marriage Heats Up in Massachusetts and Congress

Recent events in Massachusetts and California have prompted President GEORGE W. BUSH to **call** for a constitutional amendment to protect marriage. In two rulings, one in late 2003 and the other in February 2004, the Supreme Judicial Court in Massachusetts ruled that, beginning in May 2004, marriage licenses must be available to applicants of the same gender. In February 2004 in San Francisco, California, Mayor Gavin Newsom ordered the county clerk to begin issuing marriage licenses to same-sex partners. As a result, authorities in San Francisco have performed—in violation of a California code that defines marriage as a union between a man and a woman—thousands of same-sex marriages.

The Supreme Judicial Court of Massachusetts ruled on November 18, 2003, that the state cannot **deny** civil marriage to two members of the same sex who wish to marry. In *Goodridge v. Department of Public Health*, 798 N.E.2d 941 (2003), the state's high court held that the guarantee of equal treatment of citizens, a right guaranteed by the Massachusetts constitution, requires that civil marriage and its resulting protections must be available to same-sex marriages. The court **enumerated** some of the benefits of marriage, including rights in property, **probate**, tax, and evidence law that are only available to married couples. To deny civil marriage status to a certain portion of society "works a deep and scarring hardship . . . for no rational reason."

The court stayed its ruling for 180 days, in order to give the Massachusetts Legislature time to address the issue. The stay expired on May 17, 2004, at which time marriage licenses were issued to same-sex couples.

The state legislature soon crafted proposed legislation that would have prohibited same-sex marriages, but would have permitted civil unions with all the "benefits, protections, rights, and responsibilities" of marriage. In essence, the proposed legislation set up two parallel but separate devices. A civil union would be available to same-sex marriages. According to lawmakers, this would confer a "legal status equivalent to marriage." However, the bill expressly provided that marriage would only be available to couples of the opposite sex.

The state senate asked the Supreme Judicial Court for an **advisory opinion** regarding the constitutionality of the proposed legislation. The high court issued its advisory opinion in February 2004. In a 4-3 opinion dated February 3, the court concluded the proposed legislations was unconstitutional.

The Massachusetts court acknowledged in both its 2003 decision and 2004 opinion that the state may not interfere with "religious, moral, and ethical convictions" regarding marriage, "or with the decision of any religion to refuse to perform religious marriages of same-sex couples." The court went on to say, "But neither may the government, under the guise of protecting 'traditional' values, even if they be the traditional values of the majority, enshrine in law an invidious discrimination" that is forbidden by the state constitution.

The majority dismissed the notion that difference between "civil marriage" and "civil union" was a difference of semantics only, as the **dissent** argued. The court said the word choice "is a considered choice of language that reflects a demonstrable assigning of same-sex, largely homosexual, couples to second-class status."

After the Supreme Judicial Court issued its opinion, the Massachusetts legislature quickly convened a constitutional convention to consider a proposed amendment to the state constitution in order to prohibit same-sex marriages. The earliest Massachusetts citizens would vote on a proposed amendment would be in November 2006. Thirty-eight states now expressly prohibit same-sex marriages.

The dissent called the majority decision "activist." President Bush leveled the same charge when he endorsed an amendment to the U.S. Constitution. Bush said activist judges "left the people with one recourse." On February 24, 2004, the president endorsed a constitutional amendment to protect marriage as an institution only available to opposite-sex couples. In making the recommendation, Bush said, "After more than two centuries of American **jurisprudence**, and millennia of human experience, a few judges and local authorities are presuming to change the most fundamental institution of civilization. Their actions have created confusion on an issue which requires clarity."

President Bush did not endorse a specific amendment. He called upon the Congress to craft "an amendment to our Constitution defining and protecting marriage as a union of man and woman as husband and wife. The amendment should fully protect marriage, while leaving the state legislatures free to make their own choices in defining legal arrangements other than marriage." Bush said a federal amendment is necessary because activist courts may strike down the Defense of Marriage Act ("DOMA"), Pub.L. 104-99.

President BILL CLINTON signed DOMA into law in 1996. DOMA defines marriage as limited to a union between one man and one woman. The law also provides that no state is required to give legal recognition to a same-sex marriage performed in another state.

Two marriage amendments have been proposed during the 108th Congress. Representative Marilyn Musgrave (R-Co.) introduced the first one on May 21, 2003. Musgrave's proposed amendment states:

> Marriage in the United States shall consist only of the union of a man and a woman. Neither this Constitution or the constitution of any State, nor state or federal law, shall be construed to require that marital status or the legal incidents thereof be conferred upon unmarried couples or groups.

Senator A. Wayne Allard, (R-Co.), introduced a separate, identical version of the proposed amendment in the Senate in November 2003. Musgrave and Allard announced, in March 2004, that they would drop the phrase, "nor state or federal law," from the proposed amendment. Allard said the deletion would reinforce the authority of state legislatures to make decisions regarding "benefits issues related to civil unions or domestic partnerships."

A constitutional amendment would require a two-thirds majority in both the Senate and House of Representatives. It would then be passed on to the states for ratification. Thirty-eight states would need to ratify the amendment within seven years for it to become part of the U.S. Constitution. In July 2004, the Senate defeated an attempt to close debate on the amendment and send it to a vote, meaning that the vote would not happen before the November 2004 elections.

Thousands of Same-Sex Couples are Married in San Francisco After Mayor Orders Clerk to Issue Licenses

San Francisco's Mayor Gavin Newsom ignited nationwide controversy in February 2004 when he ordered the county clerk to begin to issue marriage licenses to same-sex couples. More than four thousand same-sex marriages were performed in San Francisco in a one-month period, until the California Supreme Court stopped the marriages **pending** a review of lawsuits stemming from the city's action.

Newsom, mayor of the city and county of San Francisco, sent a letter to San Francisco County Clerk Nancy Alfaro on February 10, 2004. In the letter, Newsom delineated his sworn duty to uphold the California Constitution, including the provision that requires **equal protection** of the laws. Newsom stated that California courts have ruled that the equal protection **clause** of the state constitution applies to lesbians and gay men.

Moreover, Newsom wrote, the California courts have "suggested that laws that treat homosexuals differently from heterosexuals are suspect ... and that discrimination against gay men and lesbians is invidious," and "that gender discrimination is suspect and invidious as well."

Newsom wrote, "Pursuant to my sworn duty to uphold the California Constitution, ... I request that you ... provide marriage licenses on a non-discriminatory basis, without regard to gender or sexual orientation."

Two days after Newsom's letter to Alfaro, the marriages began. Within a week, three lawsuits had been filed. These questioned the legality of the same-sex marriage licenses. Three organizations, the Campaign for California Families, the Alliance Defense Fund, and the Proposition 22 Legal Defense and Education Fund, all filed lawsuits alleging that the same-sex marriages violate California law.

San Francisco also went on the offensive. The city and county moved to sue the state, alleging that prohibiting the marriages is unconstitutional discrimination. The city seeks a ruling that the California Family Code provisions either do not apply to in-state marriages, or are "unconstitutional, void, and unenforceable." A San Francisco judge, Superior Court Judge Ronald Quidachay, combined the lawsuits. He did not, however, order that the marriage ceremonies be stopped.

On March 11, 2004, the California Supreme Court issued a temporary stay to halt the issuance of any more marriage licenses to same-sex couples. The stay went into effect immediately. San Francisco officials were commanded to enforce the family code provisions as written "without regard to respondents' personal view of the constitutionality of such provisions, and to refrain from issuing marriage licenses or certificates not authorized by such provisions."

The court did not rule on any of the underlying issues of the marriage lawsuits. The stay will remain in place until the court decides whether San Francisco officials acted beyond their authority in issuing the licenses. At that time the court will either make the stay permanent, or will allow the licenses to again be issued. The court planned on hearing the case in May or June of 2004.

By the time the California Supreme Court ordered them stopped on March 11, more than four thousand marriages had been performed. According to information compiled by the county assessor-recorder, the couples hailed from forty-six states and numerous foreign countries. The overwhelming majority came from California, however. More female couples, fifty-seven percent, were married than were male couples. The education level of the newlyweds was high; more than two-thirds held at least one college degree.

Prior to 1977, California law did not specify that marriage must be between a man and a woman. In 1977, the family code was amended to include that requirement. The law also provides that an "unmarried male" and an "unmarried female" are "capable of consenting to and consummating marriage."

In 2000, California voters passed Proposition 22, a law that defined marriage as limited to a union between a man and a woman only. Moreover, Proposition 22 provided that only marriages between a man and a woman would be recognized by the state of California. Governor Arnold Schwarzenegger announced that he believed San Francisco's same-sex marriages violated California law. He also pledged that the California **Attorney General** would defend Proposition 22.

The situation in San Francisco, as well as the fact that authorities in Massachusetts have been ordered to issue marriage licenses to same-sex partners starting in May 2004, led President GEORGE W. BUSH to **call** for a federal constitutional amendment. Although he has not endorsed a specific amendment, Bush has called for one that would define marriage as only being between a man and a woman.

The United States Supreme Court has described marriage as a being a basic civil right; it has not addressed whether it is a right that applies to gays and lesbians, or only heterosexual

San Francisco mayor Gavin Newsom stands between a pair of newlyweds during a reception in February 2004.

couples. However, in June 2003, the court ruled in *Lawrence v. Texas*, 539 U.S. 558, 123 S.Ct. 2472, 156 L.Ed.2d 506 (2003) that a state law that prohibited private consensual sex between same-sex adults was unconstitutional. The decision overturned a 1986 decision upholding a Georgia **sodomy statute**. Justice ANTHONY M. KENNEDY wrote the decision in *Lawrence*, stating the "petitioners are entitled to respect for their private lives," and "the state cannot demean their existence or control their destiny by making their private sexual conduct a crime." According to some analysts, the decision could signal that other laws pertaining to gays might be amenable to attack as well.

GUN CONTROL

Government regulation of the manufacture, sale, and possession of firearms.

Ninth Circuit Rules that the Second Amendment does not Protect an Individual's Rights to Keep and Bear Arms

The U.S. Court of Appeals for the Ninth Circuit ruled that the SECOND AMENDMENT protects only a collective right to bear arms by state militias, and does not create any sort of individual right to own or possess firearms or guns. *Silveira v. Lockyer*, 312 F.3d 1052 (9th Cir. 2002). As a result, California state residents lacked standing, under the Second Amendment, to challenge the constitutionality of California's Assault Weapons Control Act and amendments thereto.

In response to a proliferation of shootings involving semi-automatic weapons, the California legislature passed the Roberti-Roos Assault Weapons Control Act ("the AWCA") in 1989. See 1989 Cal. Stat. ch. 19, § 3, at 64, codified at CAL. PENAL CODE § 12275 **et seq.** This act significantly strengthened the state's restrictions on the possession, use, and transfer of the semi-automatic weapons popularly known as "assault weapons." California residents who either owned assault weapons, sought to acquire such weapons, or both, filed a lawsuit against the state **attorney general**, arguing that the act violated the Second Amendment to the U.S. Constitution. The U.S. District Court for the Eastern District of California, dismissed the lawsuit because the plaintiffs lacked standing (the right of a party to file a lawsuit and make a legal claim seeking to enforce the right in his or her individual **capacity**), and the Ninth Circuit affirmed.

In 1999 the legislature amended the AWCA to broaden its coverage with respect to technological developments in the manufacture of semi-automatic weapons. The 1999 amendments provide that a weapon constitutes a restricted assault weapon if it possesses certain generic characteristics listed in the **statute**, including a "semiautomatic, centerfire rifle that has a fixed magazine with the capacity to accept more than 10 rounds," as well as a semi-automatic, centerfire rifle that has the capacity to accept a detachable magazine and also features a flash suppressor, a grenade launcher, or a flare launcher. CAL. PENAL CODE § 12276.1(a)(2). The amended AWCA also restricts assault weapons equipped with "barrel shrouds," which protect the user's hands from the intense heat created by the rapid firing of the weapon, as well as semiautomatic weapons equipped with silencers.

The statute and its amendments were challenged on grounds that they violated the right to bear arms protected by the Second Amendment. The Second Amendment provides that [a] "well regulated Militia, being necessary to the security of a free State, the right of the people to keep and bear Arms, shall not be infringed." The Ninth Circuit began its analysis of the dispute by reviewing the three schools of thought on the proper **interpretation** of that amendment.

The Ninth Circuit referred to the first school of thought as the "traditional individual rights" model. It holds that the Second Amendment guarantees to individual private citizens a fundamental right to own, possess, and use firearms for any purpose at all, subject only to limited government regulation. This view, which the court said is urged by the NATIONAL RIFLE ASSOCIATION (NRA) and other firearms enthusiasts, had never been adopted by any court until the recent Fifth Circuit decision, which found that the Second Amendment does in fact protect an individual's right to use, own, and possess firearms. *United States v. Emerson*, 270 F.3d 203 (5th Cir.2001), cert. denied, 536 U.S. 907, 122 S.Ct. 2362, 153 L.Ed.2d 184 (2002).

The Ninth Circuit referred to the second school of thought as the "limited individual rights" model. Under that view, individuals maintain a constitutional right to use, own, and possess firearms, so long as that right bears a reasonable relationship to militia service.

The third school of thought, commonly called the "collective rights" model, asserts that the Second Amendment right to "bear arms" guarantees the right of the people to maintain effective state militias, but does not provide any type of individual right to use, own, or possess weapons. Under this theory of the amendment, the federal and state governments have the full authority to enact prohibitions and restrictions on the use and possession of firearms, subject only to generally applicable constitutional constraints, such as the constitutional limitations contained in the Due Process and **Equal Protection** Clauses.

According to the Ninth Circuit, the collective rights model has long been the dominant view of the Second Amendment, and widely accepted by the federal courts. However, the court noted that this school of thought has recently come under strong criticism from advocates of the individual rights model. Nonetheless, the Ninth Circuit concluded that a full analysis of the amendment, its history, and its purpose, confirms its own decision in *Hickman v. Block*, 81 F.3d 98 (9th Cir.1996), which held that the collective rights model provides the best interpretation of the Second Amendment.

The Ninth Circuit first noted the absence of any controlling U.S. SUPREME COURT precedent on the subject. Although the Supreme Court discussed the Second Amendment in *United States v. Miller*, 307 U.S. 174, 59 S.Ct. 816, 83 L.Ed. 1206 (U.S. 1939), the Ninth Circuit found that the Court's discussion did not definitively resolve the debate whether the Second Amendment supports a "collective rights" model, an "individual rights" model, or both. The most that could be said about *Miller*, the Ninth Circuit said, is that the Second Amendment does not afford a right to possess certain weapons (eg., sawed-off shotguns). *Miller* offers little guidance as to what other rights the Second Amendment does protect, the Ninth Circuit wrote.

Next the Ninth Circuit examined the history surrounding the text of the Second Amendment itself. The first **clause** is simply a **preamble**, the court of appeals found. It declares that, in the minds of the Founding Fathers, a well regulated Militia is necessary to the security of a free state. The Second Amendment reflects the American colonists' fear of standing arms being used as a tool of oppression by the central government, as the British Crown had done in the thirteen colonies before the American Revolution. JAMES MADISON and his colleagues drafted the Second Amendment, the Ninth Circuit said, to assuage fears that the new federal government would also become tyrannical, and its first move in doing so would be to dismantle the state militias.

The second clause contains the operative language of the Second Amendment, the Ninth Circuit said, prohibiting the infringement of "the right of the people to keep and bear Arms." Supporters of the individual rights model hang their hat on the use of the word "right" in this clause, since typically a right is something that can only be exercised by an individual citizen and not by a group of people. However, the Ninth Circuit found that this interpretation is not supported by the history underlying the phrase "to keep and bear arms," language that eighteenth century lawmakers usually employed to denote a military function. Specifically, this language was invoked to describe military personnel carrying rifles and other weapons, and not the private use of arms for personal purposes.

This interpretation of the second clause of the Second Amendment is reinforced by the history underlying the word "militia" in the first clause, the court continued. As mentioned earlier, the Ninth Circuit found that the original purpose of the Second Amendment was to ensure that state armies—the militia—would be maintained to defend the states against a tyrannical central government. The court supported this finding by examining the use of the word "militia" in other parts of the federal Constitution. For example, Article I states that Congress may "provide for calling forth the Militia to execute the Laws of the Union, suppress Insurrections and repel Invasions." U.S. CONST. art. I, § 8, cl. 15. The fact that the militias may be "called forth" by the federal government only in appropriate circumstances underscores their status as state institutions, the Ninth Circuit reasoned. Article II also demonstrates that the militias were conceived of as state military entities. It provides that the president is to be "Commander in Chief of the Army and Navy of the United States, and of the Militia of the several States, when called into the actual Service of the United States." Art. II, § 2, cl. 1.

"No one in the First Congress was concerned," the Ninth Circuit continued, "that federal marshals might go house-to-house taking away muskets and swords from the man on the street or on the farm." In fact, "there is not a single statement in the congressional debate about the [Second] [A]mendment that indicates that any congressman contemplated that it would establish an individual right to possess a weapon," the Ninth Circuit stressed. Finally, the Ninth Circuit noted that some of the framers explicitly disparaged the idea of creating an individual right to personal arms. For instance, in a highly influential treatise, JOHN ADAMS ridiculed the concept of such a right, asserting that the general availability of arms would "demolish every constitution, and lay the laws prostrate, so that liberty can be enjoyed by no man—it is a dissolution of the government."

The conflicting interpretations of the Second Amendment between the federal courts of **appeal** led many observers to believe that the U.S. Supreme Court would hear the appeal in *Silveira v. Lockyer*. However, the Supreme Court denied **certiorari** on December 1, 2003. *Silveira v. Lockyer*, ___ U.S. ___, 124 S.Ct. 803, 157 L.Ed.2d 693 (U.S. 2003).

HABEAS CORPUS

[*Latin, You have the body.*] A writ (court order) that commands an individual or a government official who has restrained another to produce the prisoner at a designated time and place so that the court can determine the legality of custody and decide whether to order the prisoner's release.

Habeas Petitioner's failure to "Fairly Present" his Ineffective Assistance of Counsel Claim in earlier State Court Proceedings Precluded Federal Relief

The U.S. SUPREME COURT ruled that the burden to "fairly present" a federal claim in state court lies on the prisoner seeking federal habeas relief when the prisoner is basing his request for federal habeas relief on the grounds that he has exhausted his state remedies. Thus, a state supreme court has no duty to read lower court opinions to discover the federal nature of a prisoner's claim. *Baldwin v. Reese*, ___U.S.___, 124 S.Ct. 1347, ___L.Ed. ___ (U.S. 2004).

Before seeking a federal **writ** of **habeas corpus**, a state prisoner must exhaust all available state remedies and thereby give the state an opportunity to review and correct any violations of the prisoner's federal rights. 28 U.S.C.A. 2254(b)(1). To present the state with the necessary "opportunity," the prisoner must "fairly present" his or her claim in each appropriate state court so as to alert the state court of the federal nature of a particular claim (and thus allow the prisoner to exhaust state resources before draining federal resources). *Duncan v. Henry*, 513 U.S. 364, 115 S.Ct. 887, 130 L.Ed.2d 865 (1995). The question before the U.S. Supreme Court in *Baldwin v. Reese* was whether the federal habeas petitioner had "fairly presented" his "ineffective assistance of counsel" claim to the state courts and thus exhausted his state remedies for that claim, such that a federal court could now evaluate it.

Michael Reese appealed his state court kidnapping and attempted **sodomy** convictions through Oregon's state court system. Failing on direct **appeal**, Reese then initiated collateral relief proceedings in the Oregon state courts, where he was represented by appointed **counsel**. Again denied the requested relief, Reese filed a **petition** for discretionary review with the Oregon Supreme Court.

The petition before the state supreme court alleged that Reese had received ineffective assistance from two separate attorneys: from the counsel representing him at trial and the attorney representing him on appeal. In particular, the petition alleged that *trial* counsel's negligent performance violated the Sixth Amendment of the federal Constitution, which guarantees every **defendant** the right to professionally **competent** assistance. However, the petition did not allege that his *appellate* attorney's ineffective assistance violated federal law. The Oregon Supreme Court denied relief on both claims.

Reese then filed a habeas **corpus** petition in the U.S. District Court for the District of Oregon. In this petition, he did allege that his appellate counsel's ineffectiveness violated federal law. The district court dismissed the petition on grounds that Reese had not "fairly presented" this federal claim during his state court appeals because his state supreme court **brief** did not assert that his appellate counsel had violated a federal right, only that his trial counsel had been ineffective. The U.S. Court of Appeals for the Ninth Circuit reversed. *Reese v. Baldwin*, 282 F.3d 1184 (9th Cir. 2001).

The Ninth **Circuit court** observed that the lower state court's decision had recognized Reese's ineffective assistance claim against his appellate counsel as a federal claim, and that the Oregon Supreme Court had the opportunity to read the lower court's decision. Thus, the Ninth circuit concluded that Reese had "fairly presented" the federal claim in state court, and if the Oregon Supreme Court had read the lower court's decision, it would have, or should have, recognized that the claim rested on federal law.

The U.S. Supreme Court rejected this reasoning. In an 8-1 decision written by Justice STEPHEN BREYER, the Court found that Reese had not "fairly presented," in state court, his claim that his appellate counsel's ineffectiveness violated a federal right. To say that an "appellate judge can discover [a federal] claim only by reading the lower court opinions," Breyer wrote, "is to say that those judges *must* read those opinions." Such a requirement would alter the ordinary **practice** of state appellate courts and impose a serious burden on the already overworked state appellate court judges, Breyer maintained. Appellate courts can be asked to review anywhere from five thousand appeals to more than thirty thousand in a single year, Breyer continued, and they simply do not have the time or resources to read every lower **court opinion** in the direct chain of history for the case. Instead, the burden to identify the claim as "federal" rests with the petitioner, who only needs to use the word "federal" somewhere in the petition describing the claim, or at least cite to a federal case in support of the claim, Breyer concluded.

Alternatively, Reese argued that his petition before the Oregon Supreme Court did in fact identify his ineffective-assistance claim against appellate counsel as one based on federal law. According to Reese, the phrase "ineffective assistance" is a **term of art** that only refers to one thing in Oregon, a claim based on federal law. Under Oregon state law, claims asserting an attorney's incompetence are referred to solely as "inadequate assistance of counsel," Reese said. Thus, Reese contended, the terminology by itself should have tipped off the state supreme court as to the federal nature of his claim.

The U.S. Supreme Court rejected this argument as well. Reese failed to demonstrate that in Oregon "ineffective assistance" was a term of art meaning one thing and "inadequate assistance" a term of art meaning another thing. In fact, Reese's own petition before the U.S. Supreme Court used the terms interchangeably, Breyer noted.

Death Sentence Overturned Because Prosecutors Deliberately Withheld Evidence

Litigation over **habeas corpus** petitions is a life-and-death matter for defendants sitting on death row. Old Hollywood movies sometimes pictured a prisoner sitting in the electric chair, awaiting execution, who is saved at the final instant by a phone call reprieve from the governor. This often-parodied scenario played out in real life in 2003 when the U.S. SUPREME COURT stopped the execution of Delma Banks 10 minutes before Texas authorities were to administer a lethal injection. The Court granted a stay and agreed to hear Banks' **appeal** of his habeas **petition**. In February 2004, the Court overturned the death sentence because prosecutors had deliberately withheld vital evidence from Banks during his trial. *Banks v. Dretke*, __ U.S. __, S.Ct., __ L.Ed.2d __ 2004 WL 330040 (2004).

On April 14, 1980 police in Nash, Texas, found the body of 16-year-old Richard Whitehead in a park. Whitehead had been shot three times. Willie Huff, a deputy county sheriff, received information that Whitehead and Banks had been together three nights before. Nine days later Huff got a call from a confidential informant reporting that Banks was driving to Dallas to meet someone and get a weapon. Police followed Banks and pulled him over as he left Dallas. They arrested him after they found a handgun in the car. The police went back to the residence that Banks had visited and recovered a second gun. Charles Cook, who lived in the apartment, told police that Banks had dropped off the gun with him a few days before. This gun was later identified as the weapon that was used to kill Whitehead.

Prosecutors charged Banks with **murder**. At the two-day trial, witnesses testified that they saw Whitehead and Banks together in Whitehead's Mustang automobile on April 11 and heard gunshots in the park at 4 a.m. on April 12. Charles Cook testified that Banks arrived in Dallas four hours later, driving the Mustang. Banks told Cook that he had killed "the white boy for the hell of it." Cook also said that Banks had left the car with him when he took a bus back to his home a few days later. Cook drove the car to a suburb of Dallas and abandoned it. He then sold Banks' pistol to a neighbor. Under

cross-examination Cook denied talking to anyone about his testimony. In truth, he had been "intensively coached" through his testimony by prosecutors, who allowed this misstatement to be uncorrected.

Robert Farr corroborated parts of Cook's story. He traveled with Banks to Dallas to retrieve the gun. Under cross-examination he denied that he had ever taken money from police officers or had been a police informant. Farr, like Cook, denied that he talked about the case with anyone before testifying. Again, this was untrue but the prosecutors did not try to correct this error.

Banks was convicted of murder in the course of a **robbery**, after which the jury heard testimony during the penalty phase. The prosecutors had Farr testify that Banks planned to use the gun for more robberies and that if there were any problems "he would take care of it." The jury voted in favor of the death penalty and the judge sentenced Banks to death. Banks appealed his conviction and sentence but they were upheld.

He then filed a habeas **corpus** petition in state court, alleging that prosecutors withheld information about Cook and Farr. The prosecutors told the court that they had not withheld any information. The Texas Court of Criminal Appeals rejected his petition in 1996, leading Banks to file a federal habeas petition. It was not until 1999 that Banks's attorney succeeded in forcing prosecutors to turn over all their files. In the files was a 74-page transcript of prosecutor's preparing Cook to testify. At a hearing it was disclosed for the first time that deputy sheriff Huff had paid Farr $200 for helping in the case. Farr signed an **affidavit** that claimed he made up parts of his story and had asked Banks to retrieve his gun because he wanted to use it so police could ensnare him. Based on this evidence the district court overturned the death sentence but not the conviction. The Fifth **Circuit Court** of Appeals reversed the death sentence ruling, concluding that Banks had waited too long and had not worked hard enough in his 1992 state proceeding to find this new evidence.

The Supreme Court, in a 7-2 decision, reversed the Fifth Circuit decision. The Court voided the death sentence but not Banks's conviction. Justice RUTH BADER GINSBURG, in her majority opinion, took the Texas prosecutors to task for concealing the evidence, for not correcting the false statements that Cook and Farr made, and for using this false testimony during closing arguments. Ginsburg stated that it was not up to Banks "to prove these representations false; rather Banks was entitled to treat the prosecutor's submissions as truthful." The criminal justice system could not tolerate a rule "declaring "prosecutor may hide, **defendant** must seek.'" Though the Court did not overturn Banks's conviction, it remanded the case so that he could present evidence that the prosecutorial misconduct tainted the **guilty verdict**.

Justice CLARENCE THOMAS, in a dissenting opinion joined by Justice ANTONIN SCALIA, agreed that the lower courts should reconsider the conviction. However, Thomas argued that the withheld evidence would not have made a difference in the death penalty phase if it had been presented to the jury.

Trial Judges May Not Treat Inmate Filings as Habeas Proceedings Without Notice and Warnings

Under the Antiterrorism and Effective Death Penalty Act of 1996, Pub.L.No. 104-132, 110 Stat. 1214 (1996)(AEDPA), a prisoner can only file one **petition** for **habeas corpus** as of right; a federal appeals court must approve a second filing and this determination is not appealable to the Supreme Court. The AEDPA sought to end the filing of successive habeas petitions, which had filled the federal courts and slowed down the imposition of death sentences. Therefore, prisoners must be careful not to file a habeas petition prematurely, as this will likely be the only time they have a chance to **contest** their convictions and sentences. The Supreme Court acknowledged this reality in *Castro v. United States*, __ U.S. __, 124 S.Ct. 786, __ L.Ed.2d __ (2003). The Court ruled that district courts cannot recharacterize a motion by a *pro se* (self-represented) prisoner as a habeas petition without notifying the prisoner, warning the prisoner of the consequences and giving the prisoner the opportunity to change or withdraw the motion. The Court also held that recharacterized motions that fail to follow this procedure would not be treated as habeas petitions in determining the number of habeas petitions filed by the prisoner.

A Georgia jury convicted Hernan O'Ryan Castro of drug trafficking in federal court in 1992. Sentenced to 20 years in prison, Castro unsuccessfully appealed his conviction to the Eleventh **Circuit Court** of Appeals. Following this ruling, Castro filed a *pro se* motion for a new trial with the district court in 1994. The court denied the motion, characterizing it as a request for a new trial and as a petition for habeas **corpus**. Castro appealed the denial of the motion but did not challenge the labeling of it as a habeas petition. Again the Eleventh Circuit denied his **appeal**. In 1997 Castro filed a habeas corpus petition, which was denied by the district court. When the case came up on appeal, the Eleventh Circuit questioned whether this was Castro's second habeas filing. On **remand** the district court found that the 1994 motion had been a habeas filing, which meant that the 1997 habeas petition could only proceed with the permission of Eleventh Circuit. The appeals court upheld the district court and denied Castro the right to pursue his habeas petition. The Supreme Court accepted Castro's appeals because other circuit courts refused to accept the recharacterization of a motion if the *pro se* litigant had not received prior notice.

The Supreme Court issued a unanimous **judgment** vacating the Eleventh Circuit decision, with Justices ANTONIN SCALIA and CLARENCE THOMAS joing in a concurring opinion that offered different grounds for the decision. Justice STEPHEN BREYER delivered the opinion of the Court, noting that motions by prisoners are often recharacterized as habeas petitions by the district courts. The courts recharacterize for a number of reason; these include the desire to place the motion in a different legal category, to avoid an unnecessary **dismissal** or to better match up the "substance of a *pro se* motion's claims and its underlying legal basis." Despite these legitimate reasons, Justice Breyer expressed concern that such actions prejudice prisoners, "mak[ing] it significantly more difficult for the litigant to file another such motion."

In light of the potential problems for *pro se* litigants trying to file habeas petitions, the Court adopted a set of procedures for the district courts to follow when they want to recharacterize a motion as a habeas petition. These procedures were modeled after similar ones adopted by almost every circuit court of appeals. The district court must first notify the *pro se* litigant of its intention to recharacterize the pleading. The court must also warn the prisoner that such a recharacterization would place restrictions on the ability to file a second habeas petition. Third, the court must give the prisoner time to either withdraw the motion or amend it to avoid being categorized as a habeas pleading. Justice Breyer also stated that if a court fails to follow these procedures, the motion could not be considered a habeas petition if the prisoner's later habeas petition is challenged under the AEDPA restrictions on second or successive petitions. Therefore, Castro's 1994 motion was not a habeas petition, allowing him the right to proceed with his 1997 habeas claims.

Justice Scalia, in a concurring opinion joined by Justice Thomas, argued that the district courts had no business taking it upon themselves to recharacterize *pro se* pleadings. He deemed this attitude patronizing and paternalistic; all litigants, whether or not they have legal **counsel**, should be allowed to win or lose based on their claims. The "principle of party self-determination" should govern.

Habeas Courts Must Address All Non-Defaulted Claims before Determining Whether the "Actual Innocence" Exception Applies to a Defaulted Claim

A federal habeas court faced with allegations of actual innocence must first address all non-defaulted claims for comparable **relief** before it may excuse the procedural default. *Dretke v. Haley*, ___U.S.___, 124 S.Ct. 1847, ___L.Ed.2d___ (U.S. 2004). In so holding, the U.S Supreme Court declined to determine the question on which it had granted **certiorari** from a lower court decision—whether the actual innocence exception to the procedural default rule in habeas proceedings is limited in its application to capital sentencing cases or also applies to non-capital sentencing errors. Instead, the Court vacated the **judgment** and remanded in light of the state's concession that the **respondent** had a viable and significant ineffective assistance **of counsel** claim that was not first addressed by the habeas court.

Michael Wayne Haley was indicted for misdemeanor theft, which was enhanced to a "state jail felony" (under TEX. PENAL CODE ANN. § 31.03(e)(4)(D), an offense is classified as a "state jail felony" if the **defendant** has been previously convicted of two or more thefts), because of his two prior **felony** convictions, one for delivery of amphetamines and one for aggravated **robbery**. Following his conviction on the **count** of "state jail felony," Haley was classified as a habitual felony offender, which resulted in an enhanced sentence during the punishment phase of his trial, when he was sentenced to serve 16 years and six months in a state penitentiary.

Haley appealed his conviction to the Texas Court of Criminal Appeals on several grounds, but was denied relief because the court found that he had waived his objections by failing to raise them at trial. During his state court **appeal**, Haley did not challenge the sufficiency of the evidence presented by the state to prove his prior aggravated robbery conviction. A defendant commits aggravated robbery in Texas if he "uses or exhibits a deadly weapon" during the commission of the offense. TEX. PENAL CODE ANN. § 29.03(a)(2). Haley later filed a state **habeas corpus petition**, where he did challenge the lack of evidence on the deadly weapon issue. But the state appeals courts rejected this challenge, concluding that Haley waived this claim by not raising it at trial.

In February 2000, Haley timely filed a habeas **corpus** application in the U.S. District Court for the Eastern District of Texas. In this proceeding Haley expressly alleged that there was no evidence presented to support the state's claim that he had previously been convicted of aggravated robbery. Specifically, he again argued that the state had failed to offer any evidence that he had committed the robbery with a deadly weapon. The state eventually conceded that Haley's attempted robbery conviction did not include an affirmative finding that a deadly weapon had been used.

Nonetheless, the state argued that even though there was no finding of a deadly weapon in his robbery conviction, Haley was not entitled to habeas relief because his claim was barred by the "procedural default" **doctrine**. Under this doctrine, federal courts are precluded from granting habeas relief where the last state court to consider the claims raised by petitioner expressly and unambiguously grounded its denial of relief on independent and adequate state-law procedural ground. Since Texas courts of appeals twice concluded Haley had waived the deadly-weapon issue by failing to raise it at trial, the state reasoned that Haley was now barred from raising the same issue in a federal habeas proceeding.

The district court disagreed, granting Haley's federal habeas application, and the U.S. Court of Appeals for the Fifth Circuit affirmed. Where a state court relies on procedural bar to **deny** relief on grounds that the defendant later raises as a basis for federal habeas relief, the Fifth Circuit wrote, the defendant-turned-federal-habeas petitioner may not obtain such relief absent a showing either (1) of "cause" for his default and "actual prejudice" or (2) that imposition of procedural bar would constitute a miscarriage of justice, **i.e.**, that he is actually **innocent** of the crime. In order to be "actually innocent" of a non-capital sentence within the meaning of exception to procedural default rule, the court continued, a habeas petitioner must prove that, but for constitutional error, he would not have been legally eligible for the sentence he received. The Fifth Circuit then concluded that the "actual innocence" exception to the procedural-default doctrine applied to permit Haley relief from his improperly enhanced sentence, as the state conceded that one of the convictions upon which enhancement was based had been mischaracterized as involving a deadly weapon.

The state appealed, arguing that the "actual innocence" exception to the procedural-default rule in habeas corpus proceedings applies only to capital cases and not noncapital sentencing procedures that involve a career or habitual felony offender. The petition for certiorari stated that there is a well-developed, three-way circuit split on the issue, with the seventh, eighth, and tenth circuits holding that the exception does not apply in the noncapital sentencing context, the second circuit holding that it does, and the fourth and Fifth Circuits holding that it only applies in noncapital cases involving habitual offender statutes.

Writing for the 6-3 majority, Justice SANDRA DAY O'CONNOR noted that success on the **merits** of the ineffective assistance of **counsel** claim would give Haley the relief that he sought, namely resentencing. It would also provide cause to excuse the procedural default of his sufficiency of the evidence claim.

The **avoidance** principle invoked by the Court in declining to decide the scope of the actual innocence exception in the case at bar is implicit in the **case law** establishing the actual innocence exception, Justice O'Connor noted. Thus, in *Murray v. Carrier*, 477 U.S. 478, 106 S.Ct. 2639, 91 L.Ed.2d 397 (1986), the Court expressed confidence that, "for the most part, victims of fundamental miscarriage of justice will meet the cause-and-prejudice standard." This confidence, as in the case at bar, was bolstered by the availability of ineffective assistance of counsel claims, which may act either as a ground for cause for the procedural default or as an independent **claim for relief**. "[I]t is precisely because the various exceptions to the procedural default doctrine are judge-made rules that courts as their stewards must exercise restraint, adding to or expanding them only when necessary," Justice O'Connor said.

Although sufficient **justification** for the rule of restraint is found in the availability of other remedies, "the many threshold legal questions often accompanying claims of actual innocence provide additional reason for restraint," O'Connor wrote. The Justice then noted that the Haley's sufficiency of evidence claim raised a threshold question as to whether the due process rule requiring **proof** of each **element** of a crime **beyond a reasonable doubt** extended to proof of prior convictions used to support recidivist enhancements.

Federal Judge Was Not Required to Warn Pro Se Habeas Petitioner about Effect of Procedural Choices

The U.S. SUPREME COURT held that a federal district court had no obligation to act as **counsel** to a pro se (one representing himself, rather than having a lawyer do so) habeas petitioner in a manner that required it to give two advisories crafted by the U.S. Court of Appeals for the Ninth Circuit. *Pliler v. Ford*, ___ U.S. ___, ___ S.Ct. ___, ___ L.Ed.2d ___, 2004 WL 1373174 (U.S. 2004). Thus, the Ninth Circuit erred in finding that the **dismissal** of a "mixed" habeas **petition** (see discussion in next paragraph regarding mixed petitions containing both "exhausted" and "unexhausted" claims) was improper because the habeas court did not first give warnings to the pro se petitioner about the potential consequences of the court's action.

Richard Herman Ford was convicted of **conspiracy** to commit **murder**, murder, and other crimes, and was sentenced to 36-years to life in prison. Following **affirmance** of his convictions in state appellate court, Ford filed a *pro se* **habeas corpus** petition in the U.S. District Court for the Central District of California. The habeas petition contained both "exhausted" and "unexhausted" federal claims. An "exhausted" federal claim is one in which the federal habeas petitioner exhausted all of his or her remedies in state court prior to pursuing federal habeas **relief**, as required by 28 U.S.C.A. 2254. An "unexhausted" federal claim, then, is one in which the federal habeas petitioner pursues a remedy in federal court before trying to resolve the claim through all the appropriate state channels.

Cognizant that his habeas petition contained both exhausted and unexhausted claims, Ford asked the district court to stay the petition until he first exhausted his unexhausted federal claims in state court. Instead, the district court gave Ford the choice of either (1) dismissing the petition **without prejudice** and re-filing after he exhausted the unexhausted federal claims in state court; or (2) dismissing the unexhausted claims and proceeding with only the exhausted claims. Ford chose the first option, and his habeas **corpus** petition was then dismissed. After his federal claims were then summarily denied in state court, Ford returned to federal court, filing a second habeas petition that essentially restated all of the claims from his first petition. However, the **statute of limitations** for filing a habeas claim had expired, and the district court again dismissed Ford's habeas petition, this time for being time-barred.

The U.S. Court of Appeals for the Ninth Circuit held that the dismissal of Ford's mixed petition (ie., the first habeas petition) was improper and constituted prejudicial error because the habeas court did not first inform the petitioner that it lacked the power to consider his motion for a stay unless Ford first dismissed the unexhausted claims. *Ford v. Hubbard*, 330 F.3d 1086 (9th cir 2003). The Ninth Circuit also held that the habeas court should have informed Ford that, because only days were left on the one-year limitations period, his claims likely would be time-barred upon a return to federal court. Finally, the Ninth Circuit held that the claims asserted in the second petition that had been included in the first petition related back to the date when the first petition was filed, and thus those claims were not time-barred.

The state of California appealed, arguing that the Ninth Circuit's decision conflicted with the decisions of the U.S. Supreme Court. For example, in *Rose v.Lundy*, 455 U.S. 509, 102 S.Ct. 1198, 71 L.Ed.2d 379 (U.S. 1982), the Supreme Court held that dismissal is required of mixed petitions. Thus, according to the state of California, the district court's dismissal of Ford's petition because it contained mixed claims, after the district court had given Ford the option of how to proceed, was consistent with existing precedent. Moreover, the state of California argued, the U.S. Supreme Court has never required warnings as to the effect of a dismissal or held that the absence of warnings renders the dismissal of a mixed petition erroneous. The state of California also said that the Ninth Circuit's ruling directly conflicted with decisions of at least two other circuits, including *Victor v. Hopkins*, 90 F.3d 276 (8th Cir. 1996), which held that district courts lack authority to hold mixed petitions in **abeyance**, even in capital cases.

The U.S. Supreme Court agreed with the state of California and reversed. Justice CLARENCE THOMAS wrote the opinion, in which four other Justices joined. Justices JOHN PAUL STEVENS and DAVID SOUTER concurred in the **judgment**, while Justices RUTH BADER GINSBURG and STEPHEN BREYER dissented.

"Explaining the details of federal habeas procedure and calculating statutes of limitations are tasks normally and properly performed by trained counsel as a matter of course," Justice Thomas wrote. Requiring district courts to advise a *pro se* litigant in such a manner would undermine district judges' role as **impartial** decisionmakers, Thomas reasoned. Moreover, Justice Thomas said, "to the extent that **respondent** is concerned with a district court's potential to mislead *pro se* habeas petitioners, the warnings respondent advocates run the risk of being misleading themselves."

Rose did not require that a habeas petitioner be given "the choice of returning to state court to exhaust his claims or amending or resubmitting the habeas petition to present only exhausted claims to the district court," Justice Thomas emphasized. *Rose* required only that a district court dismiss mixed petitions, which, as a practical matter, meant that a habeas petitioner must elect one of those paths if he wanted to proceed with his federal petition. However, "nothing in *Rose* requires that both of these options be equally attractive, Thomas concluded, much less suggests that district judges give specific advisements as to the availability and wisdom of these options."

Justice Thomas rejected Ford's reliance on *Castro v. United States*, 124 S.Ct. 786, 157 L.Ed.2d 778 (2003), which held that a district court cannot **sua sponte** recharacterize a *pro se* petitioner's motion to **vacate, set aside** or correct a conviction under 28 U.S.C.A. §2255, unless it first informs the petitioner of the consequences of the recharacterization and gives the petitioner the opportunity to withdraw or amend the motion. Justice Thomas noted that *Castro* concerned sua sponte actions by the court, and did not address whether a district court is required to explain a pro se litigant's options before a voluntary dismissal.

A Minor's Age and Experience Need Not Be Considered in Determining whether the Minor Is "In Custody" for *Miranda* Purposes

The U.S. SUPREME COURT ruled that a juvenile's age and experience need not be taken into account when determining whether the minor is "in custody" and thus entitled to *Miranda* warnings prior to being interrogated for his alleged role in a murder/carjacking. *Yarborough v. Alvarado*, ___U.S.___, 124 S.Ct. 2140, ___L.Ed.2d___ (U.S. 2004).

Michael Alvarado was convicted of second degree **murder** and attempted **robbery** and is currently serving a 15-year to life sentence in a California state prison. Alvarado's conviction was based in part on statements he made during a two-hour interrogation that occurred when he was 17-years-old. Following his conviction, Alvarado sought a **writ** of **habeas corpus**, alleging that he was subject to custodial police interrogation without being apprised of his Fifth Amendment rights in violation of *Miranda v. Arizona*, 384 U.S. 436, 444, 86 S.Ct. 1602, 16 L.Ed.2d 694 (1966). The U.S. District Court for the Central District of California denied the **petition**. The U.S. Court of Appeals for the Ninth Circuit reversed, granting Alvarado's requested **relief**.

In determining whether a suspect is "in custody" such that the he or she is entitled to *Miranda* warnings before being lawfully interrogated, courts must ask whether under the totality of circumstances, a reasonable person would have felt the suspect was not at liberty to terminate interrogation and leave, the ninth circuit said. The pertinent areas of inquiry in answering this question include (1) language used by the police officer to summon the individual; (2) the extent to which the individual is confronted with evidence of guilt; (3) the physical surroundings of the interrogation, (4) the duration of the **detention**, and (5) the degree of pressure applied to detain the individual.

In the case at hand, the ninth circuit ruled that Alvarado was "in custody" when he was interrogated by the police, and thus, *Miranda* warnings were required. In reaching this conclusion, the ninth circuit emphasized the following facts: (1) Alvarado's appearance at the police station was not obtained voluntarily through his own **consent**, but through his mother's authority; (2) despite the fact that Alvarado had never before been questioned by the police, his parents were refused permission to accompany him during the two-hour police interrogation; (3) although Alvarado initially denied any knowledge or involvement in a crime, the police repeatedly pressured Alvarado to tell the "truth" until he confessed; (4) Alvarado was never informed that he was not under arrest; and (5) only at the end of the interrogation was Alvarado informed that he was free to leave. Under these circumstances, the ninth circuit concluded that no reasonable 17-year-old who lacked a prior criminal record would have felt that he was at liberty to terminate interrogation and leave

Before the ninth circuit could grant the requested habeas relief, however, the court stressed that its review of the case was governed by the Anti-Terrorism and Effective Death Penalty Act of 1996 (AEDPA), which permits courts to grant federal habeas relief only if the underlying state court decision is either contrary to, or an unreasonable application of, clearly established federal law as determined by the U.S. Supreme Court. 28 U.S.C.A. section 2254(d)(1). A state court's decision involves an "unreasonable application" of federal law if it fails to extend clearly established legal principle to a new context in a way that is objectively unreasonable. Thus, the ninth circuit said that the critical factor to bear in mind when analyzing a case under the "unreasonable application" **clause** of the habeas **corpus statute** is whether the relevant Supreme Court precedents can be fairly categorized as "clearly established" federal law.

Citing *Haley v. Ohio*, 332 U.S. 596, 68 S.Ct. 302, 92 L.Ed. 224 (1948), the ninth circuit first observed that the Supreme Court established the legal principle that juvenile defendants are, in general, more susceptible to police **coercion** than adults. As such, due process demands that a defendant's juvenile status be taken into consideration when determining the proper procedural safeguards that attach to a **custodial interrogation**. At the same time, the ninth circuit noted, the Supreme Court has not directly addressed the issue of how a defendant's juvenile status modifies an "in custody" determination for the purposes of *Miranda*. However, if *Haley* and its progeny recognize that a juvenile is more susceptible to police coercion during a custodial interrogation, the ninth circuit reasoned, then the same juvenile is also more susceptible to the impression that he is, in fact, in custody in the first instance. By failing to suppress Alvarado's confession under the *Haley* line of cases, the ninth circuit held that the California state trial court failed to extend a clearly established precedent, and thus Alvarado was accordingly entitled to relief.

Writing for a 5-4 majority, Justice ANTHONY KENNEDY said that the Supreme Court has never stated that a suspect's age or experience is relevant to the *Miranda* custody analysis. "Clearly established law" as set forth in the AEDPA's standard for habeas relief refers to holdings, as opposed to **dicta**, of the Supreme Court at the time of the relevant state court decisions, Kennedy wrote..

The meaning of "unreasonable" under the AEDPA can depend in part on the specificity of the relevant legal rule, Kennedy continued. When the rule is specific the range of reasonable **judgment** will narrow. Some applications of the rule may be plainly correct or incorrect. "The more general the rule, the more leeway courts have in reaching outcomes in case by case determinations," the justice said. Under *Miranda*, Kennedy explained, the court must examine the circumstances surrounding the interrogation and, in light of those circumstances, determine whether a reasonable person would have felt free to terminate the interrogation and leave.

In this case, fair-minded jurists might disagree over whether the juvenile was in custody. The custody test is general and the state court's application of Supreme Court law fit within the Court's prior decisions, Justice Kennedy said. Nonetheless, Kennedy emphasized that there were several factors that could lead to a determination that a Miranda warning was not required. The police did not transport the juvenile to the station, they did not require him to appear at a particular time, and they did not threaten to arrest him. Rather, the detective appealed to the juvenile's interest in telling the truth.

Nor have prior Supreme Court decisions discussed the suspect's age as a factor in applying the Miranda custody test, Justice Kennedy observed. To the contrary, Supreme Court opinions have rejected reliance on the suspect's experience as a factor in determining custodial status. It was therefore improper for the ninth circuit to grant habeas relief based on the state court's failure to consider them.

Justice Kennedy noted an important "conceptual difference" between the *Miranda* line of decisions and cases in other contexts that have considered age and experience. *Miranda* involves an objective test, and thus gives clear guidance to the police as to when an interview may proceed. In contrast, consideration of a suspect's individual circumstances in determining, for example, the voluntariness of a confession, is a more subjective inquiry.

IDENTITY THEFT

Victims of Identity Theft Cannot Sue Credit Card Company for Negligence

Credit card **fraud** is the most common form of **identity theft**, comprising in 2003 more than one third of all complaints lodged by consumers to the Federal Trade Commission's Identity Theft Clearinghouse. This type of fraud often is accomplished by opening new accounts under assumed names. Though the Fair Credit Billing Act, 15 U.S.C.A. § 1601 *et seq.*, limits consumer **liability** for fraudulent credit card transactions and the Electronic Funds Transfer Act, 15 U.S.C.A. § 1693 *et seq.*, limits consumer liability for fraud arising out of bank or debit cards, consumers often are hounded by credit collection agencies. Emotional distress that arises from identify theft is not compensated for in federal law. Therefore, lawyers have sought to create a new tort, based on a bank or credit card company's negligent failure to investigate credit card applicants before issuing credit cards to them using the identity theft victim's name. Banks have aggressively fought these attempts and have been successful. In *Huggins v. Citibank, N.A.*, 355 S.C. 329, 585 S.E.2d 275 (2003), the South Carolina Supreme Court ruled that victims of identify theft could not sue credit card issuers for negligence. The court reasoned that because identify theft victims were not customers of the banks that issued the cards, the banks did not owe victims a duty of care.

Kenneth P. Huggins, Jr., sued Citibank, Capitol One Bank and Premier Bankcard in federal district court, arguing that they had negligently issued cards to a "John Doe" imposter. Doe had allegedly applied for credit cards from the three banks claiming that he was Huggins. Once the banks issued the cards, the imposter used them and then failed to make any payments. As a consequence of the fraud, Higgins claimed his credit was damaged and that he had been pursued by collection agencies. His dealings with these agencies had left him emotionally distressed and embarrassed. Huggins believed the banks were negligent because they had not done any checking into the identity of Doe nor had they in place any policies and procedures to verity the identity of credit card applicants. Adding insult to **injury**, the banks had tried to collect Doe's debts from Huggins. He contended he should be compensated for his loss of good credit, his emotional distress, and for his attempts at correcting the situation.

The banks filed a motion to dismiss the lawsuit, arguing that they had no duty to Huggins because he was not a customer. The court declined to rule on the motion because there was no clear law on this subject from the South Carolina Supreme Court. Under the Federal Rules of Procedure, federal courts may not impose their views on common law matters such as torts. Instead, the court must file a certified question with the state supreme court, requesting an answer to a legal question. The state court does not rule on the **merits** of the case but only answers the question. Once presented with the answer, the federal court may apply the law to the **controversy**. In this case, the federal court asked whether South Carolina law recognized the tort of "negligent enablement of imposter fraud." If so, the supreme court was asked to define the elements of this tort and determine if Huggins stated an **actionable** claim for tort.

The South Carolina Supreme Court, in a unanimous decision, ruled that South Carolina did not recognize an identify theft tort directed at banks issuing credit cards. Justice E.C. Burnett III, writing for the court, noted that a negligence claim will succeed only if the plaintiff can show that the **defendant** owed the plaintiff a duty of care, that the defendant breached this duty through a negligent act or omission, and the damage to the plaintiff was proximately caused by the breach. In the present case, the court focused exclusively on whether the banks owed Huggins a duty of care. In Burnett's view a duty must "arise from the relationship between the alleged **tortfeasor** and the injured party." This relationship must be recognized by the law "as the foundation of a duty of care."

The court concluded that Huggins and the banks did not have a relationship; Huggins was not their customer but merely a stranger. Huggins had argued that the rise of identify thefts made this type of credit card fraud foreseeable, but Burnett held that "forseeability alone does not suffice to create a duty of care." Though the court expressed concerns about identify theft and agreed that some fraud could be prevented by better review procedures, it ruled that the relationship between the credit card victim and the credit card issuer was "far too attenuated to rise to the level of a duty between them." Various federal consumer credit laws gave Huggins protection from having to pay the fraudulent claims. Even if these laws did not fully compensate victims for all their injuries, it was not the business of the courts to create a new tort—Congress and state legislatures should address such issues.

INSIDER TRADING

Martha Stewart Convicted for Making False Statements Regarding Stock Sale

Multimedia home decorating maven Martha Stewart was convicted in March 2004 on four counts of making false statements regarding the sale of stock that took place in December 2001. Although Stewart was not convicted of insider trading or securities **fraud**, she nevertheless received a five month prison sentence.

Stewart was the founder and chief executive officer of Martha Stewart Living Omnimedia. The business focused on four primary areas, including the production of a television show, the publication of magazines and books, merchandising, and Internet and catalog sales. Stewart was licensed to sell securities, having worked as a securities broker from 1968 through 1973. In 2002, Stewart was elected to serve on the board of the New York Stock Exchange.

Stewart held an account with the brokerage firm of Merrill Lynch. Her registered representative for the account was Peter Bacanovic, with whom Stewart had a close personal relationship, according to prosecutors. Stewart also had contact with Bacanovic's assistant, Douglas Faneuil, who was referred to as co-conspirator in Stewart's case, but was not brought up on charges along with Stewart and Bacanovic. Merrill Lynch maintained strict policies against breaching clients' confidentiality and **privacy**; revealing inside information about stocks; and a **practice** known as "piggybacking," which occurs when a broker takes advantage of a client's perceived knowledge and expertise by conducting a trade after a client has made a trade.

Stewart owned almost 4000 shares of stock in ImClone Systems Incorporated, which was based in New York. The company produced biologic medicines. Its leading product candidate was Erbitux, a treatment for a certain type of colorectal cancer. ImClone submitted an application to the Food and Drug Administration (FDA) to approve Erbitux in October 2001. The FDA had 60 days to approve or reject the drug. According to federal attorneys, Faneuil informed Bacanovic on December 27, 2001 that ImClone CEO and President Samuel Waksal was trying to sell all of his family's shares in ImClone. Waksal allegedly told Merrill Lynch that the sale of the stock was urgent. ImClone on December 28 issued a press release acknowledging that the FDA had refused to accept Erbitux for filing.

On December 27, before the ImClone's announcement, ImClone stock sold at $61.53 per share. After receiving information regarding Waksal's sale of stock, Bacanovic allegedly attempted to contact Stewart. The indictment against Stewart and Bacanovic alleges that Bacanovic left a message with Stewart's assistant, and that the assistant wrote a note that "Peter Bacanovic thinks ImClone is going to start trading downward." Later during the afternoon of December 27, Stewart sold all of her shares in ImClone at $58.43 per share. The following day, ImClone stock closed at $55.25 per share, and on December 31, 2001, a day after the FDA announced that the Erbitux filing had been declined, the stock opened at $45.39 per share.

According to prosecutors, Stewart avoided a loss of an estimated $51,222 by selling the stock on December 27. Stewart later told an interviewer that the amount she saved represented .006 percent of her net worth. .

A division of the SECURITIES AND EXCHANGE COMMISSION, along with the FEDERAL BUREAU OF INVESTIGATION and the United States Attorney's Office for the Southern District of New York began an investigation in January 2002 into the trading of ImClone prior to the FDA's announcement. Officials focused part of their investigation on the communications made between Stewart, Bacanovic, and Faneuil. Prosecutors allege that Bacanovic immediately made false statements to investigators. Bacanovic claimed that he and Stewart agreed prior to December 27 that he would sell Stewart's ImClone stock if it dropped below $60 per share. Federal authorities also claimed that Stewart changed the written message accompanying Bacanovic's telephone call on December 27 from "Peter Bacanovic thinks ImClone is going to start trading downward," to "Peter Bacanovic re imclone." Stewart then apparently directed her assistant to change the message back to its original wording.

The indictment against Stewart and Bacanovic alleged that the parties made a series of false statements from January through April in 2002. Prosecutors also alleged that Bacanovic altered documents related to Stewart's stock in ImClone and that he committed perjury when he testified under oath before the Securities and Exchange Commission. In addition to the allegations that Stewart and Bacanovic individually gave false information, prosecutors also alleged a **conspiracy** between Stewart and Bacanovic to mislead investigators. The indictment alleges conspiracy to obstruct justice, to make false statements, and to commit perjury.

Stewart and Bacanovic were indicted on nine counts related to the scandal on June 4, 2003. Stewart then resigned as CEO of Martha Stewart Living Omnimedia, though she remained as its chief creative officer and a board member. Both Stewart and Bacanovic pleaded not **guilty** to the charges. About one week later, Waksal was sentenced to seven years in prison for insider trading.

The trial against Stewart and Bacanovic began on January 27, 2004. The prosecution's case hinged on the testimony of three witnesses. Ann Armstrong, Stewart's assistant for six years, recalled Stewart's actions on December 27 and during the government investigation. Mariana Pasternak, a friend of Stewarts, testified that Stewart said about Bacanovic, "Isn't it nice to have brokers who tell you those things?", implying that Bacanovic had given Stewart inside information. Lastly, Faneuil, who pleaded guilty in October 2002 to receiving a payoff to keep quiet about the affair, confirmed the prosecution's allegations about Bacanovic's activities. Stewart's lawyers called only one witness, which was a lawyer who testified about questions that investigators asked Stewart during the probe. Stewart did not take the stand. .

On February 27, Judge Miriam Goldman Cedarbaum threw out a **count** of securities fraud against Stewart. The remaining charges went to the jury on March 3. Two days later, the jury convicted Stewart on each of the remaining charges against her and convicted Bacanovic on every charge except for one related to making false statements. On July 16, 2004, Stewart received a sentence of five months imprisonment and five months of home **detention**. Stewart was granted a stay of sentence while appealing the conviction.

Martha Stewart leaves court following a meeting with a probation officer in March 2004.

INSURANCE

A contract whereby, for specified consideration, one party undertakes to compensate the other for a loss relating to a particular subject as a result of the occurrence of designated hazards.

Aetna Health v. Davila

In June 2004, the U.S. SUPREME COURT issued its ruling in an important and closely watched matter involving the **liability** of Health

Maintenance Organizations (HMOs) for negligence in denial of benefits decisions. In *Aetna Health, Inc. v. Davila*, 542 U.S. ___, 124 S.Ct. 2488, ___ L.Ed.2d ___(2004) (consolidating two separate cases with similar issues), the high court unanimously ruled in favor of the HMOs.

Technically, the issue decided was a procedural one: whether the federal Employee Retirement Income Security Act (ERISA) preempted a Texas state law that permitted such suits. The Court ruled that the federal law prevailed, effectively prohibiting suits under state laws. Specifically, the significance of the Court's procedural decision amounted to a denial of the right of patients to sue for tort damages (e.g., pain and suffering, or scarring) caused by such HMO decisions. Instead, they would be limited to damages allowable under ERISA (e.g., the right to receive the denied treatment)

The facts before the Court were essentially straightforward. Juan Davila and (in the other case) Ruby Calad) were both provided health care benefits through ERISA-regulated employee benefit plans (Davila's through Aetna, and Calad's through CIGNA). Davila's insurance company (Aetna) rejected his doctor's prescription for an arthritis painkiller, requiring Davila to first try two less expensive drugs. When Davila began taking the less-expensive alternative medication, he suffered a severe reaction (a bleeding ulcer and heart problems) that almost cost him his life, requiring five days hospitalization in intensive care and extensive treatment. After Calad's surgery, her insurer (Cigna) would only pay for one day in the hospital. Discharged against her physician's request for a longer stay, she developed post-surgical complications.

Both plaintiffs sued their HMOs in Texas state courts, citing violations of Texas's model patient rights law, part of the Texas Health Care Liability Act (THCLA), Tex. C.P. & R. Code Ann., §§ 88.001—88.003. The separate suits alleged that the denial of benefits by each HMO was in violation of the duty "to exercise ordinary care" under the Texas act. A failure to exercise due care is grounded in **tort law** of negligence. Professional negligence is malpractice.

The respective **defendant** HMOs removed the cases to federal court, claiming that the causes of actions fell within ERISA's Section 502 and were therefore preempted by federal law. Both district courts agreed and dismissed each complaint after Davila and Calad were given the opportunity to amend their pleadings to allege violation of ERISA, but failed to do so. Both plaintiffs appealed.

The U.S. Court of Appeals for the Fifth Circuit took the opposite view. First consolidating the cases, it concluded that the claims did not fall under ERISA, which only dictated controversies involving breaches of **fiduciary** duties to a plan. Here, the appellate court concluded, plaintiffs were suing for mixed eligibility and treatment decisions that were not fiduciary in nature. Nor were they suing for recovery of wrongfully denied benefits. Rather, they were suing for personal injury and its attendant damages, such as pain and suffering. Therefore, the appeals court concluded that the plaintiffs' causes of action did not step on the toes of ERISA, and therefore that they could be brought under the Texas state law.

Justice CLARENCE THOMAS, writing for a unanimous Court, reversed and remanded the matters to the Fifth Circuit. The high court found that the causes of action were completely pre-empted by ERISA and removable to federal court.

ERISA's Section 502 provides causes of action for the recovery of wrongfully denied benefits and against a plan fiduciary for breaches of duty to that plan. The Supreme Court found the Fifth Circuit's reasoning wholly erroneous. Attempting to re-label an ERISA breach of contract claim as a tort claim for negligence did not change the essence of the claim. Justice Thomas wrote:

> [D]istinguishing between pre-empted and non-pre-empted claims based on the particular label affixed to them would "elevate form over substance and allow parties to evade" the pre-emptive scope of ERISA simply "by relabeling their contract claims as claims for **tortious** breach of contract." (quoting *Allis-Chalmers v. Lueck*, 471 U.S. 202)

The U.S. Supreme Court explained the way in which pre-emption works. (The Fifth Circuit had acknowledged that state law claims that "duplicated" or fell within the scope of an ERISA remedy would be pre-empted.) It noted that Congress intended ERISA as an exclusive remedy for alleged wrongs. Under the **doctrine** of pre-emption, if an individual could have articulated a claim under ERISA at some point in time, and there is no other independent legal duty implicated, then the individual's **cause of action** is completely pre-empted. In this case, both plaintiffs alleged violations of "the ordinary duty of care" under the Texas law, which they claimed was entirely independent of any ERISA duty. However, that argument fell on its face, according to the high court, because the plans' alleged failures to cover the requested treatments were the proximate causes of any injuries arising from such denials. Therefore, the claims for damages were *not* independent of ERISA or plan terms.

The litigants also missed the fact that the Texas law provided that an HMO was not subject to liability under the law for denials of coverage for a treatment not covered by the plans it administered.

The Court also distinguished a 2000 Supreme Court case, *Pegram v. Herdrich*, 530 U.S. 211, 120 S.Ct. 2143, 147 L.Ed.2d 164 (2000), used by the plaintiffs as supporting a claim for independent liability under state law for denial of benefits decisions. The Court noted that in *Pegram*, the plan administrator who denied the requested treatment was also the treating physician in the matter, causing a mixed eligibility and treatment decision invoking higher scrutiny. In the present case, the plan administrators were neither physicians nor employers of the treating physicians.

Justice RUTH BADER GINSBURG filed a separate concurring opinion in which she reiterated her challenge to Congress (and the Court) to "revisit what is an unjust and increasingly tangled ERISA regime." She was joined by Justice STEPHEN BREYER.

Additional implications of the decision included the fact that the Texas **statute** had been touted as a model one, copied by at least nine states in their patient's bill-of-rights statutes. The Bush administration's attempt to pass a federal patient's bill of rights was stalled in 2002 when both congressional houses differed on details, including whether to limit awards for pain and suffering and punitive damages on all malpractice cases.

INTELLECTUAL PROPERTY

Intangible rights protecting the products of human intelligence and creation, such as copyrightable works, patented inventions, trademarks, and trade secrets. Although largely governed by federal law, state law also governs some aspects of intellectual property.

Recording Industry Goes After Individuals for Sharing Music and Movie Files

The Recording Industry Association of America (RIAA) brought more than one thousand lawsuits in 2003 and 2004 against private individuals. They claimed that these individuals illegally downloaded music and movie files from the Internet. The RIAA maintains that use of programs that permit users to share files violates **copyright** laws. Many of the alleged violators are younger people, and the issues surrounding the lawsuits has affected colleges and universities, since colleges students have been targeted as the largest group that shares these files.

A Web site known as Napster was developed during the late 1990s and eventually had an estimated 16.9 million users worldwide. Napster's system accommodated about sixty-five million downloads. However, the RIAA sued Napster, and Napster eventually shut down, though other file sharing systems have retained their popularity. At the time Napster came into existence, record companies enjoyed a $14.6 billion industry that was growing at a rate of six percent per year. However, in 2002, music shipments dropped to $12.6 billion, and sales of records fell by 8.6 percent. The recording industry has blamed file sharing for the decline in these sales.

Faced with lower sales figures, the RIAA, which represents such recording companies as BMG, EMI, Sony Music, Universal Music Group, and Warner Music, began targeting individual users, many of whom were college students. In December 2002, the RIAA began to send letters and messages to colleges and universities to warn these institutions that the RIAA planned to send more notices to individuals who were found to have infringed copyrights by sharing files on peer-to-peer networks.

About three months later, at a hearing of the **intellectual property** subcommittee of the House of Representatives' Judiciary Committee, members of Congress warned three university administrators that the schools should take steps to punish students who use university networks to share music and movie files. The administrators admitted that they had never expelled a student for illegal file sharing.

Although administrators promised to work with the recording industry to put a stop to students swapping files illegally, the RIAA filed lawsuits against four students in April 2004. The students, who attended Michigan Technological University, Princeton University, and Rensselaer Polytechnic Institute, allegedly offered between twenty-seven thousand to a million songs to other students through the respective universities' networks. The students reportedly settled the cases for amounts ranging from $12,500 to $17,000. At least one of these students apparently raised the amount he owed through online donations.

In June 2003, the RIAA announced that it was targeting thousands of individuals who swap music files online. This strategy was a change in direction for the RIAA, which had previously directed most of its attacks on entities that made file-swapping programs. The RIAA planned to collect evidence of piracy, including building a list of Internet addresses of those who traded the largest number of files. The RIAA then planned to identify the individuals who swapped the files through the individuals' Internet service providers (ISPs).

By September 2003, the RIAA had filed lawsuits against an estimated 261 alleged infringers. At the same time, the recording industry announced a program that would provide amnesty for those who admit to sharing files illegally. The system, called "Clean Slate," would allow users to avoid lawsuits by promising to clean illegal files from their machines and to avoid illegal file sharing in the future. The RIAA said that it would entertain settlement proposals from defendants. During the summer of 2003, the RIAA claimed that some individuals had settled their cases for about $3,000 each.

The RIAA suffered a setback in December 2003, when the U.S. Court of Appeals for the District of Columbia ruled that the RIAA could not require an ISP to provide the identities of users who had allegedly shared files illegally. The RIAA argued that the Digital Millennium Copyright Act, 17 U.S.C. § 512(h) (2000), allowed the organization to require Verizon Internet Services to provide these identifies by way of subpoenas issued on Verizon. However, the court disagreed, finding that the law does not require the ISP to provide the identities when the ISP merely serves as a conduit for data that is transferred between two or more users. *Recording Indus. Ass'n of Am. v. Verizon Internet Servs., Inc.*, 351 F.3d 1229 (D.C. Cir. 2003)

The effect of the case has been that the RIAA must first file a lawsuit against unknown persons—known as a "John Doe" lawsuit—and then request a court to order the ISPs to reveal the identities of the individuals who traded the files. Experts noted that this would be a more time consuming and costly means for the RIAA to find the individuals who traded the files. Nevertheless, the RIAA brought suit against a record 532 people in January 2004. Although the overall effect of the lawsuits will not be known for some time, reports have indicated that the amount of file sharing decreased from June 2003, when the suits were first filed, through January 2004.

INTERNET

A worldwide telecommunications network of business, government, and personal computers.

Pop-Up Advertisements Come Under Legal Attacks

Since 2002, software companies that produce programs which create pop-up advertisements have been sued by companies for a variety of infringements related to **intellectual property**, including **copyright** and trademark infringements. Although the software companies have prevailed in some of the suits, other courts have issued injunctions prohibiting the software companies from displaying the ads when Internet users visit certain Web sites.

Gator, based in Redwood City, California, is a company that develops software that is often downloaded onto a user's machines without the user's knowledge. This software tracks the user's behavior on the Internet; it then causes advertisements to pop-up on the user's screen when the user visits a certain site. For instance, when the user visits the Web site for Dodge, a pop-up advertisement may appear for Toyota.

Gator was sued by several major publishers, including the *Washington Post*, *New York Times*, Dow Jones, for allegedly infringing on the companies' copyrights. When a user visited a Web site of one of these companies, the Gator software would cause a pop-up ad to appear on the user's screen. This pop-up ad was not tied directly with the owner of the Web site. The plaintiff's suit alleged that Gator was "essentially a parasite on the Web that free rides on the hard work and the investments of plaintiffs and other Web site owners. In short, Gator sells advertising space on the plaintiffs' Web sites without . . . authorization and pockets the profits of such sales." In July 2002, a federal judge in Virginia issued a temporary order requiring Gator to discontinue these pop-up ads on the plaintiffs' Web sites. The publishers later settled with Gator out of court in February 2003.

Another software company responsible for pop-up ads, WhenU.com, became the subject of several lawsuits in 2002 and 2003. The results in these cases varied. In October 2002, U-Haul sued WhenU.com in the U.S. District Court for the Eastern District of Virginia. They claimed that WhenU.com infringed upon U-Haul's trademark rights and copyrights. According to the suit, when a user visited U-Haul's Web site, WhenU.com's software would cause a pop-up ad to block out a user's view of the Web site. However, the advertisement did not use U-Haul's trademark in the advertisement, nor did it use any of U-Haul's copyrighted material. The judge, Gerald B. Lee, took it upon himself to test these pop-up ads by downloading software from the Internet. After experiencing these pop-up ads first-hand, the judge noted, "Computer users, like this trial judge, may wonder what we have done to warrant the punishment of **seizure** of our computer screens by pop-up advertisements for secret web cameras, insurance, travel values, and fad diets. Did we unwittingly sign up for incessant advertisements that require us to click, click, click again in order to return to our Internet work?" Nevertheless, the court found that the advertisements did not infringe upon U-Haul's rights and accordingly granted WhenU.com's motion for **summary judgment** in September 2003. *U-Haul Int'l, Inc. v. WhenU.com, Inc.*, 279 F. Supp. 2d 723 (E.D. Va. 2003)

WhenU.com prevailed in another suit brought by Wells Fargo & Co. in the U.S. District Court for the Eastern District of Michigan. In that case, Wells Fargo made many of the same arguments that U-Haul made in its case. It asserted that WhenU.com infringed upon Wells Fargo's copyrights and trademark rights through the actions of its software in having pop-up ads displayed when a user visited Wells Fargo's Web site. However, Wells Fargo was unable to prove its claims, and the court refused to issue an **injunction** against WhenU.com on November 19, 2003. *Wells Fargo & Co. v. WhenU.com, Inc.*, 293 F. Supp. 2d 734 (E.D. Mich. 2003)

A plaintiff in New York *was* able to convince a federal judge to grant a **preliminary injunction** against WhenU.com in December 2003. A company known as 1-800 Contacts, Inc. sells and markets replacement contact lenses through Internet sales and telephone and mail orders. The company registered as a trademark "1-800 CONTACTS" with the U.S. Patent and Trademark Office. It also registered the name of its Web site, 1-800Contacts.com, with the U.S. Copyright Office. One of 1-800 Contacts competitors is Vision Direct, Inc. The plaintiffs claimed that when a user with WhenU.com's software installed typed in the Web address www.1800contacts.com, the software would cause a pop-up ad for Vision Direct, Inc. to appear.

The U.S. District Court for the Southern District of New York found that 1-800 Contacts had not proven its claim of copyright infringement. However, the court found that WhenU.com used the plaintiff's trademark when it included the mark in its directory. The court determined that it was likely that when a user saw the Vision Direct pop-up ad appear at the same time that the user saw the 1-800 Contact's page, the user would click on the Vision Direct link from the pop-up window. Moreover, the court found that WhenU.com had acted in **bad faith** by ruling that WhenU.com knowingly included the plaintiff's Web address in its directory in order to give Vision Direct a competitive advantage over 1-800 Contacts. In weighing these factors, the court held that the plaintiff had established a likelihood of success in proving its trademark claim. The court issued an injunction against WhenU.com to **enjoin** WhenU.com from causing the pop-up ads to appear when users visited 1-800 Contact's site. *1-800 Contacts, Inc. v. WhenU.com*, No. 02 Civ. 8043(DAB), 2003 WL 22999270 (S.D.N.Y. Dec. 22, 2003)

IRAQ WAR

The Demise of Saddam Hussein's Iraq

In April 2003, much of the world stopped what it was doing while people from all nations stood mesmerized in front of televisions screens. What they were watching was live coverage via satellite of U.S. and coalition forces assisting Iraqi citizens in pulling down the huge statue of Saddam Hussein that had dominated the central square of Iraq's capital city, Baghdad, for decades. Photographs of the symbolic gesture appeared on the front pages of newspapers around the globe. By the end of the day, nearly every statue of Iraq's tyrannical leader had been removed, dismembered, defaced, or destroyed by a rowdy group of jubilant Iraqis. Thousands took to the streets cheering, while others burned and looted government buildings associated with Saddam's regime.

The jubilation seemed short-lived, quickly turning to anarchy. Downtown Baghdad was nearly gutted by looting and burning. Several Iraqis took advantage of the chaos to commit robberies and carry out revenge killings against fellow Iraqis. The **murder** rate in Baghdad jumped to twenty times its average. This took place in the presence of UNITED NATIONS coalition troops who had taken over control of the capital.

One year later, in April 2004, the jury was still out as to how much life had actually improved for Iraqi citizens. Most polls indicated that the majority was satisfied to see the end of Saddam's control. But anti-coalition, anti-American sentiments were on the rise as frustration over on-and-off-again utilities, high unemployment, and warring among internal factions all took their toll. Moreover, violence from Iraqi insurgents had actually escalated as the June 30, 2004, deadline for transfer of governmental control from the United Nations' Coalition Provisional Authority (CPA) to the Iraqi people drew near. In addition to military casualties, there was a palpable increase in the use of suicide bombings and sniper attacks on civilian contractors or others perceived to be assisting the coalition. (Since the beginning of the war, at least forty-eight suicide bombers had killed more than seven hundred people.) In May 2004 alone, the car bombing of the leader of the Iraqi Governing Council, as well as the beheading of an American contractor a few days earlier, served as somber reminders of the uncertain road ahead.

Almost a year earlier, on July 13, 2003, the twenty-five-member Iraqi Governing Council, which had the power to appoint ministers and approve the budget for 2004, met for the first time to discuss the future of Iraq following the demise of Saddam's Baath regime. In the interim, the United Nations had designated the CPA as the lawful government of Iraq until such time as Iraq was politically and socially stable enough to accept sovereignty. (Per the "Agreement of November 15" between the CPA and the Iraq Governing Council, the CPA was scheduled to dissolve as of June 30, 2004.) All involved remained focused on the dual objectives of searching for weapons of mass destruction and rebuilding a strong and stable Iraq.

On July 22, 2003, Saddam's sons, Uday and Qusay, were shot and killed by coalition troops in a gun battle at their Mosul hideout. The hunt for Saddam himself seemed to dominate the news of the war. A $25 million reward and all of the CIA's finest intelligence failed to find him, but alleged sightings of Saddam were common throughout the country. Finally, in December 2003, an Iraqi official in U.S. custody buckled under interrogation and blurted out Saddam's whereabouts. Within twenty-four hours, U.S. Special Forces had closed in on a farmhouse south of Tikrit, Saddam's hometown, and began looking for a hidden bunker or underground facility. At 8:15 p.m., the radio crackled and a voice announced, "We found a hole." At the base of a palm tree, a small hole was covered with a white mat and a three-pound Styrofoam block resembling a rock. A soldier pulled the pin for a hand grenade to toss into the "Spider hole," but was met with raised arms in a gesture of submissive surrender. Along with Saddam, the hole contained a gun and a briefcase. A nearby adobe hut in the palm grove was stocked with insect repellent, canned meat, fruit, Mars candy bars, and $750,000 in U.S. one hundred dollar bills. Saddam was soon removed to a jail cell in Baghdad for CIA interrogation.

Again, Iraqi citizens seemed pleased. But growing resentment over perceived American "invasion" and "occupation" eclipsed happiness over the demise of Saddam. As of April 2004, more than 105,000 U.S. troops remained in Iraq—considerably more troops than from any other nation. The United States insisted that a security presence was essential to a smooth transition. To that end, according to a draft working paper dated March 26, 2004, the U.S. Department of Defense planned to put 75,000 trained police officers on duty. Less than 3,000 Iraqis were qualified at that time, with another 13,000 partially qualified. However, close to 60,000 were on the payroll but not yet trained.

Meanwhile, the CPA ratified a new provisional constitution in March of 2004, which would need to be ratified by the elected National Assembly. Iraqi elections were to follow within six months of transfer, with the National Assembly to convene no later than December 31, 2005. However, the federated **joinder** of Iraq's various factions was tenous at best. Potentially debilitating power struggles between militants of such groups as the Shi'a and Kurds continued, as did the political question of what role Islam would play in a nation that was ninety-five percent Muslim. Caught in the center of the political and ideological struggles were the Iraqi people, who just wanted everyone to go home and leave them alone.

JUDGE

To make a decision or reach a conclusion after examining all the factual evidence presented. To form an opinion after evaluating the facts and applying the law.

A public officer chosen or elected to preside over and to administer the law in a court of justice; one who controls the proceedings in a courtroom and decides questions of law or discretion.

Louisiana Judge Removed from Bench, Charged with Perjury and Salary Extortion

A Louisiana state judge was removed from office and ordered to refrain from seeking judicial office for five years following an ethics investigation that revealed the judge had personally engaged in political fund raising and required court personnel, under threat of termination, to do the same. The judge then lied about the misconduct until confronted with irrefutable evidence in the form of audio taped conversations and transcripts. After his removal, criminal charges were then filed against the judge.

The case arose out of Judge C. Hunter King's re-election efforts in the Orleans Parish Civil District Court, Division "M," in the state of Louisiana. Judge King was first elected to the bench in October 1999 and assumed office one month later. He was re-elected to a full six-year term in October 2002; however, his 2002 re-election campaign began a year earlier.

According to a complaint received by the Louisiana Supreme Court Office of Special **Counsel** (OSC), the forty-two-year-old King had fired his court reporter, Barbara Wallace, for refusing to sell tickets to a campaign fund raising event held on behalf of the judge. The complaint also alleged that King had required other court personnel to work on his re-election campaign and prioritize their campaign efforts above the normal duties they otherwise would be performing for the court. Judge King responded to the complaint with a letter, written by his attorney, in which he characterized the allegations as little more than an "unfounded," "unprincipled," "retaliatory" attack on a "respected judge by a disgruntled former employee" who had resigned because she could not keep up with the workload.

The complaint was filed on October 4, 2001, and Judge King responded on November 20, 2001. In early December, Wallace provided the OSC with audio tapes and transcripts of four staff meetings, all made without the judge's knowledge. The evidence showed that (1) Judge King had personally engaged in political fund raising, going so far as to sell fund-raising tickets at a funeral; (2) Judge King required Wallace and other staff members to personally engage in political fund raising on his behalf; (3) Judge King derived personal benefit from public resources allotted to him for the administration of justice; (4) Judge King and his staff aggressively urged local attorneys to fund his campaign in exchange for a promise of favorable treatment when the attorneys came before him in future cases; and (5) Judge King threatened to terminate staff members who did not participate in his re-election campaign or who did participate but failed to reach certain "minimum" levels of fund-raising success.

On April 2, 2002, King appeared before the OSC. He gave a sworn statement, under oath, relating to the allegations in the complaint. Unaware of the audio tapes and transcripts, King categorically denied every accusation leveled against him.

On October 22, 2002, the Louisiana Supreme Court Judiciary Commission (the commission) filed two sets of formal charges against Judge King. They alleged that he had engaged in impermissible campaign misconduct and allowed and required his staff to do the same. They also alleged that he had given sworn testimony that he knew to be false and that was pertinent and material to the issues under investigation. The day after the charges were served upon Judge King, the OSC provided copies of the incriminating audio tapes and transcripts to Judge King's counsel.

Confronted with the evidence, Judge King jointly filed with the OSC a "Statement of Stipulated Uncontested Material Facts and Stipulated Conclusions of Law," in which he admitted most of the allegations contained in the two sets of charges. In exchange, the commission agreed to recommend that Judge King be suspended from judicial office for one year. It also ordered King to pay the commission $693.50 as reimbursement for the costs of its investigation. In making this recommendation, the commission observed that King was a new judge, that King committed the violations over fear of growing campaign debt, and that no prior complaints had been filed against King.

The Supreme Court accepted the commission's recommendation on the issue of reimbursement, but rejected the commission's recommendation on the issue of suspension. In a sternly worded opinion, the court wrote:

> One who holds a judicial office must adhere to the highest standards of personal conduct. A criminal act for which any citizen may be punished by imprisonment is much more serious when the conduct is that of a judge. Such conduct is clearly prejudicial to the administration of justice and brings the judicial office into disrepute.... When a judge, either in his official **capacity** or as a private citizen, is **guilty** of such conduct as to cause others to question his character and morals, the people not only lose respect for him as a man but lose respect for the court over which he presides as well.... the constitution vests in this court the duty to preserve the integrity of the bench for the benefit of the public by ensuring that all who don the black robe and serve as ministers of justice do not engage in public conduct which brings the judicial office in disrepute. To that end, we have recognized that the primary purpose of the Code of Judicial Conduct is to protect the public rather than to discipline judges. Likewise, the objective of a judicial disciplinary proceeding is not simply to punish an individual judge but to purge the judiciary of any taint.

Emphasizing that removal is the most severe sanction for judicial misconduct, the court concluded that removal was indeed the appropriate penalty for King. The grounds for disciplinary action against a judge are set forth in La. Const. art. V, § 25(C), the court noted. This section provides that the supreme court may "remove from office ... a judge for ... conduct while in office which would constitute a felony." Without making a finding that Judge King had actually committed two felonies, the supreme court ruled that the judge's misconduct fell within the definition of two felonies, perjury and public salary extortion.

King's categorical denials of misconduct, made while under oath and later fully admitted, fell within the definition of perjury, the court reasoned, since they represented an "intentional making of a false written or oral statement in or for use in a judicial proceeding." La. R.S. 14:123. Enlisting his court personnel, under threat of termination, as fund-raisers on his re-election campaign, fell within the definition of public salary extortion—the crime of using threats or **coercion** to derive personal benefit from a public employee—the court said. La. R.S. 14:136. Five months after the Supreme Court removed King from office, criminal charges were filed against him. On March 11, 2004, District Attorney Eddie Jordan filed a criminal complaint in the Orleans Parish Civil District Court. The complaint alleged that King had committed the offenses of perjury and public salary extortion. The maximum penalty for perjury is five years in prison, a $10,000 fine, or both, while the maximum penalty for public salary extortion is five years in prison, a $5,000 fine, or both.

JURISDICTION

The geographic area over which authority extends; legal authority; the authority to hear and determine causes of action.

Post-Filing Change in Citizenship Cannot Cure Lack of Subject-Matter Jurisdiction

A party's attempt to change its citizenship after it has filed a lawsuit in federal court cannot cure a lack of subject-matter jurisdiction that existed at the time of filing in an action premised upon **diversity of citizenship**. *Grupo Dataflux v. Atlas Global Group*, 2004 WL 1085232, ___U.S.___, ___S.Ct.___, ___L.Ed.___ (2004). Reversing the U.S. Court of Appeals for the Fifth Circuit, the U.S. SUPREME COURT emphasized that it had long adhered to the rule that subject-matter jurisdiction in diversity cases depends on the state of the facts that existed as of the time of filing.

"Diversity of citizenship" is a phrase used with reference to the jurisdiction of federal courts, which, under the U.S. Constitution, extends to civil cases between citizens of different states. U.S.C.A.Const.Art III, section 2. In the simplest terms, diversity exists when the plaintiff in a **civil action** is a citizen of one state and the **defendant** is a citizen of another state, or when one party is a citizen of one state and the other party is an alien. However, before a federal court may exercise diversity jurisdiction, the "matter in controversy" must exceed $75,000, exclusive of interests and costs. 28 USCA § 1332.

Not all diversity questions fall within the above parameters. Frequently, civil lawsuits involve more than one plaintiff and more than one defendant. In such cases, the law requires "complete diversity" before a federal court may exercise jurisdiction over the matter. This means that if a single plaintiff is a citizen of the same state as any defendant, there is no diversity and the case must be pursued in state court. If complete diversity exists and the jurisdictional amount is met, a federal court may exercise "subject matter jurisdiction" and hear the lawsuit.

Atlas Global Group, L.P., v. Grupo Dataflux raised the question whether complete diversity must exist at the time the lawsuit is filed before a federal court may exercise **subject matter jurisdiction**. The issue arose when Atlas, a Texas-based limited partnership comprised of five members, including two Mexican citizens, brought a breach of contract suit against Grupo, a Mexican corporation. Jurisdiction for the suit was based solely on diversity of citizenship, despite the fact that the partnership was deemed to be a citizen of each jurisdiction in which its partners resided. Prior to trial, the partnership completed a business transaction in which the two nondiverse Mexican citizens were removed as partners, eliminating the barrier to diversity jurisdiction. However, it was only after the jury found for the partnership that the Mexican corporation moved to dismiss for lack of jurisdiction at the time suit was filed. The district court granted the motion, but the U.S. Court of Appeals for the Fifth Circuit reversed in a 2-1 decision.

The Fifth Circuit held that a lack of diversity at the time a suit is filed may be cured after the suit has been filed if the defect is in fact cured prior to the final **verdict** or other dispositive ruling and the challenge to the jurisdictional defect is not raised until after the final verdict or other dispositive ruling has already been made. In the case at hand, the Fifth Circuit said that the judicial system, the parties, and the jurors had already committed ample resources to this matter. The case was given a full assessment of the evidence by an **impartial** jury during a six-day trial that was the culmination of several years of litigation. A verdict in the amount of $750,000 was awarded to the plaintiff, and to erase this result and start the process over by forcing the parties to re-litigate their claims in state court would undermine considerations of finality, efficiency, and economy. According to the Fifth Circuit, then, Atlas was properly allowed to cure the jurisdictional defect and Grupo was properly denied the right to challenge it.

Grupo appealed. It claimed that the Fifth Circuit's decision improperly allows a party to unilaterally alter its citizenship anytime during a lawsuit and creates an exception to the U.S. Supreme Court's longstanding limitations on diversity jurisdiction. As recently as 2003, Grupo argued, the Supreme Court reiterated a bright-line rule that diversity jurisdiction must be determined at the time suit is filed. *Dole Food Co. v. Patrickson*, 538 U.S. 468, 123 S.Ct. 1655, 155 L.Ed.2d 643. The Fifth Circuit's decision also represents an unwarranted expansion of other key Supreme Court's decisions, Grupo maintained. For example, *Caterpillar Inc. v. Lewis*, 519 U.S. 61, 117 S.Ct. 467, 136 L.Ed.2d 437 (1996), held that an improper removal of a case to federal court is not fatal if the federal diversity requirements are eventually met before the time **judgment** is entered.

In a 5-4 decision, the U.S. Supreme Court reversed the Fifth Circuit. Writing for the majority, Justice ANTONIN SCALIA said that *Caterpillar* did not augur a new approach to deciding whether a jurisdictional defect has been cured. Instead, *Caterpillar* involved an "unremarkable application" of the established exception to the time-of-filing rule under which **dismissal** of a non-diverse party may cure a defect in diversity jurisdiction. This longstanding exception, Scalia noted, has been recognized in Rule 21 of the Rules of Federal Civil Procedure, which permits the adding or dropping of parties at any stage of the litigation. In fact, as the Supreme Court held in *Newman-Green, Inc. v. Alfonzo-Larrain*, 490 U.S. 826, 109 S.Ct. 2218, 104 L.Ed.2d 893 (1989), the courts of appeals have the authority to cure a jurisdictional defect by dismissing a dispensable nondiverse party and need not **remand** the case to the district court for dismissal in that instance.

Justice Scalia said, however, that the Court had never approved a deviation from the rule, "[w]here there is no change in party, a jurisdiction depending on the condition of the party is governed by that condition, as it was at the commencement of the action." Allowing a citizenship change in a partnership to cure a jurisdictional defect existing at the time of filing would contravene this long-standing holding. "Apart from breaking with our longstanding precedent," Justice Scalia concluded, "holding that 'finality, efficiency, and judicial economy' can justify suspension of the time-of-filing rule would create an exception of indeterminate scope." The purported limitation established by the Fifth Circuit in an attempt to "cabin" the exception was both unsound in principle and "certain to be ignored in practice."

Courts Have Jurisdiction to Permit Amended Attorneys Fee Application

The U.S. judicial system generally requires each party to a lawsuit to pay their own legal fees. However, the federal Equal Access to Justice Act (EAJA), 28 U.S.C.A. § 2412 *et seq.*, authorizes the payment of fees to prevailing parties in actions against the U.S. government. However, the EAJA exempts the government from paying fees if it can show that its position in the underlying litigation was "substantially justified." The Supreme Court, in *Scarborough v. Principi*, __ U.S. __, 124 S.Ct. 1856, __ L.Ed.2d __ (2004), was called upon to decide whether an applicant who failed to allege that the government's position was not substantially justified could amend his application after the 30-day filing period had expired. The Court held that the lower federal court's did have jurisdiction to permit such an amendment.

Randall C. Scarborough sued the Department of Veterans Affairs (DVA) for disability benefits and ultimately prevailed. Eleven days after the Court of Appeals for Veterans Claims (CAVC) ruled in Scarborough's favor, his attorney applied for attorney's fees and costs. EAJA mandates that the applicant file the paperwork within 30 days, show that the applicant was the prevailing party and was eligible based on the applicant's net worth, submit a statement detailing the fees and costs sought from the government, and allege that the government's position was not substantially justified. Scarborough's attorney complied with all but the last requirement, filing a request for over $19,000 in attorney's fees and $118 in costs. The DVA filed a response, asking the CVAC to dismiss the fee application because the attorney had not included the "not substantially justified" statement. Scarborough's attorney immediately filed an amended application that included the statement and challenged the motion to dismiss. The CVAC agreed with the government that the failure to include the language was a jurisdictional defect that could not be cured once the applicant's 30-day filing period had expired. The Court of Appeals for the Federal Circuit upheld this decision. The Supreme Court agreed to hear Scarborough's **appeal** because two other circuit courts of appeals (Third and Eleventh) allowed amendments to the fee application after the 30-day filing period.

The Court, in a unanimous decision, sided with the Third and Eleventh Circuits. Justice RUTH BADER GINSBURG, writing for the Court, made clear at the outset of her opinion that the question before the Court did not concern subject-matter jurisdiction of the federal courts. Instead, the EAJA was a "mode of relief" that was "ancillary" to the **judgment** of a court that already had jurisdiction to consider a civil matter. The issue before the Court was not whether the EAJA applied to Scarborough's case, but rather when the EAJA provisions required a fee applicant to allege that the government's position was not substantially justified. The post-judgment proceedings for attorney's fees were "auxiliary to cases already within the court's ajudicatory authority."

Justice Ginsburg then examined why the EAJA required fee applicants to allege that the government's position was not substantially justified. She pointed out that the applicant did not have any **burden of proof** to back up the mere **allegation**. Instead, the government had the burden of proving its position was substantially justified. Therefore, Congress had not sought to erect barriers for litigants who raised legitimate claims. The required statement was a mere pleading requirement that was similar to requiring a signature or an oath or affirmation on a legal document. Justice Ginsburg cited previous decisions where the Court had not dismissed cases merely because the applicant had typed rather than handwrote his name or failed to verify the truthfulness of a filing through an oath or affirmation. In both situations the documents had been filed in a timely manner; the Court allowed these deficiencies to be corrected after the expiration of the filing period, finding that they could "relation back" to the original filings. This relation-back **doctrine**, which has a long history, permits courts to remedy defects by tying a later document or action to a properly made previous filing.

In Scarborough's case the ten-word statement was a "'think twice' prescription" that cautioned the applicant not to file an irresponsible claim. Justice Ginsburg also noted that the statement did not put the government on notice, as the government knows that in each case it must show that its position was substantially justified to prevail. In addition, another provision of the EAJA disallows fees where special circumstances make an award unjust. This provision gives the government an opportunity to argue that an application's defects were prejudicial. However, Scarborough's application had been timely filed and a later amended application could relate back to this original filing.

Abducted Doctor Cannot Sue U.S. Government

The U.S. government is generally immune from civil lawsuits seeking damages. However, the Federal Torts Claim Act (FTCA), 28 U.S.C.A. § 1346(b)(1), §§ 2671-2680, permits some civil lawsuits. The Supreme Court, in *Sosa v. Alvarez-Machain*, __ U.S. __, 124 S.Ct., __ L.Ed.2d __ 2004 WL 1439873(2004), ruled that a Mexican citizen could not sue under the FTCA for the alleged **tortious** acts of the Drug Enforcement Administration (DEA) in kidnapping him in Mexico and taking him to the U.S. for a criminal trial. In addition, the Court held that the plaintiff could not use a 1789 federal law to sue a Mexican citizen in U.S. courts for his participation in the **abduction**. The Court made clear that it was beyond the power of the judiciary to create jurisdiction for either **civil action**.

Humberto Alvarez-Machain, a Mexican doctor, was accused by the U.S. government of participating in the kidnapping, torture and **murder** of DEA special agent Enrique Camarena-Salazar and his airplane pilot. He was alleged to have prolonged Camarena's life so others could torture and interrogate him. On April 2, 1990, Alvarez was kidnapped from his office in Guadalajara and flown by private plane to El Paso, Texas. DEA agents were responsible for the abduction, although they did not kidnap Alvarez themselves; Jose Sosa and other Mexican citizens carried out the kidnapping. The Mexican government vehemently objected to Alvarez's abduction and sent letters to the United States government protesting the act as a violation of the extradition treaty. It asked for the arrest and extradition to Mexico of the law enforcement agents responsible for the kidnapping. The United States refused the request and prosecuted Alvarez.

Alvarez was acquitted of all charges in 1992 and returned to Mexico, where he began a civil action in California federal district court against Sosa, five unnamed Mexican citizens, four DEA agents, and the United States. He sued the U.S. under the FTCA and Sosa under the Alien Tort **Statute** (ATS), 28 U.S.C.A. § 1350, a 1789 law that gives the district courts **original jurisdiction** over "any civil action by an alien for a tort only, committed in violation of the **law of nations** or a treaty of the United States." The district court dismissed the FTCA claim but awarded Alvarez $25,000 on the ATS claim. The Ninth Circuit upheld the ATS claim but reversed on the FTCA **cause of action**, leading to the review by the Supreme Court.

The Court, in a unanimous decision, ruled that Alvarez could not sue under either federal law. Justice DAVID SOUTER, writing for the Court, noted that the FTCA contained a provision (28 U.S.C.A. § 2680(k)) that did not **waive sovereign immunity** for claims "arising in a foreign country." This provision bars claims for injuries suffered in a foreign country regardless of where the tortious act occurred. Justice Souter found that this exception "on its face" seemed to apply to the facts of Alvarez's abduction. However, the Ninth Circuit had employed the "headquarters doctrine" to sustain Alvarez's FTCA claim. Under this **doctrine**, if the DEA agents in California had planned and directed the wrongful abduction, then the FTCA claim did not arise in a foreign country.

Justice Souter rejected the headquarters doctrine based on two considerations. First, both the planning in the U.S. and the actual abduction in Mexico caused the harm. In **tort law proximate cause** is the initial act that sets off a natural and continuous sequence of events that produces **injury**. In this case the DEA actions were not the exclusive proximate cause; the actions of Sosa and his accomplices on Mexican soil were also a proximate cause of injury. Based on this analysis it was unclear that the FTCA exception did or did not apply. A second and stronger consideration was the fact that the harm (the abduction) occurred in Mexico. Souter reasoned that Congress intended "arising under" to mean an injury that occurred in a foreign country. In addition, when the FTCA was enacted courts applied the law of the place where the injury occurred in non-FTCA tort cases. The headquarters doctrine exception threatened to swallow the rule, which was contrary to what Congress sought when passing the "arising in a foreign country" provision. Therefore, Alvarez could not employ the doctrine to claim federal jurisdiction under the FTCA.

As to the Alien Tort Statute, Justice Souter concluded that Alvarez could not employ it against Sosa. The 1789 law was limited to "entertain the handful of **international law** *cum* common law clams understood to exist at that time." The ATS was a jurisdictional statute that created no new causes of action. Claims that could be raised under the ATS included offenses against ambassadors, violations of safe conducts, and piracy. The Court was unwilling to create a new cause of action, as it was the province of Congress to make such decisions legislatively. Moreover, judicial creation of such an action would have implications for U.S. foreign relations. Therefore, the Court dismissed Alvarez's claim against Sosa.

JURY

In trials, a group of people who are selected and sworn to inquire into matters of fact and to reach a verdict on the basis of the evidence presented to them.

Batson Peremptory Challenge Burden of Proof Issue Left Unresolved

The U.S. SUPREME COURT, in *Batson v. Kentucky*, 476 U.S. 79, 106 S.Ct. 1712, 90 L.Ed.2d 69 (1986), prohibited prosecutors from excluding prospective jurors on the basis of race. Under the *Batson* test, a **defendant** may object to a prosecutor's **peremptory challenge** and show an "inference of discriminatory purpose." The prosecutor then must come forward with a neutral explanation for challenging black jurors. If a neutral explanation cannot be made, the juror will not be excused. Almost twenty years after this decision, the courts are still wrestling with the administration of this test. The state of California imposed a **burden of proof** on a person making a *Batson* challenge, requiring either a "strong likelihood" or "reasonable inference" of racial bias before the opposing lawyer must explain why jurors were struck from the pool. A defendant who failed to meet this threshold appealed to the U.S. Supreme Court in *Johnson v. California*, __ U.S. __, 124 S.Ct. 1833, __ L.Ed.2d __ (2004), contending that this threshold was higher than required by *Batson*. The court heard arguments on the case in 2004, but in a surprising move, the court dismissed the case because it belatedly concluded that it did not have jurisdiction to hear it. The decision left unresolved the underlying constitutional issue.

Jay Johnson was found **guilty** of second degree **murder** of the nineteen-month-old daughter of his girlfriend by a California jury. During the selection of jurors, the prosecutor exercised twelve peremptory challenges. Unlike striking a juror for cause, jurors can be excused for no reason using peremptory challenges. A lawyer may not like the demeanor of a prospective juror or may have a "gut feeling" that the person would be sympathetic to the other side. The use of peremptory challenges is especially important to prosecutors because **felony** convictions require the unanimous vote of twelve jurors. Johnson, who is African American, objected when the prosecutor used peremptory challenges to strike three African American jurors. He then moved that the prosecutor explain his reasons for removing them. The judge denied his motion, and a jury of twelve white persons was selected.

Johnson appealed his conviction, arguing that the court's denial of his *Batson* challenge denied him a trial by a jury of his peers. Moreover, he alleged that California law placed a heavier burden of **proof** on the defendant than required by *Batson*. The California Court of Appeals agreed with Johnson and reversed his conviction. On **appeal** by the state, the California Supreme Court, in a 5-2 decision, reversed the appeals court ruling. The court held that defendants must produce a reasonable amount of proof before forcing the prosecutor to reveal the reasons for striking jurors. As to the necessary burden of proof, Justice Ming Chin concluded that the terms "reasonable inference" and "strong likelihood" were merely variations of the federal phrase "inference of discriminatory purpose." In essence, the state and federal terms required the defendant to show that the challenges were "more likely than not" based on illegal group bias. The court stated, "We believe it obvious that we considered the two terms to be different phrasing of the same standard." However, Justice Joyce Kennard, in a dissenting opinion, disagreed. She argued that the difference in phrasing was "subtle but crucial," and this produced a burden of proof that was too high and too unfair to the defendant. This stiff burden in the first part of the *Batson* challenge "short-circuits the process" and deprives the court from hearing both sides.

The U.S. Supreme Court agreed to hear Johnson's appeal to determine whether a person raising a *Batson* challenge had to "show that it is more likely than not that the other party's peremptory challenges, if unexplained, were based on impermissible group bias." Four weeks after the Court heard oral arguments, it issued a *per curiam* decision—a decision not signed by one of the justices—dismissing the appeal. The Court stated that it did not have jurisdiction to hear the matter because it can only review "final judgments or decrees rendered by the highest court of a State in which a decision could be had." In this case, the California Supreme Court had reversed the court of appeals on the *Batson* issue, but it had not addressed whether two separate issues raised on appeal—involving evidence and prosecutorial misconduct—would independently support a reversal of Johnson's conviction. In its **remand** to the court of appeals, the court directed it commence "further proceedings, consistent with [its] opinion." Therefore, it was possible that the court of appeals could overturn the conviction on one of these separate state issues. The U.S. Supreme Court declined to review the federal issue until the state courts have made final decisions on all issues. The **dismissal** did not mean that Johnson could not seek U.S. Supreme Court review in the future on his *Batson* issue. If the court of appeals affirmed his **judgment** of conviction, he could seek review again in the California Supreme Court. Assuming that court denied his claims, Johnson could **petition** the U.S. Supreme Court.

KERRY, JOHN FORBES

John Forbes Kerry

John Forbes Kerry, the DEMOCRATIC PARTY nominee for PRESIDENT OF THE UNITED STATES in 2004, was born on December 22, 1943 in Denver, Colorado. Raised by his blue-blooded mother, and lawyer and United States Foreign Service member father, Kerry "grew up in an atmosphere in which politics was passed around the table like mashed potatoes," noted the *Christian Science Monitor*. In boarding school, Kerry began to emulate President JOHN F. KENNEDY, even signing his papers, "J.F.K."- which happened to also be his monogram. This emulation continued at Yale University where Kerry joined the Yale Political Union and debated political issues. He also became a member of Yale's famed secret society, Skull and Bones.

In 1966, after graduating from Yale, Kerry enlisted in the U.S. Navy, although he had denounced the VIETNAM WAR in a commencement speech. He served as a gunboat officer on the Mekong Delta in Vietnam and became, as the Nation noted, "a believer in the war." However, after winning the Silver Star, the Bronze Star, and three Purple Hearts for his heroism, Kerry, as the Nation further noted, "returned [to the United States] full of horror." He obtained an early-release from the Navy and decided to run for Congress. After abandoning his run to support Reverend Robert F. Drinan's campaign, Kerry became a leader of Vietnam Veterans Against the War (VVAW).

For the next decade, Kerry left the political spotlight. He returned to college and earned a law degree from Boston College in 1976. Next, he worked as an assistant district attorney until he opened a law practice in 1979. During this time, Kerry also taught college classes and commentated for news programs. In 1980, it seemed as if Kerry was ready to return to politics, but he backed out of the Democratic Congressional primaries. Two years later, he successfully won the race for Massachusetts' lieutenant governor. After Senator Paul E. Tsongas vacated his Senate seat due to illness in 1984, Kerry leapt at the chance to fill the vacancy. However, he faced serious competition from Ray Shamie, an older, more conservative candidate. Voters understood where Shamie stood on the issues. With Kerry, on the other hand, most saw a John F. Kennedy wanna-be who as a Boston Globe columnist commented, "[Kerry] wrote the game plan for [his] life while he was still sitting in the sandbox." Still, Kerry, with 55 percent of the vote, won the Senate seat.

During his first term as senator, Kerry focused not on legislation, but on prosecution. From 1986 until 1989, Kerry dug into allegations that the Contras, who the United States had supported in their efforts against the Nicaraguan Sandinistas, had been trafficking drugs. During this investigation, Kerry discovered Oliver North's involvement in the effort and wrote a highly damning, but largely ignored report. Jack Blum, the lead investigator on Kerry's team recalled in the Nation that Kerry was "frustrated that so much of our work was written off by the Senate and much of the press." However, Kerry continued digging and discovered that the United States had known that Panamanian dictator Manuel Noriega was a drug lord and that the Bank of Credit and

JOHN FORBES KERRY

- **1943** Born December 11
- **1966** Enlisted in U.S. Navy
- **1976** Earned law degree from Boston University
- **1984** Elected to U.S. Senate
- **2004** Nominated as Democratic Party candidate for President

Commerce International served as a drug money launderer even for the Central Intelligence Agency (CIA).

In his third Senate term, Kerry found success by targeting environmental issues such as protecting the United States' coastlines. In July 2001, the Senate passed the Kerry Amendment that prevented President George W. Bush from opening federally-protected land to oil and gas drilling. Yet, even after 30 years of public service, Kerry maintained a mysterious appearance and is difficult to categorize, or, as the Nation quoted one voter, "[He] makes you wonder where his convictions are." For Kerry, his convictions are evident from his investigations and the amendments he has sponsored.

In July 2003, Kerry geared up for his presidential campaign by denouncing President GEORGE W. BUSH's national security efforts in the wake of the SEPTEMBER 11TH ATTACKS, telling the press "Today we still do not have a real plan and enough resources for preparedness against a terrorist attack." In September 2003, Kerry formally announced his candidacy for the Democratic Party's nomination in the 2004 election.

Kerry got off to a strong start in the primaries, winning the Iowa and New Hampshire caucuses before rolling on to victories in the Missouri, Delaware, Arizona, New Mexico, and North Dakota primaries. On the March 2, 2004 "Super Tuesday" primaries, Kerry won nine of ten contests, essentially assuring his nomination. In July, before the Democratic convention, Kerry named North Carolina senator John Edwards, one of Kerry's strongest opponents in the primaries, as his vice presidential running mate. The pair began their campaign for the presidency by attacking President Bush's actions in the invasion of Iraq, as well as targeting Bush's economic policies.

LONG, RUSSELL BILLIU

Obituary notice

Born November 3, 1918 in Shreveport, Louisiana; died on May 3, 2003, in Washington, D.C. A scion of the famed Louisiana political dynasty founded by his father Huey, Long bore the distinction of being the first American to serve in the U.S. Senate whose mother and father both had also held a seat there before him. He formally retired in 1986, after nearly 40 years of service, and at one time was considered one of Capitol Hill's most powerful lawmakers. Long graduated from Louisiana State University in 1940 and went on to earn a law degree from there, as well. He then served in the U.S. Navy during World War II, taking part in the Allied invasion of Sicily, and opened his own law firm in Baton Rouge in 1946. When one of Louisiana's U.S. senators died in office in 1948, the family political machine secured his nomination to fill the remainder of the term. He was prohibited from being sworn in for a few weeks, however, due to the constitution requirement that a senator be at least 30 years old. Long was re-elected continuously for several more six-year terms. He made a name for himself on the Senate finance committee as a tax expert, and was chosen by President JOHN F. KENNEDY to shepherd the administration's tax-reduction plan through Congress. His rise was briefly derailed by alcoholism, which he curbed on his own, but his comeback was swift and assured. He soon became the Democratic whip in the Senate, a powerful post when the party gained a majority in the chamber, and headed the Senate finance committee for 15 years after 1966. During the 1970s, Long wielded tremendous power in this post as the final arbiter on which White House tax proposals would make it to the bill stage. He also sponsored legislation himself, and his legacy includes the voluntary campaign contribution check box on federal tax forms, the earned income tax credit for families and the introduction of tax breaks to companies that gave employees stock options as part of a benefits package. Long decided to retire from the Senate when his sixth term ended in late 1986. He publicly criticized the change in campaigning that had taken hold in recent years, with its reliance on media-savvy strategists and divisive partisan politicking. Long practiced law again in Washington and Baton Rouge before his death. Married twice, he was the father of two daughters. His return to private life marked the end of the Long political machine, as well.

MANSLAUGHTER

The unjustifiable, inexcusable, and intentional killing of a human being without deliberation, premeditation, and malice. The unlawful killing of a human being without any deliberation, which may be involuntary, in the commission of a lawful act without due caution and circumspection.

U.S. Congressman Sentenced to One Hundred-Day Jail Term for Felony Manslaughter Conviction

On December 8, 2003, sixty-four-year-old William Janklow (R-S.D.) was convicted of second-degree manslaughter (a felony) for his role in the traffic death of fifty-five-year-old Randy Scott, a native of Hardwick, Minnesota. Along with the felony conviction, Janklow was also found **guilty** of running a stop sign, reckless driving, and speeding (three misdemeanors), Although Janklow faced a maximum sentence of up to ten years in prison and a $10,000 fine, Moody County Judge Rodney Steel sentenced Janklow to serve one hundred days in jail, pay a $5,400 fine, and reimburse the county $5,000 for the costs of his incarceration.

The accident happened on August 16, 2003, at the intersection of Highways 13 and 14, just south of Flandreau, South Dakota. Scott, who was heading west, was pronounced dead at the scene after his Harley Davidson motorcycle struck Janklow's vehicle, a Cadillac. Janklow was heading south toward his home in Brandon, South Dakota, after a two-day road trip that ended with a ceremony at the Brown County Fair in Aberdeen, where he gave a talk in honor of Korean War veterans and met with constituents. A cornfield apparently obstructed the views of both drivers. No pre-accident skidmarks were found at the scene, indicating that possibly neither driver applied the brakes before impact.

The case generated both national and local media attention. On the national level, Janklow was a freshman member of the U.S. House of Representatives; he had been sworn in only eight months before the accident. At the local level, Janklow had been a fixture in South Dakota politics for more than thirty years, having served one term as state **attorney general** (1974 to 1978) and two terms as governor (1979 to 1987, 1995 to 2003). After graduating from law school in 1966, Janklow also served as prosecuting attorney in several high profile cases, including the trial of AMERICAN INDIAN MOVEMENT members who were accused of seizing control of a courthouse in the Black Hills and occupying Wounded Knee, South Dakota.

Janklow's trial began on December 1, 2003, and lasted one week. The jury was comprised of eight women and four men. The prosecution introduced testimony from accident reconstruction experts showing that Janklow was traveling seventy-one miles per hour (mph) in a fifty-five mph zone, and that he was going that speed when he ran a stop sign and was struck by Scott, who was traveling at a speed of approximately fifty-six mph. The trial court precluded the prosecution from offering testimony showing that Janklow had been cited for speeding twelve times in eleven counties from 1990 to 1994. Other testimony showed that Janklow often bragged about his speeding violations. However,

U.S. Representative Bill Janklow leaves court after his conviction on manslaughter charges.

the trial court did allow a woman to testify that Janklow had run the same stop a year earlier, barely missing the woman who had to slam on the brakes to avoid colliding with him. The trial court also allowed the prosecution to offer evidence showing that Janklow had recently been stopped for speeding through a construction zone, though he was only issued a warning by the officer who stopped him.

The defense centered on the fact that Janklow was a diabetic who had not eaten any food during the entire day. The accident happened at 4:30 p.m. As a result of his severe low-blood sugar, the defense argued, Janklow suffered an unexpected bout with hypoglycemia, which caused confusion, fatigue, and possibly even a black out. Additionally, the defense put on medical testimony that Janklow, on the day of the crash, took heart medication that can mask the symptoms of a diabetic reaction. Senator Tom Daschle (D-SD) later took the stand. He testified that he had spent part of the day with Janklow and that Janklow had not eaten anything while the two were together. Janklow himself then took the stand, stating that he had not eaten any food for twenty hours prior to the accident. He denied that he had any memory of the accident. On cross examination, the prosecution got Janklow to admit that as a diabetic he was fully aware of the risks of driving a car after taking insulin on an empty stomach, an act the prosecution argued was reckless in itself.

The jury spent five hours deliberating before unanimously returning guilty verdicts on all counts. Janklow was sentenced on January 22, 2004, with his jail sentence commencing on February 7, 2004, in a Sioux Falls jail. Even before he began serving his jail sentence, Janklow appealed. He raised three issues: (1) the trial court erred in denying two proposed jury instructions; (2) the trial court erred in admitting evidence that Janklow had committed two prior acts of negligent or unlawful driving; and (3) prosecutorial misconduct in telling the jury that Janklow's medical defense had been concocted two weeks before the trial. Janklow also asked the South Dakota Supreme Court to expedite his **appeal**, a request that was denied even though it was highly likely that Janklow will have fully served his one hundred-day jail sentence before the appeal process is complete.

Janklow resigned from the House of Representatives on December 8, 2003, the day the jury announced the verdicts. Shortly thereafter, the family of Randy Scott filed a **wrongful death** action against Janklow. The lawsuit, which was filed in state court, was brought against Janklow in his individual **capacity**. However, in March of 2004 an attorney for the federal government announced that Janklow was acting in his official capacity as House member when the accident happened. The attorney filed a motion asking that the state suit be moved to federal court, since the federal government could now be named as a second **defendant**. Because punitive damages are only available in state court, the plaintiffs are expected to oppose this request.

1994 Assault Leads to 2004 Manslaughter Conviction

In February 2004, Desmon Venn was convicted of **involuntary manslaughter** and sentenced to prison for the death of Zuhair Pattah. Pattah died nearly nine years after being injured during a 1994 fistfight.

Desmon Venn and Zuhair Pattah were classmates at West Bloomfield High School in suburban Detroit, Michigan, when a fight broke out on the school grounds on May 2, 1994. The seventeen-year-old Venn threw a punch, which landed between Pattah's eyes. The sixteen-year-old then fell to the ground and lapsed into a coma after his head hit the pavement. Pattah remained in a coma until his death in January 2003.

After the fight, Venn was charged with **intent** to do great bodily harm. That charge was a **felony** and carried a possible ten-year sentence. However, the charge was reduced when a judge ruled that there was no evidence that Venn had intended to harm Pattah. The prosecution unsuccessfully appealed the reduced charge.

In 1995, Venn pleaded **guilty** to a charge of aggravated assault—a misdemeanor. He was placed on two years probation and served two months in a boot camp. He was also ordered to pay a $1,000 fine.

Pattah resided in a nursing home until his death on January 8, 2003. An autopsy indicated that his death resulted from complications caused by the head trauma sustained in the assault. Prosecutors charged Venn with involuntary **manslaughter** in February 2003. The charge was a felony and carried the possibility of a fifteen-year sentence. Venn turned himself in to authorities in West Bloomfield, and a judge set his bond at $250,000.

After Venn's arrest, his attorney argued that the new charges against his client constituted **double jeopardy**. The Fifth Amendment to the Constitution prohibits double jeopardy. It provides, "nor shall any person be subject for the same offence to be twice put in jeopardy of life or limb."

The defense argued that because the involuntary manslaughter charge came after Venn's assault conviction, double jeopardy barred the manslaughter charge because it arose from the same transaction as the assault. The prosecution responded, contending that the same transaction did not necessarily mean the same crime; the manslaughter charge could not be made until Pattah died. In the case of *Diaz v. United States*, 223 U.S.442, 32 S.Ct. 250, 56 L.Ed.2d 500 (1912), the U.S. SUPREME COURT ruled in favor of the government on a case involving similar circumstances. The court held that double jeopardy did not bar a second prosecution because "[t]he death of the injured person was the **principal element** of the homicide, but was no part of the assault and battery."

Venn entered a plea of guilty in January 2004; he was sentenced on February 10, 2004. Venn was given a sentence of twenty-nine months to thirty years. According to Venn's lawyer, twenty-nine months was the minimum amount he could have received. The thirty-year maximum was also imposed because Venn had drug convictions on his record. The judge gave Venn credit for time served, which amounted to nearly fourteen months.

At the sentencing, Pattah's younger brother spoke about the impact his brother's **injury** had on the rest of the family and how the adults in his family had never recovered from their grief. He testified that his father was rarely home and had quit his job to care for his son. Venn also spoke, reading from a prepared statement. Much of his statement was difficult to understand because he was crying.

Both the prosecutor and the defense attorney expressed satisfaction with the sentence handed down by the trial court. The prosecutor noted that both Venn and Pattah's life had been ruined by the 1994 fight. He also stated that he was impressed with the remorse expressed by Venn at the sentencing.

Desmond Venn in court prior to his sentencing for manslaughter.

Jayson Williams Acquitted of Aggravated Manslaughter; Convicted on Lesser Counts

Former pro basketball star Jayson Williams was acquitted of aggravated manslaughter, the most serious of eight charges brought against him. Williams was also acquitted on charges of possession of a weapon for an unlawful purpose, as well as **aggravated assault**. However, the jury, which was hung on one **count**, did ultimately find Williams **guilty** of four lesser counts: witness tampering, evidence tampering, hindering apprehension, and fabricating evidence. Together, his convictions carry a possible sentence of thirteen years in prison, but because the millionaire athlete does not have a criminal record, he is not likely to see any time behind bars.

The case arose out of events that began during the evening of February 13, 2002, when Williams and a group of his friends traveled to Lehigh University in Bethlehem, Pennsylvania, where they watched the Harlem Globetrotters perform in an exhibition game. Several of the Globetrotters were Williams's former teammates when he played with the New Jersey Nets in the National Basketball Association (NBA). After the game, Williams and his friends accompanied four of the Globetrotters back to their nearby hotel, where a call was placed to Seventy-Eight Limousines, a limousine service near Williams's house in Alexandria Township, New Jersey.

Costas "Gus" Christofi, a fifty-five-year-old driver for the service, was off-duty that night, but just happened to be at the office dropping off paper work when the call came in. The dispatcher, knowing that Christofi was a big sports fan, offered him the job, and Christofi jumped at the opportunity. Christofi had spent years in prison as a young man while battling drug addiction. After his release from prison, Christofi had reportedly turned his life around. Now clean and sober, he had been living a modest existence in Washington Borough, New Jersey.

Christofi picked up Williams and the eight other passengers at 10:30 p.m. He drove them to the Mountain View Chalet in Asbury, N.J., arriving at the restaurant around 11:15. During dinner, according to a witness for the prosecution, Williams teased and cursed Christofi, who was sitting alone at an adjacent table. Ultimately, Williams tried to smooth things over when the driver took offense and got up to leave the restaurant. Defense witnesses denied hearing Williams curse or tease Christofi at any point during the night.

After dinner, Williams invited everyone over to his sixty-five-acre, 30,000 square-foot estate in Alexandria. They arrived around 2:15 a.m. on February 14, 2002. During a tour of the house about thirty minutes after their arrival, Williams pulled out a loaded twelve-gauge shotgun from an unlocked gun rack in the master bedroom, and in one quick move snapped the gun shut and wheeled around. The gun then went off in his hands (the parties disputed whether the gun discharged because Williams pulled the trigger or because it malfunctioned). A spray of pellets struck Christofi in the chest. As he crumpled to his knees, blood began pooling around him on the floor. Williams attempted to stop the bleeding with a towel. He also gave Christofi mouth-to-mouth resuscitation. When those efforts failed to save Christofi's life, Williams dropped to his knees like a ton of bricks, a prosecution witness later testified, exclaiming "my God, what just happened? My life is over. How could this happen?"

Williams then attempted to wipe down the shotgun and remove his fingerprints, after which he placed the gun in Christofi's hands, a prosecution witness told the jury. According to the same witness, Williams then removed all of his clothing and jumped into his indoor pool. Returning to the bedroom dressed in different clothes, Williams allegedly ordered several guests to tell authorities that Christofi had shot himself. Transcripts of the phone call showed that Victor Williams, brother of Jayson Williams, called 911 at 2:54 a.m. and reported the shooting as a suicide.

Based on their cursory examination of the entry wounds in the victim's chest, investigators believed that the death was not a suicide. Although Williams was brought in for questioning that same day, he was not arrested until eleven days after the death. On May 1, 2002, Williams was indicted by a Hunterdon County (New Jersey) **grand jury** on charges of aggravated manslaughter, reckless manslaughter, aggravated assault, evidence tampering, witness tampering, hindering apprehension, and fabricating evidence. Aggravated manslaughter differs from reckless manslaughter in that before a **defendant** may be convicted of the former, the prosecution must prove **beyond a reasonable doubt** that the defendant was so reckless in killing the victim as to manifest an "extreme indifference to human life."

The indictment was later dismissed when Williams's attorneys challenged it on grounds that prosecutors had improperly commented to grand jurors about Williams's right to remain silent. A second indictment was then returned by another grand jury. It contained all of the charges found in the original indictment, and it added another count, unlawful possession of a weapon. Before the prosecution obtained the second indictment, the case was moved from Hunterdon County, where the shooting occurred, to Somerset County because the court found that pretrial publicity was jeopardizing Williams's chance for a fair trial.

Jury selection began on January 13, 2004, and the first witness was called a month later. The trial lasted nine weeks. Prosecutor Steven C. Lember represented the Hunterdon County, while attorneys Joseph Hayden and Billy Martin headed up the defense. Sixteen jurors, including four alternates, were eventually selected from a sixty-four-member jury pool. Twelve jurors were women and four were men. Four of the sixteen jurors were African American. Williams is biracial, his father being African American while his mother is a Caucasian Polish American.

The prosecution put forth thirty-six witnesses, while five witnesses testified for the defense. The defendant did not testify. The testimony of three witnesses was particularly important for the prosecution. Former New Jersey Net teammate Benoit Benjamin told jurors he was less than three feet away when Williams cracked open a loaded shotgun, hurled a string of profanities at Christofi, snapped the gun closed, and pulled the trigger. Kent Culuko and John Gordnick, two of Williams's house guests on the night in question, testified that, at the behest of Williams, they hid bloody clothes and wiped Williams's palm prints off the shotgun. Through the testimony of three other house guests, the jury heard that Williams had tampered with the death scene, jumped in a swimming pool to cleanse himself of evidence, and ordered witnesses to tell police that the driver had shot himself while alone in the master bedroom. One prosecution witness testified that he remembered Williams consuming a large amount of alcohol in the hours leading up to the shooting.

Defense attorneys attempted to rebut the testimony of Benjamin by calling their own witness, who testified that before trial Benjamin had offered defense investigators favorable testimony in exchange for money or a job. On **cross-examination** by the defense, Gordnick and Culuko each conceded having made deals with prosecutors to plead guilty to tampering with evidence. In return for their testimony, they were placed in a Pretrial Intervention Program instead of getting jail time. The defense also called a **forensic** expert who testified that the victim's blood had splattered across the bedroom, and that several prosecution witnesses who claimed to have seen Williams pull the trigger had no trace of blood on their clothing—raising questions as to how they could have witnessed the incident without being splattered by blood. Finally, the defense called two gun experts who testified that the shotgun could have misfired because of wear and tear, as well as debris in the firing mechanisms.

The jury deliberated twenty-three hours over four days before announcing its **verdict**. The jury could not agree on the reckless manslaughter charge. One juror, Shalisha Martin, said the vote was 8-4 in favor of acquittal. The prosecution said no decision had been made on whether Williams would be tried again on that charge. A date had not been scheduled for sentencing at the time of this writing.

During his career, Williams, who played for the Philadelphia 76ers, the Phoenix Suns, and the New Jersey Nets, was one of the NBA's leading rebounders. He also worked as an NBA analyst for NBC, and, known for his jocularity and wittiness, he appeared as a regular guest on David Letterman and Oprah Winfrey. His career ended prematurely in 2000, after he suffered a badly broken leg. However, the final years of his $94 million NBA contract were guaranteed.

Former NBA star Jayson Williams in court during his manslaughter trial.

MINE AND MINERAL LAW

The law governing the ownership, sale, and operation of mines, quarries, and wells, and the rights to natural resources found in the earth.

BedRoc Limited v. United States

The United States Supreme Court, in March 2004, determined that sand and gravel deposits on a piece of property in Nevada were not "valuable minerals" according to a federal **land grant statute**. *BedRoc Ltd. v. United States*, 124 S. Ct. 1587 (2004). The court's opinion reversed decisions by a federal district court in Nevada, as well as the Ninth **Circuit Court** of Appeals.

Since the middle of the 1800s, Congress sought to settle frontier lands by enacting a series of land-grant statutes. In the early part of the twentieth century, Nevada's population was less than one hundred thousand people. One of the difficulties in attracting a larger population to the state was the lack of surface water resources. This shortage hindered agricultural development. Congress rejected several proposals that would have called for federal funding for exploration of underground water. Instead, Congress enacted the Pittman Underground Water Act of 1919, ch. 77, 41 Stat. 293, to encourage private citizens to try to locate water in Nevada.

Under this 1919 statute, the Secretary of the Interior could issue permits of up to two years that gave the permittee the exclusive right to drill for underground water. In order to receive a permit, the applicant was required to file an **affidavit** to affirm that applications were made "honestly and in good faith" for the purposes of "reclamation and cultivation." When an applicant could prove that he or she could cultivate at least twenty acres of land, the federal government could give the applicant up to 640 acres of land. As of 1920, only about eleven percent of Nevada's 112,000 square miles of land was owned by private individuals.

Under the 1919 act, Congress retained mineral rights for the federal government. According to the statute, the United States reserved the rights to "all the coal and other valuable minerals in the lands ... together with the right to prospect for, mine, and remove" the minerals. The 1919 act was considered experimental and did not result in significant agricultural development in Nevada. In 1964, Congress repealed the statute. Pub. L. No. 88-417, 78 Stat. 398. However, the repealing statute reserved rights granted under the original 1919 statute.

Netwon and Mabel Butler obtained a patent in 1940, under the Pittman Act, for 560 acres of land located about sixty-five miles north of Las Vegas. Common sand and gravel were abundant and visible on the surface of the land. A federal surveyor had determined prior to the Butler purchase that the land was "nonmineral" in nature, meaning that the land was more valuable for purposes other than the minerals. Several changes in ownership occurred in the fifty years following the Butler's original grant.

With the meteoric growth of Las Vegas since the Butlers received their permit, a commercial market for the sand and gravel had developed. Earl Williams purchased the property in 1993 and began the process of extracting the sand and gravel from the land. After he began the extraction, the Bureau of Land Management (BLM) issued a notice of trespass. The BLM claimed that Williams was removing "valuable minerals" from federal property. In 1997, the Interior Board of Land Appeals (IBLA) affirmed the decision of the Board of Land Management. *Earl Williams*, 140 I.B.L.A. 295 (1997). Though the decisions were the same, the reasoning for the decisions differed. The BLM made its decision based on the case of *Watt v. Western Nuclear, Inc.*, 462 U.S. 36, 103 S. Ct. 2218, 76 L. Ed. 2d 400 (1983), which held that sand and gravel were minerals that were reserved to the United States under the Stock Raising **Homestead** Act of 1916, ch. 9, 39 Stat. 862. By comparison, the IBLA relied on the **legislative history** of the Pittman Act to **render** its decision.

Though Williams appealed the decision, he sold the property to BedRoc Limited, LLC in 1995. BedRoc, which in turn sold fifty-six acres to Western Elite, Inc., continued to excavate the sand and gravel under an interim agreement with the INTERIOR DEPARTMENT. After the IBLA rendered its decision, BedRoc filed an action in the U.S. District Court for the District of Nevada. In the action, BedRoc sought to quiet **title** to the land and the minerals contained on it.

The issue before the district court was whether sand and mineral deposits were considered "valuable minerals" that were reserved to the federal government. Comments made by Nevada Senator Key Pittman, the sponsor of the Pittman Act, suggested that the statute was intended to reserve all mineral rights to the federal government. During a debate about the statute in 1916, Pittman said, "it is the policy of Congress ... not to permit the acquisition of any character of minerals through any agricultural entry." 53 Cong. Rec. S707 (1916). In determining that Congress intended to retain all mineral rights when it enacted the Pittman Act, the district court held that sand and gravel were indeed valuable minerals reserved to the federal government.

BedRoc and Western Elite appealed the decision to the U.S. Court of Appeals for the Ninth Circuit. The Ninth Circuit agreed with the district court that the text and legislative history of the statute supported a finding that Congress intended to include sand and gravel as valuable minerals. Moreover, the court discovered that the Interior Department in 1914 had included a discussion of the value of sand and gravel as part of a report on mineral resources in the United States. Accordingly, the court affirmed the decision of the district court.

BecRoc and Western Elite then appealed the decision to the U.S. SUPREME COURT, which granted **certiorari** in September 2003. The government urged the Court to decide the case in a similar manner as the case of *Western Nuclear* in 1983. In that case, the Court determined that the word "mineral" as contained in the statute in question was ambiguous, and decided that Congress had intended to include sand and gravel as minerals under that statute.

However, the Court, per Justice WILLIAM REHNQUIST, distinguished the Pittman Act from the statute in *Western Nuclear* because the Pittman Act refers to "valuable minerals." Thus, Congress intended to narrow the scope of the statute by including "valuable" in the text, according to the Court's decision. The Court also refused to look at the legislative history of the Pittman Act. The Court found that the plain meaning of the text of the statute controlled the decision. According to Rehnquist's opinion, the plain meaning of the text excluded sand and gravel as valuable minerals, and the Court reversed the Ninth Circuit's decision. Justice JOHN PAUL STEVENS dissented, arguing that the Court should have followed its decision in *Western Nuclear*.

MIRANDA RIGHTS

Miranda Rights Do Not Mandate Suppression of Physical Evidence

Although the Supreme Court has refused calls to overturn its decision in *Miranda v. Arizona*, 384 U.S. 436, 86 S.Ct. 1602, 16 L.Ed.2d 694 (1966), it has limited the reach of Miranda rights in certain circumstances. In *United States v. Patane*, __ U.S. __, 124 S.Ct., __ L.Ed.2d __ 2004 WL 1431768(2004), the Court held that the failure of police officers to properly "Mirandize" a suspect (tell a suspect that he or she has the right to remain silent, that anything the suspect tells the police may be used against the suspect at trial, that the suspect is entitled to an attorney, and that if the suspect cannot afford an attorney the court will appoint one) did not require the suppression of physical evidence obtained through inadmissible questioning. In so ruling three members of the Court argued that the Fifth Amendment's **Self-Incrimination Clause** is not violated until the state seeks to introduce a defendant's self-incriminating statement. A majority of the Court declined to apply the Fourth Amendment's "fruit of the poisonous tree" **doctrine** to the Fifth Amendment.

Samuel F. Patane was arrested by Colorado Springs, Colorado, police in 2001 for harassing his former girlfriend, Linda O'Donnell. He was released on bond and the court issued a **temporary restraining order**, barring contact with the ex-girlfriend. A few days later he violated the order by trying to contact O'Donnell by phone. A probation officer told the Colorado Springs police officer investigating this conduct that federal authorities had information that Patane possessed a Glock pistol. Patane was a convicted felon who was prohibited from possessing any firearms. When the officer and a detective went to arrest Patane for violating the **restraining order**, the detective tried to Mirandize him, but Patane interrupted the detective and said he knew his rights. The officers did not advise him of his rights after this interruption. The detective then asked about the pistol. Patane hesitated but then told the detective where to retrieve the Glock. A federal district court convicted Patane on the firearms possession charge and he appealed, arguing that the introduction of the Glock as evidence should have been prohibited. He claimed that the **discovery** of the pistol was the fruit of a statement he gave without being first advised of his Miranda rights. The Tenth **Circuit Court** of Appeals agreed with this argument and reversed the district court. The Supreme Court agreed to hear the government's **appeal** because other circuit courts of appeals had ruled differently on this issue.

The Court, in a 5-4 decision, reversed the Tenth Circuit. Justice CLARENCE THOMAS, writing a **plurality** opinion joined by Chief

Justice WILLIAM REHNQUIST and Justice ANTONIN SCALIA, ruled that the suppression of the pistol as evidence was unnecessary. He based his holding on *Chavez v. Martinez*, 538 US 760, 123 S. Ct. 1994, 155 L. Ed. 2d 984 (2003). The Court in *Chavez* had ruled that the Self-Incrimination Clause was not violated until the government sought to introduce a defendant's self-incriminating statements. Justice Thomas noted that the clause "contains its own exclusionary rule," which supported "a strong presumption against expanding the *Miranda* rule any further." The introduction of physical evidence based on Patane's voluntary statement to the detective simply did not implicate his right not to testify against himself at trial. In so ruling, Thomas rejected the application of the Fourth Amendment's "fruit of the poisonous tree" doctrine. This doctrine mandates that when police illegally search and seize evidence, any additional evidence that is based on this tainted evidence cannot be used as well.

Justice ANTHONY KENNEDY, in a separate opinion joined by Justice SANDRA DAY O'CONNOR, concurred in the **judgment**. Justice Kennedy concluded that the government's case was stronger for admitting the evidence "obtained as a result of Patane's unwarned statement" than in previous cases permitting the introduction of incriminating statements. The introduction of "nontestimonial physical fruits (the Glock in question)" did not "run the risk of admitting into trial an accused's coerced incriminating statements against himself." However, these two justices declined to join Thomas's more sweeping conclusion that the Self Incrimination Clause was not implicated in cases involving physical evidence.

Justice DAVID SOUTER, in a dissenting opinion joined by Justices JOHN PAUL STEVENS, RUTH BADER GINSBURG and STEPHEN BREYER, contended that the decision gave "an evidentiary advantage to those who ignore *Miranda* and gave an "important inducement for interrogators to ignore the rule in that case." He acknowledged that a rule which excluded physical evidence obtained in violation of *Miranda* would allow some criminals to go free but "the FIFTH AMENDMENT is worth a price." Justice Stephen Breyer wrote a separate **dissent**, stating that he would extend the **fruit of the poisonous tree** doctrine to Fifth Amendment cases.

Two-Stage Interrogation Technique Violates Fifth Amendment

Law enforcement officers have chafed under the restrictions imposed by the Supreme Court in *Miranda v. Arizona*, 384 U.S. 436, 86 S.Ct. 1602, 16 L.Ed.2d 694 (1966). Reading suspects their Miranda warnings upon their arrest can discourage suspects from cooperating and confessing to their crimes. Over time police have developed a two-stage interrogation technique in which investigators interview a suspect without advising the suspect of her Miranda rights. Once the suspect gives incriminating statements the police briefly adjourn the session before "Mirandizing" the suspect and then asking her to repeat the incriminating statements. The suspect, unaware that the first statement would be inadmissible, waives these rights and repeats the incriminating statements. Courts admitted the statements made at the second stage. However, the Supreme Court in *Missouri v. Seibert*, __ U.S. __, 124 S.Ct., __ L.Ed.2d __ 2004 WL 1431864(2004), ruled that this two-stage method violated *Miranda*. The **plurality** decision left open the possibility that such a two-stage interrogation might be proper if more time elapsed between the two interviews and police had not "calculated" to evade *Miranda*.

Patrice Siebert's 12-year old son Jonathan, who had cerebral palsy, died in his sleep. Siebert, fearing that local authorities would charge her with neglect, hatched a plot with two of her teenage sons and two of their friends to burn the family's mobile home. The fire would incinerate her son so as to disguise the real cause of death. In addition, they agreed to have the fire kill a mentally ill teenager living with them to avoid the appearance that Jonathan had been left unattended. Seibert's son Darian and a friend set the fire, which killed the teenager. Five days later police arrested Patrice Siebert and took her to the Rolla, Missouri police station. The arresting officer had been told not to advise Siebert of her Miranda rights. Once at the police station an officer questioned Siebert for 40 minutes and persuaded her to admit that they had planned to kill the teenager. At that point the officer adjourned the session for a 20-minute coffee and cigarette break.

When the questioning resumed the officer turned on a tape recorder, advised Siebert of her rights and obtained a signed waiver of rights from her. He walked her through the questions he had asked before and Siebert again made incriminating statements tying her to the **murder**. Charged with murder, Siebert challenged the admission of her statements. The trial court suppressed the pre-warning statement but admitted the statements she made after being Mirandized.

Convicted of second-degree murder, Siebert challenged the admission of her statements at trial. The Missouri Court of Appeals rejected her claims but the Missouri Supreme Court ruled that none of her statements should have been admitted. The court reasoned that the second statement was the product of an invalid first statement. The U.S. SUPREME COURT agreed to hear the state's **appeal** because the federal circuit courts of appeal had divided over the constitutionality of the two-stage interrogation method.

The Supreme Court, in a 5-4 decision, ruled that the Siebert's post-warning statement was inadmissible despite the Miranda warnings given to her before she made the incriminating statements. Justice DAVID SOUTER, writing for a plurality that included Justices JOHN PAUL STEVENS, RUTH BADER GINSBURG, and STEPHEN BREYER, examined whether these Miranda warnings, when linked with the pre-warning questions and admissions, were effective in advising Siebert about her post-warning rights. The totality of the circumstances from Siebert's point of view indicated that the warnings were ineffective. The interrogation took place at the police station, the questioning was "systematic, exhaustive, and managed with psychological skill," and the prewarning statements incriminated Siebert almost completely. Another damaging fact was the officer's failure to correct Siebert's likely misimpression that her pre-warning statements would be used against her. Justice Souter concluded that the two-stage interrogation method was far different from a "good-faith *Miranda* mistake." The Court refused to endorse a method that was "draining the substance out of *Miranda*."

Justice ANTHONY KENNEDY provided the fifth vote needed to sustain the decision, but he filed a separate opinion in which he endorsed a "narrower test." A post-warning statement was admissible "unless the **deliberate** two-step strategy was employed." If this strategy had been used the confession might still be admissible if it could be shown that "a reasonable person in the suspect's situation would understand the import and effect of the *Miranda* warning and of the *Miranda* waiver."

Justice SANDRA DAY O'CONNOR, in a dissenting opinion joined by Chief Justice WILLIAM REHNQUIST and Justices ANTONIN SCALIA and CLARENCE THOMAS, argued that the post-warning statements should be admissible if they were voluntary.

Patrice Seibert, convicted of the murder of her 12-year-old son.

MURDER

The unlawful killing of another human being without justification or excuse.

Baylor University Basketball Player Allegedly Slain by Teammate

In July 2003, former Baylor University (Texas) basketball player Carlton Dotson was arrested and charged with the **murder** of his ex-teammate and roommate, Patrick Dennehy. Dotson's arrest cast further scandal upon Baylor, which was already reeling from serious National College Athletic Association (NCAA) charges relating to the recruitment and retention of Dennehy.

The body of Dennehy was found in a gravel pit near Waco, Texas, on July 25. He had been missing for six weeks. His Chevrolet Tahoe vehicle, stripped of its license plates, had previously been found in a Virginia parking lot.

From the outset, police held out hope that Dennehy would be found alive. The investigation focused on his teammates as "potential witnesses" and/or "persons of interest." Of key interest was Dotson, who was particularly close to Dennehy and often was seen with him. In early July, a friend of Dennehy's advised police that both Dotson and Dennehy may have bought guns. Later, a police informant told investigators that Dotson had told a cousin that he and Dennehy had gone to shoot guns on some property approximately twenty-one miles north of the campus. According to the informant, an argument ensued between the two men, and Dennehy pointed the gun at Dotson's head. According to the informant, Dotson said he then shot Dennehy in the head. Dotson cooperated with the police, but did not admit to any involvement in Dennehy's death. An autopsy report showed that Dennehy had been shot twice in the head.

Dotson, a former high school basketball star, was arrested by local police in his home state of Maryland four days before Dennehy's body was found. The arrest was premised upon an **affidavit** signed by the police informant.

A McLennan County (Texas) **grand jury** had indicted Dotson for the murder, and Texas Governor Rick Perry formally requested Dotson's extradition to stand trial for Dennehy's death. Maryland Governor Robert Erlick, Jr., then signed an extradition warrant in September 2003. Dotson had been held without bail in Chestertown, Maryland, **pending** the extradition decision. Trial was set for August 2004.

Concurrent with the pending criminal case, Dennehy's father, Patrick Dennehy, Sr., filed a civil suit in a Houston court for **wrongful death**. The suit essentially alleged that Baylor officials had ignored Dennehy's attempt to expose wrongdoing in the basketball program, and that coaches had attempted to cover up threats of violence made to Dennehy, which also contributed to his death. Defendants included the Baylor Board of Regents, Baylor basketball coach Dave Bliss, former athletic director Tom Stanton, and Baylor's associate athletic director for compliance, Paul Bradshaw. The suit was filed in Houston, but moved to the 19th State District Court in Waco after a judge ruled that the former location would inconvenience sixty-five witnesses, most of whom were from McLennan County.

In February 2004, all seven counts in the senior Dennehy's lawsuit were dismissed. The suit had included charges of wrongful death, negligence, misrepresentation, civil **conspiracy**, breach of contract, and **fraud**. The final dismissed **count** had alleged that "violent threats" were made against Dennehy when he tried to expose Baylor wrongdoing in the basketball program.

Meanwhile, Dennehy's girlfriend, Jessica De La Rosa, had apparently told officials at her school (University of New Mexico) that Baylor coaches had given Dennehy a large cash payment and that a basketball staff member had paid for limousine airport service for her. The school investigated and contacted the NCAA.

In February 2004, Baylor school officials released the results of their internal investigation. The in-house committee concluded that then-coach Dave Bliss wrongfully paid Dennehy's tuition, as well as that of another player. Bliss then lied to university investigators when questioned. They further found that coaches had provided for meals, transportation, lodging, and clothing for other recruits and athletes. Bliss also solicited money from at least seventeen school boosters, a violation of NCAA rules.

Following the committee's report, Baylor took several actions to rectify and prevent further abuses and wrongdoing. This included the setting of new limitations on the number of coaches who could recruit off campus and the number of recruit visits to Waco. The school initiated a self-imposed probationary period through August 2006. It also reduced the number of scholarships for the next two seasons. A new drug-testing procedure was implemented, and there was to be no postseason play for the 2004-2005 season. The NCAA was free to either accept Baylor's internal sanctions or impose additional penalties on its own.

Robert Blake Trial

Actor Robert Blake, best known for his role as "Baretta" in a 1970s television series of the same name, was arrested and held without bail in 2002 for the **murder** of his wife, Bonny Lee Bakley. In addition to criminal charges, he faced charges stemming from a **wrongful death** civil suit filed by Bakley's family. The criminal trial was repeatedly delayed or postponed because of turnover in Blake's legal representation and his difficulty in securing new **counsel**.

On the evening of May 4, 2001, Blake and his wife dined at a favorite Italian restaurant in Los Angeles. They then walked one and a half blocks to his car. According to Blake, he realized he had left his gun inside the restaurant, and he left Bakley in the car while he returned to the restaurant. When he came back to the car, he found his wife shot dead. A different gun—the murder weapon—was later recovered from a trash dumpster just a few feet from the vehicle.

Although Bakley had a sordid past, Blake was an early suspect in the murder. Apparently, no one in the restaurant recalled him retrieving anything; they do remember him coming in, appearing flustered, asking for a glass of water, then walking out of the restaurant again. One patron recalled seeing Blake vomiting in the men's restroom earlier that night. Further, it was Blake's habit to appear at the restaurant without having made reservations. He would then have a valet park his car and sit at the same table. Suspiciously, on the night of the murder, Blake called ahead for reservations, requested a different table, and parked his car a block and a half away behind a dumpster that was placed in front of a construction site.

It was well known that Blake and Bakley shared a marriage of convenience. The two had married only after DNA established that Blake was the father of Bakley's youngest child, a daughter they named Rose. Shortly after the murder, Bakley's brother told Memphis news reporters that Blake had threatened his sister many times, telling her that he "already had a bullet with her name on it."

Almost eleven months after Bakley's death, police arrested Blake and his residential handyman, Earle Caldwell, whom Blake had said was hired as a bodyguard to protect Bakley. Both were charged with **conspiracy** in the death of Bakley, but Blake was accused of pulling the trigger. Blake was also charged with two counts of solicitation to commit murder. These charges were based on statements of two former "Baretta" stuntmen who claimed that Blake had offered them money to kill his wife. Prosecutors alleged that Blake and Caldwell had plotted the murder months in advance, originally planning to take Bakley on a road trip and kill her between Arizona and California. Police found a list of supplies that Caldwell had prepared, which included old rugs, a sledgehammer, Draino, duct tape, pool acid, and a notation to "get blank gun ready."

In early 2003, while awaiting trial, Blake insisted on being interviewed by television personalities such as Diane Sawyer and Barbara Walters. This ostensibly cost him his first two attorneys, Harland Braun Jennifer Keller. Blake's third attorney, Thomas Mesereau, threatened leave his client if Blake continued to speak out.

During a **preliminary hearing** in February 2003, an audio-recorded tape was presented, secretly recorded by Bakley, in which Blake accused her of "double-crossing" him by becoming pregnant. This was followed with testimony by a stuntman alleging that Blake had offered him $10,000 to murder his wife. Other evidence included "suspicious activity" bank reports showing that Blake withdrew $126,000 from his accounts in the six months prior to his wife's death. On March 13, 2003, Superior Court Judge Lloyd Nash ruled that Blake would stand trial for murder, solicitation, conspiracy, and a special circumstance of "lying in wait." He was released on $1.5 million bail. Trial was scheduled for October 2003, but it was later rescheduled for February 2004.

In October 2003, conspiracy charges against Blake and Caldwell were dropped. In December, the court ruled that the civil case against Blake was to be delayed until after the criminal case. But in February 2004, Blake's defense attorney, Thomas Mesereau, Jr., was granted his **petition** to withdraw as counsel, citing "irreconcilable differences" with Blake. This resulted in yet another postponement of trial. As *CourtTV* reporter John Springer put it, "California's law schools turn out some great trial lawyers. And actor Robert Blake seems bent on meeting all of them, one at a time."

In March 2004, Blake appeared in court with his new counsel, M. Gerald Schwartzbach. The criminal trial was scheduled for September 2004, with the civil trial following thereafter. As of March, prosecutors still lacked **direct evidence** linking the murder weapon to Blake."

Malvo and Muhammad Convicted of Murder in Sniper Shootings

Separate juries in Virginia convicted John Allen Muhammad and Boyd Lee Malvo of **murder** and related crimes. Muhammad and Malvo are the snipers who terrorized residents in the Washington, D.C., area, including Maryland and Virginia, from September 14 to October 22, 2002. Muhammad was sentenced to death, but a jury recommended that Malvo serve a life sentence without parole.

Muhammad and Malvo are believed to be responsible for the death of thirteen people, along with the **injury** of six more, in a series of random shootings. In addition to victims in Maryland, Virginia, and Washington, D.C., they also injured or killed people in Alabama, Georgia, and Louisiana. Authorities said Malvo and Muhammad went on their killing spree as a way to extort $10 million from the United States government.

Virginia won the right to try the men first. The trials were moved to Virginia Beach and Chesapeake, Virginia, to allay concerns that an **impartial** jury could not be found nearer the crime scenes. Virginia was given the first opportunity to put Malvo on trial partly because the state permits the death penalty for defendants who were sixteen or seventeen when the crimes were committed—most states do not allow the death penalty for minors. Malvo was seventeen-years-old when he and Muhammad went on their fatal shooting spree.

The forty-two-year-old Muhammad was found **guilty** of four counts in his November 2003 trial. Initially, Muhammad sought to represent himself, but he changed his mind shortly after the trial began. The jury deliberated for just over six hours before reaching its decision.

Muhammad was convicted for the capital murder of Dean Harold Meyers. Muhammad was also convicted on another **count** that carried a possible death penalty; he became the first person convicted under a **statute** passed after September 11, 2001, for killings designed to terrorize the public. In addition, he was convicted of **conspiracy** to commit murder, as well as use of a firearm during a **felony**. Meyers, who was a Vietnam veteran, was shot with a high-powered rifle as he filled his car with gas at a service station in Manassas, Virginia, on October 9, 2002. He died of a single gunshot to his head.

Muhammad's trial lasted three weeks. The trial included grisly details from the shooting of Meyers, as well as from victims and witnesses to other shootings. Prosecutors presented ballistics evidence that showed the .223-caliber rifle found in Muhammad's car was used in the shootings. They also presented evidence to show how the defendants' 1990 Chevrolet Caprice automobile had been transformed into a "killing machine" by cutting a hole in the trunk, so that a person could sight and fire a rifle through it.

Prosecutors did not focus on proving that Muhammad actually shot Meyers. They contended that whoever pulled the trigger was **irrelevant**. Instead, they described Muhammad as the "captain" of the "killing team."

When jurors moved on to the penalty phase of the trial, they were presented with the issue of whether or not Muhammad presented a future danger or whether his crimes demonstrated a "depravity of mind." A finding of either factor meant the death penalty could be imposed.

Jurors deliberated less than six hours before recommending that Judge LeRoy Millette, Jr., impose the death penalty on Muhammad. After the trial, some of the jurors commented that they were bothered by what appeared to be Muhammad's complete lack of remorse.

Muhammad was sentenced on March 9, 2004. Although the judge could have reduced Muhammad's sentence to life in prison, he declined to do so. At the sentencing, Muhammad claimed he "had nothing to do with this." Judge Millette said he had reviewed the jury's recommendation and agreed with their conclusion that Muhammad would be a "continuing, serious threat to society" if he were permitted to live. Millette set the execution for October 14, 2004. However, the Virginia Supreme Court automatically reviews all death sentences, and other appeals will likely delay the execution for years.

In a separate trial, eighteen-year-old Lee Boyd Malvo (also known as John Lee Malvo) was convicted in December 2003 for the death of Linda Franklin. Malvo was convicted of shooting Franklin, an FBI analyst, in the parking lot of a Home Depot in Falls Church, Virginia. She was killed on October 14, 2002. Like Muhammad, Malvo was also convicted of a count of capital murder for a death that was intended to terrorize the public.

The defense painted Malvo as a victim of a mental illness known as dissociative disorder. The defense contended Muhammad had brainwashed Malvo and caused this condition. The defense introduced evidence to show that Muhammad was a father figure to Malvo. They argued that Muhammad manipulated the young man to do his bidding. The defense tried to establish that Malvo was Muhammad's puppet and that he was unable to tell right from wrong.

In light of the chilling evidence presented by the prosecution, the defense tactics were not enough to plant **reasonable doubt** in the minds of the jury, During Malvo's six-week trial, jurors heard two confessions on tape in which Malvo laughed and bragged about the killings. On one tape, he said, "I intended to kill them all." Malvo initially claimed that he was the gunman for all the shootings, although he later claimed that Muhammad had fired all the shots except in the final shooting.

After convicting Malvo, the jury rejected the prosecution's request for the death penalty. Instead, they recommended that Malvo spend the remainder of his life in prison. The decision came on December 23, 2003. On March 10, 2004, Malvo was sentenced to life in prison without the possibility of parole. By law, Judge Jane Marum Roush could not impose the death penalty.

Both Malvo and Muhammad could face more charges, not only in Virginia, but also other jurisdictions.

Millionaire Acquitted of Murder After Bizarre Aftermath of Neighbor's Death

In a dramatic ending to a bizarre trial involving alleged **identity theft**, cross-dressing disguises, and dismemberment, multimillionaire **defendant** Robert Durst was acquitted of the **murder** of his neighbor, Morris Black, whose body he admitted cutting up and throwing into Galveston

Bay. It was a decision that stunned the public, legal experts, and apparently Durst himself.

In 2000, Robert Durst, heir to a $2 billion Manhattan real estate fortune, was under renewed scrutiny over the mysterious disappearance of his first wife, Kathie, in 1982. Durst was also suspected of having a connection to the unsolved murder of a close friend, crime writer Susan Berman, who was found shot to death in her home on Christmas Eve of 2000.

Durst, whose personal quirks and eccentricities were well-documented among friends and acquaintances, claimed that he was trying to escape media hounding over the investigation into Kathie Durst's disappearance when he settled in a low-rent apartment building in Galveston, Texas. There, he posed as a mute woman, wearing a wig and communicating using handwritten notes, using the name of an old classmate of his. Seventy-one year-old Morris Black lived next door to Durst. On September 30, 2001, a boy fishing with his family found Black's headless, limbless torso floating in the bay. Trash bags recovered from nearby waters contained Black's limbs, as well as a gun, drop cloths, and tools used in the dismemberment. The head was never recovered. Durst was apprehended on a Texas highway and arrested for murder. His current wife posted bond and his **arraignment** was set for October 13, 2001. Durst did not appear for his hearing. He rented a car in Alabama using Morris Black's license, shaving his head and eyebrows to more closely resemble a seventy-one year-old man (Durst was sixty at the time). Durst was eventually arrested in Pennsylvania in late November after attempting to shoplift a sandwich from a supermarket.

Prospects for the defense looked rather bleak. Durst admitted to killing Morris Black and dismembering the body. But he claimed that the killing was a case of self-defense. Durst explained that Black, who was known for his hot temper, had broken into his apartment, picked up a hidden gun, and threatened him with it. In the ensuing struggle, Black was shot in the head. Durst then panicked, believing that suspicions surrounding the disappearance of his wife and the death of Susan Berman would ensure that no one believed his claim of self-defense. The prosecution charged that Durst murdered Black and attempted to steal his identity in order to escape questions about his wife's disappearance.

During the course of the trial, the prosecution could not establish that Durst was lying about his version of events. There were no witnesses to the incident other than Durst himself, and the prosecution could produce no contradictory evidence.

Robert Durst in court, September 2003.

Dick DeGuerin, one of three attorneys on Durst's defense team, commented: "Once we got the jury to concentrate on how Morris Black died and not what happened to his body afterward, it became a much easier case. The prosecution just didn't have the **proof** that Bob Durst voluntarily killed Morris Black."

In other words, the fact that he had dismembered the body, in and of itself, was not proof that he had committed the murder. Prosecution witnesses, on **cross-examination**, were forced to admit that there was nothing in Durst's story to indicate it was untruthful.

Durst's attorneys also seem to have made an wise choice in keeping the defense simple. Durst suffers from Asperger's Syndrome, a mild form of autism that allows the afflicted to function normally, but to have difficulty with human interactions and odd responses to stressful situations. While this could have been used to explain Durst's bizarre actions after the incident, it also would have, the defense team believed, distracted the jury from the central question of lack of compelling evidence.

By keeping the jury focused on this fact, they were able to win acquittal. But Durst is far from being free and clear of legal troubles. In early December of 2003, Durst was ordered held for trial on two counts of **felony** bail-jumping for his earlier flight to Pennsylvania. The bond for each **count** was set at an astronomical $1 billion.

Durst's attorneys have filed complaints that the bond, too much for even Durst to raise, are in violation of the Texas constitution and must be lowered. The judge justified the high bonds by saying that Durst was a proven flight risk and, having admitted to dismembering a body, a danger to the community. A ruling by Texas' 14th Court of Appeals is still **pending**. The hearing for the bail-jumping case is set for June 2004.

On February 11, 2004, Durst was indicted for evidence tampering for cutting up Morris Black's body. Durst's lawyers have called this charge "sour grapes" and are going for a **dismissal** mainly on the grounds that the **statute of limitations** on this charge have expired (the limitation is two years, and 28 months had passed since the deed was done). A ruling on the legality of this charge is also still pending.

A conviction on either bail-jumping charge or the evidence tampering charge each carries a potential ten-year prison sentence. Durst also faces future trouble if charges are eventually filed in either the disappearance of Kathie Durst or the murder of Susan Berman. In June 2004, an appeals court threw out three bond amounts of $1 billion each, ruling the amount to be unconstitutionally excessive.

Parolee Murders Wife, Kids, Days After Release

On a Sunday morning in June 2003, Daniel Franklin entered the Pontiac, Michigan, home of his ex-wife, Machekia Robinson. She lived there with her three daughters—the youngest, Danejah Franklin, age three at the time, by Daniel Franklin, and Taria Johnson, age eight and Rockell Johnson, age ten by a different father.

Police, responding to a neighbor's report, found Machekia and the two elder daughters dead. Franklin had been paroled from prison only five days earlier, where he had been serving time for various drug offenses. As it turned out, he should never have been eligible for parole, but a clerical error allowed his release.

Franklin had a long history of run-ins with the law. Beginning in 1989, when Franklin was still a teenager, he was arrested for drug delivery. He served a short sentence, but was arrested again and charged with drug possession in 1992. In 1994, he was captured after escaping from prison and sentenced to additional time. He was released in May 1998, but that same month he was arrested and charged with delivery of drugs once again. In October 1998, while awaiting sentencing on his latest conviction, he married Robinson. In November 1998 he was sentenced to up to thirty years in prison. Robinson filed for divorce in August 2002. On June 17, 2003, Franklin was released on parole. On the morning of June 22, police, responding to a report of a shooting, found Franklin at the apartment. The bodies of his ex-wife and the two elder daughters were found in their bed, dead of multiple stab wounds to the chest and neck. He had not harmed his own daughter, Danejah, but she had witnessed everything. Franklin was arrested.

Machekia Robinson had reported to a Family Independence Agency caseworker that Daniel Franklin had sent her multiple threatening letters while in prison. The day after he was released, Franklin had an altercation with the manager of the apartment complex where his ex-wife lived, demanding money he claimed he was owed. Later that day, Robinson reportedly told the manager that Franklin had raped and threatened to kill her earlier that day. Despite all of this, police claim that Robinson never reported her experiences directly to them, a statement her family disputes.

Daniel Franklin was arraigned on **murder** charges on June 25, 2003. His hearing was originally set for June 8, but postponed until August 20 on the request of his court-appointed attorney.

On July 16, Michigan state officials admitted that there had been an error, and that Daniel Franklin should have been ineligible for parole until May of 2006. On March 1, 2003, a new law

Daniel Franklin in court during his arraignment on murder charges.

had taken effect that eliminated Michigan's mandatory minimum sentences for drug offenders. Under the new law, some offenders could also be offered early parole. However, if an offender had committed other crimes while on parole or probation for other offenses, they would be automatically ineligible for early release. Due to this stipulation, Daniel Franklin was not eligible for early parole. Somewhere in the process of filing the paperwork, this fact was overlooked and Franklin received the wrong classification. After the admission of the error, Corrections Chief Patricia Caruso issued a public apology to the Robinson family;

"I would like to offer my condolences ... There is no policy change or **audit** that will bring them back, but I am committed to ensuring that the error that occurred on this file will never happen again."

On September 16th, Franklin was ordered to stand trial on three counts of first-degree murder. Franklin pleaded not **guilty** to the charges. A trial date remains **pending**. One of the most pressing questions regarding the trial is whether or not Danejah will be asked to testify against her own father. While she was only three and a half at the time of the murders, she is described as being intelligent and well spoken. A statement she gave to **forensic** examiners one day after the killings is both detailed and graphic;

"My mom and sisters got killed. Daddy got a knife from the kitchen and stabbed my mom, Rockell and Taria. Rockell asked if they could say good-bye to their mother, and he said no and killed them."

There are no hard and fast rules for using very young children's testimony in court. Much depends on how well the child is able to communicate. There are also concerns about forcing a child to relive the details of a traumatic experience. In these cases, special measures may be taken to protect the child, such as having testimony given through closed-circuit television systems so that the child does not have to face the accused. These systems also allow the child to be questioned in a more informal way, without the pressures of the courtroom surroundings.

On May 11, 2004, Franklin was convicted on three counts of first degree murder. Franklin was sentenced to life in prison without parole. The Robinson family was planning a lawsuit against the Michigan Department of Corrections for their error in releasing Franklin too early.

Washington's Green River Serial Killer Sentenced to 48 Life Terms

In December 2003, Gary Ridgway was sent to prison for the rest of his life for the **murder** of 48 women near Seattle, Washington. Ridgway received 48 consecutive life terms with no possibility of early release or parole. He received the life sentences **in lieu of** the death penalty when he agreed to cooperate with prosecutors. Ridgway confessed to more murders than any other serial killer in U.S. history.

In mid-July 1982, children at play found the first victim, 16-year old Wendy Coffield, in the Green River. A month later, four more women's bodies were found in or near the Green River. Police then set up a task force to hunt for what they suspected was a serial killer, nicknamed the Green River killer. By April 1983, Gary Leon Ridgway attracted police attention as a potential suspect. He admitted he dated prostitutes from the area where the women disappeared, but denied killing any of the women. Ridgway took a polygraph test in May 1984, and apparently passed.

By late 1984, the suspected death toll had climbed to more than 40 women. In 1987, police executed a search warrant on Ridgway's house and vehicles. They also took some body samples from Ridgway. They were unable to find evidence to connect him to the slayings.

By the early 1990s, the Green River serial killer case seemed dead. Authorities had sifted through thousands of suspects and spent more than $15 million, but were unable to charge anyone with the murders. Finally, however, technological advances gave investigators the break they needed. In late 1999, using new DNA testing, authorities were able to identify the remains of a woman who had been found near the Green River in 1986. The woman was identified as Tracy Wilson. Wilson had disappeared in 1983 when she was 19.

New DNA testing methods linked Ridgway to the slayings, and in November 2001, he was arrested in connection with four murders. Authorities claimed that DNA test results connected Ridgway to three of the four women. Ridgway entered a plea of not **guilty** in December.

Investigators worked to connect Ridgway to more of the murders, and in March 2003, he was charged with the aggravated murder of three more women. He pled not guilty to these charges as well. Authorities claimed they linked Ridgway to the crimes because of microscopic amounts of paint dust on the women's clothing. Ridgway was a truck painter.

Gary Ridgway, escorted to his sentencing in December 2003.

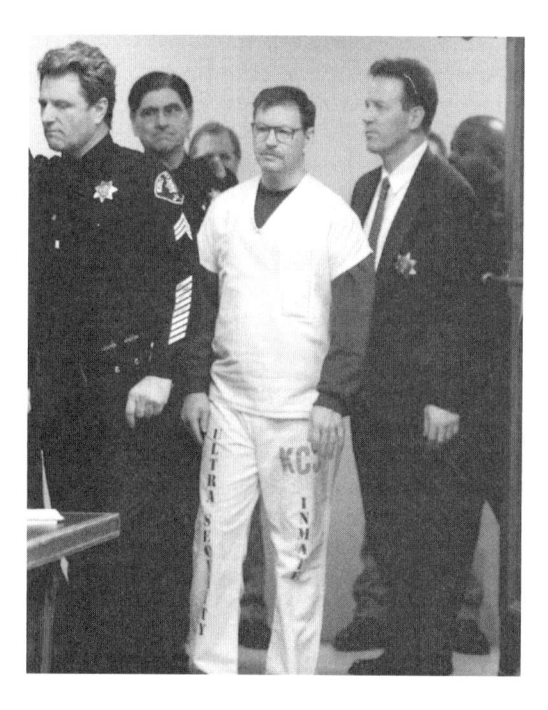

In mid-2003, Ridgway, still in custody, began to cooperate with investigators in return for a plea agreement that would spare him from the death penalty. Some of the information he provided led investigators to charge him with murders that had not yet been attributed to the Green River killer.

Ridgway entered a plea of guilty to 48 counts of murder on November 5, 2003. He provided details of the murders in his written statement entered with his guilty plea. He had a plan, and that plan was "to kill as many women I thought were prostitutes as I could." Ridgway admitted he usually did not know the names of the women when he murdered them. He said he had a hard time remembering their faces, and that, "I killed so many women I have a hard time keeping them straight."

According to his statement, Ridgway said he picked prostitutes for his victims because he hated prostitutes and because he did not want to pay them for sex. Moreover, prostitutes were "easy to pick up without being noticed. I knew they would not be reported missing right away, and might never be reported missing. I picked prostitutes because I thought I could kill as many of them as I wanted without getting caught."

Most of the women were killed in Ridgway's home. He also killed a significant number of them in his truck. All of the women were strangled to death. He told the court that he took the jewelry and clothing from the bodies before disposing of them to make them harder to identify. He then placed the bodies in groups that he called "clusters." These clusters were usually located near some landmark so that he could remember the location. He testified he liked to drive around the county past his clusters so that he could think about the women he killed.

Ridgway was sentenced in December 2003. Pursuant to the plea agreement between the prosecution and the defense, King County Superior Court Judge Richard A. Jones imposed 48 consecutive life sentences on Ridgway, age 54. The judge called Ridgway an "emissary of death" and made him turn around to face the families and friends of victims crowding the court gallery. He told Ridgway, "As you spend the balance of your life in your cell in prison, much of which will probably be in solitary confinement, I truly hope that the last thoughts you have of the free world are the faces of the people in this courtroom."

The judge's sentence came after hours of emotional testimony by the victims' families. The emotions expressed ran the gamut from rage at Ridgway to criticism of police for the investigation that took two decades, and to anger with prosecutors for not pushing for the death penalty. A small number of those testifying said they forgave Ridgway.

Ridgway read a short statement at the sentencing to apologize for his actions, but most victims' family members later said they did not believe him. Dave Reichert, the sheriff who had investigated the case from the start, also said he did not believe Ridgway. Reichert said he believed Ridgway enjoyed all the attention he received.

Police Arrest Suspect in Ohio Sniper Case

One year after the nation was terrified by the sniper shootings carried out by John Muhammad and Lee Malvo in Washington, D.C., residents of Columbus, Ohio, faced yet another sniper. An assailant fired twenty-four shots along several highways near Columbus during 2003 and 2004. One woman was killed in the shooting spree. The man suspected of carrying out the shootings, Charles A. McCoy, Jr., was captured in Las Vegas, Nevada, in March 2004. The arrest ended a ten-month reign of terror.

In May 2003, police in Columbus received a report of gun shots fired on Interstate 270. Several months later, authorities received several other reports of shots discharged in the same general area. The shots were fired at different times of the day and were apparently aimed at vehicles. Bullets broke windows and caused flat tires on several of the vehicles that were hit. Among the vehicles struck was a UPS delivery truck.

In November 2003, a shot fired by the sniper hit a driver's door and struck the passenger in the vehicle. The passenger, Gail Knisley, was killed by the shot. Authorities tested the bullet that hit Knisley with another discovered after a different shooting. The two bullets matched, confirming suspicion that a serial shooter was involved. Several other bullets from other shootings had been discovered in various vehicles, as the shooter had apparently missed the drivers of those vehicles by a matter of inches.

Immediately following Knisley's **murder**, extra patrols were stationed along the interstate, which is known as the Jack Nicklaus Highway after the famous golfer. The area along the motorway was reportedly sparsely populated and frequented by hunters. Just hours after the shooting that killed Knisley, yet another bullet struck a truck on a highway that intersects I-270.

Police officers continued their investigation, but incidents continued to occur. In February 2004, a shot broke the windshield of a minivan, though this shooting took place roughly fifteen miles south of the other shootings. Ballistics tests confirmed that the bullet that struck the van matched the bullets used in other shootings.

About one week later, authorities received their first lead when the culprit was spotted two times on the same day on different highway overpasses. The shots fired in these instances struck the hoods of a van and an automobile. Witnesses provided a general description of the suspect and of the suspect's vehicle. The news prompted a heightened state of alert in Ohio, as police hot lines received hundreds of tips regarding the shootings. Officers were stationed along highways, and agents used infrared devices to determine whether a sniper could be prowling near the highways. The scope of the area in which the sniper attacked continued to grow, with some shots being fired as far away as forty miles south of Columbus. The fright among residents near Columbus continued through March 2004, when a bullet was discovered in the siding of a house south of the city. The house was located slightly more than a mile from a bridge in which the shooter had previously fired at an automobile.

Alleged Ohio sniper Charles McCoy, Jr., right, confers with his lawyer during his preliminary hearing in March 2004.

Just weeks after the last shooting, a resident of Las Vegas, Nevada, Conrad Malsom, allegedly spotted McCoy in a sports bar while reading the newspaper *USA Today*, which featured a story about and photograph of McCoy. McCoy was apparently staying at a budget motel near the Las Vegas strip. Malsom made repeated attempts to call 911, but was transferred several times before the operator agreed to send officers to the hotel. Officers finally apprehended McCoy after making a positive identification on March 17. Days later, McCoy was extradited to Ohio, where he was charged with the twenty-four shootings and the murder of Knisley.

Several stories about the arrest arose during the weeks that followed McCoy's arrest. Some questioned the reasons why Malsom had to call 911 nearly a dozen times before finally persuading a dispatcher to send officers. Later, investigators discovered that McCoy was not present in the sports bar where Malsom said he saw McCoy. According to reports, Malsom confused McCoy with a tourist from Wisconsin who is considerably taller and heavier than McCoy.

Despite the unusual circumstances surrounding the arrest, most attention focused on charges brought against McCoy. On April 1, 2004, a **grand jury** in Franklin County, Ohio, returned a twenty-four-count indictment against McCoy that included one **count** for aggravated murder. If convicted, McCoy could face the death sentence. McCoy previously has been diagnosed with paranoid schizophrenia, and his lawyers have requested state funds to hire mental health professionals to determine whether McCoy is **competent** to stand trial. McCoy's attorneys have also asked the court for funds to hire a private investigator to review the information regarding the alleged shootings. McCoy has pleaded not **guilty** to the charges. In July 2004, McCoy was ruled fit to stand trial despite his schizophrenia, as he was able to communicate with his lawyers and understood the nature of the charges against him. McCoy's trial is set to begin in January 2005.

Scott Peterson Trial

In April 2003, the body of a full-term male baby washed ashore in the San Francisco Bay area. The following day, the badly decomposed body of a woman was found in the water nearby. DNA tests confirmed the bodies as those of twenty-seven-year-old Laci Peterson and her unborn son, Conner. **Forensic** scientists speculated that the infant could have been expelled from his mother's womb by gases created in the decomposition process. Laci Peterson had been missing since December 24, 2002, and her whereabouts had become the subject of police and private citizen searches, as well as mass media attention. By January 2003, rising suspicions surrounding her disappearance eclipsed all other national news, including that of the war in Iraq.

From the onset of his wife's disappearance, Scott Lee Peterson had been of interest to police. Peterson told detectives that he had last seen his wife at 9:30 a.m. on December 24, 2002, at which time he had left home for a solo fishing trip near Berkeley, about an hour and a half away. According to Peterson, his wife planned to go shopping and then take their golden retriever for a walk in the local East La Loma Park. When Peterson returned that night, he told investigators that he found her gone, though her purse and cell phone were still in the house. A neighbor told detectives that she had spotted the Peterson's dog running loose about 10:00 a.m., and had locked the dog in the Peterson's gated backyard.

Thousands of citizens joined police in conducting searches through woods, ditches, rivers, and farms across central and northern California. The family raised a $500,000 reward, to no avail. Concerns over Scott Peterson's behavior and conduct mounted. A local newspaper noted his smiles and laughs during a somber vigil for his wife. A neighbor told detectives she had seen Peterson loading something heavy into his truck around the time his wife disappeared. Investigators also noted that even before his wife's body was found, Peterson had sold her SUV to purchase a truck, and he reportedly had contacted real estate persons about selling the house. At a **preliminary hearing** in Modesto, a police detective testified that police found a homemade anchor, made with cement, on Peterson's boat. News of other missing homemade anchors, as well as empty bags of cement, continued to surface in various media reportings.

Approximately three weeks into the investigation, police revealed that Peterson had been having an affair with another woman, and had taken out an insurance policy on his wife. Peterson granted a rare interview, calling the allegations "a pack of lies." Unfortunately for Peterson, the other woman, Amber Frey, voluntarily came forward and identified herself to Modesto, California, police. She stated that Peterson had represented to her that he was single. Days later, Peterson granted several television interviews in which he admitted the affair but denied any connection with his wife's disappearance. At that time, he also offered explanations as to why he and his wife had taken out life insurance policies, why the drapes were pulled in the house on Christmas eve morning (when his wife was, ostensibly, last seen by him), and what his neighbor might have seen him loading in his truck.

Laci Peterson's body, as well as that of son Conner, were found approximately three miles from the marina where Peterson told police he had gone fishing. After DNA results were

Scott Peterson in court, January 2004.

known, a **probable cause** warrant for Peterson's arrest was issued on April 17, 2003. He was arrested the next day at a golf course near his parents' home. At the time of his arrest, Peterson was carrying $10,000 cash, the maximum allowable amount that can be transported across the nearby Mexican border without notification to officials. He also had lightened his hair to a reddish-blonde and had grown a beard.

Peterson was held without bail **pending** trial. A criminal complaint filed in Stanislaus County Superior Court contained two counts of **felony murder**. Special allegations contained in the complaint provided prosecutors with the latitude to request the death penalty.

In January 2004, Peterson's trial was again delayed after a change of **venue** was ordered by the Stanislaus County court. Trial was rescheduled in Redwood City, California, which is located near San Jose.

Aspiring Rapper Kills, Partially Eats Roommate

One of the more disturbing **murder** cases of recent years came to a close with the **defendant**, an up-and-coming rap musician, sentenced to consecutive life sentences without possibility of parole.

Antron Singleton, who performed under the stage name of "Big Lurch", had made a name for himself performing with local groups in his native Texas. He moved to the Compton district of Los Angeles to record an album, sharing an apartment with a 21 year-old Tynisha Ysais, a mother of two. Early in the afternoon of April 10, 2002, the police, responding to a tip from a friend of Ysais, found Singleton wandering the streets of his neighborhood, nude and covered with blood. Upon investigation, they found Ysais's mutilated corpse in the apartment, a knife blade broken off in her back, her chest torn open, her lungs partially removed, and teeth marks on her face and internal organs. An exam of Singleton revealed foreign blood and tissue in his stomach. Singleton had seemingly mutilated and partially eaten his roommate. An influence for his behavior was soon found: Ysais's boyfriend admitted that he and Singleton had spent the evening before in the apartment, smoking PCP.

Singleton was charged with Ysais's murder in early June of 2002 and held without bond. He was arraigned on June 13 and ordered to stand trial.

In April of 2003, the victim's mother, Carolyn Stinson, filed a **wrongful death** civil lawsuit against Singleton, Death Row Records, Stress Free records, and two employees of the latter company, identified as Singleton's bodyguard and Ysais's boyfriend. The suit claims that the record labels provided Singleton with PCP "to encourage him to act out in an extreme violent manner" in order to market him as a "gangsta rap" act. Suge Knight, the head of Death Row Records, came forward to point out that his company had never had any contracts or dealings with Singleton. Knight was quoted as saying "I don't know this guy ... nobody from our company knows this guy ... a lot of people ... want to have a production deal ... and they think they have (one) even if they don't." Knight went on to characterize the suit as "slander" and "fraud". Later that week, Stinson's attorney admitted that their information was erroneous. Death Row Records and Suge Knight were dropped from the suit. The suit, which is still **pending**, will go ahead against the other named parties.

Singleton entered a plea of not **guilty**, then changed the plea to not guilty by reason of insanity, saying that he was affected by the PCP and not in his right mind when the acts were committed. The trial on murder and aggravated **mayhem** charges began in June 2003 and lasted for two weeks. After closing arguments were presented, the jury needed only one hour of deliberation before returning a **verdict** of guilty on both charges, including a special circumstance of torture perpetrated on the victim.

The same jury reconvened on June 25 to consider the question of Singleton's sanity. The jury is normally charged with making the decision on whether a defendant was sane or not at the time of a crime. But after the defense had presented their evidence, including evidence of Singleton's drug use, Deputy District Attorney Drew Josfan asked for a **directed verdict** from the judge, citing section 25.5 of the California Penal Code, adopted in 1994. This section is an amendment to laws governing the temporary **insanity defense**, and states,

> "In any criminal proceeding in which a plea of not guilty by reason of insanity is entered, this defense shall not be found by the trier of fact solely on the basis of a personality or adjustment disorder, a **seizure** disorder, or addiction to, or abuse of, intoxicating substances.".

Judge Jack W. Morgan concurred and, citing Singleton's abuse of PCP, issued the directed verdict, declaring that Singleton was sane at the time of the murder. The jury was excused and a sentencing date was set for November. On November 7, 2003, Singleton was sentenced to life in prison without parole. Judge Morgan also issued an additional consecutive life sentence, citing the special circumstances of aggravated mayhem and torture.

Legendary Record Producer Charged with Murder of Actress

Rock and Roll Hall of Fame member Phil Spector was arrested on February 3, 2003, for the **murder** of Lana Clarkson. The forty-year-old actress was found dead, the victim of a gunshot wound to the head, in the foyer of Spector's Alhambra, California, mansion.

Police were alerted by Spector's driver, Adriano Desouza, who called 911 around 5:00 a.m. on February 3. Desouza later told police that he had driven Spector and Clarkson from the House of Blues nightclub to Spector's mansion, located east of Los Angeles, earlier that morning. Desouza also told police that shortly after he dropped off the couple, Spector retrieved a briefcase from the limousine. About ninety minutes later, Desouza reported that he heard a single gunshot, followed by Spector coming out of the house holding a gun. He allegedly told Desouza, "I think I just shot her."

When authorities arrived, they found Clarkson dead, her body slumped in a chair. A bloody, .38-caliber Colt revolver was found in the vicinity. In addition, Clarkson's broken teeth were found nearby. Spector stood near the body with his hands in his pockets. According to police, Spector would not show them his hands. Police then subdued Spector with a stun gun.

The sixty-two-year-old Spector was arrested shortly after 6:00 a.m. He was later freed on $1 million bail. Spector hired attorney Robert Shapiro to represent him. Shapiro, who is well known for successfully defending O.J. Simpson on 1995 murder charges, quickly issued a statement contending that Clarkson died from a self-inflicted wound and that Spector was not responsible for her death.

Lana Clarkson starred in a 1985 B-movie titled "Barbarian Queen." She also appeared in movies such as "Scarface," "Fast Times at Ridgemont High," and "Blind Date."

Spector, a long-time record producer, is perhaps best known for creating the "Wall of Sound," which gave early rock 'n' roll a symphonic sound. He is famous for producing the Beatles's final studio album, "Let It Be". During his career, Spector worked with numerous acts, ranging from the Ronettes to the Ramones. He also wrote and recorded a number one song—"To Know Him is to Love Him," with his group, the Teddy Bears—and won two Grammy awards for his work.

Spector was charged with Clarkson's murder on November 18, 2003. The **felony** complaint from Los Angeles County charges that Spector used a handgun to kill Clarkson. The complaint also alleges that the killing was done "with **malice** aforethought." Spector pleaded not **guilty** in an **arraignment** in Alhambra Superior Court.

In early February 2004, in a motion to the trial court, the prosecution demanded that the defense turn over evidence that law enforcement authorities apparently overlooked during their investigation of the crime scene. Prosecutors allege that investigators overlooked a fingernail belonging to Clarkson. Shapiro would not say if any evidence had been found by the defense. He alleged that if evidence had been found by the defense, the defense would not have a duty to turn it over to prosecutors.

Later in February 2004, Spector replace his celebrity lawyer, Robert Shapiro, with another well-known counselor, Leslie Abramson, a long-time criminal defense attorney in California. Abramson gained national fame during the 1990s for twice defending brothers Erik and Lyle Menendez, who had been charbed with the murder of their parents. In the Menendez case,

Phil Spector sits in court during his trial for murder in February 2004.

jurors in the first trial could not reach a decision, though the brothers were convicted in their second trial and sentenced to life without parole.

After taking over Spector's case from Shapiro, Abramson argued in court that the defense has no duty to turn over evidence that prosecutors may have missed. Outside of court, she claimed that the defense did not have the piece of Clarkson's nail. Superior Court Judge Carlos Uranga indicated he would probably require the defense to turn over the evidence. However, he delayed a final decision on the prosecution's motion until after an evidentiary hearing.

Binion Murder Convictions Reversed by Nevada Supreme Court

In July 2003, a divided Nevada Supreme Court overturned the convictions of Sandra Murphy and Rick Tabish in the sensationalized **murder** trial of slain casino mogul, Ted Binion. Murphy, a former stripper, was Binion's live-in girlfriend. Both she and Tabish, a Montana contractor with whom she was having an affair, were tried together and convicted of murdering Binion and stealing millions of dollars in rare coins and silver bars from his estate. Murphy had been sentenced to twenty-two years-to-life in prison. Tabish had received a sentence of twenty-five years-to-life. In ordering new trials for both, the state high court cited reversible error by prosecutors in failing to sever theft and other unrelated charges from the murder charges at the 2000 trial. The court also cited as error—an abuse of discretion—the unrestricted admission of a **hearsay** statement that unfairly prejudiced Murphy's trial. In late October 2003, the court, without comment, rejected the **petition** of prosecutors to re-hear the case.

It had taken nine months of investigation for prosecutors to even piece together a largely circumstantial case against Murphy and Tabish. The April 2000 trial became known as "the largest murder trial to hit South Nevada," and was the first ever trial to be televised live on the Internet.

The fifty-five-year-old Binion suffered from a heroin drug habit that cost him his gaming license in 1987. Nevada officials permanently revoked his license in 1998 following random drug tests that showed continued use; Binion's sister took over casino operations. Following a divorce, as well as the death of his mother, Binion met Murphy in a topless bar, and she moved in with him a few weeks later. Shortly thereafter, Binion hired Tabish to move $5 million in silver bars and rare coins from storage at the casino to an underground vault on Binion's property about sixty miles from Las Vegas. Tabish, a debt-ridden contractor, struck up a friendship with Murphy at that time; the two began spending weekends together. Murphy allegedly found Binion on the bedroom floor of his home in September 1998, with various drug paraphernalia nearby. Coroners initially ruled his death as an accidental overdose. A more thorough autopsy was later conducted, leading to the coroner's conclusion that the death was a homicide resulting from foul play.

In addition to the damaging coroner's opinion at the trial, prosecutors presented as a witness a sheriff's deputy from Pahrump, Nevada. He testified that two days after Binion's death, he came upon three men digging with a backhoe in a deserted lot at 2:00 a.m. One of the men was Tabish. When the men declared that nothing was in their tractor-trailer, the deputy took a casual look and discovered millions of dollars in rare coins and silver. Tabish then told the deputy that Binion had directed him to relocate the bounty to Binion's ranch.

At trial, prosecutors called Binion's attorney, James J. Brown, to the stand. He testified that Binion had contacted him the night before his death and directed that Murphy be removed from his will, "if she doesn't kill me tonight." He also intended to remove her from the house, and he told Brown, "If I'm dead, you'll know what happened."

The jury also heard unrelated evidence that Tabish had extorted, kidnapped, and beaten Leo Casey, with whom Tabish owned a sand pit. The jury ultimately convicted Tabish of charges relating to Casey as well.

In *Nevada v. Murphy, et al*, 119 Nev. Adv. Op 35; 72 P3d 584 (2003), the Nevada Supreme Court overturned the convictions of first-degree murder, **conspiracy**, **robbery**, and **grand larceny** for both defendants. The state high court first ruled that the jury should never have heard evidence about the Casey matter, which should have been the subject of a separate trial against Tabish. The court found this highly prejudicial to Tabish's trial on the other counts. Moreover, the court determined that the jury's hearing of the Casey allegations was especially prejudicial to Murphy as well.

The Nevada Supreme Court also ruled that the trial court had abused its discretion in allowing the hearsay statement of Binion to his attorney without a limiting instruction. Such an instruction would have guided the jury in how much evidentiary weight to give such a statement. The majority opinion noted that, "The prejudicial impact was great: the statement strongly implied Murphy killed Binion."

Four of the seven justices signed the majority opinion. Three justices dissented, believing the convictions should have been upheld. **Severance** of the Casey matter constituted a large portion of the defense **appeal**. However, Tabish remained in prison after the reversal for his conviction of **extortion** with use of a deadly weapon in the beating of Leo Casey, which the high court affirmed.

OBSCENITY

The character or quality of being obscene; an act, utterance, or item tending to corrupt the public morals by its indecency or lewdness.

Texas Woman Charged With Promoting Adult Toys

In late 2003, Joanne Webb, a former elementary school teacher, was charged with criminal **obscenity** for selling sex toys to undercover police agents. Webb was a home representative for Passion Parties, a California-based company that sells sexually-oriented products at residential gatherings similar to Tupperware parties. Following complaints received from a few neighbors in Webb's Ft. Worth, Texas, suburb, two undercover officers posed as a married couple wanting to "spice up" their love life. They visited Webb in October. Webb was not immediately arrested following the sale, but she turned herself in to authorities in November, after learning that a warrant had been issued for her arrest. Webb's violation was deemed a Class A misdemeanor, punishable by up to one year in prison and a $4,000 fine.

Texas law, specifically, Texas Penal Code 43.23, prohibits the sale or promotion of "obscene devices," defined under the law as any which are "designed or marketed as useful primarily for the stimulation of human genital organs." Texas law differs from those in other states in that it expressly includes sex toys—in addition to films, videos, books, photographs, etc.—in its description of material prohibited as **obscene**. Texas law also focuses on the promotion of such items rather than the mere sale. Many adult stores in Texas that sold the same items as Webb had avoided prosecution by labeling the sex toys as "novelties," neither promoting their sale nor suggesting their use.

Webb, an attractive forty-three-year-old mother of three, who is a Baptist churchgoer and a board member of the local Chamber of Commerce, made an unlikely **defendant**. However, police focused on the fact that she not only sold them the devices, but that Webb enthusiastically and explicitly suggested their use. According to prosecutors, it was this "promotion" of the products that offended the law.

In December 2003, Webb's Ft. Worth, Texas, attorney, BeAnne Sisemore, announced plans to challenge the constitutionality of the law. True to her word, Sisemore and her co-counsel, Steven Swander, filed suit in federal district court in February 2004. Plaintiffs in the suit did not include Webb; rather, it included the names of eight other women, who alleged that they had been afraid to have home parties or sell the products as a result of Webb's arrest. The federal suit challenged the Texas law as a violation of the right to sexual **privacy**. The suit also sought injunctive **relief** from the enforcement of the law by Texas authorities during the pendency of the federal suit.

Earlier, in June 2003, the U.S. SUPREME COURT issued a landmark decision in *Lawrence v. Texas,,* 539 U.S. 558, 123 S.Ct. 2472, 156 L.Ed.2d 508 (2003) a ruling which struck down a Texas **sodomy** law. The high court held that the constitutional right of liberty (as part of the liberty granted in the due process **clause**) included the right to "enter into [an intimate relationship] in the confines of their homes and their own private lives." That right also afforded "substantial protection to adult persons in deciding how to conduct their private lives in matters pertaining to sex." Whether Webb could assert that right on behalf of her customers (since her right to use such toys was not **at issue**) awaited **jurisprudence**.

Meanwhile, Webb's criminal trial was scheduled for the summer of 2004. Before the case could come to trial however, Johnson County attorney Bill Moore asked to have the charges dropped, claiming that pursuing the case would be a waste of county money and time, rendering the larger legal question moot for the time being. Webb thanked those who had supported her on her Web site and wrote "I have no doubt this decision was influenced by your comments and e-mails to our various governmental entities on my behalf."

OKLAHOMA CITY BOMBINGS

Trial of Terry Nichols on State Murder Charges

Following a **preliminary hearing** on the matter in May 2003, state District Court Judge Steven Taylor of Pittsburg County, Oklahoma, concluded that Terry Nichols, the federally-convicted co-conspirator in the 1995 Oklahoma City bombings, would stand trial on state **murder** charges stemming from the same incident. Both Nichols and accomplice Timothy McVeigh had been previously convicted in 1997 for the deaths of eight federal agents in the April 19, 1995, bombing of the Alfred E. Murrah Federal Building, which killed 168 persons. McVeigh, a former Army buddy of Nichols, was convicted in federal court of **conspiracy** and murder. He was executed in 2001. Nichols, also convicted on federal charges of conspiracy and **manslaughter**, is serving a life sentence.

The state trial against Nichols, who was charged with 161 state counts of first-degree murder (for the remaining 160 civilian casualties plus one unborn fetus), began in March 2004. It was expected to last four to six months. As in the previous trial, prosecutors intended to portray Nichols as a key player in the Oklahoma bombings, focusing on his loathe for the federal government. The defense **counsel** planned to show Nichols as a loving father who became an unwitting accomplice to a crafty and devious McVeigh.

Trial began with the twelve-member jury—seven men, five women—hearing hours of dry, detailed testimony involving telephone records, receipts for fertilizer, and several barrels and fuses linking Nichols to the bombings. Sales tickets from the Mid Kansas Cooperative Association showed that a man named "Mike Haven" bought a total of four thousand pounds of ammonium nitrate fertilizer (a key bomb ingredient) during a period of several months preceding the bombing. He was the third largest purchaser (behind a local experimental agri-field and a school district) and the only one to pay in cash. Three days after the bombing, FBI agents found a receipt for one two thousand-pound transaction in Nichols's Herrington, Kansas, house. The purchaser listed on the receipt was "Mike Haven." Witness Ruth Haley of Herrington, Kansas, testified that she saw a Ryder truck parked behind Nichols's house one or two days prior to the bombing. An FBI fingerprint examiner found Nichols's fingerprints on several pieces of evidence, including a box containing detonation cord like that used in the bomb. Guns and weapons, cash, a vehicle, and a cigar box filled with jade pieces stolen from a gun dealer, were found in Nichols home and a storage unit leased by him in Las Vegas.

The defense counsel countered with a defense often invoked in the federal trial: that Nichols was not present when the seven thousand pound fertilizer-and-fuel-oil bomb was detonated. The defense intended to portray Nichols as a patsy for a group of conspirators and white supremacists, and to show that Nichols was set up to take the blame for the others. On cross examination of a key prosecution witness who operated a Ryder truck leasing agency, defense counsel introduced its conspiracy theory argument. The defense succeeded in getting the prosecution witness to admit that McVeigh was accompanied by a man other than Nichols when he rented the Ryder truck used in the bombing. The witness further testified that FBI agents attempted to convince him that his memory was faulty.

Then suddenly, on April 14, the trial took an unexepcted turn. The defense counsel filed a motion seeking **dismissal** of the case in its entirety. They accused prosecutors of withholding evidence and information that could be "exculpatory" for Nichols, **i.e.**, tending to support his innocence or mitigate his guilt. Specifically, the motion for dismissal alleged that prosecutors withheld a video, taken approximately three minutes prior to the bomb's detonation, which showed images of suspects leaving the Ryder rental truck that delivered the bomb. The motion also claimed that prosecutors failed to disclose a telephone call made by McVeigh to a group of right-wing extremists in Oklahoma, known as Elohim City, after he rented the truck. Finally, the motion alleged that prosecutors failed to provide documents, previously disclosed in a series of Associated Press stories, which also hinted at the possibility of additional accomplices to the bombing.

However, after full hearing, Judge Taylor refused to dismiss the case. He commented that the defense motion to dismiss was "laced with melodrama and hyperbole, but no substance." He further stated on the record that the court found "absolutely no evidence" that the alleged videotape ever existed. He also disallowed the presentation at trial of any defense theories that other people participated in the planning and execution of the bombing, without some concrete evidence of their involvement. In short, the judge ruled that he would "not dismiss [the case] based on [defense's] speculation and guesswork."

OWNER

The person recognized by the law as having the ultimate control over, and right to use, property as long as the law permits and no agreement or covenant limits his or her rights.

Re-discovered Copy of Bill of Rights Provokes Legal Battle

In 1865, during the final days of the CIVIL WAR, a Union army under General William Tecumseh Sherman sacked Raleigh, North Carolina. One soldier took a souvenir from the state capitol building—a copy of the original Bill of Rights, affixed with the signatures of John and Samuel Adams. This priceless historical document's subsequent journey has culminated in a hotly contested legal battle of state **versus** private ownership of historical relics. After close to 140 years, assuming that the ruling is upheld, North Carolina's Bill of Rights is slated to come home.

North Carolina's Bill of Rights was one of fourteen produced by the First Federal Congress, thirteen of which were sent by George Washington to the nascent states for ratification. After being taken during the CIVIL WAR, the document was sold by the soldier to Charles Shotwell for the sum of $5. In 1925, a documents dealer tried to sell it back to North Carolina. The state refused to pay the price, saying that it would not pay for what it rightfully owned. In 1995, an attorney in Washington, D.C. showed the Bill to North Carolina archivists, saying that if they did not buy it, it would be sold to a party in the Middle East. North Carolina refused again, saying it could not meet the multimillion-dollar price tag. In 2000, noted New England antiques dealer Wayne Pratt and a Connecticut man named Bob Matthews put in equal shares and purchased the Bill from two women, descendents of Shotwell, for the sum of $200,000. Pratt then attempted to sell the Bill to a public institution. One of the museums on his

North Carolina's copy of the Bill of Rights, on display after its recovery in 2003.

list was the National Constitution Center in Philadelphia. The curator there called the police after Pratt offered the document for sale for $5 million. On March 18, 2000, an FBI agent posed as a buyer for the Center and seized the Bill in a sting operation. The document's value had since been assessed at up to $30 million.

Pratt was now the target of a criminal investigation, facing possible charges of transportation of stolen property over state lines. Pratt's attorneys fired back that both his purchase and attempted sale of the document were perfectly legal, since it could be considered spoils of war taken from an (at the time) enemy state and thus had passed out of North Carolina's rightful possession.

The case was set for a September 2003 hearing, but Pratt acted first. Concluding that there was the potential to spend a lot of money on what might well be a losing cause, and making good on his assertion that he had acquired the document with the intention of seeing it preserved in a public institution, Pratt announced that he was relinquishing the document, including all claims to ownership both for himself and for Bob Matthews. Pratt issued a statement, which reads in part:

> ... It was my goal from the beginning to have this critical piece of America's heritage go to a public institution. As it has recently been determined that this particular document was the one that was originally sent to North Carolina, the transfer of the document to that state is all the more appropriate ...

In return, North Carolina dropped its investigation of Pratt. U.S. Attorney Frank Whitney publicly praised Pratt, citing his "good citizenship" at the **dismissal** hearing. The case seemed to be drawing to an amicable and peaceful conclusion.

But on October 21, 2003, Bob Matthews filed suit against various Federal and North Carolina officials in the District Court of Connecticut in New Haven. He alleged that he had never given Pratt the authority to hand over Matthews's share of claim to the document and, in fact, prior to relinquishing claim on it, gave Matthews an additional stake in the ownership, which now constituted a majority share. Matthews's suit sought to recover the Bill or, barring that outcome, to sell it with the profits going to Matthews. The suit also sought to recover attorney's fees and expenses and asked for compensatory and punitive damages. Matthews's lawyers took the same path as Pratt had before, arguing that the Bill was taken from an enemy state as part of the spoils of war. In addition, the plaintiff's attorneys argued that North Carolina had relinquished its claim on the Bill when it left the Union and joined the Confederacy in 1861.

In January 2004, U.S. District Judge Terrence Boyle ruled that, no matter what percentage of supposed ownership Matthews might claim, the Bill was indeed the property of North Carolina. He cited a 1977 Supreme Court ruling that stated that "ownership of a public record does not change even if it is stolen or otherwise removed from a state's possession." Judge Boyle also cited the notations on the Bill's reverse side which expressly identify it as the property of the state.

Matthews appealed the decision, arguing that Boyle did not have jurisdiction to rule in the case. Matthews's suit in Connecticut remained unresolved as of July 2004. North Carolina's copy of the Bill of Rights remains in federal custody **pending** the outcome of the **appeal**.

PARTNERSHIP

An association of two or more persons engaged in a business enterprise in which the profits and losses are shared proportionally. The legal definition of a partnership is generally stated as "an association of two or more persons to carry on as co-owners a business for profit" (Revised Uniform Partnership Act § 101 [1994]).

United States v. Galletti

The U.S. SUPREME COURT, on March 23, 2004, determined that a tax assessment against a partnership extended the **statute of limitations** for collection of taxes not only against the partnership but also against the individual partners. *United States v. Galletti*, 124 S. Ct. 1548 (2004) The decision reversed an opinion from the Ninth **Circuit Court** of Appeals. The decision allows the Internal Revenue Service (IRS) to collect employment taxes, excise taxes, and penalties from partners without having to **assess** the partner's **liability** separately from the partnership.

The Internal Revenue Code (IRC) requires the IRS to make a tax assessment within three years after a tax return is filed. I.R.C. § 6501(a). Once the assessment is made, the IRS must record the liability of the taxpayer with the TREASURY DEPARTMENT. I.R.C. § 6203. The Secretary of the Treasury is required to provide notice to every person that is liable for the unpaid taxes, stating the amount of the tax and demanding payment of the amount due. I.R.C. § 6303(a). If the IRS makes a proper assessment within three years of the filing of the tax return, then the IRC extends the limitations period for collecting taxes to ten years. I.R.C. § 6502.

Abel and Sarah Galletti, along with Francesco and Angela Briguglio, were partners of Marina Cabrillo Partners. The partnership failed to pay federal employment taxes from 1992 through 1995. The IRS then assessed the unpaid taxes against the partnership from 1994 through 1996. The Gallettis filed a **petition** for Chapter 13 **bankruptcy** in October 1999, and the Briguglios filed for bankruptcy on February 2000. In the Galletti case, the IRS filed a **proof** of claim for $395,179 for the unpaid employment taxes. *In re Galletti*, No. LA 99-48587-ER, 2000 WL 1682960 (Bankr. C.D. Cal. Sept. 11, 2000) In the Briguglios' bankruptcy case, the IRS also filed a proof of claim for $427,402.

Though the INTERNAL REVENUE SERVICE had made assessments against the partnership within three years of the dates in which the taxes were due, the IRS did not make assessments against the individual partners. Under California law, partners in a partnership are jointly and severally liable for the debts of the partnership. Nevertheless, both the Gallettis and the Briguglios disputed the claims of the IRS, asserting that the IRS was required to make assessments on the individual partners within three years that the taxes were due.

The U.S. Bankruptcy Court for the Central District of California agreed with both the Gallettis and the Briguglios. Citing a series of federal district court decisions, the court held that the IRS was required to make individual assessments of the partners in order to hold the partners liable for the tax obligations of the partnership. Since the IRS had not made assessments of the individual partners within three years of the time in which the employment taxes came due, the court, in both cases, granted the petitioners' objections to the Internal Revenue Service's claims. *In re Galletti*, No. LA 99-48587-ER, 2000 WL 1682960 (Bankr. C.D. Cal. Sept. 11, 2000); *In re Briguglio*, No. LA 00-13574-ER, 2000 WL 1682978 (Bankr. C.D. Cal. Sept. 11, 2000).

The IRS appealed the decisions of the bankruptcy court to the U.S. District Court for the Central District of California. The court noted that the IRS failed to cite any cases that supported the assertion that individual assessment against the partners was not required. In contrast, the Gallettis and Briguglios cited authority that provided support for their positions, and the district court affirmed the bankruptcy court's decisions in both cases.

The IRS then appealed the decisions to the U.S. Court of Appeals for the Ninth Circuit, arguing that the partners were not separate "taxpayers" under the IRC. According to the arguments of the government, if the IRS made a timely assessment against the partnership, the government should be allowed to collect taxes directly from the individual partners, even if the IRS did not need to make assessments of the individual partners' liability. However, like the lower courts, the Ninth Circuit disagreed, noting that the court's prior decisions weighed against the government's position. The court also noted that under California law, a **judgment** against a partnership is not a judgment in itself against the individual partners. Thus, neither the Ninth Circuit's **interpretation** of the IRC nor California law supported the position of the IRS.

The government filed a petition for **writ** of **certiorari** with the U.S. Supreme Court, and the Supreme Court granted the petition on June 23, 2003. The question before the Court again focused on whether the partners were indeed separate taxpayers whose tax liability had to be assessed separately. However, the Court, per Justice CLARENCE THOMAS, pointed out that the government makes an assessment of the tax, rather than an individual taxpayer. Moreover, the Court found that nothing in the INTERNAL REVENUE CODE required the IRS "to duplicate its efforts by separately assessing the same tax against individuals or entities who are not the actual taxpayers but are, by reason of state law, liable for payment of the taxpayer's debt." Since the Service had properly assessed the partnership's tax liability within three years that the taxes came due, the Court held that IRS had sought to collect the taxes in a timely manner. Accordingly, the Court reversed the decision of the Ninth Circuit.

The Court's decision not only has significant implications as to the ability of the IRS to collect taxes, but it also could have far-reaching effects on debtors filing for bankruptcy. Employment taxes are not dischargeable in bankruptcy, and such taxes are entitled to priority status in a bankruptcy case. Thus, if a **debtor** is a partner in a partnership, and is liable for partnership taxes, a plan under Chapter 13 could be infeasible.

PATENTS

Rights, granted to inventors by the federal government, pursuant to its power under Article I, Section 8, Clause 8, of the U.S. Constitution, that permit them to exclude others from making, using, or selling an invention for a definite, or restricted, period of time.

Online Auction House eBay Sued Over Technology Use

A David vs. Goliath battle over patent infringement finally had its day in court last year, with MercExchange of Great Falls, Virginia, taking on Internet auction giant eBay over technologies at the heart of eBay's greatly successful online auction business.

In the spring of 1995, MercExchange founder and patent lawyer Thomas Woolston filed for patents on technology designed to be used on the still-nascent World Wide Web. The patents covered technology designed to use a credit card number to promise to purchase items online at a fixed price. Five months later, eBay opened for business online, using some of the patented technologies. Woolston reportedly approached eBay in June 2000, seeking to sell them the patent rights, but eBay refused. In September 2001, Woolston filed suit against eBay and Half.com, an eBay subsidiary, for infringing on three of his patents. The infringed technologies were allegedly at the heart of eBay's popular "Buy It Now" feature, which allows customers to bypass the auction process and purchas items at a higher fixed price. "Buy It Now" purchases represent close to one-third of eBay's total sales. eBay argued that others had proposed similar systems before Woolston got his patents, and that variations in their system made it different enough to constitute non-infringing use.

eBay won one early round of the battle. In October 2001, a federal judge threw out one of the three infringement claims. But a motion by eBay to dismiss the entire suit was denied.

The case went to trial on April 23, 2003. Woolston, who represented himself in court, sought triple damages for willful infringement as well as an **injunction** barring eBay from using any of the technologies for its online auctions, meaning that eBay would have to either seek a license from Woolston or shut down. Despite the danger of possibly having to lose much of their U.S. business, eBay did not seek to settle out of court. "We believe we have meritorious defenses and will defend ourselves vigorously." eBay said in a statement.

Unfortunately for eBay, the jury didn't think so. On May 27, 2003, after three days of deliberations, the federal jury unanimously found eBay **guilty** of "willful and direct" patent infringement and ordered restitution of $35 million, of which eBay was responsible for $16 million and Half.com $19 million. In post-trial motions, Woolston filed for an injunction against eBay using any of the technologies online, while eBay filed motions to overturn the **verdict** and reduce damages. On August 7, U.S. District Judge Jerome B. Friedman denied eBay's motion to overturn the verdict, but denied Woolston's **call** for triple damages for willful infringement, and reduced the damages awarded to $29.5 million, ruling that another company, ReturnBuy.com, bore some of the responsibility for infringement. (ReturnBuy had settled their responsibility with Woolston out of court.) Judge Friedman also denied Woolston's motion to block eBay from continuing with its "Buy It Now" sales, commenting that doing so would be akin to "opening Pandora's Box."

Commenting on the decision, Woolston said "We're generally pleased that the judge saw the same case the jury did ... We're ... disappointed that he did not stop eBay's continued infringement, but we're optimistic that eventually ... there will be an injunction." An executive from eBay said "We are gratified that the court rejected MercExchange's request to increase the damages ... and award a permanent injunction ... (but) it still leaves very serious questions about the jury verdict."

An **appeal** from eBay is being considered but is still **pending**. MercExchange is still mulling over whether to seek a new injunction and/or seek further damages for eBay's continued infringement. Meanwhile, now that Woolston's patent rights have been upheld, they are seeking to sell off these intellectual properties to the highest bidder. Several companies that compete with eBay in the online auction arena are being courted. eBay was also mentioned as a party of possible interest, though Woolston claims that they have made no move to acquire the patents they so bitterly disputed since Woolston offered them for sale in 2000.

Despite losing the initial ruling, eBay has escaped basically intact. $29.5 million is a significant sum, but it is not great loss to eBay, which posted a $104 million first-quarter profit in 2003. An injunction preventing them from running their online business, at least in the United States, would have been vastly more damaging. Whether Woolston seeks further damages or attempts to get a new injunction will certainly keep eBay on guard throughout the coming year.

Thomas Woolston, who won a patent lawsuit against Internet giant eBay.

PENSION

A benefit, usually money, paid regularly to retired employees or their survivors by private business and federal, state, and local governments. Employers are not required to establish pension benefits but do so to attract qualified employees.

Central Laborers Pension Fund v. Heinz

The Employee Retirement Income Security Act of 1974 (ERISA), 29 U.S.C. § 1054(g) prohibits reductions in accrued benefits that take effect after a worker has retired (the "anti-cutback" rule). In *Central Laborers Pension Fund*

v. *Heinz*, 541 U.S. __, 124 S.Ct. 2230, 159 L.Ed.2d 46 (2004), the U.S. SUPREME COURT unanimously held that expanding the categories of "disqualifying" post-retirement employment that would suspend monthly retirement benefits was in violation of the anti-cutback provision of ERISA.

In this case, Thomas Heinz was a retired construction worker who had a vested retirement benefit with the Central Laborers Pension Fund. By 1996, he had (at the age of 39) acquired enough pension credits to qualify for early retirement under a "service only" pension plan. Under Central Laborer's early retirement plan, benefits were equal to those of full retirement at the usual age, but a contingency prohibited early retirees from holding certain jobs post-retirement. If early retirees engaged in any of the prohibited post-retirement employment, their monthly benefits were suspended until they terminated the prohibited work. Accordingly, Heinz and another 39-year-old construction worker retired in 1996.

At the time of their retirement, the plan had defined "disqualifying employment" as any job as a "union or non-union construction worker." The plan did not list employment in a supervisory **capacity**. Therefore, the men accepted employment as construction supervisors after they retired. Two years after the fact, in 1998, the plan was modified to disqualify any job "in any capacity in the construction industry (either as a union or non-union construction worker)." Representatives from the benefits plan warned the men that if they continued to work as supervisors, their monthly pensions would be suspended. The two continued working, and when their benefits were suspended, they filed suit.

The suit charged that the amendment to the pension plan violated the "anti-cutback" provision in ERISA, which states that amendments to a retirement plan may not decrease the "accrued benefit of a participant" [Section 204(g)]. The pension plan administrators articulated a plausible argument that there was no cutback or reduction in benefits; that the men were still able to receive the same amount each month, —just not while working as construction supervisors.

The federal district court that first heard the case granted **summary judgment** to the pension plan on the face of the pleadings. Specifically, it held that a suspension of benefits did not amount to a reduction of an "accrued benefit," and therefore, plaintiffs had not articulated a **cognizable** claim. However, a divided Seventh **Circuit Court** of Appeals reversed. It restated the issue, holding that imposing new conditions on rights to benefits already accrued did indeed violate the anti-cutback rule.

The U.S. Supreme Court was more specific yet. Justice DAVID SOUTER, delivering the opinion for an unanimous court, held that ERISA prohibits any plan amendment that expands the categories of postretirement employment resulting in a suspension of payments of early retirement benefits already accrued. The Court explained that the anti-cutback provision was crucial to ERISA's central objective of protecting employees' justified expectations of receiving the benefits they had been promised. The Court further noted that even though the statutory language was not explicit, common sense would dictate that, in this case, the benefit expected by the men suffered as a result of the amendment. There was no way, in any practical sense, that the change of terms could not be viewed as shrinking the value of the pension rights and reducing the promised benefit.

The Court issued a wholesale rejection of the arguments forwarded by the plan administrators, who urged an **interpretation** that the cutback provision only applied to amendments directly altering a monthly payment's dollar amount. A second argument raised by the plan posited that language from an entirely different Section 203(a)(3)(B) expressly authorized suspension provisions retroactively. This was also soundly rejected by the Court as "irrelevant" because, as a technical matter, the referenced section addressed benefit forfeitures.

Said Souter in the Court's opinion, "Heinz worked and accrued retirement benefits under a plan with terms allowing him to supplement retirement income by certain employment, and he was being reasonable if he relied on those terms in planning his retirement." A concurring opinion was written by Justice STEPHEN BREYER, and Chief Justice WILLIAM H. REHNQUIST, in which Justice SANDRA DAY O'CONNOR and Justice RUTH BADER GINSBURG joined. The concurring opinion expressly noted that the justices assumed that the ruling did not foreclose a reading of ERISA that allowed the Secretaries of Labor or the Treasury to issue *regulations* allowing such plan amendment.

PRESIDENTIAL POWERS

The executive authority given to the president of the United States by Article II of the Constitution to carry out the duties of the office.

Department of Transportation v. Public Citizen

In 1982, Congress imposed a **moratorium** prohibiting Mexican motor carriers from operating in the United States. That same enactment also vested the president of the United States with the authority to lift the moratorium. Nearly twenty years later, in 2001, President GEORGE W. BUSH announced his intention to lift the moratorium in 2002. One condition precedent was that new regulations were to be created to grant (and to control) the entry and operation of Mexican motor carriers in the United States.

The promulgation of such regulations by federal agencies might or might not invoke several **corollary** federal laws, some of which were **at issue** in the case of *Department of Transportation v. Public Citizen*, 541 U.S. ___, 124 S.Ct. 2204, 159 L.Ed.2d 60 (2004). The underlying issues in the case (**i.e.**, opening U.S. roadways to Mexican trucks) sparked much **controversy** among labor organizations and environmental groups, but in fact, the U.S. SUPREME COURT ruled on narrow grounds (i.e., vested powers) to resolve the matter.

At issue in this case were provisions under the National Environmental Policy Act of 1969 (NEPA), 42 U.S.C. §§ 4321, *et seq.*, and the Clean Air Act (CAA), 42 U.S.C. §§ 7401, *et seq.* NEPA requires federal agencies to analyze the environmental impact of their proposed actions (e.g., new regulations) by preparing an Environmental Impact Statement (EIS), or (and at issue here) a more limited Environmental Assessment (EA) if the agency issues a "finding of no significant impact." In addition, the CAA allows states to develop their own plans to comply with air-quality standards, but federal agency actions must conform to those state plans, per 42 U.S.C. § 6506(c)(1).

After learning of the proposed lift of the moratorium and the president's request for appropriate regulation, the Federal Motor Carrier Safety Administration (FMCSA) published two proposed rules and invited comment. One pertained to an application form for Mexican carrier operators, and the other proposed safety inspections for carriers receiving operating authority. Acting pursuant to NEPA, the agency also issued an environmental assessment EA, concluding that the new regulations would have no significant environmental impact. In further consideration of the CAA, FMCSA reasoned that any increase in vehicle exhaust emissions coming from Mexican trucks that were authorized to enter the United States would nevertheless fall below the Environmental Protection Agency's threshold levels for triggering a CAA conformity review. Believing that it thus had met the requirements of NEPA and CAA, the FMCSA awaited congressional funds to implement its new regulations so that the moratorium could be lifted.

In fact, the contentious matter of Mexican trucks operating in the United States predated President Bush's lifting of the moratorium by several years. In 1993, President Clinton signed the NORTH AMERICAN FREE TRADE AGREEMENT (NAFTA), which, among other things, allowed Mexican trucks to use an increasingly large portion of U.S. roads. (They were initially limited to commercial border zones, but under NAFTA they were to gain full access to U.S. roads beginning in 2000.) Labor and consumer groups vehemently challenged Clinton's actions. Ultimately, the Clinton administration backed down and breached the NAFTA agreement, refusing to grant full entry and access.

The current federal suit was filed by the consumer group Public Citizen, along with the Teamsters union and others. Leery of adverse economic and environmental impact caused by Mexican trucks entering the United States, they sued on safety and environmental grounds. Seeking to avoid the lifting of the moratorium, they challenged FMCSA's proposed rules, arguing that FMCSA failed to issue an environmental impact statement (EIS) as required by NEPA. They further argued that the perfunctory EA issued by FMCSA was arbitrary and capricious in that it failed to consider the environmental effects of an increase in cross-border operations of Mexican vehicles. The U.S. Court of Appeals for the Ninth Circuit agreed and directed FMCSA to prepare an EIS and a full CAA conformity determination for its proposed regulations.

Much of the briefing and arguments raised by both sides centered around the meaning of relevant statutory language contained in NEPA and the CAA. For example, the parties waxed prolix over whether increased emissions from Mexican vehicles was an "effect" of FMCSA's proposed rules or an "effect" of the lifting of the moratorium. The answer to that question might have triggered corollary responsibilities on the part of FMCSA to consider environmental impact.

The U.S. Supreme Court essentially reduced these arguments, at least for the purpose of judicial disposition. Justice CLARENCE

THOMAS, delivering the opinion for a unanimous Court, concluded that Congress gave exclusive power to the U.S. president either to continue the moratorium or to lift it and resume the cross-border operations of Mexican motor carriers. Because FMCSA lacked the discretion to prevent such cross-border operations, neither NEPA nor CAA could require FMCSA to conduct studies or evaluate environmental effects of such operations.

Further, the high court found that the respondents (who filed the original suit) had forfeited any **objection** to the inadequacy of FMCSA's environmental assessment (EA) because in their official comments to the proposed rules, they never identified any alternatives beyond those evaluated by the EA.

Nevertheless, the Court went on to reason, through its discourse, that the causal connection between the proposed regulations and the entry of Mexican trucks was insufficient to establish responsibility, under NEPA, to consider environmental effects of such entry. Said the Court, "We hold that where an agency has no ability to prevent a certain effect due to its limited statutory authority over the relevant actions, the agency cannot be considered a legally relevant "cause" of the effect."

PRISONERS' RIGHTS

The nature and extent of the privileges afforded to individuals kept in custody or confinement against their will because they were convicted of performing an unlawful act.

No Need for Inmates to Exhaust Habeas Relief Before Filing Civil Rights Suit

42 U.S.C.A. § 1983 is recognized as one of the most important pieces of federal civil rights law, permitting a plaintiff to sue state and local government officials for damages and equitable **relief** based on the alleged deprivations by the officials of the plaintiff's constitutional rights. Prisoners have used § 1983 to **contest** prison living conditions and to seek damages for injuries that could be traced to prison officials. Sometimes prisoners in their § 1983 lawsuits also raise issues that go to the legitimacy of their underlying criminal conviction. Such issues are properly raised in **habeas corpus** suits, which led the U.S. SUPREME COURT in *Heck v. Humphrey*, 512 U.S. 477, 114 S.Ct. 2364, 129 L.Ed.2d 383 (1994), to require prisoners to succeed with a habeas action before being allowed to proceed with the § 1983 claim. However, the circuit courts of **appeal** came to contrary conclusions about the applicability of *Heck* to prison disciplinary proceedings where prisoners sought to have their prison records expunged of misconduct charges. Some circuits required the prisoner to file a habeas **petition** first, while others did not. The Supreme Court, in *Muhammad v. Close*, __ U.S. __, __ S.Ct. __, __ L.Ed.2d __ 2004 WL 344163(2004), resolved the issue, ruling that prisoners did not have to file and prevail in a habeas action if the action did not challenge the underlying criminal conviction or the duration of a sentence for that conviction.

The case arose out of a **confrontation** between Shakur Muhammad, a Michigan prison inmate and Mark Close, a prison officer. Muhammad alleged that Close stared at him while he was eating breakfast, that Muhammad stared back, and that an angry Close came within a foot of the inmate. Muhammad was handcuffed, brought to a **detention** cell and cited for violating a prison rule against threatening behavior. Muhammad was acquitted of the charge at a disciplinary hearing six days later but found **guilty** of insolence, a lesser charge. If he had been cited for insolence, prehearing detention would have been mandatory. The prison officials added seven more days of detention to Muhammad's punishment and took away his prison privileges for 30 days.

Muhammad filed a § 1983 action against Close, alleging that Close had filed the threatening behavior charge against him as retaliation for Muhammad's prior lawsuits and grievance proceedings against Close. He did not challenge his conviction for insolence nor did he seek expungement of the misconduct finding. Muhammad sought $10,000 in compensatory and punitive damages for the physical, mental and emotional injuries he sustained during his six days of prehearing detention that was mandated by Close's filing of the threatening behavior charge.

A federal **magistrate** reviewed Muhammad's lawsuit and recommended to the federal district court that the action be dismissed. The magistrate concluded that Muhammad had failed to provide enough evidence to show that Close's actions had been retaliatory. The evidence was so slim that there was no genuine issue of material fact to continue the lawsuit into the **discovery** phase. The district court agreed with the magistrate and dismissed the suit. Muhammad appealed to the Sixth Circuit of Appeals, which upheld the **dismissal** but on other grounds. The Sixth Circuit held that the lawsuit was prohibited by *Heck* because Muhammad had sought to have his misconduct charge expunged from his prison records. The appeals court invoked a Sixth Circuit precedent in making its ruling. Muhammad then filed a handwritten appeal to the Supreme Court, which accepted the case for review.

The Supreme Court, in a unanimous decision, reversed the Sixth Circuit decision. The Court issued a *per curiam* opinion (an opinion not signed by any of the justices), in which it concluded the appeals court decision was "flawed as a matter of fact and as a matter of law." The factual error was clear: Muhammad had not asked that the misconduct charge be expunged from his prison record. This error was, in the Court's view, "compounded" by the Sixth Circuit precedent that applied *Heck* "categorically to all suits challenging prison disciplinary proceedings." Prison disciplinary proceedings are administrative in nature and do not implicate "the validity of the underlying conviction." The Court found that prevailing in habeas relief first (under *Heck*) is only required if a prisoner's § 1983 suit challenges or involves the underlying conviction or affects the duration of a sentence for that underlying conviction. Muhammad's did neither (his involved a disciplinary misconduct charge at the prison), so the Court ruled that he didn't need habeas first.

The Supreme Court sent the case back to the Sixth Circuit and directed it to consider dismissing the lawsuit based on the evidentiary grounds cited by the district court.

PRIVACY

In constitutional law, the right of people to make personal decisions regarding intimate matters; under the common law, the right of people to lead their lives in a manner that is reasonably secluded from public scrutiny, whether such scrutiny comes from a neighbor's prying eyes, an investigator's eavesdropping ears, or a news photographer's intrusive camera; and in statutory law, the right of people to be free from unwarranted drug testing and electronic surveillance.

Supreme Court Limits Recovery for Privacy Act Violations

The **Privacy** Act of 1974, 5 U.S.C.A. § 552a, put in place detailed instructions for federal agencies to follow in managing their records. The act sought to limit dissemination of certain information collected from individuals. To enforce these provisions the act permitted individuals to bring civil damage suits against the federal government for violations of personal privacy. Section 552a(g)(4) states that an individual can recover "actual damages" for intentional or willful violations but "in no case shall a person entitled to recovery receive less than the sum of $1,000" and reasonable attorneys fees. Most circuit courts of appeals read this section to mean that a person who proffers any general claim of emotional harm was entitled to $1,000." However, the Supreme Court, in *Buck v. Chao*, __ U.S. __, S.Ct., __ L.Ed.2d __ 2004 WL 330043(2004), ruled otherwise, requiring that a plaintiff demonstrate an actual **injury** before recovering any money from the government.

For many years the DEPARTMENT OF LABOR (DOL) included the Social Security numbers of claimants for black lung disease compensation on all paperwork sent to claimants, employers and lawyers, including documents that contained multiple claimants. Buck Doe and six other black lung claimants objected to the disclosure and filed a federal lawsuit against DOL alleging Privacy Act violations. The plaintiffs also sought certification of a **class action** to include all claimants for black lung benefits since the enactment of the Privacy Act. The DOL admitted that the listing of Social Security numbers was incorrect and agreed to the court issuing an order prohibiting future publication of Social Security numbers on court documents that listed more than one claimant. The court denied the class action motion and dismissed all but Doe's claim because the other individuals had not raised any allegations of harm. In his pleadings Doe had stated that he had been "torn all to pieces" and "greatly concerned and worried because the disclosure of his number was potentially "devastating." Based on these allegations of harm the district court awarded him the statutory minimum of $1000.

The Fourth **Circuit Court** of Appeals reversed the award decision, concluding that the statutory minimum was available only to plaintiffs who suffered actual damages from the agency violation. In Doe's case he had not presented any evidence to **corroborate** his claim of emotional distress. The appeals court noted that Doe had not described any physical symptoms, medical treatment, loss of income or direct effect on his behavior that could be traced to the disclosure of his Social Security number. Because five other circuit courts of appeals had ruled that **proof** of actual damages was not needed, the Supreme Court agreed to hear the case to resolve the conflict.

The Supreme Court, in a 6-3 decision, agreed with the Fourth Circuit's **interpretation** of the Privacy Act provision. Justice DAVID SOUTER, in his majority opinion, disagreed with Doe's contention that nothing more than a intentional or willful statutory violation of the act justified the recovery of $1000. Justice Souter first looked to the text of § 552a(g)(4), noting that the $1000 minimum award is based on "actual damages sustained." This meant that the act made "specific provision ... for what a victim within the limited class may recover." The later **clause** that refers to guaranteeing $1000 to a "person entitled to recovery" refers back to a plaintiff who sustains "actual damages." Therefore, Doe must show actual damage to be a person entitled to the recovery of the statutory minimum.

Justice Souter acknowledged that the common law torts of **defamation** and invasion of privacy permit presumed damages, which are calculated without reference to specific harm. However, he pointed out that Congress in 1974 had deleted a presumed damages provision and had established a commission to study whether Congress should grant presumed damages in the future. These facts led the majority to conclude that actual damages must be proved before a plaintiff may recover. Souter rejected Doe's claim that other federal statutes contained remedial provisions that were similar to the Privacy Act's 552a(g)(4) and which granted presumed damages. He found that the text of these statutes was far too different to permit analogies. In addition, some of the cited laws had been passed after the Privacy Act. Therefore, a plaintiff would have to show actual damages. The majority declined to decide whether damages less than $1000 would qualify as sufficient actual damages for the plaintiff to recover the $1000 statutory minimum.

Justice RUTH BADER GINSBURG, in a dissenting opinion joined by Justices JOHN PAUL STEVENS and STEPHEN BREYER, contended that Doe's general **allegation** of harm was enough to qualify for the $1000 minimum and that there was no need for him to show an actual **pecuniary** loss. Ginsburg noted that the OFFICE OF MANAGEMENT AND BUDGET had published in 1975 a regulation that interpreted the Privacy Act provision to mean that the government must pay either actual damages or $1000, whichever is less. Moreover, the **legislative history** of the Privacy Act justified her reading of the law. Congress intended to give the law "teeth" by "deterring violations and providing remedies when violations occur." The majority's decision undermined this **intent**, for only victims of **identity theft** would seem to qualify. With no evidence that her reading of the provision would result in "massive recoveries" against the government, Justice Ginsburg concluded that the remedial effect of law the should have been preserved.

PRIVACY ACT OF 1974

Assistant U.S. Attorney Sues Justice Department

Assistant U.S. **Attorney General** Richard G. Convertino, who handled the only successful prosecution for **terrorism** following the SEPTEMBER 11TH ATTACKS, sued the Justice Department in February 2004. He alleged that the JUSTICE DEPARTMENT violated a number of federal laws, including the **Privacy** Act of 1974, in its handling of the case and surrounding circumstances. Commentators have suggested that the case may shed light on the Justice Department's handling—and mishandling—of the war on terrorism.

Convertino had been employed by the Justice Department since 1989. He prosecuted a number of complex **fraud** and gang-related cases and routinely earned high ratings for his performance as a prosecutor. Convertino received a number of awards from officers in the Department of Justice (DOJ) in the past. He trained **international law** enforcement agencies and prosecutors in Kazakhstan, Bulgaria, and Albania as part of a series of programs by the DOJ and the State Department. He has also previously been interviewed for a federal judgeship.

Six days after the September 11th attacks, agents of the FEDERAL BUREAU OF INVESTIGATION arrested Karim Koubriti, Ahmed Hannan, and Farouk Ali-Haimoud at an apartment in Detroit. The agents discovered falsified passport photos; forged visas and green cards; drawings of an American air base in Turkey and an airport in Jordan; and videotape showing several landmarks in the United States, including Disneyland and the headquarters of the *New York Times*. The Secret Service later arrested Youssef Hmimssa, who was a roommate of Koubriti and Hannan, in Iowa. In November 2001, agents arrested the group's alleged leader, Abdel-Ilah Elmardoudi.

Convertino served as the lead prosecutor on the case. From the time of the initial arrests on September 17, 2001, through January 2003, Convertino was assigned only one special agent of the FBI to assist with the case, despite having sent several requests to the DOJ for more resources. Convertino and the special agent handled many of the pretrial matters with little outside assistance from others in the Justice Department. A second assistant U.S. attorney, Keith E. Corbett, began to assist Convertino with the trial in October 2002. The trial in the case of *United States v. Koubriti* took place from March 18 through June 3 in 2003, with Convertino and Corbett presenting about one thousand exhibits and about fifty witnesses. The court convicted Kourbriti and Elmardoudi of offenses related to terrorist activities, and Hannan was convicted of fraud. Ali-Haimoud was acquitted in the case.

Attorney General JOHN ASHCROFT took credit for the prosecution on behalf of the Justice Department. However, Convertino and Corbett were both critical of the DOJ for the department's lack of assistance, support, and cooperation. According to court documents, Convertino maintains that "intra-departmental infighting ... plagued and hindered the terrorism investigation and prosecution" of the case. Officials within the DOJ allegedly responded that Convertino and Corbett were perceived as being uncooperative.

About two months after the trial, Convertino was contacted by an investigator of the Senate Finance Committee about the facts of *United States v. Koubriti*. Convertino met with investigators about the case. On September 2, 2003, he was informed that the Senate Finance Committee planned to **subpoena** him to testify at a hearing regarding identity fraud. The chair of the Finance Committee, Senator Charles E. Grassley (R-Iowa), had been a critic of both the FBI and the DOJ. Two days after Convertino was contacted by the investigator about testifying, he was removed from the terrorism case as its lead prosecutor.

Convertino testified before the Senate Finance Committee on September 9, 2003. Members of the committee, including Grassley, complimented Convertino on his handling of the case. However, after the testimony took place, officials in the DOJ allegedly ridiculed Convertino about the senators' accolades. Less than a week after giving his testimony, Convertino learned that he was being removed from his position and was being placed into a new position that handled only "simple and mundane" tasks, such as arraignments and certain pre-trial matters.

Convertino's lawsuit alleges that officials within the DOJ leaked information about him to the *Detroit Free Press* and *Detroit News* in an effort to prove that Convertino had been in contact with the Senate Finance Committee long before he gave his testimony on September 9. According to Convertino, the DOJ violated a sealing order by a court by providing the name of one of Convertino's confidential informants. Officials within the DOJ also apparently referred Convertino's files to the U.S. Department of Justice Office of **Professional Responsibility** (OPR) to investigate potential ethical violations. Following this referral, Convertino alleged that DOJ officials leaked confidential records and other information about him to people inside and outside of the department, including a reporter with the *Detroit Free Press/News*.

Convertino filed a civil lawsuit against the Department of Justice, Ashcroft, and three members of the U.S. Attorney's Office for the Eastern District of Michigan, including Jeffrey G. Collins, who serves as the U.S. attorney for that district. He alleged that the DOJ and others violated his rights under the the PRIVACY ACT OF 1974, 5 U.S.C. § 552; the Administrative Procedure Act, 5 U.S.C. §§ 701-706; the Lloyd-LaFollette Act, 5 U.S.C. § 7211; the First Amendment of the U.S. Constitution; as well as several other federal statutes.

Convertino's claims under the Privacy Act focused on his allegations that the DOJ released his confidential personnel information that was protected by the Act. This information was released to the press and eventually spread to newspapers throughout the country. Grassley later assigned Convertino to the Senate Caucus on International Narcotics Control, apparently to prevent the DOJ from firing Convertino.

The press has followed this case closely, as it may suggest that the Justice Department is in a state of disorganization in its WAR ON TERRORISM. According to an article in *U.S. News & World Report*, the case "reveals a Justice Department at war with itself, riven by petty jealousies and plagued by grandstanding that extends to Ashcroft himself, who damaged the government's **credibility** by twice violating a judge's gag order." As of May 2004, Convertino's case was still **pending** in the U.S. District Court for the DISTRICT OF COLUMBIA.

RAPE

A criminal offense defined in most states as forcible sexual relations with a person against that person's will.

New York Sex Dungeon Conviction

In a bizarre case attracting national media attention, a sixty-seven-year-old, retired New York handyman was sentenced in July 2003 for his role in kidnapping and sexually abusing five female victims who were held captive in a concrete dungeon underneath his house. An unsympathetic judge sentenced John Jamelske to eighteen years-to-life for each of the five counts in the indictment. The sentence was the result of a plea deal in which Jamelske also agreed to forfeit all of his assets—worth approximately one million dollars—to be divided among the five victims. The five women, ranging in age from thirteen to fifty, were held individually over a period of months—in one case, two years—and then released.

Jamelske had been sexually abusing women since the 1980s, apparently with impunity. The case first broke the news in the spring of 2003, when Jamelske appeared in public with one of his teenaged captives. The sixteen-year-old girl excused herself and secretly telephoned her sister from a pay telephone. The sister then called authorities. Police found Jamelske and the girl in his car a short time later. Jamelske told the police that the relationship was consensual and that the teenager was over eighteen-years-old. Neither was true. Jamelske was arrested, held without bail, and charged with kidnapping and **rape**. After police listened to the girl's story, later charges included **sodomy** and other counts of sexual abuse.

Police searching Jamelske's premises found a maze built underneath his backyard. The labyrinth led to a concrete structure containing two cell-like rooms. The bunker was accessible only by entering the basement of Jamelske's house, passing through steel doors, and then going through a crawl space. The cell rooms were windowless. One contained a toilet and washtub; the other had a foam mattress and a microwave oven.

According to authorities, Jamelske, a harmless-enough looking man, abducted women off the street. He would force them to the floor of his car, blindfold them, and take them to his ranch home, which was separated from a busy road by shrubs and trees. There, he would rape or sodomize them at least once a day, while controlling every aspect of their lives. They were forced to record on a calendar with a specified code when they bathed, brushed their teeth, ate, or had sex with him. One woman was allegedly chained to a metal grate and sexually abused daily.

Authorities further concluded that Jamelske's choice of victims was a factor in his ability to continue his assaults over the years without discovery or capture. This was true, though two of his victims had gone to the police after he released them. Police and prosecutors called his victims "disposable people"—chronic runaways, non-English speaking immigrants, and drug addicts. Such persons were not immediately missed by families, or their families lacked will or ability to come forward. For exam-

One of two rooms used by John Jamelske to imprison and rape women he had kidnapped.

ple, one fifty-three-year-old victim, an immigrant who spoke little English, told the *Syracuse Post-Standard* reporters that in 1998, Syracuse (NY) detectives discounted her story as incredulous. Another woman reported a similar story to the Onandaga sheriff's department. Both women were unable to identify the geographic location of where they were held. The agencies did not share information, and police did not publicize the women's statements.

Jamelske was able to control his victims through fear. He possessed an old police badge which he allegedly flashed at his victims, telling them that the police knew what he was doing. He would make his pet Rottweiler sniff their clothes, then he would tell them that the Rottweiler would hunt them down if they tried to escape. He also threatened to harm their relatives. One woman told authorities that Jamelske burned her with his cigar when she refused his advances after accepting a ride to her house from him. Instead, he took her to his dungeon and held her for two months as his sex slave. Two of the women never bothered to contact police after release, fearing that no one would believe them. All in all, police identified five victims, ranging in age from thirteen to fifty-three, but they believed there had been more over the years.

At his sentencing in July 2003, a tearful Jamelske apologized to his victims. However, the judge told him that he was a "sick coward, an evil man, kidnapper and rapist. Your reign of terror is over." In an interview given to *Post-Standard* reporters a few days prior to his sentencing, Jamelske referred to his victims as his "buddies," saying that he wanted to have an influence on them.

REAGAN, RONALD WILSON

Obituary notice

Born February 6, 1911, in Tampico, Illinois; died June 5, 2004, in Los Angeles, California. America's fortieth president from 1981-1989, known variously as "Dutch," the "Teflon President," "The Great Communicator," and the father of an economic system named after him ("Reaganomics"), RONALD REAGAN is one of the most controversial political figures of the twentieth century. In fact, an entire system of thought, appropriately titled "Reaganism," was coined to describe the effects of, depending on who you ask, his repositioning of American optimism and strength at the forefront of world politics or his questionable social legacy. Reagan graduated with a degree in economics from Eureka College, but became a baseball announcer in Des Moines, Iowa following graduation. Reagan then screen-tested at Warner Bros, who gave him a motion picture contract. He appeared in more than fifty films during a two-decade-plus career. Reagan served as president of the Screen Actors Guild, becoming embroiled in disputes over the issue of communism in the film industry, and his political views shifted from liberal to conservative. He toured the country as a television host, becoming a spokesman for conservatism and a company man for General Electric. Financially secure by 1962, Reagan then spent a few years delivering speeches to groups across the country, mostly about business and conservative interests and decrying big government. In 1966, he was elected governor of California by a margin of a million votes. His terms as governor were marked by conflict and controversy. Though he ran as a candidate opposed to taxes (a consideration that carried itself into his presidency), he implemented the highest tax increase in California at the time. He demanded the resignation of University of California-Berkeley chancellor Clark Kerr during the free speech demonstrations, positioning himself as the voice of moderation exasperated with "campus radicals," yet was lauded by the state for balancing the books. The early stirrings of Reaganism thus became evident during Reagan's stint as governor: a devotion to business interests (General Electric), hard-line stances against liberals seeking to expand social freedoms, attacks on Communism and the USSR, concern over America's perceived moral disintegration, a delegation of power to the point where the executive's ultimate responsibility lay in his rhetorical influence over party constituents, and finally, the entrenchment of governmental power and influence coupled with the oratorical promise of deregulation. Reagan won the Republican presidential nomination in 1980 and chose as his running mate former Texas congressman and UNITED NATIONS ambassador George Bush. Reagan set about implementing tax breaks and benefits to the wealthy that continued on long past his presidency. He coupled this with cutbacks in spending, especially on the welfare programs AFDC (Aid for Families with Dependent Children) and Medicaid. He railed against the Soviet Union and Communism as he had done throughout his Hollywood and California years, and set about increasing the budget of the Pentagon and the U.S. defense industries. At home, he implemented equally aggressive domestic policies against crime, drugs, and **pornography**; although he championed a United States free from the dictates of oppressive government control, he nevertheless used government to further his conservative social agenda, which included the banning of abortion, reinstatement of school prayer, and promotion of the nuclear, heterosexual family. His punishing stances on social disintegration came back to haunt him during the infamous Iran-Contra Hearings, in which Reagan's cabinet was caught red-handed funneling drug money into the Contras in Central America, a geographical and political zone important to the presidency for its massive drug production. A critique of Reaganism would not be complete without a consideration of the major effect Reagan had on the growth and use of media power in the United States. Politics and entertainment had finally reached the stage in their evolution where they became linked together; Reagan's persuasive use of the media in his policy implementation, as well as his economic deregulation which allowed media strategies monopolies to grow from film to publishing to sports and further, gave the media heretofore unrealized power. The Reagan presidency was undoubtedly a political success. In 1984 Reagan was reelected in a landslide amid peace and prosperity, as Americans felt that they were better off than they were four years before. In 1988 Reagan's vice-president, George Bush, was elected president in a campaign that was largely a **referendum** on Reagan's ideology and accomplishments. But this success came about largely as a result of lower taxes and higher spending, a combination that produced short-term economic growth but left huge budget deficits that threatened the long-term health of the American economy. Reagan continued to attract controversy as a former president: for retiring to a multimillion-dollar mansion in Los Angeles, for his befuddled testimony at the Iran-contra trial of John Poindexter, and for accepting millions of dollars in honoraria on a visit to Japan. In 1990 he published his autobiography, *An American Life*. His last public act was to have President BILL CLINTON inform the country of his Alzheimer's Disease.

RECUSE

To disqualify or remove oneself as a judge over a particular proceeding because of one's conflict of interest. Recusal, or the judge's act of disqualifying himself or herself from presiding over a proceeding, is based on the **maxim** that judges are charged with a duty of impartiality in administering justice.

Ashcroft Recuses Himself from Case Involving Leak of CIA Operative

Attorney General JOHN ASHCROFT, in December 2003, recused himself from the investigation of a case involving the revelation of an operative of the Central Intelligence Agency (CIA). The recusal came after months of speculation as to who was the official responsible for the leak. It marked the first time that Ashcroft had recused himself from an investigation by the Justice Department.

The controversy began with an article by Robert Novak, a syndicated journalist. Novak wrote an editorial in July 14, 2003, asserting the CIA had sent retired diplomat Joseph C. Wilson to Africa to determine whether Iraq had sought to purchase uranium in Niger. Wilson allegedly reported that such a purchase by Iraq was highly unlikely, though this information was not forwarded to CIA Director George Tenet or to President GEORGE W. BUSH. In the State of the Union address in January 2003, Bush said that the British government had information suggesting that Iraq had indeed purchased uranium from Niger. The information from the British government, however, was found to have been based on forged documents. Novak's story was run in several newspapers.

Novak's editorial focused on Wilson, but Novak made a statement that leaked the identity of a CIA operative, who turned out to be Wilson's wife. According to Novak's column, "Wilson never worked for the CIA, but his wife, Valerie Plame, is an agency operative on weapons of mass destruction. Two senior administration officials told me his wife suggested sending Wilson to Niger to investigate" an Italian report suggesting that Iraq had attempted to purchase uranium from Iraq.

The revelation of Plame as an operative sparked immediate outrage from several quarters. Shortly after the article appeared, Senator Charles E. Schumer (D-N.Y.) requested that Robert S. Mueller III, the director of the Federal Bureau of Investigation, investigate the disclosure of Plame's identity. Schumer also wanted the FBI to question Novak as part of the investigation. Several media commentators made similar suggestions.

Some speculation surfaced in September 2003 that the official who revealed Plame's identity was Karl Rove, a political consultant to Bush. Rove had previously served as an advisor to Ashcroft. However, White House press secretary Scott McClellan denied the report, indicating that it was nothing more than media speculation. McClellan also maintained that the JUSTICE DEPARTMENT, headed by Ashcroft, was in the best position to handle the investigation. Bush repeated the assertion a few days later.

Until 1999, a panel of federal judges determined when an independent prosecutor should be appointed. This power stemmed from the Ethics in Government Act of 1978, Pub. L. No. 95-921, 92 Stat. 1824. Though the law was set to expire in 1992, it was extended through 1999 by the **Independent Counsel** Reauthorization Act of 1994, Pub. L. No. 103-270, 108 Stat. 732. Several of the more controversial episodes involving government officials were handled by independent **counsel**, including Kenneth W. Starr's investigation of former President BILL CLINTON. However, the law expired in 1999. Since that time, the attorney general has been responsible for determining whether a special prosecutor should investigate the actions of federal officials.

The Justice Department, in October 2003, announced that that it had begun a full investigation into the matter. Ashcroft named John Dion, a federal prosecutor, to lead the inquiry. The probe involved not only the White House, but also the Defense Department and the STATE DEPARTMENT. Even after the investigation was announced, Democrats in Congress demanded that a full and independent investigation into the matter take place. Among the demands of these Democrats was that Ashcroft **recuse** himself from the inquiry. Some likened the controversy to the WATERGATE scandal.

On December 30, 2003, Deputy Attorney General James Comey announced that Ashcroft had recused himself from the investigation; U.S. Attorney Patrick J. Fitzgerald was appointed to head the probe. It marked the first time that Ashcroft had recused himself from a case. Ashcroft's decision came after Ashcroft reviewed evidence, which reportedly may have indicated a conflict of interest. Though several Democrats applauded the move, others cautioned that Fitzgerald was nevertheless a political appointee, and that Justice Department investigators would answer to such an appointee.

Wilson revealed in a book that he believed the possible culprit was I. Lewis Libby, chief of staff for Vice President Dick Cheney. The book, *The Politics of Truth: Inside the Lies That Led to War and Betrayed My Wife's C.I.A. Identity—A Diplomat's Memoir*, was released in April 2004. As of May 2004, federal investigators had not revealed any leads as to who may have revealed Plame as an operative.

CROSS REFERENCES
Privacy Act

Scalia Refuses to Recuse Himself in Case Involving Cheney

U.S. SUPREME COURT Justice ANTONIN SCALIA became embroiled in controversy during 2004 when he refused to **recuse** himself after journalists discovered and reported that he had embarked on a duck-hunting trip with Vice President Richard Cheney just weeks after the Supreme Court granted **certiorari** to hear a case involving Cheney (see, this volume, Discovery: *Cheney v. United States District Court for the District of Columbia*). Despite numerous calls for Scalia to recuse himself, the associate justice drafted a twenty-one page memorandum describing his reasons for refusing to do so.

In January 2001, Cheney was appointed, by President GEORGE W. BUSH, to lead the National Energy Policy Development Group (NEPDG), which provided recommendations to Bush regarding the nation's energy policy. Though the group officially consisted of officers and employees of the federal government, some critics maintained that leaders from the private sector were involved with the group. Two non-profit watchdog groups, Judicial Watch and SIERRA CLUB, demanded that the NEPDG to provide records of its meetings. When Cheney and the group declined, Judicial Watch and Sierra Club both brought lawsuits. The U.S. District Court for the District of Columbia allowed the case to proceed despite objections from Cheney and others. *Judicial Watch, Inc. v. Nat'l Energy Policy Dev. Group*, 219 F. Supp. 2d 20 (D.D.C. 2002). Cheney then appealed the decision to the U.S. Court of Appeals for the District of Columbia. However, the appellate court dismissed the **appeal**. *In re Cheney*, 334 F.3d 1096 (D.C. Cir. 2003). Cheney and others filed a **petition** for a **writ** of certiorari in September 2003, and the Supreme Court granted the petition on December 15, 2003.

LLess than a month after the Supreme Court agreed to hear the case, Scalia and Cheney went duck hunting at a private camp in southern Louisiana. . Scalia and Cheney are long-time acquaintances and reportedly have made similar trips in the past. However, several legal commentators questioned the timing of the trip and suggested that Scalia may have difficulty in deciding the case on an **impartial** basis. The *Los Angeles Times*, the newspaper that first broke the story, asked Scalia about the trip. Scalia sent a written response in which he noted, "Social contacts with high-level executive officials (including cabinet officers) have never been thought improper for judges who may have before them cases in which those people are involved in their official **capacity**, as opposed to their personal capacity."

Even before the duck-hunting incident, Cheney had been entangled in controversy regarding ethics and conflicts of interest due to his involvement with the NEPDG. The group met on a number of occasions to gather information, to **deliberate**, and to make policy recommendations to the president. Allegations arose that Kenneth L. Lay, then the chief executive officer of Enron, had been directly involved in group meetings. Enron, an energy trading company, was the seventh largest company in the United States at that time. However, at the end of 2001, the company collapsed, resulting in the largest **bankruptcy** in U.S. history. Reports claimed that Lay had been highly persuasive in Cheney's decision-making process during the time in which the energy task force had met.

Under federal law, a judge is required to disqualify himself or herself in any proceeding in which the judge's impartiality may be questioned. 28 U.S.C. § 455(a) (2000). This **statute** also demands disqualification of a judge when the judge has a personal bias or prejudice concerning a party, or where the judge has personal knowledge of the facts of the case. *Id.* § 455(b)(1). Where the latter applies, partiality on the part of the judge or justice is presumed conclusively. A second federal recusal statute applies only to federal district court judges. 28 U.S.C. § 144 (2000).

Even before the debate about Scalia's visit arose, the requirements of a judge or justice, including a Supreme Court justice, recusing himself or herself had become a topic of debate among legal commentators. Some, for instance, questioned whether certain justices should have recused themselves from the case of BUSH V. GORE, 531 U.S. 98, 121 S. Ct. 525, 148 L. Ed. 2d 388 (2000) because of political ties with the REPUBLICAN PARTY.

As the story regarding Scalia and Cheney developed, reporters discovered that the men had traveled together on a small government jet and had also been accompanied by an Air Force jet and two helicopters. This report came shortly after members of Congress had begun to question whether Scalia should remove himself from the case. Senators Patrick J. Leahy (D-Vt.) and Joe Lieberman (D-Conn.) sent letters to Chief Justice WILLIAM H. REHNQUIST, questioning whether Scalia should participate in the case.

Scalia, who had responded to several media queries regarding his decision, issued a twenty-one-page memorandum on March 18, 2004. Scalia admitted that he had made the trip with Cheney, but noted that he was never alone with the vice president during the trip. Scalia denied having discussed the case with Cheney. Regarding suggestions that he should resolve doubts about his impartiality by disqualifying himself, Scalia responded that his recusal would leave the Court with only eight justices, which could lead to a tie vote. Moreover, Scalia noted his friendship with Cheney should not be a deciding factor in whether he should recuse himself. He cited numerous instances in which Supreme Court justices regularly socialized with presidents, even though the president or other senior officials were common litigants before the Court. For these and other reasons, Scalia declined to remove himself from the case.

Scalia's refusal to recuse himself came just months after he removed himself from another **pending** case involving the question of whether "under God" should be removed from the Pledge of Allegiance. In that case, Scalia had made public comments about the specific case, which has been appealed from the U.S. Court of Appeals for the Ninth Circuit. Although the Court was also scheduled to consider other cases with similar issues, Scalia did not recuse himself from those cases.

The Supreme Court ruled 7-2 for Cheney in the case of *Cheney v. United States District Court for the District of Columbia* (03-475) on June 24, 2004.

REGAN, DONALD T.

Obituary notice

Born December 21, 1918, in Cambridge, Massachusetts; died June 10, 2003, in Williamsburg, Virginia. Donald Regan was chair and chief executive officer of the securities holders Merrill Lynch & Company, before becoming secretary of the U.S. Treasury under President RONALD REAGAN in 1981. In an unusual move, Regan swapped jobs with the White House chief of staff James A. Baker III. As treasury secretary Regan supported the idea of supply-side economics and helped promote the Economic Recovery Act, which passed in 1981 and greatly reduced federal income taxes. As chief of staff, however, he had difficulties controlling his staff, and when the Iran-contra scandal—which involved illicit U.S. government arms deals with Iran and Nicaraguan rebels—surfaced in 1986, he shouldered blame for not being more aware of the activities of the national security staff, although he denied any responsibility for the affair. The scandal led him to resign his post in 1987, and he wrote about it somewhat bitterly in his For the Record: From Wall Street to Washington (1988). In addition to For the Record, Regan was also the author of A View from the Street (1972) and The Merrill Lynch Story (1981). *For the Record* sparked controversy when Regan revealed that the First Lady relied heavily on astrology to run the President's schedule. Following his retirement, Regan took up painting, exhibiting his work on two occasions.

RIGHT TO COUNSEL

The right of a defendant in a criminal action not only to legal representation, but also to effective representation.

Defense Attorney's Closing Argument Not Deficient

The U.S. SUPREME COURT has interpreted the Sixth Amendment's right to criminal defense **counsel** to mean "effective" legal counsel. When the performance of a defendant's attorney "falls below an objective standard or reasonableness" the **right to counsel** will have been violated and the defendant's conviction must be **set aside**. The defense attorney's entire performance at trial is reviewable, including the closing argument to the jury, where the attorney is expected to put forward the strongest case for the defendant's acquittal. In *Yarborough v. Gentry*, __ U.S. __, 124 S.Ct. 1, 157 L.Ed.2d 1 (2003), the Court looked at the closing argument of a California attorney and concluded that an objective review of his performance demonstrated that he had not been so ineffective as to violate the Sixth Amendment.

A California jury convicted Lionel Gentry of assaulting his girlfriend with a knife. Gentry's defense was that he had stabbed her accidentally. At trial his girlfriend testified that she remembered being stabbed but could not recall any details. Prosecutors then confronted her with previous statements she had made that Gentry had placed his hand around her throat before stabbing her twice. A security guard also testified that he had seen the incident from a neighboring building but he vacillated as to whether the quality of light at the time was dark or light. Gentry took the stand and told the jury that he had accidentally stabbed her when he pushed her out of the way. He hurt his case when he admitted to only one criminal conviction when in fact he had several. The prosecution brought out this discrepancy, which Gentry attributed to confusion over whether a plea bargain was the same as a conviction.

In the prosecutor's closing argument, she attacked Gentry's testimony as a "pack of lies" and expressed her concern for the girlfriend, who was a drug addict, a mother of three children, and pregnant at the time. The prosecutor emphasized the girlfriend's prior statements as to how Gentry assaulted her.

Gentry's attorney then made his closing argument. He brought up the inconsistencies in the girlfriend's statements and the security guard's statements about how dark or light it was at the time of the incident. He continually emphasized that there were three versions of what had happened and that he could not tell the jury which version was correct. He argued that whether the girlfriend was pregnant and had three children did not have any bearing on deciding if Gentry had intentionally stabbed her. In addition, Gentry's prior criminal record had no bearing on the alleged assault, as there was a big difference between stealing and stabbing a girlfriend. He implored the jury to look at the evidence and make a decision.

Gentry's direct appeals of his conviction to the California courts were based on the allegedly ineffective closing argument. The courts affirmed his conviction, which then led him to file a **habeas corpus petition** in federal district court, again alleging a SIXTH AMENDMENT violation. The district court denied his petition but the Ninth **Circuit Court** of Appeals reversed.

The Supreme Court, in a unanimous decision, reversed the Ninth Circuit. The Court issued a *per curiam* opinion (an opinion not signed by any of the justices) in which it concluded that the Ninth Circuit had misapplied the constitutional standards for reviewing the effectiveness **of counsel**. The Court noted that defense attorneys have "wide latitude in deciding how best to represent a client." This deference extends to tactical decisions in the closing argument and the Court will be very careful not to second-guess decisions on the basis of hindsight.

The Supreme Court pointed out that the California state courts had rejected Gentry's claims because the closing argument made several key points about the conflicts in testimony of the three main witnesses, the irrelevancy of Gentry's criminal history and the whether the stabbing was accidental. The state courts had noted a unifying theme in the closing argument: the jury, like the prosecutor and the defense attorney, could only speculate as to what had happened and who was lying. The Ninth Circuit, however, faulted the defense attorney for not bringing up other pieces of evidence that would have helped his client. These included the girlfriend's use of drugs on the day of the stabbing and the fact that the stab wound was only one inch deep. The Supreme Court concluded that other potential arguments did not establish the unreasonableness of the closing argument. Some of these potential arguments were ambiguous and some could have backfired. For example, though the girlfriend's stab wound was not deep, it did spill "the stomach's contents into her chest cavity," which required two hours of surgery to repair.

The Supreme Court, in its review of the argument, concluded that the attorney had sound tactical reasons for making and not making arguments to the jury. It also rejected the Ninth Circuit's claim that the attorney failed his client by not expressly saying that the jury needed to find Gentry **guilty beyond a reasonable doubt**. The Court ruled that the attorney's entire presentation was built around **reasonable doubt**. Moreover, the attorney knew that the judge, when charging the jury with its duties, would voice the reasonable doubt requirement. Therefore, the attorney's conduct had not been objectively unreasonable and Gentry had not been denied the right to effective counsel.

RIGHT TO DIE

Woman in Vegetative State Subject of Right to Die Fight

Terri Schiavo, who remains in a vegetative state after suffering a heart attack more than fourteen years ago, has been in the center of a firestorm of legal **controversy** that looked to be coming to a climax in 2003. Michael, her husband, finally gained permission from the courts to cease treatment and allow her to die according to her court-certified wishes. However, Florida Governor Jeb Bush personally intervened to block the cessation of life support in a move that raised questions of constitutionality and separation of judicial and legislative powers.

In February 1990, Terri Schiavo, age 27 at the time, suffered cardiac arrest, which resulted in oxygen deprivation and brain damage. Doctors reported that while Terri's brain stem was undamaged, allowing her body to function, her cognitive abilities had been destroyed and there was no real hope of recovery. A medical mal-

Michael Schiavo, left, and his lawyer answer questions.

practice suit resulting from a misdiagnosis of a chemical imbalance which led to the cardiac arrest ended in a $1 million award to her husband, Michael Schiavo, who used the money to pay for treatment for his wife. In May 1998, Michael Schiavo filed a court **petition** asking to remove Terri's feeding tube, allowing her to die. Terri did not have a **living will**. Michael claimed that Terri had told him that in a situation such as this, she would not wish to continue life-sustaining procedures and would want to be allowed to die. However, Terri's parents, Bob and Mary Schindler, claimed that this did not sound like their daughter's wishes, and held out hope for her eventual rehabilitation. The Schindlers claimed that Terri still had some kind of consciousness and found doctors to testify that she might be able to be rehabilitated. Michael was recognized by the court as Terri's legal **guardian** and authorized to make treatment decisions for his wife, but his attempts to have Terri's feeding tube removed were undermined by appeals from the parents. The battle continued in the courts for the next four years.

In October 2002, Terri's parents tried again in court, arguing that Terri was not truly in a vegetative state. They showed a tape that supposedly shows Terri responding to vocal stimuli and tracking a moving object with her eyes. They argued that Terri's condition could be improved with further therapy. Experts for Michael Schiavo countered that Terri's responses were random and reflexive and therefore not indicative of consciousness. In November 2002, after much testimony by medical experts, the court ruled that there were no treatment options that would offer a reasonable chance of improving Terri's condition. Terri's parents appealed, and in June 2003, Florida's Second District Court upheld the trial court's ruling. The Schindlers next went to the Florida Supreme Court, which declined to review the lower court's decision.

Since the court system had already ruled that Michael's and other witness testimony regarding Terri's wishes was more credible than that presented by the Schindlers and their witnesses, Michael gave the go-ahead to remove the apparatus that supplied Terri with water and nourishment. On August 30, the Schindlers filed a federal lawsuit, which claimed, among other complaints, that denying care to Terri (who could not fend for herself) was a violation of her First, Fifth, and Fourteenth Amendment rights. The suit also alleged that Michael Schiavo had for years denied Terri proper care, instead using the money from the malpractice suit to fund his legal attempts to end her life. Also entering the battle at this point was Florida Governor Jeb Bush, who filed a friend-of-the-court **brief**. George Felos, Michael Schiavo's lawyer, motioned for **dismissal**, arguing that the lawsuit was "... yet another attempt ... to re-litigate what has been litigated many times before." U.S. District Judge Richard Lazzara agreed and dismissed the case on October 10.

On October 15, Terri's feeding tube was disconnected, and it looked as though the saga might be drawing to an end. But on October 20, the Florida Legislature passed an emergency bill which Governor Bush immediately signed into law, which allowed him to order the feeding tube restored and to appoint a new guardian for Terri. Public Law 03-418, which quickly became known as "The Terri Schiavo Law", was specifically and narrowly written for this case, as it stipulated that the governor is allowed to intervene only in cases involving a person who cannot make their wishes known, left no living will, is dependant on food and hydration tubes, and where there is a family-guardian dispute over what the person's wishes were regarding life-sustaining treatment. Bush's actions were immediately denounced by civil rights groups, citing violations of Terri's right to **privacy** and questioning the constitutionality of the legislature effectively overturning what should be a purely judicial decision. George Felos commented: "Just because the governor may believe that removal of feeding tubes is wrong, it doesn't allow him (or) … the legislature to say … "we're going to force feed you against your will because that's what we believe." Michael Schiavo requested a **restraining order** against Bush, citing the questionable constitutionality of the order, but his request was denied. On October 21, Terri's food and water supply was restored.

The battle has now partially shifted to challenging the new law, as well as fighting over getting Michael Schiavo removed as Terri's legal guardian. On November 22, Governor Bush requested that an appeals court remove Judge W. Douglas Baird from hearings on The Terri Schiavo Law, claiming bias, after Judge Baird denounced the law as "presumptively unconstitutional" at an early hearing. Baird has refused to step aside. The Schindlers have also requested that Judge George Greer disqualify himself from continued battles over appointing a new guardian for Terri, claiming that he unfairly favors Michael Schiavo's side. Judge Greer has also refused to remove himself. Michael Schiavo filed suit against Jeb Bush over Terri's Law, and the Florida Supreme Court was scheduled to hear arguments on the case beginning on August 31, 2004. Judge Baird ruled the law unconstitutional in May 2004.

SECURITIES

Evidence of a corporation's debts or property.

Fixed Rate of Return Contract Qualifies as a Security Subject to Federal Securities Laws

The Securities and Exchange Commission (SEC) regulates a wide variety of investment schemes that qualify as securities under the Securities Exchange Acts of 1933 (15 U.S.C.A. § 77b(a)(1) and 1934 (15 U.S.C.A. § 78c(a)(10). The SEC can initiate civil **fraud** enforcement actions against promoters of investment plans who bilk investors. At times those charged with fraud seek to dismiss the action, arguing that the scheme was not a security as defined by **statute** and that the SEC had no jurisdiction to pursue enforcement. The Supreme Court has been called on to decide some of these definitional issues. Such was the case in *Securities and Exchange Commission v. Edwards*, __ U.S. __, 124 S.Ct. 892, __ L.Ed.2d __ (2004). The Court held that an investment scheme that offers a fixed rate of return to investors qualifies as an investment contract and therefore is a security subject to federal securities laws.

Charles Edwards was the chairman, CEO and sole shareholder of ETS Payphones. With the deregulation of the telephone industry, Edwards saw the opportunity to sell public payphones to independent distributors. He offered the payphones in a package that included a site **lease**, a **leaseback** and management agreement, and an option for him to buy back the payphones. The purchase price was $7000, with the purchaser receiving $82 per month (a 14% annual rate of return). Once the agreement was signed the purchaser had no involvement in the day-to-day operation of the payphone; ETS selected the site, setup the phone connection, collected the money from the phone, and provided **maintenance**. ETS promised to refund the purchase price at the end of the five-year lease or within 180 days of a purchaser's request to end the agreement.

Though Edwards advertised that this scheme presented a great business opportunity, ETS could not generate enough revenue from the phones to pay the purchasers their $82 monthly installments. Faced with this shortfall, Edwards paid these purchasers from the proceeds of new investors. Finally, in September 2000 ETS filed for **bankruptcy**. The SEC became involved the same month, filing a civil fraud enforcement action. Edwards challenged the action in federal district court, arguing that the sale-and-leaseback arrangement was not an investment contract within the meaning of the federal securities laws. The court rejected his claim but the Eleventh **Circuit Court** of Appeals reversed this decision on two grounds. The appeals court concluded that the fixed rate of return offered by ETS was not an investment contract under prior Supreme Court decisions. Second, it found that Supreme Court decisions required that the return on an investment must be "derived solely from the efforts of others." In the case of ETS this requirement was not met because the purchasers had a contractual right to the return.

The Supreme Court, in a unanimous decision, reversed the Eleventh Circuit. Justice SANDRA DAY O'CONNOR, writing for the Court, noted that both the federal laws and the

Court's prior decisions had broadly defined "security" to include a variety of instruments, including investment contracts. The Court looked at whether the profits were derived solely from the efforts of others to determine if an enterprise was an investment contract. However, the Court treated this requirement with great flexibility, allowing it to be applied to "countless and variable schemes." When the Court talked about profits from the efforts of others it meant "the profits that investors seek on their investment, not the profits of the scheme in which they invest." Therefore, "profits" was used "in the sense of income, or return, to include, for example, dividends, periodic payments, or the increased value of the investment."

Justice O'Connor saw no point in distinguishing between promises of fixed returns and variable returns for the purpose of determining whether an agreement was an investment contract. ETS had invited purchasers to participate in a low-risk investment, the type that is attractive to "individuals more vulnerable to fraud, including older and less sophisticated investors." If the Court adopted the Eleventh Circuit reasoning "unscrupulous marketers" could evade the securities laws merely by promising a fixed rate of return, no matter how unrealistic the return might be. Such a result would undermine the laws' purposes.

The Court found nothing in the two securities laws or in its precedents to backup the Eleventh Circuit's conclusions. In addition, the SEC had consistently ruled that agreements with fixed rates of return were investment contracts subject to SEC jurisdiction. Therefore, it made clear that "an investment scheme promising a fixed rate of return can be an 'investment contract' and thus a 'security' subject to federal securities laws."

"FundGate" Mutual Funds Scandal

Although 2003 was a very good year for many investors, it was a better year for some (privileged) investors than for others. In September 2003, New York State **Attorney General** Elliot Spitzer rocked the investment industry when he announced a multi-million-dollar settlement with Canary Capital (a "hedge fund," usually private) for mutual fund trading abuses. Janus Capital, Strong Financial, Bank of America, and Bank One Also were also implicated at the outset of the scandal. As the trouble reverberated throughout the massive mutual fund marketplace, more and more firms were drawn into the controversy. In the end, the bruised industry was left with criminal prosecutions and multimillion-dollar penalty fines, abrupt personnel changes at the highest levels, company closings, and a promise by the Securities and Exchange Commission (SEC) and state corollaries that there would be massive regulatory clampdowns.

Mutual funds had become a popular way to attract small investors into the markets. Because mutual fund firms invested in several different stocks and securities, small investors with modest capital were ablecould to buy shares of a single mutual fund, yet but still diversify their holdings. Historically, this strategy represented a safer way to reduce loss risk. Over the years, it became increasingly popular for retirement plan administrators to invest in mutual funds as one of the main investments sources for retirement portfolio holdings.

At issue in "FundGate" were two specific practices that are peculiar to the mutual fund market: "late trading" and "market timing." Both practices result in manipulation of mutual fund prices. One is illegal (late trading), and one is unethical and against most firms' policies (market timing).

Since mutual fund prices do not fluctuate throughout the trading day as do stocks do, the value of a share of a particular fund is established at the end of each trading day, at exactly 4:00 p.m. EST. At that time, the total value of the fund's investment assets is divided by the number of outstanding shares, giving resulting in the price per share. Of particular import here, allAll orders to buy or sell mutual fund shares are held until the end of the day when the price per share is established. Thus, temporary fluctuations in the various stocks contained in a mutual fund's assets are melted down togethercompiled into one fund price per share at the end of the day.

Late trading involves the illegal attempt to place an order to buy or sell after the close of the market day, but still transact at that day's price per share. The usual motivation is based either on illegal insider information about an underlying company, or information that became available after 4:00 p.m. EST and that was expected to affect the next day's trading. Late trading is harder to detect than market timing because many transactions are legally conducted after the deadline *as long as the orders were placed prior to the deadline.* This is particularly true for intermediary transactions through brokerage firms or 401(k) plan administrators rather than direct orders to a mutual fund manager, as several hours' processing time is needed to complete the transaction. Illegal late trading involves the processing of late orders that were not in fact not placed before the deadline, for the benefit of certain investors in an attempt to capitalize on later-gained acquired information.

While market timing is not illegal *per se*, it is considered against most reputable firms' policies because it again manipulates the price per share to the detriment of the total fund's assets. Market timing essentially involves international trading that capitalizes on the time difference between closing deadlines in foreign markets. Again, the impropriety involves a handful of elite investors or clients working against the interests of all shareholders of the fund's' assets.

One month after Spitzer's September 2003 announcement, the SEC surveyed the 88 largest mutual funds firms. A shocking one-half of the firms were found to have market-timing agreements with favored clients, and ten percent may might have allowed late trading. Other major fund firms accused of wrongdoing included Prudential Securities, Putnam Investments, Strong Financial, Alliance Capital Management, and Fred Alger Management, among others.

By the end of 2003, Putnam had settled the civil lawsuit brought by the SEC, but faced a similar suit brought by the Massachusetts secretary of state. Lawrence Lasser, Putnam's CEO, was fired, as was Richard Strong, CEO of Strong Financial and chairman of Strong Mutual Funds. In December, James Connelly, the vice chairman of Fred Alger Management, was sentenced by a New York judge to one to three years in prison for tampering with market-timing evidence. Two other individuals had pleaded **guilty**, Steven Markowitz of Millennium Partners, and Nicole McDermott of Security Trust Corporation. The head of the SEC's Boston office, Juan Marcelino, also resigned after it was revealed that he had failed to act on information regarding Putnam's market-timing activities.

Janus Capital first announced that it would restore $31.5 million to the funds of its shareholders for losses likely sustained by market-timing trades. Later, in April 2004, Janus announced that it had agreed to a $226 million settlement with SEC regulators. Meanwhile, Bank of America and FleetBoston Financial offered a settlement of $515 million to New York State and the SEC in March 2004. Moreover, under the terms of the proposed agreement, eight members of the mutual funds group under Bank of America would have to relinquish their positions within a year for their alleged roles in the violations. This sanction was considered the first sanction of its kind in the $7 trillion mutual fund industry.

Another ripple effect of the scandal was the filing of private, class-action lawsuits. By mid-December 2003, 27 law firms had filed suits against ten mutual funds. Citing double standards for privileged investors, several of the suits alleged that fund managers engaged in short-term trading schemes that enabled allowed certain favored investors to gain huge profits at the expense of ordinary investors. According to Eric Zitzewitz, a finance professor at Stanford University, market timing may might have cost mutual fund investors approximately $5 billion a year.

In addition to **pending** SEC regulatory changes, as many as fifteen states were investigating mutual fund activities and their impact on resident investors. The investigators maintained low profiles, since because many state laws prohibit the disclosure of pending charges.

SENTENCING

The penalty given by a court for a criminal act.

Blakely v. Washington

The U.S. SUPREME COURT in June 2004 held that a Washington state judge had violated a defendant's Sixth Amendment right to a trial by jury by sentencing the **defendant** to sixth months above the statutory maximum range. *Blakely v. Washington*, ___ U.S. ___, 124 S.Ct. 2531, ___ L.Ed.2d ___ (2004). The case reaffirmed the case of *Apprendi v. New Jersey*, 530 U.S. 466, 120 S. Ct. 2348, 147 L. Ed. 2d 435 (2000), which established that "any fact that increases the penalty for a crime beyond the prescribed statutory maximum must be submitted to a jury, and proved beyond a reasonable doubt."

In 1995, Yolanda Blakely of Montana filed for divorce from Howard Blakely. The couple owned homes in Washington and Montana, plus an orchard, a lake home, and rental properties. To protect this property from creditors and others, the Blakelys created a trust, known as the Blakely Farms Trust. When Ms. Blakely filed for a divorce, the trustee of the Blakely Family Trust asked a court for a declaration of the validity of the trust, as well as for an accounting. A divorce court in Spokane allowed Ms. Blakely to move into one of the homes and to operate the orchard.

The trust litigation was scheduled to begin in November 1998. About two weeks prior to this scheduled litigation, Mr. Blakely accosted Ms. Blakely at her home in Washington state. He tied her up with duct tape and told her that he wanted her to end the litigation about the trust. He threw her into a trunk in the back of his truck, and then proceeded to load items from the house into the truck. When the couple's 13-year-old son, Ralphy, arrived at the house, Mr. Blakely told the boy that his mother was in danger. Ralphy heard his mother in the box, but Mr. Blakely told his son that if the boy "tried anything," Mr. Blackly would shoot the boy's mother in the box. Mr. Blakely ordered his son to drive his mother's car.

When Mr. Blakely and Ralphy stopped to get gas at a station in Washington sometime later, the boy shouted for help. Truckers at the gas station prevented Mr. Blakely from dragging the boy into the truck. Mr. Blakely nevertheless was able to escape the gas station with his wife still locked in the crate. At some point during the trip, Blakely allowed his wife to sit in the front seat of the truck. They arrived at the home of Mary Gillespie, who lived close to the Blakely's home in Montana. Ms. Blakely and Gillespie devised a scheme that allowed Gillespie to call the police. Officers arrived a short time later and arrested Mr. Blakely. Blakely was prosecuted on two counts of kidnapping involving domestic violence. He pleaded not **guilty** by reasons of insanity or **diminished capacity**.

Mr. Blakely had previously been diagnosed as a schizophrenic. During the trust litigation, the court held a hearing to determine whether Blakely was **competent**. A psychologist determined that Blakely suffered from "clear mental deficiencies," and the court appointed a **guardian ad litem** to represent Blakely. However, when the state prosecuted Blakely on kidnapping charges, two evaluators determined that Blakely did not suffer from schizophrenia, but rather suffered from a severe personality disorder. After the court determined that Blakely was competent to stand trial, the defense demanded that the court hold a criminal competency trial. This trial was held in 2000, and the jury found that Blakely was indeed competent.

Blakely agreed to a plea bargain, where the state would amend the charges to include one **count** of second degree domestic violence kidnapping and one count of second degree domestic violence assault. The prosecutors agreed to recommend a sentence in the "high end" of the standard sentencing range. In exchange, Blakely agreed to a so-called *Alford* plea of guilty, named after the case of *North Carolina v. Alford*, 400 U.S. 25, 91 S. Ct. 160, 27 L. Ed. 2d 162 (1970), which allows a defendant to plead guilty even if he disputes facts alleged by the prosecution.

Two weeks after Blakely pleaded guilty, the court held a sentencing hearing. The state recommended that the court impose the high end of a standard sentence of 49 to 53 months, which would run concurrently with a sentence of 12 to 14 months for the assault charges. However, after hearing testimony from Ms. Blakely, the court rejected the state's recommendations and ordered an exceptional sentence of 90 months for the kidnapping charge. After a second hearing in October 2000, where the court heard testimony from Ms. Blakely, Ralphy, mental health experts, and a police officer, the court again imposed a 90 month sentence for the kidnapping charge.

Blakely appealed the court's decisions to a division of the Washington Court of Appeals. Among the issues in dispute was whether the trial court violated the requirements set forth by the U.S. Supreme Court in *Apprendi v. New Jersey*, 530 U.S. 466, 120 S. Ct. 2348, 147 L. Ed. 2d 435 (2000). In *Apprendi*, the Court reviewed the constitutionality of a New Jersey hate crime **statute**, which authorized a court to increase a penalty beyond the prescribed statutory maximum sentence when a judge determined by a preponderance of the evidence that the defendant committed a crime with the purpose of intimidating a victim based on particular characteristics of the victim. The Court held that in order for a court to increase a penalty beyond the prescribed statutory maximum, evidence that prompts the increased penalty must be submitted to a jury and proven **beyond a reasonable doubt**.

Blakely argued that the Washington trial court violated the requirements of *Apprendi* because the court imposed an exceptional sentence without submitting facts that led to this sentence to the jury to be proven beyond a **reasonable doubt**. However, the court of appeals disagreed. A prior case from the Washington Supreme Court, *Washington v. Gore*, 21 P.3d 262 (Wash. 2001), determined that *Apprendi* did not apply to Washington's sentencing scheme. Washington's scheme allows a judge to impose an exceptional sentence when the judge finds aggravating factors, but the exceptional sentence remains within the maximum sentence set forth by the Washington Legislature. Thus, in applying *Gore*, the court of appeals determined that the trial court had not violated the requirements of *Apprendi* in imposing the exceptional sentence on Blakely. *Washington v. Blakely*, 47 P.3d 149 (Wash. App. 2002).

Blakely sought to **appeal** the decision to the Washington Supreme Court, but the court denied a **petition** for review in February 2003. Blakely then filed a petition for **writ** of **certiorari** with the U.S. Supreme Court, which was granted on October 20, 2003. In an opinion by Justice Antonin Sclia, the Court announced from the outset that it would apply the rule in *Apprendi*. Justice Scalia disagreed with the Washington **appellate** court's holding, stressing that under *Apprendi*, the "statutory maximum" in question is considered the "maximum sentence a judge may impose solely on the basis of the facts reflected in the jury **verdict** or admitted by the defendant." In *Blakely*, the judge could not have sentenced the defendant to 90 months in prison based on the facts that were admitted in the plea of guilty. Because the facts that led to the defendant's sentence had not been proven beyond a reasonable doubt, the Court held that the sentence was unconstitutional.

The Court's decision called into serious question the constitutionality of the Federal Sentencing Guidelines, with several federal courts of appeals taking different views about whether federal judges can constitutionally apply the Guidelines after *Blakely*. Several commentators expect the Supreme Court to rule on the constitutionality in the near future.

Federal Judiciary Opposes Legislative Restrictions on Criminal Sentencing Guidelines

In 2004, U.S. SUPREME COURT Chief Justice WILLIAM H. REHNQUIST led the fight against a new federal criminal sentencing law. The law limits federal judges in making downward departures in criminal sentencing matters. Downward departures are sentences that fall below the range prescribed by the United States Sentencing Guidelines, the rules that apply to all federal court criminal sentences.

The legislation opposed by the federal judiciary and criminal defense attorneys was enacted as part of a package called the Prosecutorial Remedies and Other Tools to End the Exploitation of Children Today Act (the "PROTECT" Act), Pub.L. 108-21. The PROTECT Act is anti-child kidnapping legislation; one of its provisions establishes a federal Amber Alert system. (Amber Alerts are used to quickly inform communities when a child is reported missing.) Representative Tom Feeney (R-Flaa.) introduced the amendment to change the Guidelines not long before passage of the PROTECT Act.

The U.S. Sentencing Guidelines provide federal judges with a structure to determine a just sentence for criminal defendants. Downward departures from the Sentencing Guidelines are permitted when unusual mitigating factors exist, such that imposition of the punishment recommended by the Guidelines guidelines would be unjust.

For example, depending upon the circumstances, a downward departure might be appropriate where a felon is in possession of a firearm. A convicted felon may not possess a firearm. To do so is a **felony**. The Sentencing Guidelines provide a sentencing range of 30 to 37 months for the offense. However, in at least one case, a judge made a downward departure and sentenced a felon in possession to 18 months where the felon had not used the firearm for a violent crime, but had only possessed it long enough to transport it to a pawnshop to exchange it for money.

According to government statistics, nearly two-thirds of all federal sentences in 2001 fell within the range of the Sentencing Guidelines for 2001. Slightly more than one-third were downward departures. However, almost half of the downward departures were attributed to cases where the defendants cooperated in preparing cases against other defendants. The new law would not affect those cases. In just slightly more than a half-percentage of cases, there was an upward departure from the guidelines in slightly more than one half of one percent of cases. The U.S. Supreme Court approved the use of downward departures in federal sentencing in 1996 in the case of *Koon v. United States*, 518 US 81, 116 S.Ct. 2035, 135 L.Ed.2d 392 (1996)

Following enactment of the PROTECT Act, **Attorney General** JOHN ASHCROFT informed all federal prosecutors that they should only agree to downward departures in rare circumstances. He also ordered prosecutors to report any downward departures made over the prosecutor's **objection** to the Department of Justice, within 14 days.

The sentencing provision was enacted without formal input from either the federal judiciary or the U.S. SENTENCING COMMISSION, the **entity** responsible for the Sentencing Guidelines. The provision orders the Sentencing Commission to amend the Sentencing Guidelines "to ensure that the incidence of downward departures are substantially reduced." Speaking shortly before Congress passed the legislation in April 2003, Rehnquist said the legislation would cause "serious harm to the basic structure of the sentencing guidelines system and would seriously impair the ability of courts to impose just and responsible sentences."

In September 2003, the Judicial Conference of the United States voted to seek **repeal** of the sentencing provisions in the PROTECT Act. The Judicial Conference is the policy-making body of the federal judiciary. Chief Justice Rehnquist is its presiding officer. Other members include the chief judge of each of the 13 courts of appeals, a district judge from each of the 12 geographic circuits, and the chief judge of the Court of International Trade. The Conference makes recommendations to Congress about legislation affecting the federal judiciary, but its input was not sought before passage of the sentencing provision of the PROTECT Act.

According to a press release, the Judicial Conference is seeking repeal for several reasons. First, the Conference objects to a requirement that would make available to the House and Senate Judiciary Committees certain documents and records that the Sentencing Commission received from courts. The Conference objects to this provision because there are no established standards on preventing inappropriate disclosure, nor standards on how ways in which sensitive and confidential documents will be handled.

The Judicial Conference also objects to the requirement that the Sentencing Commission provide the Attorney General with data specific to each judge. It also objects to the provision that requires the Attorney General to provide judge-specific sentencing information to the judiciary committees of the House and Senate. In May 2003, Rehnquist attacked these provisions, saying:

> "There can be no doubt that collecting information about how the sentencing guidelines, including downward departures, are applied in **practice** could aid Congress in making decisions about whether to legislate on these issues. There also can also be no doubt that the subject matter of the questions, and whether they target the judicial decisions of individual federal judges, could amount to an unwarranted and ill-considered effort to intimidate individ-

ual judges in the performance of their judicial duties."

One federal judge, John S. Martin of New York, announced that he would retire from the **bench** as a result of the restrictions placed on downward departures. In a June 2003 opinion piece in the *The New York Times*, Martin wrote:

> Every sentence imposed affects a human life and . . . **innocent** family members who suffer as a result of a defendant's incarceration. For a judge to be deprived of the ability to consider all of the factors that go into formulating a just sentence is completely at odds with the sentencing philosophy that has been a hallmark of the American system of justice.

A bill known as the Judicial Use of Discretion to Guarantee Equity in Sentencing (JUDGES) Act has been introduced in both houses of Congress to repeal many of the sentencing provisions of the PROTECT Act. The bill is called the Judicial Use of Discretion to Guarantee Equity in Sentencing Act ("JUDGES Act).

Life Sentence Given to 14-Year-Old Reversed on Appeal

In December 2003, a Florida appellate court reversed a life sentence without parole that had been imposed on a juvenile named Lionel Tate. Tate was convicted of murdering a six-year-old girl, Tiffany Eunick, despite claims from the defense that he had been merely engaging in "rough play." Tate had been 12 years old at the time of the killing and 14 years old when he was originally sentenced. After the reversal, Tate, now 17, pleaded **guilty** to second-degree **murder** and was sentenced to time already served.

Tate's mother, Kathleen Grossett-Tate, is a highway patrol trooper in Florida. She and the victim's mother had been long-time friends, and Grossett-Tate had reportedly watched after the girl on a number of occasions. On the day in question, she had left the children to watch television and had gone upstairs. Later that evening, the mother heard a commotion coming from the children. When she went downstairs, her son informed her that the girl had stopped breathing.

Tate claimed that he was had been merely mimicking professional wrestling moves when he had killed the young girl. He said that he had put her in a headlock and had struck her head against a black, lacquer table. However, the evidence proved that Eunick was beaten viciously, suffering a fractured skull, brain contusions, a detached liver, a rib fracture, injuries to her kidneys and pancreas, and multiple bruises. At the trial, defense attorney Jim Lewis maintained that Tate was unable to understand that professional wrestling was staged and sought to have several famous wrestling stars testify at the trial. The judge refused, although he allowed the defense to show wrestling videos to the jury.

However, none of the experts at the trial, including those called by the defense, supported the defense's assertions that Eunick's injuries were consistent with play fighting. Moreover, none of the evidence suggested that the victim's injuries were accidental. Though the defense focused much of its attention on the effect that wrestling had had on Tate, jurors reportedly were more shocked by the injuries that were had been inflicted on the girl. In January 2000, the jury convicted Tate of first-degree murder.

During the post-trial proceedings, the defense requested that the court hold a hearing to determine Tate's competency to stand trial. During the trial, a neuropsychologist testified that Tate had a mental **capacity** that was about three to four years behind his age, meaning that at age 14 he had the competency of a ten-year-old. A psychologist testified that he had the social maturity of a six-year-old. Moreover, Tate's IQ was tested as 90, which is at the low end of normal. However, the court denied the motion for a competency hearing, indicating that the defense had never questioned whether Tate was **competent** to stand trial. Judge Joel Lazarus sentenced Tate to life in prison without the possibility of parole.

The sentence prompted something of a public outcry due to Tate's age when he was sentenced. Tate appealed the conviction to Florida's Fourth District Court of Appeals. The court framed the issue as whether the trial court was constitutionally required constitutionally to "determine whether Tate had sufficient present ability to consult with his lawyer with a reasonable degree of rational understanding and whether he had a rational, as well as factual, understanding of the proceedings against him." Tate's attorney noted on **appeal** noted that Tate had rejected a favorable plea bargain, which that would have resulted in a sentence of three years in a juvenile **detention** center, followed by ten years of probation. Tate's attorney argued that since Tate did not understand that if he was convicted of the murder, he would be sentenced to life in prison without parole.

Lionel Tate at a bond hearing in January 2004.

The state's attorneys argued on appeal that Tate had told the trial court that he had understood what his attorney had told him about the plea bargain, and that after consulting with his mother, he wanted to proceed to trial. Moreover, Tate said that nobody had forced him to go to trial, and he had not asked the court any questions prior to the trial. The trial court then had ordered the trial to take place.

Despite the state's arguments, the court of appeals recognized that Tate was young and that he had had little experience with the judicial system, especially in light of the complexities of the murder trial that he faced. The court found that even if a child of Tate's age could understand less serious charges, a trial court could not determine whether the child could understand the pre-trial and trial strategies, plea offers, and various waivers that accompany a murder trial without a competency hearing. The court said that the trial court could have determined whether Tate had understood the nature of the criminal justice process, the charges brought against him, and possible penalties by conducting a pre-trial or post-trial competency hearing. Thus, the court held that Tate was entitled to a complete evaluation and hearing. Because a considerable amount of time had passed since the killing and subsequent trial had taken place, the court ordered the trial court to hold a new trial. *Tate v. Florida*, 864 So. 2d 44 (Fla. Ct. App. 2003).

In January 2004, Tate accepted a plea bargain to plead guilty to second-degree murder charges. In exchange, Tate he was sentenced to the three years that he already had served, plus one year of **house arrest**, and 10 years of probation. He must also also was required to complete 1,000 hours of community service.

SEPTEMBER 11TH ATTACKS

Shutdown of September 11th Victims Compensation Fund

December 22, 2003, was the deadline for submitting claims for benefits from the September 11th Victim Compensation Fund, which had been created under the Air Transportation Safety and System Stabilization Act of 2001 (the Act). Under the program administration regulations, the deadline could not be extended, and "[c]laims outstanding at the end of [the] program because of the claimant's failure to complete his or her filings [were to] be deemed abandoned." (28 C.F.R. § 104.35) According to Kenneth R. Feinberg, Special Administrator of the Fund, more than 98 percent of those eligible for compensation did indeed file claims. Statistics released in May 2004 indicated that a total of 7,391 claims had been submitted before the deadline, including more than 4,300 claims for personal injury. As of May 18, 2004, 6,597 of those claims had been resolved. The average deceased victim's award (after collateral source offsets) was just more than $2 million, with a range of $250,000 to $7.0 million. The median deceased victim's award was $1.59 million. The Fund's fund's official Web site had not yet released the total amount of payouts from the Fund's fund's U.S. treasury account to date.

On January 22, 2004, the Fund reached its internal deadline for processing supplemental information regarding claims and claimants, and the program transitioned into its final stage of claim disposition and settlement. By law, the final day of operation for the Fund fund program was June 15, 2004, and all claims would be either be paid or authorized for payment by that date.

Under Section 405(c)(3)(B)(i) of the Act, a claimant "waives the right to file a **civil action** (or to be a party to an action) in any Federal or State court for damages sustained as a result of the terrorist-related aircraft crashes of September 11, 2001." The only exceptions are for lawsuits to recover collateral source obligations and/or lawsuits against a **defendant** who was "a knowing participant in any **conspiracy** to hijack any aircraft or commit any terrorist act." By law, state and federal court judges must dismiss an action brought by any person(s) who had also filed for benefits under the Victims Compensation Fund. The submission of a claim for a deceased person by any beneficiary waives the rights of other beneficiaries of that victim to file a lawsuit.

Notwithstanding, approximately seventy persons (and ten companies that suffered property damage in the attacks) ostensibly waived their rights and filed civil suits against various third-party defendants in federal court. The Act had specified that all suits were to be heard by the U.S. District Court of the Southern District of New York, Manhattan, where the World Trade Center stood. The path to private suit was risky compared to the "no-fault" compensation offered by the Fund. First, Congress limited the **liability** exposure of several defendants; for example, the liability of the airlines was limited to the amount of insurance carried on each plane that was hijacked on September 11, 2001. Ultimately, those who sued instead of opting for the Fund took the chance that they might get receive the same amount, or even less, than what the Fund offered. Second, the civil suits were grounded mostly grounded in tort, necessitating requiring plaintiffs to prove fault on the parts of the various defendants airport operators, airlines, security firms, the owners and operators of the World Trade Center, and Boeing. There was very little evidence as to how the takeover of the planes actually had occurred. Since the true perpetrators had died along with the victims in the crashes, there was no way to bring them to justice. Juries might or might not be sympathetic to placing fault with other entities.

In fall 2003, the cases were consolidated for judicial economy (deciding common questions of law, and possibly common questions of fact at trial). The defendants then filed a motion to dismiss the suits. They argued that, as a **matter of law**, the plaintiffs had not pleaded a viable **cause of action** because the defendants had breached no duty to the victims. Any duty owed to victims, *if any*, had not included protecting them against the unforeseen criminal acts of third parties. Moreover, even if, **arguendo**, such a duty was owed, most of the injuries (**i.e.**, death, **injury**, and property damage) had occurred on the ground or to people and property on the ground, to whom *no* duty was had been owed.

With the clock ticking as to the deadline for filing claims under the Fundfund, U.S. District Court Judge Alvin Hellerstein ruled, in September 2003, that plaintiffs' suits articulated a **cognizable** cause of action. Finding that the defendants had owed a legal duty to protect the victims of September 11, and that the events of that day had been "foreseeable" under **tort law**, he denied the motion to dismiss.

Judge Hellerstein had previously dismissed other lawsuits stemming from the attacks. In May 2003, he dismissed three suits brought against the fund's administrator that claimed that the fund improperly limited awards to the families of high-income victims. Finding such a claim without merit, Judge Hellerstein ruled that the fund "reasonably and properly" implemented the Congressional act that created it. In April 2004, Hellerstein also dismissed **product liability** suits by firefighters' families against Motorola for defective design and/or failure to warn cross-band radio communications systems). The **dismissal** was premised on the plaintiffs' waiver of their right to sue, having also filed claims with the fund. *Vigilio v. Motorola*, S.D.N.Y., No. 03-V-10156.

Notwithstanding the existence and purpose of the Victims Compensation Fund, many other valiant acts of courage and generosity surrounded the attack victims and their survivors. On the afternoon of September 11, a special fund was set up by United Way to finance thirteen major not-for-profit organizations in efforts stemming from the disaster. United Way raised $250 million from 105 countries, of which approximately ninety percent was given as cash assistance for rent, food, and bills to victims and their families. The fund also paid for specialized mental health and counseling referrals for 20,000 people, and for mental health programs for hundreds of children who had witnessed the attacks. Columbia University research on children six months after the attacks concluded that 200,000 had developed mental health problems, including agoraphobia (fear of open spaces), separation anxiety, and generalized depression or anxiety.

Supreme Court Rules that U.S. Citizens Classified as Enemy Combatants May be Detained Indefinitely

On June 28, 2004, the United States Supreme Court issued its ruling in *Hamdi v. Rumsfeld*. The case stemmed from anti-terrorism policies implemented after the attacks on the United States on September 11, 2001. The Supreme Court ruled that the U.S. government may detain Yaser Hamdi, a United States citizen and a suspected terrorist, without charges or trial. However, the court ruled that due process demands that Hamdi be given a meaningful opportunity to challenge his **detention** in court.

Almost immediately after the September 11 attacks, Congress passed the Authorization for Use of Military Force (the "AUMF"). The AUMF authorized the president to "use all necessary and appropriate force against those nations, organizations, or persons he determines planned, authorized, committed, or aided the terrorist attacks" or "harbored such organizations or persons, in order to prevent any future acts of international **terrorism** against the United States by such nations, organizations or persons." President Bush relied on the AUMF in late 2001 when he launched military action in Afghanistan against the Taliban regime, and al Qaeda, the terrorist network responsible for the September 11 attacks.

Yaser Esam Hamdi was born in the U.S. in 1980, but grew up in Saudi Arabia. In late 2001 Hamdi was taken into custody by an Afghani group fighting the Taliban. He was turned over to U.S. custody and was transferred to the U.S. Naval Base at Guantanamo Bay in Cuba. After Hamdi's U.S. citizenship was established, he was transferred to the U.S in April 2002. He has been detained since then in a naval brig in the United States.

Hamdi's father, Esam Fouad Hamdi, filed a **petition** for **writ** of **habeas corpus** on behalf of his son. Esam Hamdi alleged that he had not been permitted to have any contact with his detained son. He asked that legal **counsel** be appointed for Yaser Hamdi, and that the government inform him of any **pending** charges. Esam Hamdi contended that Yaser Hamdi's detention violates the Fifth and Fourteenth Amendments to the Constitution, and sought his immediate release. The senior Hamdi claimed that his son was in Afghanistan doing **relief** work and was caught in the wrong place at the wrong time when the war broke out.

In response, the government contended that Hamdi's detention is authorized because he has been classified as an enemy combatant. The government argued that this classification entitles the U.S. to hold Hamdi indefinitely without pursuing formal charges. The government also contended that this status can remain in effect "unless and until" it determines that access to an attorney or further process is necessary.

As the case made its way through the lower federal court system, the government offered a declaration from Michael Mobbs, a Special Advisor to the Under Secretary of Defense for

Policy. Mobbs asserted that Hamdi had received weapons training shortly before the September 11 attacks; upon his capture, he surrendered a Kalishnikov assault rifle. Mobbs stated that individuals associated with al Qaeda and the Taliban are classified as enemy combatants, and that Hamdi was classified as such "based upon his interviews and in light of his association with the Taliban."

The first question before the Supreme Court was whether the administration has the right to detain a U.S. citizen classified as an enemy combatant. The Supreme Court noted that the government has never fully explained how it classifies persons as enemy combatants, but that it includes one who is "part of or supporting forces hostile to the United States or coalition partners" in Afghanistan and who "engaged in an armed conflict against the United States" there.

The Supreme Court agreed with the government that Hamdi's detention was explicitly authorized by Congress in the AUMF. Writing for the majority, Justice SANDRA DAY O'CONNOR explained, "We conclude that detention of individuals . . . for the duration of the particular conflict in which they were captured, is so fundamental and accepted an incident to war as to be an exercise of the 'necessary and appropriate force' Congress has authorized the President to use." She went on to explain that imprisonment is not intended as punishment, but instead is a "simple war measure" meant to prevent a combatant from returning to the battlefield. Moreover, "[t]here is no bar to this Nation's holding one of its own citizens as an enemy combatant."

Hamdi also objected to the indefinite nature of his detention. "It is a clearly established principle of the law of war that detention may last no longer than active hostilities," wrote O'Connor. The court recognized that the U.S. "war on terror" may continue indefinitely, and that as such, it could conceivably lead to Hamdi's detention for the remainder of his life. However, the court noted that at present, active hostilities continue against the Taliban in Afghanistan. As long as that is the case, detention of enemy combatants is warranted.

The court next addressed what constitutional rights are due to a citizen who disputes his enemy combatant status. After an examination of various approaches, the court held that "a citizen-detainee seeking to challenge his classification as an enemy combatant must receive notice of the factual basis for his classification, and a fair opportunity to rebut the Government's factual assertions before a neutral decision-maker." O'Connor suggested that under the unusual circumstances involved in an ongoing military conflict, it might be necessary to accept **hearsay** as reliable evidence. The court also suggested that it would be acceptable for the government to make a credible showing that a person qualified as an enemy combatant. At that point, the burden could shift to the purported combatant that he does not meet the criteria.

Finally, the court noted that Hamdi only gained access to counsel once the Supreme Court agreed to hear his case. The court stated Hamdi "unquestionably has the right to access to counsel in connection with the proceedings" as he challenges his status as an enemy combatant.

Chief Justice WILLIAM H. REHNQUIST and Justices STEPHEN BREYER and ANTHONY M. KENNEDY joined O'Connor's majority opinion. Justices DAVID H. SOUTER and RUTH BADER GINSBURG filed concurring opinions that supported Hamdi's request for a day in court. But they disagreed with the majority regarding his detention, and would have declared the detention improper.

Justices ANTONIN SCALIA, JOHN PAUL STEVENS, and CLARENCE THOMAS dissented. Scalia wrote, "the Government has failed to justify holding [Hamdi] in the absence of a further Act of Congress, criminal charges, a showing that the detention conforms to the laws of war," or any other grounds.

Moussaoui Terrorism Trial

In April 2004, the U.S. **Circuit Court** of Appeals for the Fourth Circuit issued a complicated ruling in the delayed criminal trial of Zacarias Moussaoui, alleged terrorist and self-proclaimed al-Qaeda operative. The United States intended to link Moussaoui with the September 11, 2001, terrorist attacks, charging that, but for the fact that had he not already been in federal custody as of September 11, 2001, he would have been the "20th Hijacker." Four of the six charges against him carried the death penalty. However, much of the *evidence* against him centered on alleged statements made by three other al-Qaeda members in U.S. custody. The key issue on **appeal** was the U.S. government's refusal to permit those witnesses to testify, wanting instead to submit summaries of their responses to **custodial interrogation** as substitution for **deposition** testimony. Of course, Moussaoui's defense attorneys cited Moussaoui's right to cross-examine any witness whose testimony could be used against him, the lack of which would likely result in an unfair trial.

Moussaoui alleged that the testimony of those witnesses would exonerate him and prove that he had no involvement in the SEPTEMBER 11TH ATTACKS. That very argument had been successfully used in a German court to reverse the conviction of Mounir el Motassadeq, another September 11th suspect tried in that country for aiding the three Germany-based September 11th hijackers. In February 2004, a German appeals court cited, as reason for ordering a retrial, the lack of potentially exonerating evidence from one of the same al-Qaeda witnesses as in the Moussaoui trial. The German court ruled that the lower court had failed to consider how the United States' refusal to allow access or testimony from the al-Qaeda witness (held in secret U.S. custody) affected or influenced the case. The U.S. ban on testimony was also a key factor in the acquittal of two other Germans indicted on the same charges. Moreover, the U.S. refused to allow a witness in its custody to testify in an Indonesian trial against Abu Bakar Bashir, an Islamic extremist with links to al-Qaeda links. Instead, the U.S. provided investigators' notes in which the witness implicated Bashir. The evidence was found to be inadmissible.

In the Moussaoui matter, the criminal complaint against him, filed in U.S. District Court for the Eastern District of Virginia in December 2001 (and superceded by a newer indictment in July 2002), alleged six counts of criminal **conspiracy**. According to the indictment, Moussaoui, who is of Moroccan descent, attended an al-Qaeda training camp in 1998. He arrived in the U.S. in February 2001 and began taking flight lessons in Oklahoma, but he was arrested for an immigration violation in August 2001. The indictment, highlighting similarities between Moussaoui's conduct and that of the September 11th hijackers, charged that the actions of Moussaoui, along with his co-conspirators, "result[ed] in the deaths of thousands of persons on September 11, 2001."

From the outset, Moussaoui denied any involvement in the September 11th attacks. Representing himself during early pre-trial proceedings, he demanded access to several al-Qaeda witnesses being held in custody elsewhere by U.S. officials. The district court, after consideration of the U.S. government's strong opposition, concluded that the first witness could indeed offer testimony in Moussaoui's defense.

The court further determined that the government's national security interest must yield to Moussaoui's right to a fair trial. However, the court denied a defense request for unmonitored pre-trial access to the witnesses. Balancing the interests of both sides, the court, citing Federal Rules of Criminal Procedure 15(a)(1) as authority, ordered that Moussaoui (or his standby **counsel**) take the deposition of the witnesses by remote video. In deference to national security interests, the court further ordered that the witnesses be in an undisclosed location and that counsel for both sides and/or Moussaoui, conduct the deposition in the presence of the district court (the "January 30 order").

The federal government appealed the order. On **remand**, the U.S. Fourth Circuit Court of Appeals questioned whether any substitution existed that would place Moussaoui in substantially the same position as would a deposition. Both sides presented to the district court proposed substitutions for the deposition, in the form of statements that the witness ostensibly would make if called to testify. The district court rejected the government's proposed substitute statements, and the government informed the court that it would refuse to provide access to the witness.

Meanwhile, the district court made similar rulings regarding the other witnesses to whom Moussaoui had demanded access to (the "August 29" order compelling Rule 15 depositions or approved substitutions). When the court again rejected the government's proposed substitutions, the government responded that it would not comply with the August 29 order and that it would not produce the witnesses. The defense recommended **dismissal** of the indictment. The government did not oppose, as it could always try Moussaoui in a military tribunal. It filed a **responsive pleading**, which that noted that, under the Classified Information Procedures Act, dismissal is the presumptive action a district court must take under such circumstances.

The district court sought a sanction other than dismissal. It dismissed the death notice, noting that Moussaoui had adequately demonstrated that the witnesses could provide testimony that, if believed, might preclude a jury from recommending the death penalty. The court further ordered that, since the witnesses' testimony could have exonerated Moussaoui of involvement in the September 11th attacks, the government was prohibited from introducing any evidence that suggested his involvement.

Finally, it prohibited the introduction of any evidence of cockpit voice recordings or video footage of the collapse of the World Trade Center towers, or photographs of victims.

On further appeal to the Fourth Circuit, the government objected to all of the above. The appellate court made careful note of the "grave significance" of the questions presented,

> questions that test the commitment of this nation to an independent judiciary, to the constitutional guarantee of a fair trial even to one accused of the most heinous of crimes, and to the protection of our citizens against additional terrorist attacks. These questions do not admit of easy answers.

After lengthy discourse and consideration, the Fourth Circuit ultimately affirmed in part, vacated in part, and remanded to the district court. In its April 2004 decision, it affirmed the lower court's previous orders, rejecting the government's proposed substitutions for the witnesses' testimony. It further agreed with the lower court's conclusion that the "enemy combatant witnesses" could provide material, favorable testimony on Moussaoui's behalf. However, it found that deference to the government's national security concerns was warranted. It therefore reversed the lower court's sanctions against the government, in effect, re-establishing the government's right and opportunity to pursue evidence that might support a death penalty. Finally, the **appellate** court remanded to the district court "for the crafting of substitutions for the deposition testimony of the enemy combatant witnesses." In May 2004, Moussaoui's attorney's asked the Fourth Circuit to remove the death penalty from consideration if Moussaoui did not have full access to the witnesses, arguing that he was therefore incapable of preparing his best defense.

9-11 Commission Report

The National Commission on Terrorist Attacks Upon the United States (also known as the 9-11 Commission) released its much-anticipated Commission Report in late July 2004. The findings were critical of several entities and organizations within the U.S. government, spanning both the Clinton and Bush administrations. However, the findings fell short of media speculation that the September 11, 2001 terrorist attacks could have been prevented. Instead, the report concluded,

> Since the plotters were flexible and resourceful, we cannot know whether any single step or series of steps would have defeated them. What we can say with confidence is that none of the measures adopted by the U.S. government from 1998 to 2001 disturbed or even delayed the progress of the al Qaeda plot. Across the government, there were failures of imagination, policy, capabilities, and management.

Under an Executive Summary section entitled "Who Is the Enemy?," the report identified "... Islamist extremists. The 9/11 attack was driven by Usama Bin Ladin." It went on to note, "The first phase of our post-9/11 efforts rightly included military action to topple the Taliban and pursue al Qaeda." The commission proposed a three-dimensional strategy, (1)attack terrorists and their organizations; (2)prevent the continued growth of Islamist **terrorism**; and (3) protect against and prepare for terrorist attacks.

Other key findings in the report included a determination that U.S. leaders under the Bush and Clinton administrations failed to understand the gravity of the threat, leaving the country unprepared to meet al Qaeda's challenges. According to the commission, terrorism was not the chief security concern of either administration. Further, the failure to thwart the 9/11 attacks only highlighted the inability of several government agencies to adapt to new threats or problems. A specific finding focused on the lack of coordinated information-sharing or analyses between agencies.

The commission's key recommendations included the creation of a Cabinet-level post for an intelligence director (labeled by the media as an "intelligence czar"); the establishment of a single counterterrorism center; and the establishment of a single, joint congressional committee to oversee homeland security. Although the entire 588-page report was available online at the commission's official Web site, http://www.9-11commission.gov, hard copy sales reached 150,000 on the first day, making it the No.1 seller according to Amazon.com.

The 9-11 commission was created by Congress and signed into law by President GEORGE W. BUSH (PL 107-306) in late 2002. It was set up as an independent and bipartisan initiative, fully chartered to investigate and prepare a complete account of the circumstances surrounding the September 11, 2001 terrorist attacks. The focus included not only the attack itself, but also the preparedness for, and immediate response to, the events of that day. Further, the commission's charter included a mandate to provide recommendations aimed at guarding against future attacks. Specifically, Section 604 of the law required the commission to investigate facts and circumstances relating to intelligence agencies; law enforcement agencies; immigration, nonimmigrant visas, and border patrol; commercial aviation; the flow of assets to terrorist groups; the role of congressional oversight and resource **allocation**; and other areas determined relevant to the commission in its inquiries.

To that end, the commission engaged in holding public hearings to offer public dialogue about the commission's goals and priorities. Each hearing and the topic focus were publicized several weeks beforehand. Topics included "Terrorism, Al Qaeda, and the Muslim World" (July 2003, Washington, D.C.); "Intelligence and the War on Terrorism" (October 2003, Washington, D.C.); "Emergency Preparedness" (November 2003, Drew University, New Jersey); "Security and Liberty" (December 2003 in Washington, D.C.); "Borders, Transportation, and Managing Risk" (January 2004 in Washington, D.C.); "Counter-terrorism Policy" (March 2004 in Washington, D.C.); "Testimony from Dr. Condoleezza Rice" (April 2004, Washington, D.C.); "Law Enforcement and the Intelligence Community" (April 2004 in Washington, D.C.); "Emergency Response" (May 2004 at New School University in New York City); and "National Crisis Management" plus "The 9-11 Plot" (June 2004 in Washington, D.C.).

By early 2004, the commission had taken testimony from 110 federal, state, and local officials, as well as experts from the private sector, and had interviewed more than 1,000 individuals in ten countries.

Of key interest to the media, politicians, and ultimately to the public, were the Presidential Daily Briefs (PDBs) and the testimony of Dr. Condoleezza Rice, National Security Advisor. These informational resources were considered by many to be crucial to the commission's ability to **render** a fair and accurate report, all things considered. The commission stated in its official website that its four-member Review Team had received:

> ...every single PDB item for which the Commission requested access. The Team prepared a detailed report on all PDBs of critical importance to the Commission's mandate. All Commissioners were briefed for over three hours on this 7,000-word report, joined with a supplement of complementary intelligence documents. The Commission was also given every word of the August 6, 2001, item on al Qaeda and the threat of attacks on the United States.

Moreover, the media provided television coverage of the testimony of Dr. Rice at her appearance before the commission and a public audience, which included several family members of 9/11 victims. During questioning, she offered no apology for the Bush administration's failure to prevent the attacks on the World Trade Center, but did mention several obstacles working against such preventive measures. They included structural and legal barriers to the flow of information between and within intelligence agencies, as well as a general tendency, in democratic societies, to respond slowly to gathering threats. One of the main issues to come from her testimony was the need for structural reform in domestic agencies, particularly those dealing with intelligence gathering.

Initially, the commission was to report to the President and Congress 18 months after it was established, or no later than May 27, 2004. Public Law 108-207 extended the commission's reporting deadline to July 26, 2004, after which the commission was to be terminated on August 26, 2004.

SEX OFFENSES

A class of sexual conduct prohibited by the law.

Basketball Superstar Faces Rape Charges

On June 30, 2003, near the ski resort town of Vail, a female hotel employee and a married man met in a room at a hotel in Edwards, Colorado. What happened that night is in dispute—he called it consensual sex, but she called it **rape**. What makes this case different is that the man is Los Angeles Lakers basketball star Kobe Bryant, one of the most respected and recognized athletes in the world. The build-up to the case has spawned a massive media circus of a scale not seen since the 1995 O.J. Simpson trial. As a result of the frenzied media scrutiny, many questions have been raised about the right to **privacy** of the accuser in this and other cases involving sexual assault.

The day after the alleged incident, the woman informed the police. The county sheriff issued an **arrest warrant** for Bryant. On July 4, 2003, Bryant flew back to Colorado and surrendered peacefully. He was released after posting bond of $25,000. On July 18, Bryant was charged with one **count** of sexual assault, which

Kobe Bryant (center) leaving court in March 2004.

carries a penalty of four years to life in prison or up to life on probation. Bryant admitted to having sex with the woman but insisted that the sex was consensual.

There were no witnesses to the alleged assault, so the case, which had not gone to trial as of July 2004, would pit Bryant's word against his accuser's. Most of the arguments in court will revolve around the lawyers for each side trying to build up their respective clients' **credibility**, while finding weaknesses and inconsistencies in the other side's version of events to exploit during **cross-examination**. However, the prosecution, citing Colorado's rape-shield law, challenged the depths to which Bryant's lawyers were allowed to dredge for material to build their case. Rape-shield laws, which have been enacted in many states, are designed to protect the victims of sex crimes by making any testimony regarding their previous sexual activity non-admissible in court. However, the law is only intended to prevent the defense from using such testimony merely to destroy the plaintiff's image and thus to **impeach** their credibility. The law does not apply when such testimony can be used to *directly* show that the **defendant** is **innocent**.

Bryant's lawyers worked to have the alleged victim's sexual history admitted into evidence. One of the main points in their defense is their claim that the woman framed Bryant in an attempt to win the attention of an ex-boyfriend. Her sex life is also relevant, they argue, because the genital injuries that she apparently suffered could have been caused by sex with other men. The defense claims that the woman is promiscuous and that semen stains found in her underwear are not a genetic match to Bryant. Craig Silverman, a Denver lawyer and expert on rape cases, commented that "If the defense can . . . put on evidence that she had sex with another man (besides Bryant) before going to the cops, then the chance of conviction is zero." The woman's lawyers, family, and victim-advocacy groups, meanwhile, were up in arms over the possibility that the woman could be forced to answer personal and embarrassing questions in court, something that the rape-shield law was intended to prevent.

Judge Terry Ruckriegle ordered that the plaintiff must testify about her sexual past in order to determine whether or not it was admissible in court. However, Judge Ruckriegle ordered that the hearing be held behind closed doors in order to avoid as much media scrutiny as possible. The hearings started on March 24, 2004 and continued through the next day. Proceedings were not completed, however, because several witnesses were not able to answer their subpoenas. The remainder of the hearing was scheduled for late April 2004. The woman's lawyers claim that the hearings serve no purpose but to allow the defense to intimidate their client.

Other legal maneuverings continued in preparation for the trial. The defense filed motions including a motion to suppress certain evidence (a blood-stained shirt and a tape recording of Bryant's statements to police when he was arrested), a motion to admit the accuser's mental health and medical history as evidence, and a broader challenge of Colorado's rape-shield law (possibly opening the way for the woman to be forced to testify during the case itself). The plaintiff's attorneys have filed a motion to expedite rulings on **pending** motions and to set a trial date. The woman's mother wrote a letter to the judge as well requesting that the trial be concluded as speedily as possible, citing numerous death threats that her daughter has received since news of the case broke. The mother wrote that "(the plaintiff's) life is on hold and her safety is in jeopardy until this trial is over." The woman has reportedly been moving from state to state, and job to job, trying to avoid media scrutiny and harassment from the curious and has "lived in four different states in the past six months." Reportedly, three people have been arrested so far and charged with making death threats against her. Bryant remains free and continues to play basketball for the Lakers.

With the trial set to begin in late August 2004, observers of the case were shocked to see prosecutors drop all charges against Bryant when the alleged victim refused to testify in court. Prosecutors announced that only the alleged victim's reluctance to do so caused them to drop the case, but many legal observers believed that the chances of a conviction were slim, particularly after the judge agreed to allow the alleged victim's sexual history as evidence. For his part, Bryant offered the young woman an apology, noting that "Although I truly believe this encounter between us was consensual, I recognize now that she did not and does not view this incident the same way that I did." A civil lawsuit filed against Bryant by the young woman remains to play out in court.

Conviction of Retired FBI Official

Retired Federal Bureau of Investigations (FBI) official John H. Conditt, Jr., who had headed the agency's internal investigations unit, was arrested in 2003 for sexually molesting the six-year-old daughter of two other FBI agents, one of whom was now his wife. The sexual assaults (at least ten) of his stepdaughter allegedly occurred in 2002, after Conditt retired from the FBI in June 2001. Conditt also acknowledged molesting at least two other girls prior to his two-decade law enforcement career.

Details surrounding the 2003 arrest were not the subject of media attention. However, it was known that Conditt sought treatment for sex offenders after his arrest, and also admitted that he had been attracted to other children over the years. However, according to FBI officials, there was no information to support charges of wrongdoing during the 27 years of Conditt's FBI career, and he had not been the subject of any internal investigation. Conditt also denied any abuse during those career years.

At the time of his retirement, then-50-year-old Conditt was chief of the FBI's Internal Investigations Unit 1, located within the Office of **Professional Responsibility**. The unit served as the beacon of the FBI's internal disciplinary program. Conditt held that post from 1999 until his retirement. Prior to that, he had served as an FBI special agent and a police officer. Following his retirement, Conditt headed a private consulting and investigative firm in the Dallas-Ft. Worth, Texas, area.

Of particular irony in Conditt's case is the fact that, prior to his arrest, Conditt was generally recognized as the authoritative writer of several law journal articles pertaining to the subject of internal self-policing for law enforcement agencies. One such article, published in the November 2001 FBI Law Enforcement **Bulletin**, was entitled, "Institutional Integrity: The Four Elements of Self-Policing."

In February 2004, then 53-year-old Conditt, who admitted his guilt to ostensibly spare the child from the trauma of trial, was sentenced in a Tarrant County, Ft. Worth, Texas, court to 12 years in prison. Although he could have received up to 50 years, the presiding judge cited Conditt's decision to admit guilt as one of the sentencing factors. Conditt openly wept while on the witness stand, telling the judge that his stepdaughter would need "help" for the rest of her life as a result of his conduct. Conditt's wife requested leniency in sentencing for her husband, expressing hope to remain married to him, despite his molestation of her daughter. Local members of a Colleyville church also appeared outside the courtroom to offer support.

Conditt's conviction was the latest controversy to strike within the FBI's Office of Professional Responsibility. Earlier in 2003, FBI Director Robert Mueller transferred the head of that office to another assignment outside Washington, after rebuking him for his conduct toward a whistleblower. The whistleblower had alleged that the FBI disciplinary office had a double standard when disciplining supervisors **versus** line agents. The allegations prompted investigations by Congress and the Justice Department's Inspector General. While the latter's investigation concluded that there was no *systematic* favoritism of supervisory personnel, it did find instances of a double standard in some cases involving sexual jokes or remarks.

During Conditt's **tenure** as chief, another whistleblower had complained to his office that FBI agents had failed to aggressively pursue evidence of sexual abuse in Indian territories. Conditt's office declined further review.

SEXUAL ABUSE

Illegal sex acts performed against a minor by a parent, guardian, relative, or acquaintance.

University of Colorado Football Program Marred by Rape Allegations

The football program at the University of Colorado (UC) at Boulder came under intense pressure in 2003 when three females filed lawsuits alleging that they had been raped by UC

Katie Hnida in a University of Colorado football uniform.

football players and recruits while attending an off-campus party in December 2001. Further scandal surfaced when former UC Buffalo kicker Katie Hnida told news reporters in early 2004 that she, too, had been raped and sexually harassed by her teammates during the 1999 season. The situation worsened when the UC Buffaloes' football coach Gary Barnett told reporters the media that he knew nothing of Hnida's charges, then added, "It was obvious that Katie was not very good. She was awful. You know what guys do-they respect your ability. Katie was a girl, and not only was she a girl, she was terrible. There's no other way to say it." Following Barnett's statement, the Boulder police releasing released a report that Barnett had told another woman who had alleged **rape** by a football player in 2001 that he would "back [his] player 100 percent if [she] took this forward in the criminal process." The University placed Barnett on administrative leave.

Shortly afterwards, a cascade of other less-than-desirable assertions began to tumble out. Claims that an adult entertainment company in Denver had provided strippers for recruiting parties at UC (and several other colleges) were followed by the admission of a former UC football team assistant that he had used his official UC-provided cell phone to hire prostitutes and to call sex-chat lines. These and other events prompted the district attorney (DA) in Boulder, Mary Keenan, to reopen archived investigations stemming from police reports involving two other women who had alleged rape by Colorado's football players in 2001.

When attorneys for the women in the federal lawsuits released DA Keenan's **deposition**, in which she stated that UC used women and alcohol to lure recruits, and that she had previously had put the school "on notice," the whole scandal hit the desks of state authorities' desks. Governor Bill Owens wrote to the UC Board of Regents, urging them to hasten resolution. This action prompted the UC Board of Regents to create a paneled commission to investigate the various charges.

The UC Board of Regents appointed seven members to the panel, which was to report its findings later in 2004. In addition, Keenan requested that the governor involve the state **attorney general** in order to allay concerns that her involvement in the civil suits would not interfere with any criminal investigations. In February 2004, Governor Owens appointed Colorado state Attorney General Ken Salazar as special prosecutor in the matter.

However, UC's problems were not over. In early 2004, the newly formed National College Athletic Association's (NCAA) Task Force on Recruiting began investigating the issue. In March 2004, UC President Betsy Hoffman testified before Congress on the matter (the House Energy and Commerce Committee's consumer protection subcommittee has jurisdiction over certain sports-related issues). The recruiting tactics of several other universities and colleges were scrutinized, with similar (on a smaller scale) findings to those of UC.

The UC rape lawsuits alleged that the university cultivated an environment that tolerated the sexual harassment and victimization of women in its football program, in violation of **Title** IX of the Education Amendments of 1972 (affecting institutions which receive federal funds). In late 2003, the U.S. Court of Appeals for the Eighth Circuit decided a similar case, *Ostrander v. Duggan*, 341 F.3d 745 (8th Cir. 2003), in which a University of Missouri (MU) female student alleged that she had been assaulted by a fraternity member. Her suit also invoked Title IX, claiming that MU controlled the premises upon which the assault took place, and acted with "deliberate indifference" to previous sexual assault allegations against the same fraternity. The court of appeals found that the student had insufficient evidence to support her allegations. Nevertheless, the appellate court noted that for a public university to be held liable, it must be "(1) deliberately indifferent (2) to known acts of discrimination (3) which occur under its control." The court further found that the fraternity neither owned nor controlled the property upon which the alleged assault had occurred, and so it never reached the issue of a Title IX violation.

On May 11, 2004, Colorado's attorney general announced that no criminal charges would be filed in the sexual assault cases. A lack of solid evidence and the desire of several victims to avoid the criminal justice process were cited as primary reasons for the decision.

Michael Jackson Charged With Sexual Abuse of Children

On November 20, 2003, pop singer Michael Jackson, 45, surrendered himself to Santa Barbara, California, police after learning they had issued a warrant for his arrest the previous day. Charged with child molestation ("lewd or lascivious acts with a child under age 14"), he was booked and released on $3 million bail. This incident followed a November 18, 2003, raid at his palatial residence, Neverland Ranch, which resulted in police and investigators seizing several bags of evidence that included computers, videotapes, and poems written by Jackson to his young accuser.

A formal **felony** complaint was filed in Santa Barbara on December 18, 2003. **Venue** was premised on the location of Neverland, Jackson's residence, located in the same county. Jackson was charged with seven counts of committing "lewd and lascivious act[s] upon and with the body and certain parts and members thereof of John Doe, a child under the age of fourteen," in violation of California Penal Code Section 288(a). Counts 8 and 9 accused Jackson of administering to "John Doe" certain intoxicating agents with the **intent** to enable or assist Jackson in committing the above-mentioned sexual felonies. It was further alleged that Jackson "had substantial sexual contact with John Doe." A special notice in the complaint declared that the pseudonym "John Doe" was used to protect the **privacy** of the alleged victim. Finally, the complaint contained notice that conviction of "this offense" would require that Jackson register as a sex offender, pursuant to Penal Code Section 290. The complaint was signed by Santa Barbara District Attorney Thomas W. Sneddon, Jr., who investigated Jackson in 1993 and 1994 for similar offenses.

In his first public statement following the charges, Jackson appeared in an interview with Ed Bradley on CBS's "60 Minutes" in late December 2003. During the Christmas Day interview in a Los Angeles hotel room, Jackson called the allegations "totally false" but admitted that he often shared his bed with children, including the 13-year-old accuser, a cancer patient. Jackson told Bradley the charges against him were all about "money."

In the same interview, Jackson complained of "hurting" and wanted to end the session sev-

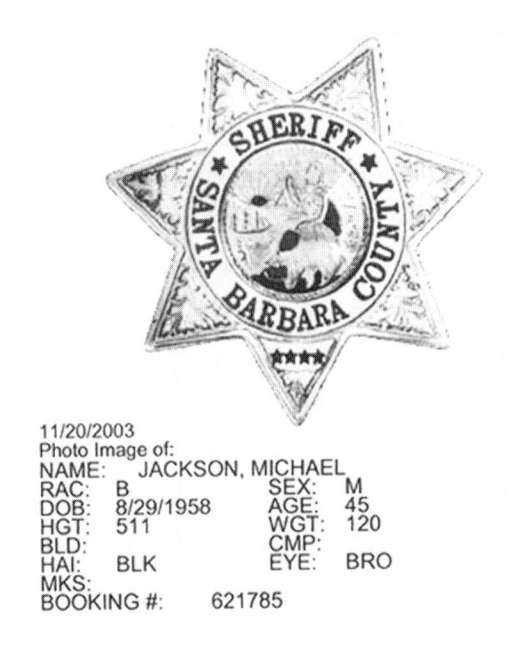

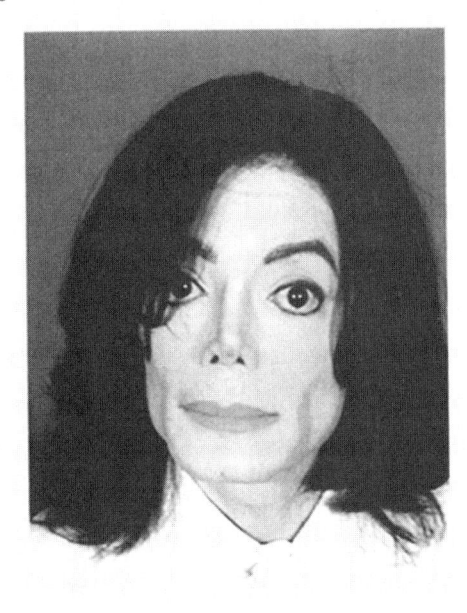

Michael Jackson's booking photo and personal information, released by the Santa Barbara County Sheriff's Department following Jackson's booking on child molestation charges.

eral times. He told Bradley that during his November 20 arrest and booking, the police "manhandled" him "very roughly," and showed Bradley marks above his wrists. He also claimed that his shoulder was "literally" dislocated, causing pain "all the time." Finally, he claimed that police "locked" him in the booking station's restroom "for, like, 45 minutes," where he endured the stench of "feces thrown all over the walls, the floor, the ceiling . . ." Santa Barbara police issued a blanket denial, and several media networks later aired a videotape of a smiling Jackson exiting the police station waving and flashing the peace sign to his fans, with both arms raised high above his shoulders.

In late 2003, the media seized upon relevant documents "leaked" from the Los Angeles County Department of Children and Family Services. Specifically, an internal memorandum, dated November 26, 2003, was disclosed on the web site thesmokinggun.com. It purported to show that a February 2003 investigation of Michael Jackson, involving alleged sexual molestation of the same child accuser, concluded that the allegations were "unfounded." Importantly, the investigation was not premised on charges made by the boy or his family, but rather, by a call to a hotline as a result of an ABC *20-20* television broadcast of a British documentary about Jackson and Neverland. In that broadcast, the boy, holding hands with Jackson, openly stated that he often slept in Jackson's bed, but that Jackson slept on the floor next to the bed. He also referred to Jackson as "Daddy." However, in private sessions with a psychiatrist later that year, the boy stated that Jackson had sexually molested him in February and March of 2003. The psychiatrist contacted authorities.

On January 16, 2004, Jackson was formally arraigned, without incident. Presiding Santa Barbara County Superior Court Judge Rodney S. Melville issued a gag order prohibiting Jackson and attorneys or witnesses involved in the case from speaking with the press. Several media outlets appealed the order in April 2004.

A **grand jury** formally indicted Jackson on all nine counts on April 21, 2004, obviating the need for a **preliminary hearing** before the judge to determine whether sufficient evidence existed to warrant a full criminal trial. The indictment was not released publicly until April 30. The published indictment contained an additional **count** for felony **conspiracy** to commit crimes of child **abduction, false imprisonment**, and **extortion**. In support thereof, the indictment **enumerated** 28 specific overt acts allegedly committed by Jackson in furtherance of the alleged conspiracy, but details of those acts were deleted from the public version of the document.

On April 30, 2004, Jackson entered his plea of not **guilty** to all charges. He appeared with his new defense attorney, Thomas Mesereau, Jr., who replaced Mark Geragos and Benjamin Brafman. Judge Melville stated that transcripts from the grand jury proceedings would be available to the attorneys but would remain under seal **pending** a hearing on May 28, 2004. He expressed hope that a trial could be completed by the end of 2004.

SEXUAL HARASSMENT

Unwelcome sexual advances, requests for sexual favors, and other verbal or physical conduct of a sexual nature that tends to create a hostile or offensive work environment.

Constructive Discharge Applies to Sexual Harassment Claims

Since the mid 1980s, the U.S. SUPREME COURT has addressed sexual harassment in the workplace claims filed under **Title** VII of the Civil Rights Act of 1964. The Court has attempted to protect employees from sexual harassment while also granting employers an **affirmative defense** if they develop harassment-reporting procedures. It sought to maintain this balance in *Pennsylvania State Police v. Suders*, __ U.S. __, 124 S.Ct., __ L.Ed.2d __ 2004 WL 1300153(2004) in ruling that a woman who had quit her job because of sexual harassment could sue her employer under the **doctrine** of constructive **discharge**. However, the Court also gave the employer the right to assert an affirmative defense to such a charge.

Nancy Drew Suders was hired by the Pennsylvania State Police (PSP) in March 1998 to work as a communications operator. Suders had three male supervisors, each of whom subjected Suders to a steady stream of sexual harassment. One supervisor constantly talked about **bestiality** in front of Suders, and another discussed his views on oral sex and young girls in front of her. Suders had to endure repeated **obscene** gestures and vulgar comments involving sex acts. In June 1998, Suders talked to the equal employment opportunity officer and indicated that she might need some help. Suders did nothing until August 1998, when she contacted the officer and reported that she was being harassed and that she was afraid. According to Suders, the officer said that she could file a complaint but did not tell her how to obtain the necessary form. Two days later, after her supervisors accused her of theft, Suders quit her job. She filed a lawsuit against PSP, alleging that the supervisors' conduct constituted sexual harassment. She claimed that her resignation amounted to constructive discharge, in violation of Title VII. The district court found that the sexual harassment had created a hostile work environment but dismissed her claim, ruling that PSP was not liable for the actions of the supervisors. On **appeal**, the U.S. Court of Appeals for the Third Circuit reversed. It agreed with Suders that her resignation was a constructive discharge. Under this doctrine, courts treat an employee's reasonable decision to quit because of extremely difficult conditions as if the employer had fired the employee. Based on this doctrine, the appeals court further held that PSP had no affirmative defense to the discharge and that it was strictly liable for the supervisors' harassing conduct.

The U.S. Supreme Court, in an 8-1 decision, agreed that constructive discharge could be applied to sexual harassment claims, but it also found that employers could assert an affirmative defense. Justice RUTH BADER GINSBURG, writing for the majority, noted that the constructive discharge concept had originated in labor law in the 1930s. The National Labor Relations Board (NLRB) developed the concept to deal with employers who coerced employees to resign by creating intolerable working conditions in retaliation for the employees' union organizing activities. Following the enactment of Title VII in 1964, the federal courts of appeal recognized constructive discharge claims based on race, religion, national origin, pregnancy and sexual harassment. In addition, the EQUAL EMPLOYMENT OPPORTUNITY COMMISSION had recognized that employers are liable for constructive discharges. Justice Ginsburg, noting that this issue was of first impression for the Court, held that constructive discharge can be used in Title VII actions.

Having settled this issue, Justice Ginsburg reviewed the ability of employers to defend themselves from **liability** for harassment attributable to a supervisor. In two 1998 decisions, *Faragher v. City of Boca Raton*, 524 U.S. 775, 118 S.Ct. 2275, 141 L.Ed.2d 662 (1998), and *Burlington Industries, Inc. v. Ellerth*, 524 U.S. 742, 118 S.Ct. 2257, 141 L.Ed.2d 663 (1998), the Court developed two categories of hostile work environment claims. The first type of claim involves harassment that "culminates in a **tangible** employment action," such as discharge or demotion. Employers are strictly liable for this type of harassment and cannot raise a defense that relieves them of responsibility for the actions of supervisors. The second claim involves harassment that does not result in a tangible employment action. In these cases, the employer may raise an affirmative defense.

The question in the present case was whether constructive discharge was a tangible employment action. Justice Ginsburg concluded that constructive discharge was "functionally the same as an actual termination in damages-enhancing respects," but it was not always based on an official act. If a plaintiff can tie the constructive discharge to an official act, then the employer will be found strictly liable. However, when no official act triggers the discharge, the employer must be given the chance to assert an affirmative defense. In such cases, the employer can escape liability by showing that it had established a sexual-harassment-reporting process and that the employee did not use this procedure.

The Court sent the case back to the lower courts so Suders could make her constructive discharge claim. If Suders cannot not show that the PSP's conduct amounted to an official act, then PSP can argue that her resignation just two days after mentioning the harassment to the equal employment opportunity officer was not justified.

Justice CLARENCE THOMAS, in a dissenting opinion, objected to the Court's definition of constructive discharge. He argued that an employee must show that the employer intended to force a resignation before constructive discharge could apply.

Nancy Suders, shown at the police barracks in McConnellsburg, Pennsylvania.

SIMON, PAUL

Obituary notice

Born November 29, 1928, in Eugene, Oregon; died December 9, 2003, in Springfield, Illinois. After beginning a career as a newspaper publisher and editor, Simon moved into politics following a stint in the U.S. Army in the early 1950s. He was elected to the Illinois House of Representatives in 1954, serving until 1963. During his time there, he won passage of forty-six major pieces of legislation and became known for his staunch ethics. Simon served as lieutenant governor after winning election in 1968, but lost a 1972 bid for the governorship of Illinois. Simon detoured into teaching following that defeat, teaching at both Sangamon State College and Harvard. In 1973, Simon won Illinois' twenty-fourth Congressional district seat, where he served for twelve years. In 1984, Simon won election to the U.S. Senate, where he voted against the MX missile, the B1 bomber, and the Strategic Defense Initiative. Simon ran for the Democratic presidential nomination in 1987, but challenged on his economic policies and acceptance of money from politcal action committees despite calling for a crackdown on those same committees, he fell out of the race early. Simon won a second term in 1990, and announced in 1994 that he would not seek third term. Following his retirement, he continued writing books, as well as starting a public policy institute at Southern Illinois University.

SIXTH AMENDMENT

Crawford v. Washington

The U.S. SUPREME COURT determined in March 2004 that a tape-recorded statement made to police officers by a criminal defendant's wife could not be used against the **defendant** at trial because the defendant could not cross-examine his wife at trial (due to **marital communications privilege**). Admission of such a statement violated the defendant's right to confront witnesses against him under the Sixth Amendment to the U.S. Constitution. The decision in *Crawford v. Washington*, 124 S. Ct. 1354 (2004) has been viewed as friendly to defense lawyers, and some commentators have suggested that the decision bars many forms of testimony that were previously admissible.

According to testimony in the case, Kenneth Lee attempted to **rape** Michael Crawford's wife, Sylvia, in 1999. Several weeks after the alleged assault, Michael Crawford became angry when Lee's name was mentioned, and Crawford and his wife went to find Lee. When they arrived at Lee's apartment, Crawford stabbed Lee in the chest. During the altercation, Crawford's hand was cut. Police officers arrested both Michael and Sylvia and read them both their *Miranda* rights. Both Michael and Sylvia were interrogated twice by the officers.

During the interrogations, which were tape-recorded. Michael's version of the story differed significantly from Sylvia's. According to Michael, he thought he saw something in Lee's hand when the fight between the men ensued. However, Michael could not state for certain that Lee indeed had a weapon or anything else in his hand at the time of the stabbing. Sylvia's story was similar to Michael's statement regarding the events that led to the stabbing, but Sylvia's account apparently differed regarding the stabbing. According to Sylvia, Lee seemed to grab for an object after the stabbing, rather than before the stabbing.

The State of Washington charged Michael Crawford with assault and attempted **murder** for stabbing Lee. Crawford claimed that he acted in self-defense. The state could not **call** Sylvia as a witness because Washington recognizes a marital privilege, which prevents one spouse from testifying against another unless the other spouse consents. Without Sylvia's testimony, the state played Sylvia's tape-recorded message to the jury. The court admitted the tape into evidence, and Crawford was convicted of assault.

Crawford objected to the admission of Sylvia's statement on the grounds that its admission violated Crawford's SIXTH AMENDMENT right to confront a witness used against him. The Supreme Court has previously clarified the Sixth Amendment's **confrontation clause** in *Ohio v. Roberts*, 448 U.S. 56, 100 S. Ct. 2531, 65 L. Ed. 2d 597 (1980), which held that the Constitution allows for the admission of a statement of an unavailable witness if the statement contains "indicia of reliability." In order to satisfy this standard, the evidence must either be admissible under a "firmly rooted **hearsay** exception" or bear "particularized guarantees of trustworthiness." The trial court allowed the tape to be entered as evidence because it found that the testimony was trustworthy.

Crawford appealed his conviction to the Washington Court of Appeals. According to the appellate court, several elements suggested that Sylvia's statement was not trustworthy. For instance, her taped statement contradicted a previous statement, and the statement was made in response to specific questions posed by police officers. Moreover, the court found that Sylvia's statement differed on critical issues related to the conviction. Accordingly, the court reversed the conviction. *State v. Crawford*, No. 25307-1-II, 2001 WL 850119 (Wash. App. July 30, 2001). However, on further **appeal**, the Washington Supreme Court reversed the court of appeals, finding that the statement indeed bore **indicia** of trustworthiness. According to the Washington Supreme Court, Sylvia's statement was virtually identical to Michael's, even though the two appeared to differ as to whether the victim had a weapon at the time of the stabbing. *State v. Crawford*, 54 P.3d 656 (Wash. 2002).

The U.S. Supreme Court granted **certiorari** to review the decision of the Washington Supreme Court. According to Justice ANTONIN SCALIA, who wrote the U.S. Supreme Court's opinion, the text of the Sixth Amendment alone could not resolve the dispute. Scalia examined, in great detail, the history of the rule regarding the right to confront witnesses. Scalia determined that the rule was principally concerned with the admission of **ex parte** examinations that occurred prior to trial. Perhaps the most famous case discussed in Scalia's opinion involved Sir Walter Raleigh, who was sentenced to death for treason in 1603. At an examination by the Privy Council prior to Raleigh's trial, one of Raleigh's accomplices, Lord Cobham, implicated Raleigh. Despite Raleigh's objections that he should be allowed to confront Cobham, the prosecutors used Cobham's testimony against Raleigh without calling Cobham himself as a witness. Due to the perceived injustices of this case, a rule in England developed that gave a criminal defendant the right to face his witnesses in court.

With this historical context in mind, the U.S. Supreme Court determined that the Sixth Amendment should bar only those statements that are "testimonial" in nature. If a statement is indeed testimonial, then it can be used against a criminal defendant only in circumstances where the witness was not able to testify and where the defendant was able to cross-examine the defendant at the time that the statement was made. On the other hand, if a statement is not testimonial, then the admissibility is determined by rules of evidence governing hearsay. The Court's opinion, however, does not define "testimonial," indicating that the Court would "leave for another day any effort to spell out a comprehensive definition of 'testimonial.'"

Significantly, the Court rejected the rule from *Ohio v. Roberts* that allowed admission of testimony if a court found "indicia of reliability." According to Scalia, the *Roberts* decision did not comport with the historical context of the rule in the confrontation clause. Although Chief Justice WILLIAM REHNQUIST agreed with the Court's **judgment**, he disagreed that the Court should have abrogated the rule in *Roberts*. In a separate concurrence, Rehnquist argued that prior precedent would require a judge to reject Sylvia's statement, and so the Court did not need to make such a dramatic change in existing law. Moreover, Rehnquist criticized Scalia's refusal to define "testimonial," noting that "thousands of federal prosecutors and tens of thousands of state prosecutors need answers" regarding the definition of this term.

Commentators have noted that the Court's decision in *Crawford* will have far-reaching implications on criminal procedure in the United States. For instance, courts will need to determine whether a call made to 911 constitutes a statement that is testimonial in nature. If such a statement is indeed testimonial, then it could be barred by the Sixth Amendment. Similarly, prosecutors in domestic violence and child abuse cases commonly do not call the victims as witnesses in trials, choosing instead to examine the police officers who took the victims' statements. Under *Crawford*, many of these victims will be required to testify in court.

Sixth Amendment Rights Under Miranda Implicated Whether or Not Police "Interrogated" Defendant

The U.S. SUPREME COURT, in *Miranda v. United States*, 384 U.S. 436, 86 S.Ct. 1602, 16 L.Ed.2d 694 (1966), required law enforcement officers to warn criminal suspects that they had a set of constitutional rights, including the right to remain silent under the Fifth Amendment and the right to legal **counsel** under the SIXTH AMENDMENT. For almost 40 years, the Court has reviewed numerous cases involving the failure of police to issue timely *Miranda* warnings to determine whether a defendant's confession may be used in a criminal trial. Many of these cases have been analyzed using the FIFTH AMENDMENT but the Sixth Amendment's **right to counsel** provision has also been used. Such was the case in *Fellers v. United States*, __ U.S. __, 124 S.Ct. 1019, __ L.Ed.2d __ (2004), in which the Court reversed a **circuit court** decision because the appeals court had incorrectly applied a Fifth Amendment rather than a Sixth Amendment analysis.

A Lincoln, Nebraska, federal **grand jury** indicted John J. Fellers for **conspiracy** to distribute methamphetamine. Following the indictment two Lincoln law enforcement officers went to Fellers' house to arrest him. He voluntarily let them into his living room. The officers told him they had an **arrest warrant** for him based on his involvement with methamphetamine distribution and that the grand jury had indicted him on the conspiracy charge. The officers referred to four individuals named in the indictment, at which point Fellers admitted that he knew them and had used methamphetamine with them. The conversation lasted about 15 minutes before the officers drove him to the county jail. It was only after arriving at the jail that the officers gave Fellers his *Miranda* warnings. Fellers signed a waiver of his rights and told the officers even more incriminating details about his association with the other alleged conspirators.

Prior to his trial, Fellers' attorney asked the court to suppress the statements that Fellers made at his house and at the jail. The judge held a hearing on the matter and agreed that any statements Fellers made at his house must be suppressed. As to the jailhouse statements the judge concluded that Fellers had knowingly and voluntarily waived his *Miranda* rights and the statements could be used at trial. The statements were used and a jury convicted Fellers of the conspiracy charge. Fellers appealed his conviction, arguing that his jailhouse statements were fruits of the suppressed house statements and should be barred as well under the Sixth Amendment. The Eighth Circuit Court of Appeals affirmed the conviction, finding that the officers had not interrogated Feller at his house. Therefore, the officers were not required to issue the *Miranda* warnings at the house. Based on this reasoning the police did not interrogate Fellers until after he waived his rights at the jail. Based on this analysis the statements made at the jail were properly admissible.

The Supreme Court unanimously reversed the Eighth Circuit decision. Justice SANDRA DAY O'CONNOR, writing for the Court, noted that the Sixth Amendment's right to counsel is triggered once a criminal proceeding begins, whether it is through indictment or some type of criminal court appearance by the **defendant**. In *Massiah v. United States*, 377 U.S. 201, 84 S.Ct. 1199, 12 L.Ed.2d 246 (1964), the Court explicitly ruled that statements must be suppressed if they are made after indictment and in the absence **of counsel**. More importantly, if law enforcement officers have "deliberately elicited" incriminating statements, they will be suppressed as a Sixth Amendment violation. This analysis is different than a Fifth Amendment **custodial interrogation** standard, which looks at whether the suspect was in custody when he was interrogated without being issued the *Miranda* warnings. Justice O'Connor made clear that the Sixth Amendment right to counsel applies even when there is no custodial interrogation.

The Eighth Circuit had incorrectly applied the Fifth Amendment standard. Finding that Fellers had not been "interrogated" at his house, the appeals court had ended the inquiry. Justice O'Connor ruled that the officers had deliberately elicited the statements at Fellers' house. Because Fellers had already been indicted, his right to counsel had been triggered prior to the officers' arrival at his house. The failure to read him his rights fatally tainted these statements and they were properly suppressed at trial.

As to the admissibility of the jailhouse statements, the Supreme Court sent the case back to the Eighth Circuit for reexamination. The Eighth Circuit was instructed to determine whether the jailhouse statements were the tainted fruits of the statements made at Fellers' house in violation of the Sixth Amendment. The appeals court was to decide whether Fellers' incriminating statements at the jail, given after a knowing and voluntary waiver of his right to counsel, were admissible.

No Precise Formula on Ways in Which Judges Advise Defendants of Their Rights

Though criminal defendants are entitled to legal **counsel** under the SIXTH AMENDMENT, defendants they may **waive** this **right to counsel**. Such waivers often occur at **arraignment** hearings, where defendants have the option of entering a **guilty** or not-guilty plea. When a **defendant** enters a guilty plea without an attorney, the judge is obligated to advise the defendant of the range of penalties that may be levied. The U.S. SUPREME COURT reaffirmed this procedure in *Iowa v. Tovar*, __ U.S. __, 124 S.Ct. 1379, 158 L.Ed.2d 209 (2004),). Their ruling overturned a state supreme court decision requiring trial judges to warn defendants of the disadvantages of not retaining a lawyer. In so ruling, the Court made clear that the Constitution does not require such a warning.

Felipe E. Tovar was a 21-year-old college student when he was arrested in Ames, Iowa, for driving under the influence of alcohol. He consented to a breath test that revealed a blood alcohol count above the legal limit. A few hours after his arrest, Tovar appeared before a judge.

He waived his right to counsel and was released. At his arraignment two weeks later, Tovar again waived his right to an attorney and pleaded guilty. The judge accepted the guilty plea only after he had explained to that Tovar that he had a right to a lawyer and a jury trial. The judge went into detail, pointing out that Tovar would lose his right to remain silent at trial, his **presumption of innocence**, and his right to **call** witnesses. The judge then informed Tovar of the maximum penalty for his crime, and Tovar stated that he understood the possible consequences of his guilty plea. He admitted to the fact that he was driving while intoxicated and again stated his desire to enter a guilty plea. The judge noted on the record that Tovar had made his plea voluntarily and that he had understood his rights and the consequences of pleading guilty. The judge then accepted his Tovar's plea.

Six weeks later, Tovar returned to court for sentencing and for arraignment on a new charge, driving with a suspended license. Tovar waived his right to counsel on the new charge, and the judge went through the same conversation as before, advising him of his rights. Again, Tovar admitted his guilt. The judge then sentenced him on both charges, giving him two days in jail and a total of $750 in fines. Sixteen months later, Tovar was convicted of driving under the influence. Though he retained an attorney for this charge, he again pleaded guilty. Tovar could not stay out of trouble. Two years later he was arrested for a third drunk-driving offense, which under Iowa law moved the charge from a gross misdemeanor to a **felony**. This third time, Tovar pleaded not guilty, and his attorney filed a motion to **set aside** the first drunk-driving conviction. He argued that the first conviction could not be used to trigger the felony charge because Tovar had not been warned by the judge of the types of disadvantages that could flow from not having legal counsel. The trial court denied the motion, ruling that such a warning was not required. Tovar was convicted of the charge and received a six-month jail sentence, three years of probation, and a $2,500 fine.

The Iowa Court of Appeals affirmed the conviction, but the Iowa Supreme Court reversed it, directing the trial court not to count the first conviction. The court reasoned that the judge's conversation with Tovar at the first arraignment had been constitutionally inadequate. The state supreme court announced a series of warnings that a trial judge must give before accepting a guilty plea from an unrepresented defendant. The court directed judges to warn defendants that they may overlook a "viable defense" by pleading guilty and that by refusing a lawyer they lose the "opportunity to obtain an independent opinion" as to whether "it is wise to plead guilty."

The U.S. Supreme Court, in a unanimous decision, overturned the Iowa Supreme Court. Justice RUTH BADER GINSBURG, writing for the Court, reaffirmed the Sixth Amendment's right to counsel at all "critical stages" of the criminal process, including arraignment and sentencing. However, a defendant may decline legal representation if the waiver of this right is "knowing, voluntary, and intelligent." Reviewing the judge's statements and questions at the first plea hearing, Justice Ginsburg concluded that the judge had satisfied these waiver requirements. The Court rejected the idea that there was a prescribed "formula or script to be read to a defendant who states that he elects to proceed without counsel." Instead, there are "case-specific factors," such as the education of the defendant and the complexity of the charges, which must be examined. In this case, Tovar understood his rights and voluntarily waived them. Justice Ginsburg questioned whether Tovar would have waived his rights if the Iowa Supreme Court's "script" had been used. In addition, she worried that such a set of warnings would give defendants false hopes and encourage them to prolong hopeless cases. Therefore, the Court rejected the constitutional need for such warnings. States are free to adopt "any guides to the acceptance of an uncounseled plea they deem useful," but they are not required to do so under the Sixth Amendment.

SOCIAL SECURITY

A federal program designed to provide benefits to employees and their dependants through income for retirement, disability, and other purposes. The social security program is funded through a federal tax levied on employers and employees equally.

Claimant Can Be Denied SSI Benefits Even If Previous Type of Work No Longer Exists

Individuals who believe they are disabled and cannot work may apply for Supplemental Security Income (SSI) through the Social Security Administration (SSA). The SSA will grant benefits only after finding that a claimant's impairment is of such severity that he or she cannot do his or her prior work and cannot, based on age, education and work experience "engage in any other kind of substantial gainful work which exists in the national economy." 42 U.S.C.A. §§ 423(d)(2)(A), 1382c(a)(3)(B). This statutory language defining a qualified "disability" has generated many administrative and judicial appeals from claimants denied SSI benefits. In *Barnhart v. Thomas*, __ U.S. __, 124 S.Ct. 376, 157 L.Ed.2d 333 (2003), the Supreme Court was called on to decide whether the SSA can **deny** benefits because the claimant can do her previous work without first investigating whether her previous work still exists in the national economy. The Court concluded that the SSA was not obligated to conduct such a review.

Pauline Thomas was an elevator operator from 1989 until 1995, when her job was eliminated. The following year she applied for SSI, claiming that she could not work because of heart disease and back problems. The SSA denied her claim and she requested a hearing before an administrative law judge (ALJ). The ALJ ruled against Thomas, finding that she did suffer from physical impairments but that these injuries did not prevent her from returning to work as an elevator operator. Thomas had argued that she was unable to do her previous work because elevator operator jobs no longer existed in the national economy. The ALJ rejected this argument, as did the SSA's Appeals Council. Thomas then filed suit in federal district court, again arguing that the scarcity of elevator operator jobs meant that she was unable to perform her previous work. Thomas lost in district court, as the judge found that under SSA regulations, the scarcity of a job was **irrelevant** in determining the award of benefits. However, the Third **Circuit Court** of Appeals reversed this decision, holding that the SSA could only deny benefits if a claimant's prior job "exists in the national economy." Four other circuit courts of **appeal** had taken a contrary position, which led the Supreme Court to accept review to resolve the conflict.

The Court, in a unanimous decision, reversed the Third Circuit decision. Justice ANTONIN SCALIA, writing for the Court, noted that the issue in the case was whether the **clause** "engag[ing] in any other kind of substantial gainful work which exists in the national economy" qualifies the earlier clause that requires that a person be unable to perform her "previous work." Justice Scalia looked at the SSA's five-step evaluation process for determining disability as a point of reference. If at any step in this process the SSA finds that a person is disabled or not disabled, then the review ends. Thomas passed the first step, as she was not gainfully employed, but at the second step, she failed to demonstrate a physical impairment that prevented her from performing basic work activities. The third step was to see if her impairment was on a list that rendered one disabled. Thomas's impairment was not on the list. The fourth step was determining whether Thomas could do her previous work. The SSA concluded that she could do that work, which then ended the inquiry. Justice Scalia pointed out that the fifth and final step was to determine whether a person was capable of performing any other work. The SSA regulations made clear that it would not move to this step unless at step 4 the claimant could not do her previous work, regardless of whether the job still existed. The Court had to determine if it should give deference to the SSA's **interpretation** of the SSI **statute**.

Justice Scalia concluded that the SSA interpretation was reasonable. The Third Circuit had disregarded the grammatical "rule of the last antecedent," in which a "a limiting clause or phrase (here, the relative clause 'which exists in the national economy') should ordinarily be read as modifying only the noun or phrase that it immediately follows (here, 'any other kind of substantial gainful work')." The Third Circuit had used the "which exists in the national economy" to limit the prior clause dealing with "previous work." Though Scalia admitted the rule was not **absolute**, it made sense in the present case. In addition, the SSA interpretation could be viewed as a reasonable interpretation of congressional **intent**. In most cases a person who was capable of performing her prior job could also perform other work. The fourth step in the SSA evaluation process was an "efficient administrative proxy" that negated an "expansive" review of the claimant's ability to find other work based in individualized factors. Therefore, the SSA reading of the statute was reasonable.

SPORTS LAW

The laws, regulations, and judicial decisions that govern sports and athletes.

Allegations of Steroid Use Tied to Several Top U.S. Athletes

A number of top American athletes, including baseball star Barry Bonds and track and field icon Marion Jones, became embroiled in a scandal involving a previously undetectable steroid, known as tetrahydrogestrinone (THG). The drug was allegedly produced by Bay Area Laboratory Co-Operative (Balco) of San Francisco under the direction of company president Victor Conte, Jr. A federal **grand jury** investigating Conte's activities distributed subpoenas to several athletes in October 2003, and the controversy has threatened the **credibility** of these athletes, including those who prepared to compete in the 2004 Summer Olympics in Athens, Greece.

In May 2003, the U.S. Anti-Doping Agency (USADA), the body that tests American athletes for illegal drugs and supplements, received an anonymous tip that several athletes were using an undetectable steroid. The tip allegedly came from a high-profile track and field coach. In June 2003, Dr. Donald H. Catlin of the University of California, Los Angeles, received a test tube of a liquid from an anonymous source, possibly the same coach who provided the information to the USADA. According to a story in *The New York Times*, Catlin believed that he had encountered a "smoking gun" that would link steroid use with some top athletes.

During the next three months, Catlin and his team of eight chemists discovered THG, which the group found to be similar to two other known steroids, gestrinone and trenbolone. The group also developed a urine test that could detect the drug. In August 2003, several elite athletes submitted urine samples. Test results showed evidence of THG in samples from Regina Jacobs, a top miler in the United States, as well as Dwain Chambers, Britain's top sprinter.

Authorities began to suspect Balco and Conte as the source of the steroid. Conte had served as a nutritional advisor to several athletes in both team sports and individual competitions. On September 3, 2003, federal and local authorities raided Balco's offices in Burlingame, California, where officers discovered banking and credit card records, e-mail messages, and similar types of evidence. The search allegedly also turned up syringes tainted with steroids in Balco's medical waste. During the next month, members of the media began to speculate that the investigation could reveal steroid use in a number of different sports. A federal grand jury was convened to determine whether Balco and Conte had violated any criminal statutes.

In October 2003, the grand jury sent subpoenas to approximately 40 amateur and professional athletes in several sports. Among those who received subpoenas were Bonds, Jones, sprinter Tim Montgomery, baseball star Jason Giambi, boxer Shane Mosley, and several professional football players. The grand jury began hearing testimony on October 30, 2003, and continued for several months. The grand jury's investigation resulted in a 42-count indictment against Conte and several other top executives from Balco, as announced by **Attorney General** JOHN ASHCROFT in February 2004. The charges allege a scheme by Balco to provide anabolic steroids, human growth hormone, and other drugs to figures in several major sports in the United States. The indictment also alleges that Balco executives engaged in **money laundering**.

Though none of the athletes that testified were charged with wrongdoing, media speculation about steroid use intensified. News agencies in March 2004 reported that Bonds, Giambi, baseball star Gary Sheffield, as well as football players Barret Robbins and Bill Romanowski, were among those athletes who had received steroids from Balco. A summary of a document prepared by an investigator of the Internal Revenue Service later revealed that Conte had named 27 individuals as those who received steroids from him.

Many commentators have speculated that the use of steroids and other performance-enhancing drugs has increased during the past decade, despite numerous efforts to curb use of these drugs. Steroid use is generally banned in most sports, although it is tested more thoroughly in some sports than in others. Olympic and other amateur athletes are subjected to intensive testing due to well-known instances

Victor Conte poses with a picture of Barry Bonds, one of the sports stars his company had dealings with.

and other allegations surrounding the use of performance-enhancing drugs. The timing of the investigation and forthcoming trial has cast a shadow over the 2004 Olympic Games in Athens, Greece, since several of the top U.S. competitors have been linked with Balco. Baseball in particular has suffered from the scandal. Bonds broke the single-season record for most home runs in a season in 2001 and surpassed Willie Mays in 2004 for third place on the list of most career home runs. However, his accomplishments have been overshadowed due to his association with the steroid allegations.

The concerns over steroid use have not been limited to sports commentators. At the State of the Union address in January 2004, President GEORGE W. BUSH singled out steroid use as a societal problem that must be addressed. "The use of performance-enhancing drugs like steroids in baseball, football, and other sports is dangerous, and it sends the wrong message—that there are shortcuts to accomplishment, and that performance is more important than character," Bush said. "So tonight I **call** on team owners, union representatives, coaches, and players to take the lead, to send the right signal, to get tough, and to get rid of steroids now."

The trial of Conte and other Balco officials was expected to begin either during the summer or the fall of 2004.

TELECOMMUNICATIONS

The transmission of words, sounds, images, or data in the form of electronic or electromagnetic signals or impulses.

Telemarketers Fight Do-Not-Call List

In January 2002, in response to consumer complaints, the Federal Trade Commission looked into the creation of a national registry for households who did not wish to receive unsolicited advertising calls, seeking to build on the precedent established by several similar initiatives passed by individual states. In May of the same year, the FEDERAL COMMUNICATIONS COMMISSION joined in. Citing updated telemarketing strategies and technologies, the FCC began researching ways to revise and update the 1991 Telephone Consumer Protection Act 47 U.S.C.A. § 227. What was eventually created became known as the Do-Not-Call Registry, and its provisions, implementation, and enforcement have been the subject of numerous court actions over the last year.

The Do-Not-Call List, as conceived, would allow households to register telephone numbers in a national registry. Companies that engaged in telemarketing practices would be required to subscribe to the list, which would be updated regularly. Money from subscription fees would be used to fund the list. If a company called a number on the list, they could be subject to fines of up to $11,000 for each violation. Most devastating to telemarketers, however, would be the removal of an estimated 60% of their potential market.

From the beginning, the Do-Not-Call List had the blessings of numerous consumer agencies and advocacy groups, who filed their comments with the FTC and FCC. In mid-December 2002, the FTC announced that it would update the Telemarketing Sales Rule already on the books to include a do-not-call list. On January 29, 2003, the nascent list received its first court challenges. In Colorado, the American Teleservices Association and two marketing companies filed suit against the FTC in U.S. District Court. Meanwhile, five telemarketing companies filed suit in Oklahoma. Both suits made basically the same allegations, the main complaint being that the list violated their First and Fifth Amendment rights by placing a "prior restraint on speech", because the government, not the individual, would have authority to determine what calls are permitted. The companies further argued that there were other options besides a government-enforced ban, such as establishing a do-not-call list regulated by the companies themselves.

On March 11, 2003, Congress passed the Do-Not-Call Implementation Act, Pub. L. 108-10, which President Bush signed, allowing the FTC to collect its subscription fees. On March 21, Stonebridge Life Insurance Company filed a suit seeking exemption from the List for insurance companies, arguing that the FTC does not have jurisdiction over the insurance industry. On June 26, the FCC announced its support of the Do-Not-Call Registry, and on June 27 the program began enrollment, with the list to go into effect on October 1. More than 730,000 telephone numbers were recorded on the very first day, and by mid-September, the list would swell to more than 50 million numbers. The FCC issued rules of its own on July 3, intended to strengthen the Do-Not-Call registry with overlapping regulations that also extended to encompass other industries not under the FTC's jurisdiction, including banks and insurance companies.

With the date of inception approaching, the judges in the Colorado and Oklahoma cases cited above issued their rulings. On September 24, Judge Lee West of the U.S. District Court in Oklahoma ruled the FTC lacked the authority to enforce the Do-Not-Call Registry. Judge West also agreed with the plaintiffs that the Registry violated the corporations' First and FIFTH AMENDMENT Rights. The response from Congress was immediate. Two days later, The House voted 412-8 and the Senate 95-0 to give the FTC a mandate to enforce the list. As Representative Billy Tauzin (R-La., House Energy and Commerce Committee Chairman) commented, "... This is not about free speech. This is about your right ... not to listen ... Fifty million Americans can't be wrong." On the same day that Congress voted, Judge Edward Nottingham of the U.S. District Court in Colorado reached the same conclusion as had Judge West. Judge Nottingham noted that he judged the Registry unfair because it did not seek to prevent calls from charities or other non-commercial solicitations by telephone. Judge Nottingham wrote in his decision: "The registry creates a burden on one type of speech based solely on its content ... (the registry) does not ... advance its interest in protecting **privacy** or curbing abusive telemarketing practices." The FTC filed emergency appeals, which were turned down, and so had to temporarily shut down the Registry.

But because the FCC had also created rules that overlapped the FTC and was not involved in the court proceedings, FCC Chairman Michael Powell affirmed that he would enforce the new rules beginning October 1. Whether the FCC could make any of the fines that might be levied stick because of the constitutional uncertainty was another matter. That problem was resolved on October 8, when a three-judge panel of the U.S. Court of Appeals for the Tenth Circuit upheld the FTC's **appeal** and allowed them to proceed with enforcing the Do-Not-Call provisions. The judges cited the "opt-in nature" of the program, finding that the **element** of private choice (whether to sign up or not) significant–in short, the consumer's right to privacy and to be free of telephonic intrusions outweighed any FIRST AMENDMENT concerns of the corporations. The telemarketing groups affected by the ruling filed an appeal.

On February 17, 2004, the Tenth Circuit upheld the earlier decision in favor of the FTC. *FTC v. Mainstream Marketing Services*, 358 F.3d 1228 (10th Cir.2004) Telemarketing firms are mulling an appeal to the Supreme Court. In the meantime, the FCC has logged more than 150,000 complaints of violations of the list, and has issued its first **citation** to California Pacific Mortgage. The rulings related to the Do-Not-Call Registry are expected to set the precedent for the inevitable battles over the national "do-not-spam" list, known as the Can-Spam Law. The FTC is expected to report their proposed ground rules for spam regulation to Congress sometime in May. From the telephone lines to the internet, it seems the battle over corporate free speech **versus** consumer privacy will continue long into the future.

Nixon v. Missouri

The issue before the U.S. SUPREME COURT, in *Nixon v. Missouri*, 541 U.S. ___ (2004), was whether a Federal Communications Commission (FCC) statutory provision preempted a conflicting Missouri state law that barred local governments from offering telecommunications services. The court, in reversing a decision from the U.S. Court of Appeals for the Eighth Circuit, found pre-emption inapplicable. As a result, private commercial providers in Missouri, as in other states with similar laws, will not face competition from subsidized local government entities. The ruling does not *require* states to bar local governments from offering local telecommunications services but rather judicially finds that states *may* bar them without fear of FCC pre-emption.

Missouri **Revised Statutes**, Section 392.410(7), with certain exceptions, prohibited local governments from providing or offering any telecommunication services or facilities for sale. Specifically, the **statute** began, in relevant part, with the words, "No political subdivisions of this state shall provide or offer for sale ..."

Conversely, 47 U.S.C. 253, part of the FCC regulatory scheme, expressly states:

> "No state or local statute or regulation, or other State or local legal requirement, may *prohibit* (emphasis added) or have the effect of prohibiting the ability *of any entity* (emphasis added) to provide any interstate or intrastate telecommunications services."

In 1998, some of Missouri's local governments, represented by the Missouri Municipal League, petitioned the FCC to pre-empt the Missouri statute under its own regulatory Section 253. Since the FCC provision declares that states cannot ban "any entity" from providing telecommunications services, the legal question was whether "any entity" meant political subdivisions of the states themselves, namely local towns or county governments.

In the case before the Supreme Court, the incumbent local carrier, Southwestern Bell, believed it unfair to be forced to compete with other service providers that were subsidized and/or favored by local governments and therefore supported the Missouri legislation.

The FCC, relying on an earlier order resolving a similar challenge to a Texas law and an earlier affirmation of an opinion from the U.S. Court of Appeals for the District of Columbia Circuit, declined to declare that section 253 pre-empted the Missouri statute. An FCC memorandum and opinion order stated:

> As we found in the *Texas Preemption Order*, the term "any entity" in section 253(a) of the Act was not intended to include political subdivisions of the state, but rather appears to prohibit restrictions on market entry that apply to independent entities subject to state regulation.

The municipal entities then filed a **petition** for review with the U.S. Court of Appeals for the Eighth Circuit. In vacating the FCC order and remanding, the Eighth Circuit held that the term "any entity" plainly included municipalities, especially because the word "entity" was modified with the word "any." Such express terms clearly met the plain-statement rule in satisfaction of the principles contained in *Gregory v. Ashcroft*, 501 U.S. 452. (Eighth Circuit Opinion at 299 F.3d 949) Therefore, the Eighth Circuit concluded that the Missouri statute could not bar local governments from providing telecommunications services because they were included under FCC protection as "any" entities.

The U.S. Supreme Court granted **certiorari** in June 2003, and consolidated the three **pending** petitions, *Nixon v. Missouri Municipal League* (Jeremiah Nixon was state **attorney general**), *FCC v. Missouri Municipal League*, and *Southwestern Bell v. Missouri Municipal League*.

Justice DAVID SOUTER, in writing for the Court, reversed the Eighth Circuit and found the Missouri law valid. Souter wrote,

> [Section] 253 would not work like a normal preemptive statute if it applied to a governmental unit. It would often accomplish nothing, it would treat States differently depending on the formal structures of their laws authorizing municipalities to function, and it would hold out no promise of a national consistency. We think it farfetched that Congress meant 253 to start down such a road in the absence of any clearer signal than the phrase, "ability of any entity."

The majority opinion included a lengthy discourse that directly addressed the sole dissenting opinion of Justice JOHN PAUL STEVENS. In short, Justice Stevens opined that the majority's use of hypothetical examples lead to a reading of Section 253 that would produce "anomalous results unnecessarily, whereas a simpler **interpretation** carrying fewer unhappy consequences is available." In analyzing the dissent's approach, the majority opinion concluded that "instead of supplying a more straightforward interpretation of Section 253, the **dissent** ends up reading it in a way that disregards its plain language and entails a policy consequence that Congress could not possibly have intended."

TELEVISION

FCC Media Ownership Rules

Under the 1996 Telecommunications Act, the Federal Communications Commission (FCC) must review its broadcast ownership rules every two years to determine "whether any of such rules are necessary in the public interest as a result of competition." If any regulation is no longer in the public interest, the Act requires the FCC to **repeal** or modify it.

On June 2, 2003, the FCC issued its Report and Order, following the most comprehensive review of media ownership regulations in the agency's history, along with a public record of over 520,000 comments. In summary, the two most controversial new rules, adopted by a 3-2 vote, increased the number of local television and radio stations that one company could own and increased the share of the listening/viewing public market that one company could reach (**i.e.**, 45 percent, up from 35 percent). The most palpable effect of this on the general public was a perceived loss of "localism," potentially caused by large, conglomerate media owners (with syndicated news and programming) buying out small, independent, local station owners.

A storm of objections, from private citizens and public lawmakers, preceded and followed the June 2, 2003, announcement. Multiple parties filed suit in various federal **appellate** courts. The cases were consolidated and assigned by lottery to the U.S. Court of Appeals for the Third Circuit, which was already the forum for one **appeal** made by the Philadelphia-based Prometheus Radio Project. On behalf of all consolidated complainants/appellants, Prometheus filed a motion to stay the implementation of the new FCC rules **pending judicial review**. On September 2, 2003, the Third Circuit issued an order granting the motion to stay the effective date of FCC's new ownership rules. It further ordered that the prior ownership rules remain in effect pending resolution of the proceedings. Oral arguments on appellate, intervenor, and **amicus curiae** briefs began in February 2004.

State of the Industry as of June 2003

As of June 2003, six conglomerates basically controlled the mass media/ mass communications market. They were Viacom-CBS-MTV, FoxTV-Murdoch-HarperCollins-Weekly Standard-NewYorkPost-LondonTimes-DirecTV, Time-Warner-CNN-AOL, Disney-ABC-ESPN, G.E.-NBC-UniversalStudios-Vivendi, and Comcast. Comcast, the largest cable company in the U.S., bid to take over Disney in a $66 billion deal in February 2004, resulting in the not-so-endearing reference by many industry-watchers to the above conglomerates as "the five sisters". Prior to 2002, cable companies such as Comcast were barred from owning broadcast stations in the same market(s) where they owned cable systems. Time-Warner successfully challenged that rule in federal court, making way for the 2004 Comcast bid for Disney.) The old FCC rules also banned cross-ownership of newspapers and television stations in the same market.

June 2003 FCC Media Ownership Rules Under Appeal

From grass-roots groups to Democratic and Republican politicians alike, the greatest **objection** to the new FCC rules was that they would make the handful of media giants even more powerful. Among other concerns (e.g., limited local voice), smaller, independent stations could not compete with the costs of buying advertising, purchasing programming, or operating stations.

The new FCC rules continued to exempt cable companies from the "common carrier" rules that governed telephone companies because cable companies did not rely on public airwaves. This effectively allowed them to circumvent requirements to open their systems to competing broadband-Internet providers and also largely exempted them from media-ownership rules.

In addition, the new rules revised the local television multiple-ownership rule. Television networks would be allowed to reach 45 percent of the national audience, up from 35 percent. Although Congress subsequently adjusted this number to 39 percent, the rule was still appealed. Prometheus, **et al.** argued that the relevant FCC provision counted only half the audience of UHF stations when determining whether a broadcaster exceeded the 39 percent limit. That **loophole** resulted in Viacom, Paxson, and others being permitted to own and to keep stations.

The new rules modified the local radio ownership rule by revising the definition of a local radio market. The radio industry replaced a signal contour method of defining local radio markets with a geographic market approach from Arbitron. Radio-ownership caps remained at the previous levels.

The new rules changed the cross-media limitations to a single limit for both radio/television and newspaper/broadcast cross-ownerships. Under the new rules, a company could own a newspaper and radio or television station in the same market. In smaller communities, companies could own two television stations in the same market, and in larger cities, they could own three television stations.

Also under fire was the FCC's internally developed "diversity index," used to measure media concentration to determine whether a particular market had enough local voices. The FCC defended its methodology by referring to it as "a more sophisticated analysis of viewpoint diversity." Labeling it as "consumer-centric," the FCC said the index was built "on data about how Americans use different media to obtain the news." However, during oral arguments before the Third Circuit in February 2004, Judge Thomas Ambro noted that the diversity index gave more weight to a community college's television station than it did to the *New York Times*. An appellate ruling was expected in mid 2004.

TERRORISM

The unlawful use of force or violence against persons or property in order to coerce or intimidate a government or the civilian population in furtherance of political or social objectives.

U.S. Prosecution of Bin Laden Aides

As of mid-2004, the search for al-Qaeda mastermind Osama bin Laden remained fruitless. Notwithstanding, several of his trained operatives had been detained at the U.S. Guantanamo Bay (Cuba) military prison for the better part of two years, but had not been formally charged with any crimes. This, in and of itself, became the subject of controversy as various human rights groups assisted sixteen detainees in moving the matter of their rights forward to the U.S. SUPREME COURT. (The Bush administration took the position that the 1948 Geneva Convention, which affords rights to "prisoners of war," did not apply to "enemy combatants" detained in the war on terrorism.)

In the wake of mounting pressure to either release the detainees or charge them, the U.S. government announced, in February 2004, that it was formally charging two of bin Laden's alleged bodyguards with **conspiracy** to commit war crimes. They were to stand trial before the special military tribunal established by President Bush after the September 11, 2001 terrorist attacks (Military Order of November 13, 2001). Their trials represented the first criminal prosecutions of enemy prisoners since the aftermath of World War II.

Ibrahim Ahmed Mahmoud al Qosi (Qosi) of Sudan was allegedly a key al Qaeda accountant who wore an explosive-packed suicide belt to thwart assassination attempts on bin Laden. He also funded monies to the al Qaeda training camps. The other detainee, Ali Hamza Ahmed Sulayman al Bahlul (Bahlul) of Yemen was an alleged propagandist who produced videos glorifying the attack on the USS Cole off the Coast of Yemen in 2000. He also was tasked with setting up a satellite communications system to enable bin Laden to view news coverage of attacks and the economic harm caused to the United States. Under the general charge of conspiracy, both men were accused of various offenses, including **terrorism**, **murder**, and destruction of property. Specifically, they were charged with "attacking civilians; attacking civilian objects; murder by an unprivileged belligerent; destruction of property by an unprivileged belligerent; and terrorism, said conduct being in the context of and associated with armed conflict."

Although no supporting documents were attached to the formal charges, the specific or overt acts that formed the basis of the charges included: participating in military training at al Qaeda sponsored camps in Afghanistan; managing and distributing monies used to provide income to al Qaeda and to provide cover for the procurement of explosives, weapons, and chemicals; and promoting bin Laden and the killing of Americans. Military prosecutors did not seek the death penalty against either man.

Military tribunals (used during times of war) parallel peacetime courts-martial, and the actual trials combine civilian **criminal law** with military procedure. Under tribunal rules, as in civilian courts, defendants enjoy the **presumption of innocence**, are entitled to defense **counsel**, and are encouraged to put on a vigorous defense. Also parallel to civilian courts, defendants must be proven **guilty beyond a reasonable doubt**. However, evidentiary rules differ and are viewed as more favorable to the government. For example, prosecutors need not establish a flawless **chain of custody** for some documents, and military officials may listen in on lawyer-client communications if security is considered to be at risk. Verdicts are the result of a consensus of at least four of six military officers serving as judges. Such verdicts are not reviewable in federal courts, but are reviewed by military officials and ultimately the president. All verdicts are subject to automatic review by the Military Commission Review Panel, composed of civilians who were commissioned major generals in the U.S. Army during their term of military service.

Trial hearings in military tribunals may be closed when classified matter is expected to be introduced. Although not guaranteed by tribunal rules, plans called for 84 media reporters plus officials from the Red Cross and the defendants' home countries to be in attendance at the Qosi/Bahlul proceedings.

No trial dates had been established for the two men as of July 2004.

Foiled Plot to Bring Down the Brooklyn Bridge

The U.S. government gained valuable ground in its continuing efforts to combat **terrorism** with the capture of al-Qaeda leader Khalid Shaikh Mohammed (referred to as KSM) in March 2003. Initially, KSM refused to divulge any information of merit while in custody. However, he acquiesced when confronted by American intelligence officials about the contents of his computer and cell phone records, and many of his subsequent references to names, places, and plots were legitimate.

One of the most disturbing realities brought to the forefront by KSM was al-Qaeda's systemic overhaul of plans to attack the United

Iyman Faris, who plotted attacks against trains and the Brooklyn Bridge, in a Justice Department photograph.

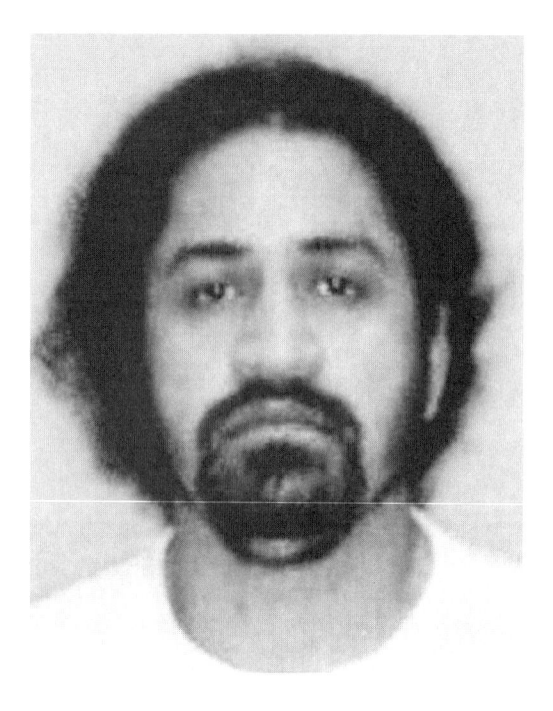

States. The September 11, 2001, hijackers were foreign nationals (mostly Saudis with the exception of one Egyptian leader and two from the United Arab Emirates) who had entered the U.S. with student or tourist visas. However, al-Qaeda intended to operate internally, using persons who were already citizens of the United States to carry out attacks. Some of the planned operations revealed by KSM included the derailing of several trains, the collapse of the Brooklyn Bridge, and the explosion of gas stations throughout the United States.

Al-Qaeda launched a concerted effort to recruit U.S. African-American Muslims in particular, believing that they would be more sympathetic to Islamic causes. Available operatives were found through recruiting efforts in mosques, universities, and prisons throughout the United States. By enlisting persons who were U.S. citizens or who had legitimate passports, al-Qaeda was able to network more freely and to move about in the United States without detection. The operatives also began using women and children as covers, or "support personnel" for the terrorists, in order to further avoid suspicion.

One such recruit was Iyman Faris (a.k.a. Mohammad Rauf), a commercial truck driver from Columbus, Ohio. A naturalized citizen of the United States, Faris, 34 at the time, was born in the Indian territory of Kashmir and came to the United States in 1994. Generally a hard worker, he allegedly led a double life in which he funneled and carried cash for al-Qaeda and served as a scout by checking out equipment that could be used to sever cables on suspension bridges or to derail trains. He also provided requested information to Osama bin Laden and KSM about "ultralight" aircraft, particularly cargo plans that could hold "more weight and more fuel."

According to papers filed under seal in the U.S. District Court for the Eastern District of Virginia, Faris, in federal custody, pleaded guilty in May 2003 to one **count** of conspiring to provide material support to terrorists, and one count of providing material support to terrorists. In cooperating with authorities (details of his arrest were not released), he admitted to researching ultralight planes on the Internet and to delivering cash, 2,000 sleeping bags, cell phones, and several plane tickets to al-Qaeda contacts. As part of the plea bargain, Faris testified to certain facts in civil courts and in military tribunals; in turn, he and his family would be placed in the witness protection program if necessary.

Faris, who became a U.S. citizen in 1999, left for Afghanistan one year later. Over the next two years, he traveled to Pakistan and Afghanistan on several occasions and met with Osama bin Laden and other senior al-Qaeda members. In 2002, he met with a senior al-Qaeda operative (identified in the court papers as "the number three man" below bin Laden) who later turned out to be KSM (arrested in Pakistan in March 2003).

According to the court papers, Faris advised KSM of his work making truck deliveries to cargo planes, which also was of interest to al-Qaeda. He was asked to research ultralight planes as a means of escape for the terrorists, to obtain gas cutters to sever the Brooklyn Bridge's cables, and to refer to them in coded communications as "gas stations." Additionally, he was asked to find tools to bend railroad tracks and to cause train derailments, referred to in code as "mechanics shops." Faris returned to the United States in 2002 and completed his research but found the terrorist plan untenable. Through a fellow operative in the United States, Faris responded in code to al-Qaeda that "the weather is too hot" to proceed.

In October 2003, a joint announcement was made by U.S. **Attorney General** JOHN ASH-CROFT, Assistant Attorney General Christopher A. Wray of the Criminal Division, and U.S. Attorney Paul McNulty of the Eastern District of Virginia, that Faris had been sentenced to 20 years in prison. Prior to sentencing, Judge

Leonie M. Brinkema denied Faris's motion to withdraw his earlier guilty plea. Faris had previously admitted to the allegations contained in the court papers.

By mid 2003, federal prosecutors invoking the "material support" **statute** (section 303 of the Antiterrorism and Effective Death Penalty Act of 1996) had obtained guilty pleas or convictions against at least six Yemeni men from western New York State, two men from Detroit, and one man from Portland, Oregon. These men allegedly either had attended al-Qaeda training camps or had otherwise planned to aid terror plots, including rendering assistance to the Taliban.

United States v. Koubriti

In June 2003, the United States government achieved convictions in its first criminal trial involving charges of **terrorism** since the September 11, 2001, attacks. In the U.S. Federal District Court for the Eastern District of Michigan, near Detroit, four men (all Middle Eastern immigrants) faced multiple terrorism-related charges. Abdel-Ilah Elmardoudi, 37, and Karim Koubriti, 24, were convicted of providing material support or resources to terrorists and of **conspiracy** to engage in **fraud** and misuse of visas, permits, and other documents. Ahmed Hannan, 34, was found **guilty** of one **count** of document fraud. Ali-Haimoud, 22, was acquitted of all charges after being held in custody for one year. The four-count criminal indictment, amended once, alleged violations under 18 U.S.C. 371, 2339A, 1546(a) and 1028(a), respectively. (Count I, Providing Material Support or Resources to Terrorists, is criminalized under the Patriot Act as part of the 1996 Anti-Terrorism and Effective Death Penalty Act, at 18 U.S.C. 2339A.)

The lengthy indictment also contained several pages of background facts. Without directly implicating the defendants as members of such groups, the complaint described "a loose, transnational network of radical Islamists" that had launched a holy war, or global *jihad* "to drive American military forces from the Arabian peninsula, erode American support for Israel, and undermine American support to moderate regimes throughout the Middle East that they viewed as insufficiently Islamic." The stated facts further alleged that in February 1998, the "World Front for Jihad Against Jews and Crusaders," led by Osama bin Laden, issued a *fatwa* (**i.e.**, religious **edict**). Leaders called upon every individual Muslim, in all countries, to acknowledge his so-called duty to "kill Americans and their allies, both civilian and military, in order to purge the infidels from the lands of Islam." The indictment purported to show specific overt acts on the part of defendants that were conducted in furtherance of the above-stated objective.

Haimoud, Hannan, and Koubriti were arrested in an apartment in Dearborn, Michigan, six days after the September 11, 2001, attacks. (The Dearborn area has the nation's highest concentration of Arab-Americans residing in the United States.) Government agents had traveled there to look for Elmardoudi, who was later arrested in a Chicago suburb. Meanwhile, agents found the remaining three men with a cache of false passports and identity papers, a day planner with sketches of alleged terrorist targets, and more than 100 audio tapes preaching holy war or other Islamic extremist views. Three of the four defendants worked at Detroit Metropolitan Airport.

Prosecutors alleged that the men had operated a sleeper terrorist cell from the Dearborn apartment and that they had conspired to help to plot terrorist attacks in the United States and abroad. The government's case relied heavily on the testimony of Youssef Hmimssa, an illegal Moroccan immigrant who had been associated with the defendants before turning against them in return for a plea deal involving charges to stolen credit cards. Defendants Elmardoudi, Koubriti, and Hannan were also Moroccan immigrants. Hmimssa testified that the defendants tried to recruit him to help to overthrow the government of Algeria. He also testified that two of the defendants had spoken of taking advantage of their jobs at the Detroit airport to poison

A court illustration of the four defendents in the first case the United States involving an alleged terror cell after September 11, 2001.

airline passengers. According to Hmimssa, Ali-Haimoud spoke of joining Osama bin Laden and of killing Jews, Christians, and errant Muslims. Prosecutors alleged that the men, who often communicated in secret code, cased both the Detroit and Chicago airports for lapses in security, and that they had considered obtaining Stinger missiles to bring down commercial airplanes.

After 26 days of testimony from 59 witnesses, the three-man, nine-woman jury deliberated for six days.Notwithstanding guilty verdicts against three men, jurors concluded there was insufficient evidence to convict Ali-Haimoud. They also denied that the ongoing campaign against terrorism had any effect on their verdict.

In December 2003, presiding District Court Judge Gerald E. Rosen issued his opinion regarding possible **contempt** of court. The defense **counsel** filed the motion in response to Attorney General John Ashcroft's public statements to the media during the the trial. In light of the substantial media coverage following the September 11, 2001, attacks, the parties stipulated and agreed to regulate public statements concerning the case. Early in the proceedings, the judge entered the stipulated "Order Concerning Public Communications by Parties or Lawyers," which generally prohibited public disclosure of any information that had a reasonable likelihood of interfering with defendants' right to a fair trial, or of otherwise being prejudicial to the case proceedings. According to the defense counsel, Ashcroft referred to the Koubriti matter at two separate briefings in Washington, D.C. The court found that the attorney general's public statements had violated the terms of the public communications order. However, the court found insufficient evidence of willful misconduct or prejudice to the rights of the defendants to warrant criminal contempt proceedings against the attorney general. It therefore concluded that a public and formal judicial admonishment of the attorney general was the appropriate sanction.

In another twist to the case, U.S. District Attorney Richard Convertino of Detroit filed suit against Attorney General JOHN ASHCROFT and the U.S. Department of Justice in February 2004, charging them with "gross mismanagement" in the handling of the case. Represented by the National Whistleblower Center, Convertino sought damages under the **Privacy** Act for leaks to the media about the Department of Justice's internal probe of him. He alleged that the probe was in retaliation for his concerns about the war on terror, which he shared in congressional testimony before a Senate subcommittee. The government later admitted that it had failed to turn over evidence during the trial that could have assisted the defense. One **allegation** involved an imprisoned drug dealer who had claimed that the government's key witness, Hmimssa, had fabricated his story.

United Nations and United States Sanctions Eased Against Libya

Restrictions and sanctions against Libya were eased or lifted in late 2003 and early 2004 by both the United States government and the UNITED NATIONS. The changes followed Libya's admission that it was responsible for blowing up Pan Am Flight 103 over Lockerbie, Scotland, in 1988, that it had agreed to settle with the Lockerbie victims' families, and that the country would dismantle its secret nuclear weapons program.

The United States first imposed sanctions on Libya in 1982. The sanctions came about as a result of deteriorating relations between the countries. The ban included imports of Libyan oil, as well as some exports from the U.S. to Libya. After a 1986 bombing of a Berlin disco that killed American servicemen, the United States expanded the ban.

On December 21, 1988, Pan Am Flight 103 exploded over Lockerbie, Scotland, while en route from London to New York. The explosion aboard the Boeing 747 killed all 259 crew and passengers, as well as 11 people in the town of Lockerbie. As a result of the **terrorism**, the United Nations Security Council imposed sanctions on Libya in 1992 and 1993. The U.N. sanctions were an effort to force the Libyan government, headed by Moammar Gadhafi, to hand over two suspects for trial under Scottish law. The United Nations sanctions involved an air and arms embargo and a ban on certain oil equipment.

The United States sanctions increased with passage of the Iran and Libya Sanctions Act of 1996; the Act was amended in 2001. The legislation was predicated on Libya's support of terrorism, the country's efforts to acquire nuclear weapons, and its noncompliance with U.N. resolutions.

In April 1999, Libya surrendered the two Lockerbie suspects to the United Nations. The U.N. Security Council immediately suspended, but did not permanently lift, its sanctions against Libya. The trial of the two suspects, Abdel Baset Ali Mohmed Al-Megrahi and Al Amin Khalifa

Fhimah, began approximately one year later in the Netherlands. In January 2001, Al Megrahi was convicted of **murder** and was sentenced to twenty years in prison. Al Amin Khalifa Fhimah was found not **guilty**.

In August 2003, lawyers representing Libya and the Lockerbie victims' families reached a settlement in civil lawsuits stemming from the bombing. Libya agreed to transfer $2.7 billion into an **escrow** account for the victims' families. The $2.7 billion represented a possible $10 million for each victim's family. In addition, the Libyan government agreed to accept responsibility for the Pan Am bombing.

In August 2003, Libya delivered a letter to the United Nations. It stated that Libya "accepts responsibility for the actions of its officials" in connection with the Lockerbie bombing. Following delivery of the letter, the United Nations Security Council voted in September to lift sanctions against Libya. The Security Council vote was 13-0; the United States and France abstained. The action by the Security Council allowed for the release of $4 million to each victim's family. Release of further compensation from the escrow fund is tied to the U.S. lifting its sanctions and dropping Libya from the list of state sponsors of terrorism.

The United States lifted its travel ban to Libya in early 2004, although U.S. air carriers still could not fly to Libya. Moreover, the U.S. retained certain restrictions on transfers of U.S. funds to the country, as well as other sanctions involving exporting goods, services, and technology to Libya. Most financial and commercial transactions with Libya remained forbidden, as did the importation of goods and services of Libyan origin.

Libya remains on the U.S. government's State Sponsors of Terrorism List. In a Consular Information Sheet dated April 4, 2004, the DEPARTMENT OF STATE acknowledged, "Libya has taken steps to cooperate in the global war on terrorism," but warned, "Although Libya appears to have curtailed its support for international terrorism, it may maintain residual contacts with some of its former terrorist clients."

In December 2003, Libya admitted that it had a secret program to amass weapons of mass destruction. At the same time, the country agreed that it would cooperate in dismantling the program. It allowed inspectors from the International Atomic Energy Agency (IAEA), the atomic agency for the United Nations, to go to the country to oversee the dismantling of the weapons program. In March 2004, Libya agreed to allow the inspectors oversight on any nuclear programs and to provide assurances that any nuclear program was peaceful.

The United States pledged its support to help Libya to dismantle its weapons program. The *Guardian* reported that a ship had left Libya in March 2004 bound for the United States. The ship was carrying 500 tons of cargo was used in the country's nuclear weapons program.

The Bush administration took other small steps to build a relationship with Libya. Steps include stationing a diplomatic presence in Libya, inviting Libya to establish an interests section in Washington, and sending a team to **assess** Libya's humanitarian situation.

Opposition to the Patriot Act

Only three weeks after the terrorist attacks of September 11, 2001, the United States Congress passed H.R. 2975, more commonly known as the USA Patriot Act (an acronym for "Uniting and Strengthening America by Providing Appropriate Tools Required to Intercept and Obstruct Terrorism"). As a bipartisan-supported bill, it passed through both houses largely unopposed, with only one "nay" vote in the Senate and 66 opposed in the House of Representatives. **Attorney General** JOHN ASHCROFT, FBI officials, and local law enforcement agencies lauded the bill for freeing their hands and opening up information to them for the purpose of fighting **terrorism**. However, the hasty nature of the bill has not sat well with everyone in the United States. Governments at the city, county, and state level have passed resolutions that refute the Patriot Act, and the list continues to grow.

The Patriot Act has many provisions, but the main powers that have been expanded (and that are under scrutiny by concerned citizens) can be summarized as follows: Federal agents have greater power to intercept communications, including reduced judicial oversight over **wiretapping**, plus increased search-and-seizure powers, with or without warrants, with or without **probable cause**, and utilizing secret evidence. The act also restricts, in certain cases, the accused party's access to legal **counsel**. The act allows increased access to formerly confidential financial, medical, and personal records, even including such details as student transcripts and books borrowed from the library. The act increases controls and restrictions on immigrants and visitors from foreign countries, including mandatory background checks and registration for citizens of certain countries. Finally, the act creates new crimes, penalties, and procedures to be used against terrorists both foreign and domestic.

The main disagreements that communities have had with the **statute** is that the powers granted to federal officials can be used for more than investigating terrorism. Moreover, the term "terrorist" is very loosely defined, thus opening the door to possible abuses. Under the Patriot Act, any individual designated a "terrorist" by the president or the U.S. Department of Justice will fall under the Patriot Act's hammer. If the individual happens to be a foreign national, he or she could be detained indefinitely, without being charged with a crime and without any kind of accountability.

Opposition to the Patriot Act has made for some odd bedfellows. Groups as politically diverse as the AMERICAN CIVIL LIBERTIES UNION, the NATIONAL RIFLE ASSOCIATION, the American Arab Institute, and the American Conservative Union have joined forces to draft resolutions against it. Individual citizens and city councilors from both sides of the ideological spectrum are writing resolutions in various towns. Most of these resolutions affirm the need for the government to protect the population against terrorism but state that the tools necessary to do this were in place before the passage of the Patriot Act and order their law enforcement agencies to refrain from enforcing the act and/or from using the expanded powers outlined in the act.

As of July 2004, four states—Alaska, Hawaii, Maine, and Vermont—have passed statewide resolutions against the Patriot Act, and 11 others are considering similar measures. In addition, 294 cities and counties across the country have passed anti-Patriot Act resolutions of varying strength. These cities, counties, and states together represent a population of more than 50 million people. Ann Arbor, Michigan (population 114,000), was the first community to approve such a resolution, in January 2002. Seattle, Washington, passed the first anti-Patriot Act **ordinance** in February 2003. Hawaii was the first state to pass a statewide resolution, which took effect of April 25, 2003. One small town in California has gone even further in its opposition measures. Arcata, population 16,000, declared it a misdemeanor for any city official to cooperate in an investigation with federal agents if such investigation violates the civil or constitutional rights of the target, levying a fine of $57 for each offense.

In February 2003, the Center for Public Integrity leaked a document outlining the Domestic Security Enhancement Act, quickly dubbed "Patriot Act II," which expanded and strengthened the powers granted in the initial act, as well as adding new powers that alarmed liberals and conservatives alike, such as the power to conduct private property searches without probable cause, warrant, or oversight, and without informing the target of the search, and for the government to strip anyone of their citizenship if he or she is found to have aided terrorists, even without their knowledge. Outcry over the DSEA was so great that the government shelved it. Facing both increasing outcry over the original Patriot Act and an ever-growing list of communities drafting legislation opposing it, Attorney General John Ashcroft spent the summer and early fall of 2003 on a whistle-stop tour of the U.S. in an attempt to explain the act and to drum up support for its provisions. The reaction he received was mixed, and the tour apparently did nothing to slow the growing tide of opposition.

Those who oppose the Patriot Act have friends in high places. Many members of Congress are supporting these local measures and encouraging their constituents to speak out. Even those members of Congress who initially supported the Patriot Act had second thoughts. Senator Orrin Hatch (R-Utah), Chairman of the Senate Judiciary Committee, put on a public forum in his state to hear the concerns of the diverse groups who are opposed to the act. Hatch, who originally helped the act to pass through Congress, said at the event, "I believe we must have both our civil liberties and national security, or we will have neither." On July 22, 2003, the House of Representatives, which had passed the Patriot Act with little opposition, enacted a measure that would block the Department of Justice from using appropriated funds for enforcing provisions concerning expanded powers over search warrants. The measure passed by a wide margin: 309 votes in favor and 118 against.

How local resolutions stand up under fire, and how any potential court cases over the law **versus** the higher calling of constitutionality will play out will be a subject of much interest in coming years.

Rasul v. Bush

In the wake of the September 11 terrorist attacks and the subsequent U.S. military actions against the Al-Qaeda terrorist network in Afghanistan, President GEORGE W. BUSH issued an Executive Order on November 13, 2001, regarding the manner in which potential military prisoners with possible terrorist affiliation were to be handled. In part, that order read:

> "... it is not practicable to apply in military commissions under this order the principles of law and the rules of evidence generally recognized in the trial of criminal cases in the United States district courts."

The United States military captured hundreds of Taliban fighters and suspected Al-Qaeda members in the military actions that followed. These captured persons have been termed "enemy combatants" by the U.S. government and were transported to Camp X-Ray at the U.S. naval base at Guantanamo Bay, Cuba, beginning in February 2002, where they have been held ever since. Information on these detainees has been slow in coming and sketchy at best, a fact that the U.S. government explains as necessary in the interests of national security. What is clear is that the detainees are being questioned by military authorities but have yet to be charged with a crime, have not appeared before a judge, and for the most part have been denied any access to legal **counsel**. The Bush administration argues that the detentions are allowable under the president's common law wartime powers, and claim the right to hold them for as long as the war on terror lasts. However, the administration is not declaring the detainees to be "prisoners of war", thus sidestepping the Geneva Convention and shielding the detainees from the jurisdiction of the WORLD COURT as well.

In early February 2002, attorneys representing three of the detainees filed a **writ** of **habeas corpus** with the U.S. District Court for the DISTRICT OF COLUMBIA, challenging the constitutionality of holding the men without charges or trial. Two of the men, Shafiq Rasul and Asif Iqbal, are citizens of the U.K. and one, David Hicks, is a citizen of Australia. In August 2002, the district court dismissed the **petition**, ruling that non-U.S. citizens held outside of U.S. territory are not subject to habeas **corpus** petitions. The ruling was appealed, but on March 11, 2003, the D.C. **Circuit Court** turned down the **appeal**, concluding that no court in the country had the authority to grant **relief** under habeas corpus. Michael Ratner, vice president of the Center for Constitutional Rights and lawyer for the detainees, responded: "The right to test the lawfulness of one's **detention** is a foundation of liberty (going back to) the Magna Carta. The U.S. ... is jeopardizing any claim that it is a country ruled by law."

On September 2, 2003, lawyers for the detainees filed a petition with the Supreme Court to review the lower court rulings. This news brought in a flood of amicus briefs filed on behalf of both sides of the argument. Former detainees of the government's internment program for Japanese Americans during WWII, retired generals and admirals, former prisoners of war, ten retired federal judges, and 175 members of the British Parliament, among many others, weighed in on the side of the detainee's cause, while former attorneys general Barr, Meese and Thornburg, former CIA director James Woolsey, and the states of Alabama, Ohio, Texas, and Virginia were among those filing briefs on the side of the administration.

On November 19, 2003, the Supreme Court agreed to review *Rasul v. Bush*. At the same time, they agreed to hear three companion cases: *Al-Odah v. United States of America*, *Hamdi v. Rumsfeld*, and *Rumsfeld v. Padilla*, dealing with the detaining of a U.S. citizen (the Hamdi case) and foreign nationals at both Guantanamo Bay and, in the Padilla case, at a U.S. Navy brig in South Carolina. The question for the court to consider in *Rasul v. Bush* was

> "Whether United States courts lack jurisdiction to consider challenges to the legality of the detention of foreign nationals captured abroad in connection with hostilities and incarcerated at the Guantanamo Bay Naval Base, Cuba."

The Supreme Court began reviewing the case on April 20, 2004. On the opening day of hearings, Chief Justice WILLIAM H. REHNQUIST questioned how a judge in Washington is supposed to deal with a detainee in Cuba. The detainees' lawyer responded by pointing out that the military, not the Cuban government, holds the only power at Guantanamo Bay, and without the U.S. court system the detainees have no way to have their cases heard. Justice STEPHEN BREYER seemed to agree, noting that without U.S. judicial oversight there were no checks and balances on the executive branch's power at Camp X-Ray.

Speaking on the **merits** of their argument, lawyers for the administration have stated that giving the detainees a public hearing would "place federal courts in the unprecedented position of micromanaging the executive's handling of captured enemy combatants ..." Solicitor General Theodore Olson added, "Every argument that's being made . . . could be made by the 2 million persons that were in custody at the end of World War II . . ." Brad Berenson, a lawyer and member of Citizens for the Common Defence, a legal think tank that filed a **brief** in support of the administration, noted that a ruling for the detainees could unleash a "flood tide of litigation" from detained suspected terrorists. Joseph Margulies, a lawyer working on behalf of the detainees, observed during the earlier cases that: "We distinguish ourselves from terrorists only by our commitment to the **rule of law**, and the law is perfectly clear that the President can't order a person locked up indefinitely, without legal process."

The Supreme Court sided with the government in another case involving the Guantanamo Bay detainees. In January 2004, the court heard an appeal to intervene in a case challenging the government's refusal to identify or give other details of the detainees, such as the charges they were being held on. The court ruled that the government was entitled to its policy of secrecy in this case.

On June 28, 2004, the Supreme Court handed down decisions on *Rasul v. Bush*, *Al-Odah v. United States*, and *Hamdi v. Rumsfeld*. The court upheld the right of the Bush administration to detain persons suspected of **terrorism** without charges or a trial. However, the Justices ruled 6-3 that both U.S. citizens and foreign nationals could not be denied legal representation or access to the courts, and were entitled to use the court system to **contest** their detentions. In her opinion on the Hamdi case, Justice SANDRA DAY O'CONNOR wrote:

> "We have no reason to doubt that courts . . . will pay proper heed both to the matters of national security . . . and to the constitutional limitations safeguarding essential liberties that remain vibrant even in times of security concerns."

TOBACCO

Tobacco Companies See Reversal In Legal Fortunes

The tobacco industry has taken some serious hits in court since the mid-1990s, being forced to pay hundreds of millions of dollars in damages to smokers made ill from years of using their products. But in 2003, a stunning reversal in a **class action** case that had threatened to bankrupt five major cigarette makers not only represented a major victory for tobacco companies, but cast into doubt the suitability and feasibility of the class-action lawsuit as a vehicle for ill smokers to seek recompense for their medical woes.

The *Engle v. Reynolds*, 853 So.2d 434 (Fla.App 3 Dist., 2003), class action suit was certified in 1996 after its scope was narrowed from a national class to only including smokers in the state of Florida. Despite the downsizing, it represented approximately 700,000 people at its zenith. The plaintiffs sought damages from five major tobacco companies: Philip Morris, RJ Reynolds, Lorillard Tobacco, Brown & Williamson, and the Ligget Group. The plaintiffs alleged that they were ensnared by a defective product that caused addiction and illness. They also alleged that the tobacco companies were **guilty** of **fraud** for using deceptive advertising and for years of covering up the true health effects of smoking. In July 2000, the jury found for the plaintiffs and awarded a staggering $145 billion in damages, by far the largest such award in class action history. The tobacco companies immediately appealed, saying that paying such a fine would result in the collapse of all of the **defendant** companies, which at the time had an approximate net worth of about $23 billion combined.

On May 21, 2003, a three-judge panel of Florida's Third District Court of Appeals threw out the damage award, citing numerous problems with the class. First, the panel noted, the class should not have been certified in the first place, because the individual health complaints of each plaintiff were unique, and thus no single person could fairly represent an "average member" of the group. As the panel noted, "In this type of . . . case where **proof** of damages is essential to **liability**, damages cannot be determined on a class-wide basis because the issue of damages requires individualized proof (for) each smoker." Jurisdiction was another problem, since a reported 65% of the plaintiffs only became Florida residents after they became smokers. Facing a situation where a review of the laws of each state where the plaintiffs had formerly lived would have to be conducted, Judge David Gersten wrote that such a requirement would be "an insuperable roadblock to smokers' class actions." The court also determined that the 1998 **Master** Settlement Agreement (MSA; a settlement between the tobacco companies and the attorneys general of forty-six states) prohibited further punitive damages being awarded in cases like *Engle v. Reynolds* where the claims made by the plaintiffs were similar to those outlined in the MSA. The court further cited problems with the trial plan, noting that money was being awarded for damages even though the harm caused to individual plaintiffs was never adequately assessed. The court further found that the damages awarded were excessive and "... it is well established that punitive damages may not be assessed in an amount which will financially destroy or bankrupt an opponent." To conclude their decision, the court roundly lambasted the plaintiff's lead attorney, Stanley Rosenblatt, for inappropriate and inflammatory language in the courtroom in an attempt to influence the jury.

The court made it clear that individual plaintiffs were free to pursue their own cases against the tobacco companies, but the idea of 700,000 individual lawsuits is unrealistic, even if lawyers could be found who would be willing to battle with the tobacco companies one-on-one. Richard Daynard, president of the Tobacco Products Liability Project, feels that the decision in *Engle* will have a chilling effect on any further class-action suits against tobacco companies. In an earlier class action case, *Broin v. Philip Morris Co. Inc.*, 641 So.2d 888 (Fla.App. 3 Dist., 1994), the same court that overturned *Engle v. Reynolds* reached the opposite conclusion about the suitability of class action suits. *Broin* was fought on behalf of plaintiffs who claimed **injury** from exposure to secondhand smoke. The court wrote in that case that a class action may proceed "if they present a question of common interest ... since it is virtually impossible to design a class whose members have identical claims." Obviously, some time between this case and *Engle*, the court's opinion on what constitutes a "common interest" had changed. Daynard commented that the court was free to take the position that the *Engle* class required individualized proof, "but then you get rid of class actions and you get rid of the realistic possibility of actually providing justice in mass tort situations."

On September 22, 2003, the 3rd District Court announced that it would not hear any further appeals on the decertification of the *Engle* class action. Whether the collapse of *Engle* will cripple or merely hinder any further class action suits against the tobacco industry is being closely watched by all sides concerned.

TORT LAW

A body of rights, obligations, and remedies that is applied by courts in civil proceedings to provide relief for persons who have suffered harm from the wrongful acts of others. The person who sustains injury or suffers pecuniary damage as the result of tortious conduct is known as the plaintiff, and the person who is responsible for inflicting the injury and incurs liability for the damage is known as the defendant or tortfeasor.

States Tackle Tort Reform Issues in 2002 and 2003

Texas and Mississippi were among several states in 2002 and 2003 that enacted legislation under the label of tort reform. The tort reform movement claims that large verdicts against such defendants as doctors and health care institutions have driven insurance costs so high that doctors cannot afford to **practice** in certain states. Among the legal changes in several of these states are provisions that limit the amount of damages a plaintiff can receive for pain and suffering.

The argument regarding tort reform has often pitted medical associations and insurance companies against trial lawyers. Proponents of tort reform note that medical malpractice premiums have steadily increased for several years, and they claim that large jury awards have caused increases in the premiums. These supporters maintain that plaintiffs—and more often attorneys for plaintiffs—abuse the civil justice system by bringing what the supporters refer to as "frivolous lawsuits." Tort reform advocates support legislation that limits certain damages that a plaintiff can collect in certain actions, such as medical malpractice cases, and they have asked legislatures for various other reforms to address such issues as **venue** and **class action** suits.

Trial lawyers and other opponents of these reform efforts claim that the civil justice system is not at fault, noting that the doctors would not be subject to the lawsuits if the they did not commit malpractice. Many opponents maintain that premium rates are not directly related to the amount of money awarded to plaintiffs and that the insurance companies are merely looking for excuses to lower their costs. Moreover, trial attorneys assert that those who suffer injuries should have the right to have their cases decided in a court of law and that tort reform efforts effectively prevent injured parties from redressing their injuries through a court action.

California was the first state to enact a major tort reform initiative, known as the Medical **Injury** Compensation Reform Act (MICRA) of 1975. The state limits recovery for certain forms of "noneconomic damages" in medical malpractice cases. These types of damages are usually associated with pain and suffering resulting from a doctor's malpractice in the plaintiff's care. The MICRA has served as a model for many other states, although the nationwide tort reform movement was sluggish during the 1970s and 1980s. States began to enact legislation to provide some **relief** for doctors in the 1990s, and the movement arrived in full force in the new millennium. The concern over malpractice premiums was the subject of a national debate, with President GEORGE W. BUSH addressing tort reform in his State of the Union address in January 2003. Bush's proposal for federal tort reform legislation was similar in many respects to California's law.

Despite the perceived success of California's tort reform efforts, parts of California, particularly Los Angeles County, remain on the American Tort Reform Association's (ATRA) list of so-called "judicial hellholes." Among the other states identified by this organization as having problems with their civil justice systems are Mississippi, Texas, Illinois, Missouri, Louisiana, West Virginia, Pennsylvania, and Florida.

Mississippi was singled out as a state with a reputation of "jackpot justice," whereby juries would **render** verdicts involving hundreds of millions of dollars in products **liability** suits against out-of-state corporations that were only connected to the state through local retailers. . Numerous businesses, not limited to the medical industry, called upon the state's legislature to enact tort reform legislation. The Mississippi Legislature passed a bill in October 2002 that limited plaintiffs' access to the courts and to recoveries in tort. Included in the legislation was a limit of $500,000 in recovery for non-economic damages to plaintiffs in medical malpractice cases.

The year 2003 saw many more efforts among the states consider tort reform efforts. According to the ATRA, at least 20 states in 2003 enacted some form of tort reform legislation, the most since 1995. Among the more comprehensive measures were those approved by the Texas Legislature. The debate in Texas over House Bill 4 was intense and lengthy, according to commentators. The arguments over this effort raged for several months in Texas's abbreviated legislative calendar, but the bill was finally signed by Governor Rick Perry on June 16, 2004. Among the changes to Texas **tort law** were limitations on **joint and several liability**, medical liability, punitive damages, venue, and liability for asbestos.

Despite the relatively widespread effort among states to enact tort reform measures, supporters maintain that more work is needed. Proponents of tort reform have continued their efforts to pressure legislatures to consider limiting damages in certain types of cases and to make other changes in the civil justice system in the interest of fairness. The insurance industry has remained one of the most outspoken advocates for this reform, claiming that the tort system in the United States costs about $200 billion per year, representing about two percent of the gross national product.

TRADEMARKS

Distinctive symbols of authenticity through which the products of particular manufacturers or the salable commodities of particular merchants can be distinguished from those of others.

Rosa Parks Entitled to Trademark Jury Trial over OutKast Song Using Her Name

Federal trademark law and state common law rights of publicity have been used by actors, musicians, professional athletes and celebrities to protect the commercial value of their names. Disputes over the use of a celebrity's name have generated many lawsuits, with courts balancing the property rights of celebrities with the First Amendment rights of creators of film and music to free expression. These issues were hotly disputed in *Parks v. LaFace Records*, 329 F.3d 437 (6th Cir. 2003), a lawsuit filed by ROSA PARKS, famous for triggering the 1955 Montgomery bus boycott and the civil rights movement of the 1950s and 1960s. Parks objected to the song entitled "Rosa Parks" by the rap/hip-hop group OutKast that was featured on its 1998 album *Aquemini*. A federal appeals court ruled that Parks was entitled to make her case to a jury that the use of her name in the song **title** constituted false advertising under the Lanham Act, 15 U.S.C.A. § 1125(a) and infringed on her right of publicity under Michigan law. The appeals court rejected the claim by OutKast that artistic freedom protected by the FIRST AMENDMENT constituted a **absolute** defense to Parks's lawsuit.

Parks became an international figure in 1955 when she refused to give up her seat to a white person and move to the back of a Montgomery, Alabama, bus. Her refusal violated state law that mandated segregated public transportation based on race. The Reverend MARTIN LUTHER KING, JR., organized a 381-day bus boycott that drew attention to racial segregation and led to the birth of the modern CIVIL RIGHTS MOVEMENT. Over the years books and television shows have celebrated Parks's courage and she became a revered figure in the civil and human rights movement. In 1995 she approved the release of a gospel album that was entitled *A Tribute to Mrs. Rosa Parks*.

André Benjamin and Antwan Patton make up the group OutKast, which releases its albums through LaFace Records. The song they wrote called "Rosa Parks" was a single off the *Aquemini* album that contained a sticker warning of "explicit content." The highly idiomatic lyrics to "Rosa Parks" made no mention of her but rather focused on the superiority of OutKast when compared to other musical groups. The sole reference to Parks was the phrase "Everybody move to the back of the bus," which was repeated a number of times. The "everybody" referred to other musicians who should give up their position to OutKast.

Parks objected to the song, which had not been approved by her, and filed a lawsuit in federal district court. She sought damages and removal of the song from the album. She argued that the use of her name constituted false advertising, as it confused buyers into believing they were purchasing a song about her and hurt the marketing of the gospel tribute album. She presented affidavits from 20 individuals claiming this type of confusion. OutKast asked that the lawsuit be dismissed on **summary judgment**, which meant that even if the facts were as Parks claimed, a reasonable jury would return a **verdict** for OutKast. OutKast asserted that as artists they had the First Amendment right of free expression. In their view the fact that the phrase "move to the back of the bus" was associated with Rosa Parks justified their "metaphorical" or "symbolic" use of her name in the title. The district court agreed and dismissed her lawsuit. She then appealed to the Sixth **Circuit Court** of Appeals.

The appeals court reversed the district court decision. Judge John Holschuh, writing for the court, applied a two-part test to see if the title was protected from legal action. A court will protect a title unless it has "no artistic relevance" to the underlying work. If there is artistic relevance, then the title will be protected if it does not explicitly mislead a person to the source or the content of the work. The appeals court focused on whether the title had artistic relevance. Judge Holschuh ruled that the artistic relationship between the title and the content of the song was open to reasonable debate. The phrase "move to the back of the bus" in the context of the entire set of song lyrics "has absolutely nothing to do with Rosa Parks." The composers admitted they did not intend to make the song about Rosa Parks; the song was about their music making abilities compared to other hip-hop artists. The appeals court found that choosing the name Rosa Parks for the song title "unquestionably enhanced the song's potential sale to the consuming public."

The court found that Parks had raised a legitimate issue of fact as to whether OutKast had misrepresented and used false advertising in titling the song after her. Outkast could make its First Amendment argument but this time to a jury. The appeals court did find, however, that if a jury found that Outkast's use of the name had artistic relevance, the group could not be liable under the second part of the test. Judge Holschuh ruled that OutKast had not explicitly mislead consumers into believing they were buying a song about the life of Rosa Parks. The group would only have been liable if the song had been titled, for example, "The True Life of Rosa Parks." The case was sent back to the district court for a trial on the issues raised in the **appeal**.

TRUTH IN LENDING ACT

Household Credit Services v. Pfennig

The issue before the U.S. SUPREME COURT in *Household Credit Services v. Pfennig*, 541 U.S. ___ (2004) was not the legitimacy or fairness of "over-limit" credit card charges, but rather the manner in which those charges appeared on consumers' credit statements. Sharon Pfennig had challenged the way the charges were listed, citing the federal Truth in Lending Act (TILA), 15 U.S.C.1601 *et seq.*, as authority.

Congress enacted the TILA to promote consumers' "informed use of credit," 15 U.S.C. 1601(a). The Act requires "meaningful disclosures of credit terms." Under TILA, credit card issuers must make certain disclosures to consumers, and consumers are provided with specific civil remedies if creditors fail to comply. In advancing the objectives of TILA, Congress delegated to the Board the responsibility of appropriating regulations that would assist consumers in understanding credit terms. **At issue** in this case was whether Board Regulation Z, which expressly excluded credit over-limit fees from the definition of "finance charges," was an unreasonable **interpretation** of TILA Section 1605.

Pfennig alleged that certain over-limit fees charged to her credit card account were essentially costs of using the card, and therefore that they should have been listed as finance charges. The U.S. Sixth **Circuit Court** of Appeals agreed with her, finding that the Board's exclusion of them conflicted with the plain language of TILA Section 1605(a). An unanimous U.S. Supreme Court decision reversed this ruling. It held that financial companies, pursuant to regulations promulgated by the FEDERAL RESERVE BOARD (Board), could list such fees separately on credit statements without violating or being inconsistent with TILA requirements. Justice CLARENCE THOMAS wrote the opinion for the Court.

The facts in this case were that Pfennig held a credit card, with a $2,000 limit, that had been issued by Household Credit Services, Inc.(Household). Household's financial portfolio was ultimately purchased by MBNA America Bank, N.A. [MBNA], also joined as party with Household. Pfennig was able to make purchases beyond the credit limit, subject to a $29 "over-limit fee" for each month that her balance exceeded $2,000. On behalf of a class of plaintiffs in a similar situation, Pfennig filed suit claiming that Household/MBNA had violated TILA by failing to classify the over-limit fees as finance charges. According to her complaint, this "misrepresented the true cost of credit."

Under Section 1605(a) of TILA, a "finance charge" is an amount "payable directly or indirectly by the person to whom the credit is extended, and imposed directly or indirectly by the creditor as an incident to the extension of credit." In interpreting this definition, the Federal Reserve Board, in its regulations (specifically in Regulation Z) expressly excluded credit over-limit fees as "finance charges." Pfennig argued that such an interpretation conflicted with the plain language of TILA's Section 1605(a) because the over-limit fees were imposed by the creditor "as an incident to the extension of credit."

The federal district court granted Household/MBNA's motion to dismiss, agreeing that Regulation Z specifically excluded such fees from the definition of "finance charges." However, the U.S. Circuit Court of Appeals for the Sixth Circuit reversed the decision on **appeal**.

Noting that TILA was a **remedial statute** to be interpreted in favor of consumers, the appellate court concluded that the over-limit fees were imposed "incident to the extension of credit" (if not caused by unilateral default on the part of the consumer) and therefore fell squarely within TILA's definition of finance charges.

The U.S. Supreme Court did not agree with the **appellate** court's rationale. It first noted that Pfennig had not challenged the Board's authority to issue binding regulations. The Court further noted that if Congress had spoken directly to the question at issue (in TILA), then courts were bound to give effect to the expressed **intent** of Congress. Conversely, if Congress had explicitly left a gap for the agency to fill (by agency regulations), those regulations were to be given controlling weight unless they were found to be arbitrary, capricious, or manifestly contrary to **statute**.

The U.S. Supreme Court noted that TILA did not explicitly address whether over-limit fees were included within the definition of "finance charge." Nevertheless, the Court, after lengthy discussion, agreed that TILA Section 1605 was ambiguous in that more than one interpretation was possible (including that of the court of appeals (although the high court found the appellate court's logic to be faulty as applied to the specific facts).

Because Section 1605 was ambiguous, the Board's Regulation Z, implementing Section 1605, was binding on the courts unless procedurally defective, arbitrary, capricious in substance, or manifestly contrary to statute. The Court's opinion concluded by noting:

> Congress has authorized the Board to make "such classifications, differentiations, or other provisions, and [to] provide for such adjustments and exceptions for any class of transactions, as in the judgment of the Board are necessary or proper to effectuate the purpose of [TILA], to prevent circumvention or evasion thereof, or to facilitate compliance therewith . . . Here, the Board has accomplished all of these objectives by setting forth a clear, easy to apply (and easy to enforce) rule that highlights the charges the Board has determined to be most relevant to a consumer's credit decisions. The judgment of the Court of Appeals is therefore reversed.

UNIFORM COMMERCIAL CODE

A general and inclusive group of laws adopted, at least partially, by all the states to further uniformity and fair dealing in business and commercial transactions.

Commissioners on Uniform Laws Approve Revised Articles 2 and 2A of the U.C.C.

After more than a decade of considering drafts and debating the various components, the National Conference of Commissioners on Uniform State Laws (NCCUSL), along with the American Law Institute (ALI), approved revised versions of Article 2 (sales) and 2A (leases) of the **Uniform Commercial Code** in 2002. The American Bar Association approved the revisions in February 2004. Despite the support from these organizations, the changes contained in these revisions have been met with fierce resistance from industries and consumer groups, among others.

The NCCUSL originally enacted a uniform law regarding the sale of goods with the enactment of the Uniform Sales Act in 1906. The uniform **sales law** was subsequently revised with the adoption of the U.C.C. by the Commissioners in 1952. For more than five decades, the text of Article 2 remained largely unchanged, though many commentators called for significant revisions. Every state, with the exception of Louisiana, has adopted Article 2 of the U.C.C. In 1987, the NCCUSL approved Article 2A, which governed leases. Although it met with some scrutiny after its initial approval—leading to a revision of Article 2A in 1990—states soon began to adopt the new law. By 1999, every state except Louisiana had adopted Article 2A.

During the early to mid 1990s, several drafts of revisions to Articles 2 and 2A were produced. A number of commentators anticipated that the revisions would be adopted by the middle or end of the decade. However, some of the revisions were viewed by critics as too extensive, and efforts to approve the changes stalled. Drafts of revised articles were submitted to the Commissioners each year from 1996 through 2002.

The NCCUSL approved the revised Article 2 and 2A at its 111th annual meeting in Tucson, Arizona, in August 2002. The American Law Institute, which shared responsibility with the NCCUSL in drafting the U.C.C., approved the changes in May 2003. The Commissioners credited the joint efforts of several organizations that were necessary to produce the new uniform laws. "The amendments to Articles 2 and 2A were the product of an exhaustive drafting process involving not just the ALI and NCCUSL, but numerous interest groups as well," said K. King Burnett, president of NCCUSL. "We believe that these amendments are fair and balanced, and an improvement over existing law."

The revised Article 2 recognizes changes in the manner in which sales take place, including sales that take place through electronic communications. Unlike the current Article 2, the revised Article 2 allows for an electronic record to serve as the equivalent of a signed writing that was necessary under the current law. The new law excludes information from its definition of the term "goods," although if an item contains a computer program that runs it, such as a digital camera, some have questioned whether this item should be considered a good. This issue has been left up to the courts.

The new Article 2 also expands the concept of **good faith**. Under the current definition, good faith is defined as honesty in fact. The new definition of good faith includes the **practice** of following reasonable commercial standards of fair dealing. Other modifications were made to provisions regarding statute of frauds, warranties, remedies, and damages. Article 2A, which is based largely upon the provisions of Article 2, has undergone similar modifications and updates.

Despite the lengthy process of drafting the revised versions of Articles 2 and 2A, the passage of these uniform laws met with substantial resistance from several camps. Many industry groups, including the NATIONAL ASSOCIATION OF MANUFACTURERS (NAM), voiced strong opposition to several aspects of the new Article 2. According to NAM, the new Article 2 represents a shift away from the goals of the U.C.C., which are to clarify the law of commercial transactions and to permit the continued expansion of commercial practices. According to NAM, "Revised Article 2 will retard and disrupt commerce, as well as impose huge additional costs, especially in the area of electronic commerce. It alters significant rules that have become the basis for customary practice and does so in a way that affirmatively harms all industries."

NAM asserts that no particular industry requested or invited the changes that have been made to Article 2. According to NAM, the revised Article 2 has received "[n]ot one letter of affirmative support . . . from any affected industry. . . ." The strong opposition to the revisions, says NAM, will lead to non-uniformity in sales law.

Despite the criticism, the revised Article 2 was scheduled to be sent to the states for their consideration in 2004. Although states are free to determine whether they will adopt a uniform law, very few states reject revised articles of the U.C.C., and commentators expected that the vast majority of states would adopt the revised Articles 2 and 2A.

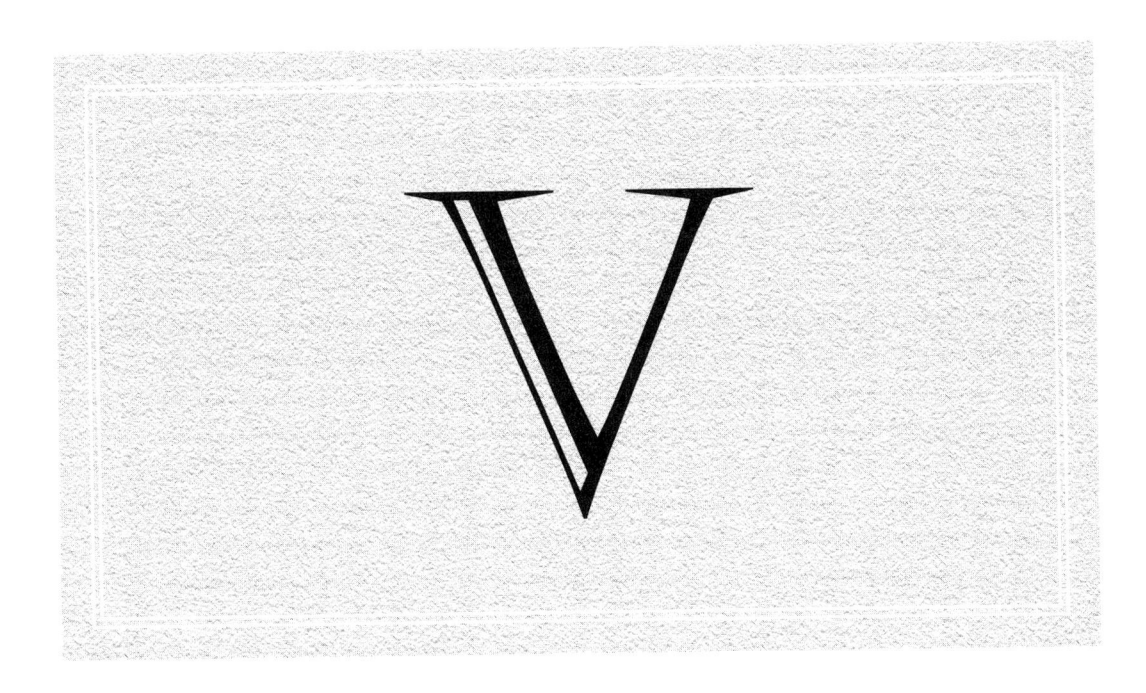

VICTIMS' RIGHTS

Generally, the rights of the victims of a criminal act, whether at trial or after conviction of the perpetrator.

Judge Rules That Iran Must Pay Victims of 1983 Bombing in Lebanon

A federal judge from the District of Columbia ruled that Iran is responsible for damages caused by the suicide bombing of a Marine barracks in Lebanon in 1983. The ruling came on May 30, 2003, in two lawsuits filed by injured servicemen and the families of servicemen killed in the attack. *Peterson v. The Islamic Republic of Iran*, Civ. No. 01-2094 (RCL) (U.S. Dist. Ct., Dist. of Columbia), and *Boulos v. The Islamic Republic of Iran*, Civ. No. 01-2684 (RCL) (U.S. Dist. Ct., Dist. of Columbia) (2003).

U.S. District Judge Royce C. Lamberth called the bombing the "most deadly state-sponsored terrorist attack against American citizens prior to September 11, 2001." While Marines slept in their barracks in Beirut on the early morning of October 23, 1983, a suicide bomber attacked in a truck loaded with explosives. Two hundred forty-one servicemen died. A similar attack at the French barracks killed 56 soldiers.

In 2001, injured survivors and victims' families filed two lawsuits. The lawsuits were filed after Congress passed the Antiterrorism and Effective Death Penalty Act of 1996 (AEDPA), Pub.L.No. 104-132, which permitted lawsuits against countries officially designated as state sponsors of **terrorism**. Iran has been on the Department of State's list since 1984. Both lawsuits named the Islamic Republic of Iran as the **defendant**. The suits sought compensatory and punitive damages for **wrongful death, battery**, assault, and for the intentional infliction of emotional distress resulting from "state-sponsored terrorism."

Iran did not file a response to either complaint, and as a consequence the trial court entered default judgments in favor of the plaintiffs in December 2002. However, federal law requires that default judgments against a foreign state are only proper where a plaintiff has established "his claim or right to **relief** by evidence that is satisfactory to the Court." Therefore, Lamberth combined the cases for a two-day **bench trial** in March 2003 to determine **liability** for the bombing.

Lamberth began by detailing the historical background of Lebanon. Lebanon did not participate in the Arab-Israeli wars of 1967 and 1973, but as a result many Palestinians took refuge in Lebanon. By 1973, 10 percent of the population were Palestinian refugees. Many of these supported the Palestine Liberation Organization (PLO) against Israel. Lamberth found that some of these supporters used bases in southern Lebanon to strike against Israel using guerilla warfare and other terrorist activities. In response, Israel retaliated against the PLO in Lebanon.

In 1975, Lebanon erupted into a civil war that lasted for 15 years. PLO supporters, including Lebanese Muslims and Palestinian refugees, fought against Lebanese Christians who opposed the PLO.

A multinational peacekeeping force arrived in Beirut, the Lebanese capital, in late 1982.

American, British, French, and Italian soldiers, under the auspices of the UNITED NATIONS, were stationed there to provide stability in Lebanon. The 24th Marine Amphibious Unit of the U.S. Marines (the "24th MAU") arrived in Beirut in May 1983.

Lamberth took testimony regarding the rules of engagement for the soldiers of the 24th MAU. These servicemen were not authorized to carry weapons with live rounds in their chambers. They could only chamber the rounds if "directly ordered to do so by a commissioned officer or they found themselves in a situation requiring the immediate use of **deadly force** in self-defense." Lamberth wrote, "the members of the 24th MAU were more restricted in their use of force than an ordinary citizen walking down a street in Washington, D.C." Lamberth concluded that the servicemen "were clearly non-combatants operating under peacetime rules of engagement." This finding was crucial because the plaintiffs would not have been allowed to recover if they had been engaged in a military action.

During the trial Lamberth examined Iran's commitment to Islamic revolution throughout the world, as expressed in its constitution and expenditures to finance terrorist organizations in the Near East, including Lebanon. He found that Hezbollah, "the party of God," the Shi'ite Muslim group that claimed responsibility for the bombing, was a tool of the Iranian government, in terms of both securing financial backing and directing terrorist operations.

Lamberth found that Iran controlled Hezbollah through the Iranian Ministry of Information and Security ("MOIS"). According to **expert testimony** at trial, the Iranian president, Ali Akbar Hashemi Rafsanjani, and Iran's supreme religious leader, Ayatollah Khomeini, would have had to approve the suicide bombing. Lamberth concluded, "Given their positions of authority, any act of these two officials must be deemed an act of the government of Iran."

Evidence at trial also included information concerning an intercepted message from September 1983, directing a leader of a terrorist group, Islamic Amal, "to take spectacular action against the United States Marines." Other testimony delineated a meeting where the attacks were planned in detail.

An explosives-laden truck, with an Iranian at the wheel, was disguised to resemble a water-delivery truck. The real water-delivery truck was then ambushed before it could arrive at the barracks. The truck arrived at the Marine barracks at about 6:25 a.m., circled a parking lot to increase its speed, and crashed through barriers to enter the barracks. Upon reaching the center, the bomb in the truck exploded.

According to the opinion, "the resulting explosion was the largest non-nuclear explosion that had ever been detonated on the face of the Earth. ... Trees located 370 feet away were shredded and completely exfoliated." Windows a half-mile away shattered. The explosion left a crater more than eight feet deep. The blast was the equivalent to that caused by 15,000 to 21,000 pounds of TNT. The explosive used was not manufactured in Lebanon at the time, but in Iran.

The testimony at the trial described the degree of planning and training that would have been necessary to make the attack a success. Lamberth concluded, "[I]t is beyond question that Hezbollah and its agents received massive material and technical support from the Iranian government."

Lamberth entered **judgment** for the plaintiffs but recognized that doing so would not "heal the pain that has become a permanent part of the lives" of the victims' families. Nevertheless, "the Court can take steps that will punish the men who carried out this unspeakable attack, and in so doing, try to achieve some small measure of justice for its survivors, and for the family members of the 241 Americans who never came home."

Lamberth had not ruled at time of publication on what damages, either compensatory or punitive, he would impose. He appointed special masters to review the claims for the damages, and then to report back to him.

Although the decision appears to be a victory for the plaintiffs, the real difficulty will come in the collection of damages. The United States has been reluctant to seize the assets of foreign countries to pay judgments. That reluctance stems at least partially from fear of retaliation. Other victims of terrorism who have won judgments against Iran have been compensated by payment from the United States TREASURY DEPARTMENT.

VOTING

New Voting Technology

Following the fiasco involving punch-card voting systems in Florida during the 2000 presidential elections, the federal government and its state counterparts moved quickly to take steps to remove doubt regarding the integrity of the systems. Employment of state-of-the-art technology has been the perceived solution that will purportedly ensure that every vote will be counted and that the American public can trust the voting results. However, a number of issues have arisen in the two years leading up the 2004 elections that raise questions as to whether this technology will actually resolve voting disputes.

Governments historically have struggled to devise voting systems that would ensure accuracy, reliability, and confidentiality. The Romans and Greeks both used systems whereby voters would drop balls or beans into containers marked for the various candidates. Similar systems survived through the settlement of North America. Beginning around the seventeenth century, many votes took place in public meeting halls, with voters shouting their selections. This method survived in many areas through the nineteenth century, until governments developed systems of voting through paper ballots, which were designed to provide confidentiality. However, this method also created an opportunity for some politicians to tamper with the actual votes.

Technology improved towards the end of the nineteenth century, as governments introduced mechanical voting booths with lever machines to count votes. By the 1960s, two new popular methods developed. Some states employed a system where voters filled in blanks on a form that could be read by an optical scanner, much like a standardized test. Many other states adopted the punch card system, whereby voters made their selections by punching holes next to the various candidates' names. While these systems were not foolproof, both provided records of the actual votes in case a dispute arose.

The results of the 2000 presidential election called into question the accuracy and reliability of some of these older voting methods. The outcome of the 2000 election came down to the votes in the state of Florida, which used a punch-card system. The results favored GEORGE W. BUSH over AL GORE, and Bush was named president. However, Gore's camp disputed the voting results. This lead to weeks of controversy in the courts, as Gore demanded a recount. Florida state courts initially ordered the recount, which required volunteers to read each punch card to determine the candidate that was actually selected on each card. Before these counters could complete the process, however, the U.S. SUPREME COURT ceased the recount. *Bush v. Gore*, 531 U.S. 98, 121 S. Ct. 525, 148 L. Ed. 2d 388 (2000)

Since the election debacle, Congress has gone so far as to pass legislation that provides funding for states to move away from the antiquated voting systems. The Help America Vote Act of 2002, Pub. L. No. 107-252, 116 Stat. 1666, provides funding to the states to replace old punch-card systems with more viable technology. The result of the legislation is that voters in about thirty states will use computers when they vote. The devices, which are similar to ATM machines, allow voters to make their selections by touching a candidate's name on a computer screen. The 2002 federal legislation created the Election Assistance Commission, which was scheduled to release $2.3 billion in aid to local governments during the summer of 2004.

Despite the promise of the computerized election methods, evidence arose that the new computer voting systems posed major security risks. In 2003, Bev Harris, a freelance writer and public relations consultant, entered a search for a book about elections on the Google search engine. She discovered a code from Diebold Election Systems, one of the leading producers of computer voting systems. Shortly thereafter, researchers at John Hopkins University determined that Harris had discovered the entire code for Diebold's voting machines. The head of that research team, Avi Rubin, said that Diebold's system is "far below even the most minimal security standards applicable in other contexts."

Other similar studies fueled the concern over the reliability of the voting systems advertised by a number of vendors, including Diebold, Sequoia Voting Systems, Election Systems & Software, and Hart InterCivic. According to these studies, computerized voting systems often have weak password control and management. On some systems, a voter could manipulate authentication methods that would allow the voter to cast more than one vote. Moreover, hackers could access some of these machines from another computer and alter or destroy votes. Since these machines generally do not provide a paper trail, if a voting controversy erupted, it would be difficult for officials to recount the actual votes that were made.

The concerns over computerized voting methods heightened in April 2004 with the release of a report from the U.S. Commission on Human Rights, which concluded that "the potential is real and present for significant problems on voting day that once again will compromise the right to vote." Several states that initially rushed to acquire computerized voting equipment are now hesitant to use these machines. The criticism has been particularly harsh in California, where computer voting caused numerous problems in elections held in March 2004.

Supporters of these voting systems note that according to several surveys, voters who use computerized methods trust the results. A number of solutions to the problems of computer voting have also been submitted. Many commentators have demanded that the system create a paper trail that would provide a means to recount the votes in the event that a dispute arose.

One solution, proposed in the early 1990s by University of Pennsylvania graduate student Rebecca Mercuri, would require the system to produce a printout of a voter's selection. The voter could verify his or her selections from this printout before leaving the voting booth.

As of May 2004, the Election Assistance Commission was deliberating over recommendations that the commission will give to the states regarding the election. However, the commission's chairperson, DeForest Soaries, acknowledged that questions about electronic voting will remain through the elections in 2004. The 2004 presidential election will take place on November 2.

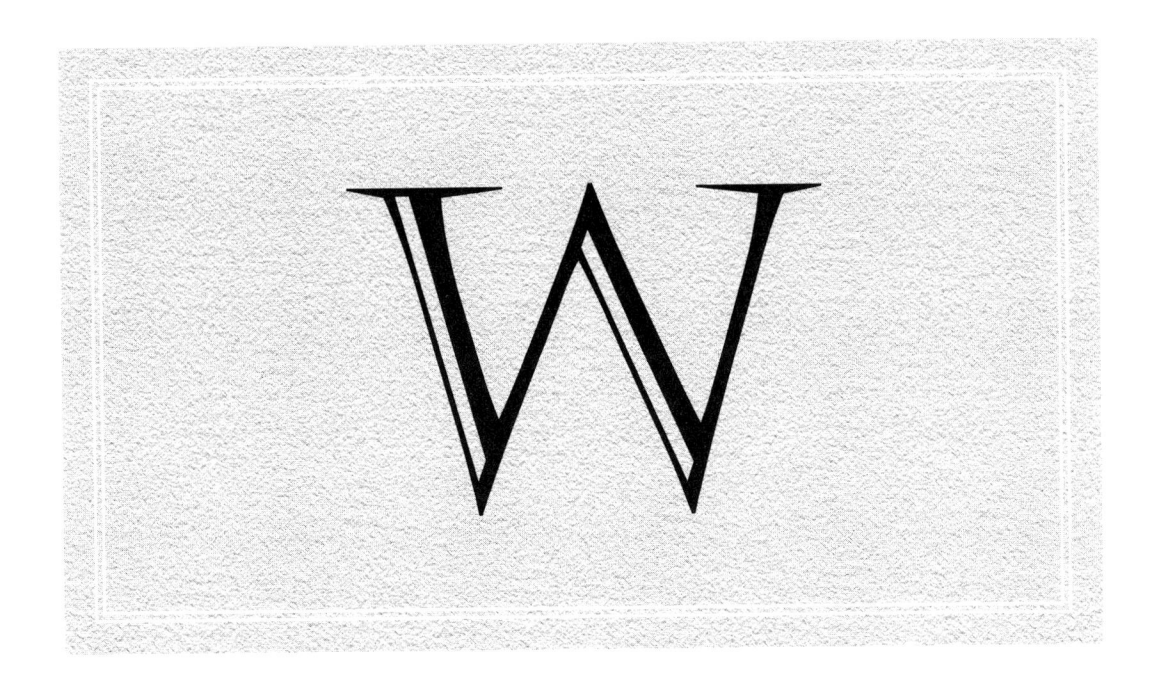

WARSAW CONVENTION

Airline Liable for Second-hand Hand Smoke Death

Article 17 of the Warsaw Convention governs **liability** issues for international air carriers. Specifically, it imposes liability on an airline for the death or bodily **injury** of a passenger if caused by an "accident" that occurs in connection with the flight. The precise meaning of the word "accident" has been heavily litigated in U.S. courts, and the U.S. SUPREME COURT has addressed Article 17. In its most recent occasion to interpret the Warsaw Convention, the Court in *Olympic Airways v. Husain*, __ U.S. __, 124 S.Ct. 1221, 1576 L.Ed.2d 1146 (2004) held that an airline is liable for willful misconduct under Article 17 for failing to move an asthmatic passenger with acute sensitivity to second hand smoke to a more remote part of the nonsmoking section of the plane. In this case, the passenger died on the airplane, and his estate was awarded $1.4 million in damages.

In December 1997, Dr. Abid M. Hanson traveled from San Francisco to Athens and Cairo with his family. When he boarded the Olympic Airways flight in New York for the trip to Athens, Dr. Hanson discovered that Olympic permitted passengers to smoke. Olympic placed Hanson and his family in the nonsmoking section, and Hanson had an uneventful trip, arriving in Cairo in good health. However, when Hanson and his family switched planes in Athens in January 1988 for his return flight, he was placed in a nonsmoking section row that was close to the smoking section. He and his wife asked the flight attendant several times to have their seats moved further away from the smokers, but the attendant refused. During the flight, Dr. Hanson's breathing became more difficult, and he had his wife administer an epinephrine injection to control his asthma attack. Hanson soon collapsed and died, in spite of the efforts of a doctor who was on the same flight.

Hanson's wife, Rubina Husain, sued Olympic Airways, arguing that the flight attendant's refusal to reseat Dr. Hanson constituted an "accident," and qualified as willful misconduct under Article 17. The judge awarded Husain and Hanson's estate $1.4 million dollars. The U.S. Court of Appeals for the Ninth Circuit upheld the **verdict**, rejecting Olympic's claim that Hanson's death was not an accident under Article 17. Olympic then appealed to the U.S. Supreme Court.

The Court, in a 6-2 decision (Justice STEPHEN BREYER did not participate), upheld the Ninth Circuit's ruling. Justice CLARENCE THOMAS, writing for the majority, relied on *Air France v. Saks*, 470 U.S] 392, 105 S.Ct. 1338, 84 L.Ed.2d 289 (1985), to determine the meaning of the word "accident." In that case, the Court concluded that the term "accident" referred to an "unexpected or unusual event or happening that is external to the passenger" and not to "the passenger's own internal reaction to the usual, normal, and expected operation of the aircraft." Armed with this definition, Justice Thomas analyzed whether the flight attendant's refusal to move Dr. Hanson's seat constituted an accident.

The parties did not **contest** the *Saks* definition of the word "accident," but did dispute which event should be the focus of the accident analysis. Olympic contended that the injury producing event was not the attendant's inaction but Dr. Hanson's internal reaction to cigarette smoke, which is permitted on Olympic's international flights. Smoking was a usual event on this flight and conformed to the usual, normal, and expected operation of the plane. In addition, the flight attendant's inaction could not be equated with Article 17, which requires an action that causes injury. Justice Thomas rejected the claim that the Court needed to focus on one injury-producing event. Instead, he proposed that there are "often multiple interrelated factual events that combine to cause any given injury." In this case the aggravating event was Dr. Hanson remaining in his assigned seat, where he was exposed to second hand smoke. The flight attendant's refusal on three different occasions to move Dr. Hanson was clearly a factual event. The events surrounding Dr. Hanson were unexpected and unusual; therefore, these external events and Dr. Hanson's reaction to them could be labeled an "accident."

Justice Thomas also rejected the claim that the attendant's failure to act could not constitute an "accident." While inaction might be a defense in **tort law** negligence cases, the Warsaw Convention's Article 17 is not based on negligence. Article 17, under the *Saks* decision, looks to an unexpected or unusual event or happening on an airplane. In this case, the attendant's rejection of an explicit request would constitute an event or happening. The attendant's conduct was unexpected and unusual, which properly led the lower courts to determine that Dr. Hanson's death was an "accident" under Article 17.

Justice ANTONIN SCALIA, in a dissenting opinion joined by Justice SANDRA DAY O'CONNOR, argued that the Court's decision contradicted judicial decisions made by other Warsaw Convention treaty partners, namely Australia and England. In these decisions the courts ruled that a failure to act could not be classified as an "accident" under the Convention.

WATER RIGHTS

A group of rights designed to protect the use and enjoyment of water that travels in streams, rivers, lakes, and ponds, gathers on the surface of the earth, or collects underground.

Virginia Establishes Rights to the Potomac River

The Potomac River flows almost 400 miles before emptying into the Chesapeake Bay. The Commonwealth of Virginia and the State of Maryland are located on either side of the Potomac, and both governments have claimed rights to the water dating back to the earliest colonial times. Disputes over these rights led Congress to pass legislation on several occasions that sought to settle matters, but control over the river remained in doubt until early in the twenty-first century. The U.S. SUPREME COURT, in *Virginia v. Maryland*, __ U.S. __, 124 S.Ct. 598, 157 L.Ed.2d 461 (2003), resolved the conflict, ruling that Maryland could not regulate Virginia's improvements along the Potomac or its right to withdraw water.

The U.S. Supreme Court has **original jurisdiction** to hear boundary disputes between states. Unlike its **appellate** jurisdiction, which consumes most of its caseload, disputes between states require the Court to act as a trial court. In this case, the Court followed its normal procedure of appointing a **special master** to conduct hearings and to take evidence from both sides. The **master** then submitted factual findings and a recommendation for the way the Court should rule.

The decisive case arose in 1997, when Maryland refused to grant permits to the Virginia water authority agency, which wanted to construct a water-intake structure 725 feet from the Virginia shore of the Potomac. The structure was designed to improve water quality for the local Virginia county. Maryland refused to issue the permit because it believed that Virginia had not provided a sufficient need for the water; some Maryland officials believed that the increased draw of water from the Potomac would encourage urban sprawl in Virginia. Virginia then made an administrative **appeal** of this decision. In 2001, the Maryland Department of Environment found that Virginia had established a sufficient need, and it issued the permit. However, the permit contained a limitation mandated by the Maryland legislature, placing a permanent flow restrictor on the intake pipe. This restrictor would limit the amount of water that Virginia could withdraw from the Potomac. Virginia filed suit in the U.S. Supreme Court, asking the court to issue a **declaratory judgment** that Maryland could not regulate its withdrawal of water from the Potomac or its construction of improvements along the shore. The special master sided with Virginia, finding that previous congressional legislation had given Virginia the right to the waters of the Potomac.

The U.S. Supreme Court, in a 7-2 decision, agreed with the special master's recommendations. Chief Justice WILLIAM REHNQUIST, writing for the majority, reviewed the history of the **controversy**. Virginia traced its rights to the Potomac back to a 1609 royal charter, while Maryland's claim was based on a charter of 1632. During the early years of the Republic, competing claims to the river led to a 1785 compact between the two states. This compact stated that the river was to be considered "as a common highway, for the purpose of navigation and commerce to the citizens of Virginia and Maryland." Article Seven granted citizens of each state "full property" rights in the shores of the Potomac and the "privilege" of building "improvements" from the shore. The compact resolved navigational and jurisdictional issues, but it did not resolve where the boundary line between the two states should be drawn. In 1874, the states submitted to binding **arbitration** on the boundary dispute. The arbitrator placed the boundary at the low-water mark on the Virginia shore, giving Maryland ownership of the entire riverbed. However, the award also stated that Virginia had the right to use the river "beyond the low-water mark as may be necessary to the full enjoyment of her riparian ownership," without impeding navigation or interfering with Maryland's use of the Potomac. Maryland established a water permitting system for the Potomac in 1933, but it was not until 1957 that Virginia applied for a permit to withdraw water. Maryland granted this permit and all others until its refusal in 1997.

Chief Justice Rehnquist noted that both sides had produced "reams of historical evidence" to support its respective view about the status of sovereignty over the Potomac as of 1785. He concluded that Maryland did not have "well-settled sovereignty" as of that date, for there would have been no point in agreeing to the compact. The arbitration award of 1874 also undercut Maryland's claim of sovereignty, as it gave Virginia the right to build improvements and the sovereign right to use the river beyond the low-water mark. Therefore, Maryland had no right to force Virginia to apply for a water-use permit. The Court also rejected Maryland's claim that Virginia had acquiesced to the Maryland regulations by applying for permits since 1957. Rehnquist stated that Maryland could claim acquiescence for "at most, 43 years." This was too short a period when measured from the 1700s.

Justice JOHN PAUL STEVENS, in a dissenting opinion joined by Justice ANTHONY KENNEDY, argued that Maryland owned virtually the entire river and that it therefore exercised sovereign jurisdiction over the use of the Potomac.

BIBLIOGRAPHY

ABORTION

ROE V. WADE CONTINUES TO MAKE HEADLINES THREE DECADES AFTER LANDMARK ABORTION DECISION

Barbash, Fred. "Blackmun's Papers Shine Light into Court; Justice's Trove Opened by Library of Congress." *The Washington Post*. March 5, 2004.

Gearan, Anne. "Private Files of Justice Blackmun, *Roe v. Wade* Author, Released." *The Associated Press State and Local Wire*. March 4, 2004.

Greenhouse, Linda. "Documents Reveal the Evolution of a Justice." *The New York Times*. March 4, 2004.

"Inadmissible." *Texas Lawyer*. March 1, 2004.

McCorvey v. Hill. Opinion and Order Denying Rule 60(b) Motion. 2003 U.S. Dist. LEXIS 12986, (U.S. Dist. Ct., N.D. Tex., June 19, 2003).

ABORTION

FIVE-WEEK-OLD FETUS IS A "MEMBER" OF THE MOTHER'S BODY FOR PURPOSES OF ATTEMPTED SEXUAL ASSAULT STATUTE

Rosen, Jeffrey. "A Viable Solution." legalaffairs.com. September-October 2003. http://www.legalaffairs.org/issues/September-October-2003/argument_rosen_sepoct03.html

AGE DISCRIMINATION

AGE DISCRIMINATION IN EMPLOYMENT ACT DOES NOT COVER REVERSE DISCRIMINATION CLAIMS

Downey, Kirstin. "High Court Backs Benefits Based on Age." *The Washington Post*. February 25, 2004.

Savage, David G. "Supreme Court Rejects Reverse Bias Claim." *Los Angeles Times*. February 24, 2004.

"Supreme Court Wades Into Reverse Age Discrimination." *Associated Press*. November 12, 2003.

ALIENS

BUSH PROPOSAL FOR TEMPORARY LEGAL STATUS OF IMMIGRANT WORKERS

Allen, Mike. "Bush Proposes Legal Status for Immigrant Labor." *The Washington Post*. January 8, 2004.

Bernstein, Aaron, et al. "This Plan May Not Get a Green Card." *Business Week*. January 19, 2004.

Lares, Angeles Negrete. "New Proposal Would Provide Legal Residency to Many Immigrants." *The Brownsville Herald*. (TX), May 10, 2004

Llorente, Elizabeth. "Bush Proposes Controversial Immigration Plan." *The Record*. (Hackersack, NJ), January 8, 2004.

O'Meara, Kelly Patricia. "Do Borders Matter to President Bush?" *Insight on the News*. March 2, 2004.

AMERICANS WITH DISABILITIES ACT

IN FOCUS: ADA COMPLIANCE OF INTERNET SITES

Texas State Library and Archives Commission. "Creating ADA-Compliant Web Sites." Available online at <http://www.tsl.state.tx.us/ld/pubs/ada/>.

U.S. Department of Justice. "Accessibility of State and Local Government Websites to People with Disabilities." June 2003. Available online at <http://www.usdoj.gov/crt/ada/websites2_scrn.pdf>.

World Wide Web Consortium. "Web Content Accessibility Guidelines 2.0." March 11, 2004. Available online at <http://www.w3.org/TR/2004/WD-WCAG20-20040311/>.

SUPREME COURT UPHOLDS ACCESS TO THE COURT FOR DISABLED PERSONS

Greenhouse, Linda. "Justices Find States Can Be Liable for Not Making Courthouses Accessible to Disabled." *New York Times*. May 18, 2004.

Holland, Gina. "Supreme Court Gets Disability Rights Case." *Kansas City Star*. June 23, 2003. Available online at <http://www.kansascity.com/mld/kansascity/news/breaking_news/6151880.htm?1c>.

Lane, Charles. "High Court Upholds Rules in Disabilities Act." *Washington Post.* May 17, 2004.

Richey, Warren. "Court Boosts Civil Rights Law for Disabled." *Christian Science Monitor.* May 18, 2004.

EMPLOYERS GRANTED MORE LEEWAY IN NOT REHIRING PERSONS WITH DRUG OR ALCOHOL ADDICTIONS

Clark, Margaret H. "High Court's ADA Ruling Leaves Some Accommodations Questions Unanswered." *HR Magazine* January 2004.

"Court Rules For Company In Workplace Rights of Recovering Addicts." *Associated Press.* December 2, 2003.

Lithwick, Dahlia. "Junkie Justice: Are Drug Addicts Covered Under The ADA?" http://slate.msn.com/id/2089534 *Slate Magazine.* October 10, 2003.

ANTITRUST

F. HOFFMAN-LAROCHE, LTD. V. EMPAGRAN, S.A.

Henning, Lily, "D.C. Circuit Opens the Door to Foreign Victims of Vitamin Price Fixing." *Legal Times*, October 13, 2003.

Henning, Lily. "Inadmissible: Take Your Vitamins." *Legal Times,* December 22, 2003.

Stoll, Neal R. and Shepard Goldfein. "Limiting the Sherman Act's Extraterritoriality." *New York Law Journal,* January 14, 2004.

SUPREME COURT LIMITS ANTITRUST LAWSUITS AGAINST PHONE COMPANIES

"Chairman Wants Antitrust Affirmed In Trinko." *Telecom Policy Report* November 12, 2003.

Holland, Gina. "Supreme Court Restricts Phone Lawsuits." *Miami Herald.* January 13, 2004.

"Supreme Court Takes Verizon Antitrust Appeal." *Associated Press.* March 10, 2003.

U.S. POSTAL SERVICE CANNOT BE SUED UNDER ANTITRUST LAWS

"Court Shields Postal Service From Suits." *Associated Press.* February 25, 2004.

Denniston, Lyle. "Ruling protects Postal Service." *Boston Globe.* February 26, 2004.

McGlinchey, David. "Supreme Court: Antitrust Suits Against Postal Service Not Allowed." *Government Executive Magazine.* http://www.govexec.com/dailyfed/0204/022604d1.htm February 26, 2004.

APPORTIONMENT

CONGRESSIONAL REDISTRICTING INCITES CONTROVERSY

Associated Press. "Texas Governor Sticks to His Guns in Political Spat." *Philadelphia Inquirer.*

Castro, April. "Texas Democrats Leave State in Protest." *Milwaukee Journal and Sentinel.* May 14, 2003.

Texas Legislative Council, *State and Federal Law Governing Redistricting in Texas* Available online at <http://www.tlc.state.tx.us/research/pdf/1799redis.pdf>.

SUPREME COURT UPHOLDS PENNSYLVANIA REDISTRICTING PLAN

Branigin, William. "High Court Upholds Pennsylvania Ruling." *Washington Post.* April 28, 2004.

Holland, Gina. "Supreme Court Upholds Pennsylvania Redistricting." *Washington Post.* April 28, 2004.

Rosenbaum, David E. "Justices Bow to Legislators In Political Gerrymander Case." *New York Times.* April 29, 2004.

Worden, Amy, and Henderson, Stephen. "Pa. Democrats Lose High Court Fight Over New Congressional District Map." *Philadelphia Inquirer.* April 29, 2004.

BANKRUPTCY

DEBTOR MUST OBJECT TO LATE FILING BEFORE CASE DECIDED ON THE MERITS

"Dealine for Objecting to Discharge is not Jurisdictional." *Bankruptcy Newsletter.* http://west.thomson.com/aboutus/newsletters/bankruptcy/bkcy012104.asp?cookie%5Ftest=1,(accessed March 22, 2004.) January 21, 2003.

"Supreme Court to Decide Four Bankruptcy Cases This Term." *National Consumer Law Center.* http://www.consumerlaw.org/initiatives/bankruptcy/sup_ct.shtml (accessed March 22, 2004.)

CHAPTER 7 ATTORNEY'S FEES MUST BE AUTHORIZED BY THE BANKRUPTCY COURT

"Attorney Compensation From Chapter 7 Estate Limited." *Bankruptcy Newsletter.* http://west.thomson.com/aboutus/newsletters/bankruptcy/bkcy020404.asp February 4, 2004.

"Notable Bankruptcy Cases of the Week." *The Legal Consultant Ezine.* http://www.lawyerassistant.com/ezine/past_issues/issue45.html February 9, 2004.

"Supreme Court to Decide Four Bankruptcy Cases This Term." *National Consumer Law Center.* http://www.consumerlaw.org/initiatives/bankruptcy/sup_ct.shtml (accessed March 22, 2004.)

DEBTORS MAY SEEK RELIEF FROM STATE-BACKED EDUCATION LOANS

Brubaker, Ralph. "On the Nature of Federal Bankruptcy Jurisdiction." *William and Mary Law Review.* March 1, 2000.

Denniston, Lyle. "Court Tackles Disputes on Student Loans, Looted Artwork." *Boston Globe.* October 1, 2003.

Holland, Gina. "Court Rules in Favor of Consumer Debtors." *Washington Post.* May 17, 2004.

TILL V. SCS CREDIT CORPORATION

"Consumers Win Supreme Court Bankruptcy Rulings." *Arizona Daily Sun*, May 18, 2004. Available online at <http://www.azdailysun.com/non_sec/nav_includes/story.cfm?storyID=87443-51K>.

"Supreme Court Justices Fail to Agree on Interest Rate in Chapter 13 Cramdown." *Bankruptcy Law Reporter*, Vol. 16, No. 21, May 20, 2004. Available online at <http://litigationcenter.bna.com/pic2/lit.nsf/id/BNAP-5Z6RAA?OpenDocument>.

Till v. SCS Credit Corporation, No. 02-1016, 542 U.S. ___ (2004). Available online at <http://www.supremecourtus.gov/opinions>.

YATES V. HENDON

Bean, Matt. "Inside the Take-Down of Andrew Luster." CourtTV.com. June 19, 2003, Available online at <http://www.courttv.com/news/2003/0618/lustermoredetails_ctv.html>.

Bean, Matt. "Luster Lassoed by Dogged Bounty Hunter." CourtTV.com, June 18, 2003, Available online at <http://www.courttv.com/news/2003/0618/lustercaught_ctv.html>

CNN.com. "Bounty Hunter Who Caught Luster Won't Get Any of Forfeited $1 Million." August 5, 2003, Available online at <http://www.cnn.com/2003/LAW/08/05/luster.hearing>

BOUNTY HUNTER

FUGITIVE GRANDSON OF MAX FACTOR CAUGHT BY BOUNTY HUNTER IN MEXICO

Bean, Matt. "Inside the Take-Down of Andrew Luster." CourtTV.com. June 19, 2003, Available online at <http://www.courttv.com/news/2003/0618/lustermoredetails_ctv.html>.

Bean, Matt. "Luster Lassoed by Dogged Bounty Hunter." CourtTV.com, June 18, 2003, Available online at http://www.courttv.com/news/2003/0618/lustercaught_ctv.html

CNN.com. "Bounty Hunter Who Caught Luster Won't Get Any of Forfeited $1 Million." August 5, 2003, Available online at <http://www.cnn.com/2003/LAW/08/05/luster.hearing>

BROADCASTING

JANET JACKSON'S BREAST EXPOSURE AT SUPER BOWL SPARKS UPROAR

Associated Press. "Senate Panel Moves on Indecency." *Houston Chronicle.*. March 10, 2004, at 10.

Salant, Jonathan D. "House Backs Stiffer Indecency Fines." *The Star-Ledger*. March 12, 2004.

CENTRAL INTELLIGENCE AGENCY

FORMER CIA AGENT'S CONVICTION OVERTURNED AFTER MORE THAN TWENTY YEARS IN PRISON

Hoppin, Jason. "DOJ Admits False Data on Ex-Agent." *National Law Journal*. June 12, 2000.

Hughes, Lynn N. (U.S. District Judge, Houston). "Opinion on Conviction, Criminal Case H-82-139 (United States of America vs. Edwin Paul Wilson)". http://www.fas.org/sgp/jud/wilson102703.pdf October 27, 2003.

Jehl, Douglas. "Ex-CIA Man Wins Verdict Reversal." *New York Times*. http://www.nytimes.com/2003/10/30/national/30INTE.html October 30, 2003.

"Judge Throws Out Ex-CIA Agent's Conviction." Associated Press. http://www.cnn.com/2003/LAW/10/29/cia.wilson.ap/ October 29, 2003.

Loeb, Vernon. "Back Channels: The Intelligence Community-Never Mind." *Washington Post*. January 20, 2000.

Ruppert, Michael C. "Ed Wilson's Revenge." *From The Wilderness*. http://www.fromthewilderness.com/cgi-bin/MasterPFP.cgi?doc=http://www.fromthewilderness.com/free/ciadrugs/Ed_Wilson_1.html January 2000.

Staff (AP). "Court Throws Out Former CIA Officer Edwin P. Wilson's Conviction". *Associated Press*. http://www.independent-media.tv/itemprint.cfm?fmedia_id=3444&fcategory_desc=Veterans%20and%20Military%20Personel October 29, 2003.

CIVIL RIGHTS

SUPREME COURT UPHOLDS FEDERAL FOUR-YEAR STATUTE OF LIMITATIONS

Anderson, Mark H. "Four-Year Limit Applies in Bias Suit." *Dow Jones Newswire*. May 3, 2004. Available online at <http://www.smartmoney.com/news/on/index.cfm?story=ON-20040503-000510-1128>.

Miller, James. "High Court Clears Path for Race Bias Suit." *Chicago Tribune*. May 4, 2004.

White, Rebecca Hanna. "Modern Discrimination Theory and the National Labor Relations Act." *William and Mary Law Review*. October 1, 1997.

INVESTIGATORS FIND THIRTY-FOUR CREDIBLE VIOLATIONS OF USA PATRIOT ACT

Bohn, Kevin. "Patriot Act Report Documents Civil Rights Complaints." CNN.com. July 31, 2003. Available online at <http://www.cnn.com/2003/LAW/07/21/justice.civil.liberties/>

Shehon, Philip. "Report on the USA Patriot Act Alleges Civil Rights Violations." *New York Times*. July 21, 2003.

U.S. Department of Justice, Office of the Inspector General. "Report to Congress on Implementation of Section 1002 of the USA PATRIOT Act." July 17, 2003.

COPYRIGHT

FEDERAL DISTRICT COURT RULES THAT DVD COPYING SOFTWARE IS ILLEGAL

321 Studios v. Metro Goldwyn Mayer Studios, Inc. et al. , Order Granting Defendants' Motion for Partial Summary Judgment and Resolving Related Motions, (U.S. Dist. Ct., No. Dist. Cal., February 19, 2004)

DVD Copy Control Association. http://www.dvdcca.org/faq.html

"321 Studios Will Appeal Court Ruling." http://www.321studios.com/PRESS/2.20.2004.htm

The Digital Millenium Copyright Act. U.S. Copyright Office Summary. www.copyright.gov/legislation/dmca.pdf

COMIC CREATORS FIGHT COPYRIGHT BATTLE OVER ORAL CONTRACT

Dean, Michael. "Gaiman vs. McFarlane Trial Transcripts." *The Comics Journal*. February 13, 2003. http://www.tcj.com/250/n_gvm.html

"Gaiman Keeps Share of Spawn Characters." ICV2.com. October 4, 2002. http://www.icv2.com/articles/news/1890.html

"Gaiman Sweep!" ICV2.com. October 3, 2002. http://www.icv2.com/articles/news/1883.html

"The Jury's Out on Gaiman vs. McFarlane." ICV2.com. October 2, 2002. http://www.icv2.com/articles/news/1880.html

Sachdev, Ameet. "Heroes Ruled Copyrightable." *Chicago Tribune*. March 5, 2004. http://www.chicagotribune.com/business/chi-0403050382mar05,1,5168100,print.story?coll=chi-business-hed

"Why Gaiman Sued McFarlane." ICV2.com. February 11, 2002. http://www.icv2.com/articles/news/1118.html

"Wisconsin Courtroom Drama, Part I." ICV2.com. October 1, 2002. http://www.icv2.com/articles/news/1878.html

"Wisconsin Courtroom Drama, Part II." ICV2.com. October 1, 2002. http://www.icv2.com/articles/news/1879.html

SCO GROUP SUES IBM, NOVELL, AND OTHERS OVER UNIX AND LINUX USE

Millard, Elizabeth, "SCO Adds Copyright Claim to IBM Lawsuit." E-Commerce News, February 6, 2004. Available online at <http://www.ecommercetimes.com/perl/story/32791.html>.

Shankland, Stephen, "IBM Denies Charges of Unix Theft." CNET News.com, May 1, 2003. Available online at <http://news.com.com/2100-1016_3-999261.html>.

Shankland, Stephen, "SCO Sues Big Blue Over Unix, Linux." CNET News.com, March 6, 2003. Available online at <http://news.com.com/2100-1016-991464.html>.

CORPORATE FRAUD

THE ROUNDUP OF ENRON EXECUTIVES CONTINUES

Associated Press. "Chronology of Fallen Energy Giant Enron." *Houston Chronicle*. http://www.chron.com/cs/CDA/story.hts/special/enron/2342585 February 19, 2004.

Flood, Mary. "Judge Delays Skilling's Trial Date." *Houston Chrionicle*. http://www.chron.com/cs/CDA/ssistory.mpl/special/enron/2445682 March 17, 2004.

Flood, Mary. "Sentencing Delayed for Enron's Andrew Fastow." *Houston Chronicle*. http://www.chron.com/cs/CDA/ssistory.mpl/business/2456007 March 18, 2004.

"Former Enron CEO Jeffrey Skilling Charged With Fraud by the SEC." SRI Media. http://www.srimedia.com/artman/publish/article_755.shtml February 19, 2004.

"Former Enron CEO Jeff Skilling Denies Any Wrongdoing; Fastow Takes the 5th." ABC News. http://abclocal.go.com/ktrk/news/20702_news_skilling.html February 7, 2002.

Hays, Kristen. "Lea Fastow Withdraws Enron Plea Agreement." Yahoo! News / Associated Press. http://news.yahoo.com/news?tmpl=story&u=/ap/20040407/ap_on_bi_ge/enron_lea_fastow_8 April 7, 2004

Iwata, Edward. "Fastow Indicted in Enron Meltdown." *USA Today*. http://www.usatoday.com/money/industries/energy/2002-10-31-enron-fastow-indicted_x.htm October 31, 2002.

Murphy, Bill. "Andrew Fastow: A Study in Contrasts." *Houston Chronicle*. http://www.chron.com/cs/CDA/story.hts/special/enron/1601330 October 2, 2002.

Rogers, Jen. "Former Enron Executive Fastow Reportedly negotiating Plea." CNN.com. http://www.cnn.com/2004/LAW/01/07/enron.fastows/ January 8, 2004.

Rogers, Jen, and others. "Fastow and His Wife Plead Guilty." CNN Money. http://money.cnn.com/2004/01/14/news/companies/enron_fastows/index.htm January 14, 2004.

"SEC Charges Jeffrey K. Skilling,, Enron's Former resident, Chief Executive Officer and Chief Operating Officer, With Fraud." SEC.gov. http://www.sec.gov/news/press/2004-18.htm February 19, 2004.

"Skilling Indicted for Fraud." CNN Money. http://money.cnn.com/2004/02/19/news/companies/skilling/ February 19, 2004.

WORLDCOM WOES

"Court Approves WorldCom Settlement with SEC." Business Law Newsletter, Law firm of KMZ Rosenman. Available online at <http://www.kmzrosenman.com>

Goldstein v. MCI WorldCom, et al., No. 02-60322, August 25. 2003. Available online at <http://www.ca5.uscourts.gov/opinions/pub/02/02=60322-cv0.pdf>.

In Re Worldcom, U.S. Bankruptcy Court for the Southern District of New York. Chapter 11 Case No. 02-13533-AJG. May 4, 2004. Available online at <http://www.findlaw.com>.

Lehman, Brian. "Misinterpretation of Fraud Statute Led WorldCom Case Dismissal." September 5, 2003. Available online at <http://www.cnn.com/2003/LAW/09/05/findlaw.analysis.lehman.worldcom/>.

"Oklahoma Files Criminal Charges Against WorldCom, Six Former Employees." Press Release from the Office of the Attorney General, State of Oklahoma. August 27, 2003. Available online at <http://www.oag.state.ok.us/oag>.

CRIMINAL PROCEDURE

UNITED STATES V. BENITEZ

Bamberger, Phylis Skloot and David J. Gottlieb, eds. *Practice Under the Federal Sentencing Guidelines*. Gaithersburg, Md.: Aspen Law & Business, 2001.

Lash, Steve. "Court Ponders Whether Defendant Can Withdraw Plea When Judge Fails To Warn." *Chicago Daily Law Bulletin.* April 22, 2004, at 3.

DISCOVERY

CHENEY V. UNITED STATES DISTRICT COURT FOR THE DISTRICT OF COLUMBIA

Epstein, Lee and Thomas G. Walker. *Constitutional Law for a Changing America : Institutional Powers and Constraints.* Washington, D.C.: CQ Press, 2004.

Fisher, Louis. *The Politics of Executive Privilege.* Durham, N.C.: Carolina Academic Press, 2004.

DISCOVERY

U.S. COURTS MAY ORDER DISCOVERY FOR FOREIGN TRIBUNALS

Holland, Gina. "U.S. Courts Can Help Foreign Regulators: June 21, 2004. http://www.cnn.com/2004/LAW/06/21/scotus.intel.ap/ *CNN.com*

Waldmeir, Patti. "Alarm Over Ruling on Documents Discovery." June 22, 2004. http://news.ft.com/servlet/ContentServer?pagename=FT.com/StoryFT/FullStory&c=StoryFT&cid=1087373167873 *Financial Times.*

Kessler, Michelle. "High Court: Intel Can Be Forced to Give Documents." June 22, 2004. http://www.usatoday.com/tech/techinvestor/techcorporatenews/2004-06-22-amd-intel_x.htm*USA Today.*

Jones, Terill Yue Jones. "AMD Can Seek Documents From Intel Via U.S. Courts." June 22, 2004. *Los Angeles Times.*

DNA TESTING

MANDATORY DNA TESTING IN NEW JERSEY FACES COURT CHALLENGES

Jost, Kenneth. "DNA Databases: Does Expanding Them Threaten Civil Liberties?" *CQ Researcher.* May 28, 1999.

Toutant, Charles. "Suit Challenges Expanded DNA Law." *New Jersey Law Journal.* January 28, 2004.

DOUBLE JEOPARDY

TRIBAL PROSECUTIONS DO NOT BAR FEDERAL CRIMINAL PROCEEDINGS

Greenhouse, Linda. "Court Upholds Tribal Power it Once Denied." *New York Times.* April 20, 2004.

Henderson, Stephen. "U.S. Supreme Court: 'The Color of Authority.'" *Grand Forks Herald.* January 22, 2004. Available online at <http://www.grandforks.com/mld/grandforks/7766995.htm>

"Lara and the Persistence of Tribal Sovereignty." *Indian Country Today.* April 29, 2004. Available online at <http://www.indiancountry.com/?1083269726>

Tedlock, Jennifer. "Ruling Upholds Tribal Sovereignty." *Native American Times.* April 22, 2004. Available online at <http://nativetimes.com/index.asp?action=displayarticle&article_id=4327>.

DRUGS

FDA BANS EPHEDRA

"FDA Plans Warning Labels for Ephedra." *www.cnn.com.* March 2, 2003. Available online at <http://www.cnn.com/2003/HEALTH/diet.fitness/02/28/ephedra.fda/>

Hurley, Dan. "Judge Clears the Way for U.S. Ban on Ephedra." *New York Times.* April 13, 2004.

Kaufman, Marc. "U.S. to Stop Ephedra Sales." *Washington Post.* December 31, 2004.

Mitchell, Lesley. "A Rush to Beat Ephedra Ban." *Salt Lake Tribune.* April 13, 2004. Available online at <http://www.sltrib.com/2004/Apr/04132004/business/156612.asp>

EDUCATION

NUMEROUS GROUPS OPPOSE FEDERAL NO CHILD LEFT BEHIND ACT

Associated Press. "States Rebelling Against No Child Left Behind." FOX News.com. February 17, 2004. Available online at <http://www.foxnews.com/story/0,2933,111675,00.html>.

Sunderman, Gail L. and Jimmy Kim. *Inspiring Vision, Disappointing Results: Four Studies on Implementing the No Child Left Behind Act.* Cambridge, Mass.: The Civil Rights Project, Harvard University, 2004. Available online at <http://www.civilrightsproject.harvard.edu/research/esea/nclb.php>.

ELECTIONS

CALIFORNIA GUBERNATORIAL RECALL SURVIVES NUMEROUS LEGAL CHALLENGES

Associated Press. "Davis Asks Court to Delay Recall, Make Him a Candidate." FOXNews.com. http://www.foxnews.com/story/0,2933,93672,00.html August 4, 2003.

Brownfeld, Peter. "ACLU: Accuracy of California Recall in Danger." FOXNews.com. http://www.foxnews.com/story/0,2933,97006,00.html September 11, 2003.

Chorney, Jeff. "Supreme Court Rejects Bid to Halt Gray Davis Recall Vote." Law.com. http://www.law.com/servlet/ContentServer?pagename=Open Market/Xcelerate/Preview&c=PubArticle&cid=1058416429340 July 28, 2003.

"Court Clears Road to Calif. Recall." CBSNews.com. http://www.cbsnews.com/stories/2003/08/08/politics/main567289.shtml August 8, 2003.

"Court Rules for Davis Recall Proponents." NBCSandiego.com. http://www.nbcsandiego.com/politics/2343704/detail.html July 18, 2003.

Franken, Bob, Kelly Wallace, and others. "Appeals Court Blocks California Recall." CNN.com. http://www.cnn.com/2003/ALLPOLITICS/09/15/recall.delay/ September 15, 2003.

Lakely, James G. "Court Affirms Oct. 7 California Recall Election." *The Washington Times* http://www.washtimes.com/national/20030923-114945-2889r.htm September 24, 2003.

Mercurio, John. "California Recall Bid Succeeds." CNN.com. http://www.cnn.com/2003/ALLPOLITICS/07/23/davis.recall/ July 29, 2003

Mintz, Howard. "Recall Revived." *The Miami Herald* http://www.miami.com/mld/miamiherald/news/special_packages/recall/6847473.htm?1c September 24, 2003.

"Recall Gray Davis Committee, et al., vs. Kevin Shelley, etc., et al." (Case C044487, Sacramento County)" Findlaw.com. http://news.findlaw.com/hdocs/docs/elections/recallshlly71803ord.pdf July 18, 2003.

"Voting Rights." *Center for Voting and Democracy.* http://www.fairvote.org/vra/#background

Wallace, Kelly and others. "Federal Judges Refuse to Postpone California Recall." Cnn.com. http://www.cnn.com/2003/ALLPOLITICS/09/05/calif.recall/index.html September 5, 2003.

Wasserman, Jim. "Davis Recall Backers Sue Calif. Official." *The Mercury News.* http://www.mercurynews.com/mld/mercurynews/news/politics/6277168.htm July 10, 2003.

MAJOR PROVISIONS OF FEDERAL CAMPAIGN FINANCE LAW ARE CONSTITUTIONAL

Barbash, Fred. "Supreme Court Upholds Political Money Law." *Washington Post.* December 10, 2003.

Lane, Charles. "Justices Uphold Campaign Finance Law." *Washington Post.* December 11, 2003.

Richey, Warren. "Court Upholds 'Soft Money' Ban." *Christian Science Monitor.* December 11, 2003.

Stout, David. "Divided Court Says Government Can Ban 'Soft Money'." *New York Times.* December 10, 2003.

ELEVENTH AMENDMENT

LAWSUIT AGAINST STATE TO ENFORCE CONSENT DECREE DOES NOT VIOLATE THE ELEVENTH AMENDMENT

Gearan, Ann. "Justices Hold States To Consent Agreements." Cleveland.com. http://www.cleveland.com/news/plaindealer/index.ssf?/base/news/107416771994100.xml January 15, 2004.

Mears, Bill. "Justices Hear First Case Of Term Concerning State Agreements." CNN.com. http://www.cnn.com/2003/LAW/10/07/scotus.state.sovreignty/ October 7, 2003.

Mears, Bill. "Supreme Court Refuses To Let States Out Of Lawsuit Settlements." CNN.com. http://www.cnn.com/2004/LAW/01/14/scotus.consent.decree/ January 14, 2004.

E-MAIL

ACTUAL DAMAGE TO COMPUTER E-MAIL SYSTEM REQUIRED IN TRESPASS ACTION

Oreskovic, Alexei. "Calif. Supreme Court Rules Intel Can't Stop E-Mail With Trespass Law." *The Recorder.* http://www.law.com/jsp/article.jsp?id=1056139916236 July 1, 2003.

Farmer, John. "Law Column." *Richmond Times-Dispatch.* July 29, 2003.

Cramer, Michael H. "Mass E-Mail Alone is Not Trespass." *HR Magazine.* September 1, 2003.

"California Supreme Court says anti-Intel e-mail not trespassing." *USA Today.* http://www.usatoday.com/tech/news/2003-07-01-spam-shocker_x.htm July 1, 2003.

CONGRESS AND STATES ENACT LEGISLATION TO FIGHT SPAM

Flores, Chris. "Some Say Va. Spam Law Isn't Enough." *Daily Press.* July 13, 2003.

Wright, Brad. "Virginia Indicts Two on Spam Felony Charges." CNN.com. December 12, 2003. Available online at <http://www.cnn.com/2003/TECH/internet/12/12/spam.charges/>.

ENVIRONMENTAL LAW

SUPREME COURT DELIVERS MIXED RULING OVER WATER REGULATION IN EVERGLADES

Davies, Frank. "High Court Takes on Everglades Water Dispute." *San Jose Mercury News.* January 15, 2004. Available online at <http://www.mercurynews.com/mld/mercurynews/sports/7713215.htm?1c>.

Holland, Gina. "Supreme Court Takes Up Air And Water Pollution Cases." *Miami Herald.* January 14, 2004. Available online at <http://www.miami.com/mld/miamiherald/7708232.htm?1c>.

Lane, Charles. "Court Urged to Require EPA Role in Everglades Shift of Polluted Water." *Washington Post.* January 15, 2004.

Sachs, Noah. "Muddy Waters." April 1, 2004. *findlaw.com*. Available online at <http://www.findlaw.com>.

ENVIRONMENTAL LAW

ENVIRONMENTAL GROUPS MAY NOT SUE TO COMPEL FEDERAL AGENCY TO TAKE ACTION

Gehrke, Robert. "Supreme Court Slaps Down Attempt to Restrict Off-Road Vehicles in Utah." *Salt Lake Tribune.* June 15, 2004. http://www.sltrib.com/2004/jun/06152004/utah/175528.asp

Reuters. "High Court: Groups Can't Sue Over Public Lands." *Washington Post.* June 14, 2004.

Weinstein, Henry. "Off-Road Vehicle Case is Rejected." *Los Angeles Times.* June 15, 2004.

ESPIONAGE

NATIONAL GUARDSMAN CHARGED WITH ESPIONAGE, GUANTANAMO BAY CHAPLAIN IS RELEASED

Ammons, David. "Guard member charged in al-Qaeda case." Press release. *The Columbian.* February 19, 2004.

"U.S. soldier charged with offering information to al-Qaeda." *Canadian Press.* 2004 WL 69755755. February 19, 2004.

ESTABLISHMENT CLAUSE

STATE TAX LAW INVOLVING RELIGION MAY BE CHALLENGED IN FEDERAL COURT

Greenhouse, Linda. "Supreme Court Roundup. June 14, 2004. *New York Times.*

Holland, Gina. "High Court: Challenging Taxes OK." June 14, 2004. *Washington Post.*

Richey, Warren. "Case Could Boost Funding for Private Schools." January 20, 2004. *Christian Science Monitor.*

ALABAMA'S CHIEF JUSTICE CONTINUES FIGHT OVER TEN COMMANDMENTS

Gaustad, Edwin S. *Church and State in America.* New York: Oxford University Press, 2003.

Perry, Michael J. *Under God?: Religious Faith and Liberal Democracy.* New York: Cambridge University Press, 2003.

FOREIGN SOVEREIGN IMMUNITIES ACT

SUPREME COURT PERMITS LAWSUIT AGAINST AUSTRIA TO RECLAIM ART TREASURES

Barbash, Fred. "Supreme Court Clears Lawsuits for Art Stolen by the Nazis." *Washington Post.* June 7, 2004.

Greenhouse, Linda. "Justices Allow Suit Against Austria to Regain Art." *New York Times.* June 7. 2004.

Lane, Charles. "Justices Allow Lawsuit on Art Taken by Nazis." *Washington Post.* June 8, 2004.

Weinstein, Henry. "Woman Can Sue Austria Over Art Seized by Nazis." *Los Angeles Times.* June 8, 2004.

FEDERALISM

SUPREME COURT ENDORSES FEDERAL ENVIRONMENTAL REGULATORY POWERS

Greenhouse, Linda. "Court Upholds E.P.A. Role in Alaska Case." *New York Times.* January 22, 2004.

Lane, Charles. "Justices Decide EPA Can Overrule States." *Washington Post.* January 22, 2004.

Mears, Bill. "Justices Rule For Federal Government In Clean Air Case." January 21, 2004. http://www.cnn.com/2004/LAW/01/21/scotus.cleanair.ruling/ CNN.com

Ruskin, Liz. "Justices Rule Against State, Mine." *Anchorage Daily News.* January 22, 2004.

FETAL RIGHTS

UNBORN VICTIMS OF VIOLENCE ACT

Canham, Matt. "Prosecutors Drop Murder Charge in C-section Case." *The Salt Lake Tribune.* April 8, 2004. Available online at <http://www.sltrib.com/2004/Apr/04082004/utah/155254.asp>.

Childress, Sarah. "A New Controversy in the Fetal Rights Wars." *Newsweek.* March 29, 2004.

Goldstein, Amy. "Bush Signs Unborn Victims Act." *Washington Post.* April 2, 2004

"Laci and Conner's Law, H.R. 1997." Available online at <http://news.findlaw.com/hdocs/docs/abortion/unbornbill32504.html>.

"Supreme Court Denies Stillborn Appeal." *Community CustomWire.* October 6, 2003.

"U.S. Senate Passes Fetal Protection Bill." *Women's Health Weekly.* April 15, 2004.

FIRST AMENDMENT

SUPREME COURT CLARIFIES ADULT BUSINESS LICENSING REQUIREMENTS

"Court Backs Colo. City's Adult Ordinance." *Los Angeles Times.* June 7, 2004.

Merritt, George. "U.S. High Court Says Littleton Can Force Christal's to Seek License." *Denver Post.* June 8, 2004. http://www.denverpost.com/Stories/0,1413,36-53-2198941,00.html

Kelly, Eric D. and Cooper, Connie. *Everything You Always Wanted to Know About Regulating Sex Businesses.* Chicago: American Planning Association, 2001.

STATES MAY DENY SCHOLARSHIPS TO THEOLOGY STUDENTS

Barbash, Fred. "High Court Allows States to Deny Scholarships for Religious Study." *Washington Post.* February 25, 2004.

Lane, Charles. "A Case of Church and State and the States." *Washington Post.* December 1, 2003.

Richey, Warren. "On The Docket: Church-State Case, Political Battles." *Christian Science Monitor.* October 6, 2003.

"Supreme Court Approves Denial of Divinity Scholarships." *New York Times.* February 25, 2004.

SUPREME COURT SETS REASONABLE WAITING PERIOD FOR FORCED ENTRY INTO HOUSE

Batt, Tony. "Las Vegas Man Ready To Take Argument To Supreme Court." http://www.reviewjournal.com/lvrj_home/2003/Oct-13-Mon-2003/news/22347895.html *Las Vegas Review-Journal.* October 13, 2003.

Richey, Warren." Should Police Wait After Knocking?" *Christian Science Monitor.* October 15, 2003.

"Supreme Court Gives Police Victory In Home Searches Of Drug Suspects." December 2, 2003. Associated Press. http://www.cnn.com/2003/LAW/12/02/scotus.police.searches.ap/*CNN.com*

FOURTH AMENDMENT

GAS TANK BORDER SEARCHES ARE CONSTITUTIONAL

Anderson, Mark H. and Block, Robert. "High Court Backs Customs Power to Conduct Searches at Borders." *Wall Street Journal.* March 31, 2004.

Holland, Gina. "Supreme Court Oks Gas Tank Border Searches." *Associated Press.* March 30, 2004.

Richey, Warren. "Can Border Agents Search a Gas Tank?" *Christian Science Monitor.* February 25, 2004.

SUPREME COURT FAILS TO RESOLVE AUTOMOBILE SEARCH ISSUE

Davies, Thomas Y. "Recovering the Original Fourth Amendment." December 1, 1999. *Michigan Law Review*.

Decker, John. "Emergency Circumstances, Police Responses and Fourth Amendment Restrictions." January 1, 1999. *Journal of Criminal Law and Criminology*.

Greenhouse, Linda. "Justices Will Revisit Rules Governing Use of Evidence." April 21, 2003. *New York Times*.

LAW ENFORCEMENT OFFICER CAN BE LIABLE FOR PREPARING FAULTY SEARCH WARRANT

Gearan, Ann. "Court Eyes Liability for Faulty Warrant." *Philly.com* http://www.philly.com/mld/philly/news/columnists/jane_eisner/7183393.htm?1c November 4, 2003.

Greenhouse, Linda. "Supreme Court Roundup." *New York Times*. February 25, 2004.

Lane, Charles. "High Court Underscores Warrant Rules." *Washington Post*. February 25, 2004.

REFUSING TO GIVE NAME TO POLICE IS A CRIME

Greenhouse, Linda. "Justices Uphold a Nevada Law Requiring Citizens to Identify Themselves to Police." June 22, 2004. *New York Times*.

Lane, Charles. "Refusing to Give Name a Crime." June 22, 2004. *Washington Post*.

Richey, Warren. "Court: If Police Ask, You Must Give Your Name." June 22, 2004. *Christian Science Monitor*.

Savage, David G. "High Court Says IDs Can Be Required in Police Stops." June 22, 2004. *Los Angeles Times*.

HIGHWAY CHECKPOINTS NOT PRESUMPTIVELY UNCONSTITUTIONAL

Lane, Charles. "Informational Roadblocks Do Not Violate Fourth Amendment." *The Washington Post*. January 13, 2004.

Stout, David. "Court Upholds Roadblock Use to Seek Witnesses." *New York Times*. January 13, 2004.

"Supreme Court Approves 'Informational Roadblocks' by Police." CNN.com. http://www.cnn.com/2004/LAW/01/13/scotus.roadblocks.ap/ January 13, 2004.

POLICE HAD PROBABLE CAUSE TO ARREST PASSENGER OF VEHICLE IN WHICH DRUGS WERE FOUND

Holland, Gina. "Court Allows Arrest of All in Drug Stop." *Associated Press*. http://www.alabamastatetrooper.com/court_allows_arrests_of_all_in_drug%20stops.htm December 19, 2003.

Richey, Warren. "Court Import: Be Careful Whom You Get In A Car With." *Christian Science Monitor*. December 19, 2003.

SEARCH INCIDENT TO ARREST OF DRIVER WHO HAS EXITED VEHICLE DOES NOT VIOLATE THE FOURTH AMENDMENT

Americans United for Separation of Church and State. "Federal Judge Strikes Down Louisiana School Prayer Law." Press release. <http://www.au.org/press/pr61400.htm>. June 14, 2000.

"Louisiana School District Agrees to Stop Official School Prayer." Press release. <http://www.au.org/press/pr62700.htm> June 27, 2000.

"Louisiana School Prayer Law Challenged in Federal Court." Press release. <http://www.au.org/press/pr12399.htm>. December 3, 1999.

"Nation in Brief." *Washington Post*. December 12, 2001.

FREEDOM OF INFORMATION ACT

PRIVACY RIGHTS OF SURVIVORS TRUMPS PUBLIC'S RIGHT TO KNOW

Greenhouse, Linda. "Justices Unanimously Bar Release of Photos From the Suicide of a Top Clinton Aide." March 31, 2004. *New York Times*.

Holland, Gina. "High Court Permits Foster Photos Withheld." March 30, 2004. *Los Angeles Times*.

Mauro, Tony. "Supreme Court's Ruling Marks Blow to Public's Right to Know." April 6, 2004. *USA Today*.

Lane, Charles. "Court Bars Release of Foster Photos." March 30, 2004. *Washington Post*.

GAY AND LESBIAN RIGHTS

BATTLE OVER GAY MARRIAGE HEATS UP IN MASSACHUSETTS AND CONGRESS

Abraham, Yvonne. "Weeks Ahead Crucial for Foes, Supporters of Gay Marriage." *The Boston Globe*, April 11, 2004, Available online at <http://www.boston.com/news/local/articles/2004/04/11/weeks_ahead_crucial_for_foes_supporters_of_gay_marriage/>.

Burge, Kathleen. "Justices' Opinions Reveal Deep Division." *The Boston Globe*. February 5, 2004. Available online at <http://www.boston.com/news/local/massachusetts/articles/2004/02/05/justices_opinions_reveal_deep_division/>.

"Bush Amendment Proposal Prompts Strong Reaction." *CNN.com*. February 25, 2004. Available online at <http://www.cnn.com/2004/ALLPOLITICS/02/24/elec04.marriage.reacts/index.html>.

Bush, George W. Remarks by the President: President Calls for Constitutional Amendment Protecting Marriage. February 24, 2004. Available online at <http://www.whitehouse.gov/news/releases/2004/02/20040224-2.html>.

Curry, Tom. "A Guide to the Marriage Furor." *MSNBC*. March 12, 2004. Available online at <http://www.msnbc.msn.com/id/4473785/>.

Lewis, Raphael. "SJC Affirms Gay Marriage: Court Deems Civil Unions Insufficient." *The Boston Globe*. February 5, 2004. Available online at <http://www

.boston.com/news/local/massachusetts/articles/2004/
02/05/sjc_affirms_gay_marriage/>.

Opinions of the Justices to the Senate. Massachusetts Supreme Judicial Court (SJC-09163). February 3, 2004. Available online at <http://news.findlaw.com/hdocs/docs/conlaw/maglmarriage20304.html>.

"Proposal to Ban Gay Marriage Gets New Language." *CNN.com*. March 22, 2004. Available online at <http://www.cnn.com/2004/ALLPOLITICS/03/22/congress.gay.marriage.ap/>.

"Same-Sex Marriage: A History of the Law." *Nolo, Inc..* 2002. Available online at <http://public.findlaw.com/family/nolo/ency/6DF0766E-C4A3-4952-A542F5997196E8B5.html>.

Status of Proposed Federal Marriage Amendments. Library of Congress. Available online at <http://thomas.loc.gov/bss/d108query.html>.

THOUSANDS OF SAME-SEX COUPLES ARE MARRIED IN SAN FRANCISCO AFTER MAYOR ORDERS CLERK TO ISSUE LICENSES

"California Supreme Court Takes Action in Same-Sex Marriage Cases." Press Release from the California Supreme Court. March 11, 2004. Available online at <http://www.courtinfo.ca.gov/presscenter/newsreleases/NR15-04.HTM>.

City and County of San Francisco's Cross-Complaint for Declaratory Relief. California Superior Court, Case No. 503943. February 19, 2004.

Curry, Tom. "A Guide to the Marriage Furor." *MSNBC*. March 12, 2004. Available online at <http://www.msnbc.msn.com/id/4473785/>.

"Judge Combines Same-Sex Marriage Cases." *CNN.com*. February 20, 2004. Available online <http://www.cnn.com/2004/LAW/02/20/samesex.marriage/>.

Murphy, Dean E. "San Francisco Forced to Halt Gay Marriages." *The New York Times*. March 12, 2004.

Murphy, Dean E. "San Francisco Married 4,037 Same-Sex Pairs From 46 States." *The New York Times*. March 18, 2004.

"Same-Sex Marriage: A History of the Law." *Nolo, Inc..* 2002. Available online at <http://public.findlaw.com/family/nolo/ency/6DF0766E-C4A3-4952-A542F5997196E8B5.html>.

"San Francisco Challenges State's Same-Sex Marriage Ban in Court." *CNN.com*. February 19, 2004. Available online at <http://www.cnn.com/2004/LAW/02/19/samesex.marriage/index.html>.

San Francisco Mayor Gavin Newsom's Letter to County Clerk Nancy Alfaro. February 10, 2004. Available online at <http://news.findlaw.com/hdocs/docs/glrts/sfmayor21004ltr.html>.

"Supreme Court Strikes Down Texas Sodomy Law." *CNN.com*. November 18, 2003. Available online at <http://www.cnn.com/2003/LAW/06/26/scotus.sodomy/index.html>.

HABEAS CORPUS

DEATH SENTENCE OVERTURNED BECAUSE PROSECUTORS DELIBERATELY WITHHELD EVIDENCE

Gearan, Ann. "Court Blocks Execution of Texas Inmate." http://apnews.myway.com/article/20040224/D80TO5JO2.html Associated Press. February 24, 2004.

Greenhouse, Linda. "Supreme Court Overturns Death Sentence in Texas Case." *New York Times*. February 24, 2004.

Lane, Charles. "Justices Overturn Texas Death Sentence." *Washington Post*. February 25, 2004.

Richey, Warren. "High-Level Rebuke To Courtroom Deceit." *Christian Science Monitor*. February 25, 2004.

TRIAL JUDGES MAY NOT TREAT INMATE FILINGS AS HABEAS PROCEEDINGS WITHOUT NOTICE AND WARNINGS

"U.S. Supreme Court's Last Term Was Heavy With Habeas Corpus Cases." *BNA Criminal Law Reporter*. http://litigationcenter.bna.com/pic2/lit.nsf/id/BNAP-5QTHY6?OpenDocument August 27, 2003.

IDENTITY THEFT

VICTIMS OF IDENTITY THEFT CANNOT SUE CREDIT CARD COMPANY FOR NEGLIGENCE

"Court Issues Identity Theft Decision." Privacy.org. http://www.privacy.org/archives/001103.html. August 14, 2003.

Duffy, Shannon. "South Carolina High Court Hands Down Major Identity Theft Decision." *The Legal Intelligencer*. August 12, 2003.

"Victory for Banks in Identity Theft Ruling." Legalbrief.com. http://www.legalbrief.co.za/view_1.php?artnum=11668

INSIDER TRADING

MARTHA STEWART CONVICTED FOR MAKING FALSE STATEMENTS REGARDING STOCK SALE

Associated Press. "Timeline of Martha Stewart Scandal." *USA Today*. March 5, 2004, <http://www.usatoday.com/money/media/2004-03-05-stewart-timeline_x.htm>

Naughton, Keith and Barney Gimbel. "Martha's Fall." *Newsweek*. March 15, 2004, at 28

INSURANCE

AETNA HEALTH V. DAVILA

Aetna Health v. Davila, No. 02-1845, 542 U.S. ___ (2004) http:// www.supremecourtus.gov/opinions.

Greenhouse, Linda "Justices Limit Ability to Sue Health Plans." *New York Times*. June 22, 2004.

"HMOs Win, Patients Lose and Congress Stays in a Coma." *USA Today*. June 21, 2004.

INTELLECTUAL PROPERTY

RECORDING INDUSTRY GOES AFTER INDIVIDUALS FOR SHARING MUSIC AND MOVIE FILES

Bay, Hiawatha. "Music Industry to Sue File-Swappers Targeting Thousands of High-Volume Users." *The Boston Globe*. June 26, 2003.

Carlson, Scott. "A President Tries to Settle the Controversy Over File Sharing." *The Chronicle of Higher Education*. May 23, 2003.

INTERNET

POP-UP ADVERTISEMENTS COME UNDER LEGAL ATTACKS

Klug, Foster. "Judge OKs Internet Company's Pop-Up Ads." SiliconValley.com. December 16, 2003. Available online at <http://www.siliconvalley.com/mld/siliconvalley/news/7499325.htm>

Lewis, Shari Claire. "Latest Legal Challenge May Be Opening Salvo in Web War." *New York Law Journal*. March 30, 2004.

IRAQ WAR

THE DEMISE OF SADDAM HUSSEIN'S IRAQ

"Baghdad Blast Kills Iraq Leader." BBC News, May 17, 2004. Available online at <http://news.bbc.co.uk/l/hi/world/middle_east/3720161.stm>.

"Iraq/Anniversary." *Government CustomWire*, April 10, 2004. Available online at <http://search.epnet.com/direct.asp?an=CX2004101X0212&db=15h>.

Nordland, Rod, et al. "The Road Ahead." *Newsweek*. April 12, 2004.

Thomas, Evan, et al. "Inside Red Dawn; Saddam Up Close." *Newsweek*. December 29, 2003.

Valenti, Peter C. "Provisional Constitution, Attacks on Iraqi Shi'I Seen in Context of U.S. Occupation." *Washington Report on Middle East Affairs*. May 2004.

"Welcome to Countdown to Sovereignty." Coalition Provisional Authority. Available online at <http://countdowntosovereignty.org/> and <http://www.cpa.gov>.

JURISDICTION

COURTS HAVE JURISDICTION TO PERMIT AMENDED ATTORNEYS FEE APPLICATION

Stichman, Barton F. *Veterans Benefits Manual 2003*. 2004. Lexis Law Publications: Dayton, OH.

ABDUCTED DOCTOR CANNOT SUE U.S. GOVERNMENT

Holland, Gina. "Court Throws Out Human Rights Lawsuit." June 29, 2004. *Washington Post*.

Thadhani, Pia Zara. "Regulating Corporate Human Rights Abuses." December 1, 200. *William and Mary Law Review*.

Lane, Charles. "Court Hears Cases on Agents' Actions Abroad." March 31, 2004. *Washington Post*.

Greenhouse, Linda. "Use of Federal Courts by Foreigners at Issue." April 1, 2004 *New York Times*.

JURY

BATSON PEREMPTORY CHALLENGE BURDEN OF PROOF ISSUE LEFT UNRESOLVED

Alfieri, Alfred. "Retrying Race." *Michigan Law Review*. March 1, 2003.

Muller, Eric L. "Solving the Batson Paradox." *Yale Law Journal*. October 1, 1996.

McCaffrey, Shannon. "High Court Test: Can Jurors Be Ruled Out by Race." *Fort Wayne News Sentinel*. October 15, 2002. Available online at <http://www.fortwayne.com/mld/newssentinel/4291806.htm>

Lazarus, Edward. "Race-Based Jury Selection And The Supreme Court." Findlaw.com. February 19, 2002. Available online at <http://writ.news.findlaw.com/lazarus/20020219.html>

JOHN FORBES KERRY

"John Forbes Kerry. *Biography Resource Center*. Gale, 2004.

MANSLAUGHTER

U.S. CONGRESSMAN SENTENCED TO ONE HUNDRED-DAY JAIL TERM FOR FELONY MANSLAUGHTER CONVICTION

Kranz, David. "Janklow will waive hearing for new trial." *ArgusLeader*. February 10, 2004.

Walker, Carson. S. "Dakota congressman takesstandathismanslaughtertrial." *TheSanDiegoUnion-Tribune*. December7,2003.

1994 ASSAULT LEADS TO 2004 MANSLAUGHTER CONVICTION

"Desmon Venn Re-Charged in 1994 West Bloomfield School Beating." February 12, 2003. Available online at <http://www.co.oakland.mi.us/prosatty/news/03_pressrelease/02_venn.html>.

Gilbert, Matthew. "A Coma Victim Dies, Bringing New Charges For His Attacker." *Court TV*. March 29, 2003. Available online at <http://edition.cnn.com/2003/LAW/03/29/ctv.venn/index.html>.

Karush, Sarah. "Man Sentenced for Involuntary Manslaugher in School Fight." *The Detroit News*. February 10, 2004. Available online at <http://www.detnews.com/2004/metro/0402/11/metro-60621.htm>.

"Man Pleads Guilty in Classmate's Death." *CNN.com*. January 27, 2004. Available online at <http://edition.cnn.com/2004/US/Midwest/01/27/school.fight.death.ap/>.

"Man Turns Himself in For 1994 Assault." *Click on Detroit*. February 19, 2003. Available online at <http://www.clickondetroit.com/news/1991117/detail.html>.

JAYSON WILLIAMS ACQUITTED OF AGGRAVATED MANSLAUGHTER; CONVICTED ON LESSER COUNTS

Gold, Jeffrey. "Williams jury sent home as lawyers argue about evidence." *The Philadelphia Daily News*. April 2, 2004.

Gold, Jeffrey. "Confident in jury, Williams says he will not testify; The ex-NBA star's defense rested in his manslaughter trial. Up next: The prosecution's rebuttal witnesses." April 1, 2004.

MINES AND MINERAL LAW

BEDROC LIMITED V. UNITED STATES

Braunstein, Michael. *Mineral Rights on the Public Domain*. Cincinnati, Ohio: Anderson Publishing Co., 1987.

"Nevada Sand and Gravel Case Defines U.S. Land Grant Law." *Engineering News-Record*. April 12, 2004.

MIRANDA RIGHTS

MIRANDA RIGHTS DO NOT MANDATE SUPPRESSION OF PHYSICAL EVIDENCE

Greenhouse, Linda. "Tactic of Delayed Miranda Warning Is Barred." June 29, 2004. *New York Times*.

Knickerbocker, Brad and Marks, Alexandra. "Two Court Rulings Highlight a delicate Balance on Miranda." June 29, 2004. *Christian Science Monitor*.

Markon, Jerry. "Police Tactic to Sidestep Miranda Rights Rejected." June 29, 2004. *Washington Post*.

Savage, David. G. "Divided High Court Upholds Miranda Warnings." June 29, 2004. *Los Angeles Times*.

TWO-STAGE INTERROGATION TECHNIQUE VIOLATES FIFTH AMENDMENT

Greenhouse, Linda. "Tactic of Delayed Miranda Warning Is Barred." June 29, 2004. *New York Times*.

Knickerbocker, Brad and Marks, Alexandra. "Two Court Rulings Highlight a delicate Balance on Miranda." June 29, 2004. *Christian Science Monitor*.

Markon, Jerry. "Police Tactic to Sidestep Miranda Rights Rejected." June 29, 2004. *Washington Post*.

Savage, David. G. "Divided High Court Upholds Miranda Warnings." June 29, 2004. *Los Angeles Times*.

MURDER

BAYLOR UNIVERSITY BASKETBALL PLAYER ALLEGEDLY SLAIN BY TEAMMATE

Caplan, Jeff. "Dotson's Murder Trial Set for August." *Fort Worth Star-Telegram*, February 28, 2004.

Gaar, Brian. "BU Alum to Hear Dennehy Lawsuit." *Waco Tribune-Herald*, 2003.

Kennedy, Kostya and March Bechtel, Eds. "Arresting Developments Breakthroughs in the Dennehy Case." *Sports Illustrated*, July 28, 2003.

Miller, Jeff. "6 of 7 Counts Dismissed . . ." *Dallas Morning News*, February 7, 2004.

Miller, Jeff. "Dotson's Murder Trial Set for August." *Fort Worth Star-Telegram*, February 28, 2004.

Montgomery, Dave and Bill Hanna. "Maryland Governor Signs Dotson's Extradition." *Fort Worth Star-Telegram*, September 25, 2003.

Pearce, Ellise and Stephanie Franks. "A Question of Foul Play Off the Court." *Newsweek*, July 14, 2003.

Riggs, Randy. "Bliss Paid Tuition for Dennehy, Teammate." *Austin American-Statesman*, February 27, 2004.

ROBERT BLAKE TRIAL

Bickel, Bill. "Robert Blake and the Murder of Bonny Lee Bakley." Available online at <http://crime.about.com/library/blfiles/blrobertblake.htm>.

Grossberg, Josh. "Robert Blake's World Turns." *E! Online News*, January 15, 2003. Available online at <http://www.eonline.com/News/Items/0,1,11125,00.html>.

Steinhaus, Rochelle. "'Baretta Star's Real-Life Murder Rap." *Court TV*, April 30, 2002. Available online at <http://courttv.com/news/blake/background_ctv.html>."

MALVO AND MUHAMMAD CONVICTED OF MURDER IN SNIPER SHOOTINGS

"Jury Recommends Death for Muhammad." *CNN.com*, November 25, 2003, Available online at <http://www.cnn.com/2003/LAW/11/24/sprj.dcsp.muhammad.trial/index.html>.

"Jury Spares Malvo's Life in Washington Sniper Case." *CNN.com*, December 25, 2003. Available online at <http://www.cnn.com/2003/LAW/12/23/sprj.dcsp.malvo.trial/index.html>.

"Malvo Convicted; Faces Death." *CourtTV.com*, December 18, 2003. Available online at <http://www.courttv.com/trials/sniper/121803_guilty_ap.html>.

"Sniper Malvo Sentenced to Life Without Parole." *CourtTV.com*, March 11, 2004. Available onlinet at <http://www.cnn.com/2004/LAW/03/10/sniper.malvo/>.

"Sniper Muhammad Sentenced to Death." *CNN.com*, March 9, 2004. Available online at <http://www.cnn.com/2004/LAW/03/09/sniper/index.html>.

"Sniper Suspect Muhammad Guilty of Murder." *CourtTV.com*, November 17, 2003. Available online at <http://www.courttv.com/trials/sniper/muhammad-verdict.html>.

"Victims' Families Cheer Sniper Death Sentence." *CNN.com*, March 9, 2004. Available online at <http://www.cnn.com/2004/LAW/03/09/sniper.reax/index.html>.

MILLIONAIRE ACQUITTED OF MURDER AFTER BIZARRE AFTERMATH OF NEIGHBOR'S DEATH

Bruno, Anthony. "Robert Durst- Millionaire Murderer." Crimelibrary.com. http://www.crimelibrary.com/notorious_murders/classics/robert_durst/1.html?sect=13 Accessed May 2004.

"Durst Bail-Jumping Bond Set At $2 Billion." Click2Houston.com. http://www.click2houston.com/news/2679715/detail.html December 3, 2003.

Hays, Kristen. "Robert Durst Faces Tampering Indictment." Newsday.com. http://www.newsday.com/news/nationworld/wire/sns-ap-fugitive-heir,0,4696130.story?coll=sns-ap-nationworld-headlines February 12, 2004.

Moran, Kevin. "Durst Lawyers Want Indictment Quashed." Houstonchronicle.com. http://www.chron.com/cs/CDA/printstory.mpl/front/2447225 March 13, 2004

"Mystery of Robert Durst." CBSNews.com. http://www.cbsnews.com/stories/2004/03/15/48hours/printable606443.shtml March 17, 2004.

"N.Y. millionaire Durst not guilty of murder." CNN.com http://www.cnn.com/2003/LAW/11/11/durst.verdict/ November 11, 2003.

Tolson, Mike and Andrew Tilghman. "It was all or nothing." *The Houston Chronicle* http://www.chron.com/cs/CDA/printstory.mpl/topstory/2216703 November 12, 2003.

PAROLEE MURDERS WIFE, KIDS, DAYS AFTER RELEASE

Brasier, L.L. and Hugh McDiarmid Jr. "'Daddy got a knife': 3½ year old Gives Chilling Account of Pontiac Slaying." *Detroit Free Press.* http://www.freep.com/news/locoak/pont25_20030625.htm June 25, 2003.

Brasier, L.L. "Hearing Postponed for Pontiac Murder Suspect." *Detroit Free Press.* http://www.freep.com/news/latestnews/pm15292_20030708.htm July 8, 2003.

Cain, Charlie. "Error Frees Accused Killer." *The Detroit News.* http://www.detnews.com/2003/metro/0307/20/a01-220296.htm July 17, 2003.

"Evidence Sends Ex-Husband To Trial For Pontiac Murders." ClickOnDetroit.com. http://www.clickondetroit.com/news/2488048/detail.html

"Pontiac Murder Suspect Faces Preliminary Exam." ClickOnDetroit.com. http://www.clickondetroit.com/news/2419432/detail.html, August 20, 2003.

WASHINGTON'S GREEN RIVER SERIAL KILLER SENTENCED TO 48 LIFE TERMS

Comments by Judge Richard Jones at the Ridgway Sentencing. *State of Washington v. Gary Leon Ridgway*, (Superior Court of Washington, King County, Case 01-1-10270-9). http://www.metrokc.gov/kcsc/ridgway.htm. December 19, 2003.

"Green River Killer Avoids Death in Plea Deal." *CNN.com.* http://www.cnn.com/2003/LAW/11/05/green.river.killings/. November 6, 2003.

"'I Forgive You,' Some Families Tell Ridgway; Others Wish Him 'Long, Suffering, Cruel Death.'" *The Seattle Times.* http://archives.seattletimes.nwsource.com/cgi-bin/texis.cgi/web/vortex/display?slug=families19m&date=20031219. December 19, 2003.

Ith, Ian. "'Emissary of Death' Sentenced to Life." *The Seattle Times.* http://archives.seattletimes.nwsource.com/cgi-bin/texis.cgi/web/vortex/display?slug=ridgway19m&date=20031219. December 19, 2003.

"Ridgway's Statement." *The Seattle Times.* http://archives.seattletimes.nwsource.com/cgi-bin/texis.cgi/web/vortex/display?slug=ridgwaystatement19m&date=20031219. December 19, 2003.

Statement of Defendant Gary Ridgway on Plea of Guilty. *State of Washington v. Gary Leon Ridgway.* (Superior Court of Washington, King County, Case 01-1-10270-9). http://www.metrokc.gov/kcsc/ridgway.htm. December 19, 2003.

"Timeline: DNA Testing Helped Lead Investigators to Green River Killer." *The Seattle Times.* http://seattletimes.nwsource.com/html/greenriverkillings/2001784443_greenline06m.html. November 06, 2003.

Wilson, Duff, and Michael Ko. "Ridgway Gave Tips to Police in '83." *The Seattle Times.* http://seattletimes.nwsource.com/html/greenriverkillings/2001869963_ridgway03m.html. March 03, 2004.

POLICE ARREST SUSPECT IN OHIO SNIPER CASE

Fox, James Alan and Jack Levin. "Media Exaggerate Sniper Threat." *USA Today.* December 9, 2003.

Ludlow, Randy. "Victim's Family Awaiting Closure." *Columbus Dispatch.* March 17, 2004.

SCOTT PETERSON TRIAL

"Criminal Complaint No. 1056770," Stanislaus County Superior Court, April 21, 2003. Available online at <http://www.findlaw.com>.

"Pre-Booking/Probable Cause Declaration," attachment to Criminal Complaint No. 1056770, Stanislaus County Superior Court, April 21, 2003. Available online at <http://www.findlaw.com>.

Ryan, Harriet. "From Start, Suspicion Falls on Peterson." *Court TV*, Undated. Available online at <http://www.courttv.com/trials/peterson/background.html>.

Seyfer, Jessie. "Judge Says GPS Evidence Admissible in Scott Peterson Trial." *San Jose Mercury News.* February 17, 2004.

Sulek, Julia Prodis. "Judge Orders Change of Venue for Scott Peterson Trial." *San Jose Mercury News.* January 8, 2004.

Warrant for Arrest, attachment to Criminal Complaint No. 1056770, Stanislaus County Superior Court, April 21, 2003. Available online at <http://www.findlaw.com>.

ASPIRING RAPPER KILLS, PARTIALLY EATS ROOMMATE

Creekmur, Chuck "Jigsaw". "Rapper Charged With Murder After Human Flesh Found in Stomach." BET.com. http://www.bet.com/articles/0,,c3gb2980-3641,00.html June 7, 2002.

Creekmur, Chuck "Jigsaw". "Suge Knight Denial 'Cannibal' Claim." BET.com. http://www.bet.com/articles/0%2C1048%2Cc2gb6037-6786-1%2C00.html#boardsAnchor April 15, 2003.

Malo, Aaron, Matthew P. Barach, and Joseph A. Levin. "The Temporary Insanity Defense in California." Public Law Research Institute. http://www.uchastings.edu/plri/spring95/tmpinsan.html

"Rapper Killed to Boost image." *BBC News.* http://news.bbc.co.uk/1/hi/entertainment/music/2945997.stm April 14, 2003.

Scott, Joe. "Aspiring Rapper Found Sane in Roommate's Murder." Los Angeles County District Attorney's Office. http://da.co.la.ca.us/mr/070103a.htm July 1, 2003.

Scott, Joe. "Aspiring Rapper to Spend Remainder of Life in Prison for Roommate's Murder." Los Angeles County District Attorney's Office. http://da.co.la.ca.us/mr/110703c.htm November 7, 2003.

Scott, Joe. "Man Convicted of Killing Roommate While on PCP." Los Angeles County District Attorney's Office. http://da.co.la.ca.us/mr/062503b.htm June 25, 2003.

Strong, Nolan. "Death Row Removed From Wrongful Death Lawsuit." AllHipHop.com. http://www.allhiphop.com/hiphopnews/?ID=1786

LEGENDARY RECORD PRODUCER CHARGED WITH MURDER OF ACTRESS

Deutsch, Linda. "Phil Spector Defense Says it Doesn't Have Purported Evidence." February 17, 2004. Available online at <http://www.signonsandiego.com/news/state/20040217-1759-ca-philspector.html>.

Felony Complaint. California v. Phillip Spector. Case No. GA048824. Superior Court, County of Los Angeles. November 18, 2003.

"Judge Demands Evidence from Phil Spector Defense." cnn.com, February 4, 2004. Available online at <http://www.cnn.com/2004/LAW/02/04/phil.spector.ap/>.

"Phil Spector Replaces Lawyer, Hires Leslie Abramson to Defend Him." cnn.com, February 3, 2004. Available online at <http://us.cnn.com/2004/LAW/02/03/phil.spector.ap/>.

"Record Producer Phil Spector Charged with Murder." cnn.com, November 20, 2003. Available online at <http://www.cnn.com/2003/LAW/11/20/spector.charges/>.

"Record Producer Spector Arrested in Woman's Death." cnn.com, December 11, 2003. Available online at <http://www.cnn.com/2003/SHOWBIZ/Music/02/04/spector.arrest/index.html>.

"Spector Records Describe Grisly Scene." cnn.com, December 10, 2003. Available online at <http://us.cnn.com/2003/LAW/12/10/spector.killing.ap/" http://us.cnn.com/2003/LAW/12/10/spector.killing.ap/>.

BINION MURDER CONVICTIONS REVERSED BY NEVADA SUPREME COURT

"Casino Owner Ted Binion Killed for "Buried Treasure." *American Law Yearbook*, 2000. Farmington Hills: The Gale Group.

Puit, Glenn and J.M Kalil. "Murder Convictions in Binion Case Overturned." *Review-Journal*, July 15, 2003. Available online at <http://www.reviewjournal.com/lvrj_home/2003/Jul-15-Tue-2003/news/21731396.html>.

Ryan, Cy. "High Court Upholds New Trial for Murphy." *Las Vegas Sun*, October 24, 2003. Available online at <http://www.lasvegassun.com/sunbin/stories/lv-crime/2003/oct/24/515778190.html>.

OBSCENITY

TEXAS WOMAN CHARGED WITH PROMOTING ADULT TOYS

Deller, Martha. "Burleson Texas Woman Agrees to Limited Gag Order in Sex-Toy Case." *Forth Worth Star-Telegram*, February 13, 2004.

Fox, Laurie. "Saleswoman Finds Texas Law Obscene." *Dallas Morning News*, December 22, 2003.

Grossman, Joanne. "Is There a Constitutional Right to Promote the Use of Sex Toys?" Available at HYPERLINK "http://writ.news.findlaw.com/grossman/20040127.html" http://writ.news.findlaw.com/grossman/20040127.html

"Texas Mom Faces Trial for Selling Sex Toys." February 11, 2004. Available at HYPERLINK "http://www.cnn.com/2004?LAW/02/11/obscenity/trial.reut/" http://www.cnn.com/2004?LAW/02/11/obscenity/trial.reut/

OKLAHOMA CITY BOMBINGS

TRIAL OF TERRY NICHOLS ON STATE MURDER CHARGES

Candiotti, Susan and Jim Polk, CNN contributors. "Nichols' Defense Challenges State's Key Witness." Available at online at http://www.cnn.com/2004/LAW/04/21/nichols/trial/].

Hamilton, Arnold. "For Second Time, Nichols Faces Life-or-Death Trial." *Dallas Morning News*, March 22, 2004.

Talley, Tim. "Fertilizer Purchases Focus in Nichols Case." *Community CustomWire*, March 30, 2004.

Talley, Tim. "Nichols Defense Suggests Wider Conspiracy." *Community CustomWire*, April 6, 2004.

Talley, Tim. "Prosecutors Build Case in Nichols' Trial." *Community CustomWire*, March 29, 2004.

Talley, Tim. "Terry Nichols' Attorneys Seek Dismissal." *Community CustomWire*, April 13, 2004.

"Witness: Weapons Found in Nichols' House Stolen From Gun Dealer." *Boston Herald*, April 14, 2004. Available online at <http://news.bostonherald.com/national/view.bg?aricleid+1750&format>.

OWNERSHIP

RE-DISCOVERED COPY OF BILL OF RIGHTS PROVOKES LEGAL BATTLE

Dalesio, Emery P. "Authorities could charge antiques dealer in Bill of Rights case." *The Charlotte Observer*, courtesy of Associated Press. http://www.charlotte.com/mld/observer/news/local/5527551.htm?ERIGHTS=848149771689698426charlotte::hatrax@yahoo.com&KRD_RM=8oovovoswquwwqwvrptooooooo|Jeffrey|Y March 31, 2003.

Hewett, David. "Further Twists to the Case of the Bill of Rights." *Maine Antique Digest*. http://www.maineantiquedigest.com/articles/dec03/bill1203.htm

"Home of the Bill; A federal judge says N.C.'s copy belongs in Raleigh." *The Charlotte Observer*. http://www.charlotte.com/mld/observer/2004/01/29/news/7821956.htm?template=contentModules/printstory.jsp January 29, 2004.

Jonsson, Patrik. "A Bill of Rights, looted long ago, is stolen back." *The Christian Science Monitor*. http://www.csmonitor.com/2003/0422/p01s01-usgn.html April 22, 2003

Kinsella, James. "Antiques dealer withdraws claim on NC Bill of Rights." *The Inquirer and Mirror.* http://www.ack.net/IM/current/4255news_storypage.html

PR Newswire. "Connecticut Antiques Dealer Exonerated in North Carolina Bill of Rights Case" ForRelease.com. http://www.forrelease.com/D20031007/netu050.P2.10072003170427.06597.html October 7, 2003.

PARTNERSHIP

UNITED STATES V. GALLETTI

Gargotta, Craig A. "United States v. Galletti Will Affect IRS'S Ability To Collect Obligations." *Texas Lawyer.* January 26, 2004.

"Supreme Court Allows Collection of Employment Taxes Against Partners Based Only on Timely Assessment Against Partnership." *Standard Federal Tax Reports: Taxes on Parade.* March 25, 2004.

PATENTS

ONLINE AUCTION HOUSE EBAY SUED OVER TECHNOLOGY USE

Cox, Beth. "Trial Date Nears in eBay Patent Case." Ecommerce News, Internetnews.com. http://ecommerce.internet.com/news/news/article/0,,10375_2172161,00.html March 31, 2003.

Decker, Susan. "eBay Loses Bid to Overturn Verdict, Wins Cut in Award." *The Detroit News.* http://www.detnews.com/2003/technology/0308/08/technology-238269.htm August 7, 2003.

"eBay Must Pay $35 Million in Patent Case." CNN.com. http://www.cnn.com/2003/TECH/biztech/05/28/ebay.lawsuit.ap/ May 28, 2003.

Haley, Colin C. "Expert: MercExchange Must Beat eBay Twice." Internet News.com. http://www.internetnews.com/ec-news/article.php/2196951 April 25, 2003.

"MercExchange, L.L.C. v. eBay, Inc., et al." MoreLaw.com. http://www.morelaw.com/verdicts/case.asp?n=01-CV-736&s=VA%20%20%20%20%20%20%20%20&d=25474 August 12, 2003.

Partlow, Joshua. "eBay Told to Pay $29.5 Million in Patent Case." *The Washington Post.* http://www.washingtonpost.com/ac2/wp-dyn?pagename=article&node=&contentId=A25706-2003Aug6&notFound=true August 7, 2003.

Rosencrance, Linda. "eBay Goes to Court Over Patent Infringement." Computerworld.com. http://www.computerworld.com/printthis/2003/0,4814,80578,00.html April 22, 2003.

Singer, Michael. "eBay Ordered to Pay $35M Patent Claim." Internetnews.com. http://siliconvalley.internet.com/news/article.php/2212871 May 27, 2003.

Steiner, Ina. "eBay-Contested MercExchange Patents Are on the Block." *Auction Bytes.* http://www.auctionbytes.com/cab/abn/y03/m05/i30/s01 May 30, 2003.

Verdict Form, Case No. 2:01cv736, In the United States District Court For the Eastern District of Virginia, Norfolk Division. Findlaw.com. http://news.findlaw.com/wp/docs/ebay/mercebay52603vrdct.pdf

PENSION

CENTRAL LABORERS PENSION FUND V. HEINZ

Central Laborers Pension Fund v. Heinz, 541 U.S. ___, 124 S.Ct. 2230, 159 L.Ed.2d 46 (2004), http://www.supremecourtus.gov/opinions

Grenier, B. Janell. "Supreme Court Issues Opinion in Central Laborers'..." *enefitsblog*, June 8, 2004.

"High Court: Pension Can't be Cut Post-retirement." *Boston Globe*, June 8, 2004. http://www.bonston.com/dailyglobe.../High_court_Pension_can_t_be_cut_post_retirement+shtm (Accessed June 15, 2004)

PRESIDENTIAL POWERS

DEPARTMENT OF TRANSPORTATION V. PUBLIC CITIZEN

Department of Transportation v. Public Citizen, No. 03-358, 541 U.S. ___, 124 S.Ct. 2204, 159 L.Ed.2d 60 (2004), http://www.supremecourtus.gov/opinions

Gearan, Anne. "Path Clear for Mexican Trucks." *Boston Globe.* June 8, 2004.

PRISONERS' RIGHTS

NO NEED FOR INMATES TO EXHAUST HABEAS RELIEF BEFORE FILING CIVIL RIGHTS SUIT

Holland, Gina. "Supreme Court Accepts Handwritten Appeal from Poor, Michigan Inmate." *The Detroit News.* June 16, 2003.

PRIVACY ACT

ASSISTANT U.S. ATTORNEY SUES JUSTICE DEPARTMENT

"Prosecutor in Terror Case Controversy Sues Ashcroft." *USA Today*, February 17, 2004. Available online at <http://www.usatoday.com/news/washington/2004-02-17-ashcroft-sued_x.htm>.

Ragavan, Chitra, Nancy Bentrup, Carol Hook, and Monica Ekman, "A Real Case of Snakebite." *U.S. News and World Report*, March 22, 2004.

"U.S. Prosecutor Sues Ashcroft." CBSNews.com, February 17, 2004. Available online at <http://www.cbsnews.com/stories/2004/02/17/terror/main600677.shtml>.

PRIVACY

SUPREME COURT LIMITS RECOVERY FOR PRIVACY ACT VIOLATIONS

"Court Protects Government from Privacy Suits." *Guardian Unlimited.* http://www.guardian.co.uk/uslatest/story/0,1282,-3784548,00.html February 24, 2004,

Gearan, Anne Gearan. "Supreme Court Will Settle Privacy Case." *New York Times*. June 27, 2003.

RAPE

NEW YORK SEX DUNGEON CONVICTION

Hampson, Rick. "Abductions Spark 'Disbelief.'" *USA Today*, May 1, 2003.

"N.Y. Police Build Case Against Man Accused of Raping Captive Women." April 29, 2003. Available online at <http://www.cnn.com>.

Pieklik, Dave, ed. "Jamelske Speaks of Sex Chamber." July 15, 2003. Available online at <http://www.wstm.com/Global/story.asp?=1361363>.

Pieslik, Dave, ed. "Jamelske Gets 18 to Life for Sex Chamber Kidnappings." July 15, 2003. Available online at <http://www.wstm.com/Global/story.asp?=1361363>.

Smalley, Suzanne and Seth Mnookin. "House of Horrors." *Newsweek*, May 5, 2003.

RONALD REAGAN

OBITUARY NOTICE

"Ronald Reagan." *St. James Encyclopedia of Popular Culture*. 5 vols. St. James Press, 2000. Reproduced in *Biography Resource Center*. Farmington Hills, Mich.: The Gale Group. 2004. http://galenet.galegroup.com/servlet/BioRC

"Ronald Wilson Reagan." *Gale Encyclopedia of U.S. Economic History*. Gale Group, 1999. Reproduced in *Biography Resource Center*. Farmington Hills, Mich.: The Gale Group. 2004. http://galenet.galegroup.com/servlet/BioRC

RECUSAL

ASHCROFT RECUSES HIMSELF FROM CASE INVOLVING LEAK OF CIA OPERATIVE

Branch-Brioso, Karen. "Justice Delayed? Ashcroft's Recusal from Case Has Many Benefits." *St. Louis Post-Dispatch*. January 4, 2004.

"New Boss for CIA Leak Probe." CBSNews.com. December 31, 2003. Available online at <http://www.cbsnews.com/stories/2003/09/30/national/main575925.shtml>.

SCALIA REFUSES TO RECUSE HIMSELF IN CASE INVOLVING CHENEY

Federal Judicial Center. *Recusal: Analysis of Case Law Under 28 U.S.C. §§ 455 & 144*. Washington, D.C.: Federal Judicial Center, 2002.

Neumann, Richard K. "Conflicts of Interest in Bush v. Gore: Did Some Justices Vote Illegally?" *Georgetown Journal of Legal Ethics*. Spring 2003.

DONALD REGAN

OBITUARY NOTICE

"Donald Regan." In *Contemporary Authors Online*, Gale, 2004. Reproduced in *Biography Resource Center*. Farmington Hills, Mich.: The Gale Group, 2004. http://galenet.galegroup.com/servlet/BioRC

RIGHT TO DIE

WOMAN IN VEGETATIVE STATE SUBJECT OF RIGHT TO DIE FIGHT

"Another Chapter in Legal Fight for Terri Schiavo's Life." *American Morning*. (on-air transcript) CNN.com. http://www.cnn.com/TRANSCRIPTS/0310/22/ltm.18.html Aired October 22, 2003.

Associated Press. "Bush Seeks Removal of Judge in Schiavo Case." *Tallahassee Democrat*. http://www.tallahassee.com/mld/democrat/news/local/7323525.htm November 22, 2003.

Associated Press. "Terri Schiavo's Feeding Tube Replaced." *The Oracle*. http://www.usforacle.com/vnews/display.v/ART/2003/10/24/3f991d9d472bf?template=pda%22 October 24, 2003.

Campisi, Gloria. "Terri Schiavo's Family Insists She's Not Comatose." Philly.com. http://www.philly.com/mld/dailynews/news/local/7090958.htm?1c October 24, 2003.

Conigliaro, Matt. *Abstract Appeal*. http://abstractappeal.com/schiavo/infopage.html

Johnson, Jeff. "Federal Judge Dismisses Parents' Lawsuit in Terri Schiavo Case." CNSNews.com. http://www.propertyrightsresearch.org/articles5/federal_judge_dismisses_parents.htm October 10, 2003.

Martin, Marisa. "In Re Schiavo: The Saga Continues." Univerity of Houston Law Center. http://www.law.uh.edu/healthlawperspectives/Death/040229 Schiavo.html February 29, 2004.

Shepherd, Lois. "Gov. Bush: Health-care Surrogate?" *Talahassee Democrat*. http://www.tallahassee.com/mld/democrat/news/opinion/7086970.htm October 26, 2003.

Somers, Andrew. "Does Terri's Husband Have the Right to End Her Life?" About.com/Civil Liberties. http://civilliberty.about.com/cs/humaneuthinasia/a/bgTerri_p.htm

terrisfight.org (website run by the family of Terri Schiavo). http://www.terrisfight.org/

United Press International. "Analysis: Schiavo Case Back in Court." *ClariNet*. http://quickstart.clari.net/qs_se/webnews/wed/bm/Uus-coma.RcwP_DNB.html November 11, 2003.

RIGHT TO COUNSEL

DEFENSE ATTORNEY'S CLOSING ARGUMENT NOT DEFICIENT

"Lawyer's Insult Not Appeal-ing." CBSnews.com. http://www.cbsnews.com/stories/2003/10/20/supremecourt/main579001.shtml October 20, 2003.

"With a 6-5 Split, 9th Circuit Treads Familiar Ground," www.law.com/jsp/article.jsp?id=1066605408649*Law.com*. October 21, 2003.

SECURITIES

FIXED RATE OF RETURN CONTRACT QUALIFIES AS A SECURITY SUBJECT TO FEDERAL SECURITIES LAWS

Anderson, Cerisse. "N.Y. Court Rules on Pay Phone Sale and Leaseback." *New York Law Journal.* http://www.law.com/jsp/article.jsp?id=1071091309656 December 12, 2003.

"Supreme Court Will Decide Whether SEC Can Pursue Georgia Pay Phone Company." *Macon Telegraph.* http://www.macon.com/mld/macon/news/breaking_news/5682402.htm April 21, 2003.

"FUNDGATE" MUTUAL FUNDS SCANDAL

"2 Banks Pay $515M in Mutual Fund Scandal." *Business CustomWire.* March 16, 2004.

Barney, Lee. "Ex-Alger Vice Chair Gets Jail Time." *Investment Management Weekly.* December 22, 2003.

Elstein, Aaron. "Lawyers Unleash Mutual Funds Suits." *Crain's New York Business.* December 1, 2003.

Fulman, Ricki. "Pension Funds Hit Two or Three Times." *Pensions & Investments.* December 22, 2003.

"Janus Agrees to a Settlement of $226 Million." *Business CustomWire.* April 26, 2004.

"Many States Ready to File Funds Charges." *Community CustomWire.* December 28, 2003.

Waggoner, John. "Scandal Outrage Keeps Growing." *USA Today.* November 3, 2003.

SENTENCING GUIDELINES

FEDERAL JUDICIARY OPPOSES LEGISLATIVE RESTRICTIONS ON CRIMINAL SENTENCING GUIDELINES

Allenbaugh, Mark. "Sentencing Provisions and Ashcroft: An Assault Against Federal Courts." *CNN.com,* August 15, 2003, http://www.cnn.com/2003/LAW/08/15/findlaw.analysis.allenbaugh.sentencing/.

Bill Summary & Status for the 108th Congress. Library of Congress, http://thomas.loc.gov/cgi-bin/bdquery/z?d108:SN01086:@@@K.

Christensen, Dan. "Sentencing Guidelines Face Test Case." *Miami Daily Business Review,* December 24, 2003, http://www.law.com/jsp/article.jsp?id=1071719732346.

"In Their Words: Judges' Views on Federal Sentencing." The Federal Judiciary. http://www.uscourts.gov/judicary2003/judgesview.pdf.

"Judicial Conference Seeks Restoration of Judges' Sentencing Authority." Press Release, Administrative Office of the U.S. Courts. September 23, 2003, http://www.uscourts.gov/Press_Releases/jc903.pdf

Kirkland, Michael. "Rehnquist Rips PROTECT Act." *United Press International.* January 1, 2004, http://www.upi.com/view.cfm?StoryID=20031231-104741-6525r.

Martin, Jr., John S. "Let Judges Do Their Jobs." *New York Times,* June 24, 2003, reprinted at http://www.nacdl.org/public.nsf/legislation/ci_03_28?OpenDocument.

Mears, Bill. "Rehnquist Slams Congress Over Reducing Sentencing Discretion." *CNN.com,* January 1, 2004, http://www.cnn.com/2004/LAW/01/01/rehnquist.judiciary/.

SENTENCE

BLAKELY V. WASHINGTON

Gearan, Anne. "Court To Rule Whether Judges Can Give Extra-Long Sentences." *Houston Chronicle.* October 21, 2003, at 5.

Johnson, Tracy. "Judges' Authority To Mete Out Harsher Sentence is Challenged." *Seattle Post-Intelligencer.* March 22, 2004, at A1.

LIFE SENTENCE GIVEN TO 14-YEAR-OLD REVERSED ON APPEAL

"Lionel Tate Pleads Guilty in Wrestling Death." USAToday.com. January 29, 2004, <http://www.usatoday.com/news/nation/2004-01-29-lionel-tate_x.htm>.

"Lionel Tate Released." CNN.com. January 27, 2004, <http://www.cnn.com/2004/LAW/01/26/wrestling.death/>

SEPTEMBER 11TH ATTACKS

SHUTDOWN OF SEPTEMBER 11TH VICTIMS COMPENSATION FUND

Feinberg, Kenneth. "Policy Statement on Program Shutdown Schedule." September 11th Victim Compensation Fund of 2001. http://www/usdoj.gov/victimscompensation/payments_deceased.html

"Frequently Asked Questions 9.8." September 11th Victim Compensation Fund of 2001. Official Website at http://www/usdoj.gov/victimscompensation.html

Harras, Steven. "9/11 Firefighters' Families Sue Motorola, But Court Finds They Waived Right to Sue." *BNA Product Safety & Liability Reporter.* April 5, 2004. http://llitigationcenter.bna.com/pic2/lit.nsf/id/BNAP-5XNNFK?OpenDocument

Lin, Anthony. "Suit Challenging 9/11 Victims' Fund Dismissed." http://lawhelp.org/info/news/NYLJ.htm

Sebok, Anthony. "The Hardest Job in the Law: Judge Who Hears 9/11 Suits." http://cnn.com/2003/LAW/09/25/findlaw.analysis.sebok.911.compensation/

MOUSSAOUI TERRORISM TRIAL

Brickel, Bill. "The 20th Hijacker: The Trial of Zacarias Moussaoui." May 6, 2004. http://crime.about.com/library/weekly/aa20thHijacker.htm

Rising, David. "War on Terror is {AU: Cap. in source?} Suffering in Courtrooms." *Community CustomWire.* March 22, 2004.

United States v. Moussaoui, U.S. District Court for the Eastern District of Virginia at Alexandria, Case No. CR-01-455. http://www.usdoj.gov/ag/moussaouiindictment.htm

United States v. Moussaoui, U.S. Court of Appeals for the Fourth Circuit,Fourth Circuit Court of Appeals

Case No. 03-4792, April 22, 2004, http://www
.findlaw.com

9-11 COMMISSION REPORT

"9/11 Commission Full Report." 22 July 2004. http://www.cnn.com/2004/US/07/22/9.11.full.report/

"About the Commission." The National Commission on Terrorist Attacks Upon the United States. Official Web site at http://www.9-11commission.gov/about/index.htm

"Frequently Asked Questions." The National Commission on Terrorist Attacks Upon the United States. Official Web site at http://www.9-11commission.gov/about/index.htm

Marlantes, Liz, et al. "On Stand, Rice Strikes Back." *Christian Science Monitor*, April 9, 2004.

The 9/11 Commission Report, Executive Summary, p.9, 22 July 2004, published online at http://www.9-11commission.gov/report/911ReportExec.pdf

SEX OFFENSES

BASKETBALL SUPERSTAR FACES RAPE CHARGES

"Bryant, Accuser Face Each Other in Courtroom." CNN.com. March 24, 2004. http://www.cnn.com/2004/LAW/03/24/bryant.heaing/index.html

"Bryant's Accuser Must Testify at Hearing." CNN.com. March 11, 2004. http://www.cnn.com/2004/LAW/03/11/bryant.case.ap/index.html

Dorf, Michael C. "Can Kobe Bryant Be Convicted on 'He Said / She Said' Evidence Alone?" CNN.com. July 24, 2003. http://www.cnn.com/2003/LAW/07/24/findlaw.analysis.dorf.kobe.bryant/

"Judge Closes Key Hearing in Kobe Case." *Fox News* January 21, 2004. http://www.foxnews.com/story/0,2933,109096,00.html

"Kobe Bryant Charged With {AU: Capitalized in source?} Sexual Assault." CNN.com. December 16, 2003. http://www.cnn.com/2003/LAW/07/18/kobe.bryant/

O'Driscoll, Patrick. "Kobe Bryant to Face His Accuser Today." *USA Today*. March 23, 2004. http://www.usatoday.com/sports/basketball/nba/2004-03-23-kobe-accuser_x.htm

Sarche, John. "Bryant Accuser Urges Trial Date." CNN.com. March 26, 2004. http://news.findlaw.com/ap_stories/s/2030/3-26-2004/20040326041503_21.html

"Why the Kobe Case is Moving Slowly." CBSNews.com. March 25, 2004. http://www.cbsnews.com/stories/2004/03/25/opinion/courtwatch/main608773.shtml

CONVICTION OF RETIRED FBI OFFICIAL

Conditt, John H. Jr. "Institutional Integrity: The Four Elements of Self-Policing." *The FBI Law Enforcement Bulletin*, 2001.

"Ex-FBI Official Pleads Guilty to Child Molestation." http://www.cnn.com/2004/LAW/02/17/bc.fbi.child molester.ap/

Kelly, Karin. "Former FBI Agent Sentenced in Sexual Assault." WFAA-TV, February 13, 2004

"Washington in Brief." *Washington Post*, February 18, 2004.

SEXUAL ABUSE

UNIVERSITY OF COLORADO FOOTBALL PROGRAM MARRED BY RAPE ALLEGATIONS

"Colorado AG to Probe Recruiting Scandal." *Community CustomWire*, February 28, 2004.

Hoffman, Dr. Elizabeth "Betsy." "Recruiting of College Student Athletes." *FDCH Congressional Testimony*, March 11, 2004.

Jacobson, Jennifer and Welch Suggs. "Sex and Football." *Chronicle of Higher Education*, February 27, 2004

Ostrander v. Duggan, et al., No. 02-2288, 8th8th Circuit Court of Appeals (2003). Citation only.

"Sexual Assault and Title IX." *National On-Campus Report*, January 1, 2004.

Whiteside, Kelly. "College Sports Recruiting to be Scrutinized Today at Hearing." *USA Today*, March 11, 2004.

MICHAEL JACKSON CHARGED WITH SEXUAL ABUSE OF CHILDREN

Bickel, Bill. "Michael Jackson Arrested." November 20, 2003. http://crime.about.com/cs/celebrity criminal/a/mjacksonarrest.htm

Bickel, Bill. "Michael Jackson: Background and Updates." http://crime.about.com/cs/currentcases/a/jackson.htm

Deutsch, Linda. "Michael Jackson Indicted on Counts Including Molestation, Conspiracy; Pleads Not Guilty." AP Breaking News. April 30, 2004. Available at http://sfgate.com/cgi-bin/article.cgi?f=/news/archive/2004/04/30/national1150EDT0563.DTL

Felony Complaint. *People v. Michael Joe Jackson*, DA No. 03-12-098996. http://news.findlaw.com/hdocs/docks/jacko/cajackson121803cmp.html

Hottenroth, Jennifer. Memorandum to Dr. Charles Sophy. Los Angeles Department of Children & Family Services. November 26, 2003. Available at http://www.thesmokinggun.com/archive/dcfs memo2.html

Indictment. *People v. Michael Joe Jackson*, No. 1133603. Santa Barbara County Superior Court. http://news.findlaw.com/hdocs/docks/jacko/camj43004ind.html

Kaisindorf, Martin and Cesar G. Soviano. "Jackson Accuser's Story Changed." *USA Today*, December 10, 2003.

Oldenburg, Ann. "Jackson: Charges 'Totally False.'" *USA Today*, December 29, 2003.

Smolowe, Jill, et al. "His Story." *People*, January 12, 2004

SEXUAL HARASSMENT

CONSTRUCTIVE DISCHARGE APPLIES TO SEXUAL HARASSMENT CLAIMS

Greenhouse, Linda. "Rules are Set for Some Harassment Cases." June 15, 2004. *New York Times*.

Savage, David G. "Supreme Court Clarifies Law on Sex Harassment." June 15, 2004. *Los Angeles Times.*

Associated Press. "Workers Who Quit Over Sexual Harassment Can Sue Former Employers." June 14, 2004. *Washington Post.*

SEXUAL HARASSMENT

OBITUARY NOTICE

"Former Senator Paul Simon Dies After Surgery." CNN.com. December 9, 2003. http://www.cnn.com/2003/ALLPOLITICS/12/09/simon.obit.ap/

"Paul Simon." In *Contemporary Authors Online.* Reproduced in Biography Resource Center. Gale Group, 2004. http://galenet.galegroup.com/servlet/BioRC

SIXTH AMENDMENT

CRAWFORD V. WASHINGTON

"911 Call is Admissible as Trial Evidence if It Meets 'Excited Utterance' or Other Hearsay Exceptions." *New York Law Journal.* April 23, 2004, at 20.

Franzen, Robin. "Ruling on Hearsay Evidence Guts Cases." *The Oregonian.* March 11, 2004, at A1.

SIXTH AMENDMENT RIGHTS UNDER MIRANDA IMPLICATED WHETHER OR NOT POLICE "INTERROGATED" DEFENDANT

Holland, Gina. "Supreme Court Reaffirms Miranda Ruling." *Miami Herald.* January 26, 2004.

Mauro, Tony. "A Look Ahead to Next Term." Law.Com. http://www.law.com/jsp/article.jsp?id=1056139907048 June 30, 2003.

NO PRECISE FORMULA ON WAYS IN WHICH JUDGES ADVISE DEFENDANTS OF THEIR RIGHTS

Greenhouse, Linda. "Supreme Court Roundup." *New York Times.* March 9, 2004.

Holland, Gina. "Court Rules on Defendant-Counsel Rights." *Washington Post.* March 8, 2004.

SOCIAL SECURITY

CLAIMANT CAN BE DENIED SSI BENEFITS EVEN IF PREVIOUS TYPE OF WORK NO LONGER EXISTS

Kirkland, Michael. "High Court Narrows 'Disabled Claims.'" http://www.upi.com/view.cfm?StoryID=20031112-103640-8691r United Press International. November 12, 2003.

SPORTS LAW

ALLEGATIONS OF STEROID USE TIED TO SEVERAL TOP U.S. ATHLETES

Associated Press. "Report: Bonds, Giambi, Sheffield Among Pro Athletes Who Received Steroids," *Boston Herald,* March 2, 2004, <http://news.bostonherald.com/national/view.bg?articleid=5105&format=>.

Longman, Jere and Joe Drape. "How a New Steroid was Decoded." *New York Times.* November 2, 2003.

TELECOMMUNICATIONS

TELEMARKETERS FIGHT DO-NOT-CALL LIST

"ATA Launches Legal Challenge Against New Rules." American Teleservices Association web site. http://www.ataconnect.org/ataconnect.org-asp//newsrelease.asp?ID=2 January 3, 2003.

"Bush Signs 'Do Not Call' Bill." CBSNews.com. http://www.cbsnews.com/stories/2003/07/07/tech/main561876.shtml September 29, 2003.

"Court Upholds Do-Not-Call List." CBSNews.com. http://www.cbsnews.com/stories/2004/01/29/national/main596573.shtml February 17, 2004.

Davidson, Paul and Theresa Howard. "It's the FCC to the Rescue of Do-Not-Call List." *USA Today.* http://www.usatoday.com/money/industries/telecom/2003-09-29-do-not-call-back_x.htm September 29, 2003.

"'Do Not Call' List Unplugged." CNNMoney.com. http://money.cnn.com/2003/09/24/technology/ftc_donotcall/ September 24, 2003.

"Do-Not-Call Registry Faces Tougher Challenge." CNN.com. http://www.cnn.com/2003/ALLPOLITICS/09/25/congress.no.call/ September 26, 2003.

Hudson, David L. Jr. "Federal Trade Commission Creates National Do-Not-Call Registry." The Media Institute Homepage. http://www.mediainstitute.org/ONLINE/FAM2003/4-b.html

Mayer, Caroline E. "Court Says Do-Not-Call List Can Be Enforced." *Washington Post.* http://www.washingtonpost.com/wp-dyn/articles/A58828-2003Oct7.html October 8, 2003.

McCullagh, Declan. "Court Upholds Do Not Call List." CNET News.com http://news.com.com/2100-1028-5160690.html February 17, 2004.

National Do-Not-Call Registry (FCC Website). http://www.fcc.gov/cgb/donotcall/

"Timeline of Do-Not-Call Registry" (dates, links and other information). ReclaimDemocracy.org. http://www.reclaimdemocracy.org/corporate_speech/timeline_do_not_call_registry.html

Witte, Griff. "FCC Issues Its First 'Do Not Call' Citation." *Washington Post.* http://www.washingtonpost.com/ac2/wp-dyn?pagename=article&node=&contentId=A13420-2003Dec18&notFound=true December 19, 2003.

NIXON V. MISSOURI

Nixon v. Missouri, No. 02-1238, 541 U.S. ___ (2004). Syllabus and Slip Opinion available at <http://www.supremecourtus.gov/opinions/>

"Supreme Court Reverses in Nixon v. Missouri." *Tech Law Journal,* March 24, 2004. Available online at http://www.techlawjournal.com/topstories/2004/20040324b.asp

TELEVISION

FCC MEDIA OWNERSHIP RULES

Ahrens, Frank. "Court Blocks Media Rules." *Washington Post,* September 4, 2003, p. A01.

Davidson, Paul. "Media Ownership Rules Put Under Microscope." *USA Today*, February 11, 2004. http://www.usatoday.com/money/media/2004-02-11-mediaown_x.htm

"FCC Sets Limits on Media Concentration." FCC Press Release, June 2, 2003. http://www.fcc.gov

Gelles, Jeff. "Cable's Clear Shot at Media." *Philadelphia Inquirer*, February 15, 2004.

"Media Ownership Policy Reexamination." http://www.fcc.gov

Order, *Prometheus Radio Project v. FCC*, No. 03-3388. U.S. Court of Appeals for the Third Circuit. http://www.findlaw.com

Safire, William. "The Five Sisters." *New York Times*, February 16, 2004.

TERRORISM

U.S. PROSECUTION OF BIN LADEN AIDES

"2 Gitmo Prisoners to Stand Trial." CBS News. February 24, 2004. http://www.cbsnews.com/stories/2004/02/24/terror/main602018.shtml

Marek, Angie C. "The First to Face Tribunals." *U.S. News & World Report*, March 8, 2004.

Mintz, John. "U.S. Charges 2 as Bin Laden Aides." *Washington Post*. February 25, 2004.

U.S. v. al Qosi, http://www.findlaw.com/hdocs/docs/dod/alqosi22404chrg.pdf

SUPREME COURT RULES THAT U.S. CITIZENS CLASSIFIED AS ENEMY COMBATANTS MAY BE DETAINED INDEFINITELY

A Mixed Verdict on the Terror War CNN.com. http://www.cnn.com/2004/LAW/06/28/scotus.enemy.combatants.ap/index.html (June 28, 2004).

Hamdi v. Rumsfeld, 542 U.S. __ (2004).

FOILED PLOT TO BRING DOWN THE BROOKLYN BRIDGE

Agency Group 7. "Iyman Faris Sentenced for Providing Material Support to Al {AU: Capital "A" in source? Hyphen?} Qaeda." *FDCH Regulatory Intelligence Database*, October 28, 2003

"Imposition and Expansion of Controls on Designated Terrorists . . ." *Federal Register [Rules and Regulations]*, Vol. 68, No. 109, June 6, 2003, pp. 34191-34192. http://wais.access.gpo.gov.

Locy, Toni. "Ohio Man Served as al-Qaeda's U.S. Scout." *USA Today*, June 20. 2003

Schmidt, Susan. "Trucker Pleads Guilty in Plot by {AU: Capital "A" in source?} Al-Qaeda." *Washington Post*, June 20, 2003.

Thomas, Evan, et al. "Al-Qaeda in America." *Newsweek*. June 23, 2003.

UNITED STATES V. KOUBRITI

Hakim, Danny. "Terrorist Trial Nets Convictions." *Salt Lake Tribune*, June 4, 2003. http://www.sltrib.com/2003/Jun/06042003/nation_w/nation_w.asp

"Opinion and Order Regarding Defendants' Motion to Require Attorney General to Show Cause Why He Should Not Be Held in Contempt." Case No. 01-80778. Court Records, U.S. District Court, Eastern District of Michigan. Available at http://news.findlaw.com/hdocs/docs/terrorism/uskoubriti

"Second Superceding Indictment." Case No. 01-80778. Court Records, U.S. District Court, Eastern District of Michigan. Available at http://news.findlaw.com/hdocs/docs/terrorism/uskoubriti82802ind.pdf

"Two Guilty in Detroit Terror Trial." *NewsMax Wires*. June 4, 2003. Http://www.newsmax.com/archives/articles/2003/6/3/185254.shtml

"U.S. Prosecutor Sues Ashcroft." February 17, 2004. Available at http://www.cbs.news.com/stories/2004/02/17/terror/main600677.html

UNITED NATIONS AND UNITED STATES SANCTIONS EASED AGAINST LIBYA

Consular Information Sheet. U.S. Department of State. April 4, 2004. http://travel.state.gov/libya.html.

Jahn, George. "Dossier on Libya Nuclear Program to Close." *The Guardian*. March 10, 2004. http://www.guardian.co.uk/worldlatest/story/0,1280,-3846171,00.html.

"Key Facts: Libya Sanctions." *CNN.com*. September 12, 2003. http://www.cnn.com/2003/WORLD/africa/09/01/libya.uta.facts.reut/index.html.

King, John. "U.S. Lifts Travel Ban to Libya." *CNN.com*. February 27, 2004. http://www.cnn.com/2004/US/02/26/libya/.

"Lockerbie Crash Timeline." *CNN.com*. September 12, 2003. http://www.cnn.com/2003/WORLD/europe/08/14/lockerbie.timeline/index.html.

"U.S.: Libya Takes Lockerbie Blame." *CNN.com*. February 10, 2004. http://www.cnn.com/2003/US/08/15/lockerbie.delay/.

OPPOSITION TO THE PATRIOT ACT

Brownfeld, Peter. "Patriot Act Opponents Say Law Endangers Rights." FOXNews.com. http://www.foxnews.com/story/0,2933,97003,00.html September 11, 2003.

Colson, Nicole. "The Sequel is Worse Than the Original: Patriot Act II." *International Socialist Review* (available at thirdworldtraveller.com) http://www.thirdworldtraveler.com/Civil_Liberties/Sequel Worse_PatriotII.html May-June, 2003.

Davidson, Lee. "Patriot Act Takes Hard Hits From the Right and Left." *Deseret Morning News*. http://deseretnews.com/dn/view/0,1249,525038886,00.html November 19, 2003.

Gaddy, Michael. "Conservatives and Liberals Unite in Opposition to Patriot II." *Sierra Times* http://www.citizenreviewonline.org/mar_2003/conservatives.htm March 15, 2003.

Huang, Josie and Kelley Bouchard. "Councilors Denounce Patriot Act Provisions." *Portland Press Herald*. http://www.pressherald.com/news/local/040316portcouncil.shtml?survey44182 March 16, 2004.

Judd, Ron C. "A Tiny Town Shouts 'Whoa' to Patriot Act." *The Seattle Times* http://archives.seattletimes.nwsource.com/cgi-bin/texis.cgi/web/vortex/display?slug=patriot10m&date=20030810 August 10, 2003.

Schabner, Dean. "War On Terror Walkouts." ABSNews.com. http://abcnews.go.com/sections/us/DailyNews/usapatriot_oakland021217.html December 17, 2003.

Struzzi, Diane. "Legality of Patriot Act Questioned." *Hartford Courant* (text available at refuseandresist.org) http://www.refuseandresist.org/police_state/art.php?aid=640 March 23, 2003.

Taylor, Guy. "Communities Shun Patriot Act." *The Washington Times*. http://www.washtimes.com/national/20030720-115938-3269r.htm July 21, 2003.

"Victories in Four States and 295 Cities, Towns and Counties." Bill of Rights Defense Committee Website. http://www.bordc.org/

RASUL V. BUSH

Gearan, Anne. "Supreme Court Rejects Appeal Over Secret Sept. 11 Detentions." *USA Today*. http://www.usatoday.com/news/washington/judicial/supremecourtopinions/2004-01-12-detainees_x.htm January 12, 2004.

McCutcheon, Chuck. "Guantanamo Case Draws Wide Range of 'Amicus' Briefs to Supreme Court." *Newhouse News Service*. http://www.newhousenews.com/archive/mccutcheon031004.html March 10, 2004.

"Military Order of November 13, 2001." *Federal Register*, Volume 66, Number 222. http://www.fas.org/irp/offdocs/eo/mo-111301.htm November 16, 2001.

"A Mixed Verdict on the Terror War". CNN.com. http://www.cnn.com/2004/LAW/06/28/scotus.enemy.combatants.ap/ June 28, 2004.

"Rasul v. Bush: Synopsis." Center for Constitutional Rights. http://www.ccr-ny.org/v2/legal/september_11th/sept11Article.asp?ObjID=ytOOAV96a7&Content=91 2004.

Supreme Court Docket, April 2004. Findlaw.com. http://supreme.lp.findlaw.com/supreme_court/docket/2003/april.html

"Supreme Court Hears First Test of Bush Anti-Terror Tactics." CNN.com. http://www.cnn.com/2004/LAW/04/20/scotus.detainees.ap/ April 20, 2004.

Willing, Richard. "High Court to Rule on Cuba Detainees." *USA Today* http://www.usatoday.com/news/washington/2003-11-10-scotus-gitmo_x.htm November 10, 2003.

TOBACCO

TOBACCO COMPANIES SEE REVERSAL IN LEGAL FORTUNES

Choe, Howard. "The Smoke Around Big Tobacco Clears." *Business Week*. (online edition) http://www.businessweek.com/investor/content/may2003/pi20030522_2840_pi041.htm May 22, 2003.

Cunningham, Laurie. "Appeals Court Refuses to Rehear 'Engle' Tobacco Suit." *Miami Daily Business Review*. (available at Law.com) http://www.law.com/jsp/article.jsp?id=1063212077718 September 29, 2003.

"Engle." British American Tobacco. http://www.bat.com/oneweb/sites/uk__3mnfen.nsf/vwlivelookup HomePageText/9A1DEAC7DD4290D048256C5A0058A4D0?opendocument

"Florida Appeals Court Throws Out $145 Billion Tobacco Verdict." CNN.com. http://www.cnn.com/2003/LAW/05/21/tobacco.ruling.overturned/ May 27, 2003.

"History of Tobacco Litigation 1999 - Present." Altria.com. http://www.altria.com/media/03_06_01_02_04_1998-Present.asp

"Huge Tobacco Ruling Overturned." BBC News. http://news.bbc.co.uk/2/hi/business/3048053.stm May 21, 2003.

"Tobacco Class Action Goes Up In Smoke; Individual and Government Cases Proceed." *TRIAL*. (Available at VanDerGinst Law, P.C. web site.) http://thepeoplesfirm.com/stores/190/nh_article_080103_b.htm August 2003.

TORT LAW

STATES TACKLE TORT REFORM ISSUES IN 2002 AND 2003

American Tort Reform Association. *Bringing Justice to Judicial Hellholes 2003*. <http://www.atra.org/reports/hellholes/report.pdf>.

Hofmann, Mark A. "Busy Year for State Tort Reform." *Business Insurance.*. July 21, 2003, at 4.

Kirkland, Elizabeth, "Tort Reform as Important for Banks as Doctors, Insurance." *Mississippi Business Journal.*. November 11, 2002, at 24.

TRADEMARK

ROSA PARKS ENTITLED TO TRADEMARK JURY TRIAL OVER OUTKAST SONG USING HER NAME

"Rosa Parks asks court to reinstate lawsuit against rappers." *Detroit News*. http://www.detnews.com/2001/metro/0105/05/metro-220433.htm May 5, 2001.

Rosen, Craig. "OutKast Beats Rosa Parks In Federal Lawsuit." http://launch.yahoo.com/read/news.asp?contentID=163600 November 19, 1999.

"Supreme Court allows Rosa Parks to sue OutKast." CNN.com. http://www.cnn.com/2003/LAW/12/08/scotus.parks.ap/ December 8, 2003.

TRUTH IN LENDING ACT

HOUSEHOLD CREDIT SERVICES V. PFENNIG

Goch, David. "Supreme Court Decides Household Credit Services v. Pfennig." April 22, 2004. http://www.clla.org/newswire/Washington_Hot_news.cfm?newsID=28

Household Credit Services v. Pfennig, No. 02-857, 541 U.S. ___ (2004). Syllabus and slip opinion available at http://www.supremecourtus.gov/opinions/03

UNIFORM COMMERCIAL CODE

COMMISSIONERS ON UNIFORM LAWS APPROVE REVISED ARTICLES 2 AND 2A OF THE U.C.C.

McLaughlin, Gerald T. and Neil B. Cohen. "Summarizing Key Revisions to UCC Article 2." *New York Law Journal*. July 9, 2003, at 3.

National Association of Manufacturers. "Industry Concerns About Final Article 2." Press Release, <http://www.nam.org/>

VICTIMS' RIGHTS

JUDGE RULES THAT IRAN MUST PAY VICTIMS OF 1983 BOMBING IN LEBANON

"Iran Responsible for 1983 Marine Barracks Bombing, Judge Rules. *CNN.com*. May 30, 2003. http://www.cnn.com/2003/LAW/05/30/iran.barracks.bombing/index.html.

"Judge: Iranian Government Responsible for 1983 Beirut Bombing." *USA Today*. May 30, 2003. http://www.usatoday.com/news/world/2003-05-30-bombing-lawsuit_x.htm.

Memorandum Opinion. Peterson v. The Islamic Republic of Iran, Civ. No. 01-2094 (RCL) (U.S. Dist. Ct., Dist. of Columbia), and Boulos v. The Islamic Republic of Iran, Civ. No. 01-2684 (RCL) (U.S. Dist. Ct., Dist. of Columbia) May 30, 2003, htttp://www.dcd.uscourts.gov/01-2094.pdf.

"Twenty Years Later, Lebanon Bombing Haunts." *CNN.com*. October 23, 2003. http://www.cnn.com/2003/WORLD/meast/10/21/lebanon.anniv.ap/index.html.

VOTING

NEW VOTING TECHNOLOGY

Hamman, Henry. "Security Fears Grow Over Electronic Voting Systems." *Financial Times*. September 12, 2003.

Levy, Steven. "Ballot Boxes Go High Tech." *Newsweek*. March 29, 2004.

Office of Civil Rights Evaluation, U.S. Commission on Human Rights. *Is America Ready to Vote: Election Readiness Briefing Paper*. April 2004.

WARSAW CONVENTION

AIRLINE LIABLE FOR SECOND-HAND HAND SMOKE DEATH

Hoppin, Jason. "9th Circuit Upholds $1.4M Secondhand Smoke Award." December 13, 2002. wwww.law.com. http://www.law.com/jsp/article.jsp?id=1039054444545

"US Court Ruling May Review Airline Lawsuits." March 14, 2004. http://news.airwise.com/stories/2004/03/1079245328.html *Reuters*.

Wald, Matthew L. "Justices Say Airline Is Liable For a Fatal Reaction to Smoking ." *New York Times*. February 25, 2004.

WATER RIGHTS

VIRGINIA ESTABLISHES RIGHTS TO THE POTOMAC RIVER

Masters, Brooke A. "1785 Deal Floats to Top of Potomac Pipe Battle." April 17, 2001. *Washington Post*.

Siler, Jeanne. "Raphael Wins One for the Commonwealth." Spring, 2004. http://www.law.virginia.edu/home2002/html/alumni/uvalawyer/sp04/raphael.htm *UVA Lawyer*.

"Supreme Court Approves Virginia Claim to River Water." December 2003. http://www.uswaternews.com/archives/arcrights/3supcou12.html *U.S. Water News Online*.

Appendix

Elections

The Bipartisan Campaign Finance Reform Act of 2002

The Bipartisan Campaign Finance Reform Act sought to ban "soft money" contributions to political candidates and to restrict corporations, labor unions, and advocacy groups from spending their funds to finance "electioneering communications" that seek to influence a federal election.

H.R. 2356

SEC. 101. SOFT MONEY OF POLITICAL PARTIES.

(a) In General.—Title III of the Federal Election Campaign Act of 1971 (2 U.S.C. 431 et seq.) is amended by adding at the end the following:

SEC. 323. NOTE: 2 USC 441i. SOFT MONEY OF POLITICAL PARTIES.

(a) National Committees.—

(1) In general.—A national committee of a political party (including a national congressional campaign committee of a political party) may not solicit, receive, or direct to another person a contribution, donation, or transfer of funds or any other thing of value, or spend any funds, that are not subject to the limitations, prohibitions, and reporting requirements of this Act.

(2) Applicability.—The prohibition established by paragraph (1) applies to any such national committee, any officer or agent acting on behalf of such a national committee, and any entity that is directly or indirectly established, financed, maintained, or controlled by such a national committee.

(b) State, District, and Local Committees.—

(1) In general.—Except as provided in paragraph (2), an amount that is expended or disbursed for Federal election activity by a State, district, or local committee of a political party (including an entity that is directly or indirectly established, financed, maintained, or controlled by a State, district, or local committee of a political party and an officer or agent acting on behalf of such committee or entity), or by an association or similar group of candidates for State or local office or of individuals holding State or local office, shall be made from funds subject to the limitations, prohibitions, and reporting requirements of this Act.

(2) Applicability.—

(A) In general.—Notwithstanding clause (i) or (ii) of section 301(20)(A), and subject to subparagraph (B), paragraph (1) shall not apply to any amount expended or disbursed by a State, district, or local committee of a political party for an activity described in either such clause to the extent the amounts expended or disbursed for such activity are allocated (under regulations prescribed by the Commission) among amounts—

(i) which consist solely of contributions subject to the limitations, prohibitions, and reporting requirements of this Act (other than amounts described in subparagraph (B)(iii)); and

(ii) other amounts which are not subject to the limitations, prohibitions, and reporting requirements of this Act (other than any requirements of this subsection).

(B) Conditions.—Subparagraph (A) shall only apply if—

(i) the activity does not refer to a clearly identified candidate for Federal office;

(ii) the amounts expended or disbursed are not for the costs of any broadcasting, cable, or satellite communication, other than a communication which refers solely to a clearly identified candidate for State or local office;

(iii) the amounts expended or disbursed which are described in subparagraph (A)(ii) are paid from amounts which are donated in accordance with State law and which meet the requirements of subparagraph (C), except that no person (including any person established, financed, maintained, or controlled by such person) may donate more than $10,000 to a State, district, or local committee of a political party in a calendar year for such expenditures or disbursements; and

(iv) the amounts expended or disbursed are made solely from funds raised by the State, local, or district committee which makes such expenditure or disbursement, and do not include any funds provided to such committee from—

(I) any other State, local, or district committee of any State party,

(II) the national committee of a political party (including a national congressional campaign committee of a political party),

(III) any officer or agent acting on behalf of any committee described in subclause (I) or (II), or

(IV) any entity directly or indirectly established, financed, maintained, or controlled by any committee described in subclause (I) or (II).

(C) Prohibiting involvement of national parties, federal candidates and officeholders, and state parties acting jointly.—Notwithstanding subsection (e) (other than subsection (e)(3)), amounts specifically authorized to be spent under subparagraph (B)(iii) meet the requirements of this subparagraph only if the amounts—

(i) are not solicited, received, directed, transferred, or spent by or in the name of any person described in subsection (a) or (e); and

(ii) are not solicited, received, or directed through fundraising activities conducted jointly by 2 or more State, local, or district committees of any political party or their agents, or by a State, local, or district committee of a political party on behalf of the State, local, or district committee of a political party or its agent in one or more other States.

(c) Fundraising Costs.—An amount spent by a person described in subsection (a) or (b) to raise funds that are used, in whole or in part, for expenditures and disbursements for a Federal election activity shall be made from funds subject to the limitations, prohibitions, and reporting requirements of this Act.

(d) Tax-Exempt Organizations.—A national, State, district, or local committee of a political party (including a national congressional campaign committee of a political party), an entity that is directly or indirectly established, financed, maintained, or controlled by any such national, State, district, or local committee or its agent, and an officer or agent acting on behalf of any such party committee or entity, shall not solicit any funds for, or make or direct any donations to—

(1) an organization that is described in section 501(c) of the Internal Revenue Code of 1986 and exempt from taxation under section 501(a) of such Code (or has submitted an application for determination of tax exempt status under such section) and that makes expenditures or disbursements in connection with an election for Federal office (including expenditures or disbursements for Federal election activity); or

(2) an organization described in section 527 of such Code (other than a political committee, a State, district, or local committee of a political party, or the authorized campaign committee of a candidate for State or local office).

(e) Federal Candidates.—

(1) In general.—A candidate, individual holding Federal office, agent of a candidate or an individual holding Federal office, or an entity directly or indirectly established, financed, maintained or controlled by or acting on behalf of 1 or more candidates or individuals holding Federal office, shall not—

(A) solicit, receive, direct, transfer, or spend funds in connection with an election for Federal office, including funds for any Federal election activity, unless the funds are subject to the limitations, prohibitions, and reporting requirements of this Act; or

(B) solicit, receive, direct, transfer, or spend funds in connection with any election other than an election for Federal office or disburse funds in connection with such an election unless the funds—

(i) are not in excess of the amounts permitted with respect to contributions to candidates and political committees under paragraphs (1), (2), and (3) of section 315(a); and

(ii) are not from sources prohibited by this Act from making contributions in connection with an election for Federal office.

(2) State law.—Paragraph (1) does not apply to the solicitation, receipt, or spending of funds by an individual described in such paragraph who is or was also a candidate for a State or local office solely in connection with such election for State or local office if the solicitation, receipt, or spending of funds is permitted under State law and refers only to such State or local candidate, or to any other candidate for the State or local office sought by such candidate, or both.

(3) Fundraising events.—Notwithstanding paragraph (1) or subsection (b)(2)(C), a candidate or an individual holding Federal office may attend, speak, or be a featured guest at a fundraising event for a State, district, or local committee of a political party.

(4) Permitting certain solicitations.—

(A) General solicitations.—Notwithstanding any other provision of this subsection, an individual described in paragraph (1) may make a general solicitation of funds on behalf of any organization that is described in section 501(c) of the Internal Revenue Code of 1986 and exempt from taxation under section 501(a) of such Code (or has submitted an application for determination of tax exempt status under such section) (other than an entity whose principal purpose is to conduct activities described in clauses (i) and (ii) of section 301(20)(A)) where such solicitation does not specify how the funds will or should be spent.

(B) Certain specific solicitations.—In addition to the general solicitations permitted under subparagraph (A), an individual described in paragraph (1) may make a solicitation explicitly to obtain funds for carrying out the activities described in clauses (i) and (ii) of section 301(20)(A), or for an entity whose principal purpose is to conduct such activities, if—

(i) the solicitation is made only to individuals; and

(ii) the amount solicited from any individual during any calendar year does not exceed $20,000.

(f) State Candidates.—

(1) In general.—A candidate for State or local office, individual holding State or local office, or an agent of such a candidate or individual may not spend any funds for a communication described in section 301(20)(A)(iii) unless the funds are subject to the limitations, prohibitions, and reporting requirements of this Act.

(2) Exception for certain communications.—Paragraph (1) shall not apply to an individual described in such paragraph if the communication involved is in connection with an election for such State or local office and refers only to such individual or to any other candidate for the State or local office held or sought by such individual, or both.

SEC. 303. STRENGTHENING FOREIGN MONEY BAN.

Section 319 of the Federal Election Campaign Act of 1971 (2 U.S.C. 441e) is amended—

(1) by striking the heading and inserting the following:

contributions and donations by foreign nationals; and

(2) by striking subsection (a) and inserting the following:

(a) Prohibition.—It shall be unlawful for—

(1) a foreign national, directly or indirectly, to make—

(A) a contribution or donation of money or other thing of value, or to make an express or implied promise to make a contribution or donation, in connection with a Federal, State, or local election;

(B) a contribution or donation to a committee of a political party; or

(C) an expenditure, independent expenditure, or disbursement for an electioneering communication (within the meaning of section 304(f)(3)); or

(2) a person to solicit, accept, or receive a contribution or donation described in subparagraph (A) or (B) of paragraph (1) from a foreign national.

SEC. 307. MODIFICATION OF CONTRIBUTION LIMITS.

(a) Increase in Individual Limits for Certain Contributions.— Section 315(a)(1) of the Federal Election Campaign Act of 1971 (2 U.S.C. 441a(a)(1)) is amended—

(1) in subparagraph (A), by striking

$1,000 and inserting

$2,000; and

(2) in subparagraph (B), by striking

$20,000 and inserting

$25,000.

(b) Increase in Annual Aggregate Limit on Individual Contributions.—Section 315(a)(3) of the Federal Election Campaign Act of 1971 (2 U.S.C. 441a(a)(3)) is amended to read as follows:

(3) During the period which begins on January 1 of an odd-numbered year and ends on December 31 of the next even-numbered year, no individual may make contributions aggregating more than—

(A) $37,500, in the case of contributions to candidates and the authorized committees of candidates;

(B) $57,500, in the case of any other contributions, of which not more than $37,500 may be attributable to contributions to political committees which are not political committees of national political parties.

(c) Increase in Senatorial Campaign Committee Limit.—Section 315(h) of the Federal Election Campaign Act of 1971 (2 U.S.C. 441a(h)) is amended by striking

$17,500 and inserting $35,000.

(d) Indexing of Contribution Limits.—Section 315(c) of the Federal Election Campaign Act of 1971 (2 U.S.C. 441a(c)) is amended—

(1) in paragraph (1)—

(A) by striking the second and third sentences;

(B) by inserting

(A)" before

At the beginning"; and

(C) by adding at the end the following:

(B) Except as provided in subparagraph (C), in any calendar year after 2002—

(i) a limitation established by subsections (a)(1)(A),

(a)(1)(B), (a)(3), (b), (d), or (h) shall be increased by the percent difference determined under subparagraph (A);

(ii) each amount so increased shall remain in effect for the calendar year; and

(iii) if any amount after adjustment under clause (i) is not a multiple of $100, such amount shall be rounded to the nearest multiple of $100.

(e) Effective *NOTE: 2 USC 441a note.* Date.—The amendments made by this section shall apply with respect to contributions made on or after January 1, 2003.

E-MAIL

The CAN SPAM Act of 2003

In response to the flood of unwanted emails swamping Internet users' mailboxes on a daily basis, Congress passed the CAN SPAM Act of 2003, which sought to make such actions illegal.

Bill S.630 "CAN SPAM Act of 2003 (Introduced in Senate) Sec. 1037. Fraud and related activity in connection with electronic mail

(a) IN GENERAL- Whoever, in or affecting interstate or foreign commerce, knowingly—

(1) accesses a protected computer without authorization, and intentionally initiates the transmission of multiple commercial electronic mail messages from or through such computer,

(2) uses a protected computer to relay or retransmit multiple commercial electronic mail messages, with the intent to deceive or mislead recipients, or any Internet access service, as to the origin of such messages,

(3) materially falsifies header information in multiple commercial electronic mail messages and intentionally initiates the transmission of such messages,

(4) registers, using information that materially falsifies the identity of the actual registrant, for five or more electronic mail accounts or online user accounts or two or more domain names, and intentionally initiates the transmission of multiple commercial electronic mail messages from any combination of such accounts or domain names, or

(5) falsely represents oneself to be the registrant or the legitimate successor in interest to the registrant of 5 or more Internet Protocol addresses, and intentionally initiates the transmission of multiple commercial electronic mail messages from such addresses, or conspires to do so, shall be punished as provided in subsection (b).

(b) PENALTIES- The punishment for an offense under subsection (a) is—

(1) a fine under this title, imprisonment for not more than 5 years, or both, if—

(A) the offense is committed in furtherance of any felony under the laws of the United States or of any State; or

(B) the defendant has previously been convicted under this section or section 1030, or under the law of any State for conduct involving the transmission of multiple commercial electronic mail messages or unauthorized access to a computer system;

(2) a fine under this title, imprisonment for not more than 3 years, or both, if—

(A) the offense is an offense under subsection (a)(1);

(B) the offense is an offense under subsection (a)(4) and involved 20 or more falsified electronic mail or online user account registrations, or 10 or more falsified domain name registrations;

(C) the volume of electronic mail messages transmitted in furtherance of the offense exceeded 2,500 during any 24-hour period, 25,000 during any 30-day period, or 250,000 during any 1-year period;

(D) the offense caused loss to one or more persons aggregating $5,000 or more in value during any 1-year period;

(E) as a result of the offense any individual committing the offense obtained anything of value aggregating $5,000 or more during any 1-year period; or

(F) the offense was undertaken by the defendant in concert with three or more other persons with respect to whom the defendant occupied a position of organizer or leader; and

(3) a fine under this title or imprisonment for not more than 1 year, or both, in any other case.

FETAL RIGHTS

Unborn Victims of Violence Act

The Unborn Victims of Violence Act, also known as Laci and Conner's Law, was passed during the highly publicized murder trial of Scott Peterson, who was accused of murdering his wife Lacy and their unborn son Conner. The new law effectively established two separate crimes committed against a pregnant woman: one against her and one against her unborn child. This was significant in that it represented the first time ever that federal law recognized an embryo or fetus as a distinct person.

H.R.1997

An Act

To amend title 18, United States Code, and the Uniform Code of Military Justice to protect unborn children from assault and murder, and for other purposes.

SECTION 1. SHORT TITLE.

This Act may be cited as the 'Unborn Victims of Violence Act of 2004' or Laci and Conner's Law'.

SEC. 2. PROTECTION OF UNBORN CHILDREN.

(a) IN GENERAL- Title 18, United States Code, is amended by inserting after chapter 90 the following:

CHAPTER 90A—PROTECTION OF UNBORN CHILDREN

Sec. 1841. Protection of unborn children

(a)(1) Whoever engages in conduct that violates any of the provisions of law listed in subsection (b) and thereby causes the death of, or bodily injury (as defined in section 1365) to, a child, who is in utero at the time the conduct takes place, is guilty of a separate offense under this section.

(2)(A) Except as otherwise provided in this paragraph, the punishment for that separate offense is the same as the punishment provided under Federal law for that conduct had that injury or death occurred to the unborn child's mother.

(B) An offense under this section does not require proof that—

(i) the person engaging in the conduct had knowledge or should have had knowledge that the victim of the underlying offense was pregnant; or

(ii) the defendant intended to cause the death of, or bodily injury to, the unborn child.

(C) If the person engaging in the conduct thereby intentionally kills or attempts to kill the unborn child, that person shall instead of being punished under subparagraph (A), be punished as provided under sections 1111, 1112, and 1113 of this title for intentionally killing or attempting to kill a human being.

(D) Notwithstanding any other provision of law, the death penalty shall not be imposed for an offense under this section.

(c) Nothing in this section shall be construed to permit the prosecution—

(1) of any person for conduct relating to an abortion for which the consent of the pregnant woman, or a person authorized by law to act on her behalf, has been obtained or for which such consent is implied by law;

(2) of any person for any medical treatment of the pregnant woman or her unborn child; or

(3) of any woman with respect to her unborn child.

(d) As used in this section, the term 'unborn child' means a child in utero, and the term 'child in utero' or 'child, who is in utero' means a member of the species homo sapiens, at any stage of development, who is carried in the womb.'.

SEC. 3. MILITARY JUSTICE SYSTEM.

(a) PROTECTION OF UNBORN CHILDREN- Subchapter X of chapter 47 of title 10, United States Code (the Uniform Code of Military Justice), is amended by inserting after section 919 (article 119) the following new section:

Sec. 919a. Art. 119a. Death or injury of an unborn child

(a)(1) Any person subject to this chapter who engages in conduct that violates any of the provisions of law listed in subsection (b) and thereby causes the death of, or bodily injury (as defined in section 1365 of title 18) to, a child, who is in utero at the time the conduct takes place, is guilty of a separate offense under this section and shall, upon conviction, be punished by such punishment, other than death, as a court-martial may direct, which shall be consistent with the punishments prescribed by the President for that conduct had that injury or death occurred to the unborn child's mother.

(2) An offense under this section does not require proof that—

(i) the person engaging in the conduct had knowledge or should have had knowledge that the victim of the underlying offense was pregnant; or

(ii) the accused intended to cause the death of, or bodily injury to, the unborn child.

(3) If the person engaging in the conduct thereby intentionally kills or attempts to kill the unborn child, that person shall, instead of being punished under paragraph (1), be punished as provided under sections 880, 918, and 919(a) of this title (articles 80, 118, and 119(a)) for intentionally killing or attempting to kill a human being.

(4) Notwithstanding any other provision of law, the death penalty shall not be imposed for an offense under this section.

(c) Nothing in this section shall be construed to permit the prosecution—

(1) of any person for conduct relating to an abortion for which the consent of the pregnant woman, or a person authorized by law to act on her behalf, has been obtained or for which such consent is implied by law;

(2) of any person for any medical treatment of the pregnant woman or her unborn child; or

(3) of any woman with respect to her unborn child.

(d) In this section, the term 'unborn child' means a child in utero, and the term 'child in utero' or 'child, who is in utero' means a member of the species homo sapiens, at any stage of development, who is carried in the womb.'.

TELECOMMUNICATIONS

Do-Not-Call Implementation Act

In an attempt to reduce the amount of unwanted solicitation phone calls citizens received from businesses, Congress passed the Do-Not-Call Implementation Act, which created a list for those wishing to be removed from telemarketing call lists. Companies who called people on the list would be penalized.

H. R. 395

AN ACT

To authorize the Federal Trade Commission to collect fees for the implementation and enforcement of a 'do-not-call' registry, and for other purposes.

Be it enacted by the Senate and House of Representatives of the United States of America in Congress assembled,

SECTION 1. SHORT TITLE.

This Act may be cited as the 'Do-Not-Call Implementation Act'.

SEC. 2. TELEMARKETING SALES RULE; DO-NOT-CALL REGISTRY FEES.

The Federal Trade Commission may promulgate regulations establishing fees sufficient to implement and enforce the provisions relating to the 'do-not-call' registry of the Telemarketing Sales Rule (16 CFR 310.4(b)(1)(iii)), promulgated under the Telemarketing and Consumer Fraud and Abuse Prevention Act (15 U.S.C. 6101 et seq.). Such regulations shall be promulgated in accordance with section 553 of title 5, United States Code. Fees may be collected pursuant to this section for fiscal years 2003 through 2007, and shall be deposited and credited as offsetting collections to the account, Federal Trade Commission—Salaries and Expenses, and shall remain available until expended. No amounts shall be collected as fees pursuant to this section for such fiscal years except to the extent provided in advance in appropriations Acts. Such amounts shall be available for expenditure only to offset the costs of activities and services related to the implementation and enforcement of the Telemarketing Sales Rule, and other activities resulting from such implementation and enforcement.

SEC. 3. FEDERAL COMMUNICATIONS COMMISSION DO-NOT-CALL REGULATIONS.

Not later than 180 days after the date of enactment of this Act, the Federal Communications Commission shall issue a final rule pursuant to the rulemaking proceeding that it began on September 18, 2002, under the Telephone Consumer Protection Act (47 U.S.C. 227 et seq.). In issuing such rule, the Federal Communications Commission shall consult and coordinate with the Federal Trade Commission to maximize consistency with the rule promulgated by the Federal Trade Commission (16 CFR 310.4(b)).

SEC. 4. REPORTING REQUIREMENTS.

(a) REPORT ON REGULATORY COORDINATION- Within 45 days after the promulgation of a final rule by the Federal Communications Commission as required by section 3, the Federal Trade Commission and the Federal Communications Commission shall each transmit to the Committee on Energy and Commerce of the House of Representatives and the Committee on Commerce, Science, and Transportation of the Senate a report which shall include—

(1) an analysis of the telemarketing rules promulgated by both the Federal Trade Commission and the Federal Communications Commission;

(2) any inconsistencies between the rules promulgated by each such Commission and the effect of any such inconsistencies on consumers, and persons paying for access to the registry; and

(3) proposals to remedy any such inconsistencies.

(b) ANNUAL REPORT- For each of fiscal years 2003 through 2007, the Federal Trade Commission and the Federal Communications Commission shall each transmit an annual report to the Committee on Energy and Commerce of the House of Representatives and the Committee on Commerce, Science, and Transportation of the Senate a report which shall include—

(1) an analysis of the effectiveness of the 'do-not-call' registry as a national registry;

(2) the number of consumers who have placed their telephone numbers on the registry;

(3) the number of persons paying fees for access to the registry and the amount of such fees;

(4) an analysis of the progress of coordinating the operation and enforcement of the 'do-not-call' registry with similar registries established and maintained by the various States;

(5) an analysis of the progress of coordinating the operation and enforcement of the 'do-not-call' registry with the enforcement activities of the Federal Communications Commission pursuant to the Telephone Consumer Protection Act (47 U.S.C. 227 et seq.); and

(6) a review of the enforcement proceedings under the Telemarketing Sales Rule (16 CFR 310), in the case of the Federal Trade Commission, and under the Telephone Consumer Protection Act (47 U.S.C. 227 et seq.), in the case of the Federal Communications Commission.

Passed the House of Representatives February 12, 2003.

GLOSSARY OF LEGAL TERMS

This section includes difficult or uncommon legal terms (**bolded** in the essays) *and their definitions from West's Encyclopedia of American Law (WEAL). Simple or common legal terms such as "lawsuit" and "plaintiff" are not* **bolded** *in the text and do not appear in this glossary; they do, however, have full entries in WEAL. Furthermore, terms that appear in* SMALL CAPS *within the essays—such as acts, cases, events, organizations, and persons—also appear in WEAL.*

A

Abduction: The act of restraining another through the use or threat of deadly force or through fraudulent persuasion. The requisite restraint generally requires that the abductor intend to prevent the liberation of the abductee. Some states require that the abductee be a minor or that the abductor intend to subject the abductee to prostitution or illicit sexual activity.

Abeyance: A lapse in succession during which there is no person in whom title is vested. In the law of estates, the condition of a freehold when there is no person in whom it is vested. In such cases the freehold has been said to be *in nubibus* (in the clouds), *in pendenti* (in suspension), and *in gremio legis* (in the bosom of the law). Where there is a tenant of the freehold, the remainder or reversion in fee may exist for a time without any particular owner, in which case it is said to be in abeyance. A condition of being undetermined or in a state of suspension or inactivity. In regard to sales to third parties of property acquired by county at tax sale, being held in *abeyance* means that certain rights or conditions are in expectancy.

Absolute: Complete; perfect; final; without any condition or encumbrance; as an absolute bond in distinction from a conditional bond. Unconditional; complete and perfect in itself; without relation to or dependence on other things or persons.

Free from conditions, limitations or qualifications, not dependent, or modified or affected by circumstances; that is, without any condition or restrictive provisions.

Actionable: Giving sufficient legal grounds for a lawsuit; giving rise to a cause of action.

Adjudication: The legal process of resolving a dispute. The formal giving or pronouncing of a judgment or decree in a court proceeding; also the judgment or decision given. The entry of a decree by a court in respect to the parties in a case. It implies a hearing by a court, after notice, of legal evidence on the factual issue(s) involved. The equivalent of a determination. It indicates that the claims of all the parties thereto have been considered and set at rest.

Adversary proceeding: Any action, hearing, investigation, inquest, or inquiry brought by one party against another in which the party seeking relief has given legal notice to and provided the other party with an opportunity to contest the claims that have been made against him or her.

Advisory opinion: An opinion by a court as to the legality of proposed legislation or conduct, given in response to a request by the government, legislature, or some other interested party.

Affidavit: A written statement of facts voluntarily made by an affiant under an oath or affirmation administered by a person authorized to do so by law.

Affirmance: A declaration by an appellate court that a judgment, order, or decree of a lower court that has been brought before it for review is valid and will be upheld.

Affirmative defense: A new fact or set of facts that operates to defeat a claim even if the facts supporting that claim are true.

Aggravated assault: A person is guilty of aggravated assault if he or she attempts to cause serious bodily injury to another or causes such injury purposely, knowingly, or recklessly under circumstances manifesting extreme indifference to the value of human life; or attempts to cause or purposely or knowingly causes bodily injury to another with a deadly weapon. In all jurisdictions, statutes punish such aggravated assaults as assault with intent to murder (or rob or kill or rape) and assault with a dangerous (or deadly) weapon more severely than "simple" assaults.

Aliens: Foreign-born persons who have not been naturalized to become U.S. citizens under federal law and the Constitution.

Allegation: The assertion, claim, declaration, or statement of a party to an action, setting out what he or she expects to prove.

Allocation: The apportionment or designation of an item for a specific purpose or to a particular place.

Amicus curiae: [*Latin, Friend of the court.*] A person with strong interest in or views on the subject matter of an action, but not a party to the action, may petition the court for permission to file a brief, ostensibly on behalf of a party but actually to suggest a rationale consistent with its own views. Such amicus curiae briefs are commonly filed in appeals concerning matters of a broad public interest; e.g., civil rights cases. They may be filed by private persons or the government. In appeals to the U.S. courts of appeals, an amicus brief may be filed only if accompanied by written consent of all parties, or by leave of court granted on motion or at the request of the court, except that consent or leave shall not be required when the brief is presented by the United States or an officer or agency thereof.

Appeal: Timely resort by an unsuccessful party in a lawsuit or administrative proceeding to an appropriate superior court empowered to review a final decision on the ground that it was based upon an erroneous application of law.

Appellate: Relating to appeals; reviews by superior courts of decisions of inferior courts or administrative agencies and other proceedings.

Apportionment: The process by which legislative seats are distributed among units entitled to representation. Determination of the number of representatives that a state, county, or other subdivision may send to a legislative body. The U.S. Constitution provides for a census every ten years, on the basis of which Congress apportions representatives according to population; but each state must have at least one representative. *Districting* is the establishment of the precise geographical boundaries of each such unit or constituency. Apportionment by state statute that denies the rule of one-person, one-vote is violative of equal protection of laws.

Also, the allocation of a charge or cost such as real estate taxes between two parties, often in the same ratio as the respective times that the parties are in possession or ownership of property during the fiscal period for which the charge is made or assessed.

Arbitration: The submission of a dispute to an unbiased third person designated by the parties to the controversy, who agree in advance to comply with the award—a decision to be issued after a hearing at which both parties have an opportunity to be heard.

Arguendo: In the course of the argument.

Arraignment: A criminal proceeding at which the defendant is officially called before a court of competent jurisdiction, informed of the offense charged in the complaint, information, indictment, or other charging document, and asked to enter a plea of guilty, not guilty, or as otherwise permitted by law. Depending on the jurisdiction, arraignment may also be the proceeding at which the court determines whether to set bail for the defendant or release the defendant on his or her own recognizance.

Arrest warrant: A written order issued by authority of the state and commanding the seizure of the person named.

Assess: To determine financial worth. To ascertain the amount of damages. To fix and adjust the individual shares to be contributed by several persons toward a common beneficial objective in proportion to the benefit each person will receive. To tax by having qualified experts estimate the value of property by considering the nature of the property, its size, the value of other comparable property, and the proportionate share of services that is used by that property. To levy a charge on the owner of property that has been improved at the expense of the local government unit, such as when sewers or sidewalks are installed.

At issue: A phrase that describes the status of parties in a lawsuit when they make contradictory statements about a point specified in their pleadings.

Audit: A systematic examination of financial or accounting records by a specialized inspector, called an auditor, to verify their accuracy and truthfulness. A hearing during which financial data are investigated for purposes of authentication.

Avoidance: An escape from the consequences of a specific course of action through the use of legally acceptable means. Cancellation; the act of rendering something useless or legally ineffective.

B

Bad faith: The fraudulent deception of another person; the intentional or malicious refusal to perform some duty or contractual obligation.

Bankruptcy: A federally authorized procedure by which a debtor—an individual, corporation, or municipality—is relieved of total liability for its debts by making court-approved arrangements for their partial repayment.

Battery: At common law, an intentional unpermitted act causing harmful or offensive contact with the person of another.

Bench: A forum of justice comprised of the judge or judges of a court. The seat of the court occupied by the judges.

Bench trial: A trial conducted before a judge presiding without a jury.

Bequeath: To dispose of personal property owned by a decedent at the time of death as a gift under the provisions of the decedent's will.

Bestiality: Sexual relations between a human being and an animal.

Beyond a reasonable doubt: The standard that must be met by the prosecution's evidence in a criminal prosecution: that no other logical explanation can be derived from the facts except that the defendant committed the crime, thereby over-coming the presumption that a person is innocent until proven guilty.

Bona fide: [*Latin, In good faith.*] Honest; genuine; actual; authentic; acting without the intention of defrauding.

Bounty hunter: Name for a category of persons who are offered a promised gratuity in return for "hunting" down and capturing or killing a designated target, usually a person or animal.

Brief: A summary of the important points of a longer document. An abstract of a published judicial opinion prepared by a law student as part of an assignment in the case method study of law. A written document drawn up by an attorney for a party in a lawsuit or by a party himself or herself appearing pro se that concisely states the (1) issues of a lawsuit; (2) facts that bring the parties to court; (3) relevant laws that can affect the subject of the dispute; and (4) arguments that explain how the law applies to the particular facts so that the case will be decided in the party's favor.

Bulletin: A printing of public notices and announcements that discloses the progress of matters affecting the general public and which usually includes provisions for public comment. A summarized report of a newsworthy item for immediate release to the public. The official publication of an association, business, or institution.

Burden of proof: A duty placed upon a civil or criminal defendant to prove or disprove a disputed fact.

Burglary: The criminal offense of breaking and entering a building illegally for the purpose of committing a crime therein.

C

Call: To convoke or summon by public announcement; to request the appearance and participation of several people—such as a call of a jury to serve, a roll call, a call of public election, or a call of names of the members of a legislative body.

In contract law, the demand for the payment of money according to the contract terms, usually by formal notice.

As applied to corporation law, the demand of the board of directors that subscribers pay an installment or portion of the amount that is still owed on shares that they have agreed to buy. A call price is the price paid by a corporation for the redemption of its own securities.

In securities, a contract that gives a person the right to demand payment of a certain specified number of shares of stock at a stated price or upon a fixed date.

Capacity: The ability, capability, or fitness to do something; a legal right, power, or competency to perform some act. An ability to comprehend both the nature and consequences of one's acts.

Caption: The standardized heading of a legal instrument, such as a motion or a complaint, which sets forth the names of the parties in controversy, the name of the court, the docket number, and the name of the action.

Cartel: A combination of producers of any product joined together to control its production, sales, and price, so as to obtain a monopoly and restrict competition in any particular industry or commodity. Cartels exist primarily in Europe, being illegal in the United States by virtue of antitrust laws. Also, an association by agreement of companies or sections of companies having common interests, designed to prevent extreme or unfair competition and allocate markets, and to promote the interchange of knowledge resulting from scientific and technical research, exchange of patent rights, and standardization of products.

In war, an agreement between two hostile powers for the delivery of prisoners or deserters, or authorizing certain nonhostile intercourse between each other that would otherwise be prevented by the state of war, for example, agreements between enemies for intercommunication by post, telegraph, telephone, or railway.

Case law: Legal principles enunciated and embodied in judicial decisions that are derived from the application of particular areas of law to the facts of individual cases.

Cause of action: The fact or combination of facts that gives a person the right to seek judicial redress or relief against another. Also, the legal theory forming the basis of a lawsuit.

Censorship: The suppression or proscription of speech or writing that is deemed obscene, indecent, or unduly controversial.

Certiorari: [*Latin, To be informed of.*] At common law, an original writ or order issued by the Chancery of King's Bench, commanding officers of inferior courts to submit the record of a cause pending before them to give the party more certain and speedy justice.

A writ that a superior appellate court issues on its discretion to an inferior court, ordering it to produce a certified record of a particular case it has tried, in order to determine whether any irregularities or errors occurred that justify review of the case.

A device by which the Supreme Court of the United States exercises its discretion in selecting the cases it will review.

Chain of custody: The movement and location of physical evidence from the time it is obtained until the time it is presented in court.

Circuit court: A specific tribunal that possesses the legal authority to hear cases within its own geographical territory.

Citation: A paper commonly used in various courts—such as a probate, matrimonial, or traffic court—that is served upon an individual to notify him or her that he or she is required to appear at a specific time and place.

Reference to a legal authority—such as a case, constitution, or treatise—where particular information may be found.

Civil action: A lawsuit brought to enforce, redress, or protect rights of private litigants (the plaintiffs and the defendants); not a criminal proceeding.

Claim for relief: The section of a modern complaint that states the redress sought from a court by a person who initiates a lawsuit.

Class action: A lawsuit that allows a large number of people with a common interest in a matter to sue or be sued as a group.

Clause: A section, phrase, paragraph, or segment of a legal document, such as a contract, deed, will, or constitution, that relates to a particular point.

Coercion: The intimidation of a victim to compel the individual to do some act against his or her will by the use of psychological pressure, physical force, or threats. The crime on intentionally and unlawfully restraining another's freedom by threatening to commit a crime, accusing the victim of a crime, disclosing any secret that would seriously impair the victim's reputation in the community, or by performing or refusing to perform an official action lawfully requested by the victim, or by causing an official to do so.

A defense asserted in a criminal prosecution that a person who committed a crime did not do so of his or her own free will, but only because the individual was compelled by another through the use of physical force or threat of immediate serious bodily injury or death.

Cognizable: The adjective "cognizable" has two distinct (and unrelated) applications within the field of law. A cognizable claim or controversy is one that meets the basic criteria of viability for being tried or adjudicated before a particular tribunal. The term means that the claim or controversy is within the power or jurisdiction of a particular court to adjudicate. Conversely, a "cognizable group" of jurors or potential jurors refers to that common trait or characteristic among them that is recognized as distinguishing them from others, such as race, ethnicity, and gender. Trial counsel are generally prohibited from eliminating jurors who are in the same cognizable group as that of a party or litigant through discriminatory peremptory challenges when that distinction is the basis for the challenge. In *Batson v. Kentucky*, 476 U.S. 79, 106 S.Ct. 1712, 90 L.Ed.2d 69, 54 USLW 4425 (U.S.Ky., Apr 30, 1986) (NO. 84-6263), the U.S. Supreme Court ruled that prosecutors may not use peremptory challenges to exclude African Americans from a jury solely on the basis of race. Over the years, other cases have expanded the scope of protected or "cognizable groups" of jurors to include gender, religion, and socioeconomic status.

Commerce clause: The provision of the U.S. Constitution that gives Congress exclusive power over trade activities between the states and with foreign countries and Indian tribes.

Competent: Possessing the necessary reasoning abilities or legal qualifications; qualified; capable; sufficient.

Complainant: A plaintiff; a person who commences a civil lawsuit against another, known as the defendant, in order to remedy an alleged wrong. An individual who files a written accusation with the police charging a suspect with the commission of a crime and providing facts to support the allegation and which results in the criminal prosecution of the suspect.

Concurrent: Simultaneous; converging; of equal or joint authority.

Confrontation: A fundamental right of a defendant in a criminal action to come face to face with an adverse witness in the court's presence so the defendant has a fair chance to object to the testimony of the witness and the opportunity to cross-examine the witness.

Consent: Voluntary acquiescence to the proposal of another; the act or result of reaching an accord; a concurrence of minds; actual willingness that an act or an infringement of an interest shall occur.

Conspiracy: An agreement between two or more persons to engage jointly in an unlawful or criminal act, or an act that is innocent in itself but becomes unlawful when done by the combination of actors.

Constitutional law: The written text of the state and federal constitutions. The body of judicial PRECEDENT that has gradually developed through a process in which courts interpret, apply, and explain the meaning of particular constitutional provisions and principles during a legal proceeding. Executive, legislative, and judicial actions that conform with the norms prescribed by a constitutional provision.

Contempt: An act of deliberate disobedience or disregard for the laws, regulations, or decorum of a public authority, such as a court or legislative body.

Contest: To defend against an adverse claim made in a court by a plaintiff or a prosecutor; to challenge a position asserted in a judicial proceeding, as to contest the probate of a will.

Controversy: An actual dispute between individuals who seek judicial resolution of their grievances that have arisen from a conflict of their alleged legal rights.

Conveyance: The transfer of ownership or interest in real property from one person to another by a document, such as a deed, lease, or mortgage.

Copyright: An intangible right granted by statute to the author or originator of certain literary or artistic productions, whereby, for a limited period, the exclusive privilege is given to the person to make copies of the same for publication and sale.

Corollary: A consequence or result that can be logically drawn from the existence of a set of facts by the exercise of common sense and reason.

Corpus: [*Latin, Body, aggregate, or mass.*].

Corroborate: To support or enhance the believability of a fact or assertion by the presentation of additional information that confirms the truthfulness of the item.

Counsel: An attorney or lawyer. The rendition of advice and guidance concerning a legal matter, contemplated form of argument, claim, or action.

Count: In common-law pleading or code pleading, the initial statements made by a plaintiff that set forth a cause of action to commence a civil lawsuit; the different points of a plaintiff's declaration, each of which constitute a basis for relief. In criminal procedure, one of several parts or charges of an indictment, each accusing the defendant of a different offense.

Court of Appeal: An intermediate federal judicial tribunal of review that is found in thirteen judicial districts, called circuits, in the United States.

A state judicial tribunal that reviews a decision rendered by an inferior tribunal to determine whether it made errors that warrant the reversal of its judgment.

Court opinion: A statement that is prepared by a judge or court announcing the decision after a case is tried; includes a summary of the facts, a recitation of the applicable law and how it relates to the facts, the rationale supporting the decision, and a judgment; and is usually presented in writing, though occasionally an oral opinion is rendered.

Credibility: Believability. The major legal application of the term *credibility* relates to the testimony of a witness or party during a trial. Testimony must be both competent and credible if it is to be accepted by the trier of fact as proof of an issue being litigated.

Criminal law: A body of rules and statutes that defines conduct prohibited by the government because it threatens and harms public safety and welfare and that establishes punishment to be imposed for the commission of such acts.

Cross-examination: The questioning of a witness or party during a trial hearing, or deposition by the party opposing the one who asked the person to testify in order to evaluate the truth of that person's testimony, to develop the testimony further, or to accomplish any other objective. The interrogation of a witness or party by the party opposed to the one who called the witness or party, upon a subject raised during direct examination—the initial questioning of a witness or party—on the merits of that testimony.

Cruel and unusual punishment: Such punishment as would amount to torture or barbarity, and cruel and degrading punishment not known to the common law, or any fine, penalty, confinement, or treatment so disproportionate to the offense as to shock the moral sense of the community.

Culpable: Blameworthy; involving the commission of a fault or the breach of a duty imposed by law.

Custodial interrogation: Questioning initiated by law enforcement officers after a person is taken into custody or otherwise deprived of his or her freedom in any significant way, thus requiring that the person be advised of his or her constitutional rights.

D

Deadly force: An amount of force that is likely to cause either serious bodily injury or death to another person.

Debtor: One who owes a debt or the performance of an obligation to another, who is called the creditor; one who may be compelled to pay a claim or demand; anyone liable on a claim, whether due or to become due.

In bankruptcy law, a person who files a voluntary petition or person against whom an involuntary petition is filed. A person or municipality concerning which a bankruptcy case has been commenced.

Decision on the merits: An ultimate determination rendered by a court in an action that concludes the status of legal rights contested in a controversy and precludes a later lawsuit on the same cause of action by the parties to the original lawsuit.

Declaratory judgment: Statutory remedy for the determination of a justiciable controversy where the plaintiff is in doubt as to his or her legal rights. A binding adjudication of the rights and status of litigants even though no consequential relief is awarded.

Defamation: Any intentional false communication, either written or spoken, that harms a person's reputation; decreases the respect, regard, or confidence in which a person is held; or induces disparaging, hostile, or disagreeable opinions or feelings against a person.

Defendant: The person defending or denying; the party against whom relief or recovery is sought in an action or suit, or the accused in a criminal case.

Deliberate: Willful; purposeful; determined after thoughtful evaluation of all relevant factors; dispassionate. To act with a particular intent, which is derived from a careful consideration of factors that influence the choice to be made.

Deny: To refuse to acknowledge something; to disclaim connection with or responsibility for an action or statement. To deny someone of a legal right is to deprive him or her of that right.

Deposition: The testimony of a party or witness in a civil or criminal proceeding taken before trial, usually in an attorney's office.

Detention: The act of keeping back, restraining, or withholding, either accidentally or by design, a person or thing.

Dicta: Opinions of a judge that do not embody the resolution or determination of the specific case before the court. Expressions in a court's opinion that go beyond the facts before the court and therefore are individual views of the author of the opinion and not binding in subsequent cases as legal precedent. The plural of *dictum*.

Diminished capacity: This doctrine recognizes that although, at the time the offense was committed, an accused was not suffering from a mental disease or defect sufficient to exonerate him or her from all criminal responsibility, the accused's mental capacity may have been diminished by intoxication, trauma, or mental disease so that he or she did not possess the specific mental state or intent essential to the particular offense charged.

Direct evidence: Evidence in the form of testimony from a witness who actually saw, heard, or touched the subject of questioning. Evidence that, if believed, proves existence of the fact in issue without inference or presumption. That means of proof which tends to show the existence of a fact in question, without the intervention of the proof of any other fact, and which is distinguished from circumstantial evidence, often called *indirect*.

Evidence that directly proves a fact, without an inference or presumption, and which in itself, if true, conclusively establishes that fact.

Directed verdict: A procedural device whereby the decision in a case is taken out of the hands of the jury by the judge.

Discharge: To liberate or free; to terminate or extinguish. A discharge is the act or instrument by which a contract or agreement is ended. A mortgage is discharged if it has been carried out to the full extent originally contemplated or terminated prior to total execution.

Discharge also means to release, as from legal confinement in prison or the military service, or from some legal obligation such as jury duty, or the payment of debts by a person who is bankrupt. The document that indicates that an individual has been legally released from the military service is called a discharge.

Discovery: A category of procedural devices employed by a party to a civil or criminal action, prior to trial, to require the adverse party to disclose information that is essential for the preparation of the requesting party's case and that the other party alone knows or possesses.

Dismissal: A discharge of an individual or corporation from employment. The disposition of a civil or criminal proceeding or a claim or charge made therein by a court order without a trial or prior to its completion which, in effect, is a denial of the relief sought by the commencement of the action.

Dissent: An explicit disagreement by one or more judges with the decision of the majority on a case before them.

Diversity of citizenship: A phrase used with reference to the jurisdiction of the federal courts which, under the U.S. Constitution, Art. III, § 2, extends to cases between citizens of different states designating the condition existing when the party on one side of a lawsuit is a citizen of one state and the party on the other side is a citizen of another state, or between a citizen of a state and an alien. The requisite jurisdictional amount must, in addition, be met.

Doctrine: A legal rule, tenet, theory, or principle. A political policy.

Double jeopardy: A second prosecution for the same offense after acquittal or conviction or multiple punishments for same offense. The evil sought to be avoided by prohibiting double jeopardy is double trial and double conviction, not necessarily double punishment.

Due process of law: A fundamental, constitutional guarantee that all legal proceedings will be fair and that one will be given notice of the proceedings and an opportunity to be heard before the government acts to take away one's life, liberty, or property. Also, a constitutional guarantee that a law shall not be unreasonable, arbitrary, or capricious.

E

Edict: A decree or law of major import promulgated by a king, queen, or other sovereign of a government.

Element: A material factor; a basic component.

Eminent domain: The power to take private property for public use by a state, municipality, or private person or corporation authorized to exercise functions of public character, following the payment of just compensation to the owner of that property.

En banc: [*Latin, French. In the bench.*] Full bench. Refers to a session where the entire membership of the court will participate in the decision rather than the regular quorum. In other countries, it is common for a court to have more members than are usually necessary to hear an appeal. In the United States, the Circuit Courts of Appeal usually sit in panels of judges but for important cases may expand the bench to a larger number, when the judges are said to be sitting *en banc*. Similarly, only one of the judges of the U.S. Tax Court will typically hear and decide on a tax controversy. However, when the issues involved are unusually novel or of wide impact, the case will be heard and decided by the full court sitting *en banc*.

Enjoin: To direct, require, command, or admonish.

Entity: A real being; existence. An organization or being that possesses separate existence for tax purposes. Examples would be corporations, partnerships, estates, and trusts. The accounting entity for which accounting statements are prepared may not be the same as the entity defined by law.

Entity includes corporation and foreign corporation; not-for-profit corporation; profit and not-for-profit unincorporated association; business trust, estate, partnership, trust, and two or more persons having a joint or common economic interest; and state, U.S., and foreign governments.

An existence apart, such as a corporation in relation to its stockholders.

Entity includes person, estate, trust, governmental unit.

Enumerated: This term is often used in law as equivalent to *mentioned specifically, designated,* or *expressly named or granted;* as in speaking of enumerated governmental powers, items of property, or articles in a tariff schedule.

Equal protection: The constitutional guarantee that no person or class of persons shall be denied the same protection of the laws that is enjoyed by other persons or other classes in like circumstances in their lives, liberty, property, and pursuit of happiness.

Escrow: Something of value, such as a deed, stock, money, or written instrument, that is put into the custody of a third person by its owner, a grantor, an obligor, or a promisor, to be retained until the occurrence of a contingency or performance of a condition.

Et al.: An abbreviated form of *et alia*, Latin for "and others." When affixed after the name of a person, *et al.* indicates that additional persons are acting in the same manner, such as several plaintiffs or grantors.

Et seq.: An abbreviation for the Latin *et sequentes* or *et sequentia*, meaning "and the following."

Ex parte: [*Latin, On one side only.*] Done by, for, or on the application of one party alone.

Executive privilege: The right of the president of the United States to withhold information from Congress or the courts.

Expert testimony: Testimony about a scientific, technical, or professional issue given by a person qualified to testify because of familiarity with the subject or special training in the field.

Extortion: The obtaining of property from another induced by wrongful use of actual or threatened force, violence, or fear, or under color of official right.

F

False imprisonment: The illegal confinement of one individual against his or her will by another individual in such a manner as to violate the confined individual's right to be free from restraint of movement.

Felony: A serious crime, characterized under federal law and many state statutes as any offense punishable by death or imprisonment in excess of one year.

Fiduciary: An individual in whom another has placed the utmost trust and confidence to manage and protect property or money. The relationship wherein one person has an obligation to act for another's benefit.

Forensic: Belonging to courts of justice.

Fraud: A false representation of a matter of fact—whether by words or by conduct, by false or misleading allegations, or by concealment of what should have been disclosed—that deceives and is intended to deceive another so that the individual will act upon it to her or his legal injury.

Fruit of the poisonous tree: The principle that proscribes the use of evidence directly derived from an illegal search and seizure.

G

General Welfare: The concern of the government for the health, peace, morality, and safety of its citizens.

Gerrymander: The process of dividing a particular state or territory into election districts in such a manner as to accomplish an unlawful purpose, such as to give one party a greater advantage.

Good faith: Honesty; a sincere intention to deal fairly with others.

Grand jury: A panel of citizens that is convened by a court to decide whether it is appropriate for the government to indict (proceed with a prosecution against) someone suspected of a crime.

Grand larceny: A category of larceny—the offense of illegally taking the property of another—in which the value of the property taken is greater than that set for petit larceny.

Guardian: A person lawfully invested with the power, and charged with the obligation, of taking care of and managing the property and rights of a person who, because of age, understanding, or self-control, is considered incapable of administering his or her own affairs.

Guardian ad litem: A guardian appointed by the court to represent the interests of infants, the unborn, or incompetent persons in legal actions.

Guilty: Blameworthy; culpable; having committed a tort or crime; devoid of innocence.

H

Habeas corpus: [*Latin, You have the body.*] A writ (court order) that commands an individual or a government official who has restrained another to produce the prisoner at a designated time and place so that the court can determine the legality of custody and decide whether to order the prisoner's release.

Harmless error: A legal doctrine in criminal law that allows verdicts to stand without new trials being ordered despite errors of law at trial as long as all errors were insufficient to affect the final outcome. Rule 52(a) of the Federal Code of Criminal Procedure explains it as, "Any error, defect, irregularity or variance which does not affect substantial rights shall be disregarded."

Hearsay: A statement made out of court that is offered in court as evidence to prove the truth of the matter asserted.

Homestead: The dwelling house and its adjoining land where a family resides. Technically, and pursuant to the modern homestead exemption laws, an artificial estate in land, created to protect the possession and enjoyment of the owner against the claims of creditors by preventing the sale of the property for payment of the owner's debts so long as the land is occupied as a home.

House arrest: Confinement to one's home or another specified location instead of incarceration in a jail or prison.

I

I.e.: An abbreviation for the Latin *id est*, "that is to say, meaning."

Identity theft: Identity theft is the assumption of a person's identity in order, for instance, to obtain credit; to obtain credit cards from banks and retailers; to steal money from existing accounts; to rent apartments or storage units; to apply for loans; or to establish accounts using another's name.

Immunity: Exemption from performing duties that the law generally requires other citizens to perform, or from a penalty or burden that the law generally places on other citizens.

Impartial: Favoring neither; disinterested; treating all alike; unbiased; equitable, fair, and just.

Impeach: To accuse; to charge a liability upon; to sue. To dispute, disparage, deny, or contradict; as in to impeach a judgment or decree, or impeach a witness; or as used in the rule that a jury cannot *impeach its verdict*. To proceed against a public officer for crime or misfeasance, before a proper court, by the presentation of a written accusation called articles of impeachment.

In lieu of: Instead of; in place of; in substitution of. It does not mean *in addition to*.

Independent counsel: An attorney appointed by the federal government to investigate and prosecute federal government officials.

Indicia: Signs; indications. Circumstances that point to the existence of a given fact as probable, but not certain. For example, *indicia of partnership* are any circumstances which would induce the belief that a given person was in reality, though not technically, a member of a given firm.

Inference: In the law of evidence, a truth or proposition drawn from another that is supposed or admitted to be true. A process of reasoning by which a fact or proposition sought to be established is deduced as a logical consequence from other facts, or a state of facts, already proved or admitted. A logical and reasonable conclusion of a fact not presented by direct evidence but which, by process of logic and reason, a trier of fact may conclude exists from the established facts. Inferences are deductions or conclusions that with reason and common sense lead the jury to draw from facts which have been established by the evidence in the case.

Injunction: A court order by which an individual is required to perform or is restrained from performing a particular act. A writ framed according to the circumstances of the individual case.

Injury: A comprehensive term for any wrong or harm done by one individual to another individual's body, rights, reputation, or property. Any interference with an individual's legally protected interest.

Innocent: Absent guilt; acting in good faith with no knowledge of defects, objections, or inculpative circumstances.

Insanity defense: A defense asserted by an accused in a criminal prosecution to avoid liability for the commission of a crime because, at the time of the crime, the person did not appreciate the nature or quality or wrongfulness of the acts.

Intellectual property: Intangible rights protecting the products of human intelligence and creation, such as copyrightable works, patented inventions, trademarks, trade secrets, and rights against unfair competition. Although largely governed by federal law, state law also governs some aspects of intellectual property.

Intent: A determination to perform a particular act or to act in a particular manner for a specific reason; an aim or design; a resolution to use a certain means to reach an end.

International law: The body of law governing the legal relations between states or nations.

Interpretation: The art or process of determining the intended meaning of a written document, such as a constitution, statute, contract, deed, or will.

Involuntary manslaughter: The act of unlawfully killing another human being unintentionally.

Irrelevant: Unrelated or inapplicable to the matter in issue.

J

Joinder: The union in one lawsuit of multiple parties who have the same rights or against whom rights are claimed as coplaintiffs or codefendants. The combination in one lawsuit of two or more causes of action, or grounds for relief. At common law the acceptance by opposing parties that a particular issue is in dispute.

Joint and several liability: A designation of liability by which members of a group are either individually or mutually responsible to a party in whose favor a judgment has been awarded.

Joint venture: An association of two or more individuals or companies engaged in a solitary business enterprise for profit without actual partnership or incorporation; also called a joint adventure.

Judgment: A decision by a court or other tribunal that resolves a controversy and determines the rights and obligations of the parties.

Judicial assistance: Aid offered by the judicial tribunals of one state to the judicial tribunals of a second state.

Judicial review: A court's authority to examine an executive or legislative act and to invalidate that act if it is contrary to constitutional principles.

Jurisprudence: From the Latin term *juris prudentia*, which means "the study, knowledge, or science of law"; in the United States, more broadly associated with the philosophy of law.

Justiciable: Capable of being decided by a court.

Justification: A sufficient or acceptable excuse or explanation made in court for an act that is otherwise unlawful; the showing of an adequate reason, in court, why a defendant committed the offense for which he or she is accused that would serve to relieve the defendant of liability.

A legal excuse for the performance or nonperformance of a particular act that is the basis for exemption from guilt. A classic example is the excuse of self-defense offered as justification for the commission of a murder.

K

Kickback: The seller's return of part of the purchase price of an item to a buyer or buyer's representative for the purpose of inducing a purchase or improperly influencing future purchases.

L

Land grant: A conveyance of public property to a subordinate government or corporation; a muniment of title issued by a state or government for the donation of some part of the public domain.

Law of nations: The body of customary rules that determine the rights and that regulate the intercourse of independent countries in peace and war.

Lease: A contractual agreement by which one party conveys an estate in property to another party, for a limited period, subject to various conditions, in exchange for something of value, but still retains ownership.

Leaseback: A transaction whereby land is sold and subsequently rented by the seller from the purchaser who is the new owner.

Legislative history: The discussions and documents, including committee reports, hearings, and floor debates, surrounding and preceding the enactment of a law.

Levy: To assess; raise; execute; exact; tax; collect; gather; take up; seize. Thus, to levy a tax; to levy a nuisance; to levy a fine; to levy war; to levy an execution, *i.e.*, to levy or collect a sum of money on an execution.

A seizure. The obtaining of money by legal process through seizure and sale of property; the raising of the money for which an execution has been issued.

Liability: A comprehensive legal term that describes the condition of being actually or potentially subject to a legal obligation.

Lien: A right given to another by the owner of property to secure a debt, or one created by law in favor of certain creditors.

Liquidation: The collection of assets belonging to a debtor to be applied to the discharge of his or her outstanding debts.

A type of proceeding pursuant to federal bankruptcy law by which certain property of a debtor is taken into custody by a trustee to be sold, the proceeds to be distributed to the debtor's creditors in satisfaction of their claims.

The settlement of the financial affairs of a business or individual through the sale of all assets and the distribution of the proceeds to creditors, heirs, or other parties with a legal claim.

Living will: A written document that allows a patient to give explicit instructions about medical treatment to be administered when the patient is terminally ill or permanently unconscious; also called an advance directive.

Loophole: An omission or ambiguity in a legal document that allows the intent of the document to be evaded.

M

Magistrate: Any individual who has the power of a public civil officer or inferior judicial officer, such as a justice of the peace.

Maintenance: Unauthorized intervention by a nonparty in a lawsuit, in the form of financial or other support and assistance to prosecute or defend the litigation. The preservation of an asset or of a condition of property by upkeep and necessary repairs.

A periodic monetary sum paid by one spouse for the benefit of the other upon separation or the dissolution of marriage; also called alimony or spousal support.

Malfeasance: The commission of an act that is unequivocally illegal or completely wrongful.

Malice: The intentional commission of a wrongful act, absent justification, with the intent to cause harm to others; conscious violation of the law that injures another individual; a mental state indicating a disposition in disregard of social duty and a tendency toward malfeasance.

Mandamus: [*Latin, We command.*] A writ or order that is issued from a court of superior jurisdiction that commands an inferior tribunal, corporation, municipal corporation, or individual to perform, or refrain from performing, a particular act, the performance or omission of which is required by law as an obligation.

Manslaughter: The unjustifiable, inexcusable, and intentional killing of a human being without deliberation, premeditation, and malice. The unlawful killing of a human being without any deliberation, which may be involuntary, in the commission of a lawful act without due caution and circumspection.

Marital communications privilege: The right given to a husband and wife to refuse to testify in a trial as to confidential statements made to each other within and during the framework of their spousal relationship.

Master: An individual who hires employees or servants to perform services and who directs the manner in which such services are performed.

A court officer appointed by a judge to perform such jobs as examining witnesses, taking testimony, computing damages, or taking oaths, affidavits, or acknowledgments of deeds.

Matter of law: That which is determined or ascertained through the use of statutes, rules, court decisions, and interpretations of legal principles.

Maxim: A broad statement of principle, the truth and reasonableness of which are self-evident. A rule of equity, the system of justice that complements the common law.

Mayhem: Mayhem at common law required a type of injury that permanently rendered the victim less able to fight offensively or defensively; it might be accomplish either by the removal of (dismemberment), or by the disablement of, some bodily member useful in fighting. Today, by statute, permanent disfigurement has been added; and as to dismemberment and disablement, there is no longer a requirement that the member have military significance. In many states the crime of mayhem is treated as aggravated assault.

Meeting of creditors: One of the first steps in federal bankruptcy proceedings whereby the creditors of a debtor meet in court to present their claims against him or her and a trustee is named to handle the application of the debtor's assets to pay his or her debts.

Merits: The strict legal rights of the parties to a lawsuit.

Mitigating circumstances: Circumstances that may be considered by a court in determining culpability of a defendant or the extent of damages to be awarded to a plaintiff. Mitigating circumstances do not justify or excuse an offense but may reduce the severity of a charge. Similarly, a recognition of mitigating circumstances to reduce a damage award does not imply that the damages were not suffered but that they have been partially ameliorated.

Money laundering: The process of taking the proceeds of criminal activity and making them appear legal.

Moratorium: A suspension of activity or an authorized period of delay or waiting. A moratorium is sometimes agreed upon by the interested parties, or it may be authorized or imposed by operation of law. The term also is used to denote a period of time during which the law authorizes a delay in payment of debts or performance of some other legal obligation. This type of moratorium is most often invoked during times of distress, such as war or natural disaster.

Murder: The unlawful killing of another human being without justification or excuse.

N

Naturalization: The process under federal law whereby a foreign-born person may be granted citizenship. In order to qualify for naturalization, an applicant must meet a number of statutory requirements, including those related to residency, literacy, and education, as well as an exhibition of "good moral character" and a demonstration of an attachment to constitutional principles upon which the United States is based.

Navigable waters: Waters that provide a channel for commerce and transportation of people and goods.

North american free trade agreement: A trade agreement between the United States, Canada, and Mexico, which took effect January 1, 1994. Its purpose is to increase the efficiency and fairness of trade between the three nations.

Null: Of no legal validity, force, or effect; nothing.

O

Objection: A formal attestation or declaration of disapproval concerning a specific point of law or procedure during the course of a trial; a statement indicating disagreement with a judge's ruling.

Obscene: Offensive to recognized standards of decency.

Obscenity: The character or quality of being obscene; an act, utterance, or item tending to corrupt the public morals by its indecency or lewdness.

Of Counsel: A term commonly applied in the practice of law to an attorney who has been employed to aid in the preparation and management of a particular case but who is not the principal attorney in the action.

One person, one vote: The principle that all citizens, regardless of where they reside in a state, are entitled to equal legislative representation.

Open court: Common law requires a trial in open court; "open court" means a court to which the public has a right to be admitted. This term may mean either a court that has been formally convened and declared open for the transaction of its proper judicial business or a court that is freely open to spectators.

Ordinance: A law, statute, or regulation enacted by a municipal corporation.

Original jurisdiction: The authority of a tribunal to entertain a lawsuit, try it, and set forth a judgment on the law and facts.

Outstanding warrant: An order that has not yet been carried out; an order for which the action commanded has not been taken.

Overrule: The refusal by a judge to sustain an objection set forth by an attorney during a trial, such as an objection to a particular question posed to a witness. To make void, annul, supersede, or reject through a subsequent decision or action.

P

Pander: To pimp; to cater to the gratification of the lust of another. To entice or procure a person, by promises, threats, fraud, or deception to enter any place in which prostitution is practiced for the purpose of prostitution.

Pecuniary: Monetary; relating to money; financial; consisting of money or that which can be valued in money.

Pending: Begun, but not yet completed; during; before the conclusion of; prior to the completion of; unsettled; in the process of adjustment.

Peremptory challenge: The right to challenge a juror without assigning, or being required to assign, a reason for the challenge.

Petition: A written application from a person or persons to some governing body or public official asking that some authority be exercised to grant relief, favors, or privileges.

A formal application made to a court in writing that requests action on a certain matter.

Plurality: The opinion of an appellate court in which more justices join than in any concurring opinion.

The excess of votes cast for one candidate over those votes cast for any other candidate.

Police power: The authority conferred upon the states by the Tenth Amendment to the U.S. Constitution and which the states delegate to their political subdivisions to enact measures to preserve and protect the safety, health, welfare, and morals of the community.

Pornography: The representation in books, magazines, photographs, films, and other media of scenes of sexual behavior that are erotic or lewd and are designed to arouse sexual interest.

Practice: Repeated or customary action; habitual performance; a succession of acts of similar kind; custom; usage. The exercise of any profession.

The form or mode or proceeding in courts of justice for the enforcement of rights or the redress of wrongs, as distinguished from the substantive law that gives the right or denounces the wrong. The form, manner, or order of instituting and conducting an action or other judicial proceeding, through its successive stages to its end, in accordance with the rules and principles laid down by law or by the regulations and precedents of the courts.

Preamble: A clause at the beginning of a constitution or statute explaining the reasons for its enactment and the objectives it seeks to attain.

Preliminary hearing: A proceeding before a judicial officer in which the officer must decide whether a crime was committed, whether the crime occurred within the territorial jurisdiction of the court, and whether there is probable cause to believe that the defendant committed the crime.

Preliminary injunction: A temporary order made by a court at the request of one party that prevents the other party from pursuing a particular course of conduct until the conclusion of a trial on the merits.

Presumption of innocence: A principle that requires the governmment to prove the guilt of a criminal defendant and relieves the defendant of any burden to prove his or her innocence.

Price-fixing: The organized setting of what the public will be charged for certain products or services agreed to by competitors in the marketplace in violation of the Sherman Anti-Trust Act (15 U.S.C.A. § 1 et seq.).

Principal: A source of authority; a sum of a debt or obligation producing interest; the head of a school. In an agency relationship, the principal is the person who gives authority to another, called an agent, to act on his or her behalf. In criminal law, the principal is the chief actor of perpetrator of a crime; those who aid, abet, counsel, command, or induce the commission of a crime may also be principals. In investments and banking, the principal refers to the person for whom a broker executes an order; it may also mean the capital invested or the face amount of a loan.

Privacy: In constitutional law, the right of people to make personal decisions regarding intimate matters; under the common law, the right of people to lead their lives in a manner that is reasonably secluded from public scrutiny, whether such scrutiny comes from a neighbor's prying eyes, an investigator's eavesdropping ears, or a news photographer's intrusive camera; and in statutory law, the right of people to be free from unwarranted drug testing and electronic surveillance.

Privileges and immunities: Concepts contained in the U.S. Constitution that place the citizens of each state on an equal basis with citizens of other states in respect to advantages resulting from citizenship in those states and citizenship in the United States.

Pro se: For one's own behalf; in person. Appearing for oneself, as in the case of one who does not retain a lawyer and appears for himself or herself in court.

Probable cause: Apparent facts discovered through logical inquiry that would lead a reasonably intelligent and prudent person to believe that an accused person has committed a crime, thereby warranting his or her prosecution, or that a cause of action has accrued, justifying a civil lawsuit.

Probate: The court process by which a will is proved valid or invalid. The legal process wherein the estate of a decedent is administered.

Product liability: The responsibility of a manufacturer or vendor of goods to compensate for injury caused by a defective good that it has provided for sale.

Professional responsibility: The obligation of lawyers to adhere to rules of professional conduct.

Proof: The establishment of a fact by the use of evidence. Anything that can make a person believe that a fact or proposition is true or false. It is distinguishable from evidence in that proof is a broad term comprehending everything that may be adduced at a trial, whereas evidence is a narrow term describing certain types of proof that can be admitted at trial.

Protocol: A brief summary; the minutes of a meeting; the etiquette of diplomacy.

Proximate cause: An act from which an injury results as a natural, direct, uninterrupted consequence and without which the injury would not have occurred.

Q

Quid pro quo: [*Latin, What for what or Something for something.*] The mutual consideration that passes between two parties to a contractual agreement, thereby rendering the agreement valid and binding.

Quorum: A majority of an entire body; e.g., a quorum of a legislative assembly.

R

Rape: A criminal offense defined in most states as forcible sexual relations with a person against that person's will.

Re: [Latin, *In the matter of; in the case of.*].

Reasonable doubt: A standard of proof that must be surpassed to convict an accused in a criminal proceeding.

Reasonable time: In the absence of an express or fixed time established by the parties to an agreement or contract (especially one that falls under the purview of the Uniform Commercial Code [UCC]), any time which is not manifestly *unreasonable* under the circumstances. For example, if a contract does not fix a specific time for performance, the law will infer (and impose) a reasonable time for such performance. This is defined as that amount of time which is fairly necessary, conveniently, to do what the contract requires to be done, as soon as circumstances permit. The term "reasonable time" has other (related) applications: UCC 2-206(2) requires that acceptance of an offer be made within a "reasonable time" if no time is specified. The reasonableness or unreasonableness of time used or taken by a party may be the subject of judicial review in light of the nature, purpose, and circumstances of each case. In considering whether there has been unreasonable delay in performance, a court may also consider other factors such as prior dealings between the parties, business routine or custom within the trade, and whether there were any objective manifestations of expectation expressed between the parties.

Recuse: To disqualify or remove oneself as a judge over a particular proceeding because of one's conflict of interest. Recusal, or the judge's act of disqualifying himself or herself from presiding over a proceeding, is based on the maxim that judges are charged with a duty of impartiality in administering justice.

Referendum: The right reserved to the people to approve or reject an act of the legislature, or the right of the people to approve or reject an act of the legislature, or the right of the people to approve or reject legislation that has been referred to them by the legislature.

Relief: Financial assistance provided to the indigent by the government. The redress, or benefit, given by a court to an individual who brings a legal action.

Remand: To send back.

Remedial statute: A law enacted for the purpose of correcting a defect in a prior law, or in order to provide a remedy where none previously existed.

Render: Return; yield; pay or perform, as in charges or services.

Repeal: The annulment or abrogation of a previously existing statute by the enactment of a later law that revokes the former law.

Respondent: In equity practice, the party who answers a bill or other proceeding in equity. The party against whom an appeal or motion, an application for a court order, is instituted and who is required to answer in order to protect his or her interests.

Responsive pleading: A formal declaration by a party in reply to a prior declaration by an opponent.

Restraining order: A command of the court issued upon the filing of an application for an injunction, prohibiting the defendant from performing a threatened act until a hearing on the application can be held.

Retroactive: Having reference to things that happened in the past, prior to the occurrence of the act in question.

Revised statutes: A body of statutes that have been revised, collected, arranged in order, and reenacted as a whole. The legal title of the collection of compiled laws of the United States, as well as some of the individual states.

Right to counsel: The right of a defendant in a criminal action not only to legal representation, but also to *effective* representation.

Robbery: The taking of money or goods in the possession of another, from his or her person or immediate presence, by force or intimidation.

Rule of law: Rule according to law; rule under law; or rule according to a higher law.

S

Sales law: The law relating to the transfer of ownership of property from one person to another for value, which is codified in article 2 of the UNIFORM COMMERCIAL CODE (UCC), a body of law governing mercantile transactions adopted in whole or in part by the states.

Search and seizure: In international law, the right of ships of war, as regulated by treaties, to examine a merchant vessel during war in order to determine whether the ship or its cargo is liable to seizure.

A hunt by law enforcement officials for property or communications believed to be evidence of crime, and the act of taking possession of this property.

Sedition: A revolt or an incitement to revolt against established authority, usually in the form of treason or defamation against government.

Seizure: Forcible possession; a grasping, snatching, or putting in possession.

Self-incrimination: Giving testimony in a trial or other legal proceeding that could subject one to criminal prosecution.

Set aside: To cancel, annul, or revoke a judgment or order.

Severance: The act of dividing, or the state of being divided.

Sodomy: Anal or oral intercourse between human beings, or any sexual relations between a human being and an animal, the act of which may be punishable as a criminal offense.

Sovereign immunity: The legal protection that prevents a sovereign state or person from being sued without consent.

Statute: An act of a legislature that declares, proscribes, or commands something; a specific law, expressed in writing.

Statute of limitations: A type of federal or state law that restricts the time within which legal proceedings may be brought.

Stop and frisk: The situation where a police officer who is suspicious of an individual detains the person and runs his hands lightly over the suspect's outer garments to determine if the person is carrying a concealed weapon.

Strict scrutiny: A standard of judicial review for a challenged policy in which the court presumes the policy to be invalid unless the government can demonstrate a compelling interest to justify the policy.

Sua sponte: [*Latin, Of his or her or its own will; voluntarily.*].

Subject matter jurisdiction: The power of a court to hear and determine cases of the general class to which the proceedings in question belong.

Subpoena: [*Latin, Under penalty.*] A formal document that orders a named individual to appear before a duly authorized body at a fixed time to give testimony.

Summary judgment: A procedural device used during civil litigation to promptly and expeditiously dispose of a case without a trial. It is used when there is no dispute as to the material facts of the case and a party is entitled to judgment as a matter of law.

T

Tangible: Possessing a physical form that can be touched or felt.

Temporary restraining order: A court order that lasts only until the court can hear further evidence.

Tenure: A right, term, or mode of holding or occupying something of value for a period of time.

In feudal law, the principal mode or system by which a person held land from a superior in exchange for the rendition of service and loyalty to the grantor. See also feudalism.

The status given to an educator who has satisfactorily completed teaching for a trial period and is, therefore, protected against summary dismissal by the employer.

A length of time during which an individual has a right to occupy a public or private office.

Term of art: A word or phrase that has special meaning in a particular context.

Terrorism: The unlawful use of force or violence against persons or property in order to coerce or intimate a government or the civilian population in furtherance of political or social objectives.

Title: In property law, a comprehensive term referring to the legal basis of the ownership of property, encompassing real and personal property and intangible and tangible interests therein; also a document serving as evidence of ownership of property, such as the certificate of title to a motor vehicle.

In regard to legislation, the heading or preliminary part of a particular statute that designates the name by which that act is known.

In the law of trademarks, the name of an item that may be used exclusively by an individual for identification purposes to indicate the quality and origin of the item.

Tort law: A body of rights, obligations, and remedies that is applied by courts in civil proceedings to provide relief for persons who have suffered harm from the wrongful acts of others. The person who sustains injury or suffers pecuniary damage as the result of tortious conduct is known as the plaintiff, and the person who is responsible for inflicting the injury and incurs liability for the damage is known as the defendant or tortfeasor.

Tortfeasor: A wrongdoer; an individual who commits a wrongful act that injures another and for which the law provides a legal right to seek relief; a defendant in a civil tort action.

Tortious: Wrongful; conduct of such character as to subject the actor to civil liability under tort law.

U

U.S. Code: A multivolume publication of the text of statutes enacted by Congress.

Undue influence: A judicially created defense to transactions that have been imposed upon weak and vulnerable persons that allows the transactions to be set aside.

Uniform Commercial Code: A general and inclusive group of laws adopted, at least partially, by all the states to further uniformity and fair dealing in business and commercial transactions.

V

Vacate: To annul, set aside, or render void; to surrender possession or occupancy.

Vague: Imprecise; uncertain; indefinite.

Venue: A place, such as the territory from which residents are selected to serve as jurors.

A proper place, such as the correct court to hear a case because it has authority over events that have occurred within a certain geographical area.

Verdict: The formal decision or finding made by a jury concerning the questions submitted to it during a trial. The jury reports the verdict to the court, which generally accepts it.

Versus: [*Latin, Against.*] A designation used in the caption of a lawsuit to indicate the opposite positions taken by the parties.

W

Waive: To intentionally or voluntarily relinquish a known right or engage in conduct warranting an inference that a right has been surrendered.

Wiretapping: A form of electronic eavesdropping accomplished by seizing or overhearing communications by means of a concealed recording or listening device connected to the transmission line.

Without prejudice: Without any loss or waiver of rights or privileges.

Writ: An order issued by a court requiring that something be done or giving authority to do a specified act.

Wrongful death: The taking of the life of an individual resulting from the willful or negligent act of another person or persons.

ABBREVIATIONS

A.	Atlantic Reporter
A. 2d	Atlantic Reporter, Second Series
AA	Alcoholics Anonymous
AAA	American Arbitration Association; Agricultural Adjustment Act of 1933
AALS	Association of American Law Schools
AAPRP	All African People's Revolutionary Party
AARP	American Association of Retired Persons
AAS	American Anti-Slavery Society
ABA	American Bar Association; Architectural Barriers Act of 1968; American Bankers Association
ABC	American Broadcasting Companies, Inc. (formerly American Broadcasting Corporation)
ABM	Antiballistic missile
ABM Treaty	Anti-Ballistic Missile Treaty of 1972
ABVP	Anti-Biased Violence Project
A/C	Account
A.C.	Appeal cases
ACAA	Air Carrier Access Act
ACCA	Armed Career Criminal Act of 1984
ACF	Administration for Children and Families
ACLU	American Civil Liberties Union
ACRS	Accelerated Cost Recovery System
ACS	Agricultural Cooperative Service
ACT	American College Test
Act'g Legal Adv.	Acting Legal Advisor
ACUS	Administrative Conference of the United States
ACYF	Administration on Children, Youth, and Families
A.D. 2d	Appellate Division, Second Series, N.Y.
ADA	Americans with Disabilities Act of 1990
ADAMHA	Alcohol, Drug Abuse, and Mental Health Administration
ADC	Aid to Dependent Children
ADD	Administration on Developmental Disabilities
ADEA	Age Discrimination in Employment Act of 1967
ADL	Anti-Defamation League
ADR	Alternative dispute resolution
AEC	Atomic Energy Commission

AECB	Arms Export Control Board
AEDPA	Antiterrorism and Effective Death Penalty Act
A.E.R.	All England Law Reports
AFA	American Family Association; Alabama Freethought Association
AFB	American Farm Bureau
AFBF	American Farm Bureau Federation
AFDC	Aid to Families with Dependent Children
aff'd per cur.	Affirmed by the court
AFIS	Automated fingerprint identification system
AFL	American Federation of Labor
AFL-CIO	American Federation of Labor and Congress of Industrial Organizations
AFRes	Air Force Reserve
AFSC	American Friends Service Committee
AFSCME	American Federation of State, County, and Municipal Employees
AGRICOLA	Agricultural Online Access
AIA	Association of Insurance Attorneys
AIB	American Institute for Banking
AID	Artificial insemination using a third-party donor's sperm; Agency for International Development
AIDS	Acquired immune deficiency syndrome
AIH	Artificial insemination using the husband's sperm
AIM	American Indian Movement
AIPAC	American Israel Public Affairs Committee
AIUSA	Amnesty International, U.S.A. Affiliate
AJS	American Judicature Society
ALA	American Library Association
Alcoa	Aluminum Company of America
ALEC	American Legislative Exchange Council
ALF	Animal Liberation Front
ALI	American Law Institute
ALJ	Administrative law judge
All E.R.	All England Law Reports
ALO	Agency Liaison
A.L.R.	American Law Reports
ALY	*American Law Yearbook*
AMA	American Medical Association
AMAA	Agricultural Marketing Agreement Act
Am. Dec.	American Decisions
amdt.	Amendment
Amer. St. Papers, For. Rels.	American State Papers, Legislative and Executive Documents of the Congress of the U.S., Class I, Foreign Relations, 1832–1859
AMS	Agricultural Marketing Service
AMVETS	American Veterans (of World War II)
ANA	Administration for Native Americans
Ann. Dig.	Annual Digest of Public International Law Cases
ANRA	American Newspaper Publishers Association
ANSCA	Alaska Native Claims Act
ANZUS	Australia-New Zealand-United States Security Treaty Organization
AOA	Administration on Aging
AOE	Arizonans for Official English
AOL	America Online
AP	Associated Press
APA	Administrative Procedure Act of 1946
APHIS	Animal and Plant Health Inspection Service
App. Div.	Appellate Division Reports, N.Y. Supreme Court

Arb. Trib., U.S.-British	Arbitration Tribunal, Claim Convention of 1853, United States and Great Britain Convention of 1853
Ardcor	American Roller Die Corporation
ARPA	Advanced Research Projects Agency
ARPANET	Advanced Research Projects Agency Network
ARS	Advanced Record System
Art.	Article
ARU	American Railway Union
ASCME	American Federation of State, County, and Municipal Employees
ASCS	Agriculture Stabilization and Conservation Service
ASM	Available Seatmile
ASPCA	American Society for the Prevention of Cruelty to Animals
Asst. Att. Gen.	Assistant Attorney General
AT&T	American Telephone and Telegraph
ATFD	Alcohol, Tobacco and Firearms Division
ATLA	Association of Trial Lawyers of America
ATO	Alpha Tau Omega
ATTD	Alcohol and Tobacco Tax Division
ATU	Alcohol Tax Unit
AUAM	American Union against Militarism
AUM	Animal Unit Month
AZT	Azidothymidine
BAC	Blood alcohol concentration
BALSA	Black-American Law Student Association
BATF	Bureau of Alcohol, Tobacco and Firearms
BBS	Bulletin Board System
BCCI	Bank of Credit and Commerce International
BEA	Bureau of Economic Analysis
Bell's Cr. C.	Bell's English Crown Cases
Bevans	United States Treaties, etc. *Treaties and Other International Agreements of the United States of America, 1776–1949* (compiled under the direction of Charles I. Bevans, 1968–76)
BFOQ	Bona fide occupational qualification
BI	Bureau of Investigation
BIA	Bureau of Indian Affairs; Board of Immigration Appeals
BID	Business improvement district
BJS	Bureau of Justice Statistics
Black.	Black's United States Supreme Court Reports
Blatchf.	Blatchford's United States Circuit Court Reports
BLM	Bureau of Land Management
BLS	Bureau of Labor Statistics
BMD	Ballistic missile defense
BNA	Bureau of National Affairs
BOCA	Building Officials and Code Administrators International
BOP	Bureau of Prisons
BPP	Black Panther Party for Self-defense
Brit. and For.	British and Foreign State Papers
BSA	Boy Scouts of America
BTP	Beta Theta Pi
Burr.	James Burrows, *Report of Cases Argued and Determined in the Court of King's Bench during the Time of Lord Mansfield* (1766–1780)
BVA	Board of Veterans Appeals
c.	Chapter
C^3I	Command, Control, Communications, and Intelligence
C.A.	Court of Appeals
CAA	Clean Air Act
CAB	Civil Aeronautics Board; Corporation for American Banking

CAFE	Corporate average fuel economy
Cal. 2d	California Reports, Second Series
Cal. 3d	California Reports, Third Series
CALR	Computer-assisted legal research
Cal. Rptr.	California Reporter
CAP	Common Agricultural Policy
CARA	Classification and Ratings Administration
CATV	Community antenna television
CBO	Congressional Budget Office
CBS	Columbia Broadcasting System
CBOEC	Chicago Board of Election Commissioners
CCC	Commodity Credit Corporation
CCDBG	Child Care and Development Block Grant of 1990
C.C.D. Pa.	Circuit Court Decisions, Pennsylvania
C.C.D. Va.	Circuit Court Decisions, Virginia
CCEA	Cabinet Council on Economic Affairs
CCP	Chinese Communist Party
CCR	Center for Constitutional Rights
C.C.R.I.	Circuit Court, Rhode Island
CD	Certificate of deposit; compact disc
CDA	Communications Decency Act
CDBG	Community Development Block Grant Program
CDC	Centers for Disease Control and Prevention; Community Development Corporation
CDF	Children's Defense Fund
CDL	Citizens for Decency through Law
CD-ROM	Compact disc read-only memory
CDS	Community Dispute Services
CDW	Collision damage waiver
CENTO	Central Treaty Organization
CEO	Chief executive officer
CEQ	Council on Environmental Quality
CERCLA	Comprehensive Environmental Response, Compensation, and Liability Act of 1980
cert.	*Certiorari*
CETA	Comprehensive Employment and Training Act
C & F	Cost and freight
CFC	Chlorofluorocarbon
CFE Treaty	Conventional Forces in Europe Treaty of 1990
C.F. & I.	Cost, freight, and insurance
C.F.R	Code of Federal Regulations
CFNP	Community Food and Nutrition Program
CFTA	Canadian Free Trade Agreement
CFTC	Commodity Futures Trading Commission
Ch.	Chancery Division, English Law Reports
CHAMPVA	Civilian Health and Medical Program at the Veterans Administration
CHEP	Cuban/Haitian Entrant Program
CHINS	Children in need of supervision
CHIPS	Child in need of protective services
Ch.N.Y.	Chancery Reports, New York
Chr. Rob.	Christopher Robinson, *Reports of Cases Argued and Determined in the High Court of Admiralty* (1801–1808)
CIA	Central Intelligence Agency
CID	Commercial Item Descriptions
C.I.F.	Cost, insurance, and freight
CINCNORAD	Commander in Chief, North American Air Defense Command
C.I.O.	Congress of Industrial Organizations

CIPE	Center for International Private Enterprise
C.J.	Chief justice
CJIS	Criminal Justice Information Services
C.J.S.	Corpus Juris Secundum
Claims Arb. under Spec. Conv., Nielsen's Rept.	Frederick Kenelm Nielsen, *American and British Claims Arbitration under the Special Agreement Concluded between the United States and Great Britain, August 18, 1910* (1926)
CLASP	Center for Law and Social Policy
CLE	Center for Law and Education; Continuing Legal Education
CLEO	Council on Legal Education Opportunity; Chief Law Enforcement Officer
CLP	Communist Labor Party of America
CLS	Christian Legal Society; critical legal studies (movement); Critical Legal Studies (membership organization)
C.M.A.	Court of Military Appeals
CMEA	Council for Mutual Economic Assistance
CMHS	Center for Mental Health Services
C.M.R.	Court of Military Review
CNN	Cable News Network
CNO	Chief of Naval Operations
CNOL	Consolidated net operating loss
CNR	Chicago and Northwestern Railway
CO	Conscientious Objector
C.O.D.	Cash on delivery
COGP	Commission on Government Procurement
COINTELPRO	Counterintelligence Program
Coke Rep.	Coke's English King's Bench Reports
COLA	Cost-of-living adjustment
COMCEN	Federal Communications Center
Comp.	Compilation
Conn.	Connecticut Reports
CONTU	National Commission on New Technological Uses of Copyrighted Works
Conv.	Convention
COPA	Child Online Protection Act (1998)
COPS	Community Oriented Policing Services
Corbin	Arthur L. Corbin, *Corbin on Contracts: A Comprehensive Treatise on the Rules of Contract Law* (1950)
CORE	Congress on Racial Equality
Cox's Crim. Cases	Cox's Criminal Cases (England)
COYOTE	Call Off Your Old Tired Ethics
CPA	Certified public accountant
CPB	Corporation for Public Broadcasting, the
CPI	Consumer Price Index
CPPA	Child Pornography Prevention Act
CPSC	Consumer Product Safety Commission
Cranch	Cranch's United States Supreme Court Reports
CRF	Constitutional Rights Foundation
CRR	Center for Constitutional Rights
CRS	Congressional Research Service; Community Relations Service
CRT	Critical race theory
CSA	Community Services Administration
CSAP	Center for Substance Abuse Prevention
CSAT	Center for Substance Abuse Treatment
CSC	Civil Service Commission
CSCE	Conference on Security and Cooperation in Europe
CSG	Council of State Governments

CSO	Community Service Organization
CSP	Center for the Study of the Presidency
C-SPAN	Cable-Satellite Public Affairs Network
CSRS	Cooperative State Research Service
CSWPL	Center on Social Welfare Policy and Law
CTA	*Cum testamento annexo* (with the will attached)
Ct. Ap. D.C.	Court of Appeals, District of Columbia
Ct. App. No. Ireland	Court of Appeals, Northern Ireland
Ct. Cl.	Court of Claims, United States
Ct. Crim. Apps.	Court of Criminal Appeals (England)
Ct. of Sess., Scot.	Court of Sessions, Scotland
CTI	Consolidated taxable income
CU	Credit union
CUNY	City University of New York
Cush.	Cushing's Massachusetts Reports
CWA	Civil Works Administration; Clean Water Act
DACORB	Department of the Army Conscientious Objector Review Board
Dall.	Dallas's Pennsylvania and United States Reports
DAR	Daughters of the American Revolution
DARPA	Defense Advanced Research Projects Agency
DAVA	Defense Audiovisual Agency
D.C.	United States District Court; District of Columbia
D.C. Del.	United States District Court, Delaware
D.C. Mass.	United States District Court, Massachusetts
D.C. Md.	United States District Court, Maryland
D.C.N.D.Cal.	United States District Court, Northern District, California
D.C.N.Y.	United States District Court, New York
D.C.Pa.	United States District Court, Pennsylvania
DCS	Deputy Chiefs of Staff
DCZ	District of the Canal Zone
DDT	Dichlorodiphenyltricloroethane
DEA	Drug Enforcement Administration
Decl. Lond.	Declaration of London, February 26, 1909
Dev. & B.	Devereux & Battle's North Carolina Reports
DFL	Minnesota Democratic-Farmer-Labor
DFTA	Department for the Aging
Dig. U.S. Practice in Intl. Law	Digest of U.S. Practice in International Law
Dist. Ct.	D.C. United States District Court, District of Columbia
D.L.R.	Dominion Law Reports (Canada)
DMCA	Digital Millennium Copyright Act
DNA	Deoxyribonucleic acid
Dnase	Deoxyribonuclease
DNC	Democratic National Committee
DOC	Department of Commerce
DOD	Department of Defense
DODEA	Department of Defense Education Activity
Dodson	Dodson's Reports, English Admiralty Courts
DOE	Department of Energy
DOER	Department of Employee Relations
DOJ	Department of Justice
DOL	Department of Labor
DOMA	Defense of Marriage Act of 1996
DOS	Disk operating system
DOT	Department of Transportation
DPT	Diphtheria, pertussis, and tetanus
DRI	Defense Research Institute

DSAA	Defense Security Assistance Agency
DUI	Driving under the influence; driving under intoxication
DVD	Digital versatile disc
DWI	Driving while intoxicated
EAHCA	Education for All Handicapped Children Act of 1975
EBT	Examination before trial
E.coli	Escherichia coli
ECPA	Electronic Communications Privacy Act of 1986
ECSC	Treaty of the European Coal and Steel Community
EDA	Economic Development Administration
EDF	Environmental Defense Fund
E.D.N.Y.	Eastern District, New York
EDP	Electronic data processing
E.D. Pa.	Eastern-District, Pennsylvania
EDSC	Eastern District, South Carolina
EDT	Eastern daylight time
E.D. Va.	Eastern District, Virginia
EEC	European Economic Community; European Economic Community Treaty
EEOC	Equal Employment Opportunity Commission
EFF	Electronic Frontier Foundation
EFT	Electronic funds transfer
Eliz.	Queen Elizabeth (Great Britain)
Em. App.	Temporary Emergency Court of Appeals
ENE	Early neutral evaluation
Eng. Rep.	English Reports
EOP	Executive Office of the President
EPA	Environmental Protection Agency; Equal Pay Act of 1963
ERA	Equal Rights Amendment
ERDC	Energy Research and Development Commission
ERISA	Employee Retirement Income Security Act of 1974
ERS	Economic Research Service
ERTA	Economic Recovery Tax Act of 1981
ESA	Endangered Species Act of 1973
ESF	Emergency support function; Economic Support Fund
ESRD	End-Stage Renal Disease Program
ETA	Employment and Training Administration
ETS	Environmental tobacco smoke
et seq.	*Et sequentes* or *et sequentia* ("and the following")
EU	European Union
Euratom	European Atomic Energy Community
Eur. Ct. H.R.	European Court of Human Rights
Ex.	English Exchequer Reports, Welsby, Hurlstone & Gordon
Exch.	Exchequer Reports (Welsby, Hurlstone & Gordon)
Ex Com	Executive Committee of the National Security Council
Eximbank	Export-Import Bank of the United States
F.	Federal Reporter
F. 2d	Federal Reporter, Second Series
FAA	Federal Aviation Administration; Federal Arbitration Act
FAAA	Federal Alcohol Administration Act
FACE	Freedom of Access to Clinic Entrances Act of 1994
FACT	Feminist Anti-Censorship Task Force
FAIRA	Federal Agriculture Improvement and Reform Act of 1996
FAMLA	Family and Medical Leave Act of 1993
Fannie Mae	Federal National Mortgage Association
FAO	Food and Agriculture Organization of the United Nations
FAR	Federal Acquisition Regulations

FAS	Foreign Agricultural Service
FBA	Federal Bar Association
FBI	Federal Bureau of Investigation
FCA	Farm Credit Administration
F. Cas.	Federal Cases
FCC	Federal Communications Commission
FCIA	Foreign Credit Insurance Association
FCIC	Federal Crop Insurance Corporation
FCLAA	Federal Cigarette Labeling and Advertising Act
FCRA	Fair Credit Reporting Act
FCU	Federal credit unions
FCUA	Federal Credit Union Act
FCZ	Fishery Conservation Zone
FDA	Food and Drug Administration
FDIC	Federal Deposit Insurance Corporation
FDPC	Federal Data Processing Center
FEC	Federal Election Commission
FECA	Federal Election Campaign Act of 1971
Fed. Cas.	Federal Cases
FEHA	Fair Employment and Housing Act
FEHBA	Federal Employees Health Benefit Act
FEMA	Federal Emergency Management Agency
FERC	Federal Energy Regulatory Commission
FFB	Federal Financing Bank
FFDC	Federal Food, Drug, and Cosmetics Act
FGIS	Federal Grain Inspection Service
FHA	Federal Housing Administration
FHAA	Fair Housing Amendments Act of 1998
FHWA	Federal Highway Administration
FIA	Federal Insurance Administration
FIC	Federal Information Centers; Federation of Insurance Counsel
FICA	Federal Insurance Contributions Act
FIFRA	Federal Insecticide, Fungicide, and Rodenticide Act
FIP	Forestry Incentives Program
FIRREA	Financial Institutions Reform, Recovery, and Enforcement Act of 1989
FISA	Foreign Intelligence Surveillance Act of 1978
FISC	Foreign Intelligence Surveillance Court of Review
FJC	Federal Judicial Center
FLSA	Fair Labor Standards Act
FMC	Federal Maritime Commission
FMCS	Federal Mediation and Conciliation Service
FmHA	Farmers Home Administration
FMLA	Family and Medical Leave Act of 1993
FNMA	Federal National Mortgage Association, "Fannie Mae"
F.O.B.	Free on board
FOIA	Freedom of Information Act
FOMC	Federal Open Market Committee
FPA	Federal Power Act of 1935
FPC	Federal Power Commission
FPMR	Federal Property Management Regulations
FPRS	Federal Property Resources Service
FR	Federal Register
FRA	Federal Railroad Administration
FRB	Federal Reserve Board
FRC	Federal Radio Commission
F.R.D.	Federal Rules Decisions

FSA	Family Support Act
FSB	Federal'naya Sluzhba Bezopasnosti (the Federal Security Service of Russia)
FSLIC	Federal Savings and Loan Insurance Corporation
FSQS	Food Safety and Quality Service
FSS	Federal Supply Service
F. Supp.	Federal Supplement
FTA	U.S.-Canada Free Trade Agreement of 1988
FTC	Federal Trade Commission
FTCA	Federal Tort Claims Act
FTS	Federal Telecommunications System
FTS2000	Federal Telecommunications System 2000
FUCA	Federal Unemployment Compensation Act of 1988
FUTA	Federal Unemployment Tax Act
FWPCA	Federal Water Pollution Control Act of 1948
FWS	Fish and Wildlife Service
GAL	Guardian ad litem
GAO	General Accounting Office; Governmental Affairs Office
GAOR	General Assembly Official Records, United Nations
GAAP	Generally accepted accounting principles
GA Res.	General Assembly Resolution (United Nations)
GATT	General Agreement on Tariffs and Trade
GCA	Gun Control Act
Gen. Cls. Comm.	General Claims Commission, United States and Panama; General Claims United States and Mexico
Geo. II	King George II (Great Britain)
Geo. III	King George III (Great Britain)
GHB	Gamma-hydroxybutrate
GI	Government Issue
GID	General Intelligence Division
GM	General Motors
GNMA	Government National Mortgage Association, "Ginnie Mae"
GNP	Gross national product
GOP	Grand Old Party (Republican Party)
GOPAC	Grand Old Party Action Committee
GPA	Office of Governmental and Public Affairs
GPO	Government Printing Office
GRAS	Generally recognized as safe
Gr. Br., Crim. Ct. App.	Great Britain, Court of Criminal Appeals
GRNL	Gay Rights-National Lobby
GSA	General Services Administration
Hackworth	Green Haywood Hackworth, *Digest of International Law* (1940–1944)
Hay and Marriott	Great Britain. High Court of Admiralty, *Decisions in the High Court of Admiralty during the Time of Sir George Hay and of Sir James Marriott, Late Judges of That Court* (1801)
HBO	Home Box Office
HCFA	Health Care Financing Administration
H.Ct.	High Court
HDS	Office of Human Development Services
Hen. & M.	Hening & Munford's Virginia Reports
HEW	Department of Health, Education, and Welfare
HFCA	Health Care Financing Administration
HGI	Handgun Control, Incorporated
HHS	Department of Health and Human Services
Hill	Hill's New York Reports
HIRE	Help through Industry Retraining and Employment
HIV	Human immunodeficiency virus

H.L.	House of Lords Cases (England)
H. Lords	House of Lords (England)
HMO	Health Maintenance Organization
HNIS	Human Nutrition Information Service
Hong Kong L.R.	Hong Kong Law Reports
How.	Howard's United States Supreme Court Reports
How. St. Trials	Howell's English State Trials
HUAC	House Un-American Activities Committee
HUD	Department of Housing and Urban Development
Hudson, Internatl. Legis.	Manley Ottmer Hudson, ed., *International Legislation: A Collection of the Texts of Multipartite International Instruments of General Interest Beginning with the Covenant of the League of Nations* (1931)
Hudson, World Court Reps.	Manley Ottmer Hudson, ea., *World Court Reports* (1934–)
Hun	Hun's New York Supreme Court Reports
Hunt's Rept.	Bert L. Hunt, *Report of the American and Panamanian General Claims Arbitration* (1934)
IAEA	International Atomic Energy Agency
IALL	International Association of Law Libraries
IBA	International Bar Association
IBM	International Business Machines
ICA	Interstate Commerce Act
ICBM	Intercontinental ballistic missile
ICC	Interstate Commerce Commission; International Criminal Court
ICJ	International Court of Justice
ICM	Institute for Court Management
IDEA	Individuals with Disabilities Education Act of 1975
IDOP	International Dolphin Conservation Program
IEP	Individualized educational program
IFC	International Finance Corporation
IGRA	Indian Gaming Regulatory Act of 1988
IJA	Institute of Judicial Administration
IJC	International Joint Commission
ILC	International Law Commission
ILD	International Labor Defense
Ill. Dec.	Illinois Decisions
ILO	International Labor Organization
IMF	International Monetary Fund
INA	Immigration and Nationality Act
IND	Investigational new drug
INF Treaty	Intermediate-Range Nuclear Forces Treaty of 1987
INS	Immigration and Naturalization Service
INTELSAT	International Telecommunications Satellite Organization
Interpol	International Criminal Police Organization
Int'l. Law Reps.	International Law Reports
Intl. Legal Mats.	International Legal Materials
IOC	International Olympic Committee
IPDC	International Program for the Development of Communication
IPO	Intellectual Property Owners
IPP	Independent power producer
IQ	Intelligence quotient
I.R.	Irish Reports
IRA	Individual retirement account; Irish Republican Army
IRC	Internal Revenue Code
IRCA	Immigration Reform and Control Act of 1986
IRS	Internal Revenue Service
ISO	Independent service organization

ISP	Internet service provider
ISSN	International Standard Serial Numbers
ITA	International Trade Administration
ITI	Information Technology Integration
ITO	International Trade Organization
ITS	Information Technology Service
ITT	International Telephone and Telegraph Corporation
ITU	International Telecommunication Union
IUD	Intrauterine device
IWC	International Whaling Commission
IWW	Industrial Workers of the World
JAGC	Judge Advocate General's Corps
JCS	Joint Chiefs of Staff
JDL	Jewish Defense League
JNOV	Judgment *non obstante veredicto* ("judgment nothing to recommend it" or "judgment notwithstanding the verdict")
JOBS	Jobs Opportunity and Basic Skills
John. Ch.	Johnson's New York Chancery Reports
Johns.	Johnson's Reports (New York)
JP	Justice of the peace
K.B.	King's Bench Reports (England)
KFC	Kentucky Fried Chicken
KGB	Komitet Gosudarstvennoi Bezopasnosti (the State Security Committee for countries in the former Soviet Union)
KKK	Ku Klux Klan
KMT	Kuomintang (Chinese, "national people's party")
LAD	Law Against Discrimination
LAPD	Los Angeles Police Department
LC	Library of Congress
LCHA	Longshoremen's and Harbor Workers Compensation Act of 1927
LD50	Lethal dose 50
LDEF	Legal Defense and Education Fund (NOW)
LDF	Legal Defense Fund, Legal Defense and Educational Fund of the NAACP
LEAA	Law Enforcement Assistance Administration
L.Ed.	Lawyers' Edition Supreme Court Reports
LI	Letter of interpretation
LLC	Limited Liability Company
LLP	Limited Liability Partnership
LMSA	Labor-Management Services Administration
LNTS	League of Nations Treaty Series
Lofft's Rep.	Lofft's English King's Bench Reports
L.R.	Law Reports (English)
LSAC	Law School Admission Council
LSAS	Law School Admission Service
LSAT	Law School Aptitude Test
LSC	Legal Services Corporation; Legal Services for Children
LSD	Lysergic acid diethylamide
LSDAS	Law School Data Assembly Service
LTBT	Limited Test Ban Treaty
LTC	Long Term Care
MAD	Mutual assured destruction
MADD	Mothers against Drunk Driving
MALDEF	Mexican American Legal Defense and Educational Fund
Malloy	William M. Malloy, ed., *Treaties, Conventions International Acts, Protocols, and Agreements between the United States of America and Other Powers* (1910–1938)

Martens	Georg Friedrich von Martens, ea., *Noveau recueil général de traités et autres actes relatifs aux rapports de droit international* (Series I, 20 vols. [1843–1875]; Series II, 35 vols. [1876–1908]; Series III [1909–])
Mass.	Massachusetts Reports
MCC	Metropolitan Correctional Center
MCCA	Medicare Catastrophic Coverage Act of 1988
MCH	Maternal and Child Health Bureau
MCRA	Medical Care Recovery Act of 1962
MDA	Medical Devices Amendments of 1976
Md. App.	Maryland, Appeal Cases
M.D. Ga.	Middle District, Georgia
Mercy	Movement Ensuring the Right to Choose for Yourself
Metc.	Metcalf's Massachusetts Reports
MFDP	Mississippi Freedom Democratic party
MGT	Management
MHSS	Military Health Services System
Miller	David Hunter Miller, ea., *Treaties and Other International Acts of the United States of America* (1931–1948)
Minn.	Minnesota Reports
MINS	Minors in need of supervision
MIRV	Multiple independently targetable reentry vehicle
MIRVed ICBM	Multiple independently targetable reentry vehicled intercontinental ballistic missile
Misc.	Miscellaneous Reports, New York
Mixed Claims Comm., Report of Decs	Mixed Claims Commission, United States and Germany, Report of Decisions
M.J.	Military Justice Reporter
MLAP	Migrant Legal Action Program
MLB	Major League Baseball
MLDP	Mississippi Loyalist Democratic Party
MMI	Moslem Mosque, Incorporated
MMPA	Marine Mammal Protection Act of 1972
Mo.	Missouri Reports
MOD	Masters of Deception
Mod.	Modern Reports, English King's Bench, etc.
Moore, Dig. Intl. Law	John Bassett Moore, *A Digest of International Law*, 8 vols. (1906)
Moore, Intl. Arbs.	John Bassett Moore, *History and Digest of the International Arbitrations to Which United States Has Been a Party*, 6 vols. (1898)
Morison	William Maxwell Morison, *The Scots Revised Report: Morison's Dictionary of Decisions* (1908–09)
M.P.	Member of Parliament
MP3	MPEG Audio Layer 3
MPAA	Motion Picture Association of America
MPAS	Michigan Protection and Advocacy Service
MPEG	Motion Picture Experts Group
mpg	Miles per gallon
MPPDA	Motion Picture Producers and Distributors of America
MPRSA	Marine Protection, Research, and Sanctuaries Act of 1972
M.R.	Master of the Rolls
MS-DOS	Microsoft Disk Operating System
MSHA	Mine Safety and Health Administration
MSPB	Merit Systems Protection Board
MSSA	Military Selective Service Act
N/A	Not Available
NAACP	National Association for the Advancement of Colored People
NAAQS	National Ambient Air Quality Standards

NAB	National Association of Broadcasters
NABSW	National Association of Black Social Workers
NACDL	National Association of Criminal Defense Lawyers
NAFTA	North American Free Trade Agreement of 1993
NAGHSR	National Association of Governors' Highway Safety Representatives
NALA	National Association of Legal Assistants
NAM	National Association of Manufacturers
NAR	National Association of Realtors
NARAL	National Abortion and Reproductive Rights Action League
NARF	Native American Rights Fund
NARS	National Archives and Record Service
NASA	National Aeronautics and Space Administration
NASD	National Association of Securities Dealers
NATO	North Atlantic Treaty Organization
NAVINFO	Navy Information Offices
NAWSA	National American Woman's Suffrage Association
NBA	National Bar Association; National Basketball Association
NBC	National Broadcasting Company
NBLSA	National Black Law Student Association
NBS	National Bureau of Standards
NCA	Noise Control Act; National Command Authorities
NCAA	National Collegiate Athletic Association
NCAC	National Coalition against Censorship
NCCB	National Consumer Cooperative Bank
NCE	Northwest Community Exchange
NCF	National Chamber Foundation
NCIP	National Crime Insurance Program
NCJA	National Criminal Justice Association
NCLB	National Civil Liberties Bureau
NCP	National contingency plan
NCSC	National Center for State Courts
NCUA	National Credit Union Administration
NDA	New drug application
N.D. Ill.	Northern District, Illinois
NDU	National Defense University
N.D. Wash.	Northern District, Washington
N.E.	North Eastern Reporter
N.E. 2d	North Eastern Reporter, Second Series
NEA	National Endowment for the Arts; National Education Association
NEH	National Endowment for the Humanities
NEPA	National Environmental Protection Act; National Endowment Policy Act
NET Act	No Electronic Theft Act
NFIB	National Federation of Independent Businesses
NFIP	National Flood Insurance Program
NFL	National Football League
NFPA	National Federation of Paralegal Associations
NGLTF	National Gay and Lesbian Task Force
NHL	National Hockey League
NHRA	Nursing Home Reform Act of 1987
NHTSA	National Highway Traffic Safety Administration
Nielsen's Rept.	Frederick Kenelm Nielsen, *American and British Claims Arbitration under the Special Agreement Concluded between the United States and Great Britain, August 18, 1910* (1926)
NIEO	New International Economic Order
NIGC	National Indian Gaming Commission
NIH	National Institutes of Health

NIJ	National Institute of Justice
NIRA	National Industrial Recovery Act of 1933; National Industrial Recovery Administration
NIST	National Institute of Standards and Technology
NITA	National Telecommunications and Information Administration
N.J.	New Jersey Reports
N.J. Super.	New Jersey Superior Court Reports
NLEA	Nutrition Labeling and Education Act of 1990
NLRA	National Labor Relations Act
NLRB	National Labor Relations Board
NMFS	National Marine Fisheries Service
No.	Number
NOAA	National Oceanic and Atmospheric Administration
NOC	National Olympic Committee
NOI	Nation of Islam
NOL	Net operating loss
NORML	National Organization for the Reform of Marijuana Laws
NOW	National Organization for Women
NOW LDEF	National Organization for Women Legal Defense and Education Fund
NOW/PAC	National Organization for Women Political Action Committee
NPDES	National Pollutant Discharge Elimination System
NPL	National priorities list
NPR	National Public Radio
NPT	Nuclear Non-Proliferation Treaty of 1970
NRA	National Rifle Association; National Recovery Act
NRC	Nuclear Regulatory Commission
NRLC	National Right to Life Committee
NRTA	National Retired Teachers Association
NSA	National Security Agency
NSC	National Security Council
NSCLC	National Senior Citizens Law Center
NSF	National Science Foundation
NSFNET	National Science Foundation Network
NSI	Network Solutions, Inc.
NTIA	National Telecommunications and Information Administration
NTID	National Technical Institute for the Deaf
NTIS	National Technical Information Service
NTS	Naval Telecommunications System
NTSB	National Transportation Safety Board
NVRA	National Voter Registration Act
N.W.	North Western Reporter
N.W. 2d	North Western Reporter, Second Series
NWSA	National Woman Suffrage Association
N.Y.	New York Court of Appeals Reports
N.Y. 2d	New York Court of Appeals Reports, Second Series
N.Y.S.	New York Supplement Reporter
N.Y.S. 2d	New York Supplement Reporter, Second Series
NYSE	New York Stock Exchange
NYSLA	New York State Liquor Authority
N.Y. Sup.	New York Supreme Court Reports
NYU	New York University
OAAU	Organization of Afro American Unity
OAP	Office of Administrative Procedure
OAS	Organization of American States
OASDI	Old-age, Survivors, and Disability Insurance Benefits
OASHDS	Office of the Assistant Secretary for Human Development Services

OCC	Office of Comptroller of the Currency
OCED	Office of Comprehensive Employment Development
OCHAMPUS	Office of Civilian Health and Medical Program of the Uniformed Services
OCSE	Office of Child Support Enforcement
OEA	Organización de los Estados Americanos
OEM	Original Equipment Manufacturer
OFCCP	Office of Federal Contract Compliance Programs
OFPP	Office of Federal Procurement Policy
OIC	Office of the Independent Counsel
OICD	Office of International Cooperation and Development
OIG	Office of the Inspector General
OJARS	Office of Justice Assistance, Research, and Statistics
OMB	Office of Management and Budget
OMPC	Office of Management, Planning, and Communications
ONP	Office of National Programs
OPD	Office of Policy Development
OPEC	Organization of Petroleum Exporting Countries
OPIC	Overseas Private Investment Corporation
Ops. Atts. Gen.	Opinions of the Attorneys-General of the United States
Ops. Comms.	Opinions of the Commissioners
OPSP	Office of Product Standards Policy
O.R.	Ontario Reports
OR	Official Records
OSHA	Occupational Safety and Health Act
OSHRC	Occupational Safety and Health Review Commission
OSM	Office of Surface Mining
OSS	Office of Strategic Services
OST	Office of the Secretary
OT	Office of Transportation
OTA	Office of Technology Assessment
OTC	Over-the-counter
OTS	Office of Thrift Supervisors
OUI	Operating under the influence
OVCI	Offshore Voluntary Compliance Initiative
OWBPA	Older Workers Benefit Protection Act
OWRT	Office of Water Research and Technology
P.	Pacific Reporter
P. 2d	Pacific Reporter, Second Series
PAC	Political action committee
Pa. Oyer and Terminer	Pennsylvania Oyer and Terminer Reports
PATCO	Professional Air Traffic Controllers Organization
PBGC	Pension Benefit Guaranty Corporation
PBS	Public Broadcasting Service; Public Buildings Service
P.C.	Privy Council (English Law Reports)
PC	Personal computer; politically correct
PCBs	Polychlorinated biphenyls

PCIJ	Permanent Court of International Justice
	    Series A-Judgments and Orders (1922–30)
	    Series B-Advisory Opinions (1922–30)
	    Series A/B-Judgments, Orders, and Advisory Opinions (1931–40)
	    Series C-Pleadings, Oral Statements, and Documents relating to Judgments and Advisory Opinions (1923–42)
	    Series D-Acts and Documents concerning the Organization of the World Court (1922 –47)
	    Series E-Annual Reports (1925–45)

PCP	Phencyclidine

P.D.	Probate Division, English Law Reports (1876–1890)
PDA	Pregnancy Discrimination Act of 1978
PD & R	Policy Development and Research
Pepco	Potomac Electric Power Company
Perm. Ct. of Arb.	Permanent Court of Arbitration
PES	Post-Enumeration Survey
Pet.	Peters' United States Supreme Court Reports
PETA	People for the Ethical Treatment of Animals
PGA	Professional Golfers Association
PGM	Program
PHA	Public Housing Agency
Phila. Ct. of Oyer and Terminer	Philadelphia Court of Oyer and Terminer
PhRMA	Pharmaceutical Research and Manufacturers of America
PHS	Public Health Service
PIC	Private Industry Council
PICJ	Permanent International Court of Justice
Pick.	Pickering's Massachusetts Reports
PIK	Payment in Kind
PINS	Persons in need of supervision
PIRG	Public Interest Research Group
P.L.	Public Laws
PLAN	Pro-Life Action Network
PLC	Plaintiffs' Legal Committee
PLE	Product liability expenses
PLI	Practicing Law Institute
PLL	Product liability loss
PLLP	Professional Limited Liability Partnership
PLO	Palestine Liberation Organization
PLRA	Prison Litigation Reform Act of 1995
PNET	Peaceful Nuclear Explosions Treaty
PONY	Prostitutes of New York
POW-MIA	Prisoner of war-missing in action
Pratt	Frederic Thomas Pratt, *Law of Contraband of War, with a Selection of Cases from Papers of the Right Honourable Sir George Lee* (1856)
PRIDE	Prostitution to Independence, Dignity, and Equality
Proc.	Proceedings
PRP	Potentially responsible party
PSRO	Professional Standards Review Organization
PTO	Patents and Trademark Office
PURPA	Public Utilities Regulatory Policies Act
PUSH	People United to Serve Humanity
PUSH-Excel	PUSH for Excellence
PWA	Public Works Administration
PWSA	Ports and Waterways Safety Act of 1972
Q.B.	Queen's Bench (England)
QTIP	Qualified Terminable Interest Property
Ralston's Rept.	Jackson Harvey Ralston, ed., *Venezuelan Arbitrations of 1903* (1904)
RC	Regional Commissioner
RCRA	Resource Conservation and Recovery Act
RCWP	Rural Clean Water Program
RDA	Rural Development Administration
REA	Rural Electrification Administration
Rec. des Decs. des Trib. Arb. Mixtes	G. Gidel, ed., *Recueil des décisions des tribunaux arbitraux mixtes, institués par les traités de paix* (1922–30)

Redmond	Vol. 3 of Charles I. Bevans, *Treaties and Other International Agreements of the United States of America, 1776–1949* (compiled by C. F. Redmond) (1969)
RESPA	Real Estate Settlement Procedure Act of 1974
RFC	Reconstruction Finance Corporation
RFRA	Religious Freedom Restoration Act of 1993
RIAA	Recording Industry Association of America
RICO	Racketeer Influenced and Corrupt Organizations
RLUIPA	Religious Land Use and Institutionalized Persons Act
RNC	Republican National Committee
Roscoe	Edward Stanley Roscoe, ed., *Reports of Prize Cases Determined in the High Court Admiralty before the Lords Commissioners of Appeals in Prize Causes and before the judicial Committee of the Privy Council from 1745 to 1859* (1905)
ROTC	Reserve Officers' Training Corps
RPP	Representative Payee Program
R.S.	Revised Statutes
RTC	Resolution Trust Corp.
RUDs	Reservations, understandings, and declarations
Ryan White CARE Act	Ryan White Comprehensive AIDS Research Emergency Act of 1990
SAC	Strategic Air Command
SACB	Subversive Activities Control Board
SADD	Students against Drunk Driving
SAF	Student Activities Fund
SAIF	Savings Association Insurance Fund
SALT	Strategic Arms Limitation Talks
SALT I	Strategic Arms Limitation Talks of 1969–72
SAMHSA	Substance Abuse and Mental Health Services Administration
Sandf.	Sandford's New York Superior Court Reports
S and L	Savings and loan
SARA	Superfund Amendment and Reauthorization Act
SAT	Scholastic Aptitude Test
Sawy.	Sawyer's United States Circuit Court Reports
SBA	Small Business Administration
SBI	Small Business Institute
SCCC	South Central Correctional Center
SCLC	Southern Christian Leadership Conference
Scott's Repts.	James Brown Scott, ed., *The Hague Court Reports*, 2 vols. (1916–32)
SCS	Soil Conservation Service; Social Conservative Service
SCSEP	Senior Community Service Employment Program
S.Ct.	Supreme Court Reporter
S.D. Cal.	Southern District, California
S.D. Fla.	Southern District, Florida
S.D. Ga.	Southern District, Georgia
SDI	Strategic Defense Initiative
S.D. Me.	Southern District, Maine
S.D.N.Y.	Southern District, New York
SDS	Students for a Democratic Society
S.E.	South Eastern Reporter
S.E. 2d	South Eastern Reporter, Second Series
SEA	Science and Education Administration
SEATO	Southeast Asia Treaty Organization
SEC	Securities and Exchange Commission
Sec.	Section
SEEK	Search for Elevation, Education and Knowledge
SEOO	State Economic Opportunity Office
SEP	Simplified employee pension plan

Ser.	Series
Sess.	Session
SGLI	Servicemen's Group Life Insurance
SIP	State implementation plan
SLA	Symbionese Liberation Army
SLAPPs	Strategic Lawsuits Against Public Participation
SLBM	Submarine-launched ballistic missile
SNCC	Student Nonviolent Coordinating Committee
So.	Southern Reporter
So. 2d	Southern Reporter, Second Series
SPA	Software Publisher's Association
Spec. Sess.	Special Session
SPLC	Southern Poverty Law Center
SRA	Sentencing Reform Act of 1984
SS	*Schutzstaffel* (German, "Protection Echelon")
SSA	Social Security Administration
SSI	Supplemental Security Income
START I	Strategic Arms Reduction Treaty of 1991
START II	Strategic Arms Reduction Treaty of 1993
Stat.	United States Statutes at Large
STS	Space Transportation Systems
St. Tr.	State Trials, English
STURAA	Surface Transportation and Uniform Relocation Assistance Act of 1987
Sup. Ct. of Justice, Mexico	Supreme Court of Justice, Mexico
Supp.	Supplement
S.W.	South Western Reporter
S.W. 2d	South Western Reporter, Second Series
SWAPO	South-West Africa People's Organization
SWAT	Special Weapons and Tactics
SWP	Socialist Workers Party
TDP	Trade and Development Program
Tex. Sup.	Texas Supreme Court Reports
THAAD	Theater High-Altitude Area Defense System
THC	Tetrahydrocannabinol
TI	Tobacco Institute
TIA	Trust Indenture Act of 1939
TIAS	Treaties and Other International Acts Series (United States)
TNT	Trinitrotoluene
TOP	Targeted Outreach Program
TPUS	Transportation and Public Utilities Service
TQM	Total Quality Management
Tripartite Claims Comm., Decs. and Ops.	Tripartite Claims Commission (United States, Austria, and Hungary), Decisions and Opinions
TRI-TAC	Joint Tactical Communications
TRO	Temporary restraining order
TS	Treaty Series, United States
TSCA	Toxic Substance Control Act
TSDs	Transporters, storers, and disposers
TSU	Texas Southern University
TTBT	Threshold Test Ban Treaty
TV	Television
TVA	Tennessee Valley Authority
TWA	Trans World Airlines

UAW	United Auto Workers; United Automobile, Aerospace, and Agricultural Implements Workers of America
U.C.C.	Uniform Commercial Code; Universal Copyright Convention
U.C.C.C.	Uniform Consumer Credit Code
UCCJA	Uniform Child Custody Jurisdiction Act
UCMJ	Uniform Code of Military Justice
UCPP	Urban Crime Prevention Program
UCS	United Counseling Service
UDC	United Daughters of the Confederacy
UFW	United Farm Workers
UHF	Ultrahigh frequency
UIFSA	Uniform Interstate Family Support Act
UIS	Unemployment Insurance Service
UMDA	Uniform Marriage and Divorce Act
UMTA	Urban Mass Transportation Administration
U.N.	United Nations
UNCITRAL	United Nations Commission on International Trade Law
UNCTAD	United Nations Conference on Trade and Development
UN Doc.	United Nations Documents
UNDP	United Nations Development Program
UNEF	United Nations Emergency Force
UNESCO	United Nations Educational, Scientific, and Cultural Organization
UNICEF	United Nations Children's Fund (formerly United Nations International Children's Emergency Fund)
UNIDO	United Nations Industrial and Development Organization
Unif. L. Ann.	Uniform Laws Annotated
UN Repts. Intl. Arb. Awards	United Nations Reports of International Arbitral Awards
UNTS	United Nations Treaty Series
UPI	United Press International
URESA	Uniform Reciprocal Enforcement of Support Act
U.S.	United States Reports
U.S.A.	United States of America
USAF	United States Air Force
USA PATRIOT Act	Uniting and Strengthening America by Providing Appropriate Tools Required to Intercept and Obstruct Terrorism Act
USF	U.S. Forestry Service
U.S. App. D.C.	United States Court of Appeals for the District of Columbia
U.S.C.	United States Code; University of Southern California
U.S.C.A.	United States Code Annotated
U.S.C.C.A.N.	United States Code Congressional and Administrative News
USCMA	United States Court of Military Appeals
USDA	U.S. Department of Agriculture
USES	United States Employment Service
USFA	United States Fire Administration
USGA	United States Golf Association
USICA	International Communication Agency, United States
USMS	U.S. Marshals Service
USOC	U.S. Olympic Committee
USSC	U.S. Sentencing Commission
USSG	United States Sentencing Guidelines
U.S.S.R.	Union of Soviet Socialist Republics
UST	United States Treaties
USTS	United States Travel Service
v.	*Versus*
VA	Veterans Administration
VAR	Veterans Affairs and Rehabilitation Commission

VAWA	Violence against Women Act
VFW	Veterans of Foreign Wars
VGLI	Veterans Group Life Insurance
Vict.	Queen Victoria (Great Britain)
VIN	Vehicle identification number
VISTA	Volunteers in Service to America
VJRA	Veterans Judicial Review Act of 1988
V.L.A.	Volunteer Lawyers for the Arts
VMI	Virginia Military Institute
VMLI	Veterans Mortgage Life Insurance
VOCAL	Victims of Child Abuse Laws
VRA	Voting Rights Act
WAC	Women's Army Corps
Wall.	Wallace's United States Supreme Court Reports
Wash. 2d	Washington Reports, Second Series
WAVES	Women Accepted for Volunteer Service
WCTU	Women's Christian Temperance Union
W.D. Wash.	Western District, Washington
W.D. Wis.	Western District, Wisconsin
WEAL	*West's Encyclopedia of American Law*; Women's Equity Action League
Wend.	Wendell's New York Reports
WFSE	Washington Federation of State Employees
Wheat.	Wheaton's United States Supreme Court Reports
Wheel. Cr. Cases	Wheeler's New York Criminal Cases
WHISPER	Women Hurt in Systems of Prostitution Engaged in Revolt
Whiteman	Marjorie Millace Whiteman, *Digest of International Law*, 15 vols. (1963–73)
WHO	World Health Organization
WIC	Women, Infants, and Children program
Will. and Mar.	King William and Queen Mary (Great Britain)
WIN	WESTLAW Is Natural; Whip Inflation Now; Work Incentive Program
WIPO	World Intellectual Property Organization
WIU	Workers' Industrial Union
W.L.R.	Weekly Law Reports, England
WPA	Works Progress Administration
WPPDA	Welfare and Pension Plans Disclosure Act
WTO	World Trade Organization
WWI	World War I
WWII	World War II
Yates Sel. Cas.	Yates's New York Select Cases
YMCA	Young Men's Christian Association
YWCA	Young Women's Christian Association

TABLE OF CASES CITED BY NAME

1

1-800 Contacts, Inc. v. WhenU.com, 121

3

321 Studios v. Metro Goldwyn Mayer Studios, 41–43

A

Access Now, Inc. v. Claire's Stores, Inc., 9
Access Now, Inc. v. Southwest Airlines Co., 9
Adams v. R.R. Donnelley & Sons Co., 39
Advanced Micro Devices, Inc. v. Intel Corp., 53
Aetna Health, Inc. v. Davila, 117–119
Air France v. Saks, 229
Alaska Department of Environmental Conservation v. Environmental Protection Agency, 77–78
Alaska Department of Environmental Conservation v. United States Environmental Protection Agency, 78
Allis-Chalmers v. Lueck, 118
Al-Odah v. United States, 218, 217
American Civil Liberties Union v. Ashcroft, 80
American Civil Liberties Union v. Reno, 80
Apprendi v. New Jersey, 183, 184
Arizona v. Dean, 89
Arizona v. Gant, 89
Ashcroft v. American Civil Liberties Union, 79–80
Atkins v. Virginia, 37
Atlas Global Group, L.P., v. Grupo Dataflux, 125

B

Baker v. Carr, 17
Balderas v. Texas, 15–16
Baldwin v. Reese, 107–108
Banks, United States v., 86–87
Banks v. Dretke, 108–109
Banks v. Horn, 31
Barnhart v. Thomas, 203–204
Batson v. Kentucky, 128–129
Beard v. Banks, 31
BedRoc Limited v. United States, 140–141
Blakely v. Washington, 183–185
Boulos v. The Islamic Republic of Iran, 225
Broin v. Philip Morris Co. Inc., 219
Brown v. Texas, 93
Buckley v. Valeo, 62
Buck v. Chao, 167–168
Burlington Industries, Inc. v. Ellerth, 199
Bush v. Gore, 175, 227

C

Carparts Distribution Ctr. v. Automotive Wholesaler's Ass'n of New England, Inc., 9
Castro v. United States, 109–110, 113
Caterpillar Inc. v. Lewis, 125
Central Laborers Pension Fund v. Heinz, 163–164
Chavez v. Martinez, 142
Cheney v. United States District Court for the District of Columbia, 51–52, 176
City of Littleton, Colorado v. Z.J. Gifts D-4, L.L.C., 80–81
Cline v. General Dynamics Land Systems, Inc., 5
Commonwealth v. Banks, 31
Crawford v. Washington, 200–201

D

Davey v. Locke, 82
Davis v. Bandemer, 16–17
Den Norske Stats Oljeselskap AS v. HeereMac Vof, 12
Department of Transportation v. Public Citizen, 164–166
Diaz v. United States, 137
Dole Food Co. v. Patrickson, 125
Dretke v. Haley, 110–112
Duncan v. Henry, 107

E

Earl Williams, 140
Eddings v. Oklahoma, 32
Empagran S.A. v. F. Hoffman-LaRoche, Ltd., 11
Engine Manufacturers Association v. South Coast Air Quality Management District, 67–69
Engle v. Reynolds, 218–219
Ex parte Young, 64

F

Faragher v. City of Boca Raton, 199
FCC v. Missouri Municipal League, 209
FDIC v. Meyer, 14
Fellers v. United States, 201–202
Flamingo Industries (USA) Ltd. v. United States Postal Service, 14
Flores-Montano, United States v., 87–88
Ford v. Hubbard, 112
Frazar v. Gilbert, 64
Frew v. Hawkins, 63–64
FTC v. Mainstream Marketing Services, 208
Fugate v. Department of Corrections, 34
FW/PBS, Inc. v. Dallas, 81

G

Galletti, United States v., 161–162
General Dynamics Land Systems, Inc. v. Cline, 5
Glassroth v. Moore, 74–75, 74
Glassroth v. Moore 242 F. Supp. 2d 1068 (M.D. Ala. 2002), 74
Goldstein v. MCI WorldCom, 48, 47
Goodridge v. Department of Public Health, 101–102
Gregory v. Ashcroft, 209
Groh v. Ramirez, 89–91
Grupo Dataflux v. Atlas Global Group, 124–126

H

Haley v. Ohio, 114
Hamdi v. Rumsfeld, 189–190, 217, 218
Hansen v. Ann Arbor Public Schools, 97–99
Heck v. Humphrey, 166
Hibbs v. Winn, 73–74
Hickman v. Block, 105
Hiibel v. Sixth Judicial District Court of Nevada, Humboldt County, 91
Horn v. Banks, 31
Household Credit Services v. Pfennig, 221–222
Hudgins, United States v., 95
Huggins v. Citibank, N.A., 115–116

I

Illinois v. Lidster, 92–93
In re Cheney, 52, 175
In re Equipment Services, Inc., 20
In re Galletti, 161
In re Hood, 21
In re Till, 23
In re Yates, 24
Indianapolis v. Edmund, 92
In re Briguglio, 162
Intel Corporation v. Hamidi, 64–65
Intel Corp. v. Advanced Micro Devices, Inc., 52–54
Iowa v. Tovar, 202–203

J

Johnson v. California, 128
Jones v. R.R. Donnelley & Sons Co., 39–40
Judicial Watch, Inc. v. Nat'l Energy Policy Dev. Group, 51, 175

K

Kontrick v. Ryan, 19–20
Koon v. United States, 185
Koubriti, United States v., 169, 213, 214
Kruman v. Christie's International PLC, 12

L

Lamie v. U.S. Trustee, 20–21
Law Offices of Curtis V. Trinko, LLP v. Bell Atlantic Corp., 13
Lawrence v. Texas, 104, 157
Lemon v. Kurtzman, 98
Lockett v. Ohio, 32
Locke v. Davey, 81–83

M

Maryland v. Pringle, 93–94
Massiah v. United States, 202
McConnell v. Federal Election Commission, 62–63
McFarlane v. Gaiman, 43–44

McGinley v. Houston, 75
McKnight v. South Carolina, 79
Miccosukee Tribe of Indians v. South Florida Water Management District, 70
Mills v. Maryland, 31
Miranda v. Arizona, 113, 141, 142
Miranda v. United States, 201
Missouri v. Seibert, 142–143
Muhammad v. Close, 166–167
Murray v. Carrier, 111

N

National Archives and Records Administration v. Favish, 95–97
Nelson v. Alabama, 34
Nelson v. Campbell, 33–34
Nevada v. Murphy, et al, 155
Newdow v. U.S. Congress, 83–85
Newman-Green, Inc. v. Alfonzo-Larrain, 126
New York v. Belton, 88–89, 95
Nixon v. Missouri, 208–209
Noah v. AOL Time Warner, Inc., 9
North Carolina v. Alford, 184
Norton v. Southern Utah Wilderness Alliance, 70–71

O

Ohio v. Roberts, 200, 201
Olympic Airways v. Husain, 229–230
Ostrander v. Duggan, 196

P

Parks v. LaFace Records, 220–221
Patane, United States v., 141–142
Pegram v. Herdrich, 119
Pennsylvania State Police v. Suders, 198–199
Penry v. Johnson, 36
Penry v. Lynaugh, 36
People v. Luster, 26
Peterson v. The Islamic Republic of Iran, 225–226
Planned Parenthood v. Casey, 2
Pliler v. Ford, 112–113

R

Rasul v. Bush, 216–218
Raytheon Co. v. Hernandez, 10–11
Recording Indus. Ass'n of Am. v. Verizon Internet Servs., Inc., 120
Reese v. Baldwin, 108
Republic of Austria v. Altmann, 85–86
Richmond Medical Center v. Hicks, 4, 5
Ring v. Arizona, 34–36

Roe v. Wade, 1–2
Rose v.Lundy, 112
Rumsfeld v. Padilla, 217

S

Sabri v. United States, 26–27
Sabri v. U.S., 26
Scarborough v. Principi, 126–127
Schriro v. Summerlin, 34–36
Securities and Exchange Commission v. Edwards, 181–182
SEC v. WorldCom, Inc., 47
Silveira v. Lockyer, 104–106
Smith v. Cockrell, 36
Sosa v. Alvarez-Machain, 127–128
Southern Utah Wilderness Alliance v. Norton, 71
South Florida Water Management District v. Miccosukee Tribe of Indians, 69–70
Southwestern Bell v. Missouri Municipal League., 209
State v. Crawford, 201
State v. Sandoval, 2–4
State v. Towery, 35
Stenberg v. Carhart, 4
Strahan, United States v., 95

T

Tate v. Florida, 186–188
Teague v. Lane, 31, 35
Tennard v. Cockrell, 37
Tennard v. Dretke, 36–37
Tennessee Student Assistance Corporation v. Hood, 21–22
Tennessee v. Lane, 7–10
Terry v. Ohio, 91–92
Thornton v. United States, 94–95
Thornton v. U.S., 94
Till v. SCS Credit Corporation, 22–23

U

U-Haul Int'l, Inc. v. WhenU.com, Inc., 120–121
United States Postal Service v. Flamingo Industries (USA) Ltd., 14–15
United States v. Benitez, 48–50
United States v. Elcom Ltd., 42
United States v. Emerson, 104
United States v. Lara, 55–56
United States v. Lopez, 27
United States v. Miller, 105
United States v. Morrison, 27
United States v. Olano, 49
United States v. Sabri, 27
Universal City Studios, Inc. v. Corley, 42

V

Verizon Communications Inc. v. Law Offices of Curtis V. Trinko, LLP, 12–14
Victor v. Hopkins, 112
Vieth v. Jubelirer, 16
Vieth v. Pennsylvania, 17
Vigilio v. Motorola, S.D.N.Y., 189
Virginia v. Maryland, 230–231

W

Washington v. Blakely, 185
Washington v. Gore, 184
Watt v. Western Nuclear, Inc., 140
Wells Fargo & Co. v. WhenU.com, Inc., 121
West Virginia State Board of Education v. Barnette, 84
Winn v. Killian, 73
Woodson v. North Carolina, 32

Y

Yarborough v. Alvarado, 113–114
Yarborough v. Gentry, 176–177
Yates v. Hendon, 23–24

Z

Z.J. Gifts D-4, L.L.C. v. City of Littleton, Colorado, 81

INDEX
BY NAME AND SUBJECT

Page numbers appearing in boldface indicate major treatment of entries. Italicized page numbers refer to photos.

A

Abortion, **1–5**
ACLU (American Civil Liberties Union), 54–55, 61–62, 79–80
ADA (Americans With Disabilities Act), **7–11**
ADEA (Age Discrimination in Employment Act), 5–6
ADEC (Alaska Department of Environmental Conservation), 77–78
Administrative Procedure Act (APA), 71
Adult business requirements, 80–81
Advanced Micro Devices Inc. (AMD), 53–54
Aetna, 118
Age discrimination, **5–6**
Age Discrimination in Employment Act (ADEA), 5–6
Air pollution, 67–69, 77–78, 165–166
al Qaeda, 192–193, 211
Alabama, cases in, 33–34, 74–75
Alaska Department of Environmental Conservation (ADEC), 77–78
Aliens, **6–7**
Altmann, Maria V., 85–86, *86*
Alvarado, Michael, 113–114
Alvarez-Machain, Humberto, 127–128
AMD (Advanced Micro Devices Inc.), 53–54
American Civil Liberties Union (ACLU), 54–55, 61–62, 79–80
American Indian tribes, 55–56
Americans With Disabilities Act (ADA), **7–11**
Anderson, Ryan G., 72
Antiterrorism and Effective Death Penalty Act of 1996, 109, 113–114
Antitrust law, **11–15**, 53–54
APA (Administrative Procedure Act), 71
Apportionment, **15–17**
Arizona, cases in, 34–36, 73–74, 88–89

Ashcroft, John, 173–174
Assault Weapons Control Act (AWCA), 104–106
Athletes
  Bryant, Kobe, 193–195, *194*
  Dennehy, Patrick, 143–144
  steroid use, 204–206
  University of Colorado Football Program, 195–197
  Williams, Jayson, 138–139, *139*
Attorney's fees, 20–21
AUMF (Authorization for Use of Military Force), 189–190
Austria, sovereign immunity, 85–86
Authorization for Use of Military Force (AUMF), 189–190
Automobile searches, 88–89
AWCA (Assault Weapons Control Act), 104–106

B

Bacanovic, Peter, 116–117
BACT (best available control technology) standard, 77–78
Bakley, Bonny Lee, 144–145
Balco (Bay area Laboratory Co-Operative), 205
Bankruptcy, **19–24**, 161–162
Banks, Delma, 108–109
Banks, George, 31–33
Banks, Lawshawn L., 86–87, *87*
Banks and credit card fraud, 115–116
Banning, Sandra, 84–85
Batson challenges, 128–129
BCRA (Bipartisan Campaign Reform Act of 2002), 62–63

BedRoc Limited, LLC, 140–141
Benitez, Carlos Dominguez, 48–50
Big Lurch (rapper), 153–154
Bill of Rights, ownership of, *159*, 159–160
Binion, Ted, 155–156
Bipartisan Campaign Reform Act of 2002 (BCRA), 62–63
Black, Morris, 146–148
Blackmun, Harry A., 1–2
Blake, Robert, 144–145
Blakely, Howard and Yolanda, 183–185
BLM (Bureau of Land Management), 71
Border crossings, 88
Bounty Hunters, **24–26**
Breyer, Stephen G., 53–56, 80–81, 91–93
Bribery, **26–27**
Briguglio, Francesco and Angela, 161–162
Broadcasting, **27–29**
Brooklyn Bridge, plan to destroy, 211–213
Bryant, Kobe, 193–195, *194*
Bureau of Land Management (BLM), 71
Bush, George W., 6–7, 101–104, 165–166, 216–218
Butler, Netwon and Mabel, 140–141

C

Calad, Ruby, 118
California
    Assault Weapons Control Act, 104–106
    "Big Lurch" murder case, 153–154
    bounty hunter case, 24–26
    Clean Air Act, 67–69
    e-mail case, 64–65
    gay marriage, 102–104
    governor recall election, 60–62
    habeas corpus, 112–113
    Michael Jackson child molestation case, 197
    peremptory challenges based on race, 128–129
    Phil Spector murder case, 154–155
    Pledge of Allegiance case, 83–85
    right to counsel case, 176–177
    Scott Peterson murder trial, 152–153
    tax assessments on partnerships, 161–162
    tort reform, 219–220
Campaign Finance Law, 61–63
Capital punishment, **31–37**, 108–109
Castro, Hernan O'Ryan, 109–110
CAVC (Court of Appeals for Veterans Claims), 126–127
Celebrities in the news
    "Big Lurch" (rapper), 153–154
    Blake, Robert, 144–145
    Bryant, Kobe, 193–195, *194*
    Dennehy, Patrick, 143–144

    Jackson, Janet, 27–29, *28*
    OutKast, 220–221
    Spector, Phil, 154–155
    Stewart, Martha, 116–117, *117*
    Timberlake, Justin, 27–29, *28*
    Williams, Jayson, 138–139, *139*
Central Intelligence Agency (CIA), **38–39**
Central Laborers Pension Fund, 163–164
Chapman, Duane "Dog," 24–26
Cheney, Richard, 51–52, 175–176
Child molestation, 195, 197–198
Child Online Protection Act (COPA), 79–80
Christofi, Costas "Gus," 138
CIA (Central Intelligence Agency), **38–39**, 174
Cigna, 118
Civil rights, **39–41**, 166–167
Civil Rights Acts, 39–40
Clarkson, Lana, 154–155
Class-action lawsuits, 218–219
Clean Air Act, 67–69, 77–78
Colorado, cases in, 193–195
Conditt, John H. Jr., 195
Congressional redistricting, 15–17
Connecticut, ruling on status of fetus, 2–4
Conte, Victor Jr., 205, *205*
Contents Scramble System (CSS), 42
Contracts, verbal, 43–44
Convertino, Richard G., 168–169, 214
Cook, Charles, 108–109
COPA (Child Online Protection Act), 79–80
Copyright, **41–43**, 119–120, 120–121
Corporate fraud, **45–48**
Court of Appeals for Veterans Claims (CAVC), 126–127
Cram-down provision of Bankruptcy Code, 22–23
Crawford, Michael, 200–201
Crawford, Sylvia, 200–201
Credit card charges, 221–222
Credit card fraud, 115–116
Criminal procedure, 48–50
"Cut-down" procedure, 33–34

D

Date rape drug, 25
Davey, Joshua, 81–83, *82*
Davila, Juan, 118
Davis, Gray, 60–62, *61*
D&E procedure, 4–5
Dean, Donald, 89
Death penalty, **31–37**, 108–109
Defense of Marriage Act (DOMA), 102
Democratic Party and redistricting, 15–16
Dennehy, Patrick, 143–144
Digital Millennium Copyright Act, 41–43

Disabled persons, 7–11, 203–204
Discovery, **51–52**
Diversity of citizenship, 125–126
DNA testing, **54–55**
Do-Not-Call Registry, 207–208
DOMA (Defense of Marriage Act), 102
Dotson, Carlton, 143–144
Double jeopardy, **55–56**, 137
Downward departures, 185–186
Drugs and narcotics, **56–57**
    addiction and ADA, 10–11
    cases involving probable cause requirement, 93–94
    Ephedra ban, 56–57
    steroid use in sports, 204–206
    use in sexual assault, 2–4, 25
Durst, Robert, 146–148, *147*
DVD copying software, 41–43

E

E-mail, **64–65**
Early Periodic Screening Diagnosis (EPSDT), 64
eBay, 162–163
Ebbers, Bernard J., 47–48
Education law, **59–60**
Edwards, Charles, 181–182
EEOC (Equal Employment Opportunity Commission), 5–6
Elections, **60–63**, 226–228
Eleventh amendment, 7, 21–22, **63–64**
Elmardoudi, Abdel-Ilah, 213–214
EMA (Engine Manufacturers Association), 67–69
Employee Retirement Income Security Act (ERISA), 23–24, 117–119, 163–164
Enemy combatants, 189–190, 216–218
Energy policy, 51–52, 175–176
Engine Manufacturers Association (EMA), 67–69
Enron Corp., 45–47
Environmental law, **67–71**, 77–78, 165–166
Environmental Protection Agency, 77–78
Ephedra ban, 56–57
EPSDT (Early Periodic Screening Diagnosis), 64
Equal Access to Justice Ace (EAJA), 126–127
Equal Employment Opportunity Commission (EEOC), 5–6
Equal Protection Clause, 98–99
Equipment Services Inc. (ESI), 20–21
ERISA (Employee Retirement Income Security Act), 23–24, 117–119, 163–164
Espionage, **72–73**
Establishment Clause, **73–75**, 81–83, 83–85, 98

ETS Payphones, 181–182
Everglades, 69–70
Evidence, withholding, 108–109
Ex parte Young, 64

F

FACA (Federal Advisory Committee Act), 52
"Fairly present" in state court, 107–108
Faris, Lyman, 211, *211*
Farr, Robert, 109
Fastow, Andrew, 46–47
Favish, Allan, 96, *96*
FCC (Federal Communications Commission), 27–29, 207–208, 209–210
FDA (Food and Drug Administration), 56–57
Federal Motor Carrier Safety Administration (FMCSA), 165–166
Federal Rules of Civil Procedure, 1–2
Federal Torts Claim Act (FTCA), 127–128
Federalism, **77–78**
Fellers, John J., 201–202
Fetal rights, 2–4, **78–79**
Fifth amendment, 141–142
File sharing, 119–120
First amendment, **79–85**
    adult business requirements, 80–81
    Child Online Protection Act (COPA), 79–80
    freedom of speech, **97–99**
    Internet pornography, 79–80
    Pledge of Allegiance, 83–85
    scholarships to theology students, 81–83
    use of Rosa Parks' name in song, 220–221
Fixed rate of return contract, 181–182
Flamingo Industries, 14–15
Flores-Montano, Manuel, 88
Florida, cases in, 177–179, 186–188, 218–219
FMCSA (Federal Motor Carrier Safety Administration), 165–166
Food and Drug Administration (FDA), 56–57
Forced entry, 86–87
Ford, Richard Herman, 112–113
Foreign Sovereign Immunities Act, **85–86**
Foreign Trade Antitrust Improvements Act (FTAIA), 12
Foster, Vince, 96–97
Fourteenth amendment, 8–9
Fourth amendment, **86–95**
    automobile searches, 88–89
    border searches, 88
    faulty search warrants, 88–90
    forced entry, 86–87
    highway checkpoints, 92–93
    probable cause, 93–94
    refusing to give name to police, 91–92
    search incident to arrest of driver, 94–95

Franklin, Daniel, *148*, 148–149
Free Exercise clause, 81–83
Freedom of Information Act (FOIA), **95–97**
Freedom of Speech, **97–99**. *See also* First amendment
Frew, Linda, 64
FTAIA (Foreign Trade Antitrust Improvements Act), 12
FTC (Federal Trade Commission), 207–208
FTCA (Federal Torts Claim Act), 127–128
"FundGate," 182–183

G

Gaiman, Neil, *43*, 43–44
Galletti, Abel and Sarah, 161–162
Gator, 120
Gay and lesbian rights, **101–104**
Gay marriage, 101–104
General Dynamics, 5–6
Gentry, Lionel, 176–177
Georgia, cases in, 109–110
Gerrymandering, 15–17
GHB (date rape drug), 25
Ginsburg, Ruth Bader
　bankruptcy cases, 20, 24
　criminal procedure case, 50
　discovery case, 53–54
　Equal Access to Justice Act (EAJA) opinion, 126–127
　Establishment Clause opinion, 73–74
　federal environmental regulatory powers opinion, 78
　habeas corpus, 109
　insurance negligence, 118–119
　privacy and Social Security numbers opinion, 168
　sexual harassment opinion, 198–200
　sixth amendment, 202–203
Godbey, David C., 1–2
Goodwin, Alfred T., 84–85
Green River serial killer, 149–150
Groh, Jeff, 89–90
Grupo, 125–126
Guantanamo Bay detention center, 72–73, 211, 216–218
Gun control, **104–106**

H

Habeas corpus, **107–114**
　burden to "fairly present" federal claim in state court, 107–108
　Miranda warning to minor, 113–114
　mixed habeas petition, 112–113
　non-defaulted claims, 110–112
　notice and warnings, 109–110
　prisoners' rights, 166–167
　withholding evidence, 108–109
Haimoud, Ali, 213–214
Haley, Michael Wayne, 110–112
Hamdi, Yaser Esam, 189–190
Hamidi, Kourosh K., 64–65
Hannan, Ahmed, 213–214
Hansen, Elisabeth "Betsy," 97–99
Hanson, Abid M., 229–230
Health and Human Services, Dept. of (HHS), 57
Health maintenance organizations (HMOs), 117–119
Helerstein, Alvin, 188–189
Hernandez, Joel, 10–11, *11*
HHS (Health and Human Services, Dept. of), 57
High school students, legal issues of, 97–99, 137
Highway checkpoints, constitutionality of, 92–93
Hiibel, Larry D., 91–92
HMOs (Health Maintenance Organizations), 117–119
Hnida, Katie, 196, *196*
Holschuh, John, 221
Homosexuality, 97–99, 101–104
Hood, Pamela, 21–22
Household Credit Services, Inc., 222
Hughes, Lynn N., 39
Hussein, Saddam, 121–122

I

IBM, 44–45
Identity theft, **115–116**
Illegal aliens, 6–7
Illinois, cases in, 92–93
Illston, Susan, 41–43
ImClone Systems, 116–117
Indecent exposure, 27–29
Insider trading, **116–117**
Inspector General, 40–41
Insurance, **117–119**
Intact D&E procedure, 4–5
Intel Corp., 53–54, 64–65
Intellectual property, 41–43, 53–54, **119–120**, 120–121, 220–221
Internal Revenue Service (IRS), 161–162
Internet, 8–9, 79–80, 119–120, **120–121**
Internet Service Providers (ISPs), 65–67, *66*
Interrogation, 142–143
Iowa, cases in, 202–203
Iran's role in 1983 Lebanon bombing, 225–226
Iraq War, **121–122**

J

Jackson, Janet, 27–29, *28*
Jackson, Michael, *197*, 197–198
Jamelske, John, 171–172
Janklow, William, 135–137, *136*
Johnson, Jay, 128–129
Jones, Beverly, 7–10
Judges, **123–124**
Judicial misconduct, 123–124
Juries, **128–129**
Jurisdiction, **124–128**
Jury selection, racial bias in, 128–129
Justice Department, 168–169, 173–174

K

Kennedy, Anthony M.
   antitrust case, 14–15
   bankruptcy case, 21
   Child Online Protection Act (COPA), 79–80
   discovery opinion, 52
   double jeopardy clause, 56
   eleventh amendment, 64
   faulty search warrants opinion, 90
   federal environmental regulatory powers opinion, 78
   Foreign Sovereign Immunities Act, 85–86
   Freedom of Information Act, 96–97
   habeas corpus, 114
   Miranda rights opinion, 141–142, 142–143
   refusing to give name to police case, 91–92
Kerry, John F., **131–132**
Koubriti, Karim, 213–214

L

Laci and Conner's Law, 78
LaFace Records, 220–221
Lamberth, Royce C., 225–226
Lamie, John M., 20–21
Lane, George, 7–10, *10*
Lara, Billy Jo, 55–56
Lay, Kenneth, 47
Lee, Kenneth, 200–201
Legal fees, 126–127
Libya, sanctions against, 214–215
Lidster, Robert, 92–93
Life sentence for juvenile, 186–188
Linux operating system, 44–45
Local exchange carriers (LEC), 13–14
Long, Russell Billiu, **133**
Louisiana, judicial misconduct in, 123–124
Lucier, Laurence and Laurie
Luster, Andrew Stuart, 24–26, *25*

M

Malvo, Lee, 145–146
Manslaughter, **135–140**. *See also* murder
Marina Cabrillo Partners, 161–162
Marital privilege, 200–201
Maryland, cases in, 93–94, 230–231
Massachusetts, gay marriage in, 101–102
Matthews, Bill, 159–160
MBNA America Bank, N.A., 222
McCain-Feingold Law, 62–63
McConnel, Mitch, 62–63, *63*
McCorvey, Norma, 1–2
McCoy, Charles A. Jr., 150–152, *151*
McFarlane, Todd, 43–44
Media ownership, 209–210
Mental retardation, 36–37
MercExchange, 162–163
Mexican trucks operating in the U.S., 165–166
Miccosukee Indian Tribe, 69–70
Michigan, cases in, 137, 148–149, 166–167
Mine and mineral law, **140–141**
Miranda rights, 113–114, **141–143**, 201–202
Mississippi, cases in, 220
Missouri, cases in, 208–209
Mixed habeas petition, 112–113
Mohammed, Khalid Shaikh, 211–212
Moore, Roy S., 74–75
Moussaoui, Zacarias, 190–192
Muhammed, John Allen, 145–146
Muhammed, Shakur, 166–167
Murder, **143–156**. *See also* manslaughter
   "Big Lurch" rapper case, 153–154
   Daniel Franklin case, 148–149
   Green River serial killer, 149–150
   Lionel Tate case, 186–188
   Ohio sniper case, 150–152
   Oklahoma City bombings, 158–159
   of Patrick Dennehy, 143–144
   Phil Spector case, 154–155
   Robert Blake case, 144–145
   Robert Durst case, 146–148
   Scott Peterson case, 152–153
   Ted Binion convictions reversed, 155–156
   Washington D.C. snipers, 145–146
Murphy, Sandra, 155–156
Music, lawsuits about, 119–120, 220–221
Mutual funds scandal, 182–183

N

National Conference of Commissioners on Uniform State Laws (NCCUSL), 223–224
National Education Association (NEA), 59–60
National Energy Policy Development Group (NEPDG), 51–52, 175–176

National Environmental Policy Act of 1969 (NEPA), 165–166
NCCUSL (National Conference of Commissioners on Uniform State Laws), 223–224
NEA (National Education Association), 59–60
Nebraska, cases in, 4–5, 201–202
Nelson, David Larry, 33–34
NEPA (National Environmental Policy Act of 1969), 165–166
NEPDG (National Energy Policy Development Group), 51–52, 175–176
Nevada, cases in, 91–92, 140–141, 155–156
New Jersey, mandatory DNA testing in, 54–55
Newdow, Michael, 83–85
Newsom, Gavin, 102–104, *103*
Nichols, Deion, 94–95
Nichols, Terry, 158–159
9-11 Commission Report, 192–193
No Child Left Behind Act (NCLBA), 59–60
Non-defaulted claims in habeas corpus proceedings, 110–112
North Carolina, bill of rights ownership, 159–160
Notice and warnings in habeas corpus proceedings, 109–110
Novak, Robert, 174

O

Obituaries
  Long, Russell Billiu, **133**
  Reagan, Ronald Wilson, **172–173**
  Regan, Donald T., **176**
  Simon, Paul, **200**
Obscenity, 27–29, 79–81, **157–158**
O'Connor, Sandra Day
  campaign finance law, 62–63
  capital punishment case, 37
  enemy combatants opinion, 190, 216–218
  habeas corpus, 111–112
  Miranda rights opinions, 142–143, 202
  securities law opinion, 181–182
  water regulation opinion, 70
Off-road vehicles (ORVs), 71
Ohio sniper case, 150–152
Oklahoma City bombings, **158–159**
Olson, Jim, *32*
Olympic Airways, 229–230
Oregon, cases in, 107–108
ORVs (Off-road vehicles), 71
OutKast, 220–221
Ownership, **159–160**

P

PACs (Political Action Committees), 62–63
Pan Am Flight 103, 214–215
Parks, Rosa, 220–221
Partial birth abortion, 4–5
Partnerships (business), **161–162**
Patane, Samuel F., 141–142
Patents, **162–163**
Patriot Act, 40–41, 215–216
Pattah, Zuhair, 137
Pennsylvania, cases in, 16–17, 198–200
Pennsylvania State Police, 198–200
Pension plans, 23–24, **163–164**
Peremptory challenges, 128–129
Perry, Rick, 16
Peterson, Laci, 152
Peterson, Scott, *152*, 152–153
Pfennig, Sharon, 221–222
Pioneer High School (Ann Arbor, Michigan), 97–99
Pittman Underground Water Act of 1919, 140–141
Plame, Valeria, 174
Plea bargains, 48–50
Pledge of Allegiance, 83–85
Political Action Committees (PAC), 62–63
Pornography, 79–80. *See also* Obscenity
Postal Reorganization Act (PRA), 14–15
Potomac River, 230–231
Pratt, Wayne, 159–160
Presidential elections, 62–63, 131–132, 226–228
Presidential powers, **164–166**
Price-fixing, 11–12
Pringle, Joseph, 93–94
Prisoners' rights, **166–167**
Privacy, 54–55, 95–97, **167–168**
Privacy Act of 1974, 167–168, **168–169**
Probable cause, 93–94
Promise Scholarship program, 81–83
Prosecutorial Remedies and Other Tools to End the Exploitation of Children Today Act (PROTECT), 185–186
PROTECT (Prosecutorial Remedies and Other Tools to End the Exploitation of Children Today Act), 185–186

Q

Qadaffy, Moammar, 38

R

R. R. Donnelley & Sons, 39–40
Racial bias in jury selection, 128–129
Ramirez, Joseph, 89–90
Rape, **171–172**, 193–197

Raytheon, 10–11
Reagan, Ronald Wilson, **172–173**
Recall election, California, 60–62
Recusal, **173–176**
Reese, Michael, 107–108
Regan, Donald T., **176**
Rehnquist, William H.
    ADA case, 9–10
    bankruptcy case, 21–22
    campaign finance law, 62–63
    criminal procedure case, 50
    gas tank searches opinion, 88
    mine and mineral rights opinion, 141
    probable cause requirement opinion, 93–94
    scholarships to theology students case, 82–83
    search incident to arrest rule, 95
    sixth amendment and marital privilege, 200–201
    water rights case, 231
Republican Party and redistricting, 15–16
RIAA (Recording Industry Association of America), 119–120
Ridgway, Gary, 149–150, *150*
Right to counsel, **176–177**, 202–203
Right to die, **177–179**
Robinson, Machekia, 148–149
Roe v. Wade, 1–2
Rosen, Gerald, 98–99

S

Sabri, Basim Omar, 26–27
Safe, Orderly Legal Visas and Enforcement (SOLVE), 7
Sales law, 223–224
San Francisco, gay marriage in, 102–104
Sandoval, Edwin, 2–3
Scalia, Antonin
    ADA case, 10
    antitrust case, 13–14
    bankruptcy opinion, 23–24
    campaign finance law, 62–63
    capital punishment case, 35–56
    diversity of citizenship opinion, 125–126
    enemy combatants opinion, 190
    environmental law, 67–69
    habeas corpus, 110
    ORVs' effect on environment opinion, 71
    redistricting case, 17
    refusal to recuse in Cheney case, 175–176
    scholarships to theology students case, 83
    second-hand smoke opinion, 230
    sentencing beyond maximum range, 185
    sixth amendment and marital privilege, 200–201
    Social Security case, 203–204

SCAQMD (South Coast Air quality Management District), 67–69
Scarborough, Randall C., 126–127
Schiavo, Michael, 177–179, *178*
Schiavo, Terri, 177–179
SCO Group, 44–45
SCS Credit Corporation, 22–23
Search incident to arrest rule, 94–95
Search warrants, faulty, 89–90
SEC (Securities and Exchange Commission), 182–183
Second amendment, 104–106
Second-hand smoke, 229–230
Securities, **181–183**
Securities and Exchange Commission (SEC), 182–183
Seibert, Patrice, 142–143, *143*
Sentencing, **183–188**
Sentencing guidelines, 185–186
September 11th attacks, **188–193**
September 11th Victims Compensation Fund, 188–189
Sex offenses, 2–4, 171–172, **193–195**, 195–198
Sex toys, promotion of, 157–158
Sexual abuse, 195, **195–198**
Sexual harassment, **198–200**
SFWMD (South Florida Water Management District), 69–70
Sherman Antitrust Act, 12–14
Siebert, Patrice, 142–143
Simon, Paul, **200**
Singleton, Antron, 153–154
Sixth amendment, 176–177, **200–203**
Skilling, Jeffrey, *46*, 46–47
Smoking, 218–219, 229–230
Social Security, **203–204**
Social Security numbers, disclosure of, 167–168
Souter, David H.
    age discrimination opinion, 6
    bribery case, 27
    civil suits against U.S. government opinion, 127–128
    criminal procedure case, 50
    forced entry opinion, 87
    Miranda rights opinion, 141–142, 142–143
    pension plan opinion, 163–164
    privacy and Social Security numbers, 168
South Carolina, cases in, 115–116
South Coast Air Quality Management District (SCAQMD), 67–69
South Dakota Congressman convicted of manslaughter, 135–137
South Florida Water Management District (SFWMD), 69–70

Southern Utah Wilderness Alliance (SUWA), 71
Sovereign immunity, 7–11, 21–22, 63–64, 85–86
Spam (email), 65–67
Spector, Phil, *154*, 154–155
Spitzer, Elliot, 182–183
Sports, 27–29, 204–206. *See also* Athletes
Sports law, **204–206**
Statutes of limitations, 39–40
Steroids, athletes' use of, 204–206
Stevens, John Paul
    ADA case, 8–9
    bankruptcy case, 21, 23
    campaign finance law, 62–63
    criminal procedure case, 50
    double jeopardy clause, 56
    faulty search warrants opinion, 90
    Foreign Sovereign Immunities Act, 85–86
    highway checkpoints opinion, 93
    mine and mineral rights opinion, 141
    Pledge of Allegiance opinion, 84–85
    redistricting case, 17
    refusing to give name to police, 91–92
    telecommunications services and local governments, 208–209
    water rights case, 231
Stewart, Martha, 116–117, *117*
Stock transactions, 116–117
Student loans, 21–22
Suders, Nancy Drew, 198–200, *199*
Sullivan, Scott, 47–48
Summerlin, Warren, 34–36, *35*
Super Bowl halftime show, 27–29
Supreme Court, United States
    abortion cases, 1–2
    ADA cases, 7–11
    adult business requirements, first amendment rights, 80–81
    age discrimination case, 5–6
    antitrust cases, 11–15
    bankruptcy cases, 20, 21–22, 23, 24
    bribery case, 27
    campaign finance law, 62–63
    capital punishment cases, 32–37
    Child Online Protection Act (COPA), 79–80
    civil rights cases, 39–40
    civil suits against U.S. government, 127–128
    Clean Air Act, 67–69
    credit card charges case, 222
    criminal procedure, 48–50
    discovery cases, 51–54
    diversity of citizenship, 125–126
    double jeopardy case, 55–56
    eleventh amendment, 64
    enemy combatants, 190, 211, 216–218
    Equal Access to Justice Act (EAJA), 126–127
    Establishments Clause, 73–74
    faulty search warrants case, 90–91
    federal environmental regulatory powers, 77–78
    forced entry case, 87
    Foreign Sovereign Immunities Act, 85–86
    Freedom of Information Act, 96–97
    gas tank searches case, 88
    gay marriage, 103–104
    habeas corpus, 107–114
    highway checkpoints case, 92–93
    insurance negligence, 118–119
    Legal fees case, 126–127
    Mexican trucks operating in the U.S., 165–166
    mine and mineral rights, 141
    Miranda rights, 141–142, 142–143, 202
    ORVs' effect on environment, 71
    pension plan case, 163–164
    Pledge of Allegiance case, 83–85
    prisoners' rights, 166–167
    privacy and Social Security numbers, 168
    probable cause requirement, 93–94
    redistricting, 16–17
    refusing to give name to police, 91–92
    right to counsel, 176–177
    Scalia's refusal to recuse in Cheney case, 175–176
    scholarships to theology students case, 82–83
    search incident to arrest rule, 95
    second-hand smoke case, 229–230
    securities law, 181–182
    sentencing beyond maximum range, 185
    sexual harassment case, 198–200
    sixth amendment, 200–201, 202–203
    Social Security case, 203–204
    telecommunications services and local governments, 208–209
    Texas sodomy law, 157–158
    water rights and regulation cases, 70, 230–231
SUWA (Southern Utah Wilderness Alliance), 71

T

Tabish, Rick, 155–156
Tate, Lionel, 186–188, *187*
Tax assessments, 161–162
Tax Injunction Act (TIA), 73–74
Taylor, Steven, 158–159
Telecommunications, **207–209**
Telephone companies, 12–14

Television, **209–210**
Ten commandments monument, 74–75
Tennard, Robert James, 36–37, *37*
Tennessee, cases in, 7–10, 21–22
Terrorism, **210–218**
    1983 bombing in Lebanon, 225–226
    Brooklyn Bridge plot foiled, 211–213
    Detroit terror cell, 213–214
    enemy combatants at Guantanomo Bay, Cuba, 211, 216–218
    Patriot Act opposition, 215–216
    sanctions against Libya eased, 214–215
    September 11th attacks, **188–193**
Texas
    capital punishment case, 36–37
    eleventh amendment, 63–64
    habeas corpus, 108–109, 110–112
    murder of Patrick Dennehy, 143–144
    promotion of sex toys case, 157–158
    redistricting, 15–16
    Robert Durst murder trial, 148–149
    tort reform, 220
Thomas, Clarence
    ADA case, 11
    age discrimination opinion, 6
    bankruptcy opinions, 22, 23, 24
    capital punishment opinion, 32–33
    double jeopardy clause, 56
    faulty search warrants opinion, 90–91
    habeas corpus, 109, 110, 112–113
    insurance negligence, 118–119
    Mexican trucks operating in the U.S., 165–166
    Miranda rights opinion, 141–142
    second-hand smoke opinion, 229–230
Thomas, Pauline, 203–204
Thornton (defendant), 94–95
Tiger, William Buffalo, *70*
TILA (Truth in Lending Act), **221–222**
Timberlake, Justin, *28*, 28–29
Tobacco lawsuits, **218–219**
Tort law, **219–220**
Tovar, Felipe, 202–203
Trademarks, **220–221**
Tribal sovereignty, 55–56
Truck fleets, 67–69
Truth in Lending Act (TILA), **221–222**

U

Unborn Victims of Violence Act, 78–79

Uniform Commercial Code, **223–224**
United Nations, 214–215
University of Colorado Football Program, 195–197
Unix operating system, 44–45
U.S. government, civil suits against, 127–128
U.S. Postal Service, 14–15
USA Patriot Act, 40–41, 215–216

V

Venn, Desmon, 137, *137*
Victims Compensation Fund, 188–189
Victims' rights, 78–79, 188–189, **225–226**
Virginia, 4–5, 65–67, 145–146, 230–231
Vitamin producers, 11–12
Voting, **226–228**

W

War on Terrorism, 168–169
Warsaw Convention, **229–230**
Washington D.C. snipers, 145–146
Washington (state), cases in, 81–83, 149–150, 183–185, 200–201
Water regulation and rights, 69–70, **230–231**
Webb, Joanne, 157–158
Werdegar, Kathryn Mickle, 65
West Bloomfield High School (West Bloomfield, Michigan), 137
Western Elite, Inc., 140–141
Western States Petroleum Association (WSPA), 67–69
WhenU.com, 120–121
Williams, Jayson, 138–139, *139*
Williams, Richard L., 4–5
Wilson, Edwin P., *38*, 38–39
Woolston, Thomas, 162–163, *163*
WSPA (Western States Petroleum Association), 67–69

Y

Yates, Raymond, 23–24
Yee, James, 72–73
Ysais, Tynisha, 153

Z

Z.J. Gifts, 80–81

ISBN 0-7876-9027-9